HUDSONS

HUDSON'S

At the heart of Britain's heritage

Published by Hudson's Heritage Group
35 Thorpe Road, Peterborough PE3 6AG
Telephone: 01733 296910
Email: hudsons@hhgroup.co.uk
www.hudsonsheritage.com

Front Cover: Buckingham Palace © Getty Images

2012

HUDSON'S celebrate 25 years with us

CLARENCE HOUSE

After the Second World War, many great houses fell into disrepair and, tragically, were demolished. A reasonable number of others, however, survived the period of austerity that followed, and opened their doors to the public for the first time.

Today, great houses, castles, museums, gardens and sites of important historical significance continue to fascinate visitors from home and overseas, reaffirming their importance and value to the nation and the wider world.

In this directory, Hudsons, now celebrating its twenty-fifth anniversary, continues to provide a comprehensive, entertaining and accessible guide to this area of the nation's precious heritage.

I wish it continued success into the future.

Daniel Mihailescu/AFP/Getty Images

WELCOME to *Hudson's* in its 25th anniversary year

'2012 is a special year for the UK: we're celebrating the Queen's Diamond Jubilee, we're hosting the 30th Olympic Games – and we are also launching a new-look ***Hudson's!*** *I hope you find it as useful as it's always been, with the added attraction of more extensive, and I hope, more stimulating editorial. In the following pages we have some familiar household names – as well as a few new faces. As a nation, we're not always forthcoming about our achievements and everything the UK has to offer its visitors and public. It's my mission to bring our heritage alive in the most accessible and entertaining ways possible.*
I hope you enjoy what we've done so far.'
Nick McCann Editor

our *Hudson's* *heroes & heroines*

bringing Britain's brilliant heritage alive

NORMAN HUDSON OBE was *Hudson's* creator and original Editor. To celebrate 25 years of the Directory, he tells us what gave rise to his big idea on a trip down memory lane at a favourite haunt; Broughton Castle. **Page 6**

THE DUCHESS OF RUTLAND's Belvoir Castle plays host to the 2012 CLA Game Fair. Not just for the shooting n' hunting fraternity, this once modest country pursuits event has grown into a 'must-go' for the family. **Page 15**

IAN VASEY lends *Hudson's* his Location Manager expertise on film and television production. Britain's historic houses and gardens are the true stars of so many UK and Hollywood blockbusters. **Page 20**

BRIAN SEWELL needs little introduction. The 'Marmite' of the arts world (we like him on toast) views London's great houses and at Apsley, admires Wellington's home and Napoleon's statue. **Page 24**

SIMON FOSTER is one of the UK's leading heritage gurus. Providing advice and business savvy to historic houses up and down the land, he opens up his portfolio to give *Hudson's* his thoughts on current trends in 'Simon Says'. **Page 31**

ROBERT SEATTER has a special position as Head of BBC History. With exciting developments at the Corporation and relocations underway, Robert provides a privileged insight into the BBC's historic buildings. **Page 43**

LORD MELVYN BRAGG is famously loyal to his native Cumbria. A prolific writer, broadcaster and lifelong champion of the arts, he is Patron of the Lowther Castle & Gardens Trust; 'Work in Progress'. **Page 50**

TIM KNOX leads a dedicated and expert team as Director of London's extraordinary and fascinating Soane Museum. The 'Opening Up The Soane' initiative is on target to raise the millions necessary to maintain this national treasure. **Page 54**

GEOFFREY BOND OBE has been very busy: variously broadcaster, lawyer, fund-raiser and recently Sheriff of the City of London. A great heritage enthusiast and supporter, he finally relaxes over coffee with Tim Knox. **Page 54**

THE RT HON MICHAEL PORTILLO is rarely off our TV screens these days. After a First at Cambridge, a high profile political career and much else besides, he takes *Hudson's* (by train of course) to the little known gem of Wotton House, Buckinghamshire. **Page 58**

DAVID GLADSTONE the direct descendant of Queen Victoria's Prime Minister is the custodian of Wotton's rich heritage. In 'House Party' with pasta made with Portillo, he extends his charming hospitality to *Hudson's*. **Page 58**

DEREK TARR is a lifelong member of the National Trust and English Heritage. As an Accountant he is able to balance his life between spreadsheets and walking in the UK. This time it's Wiltshire's great houses and pubs on the agenda. **Page 66**

VISCOUNT COKE has the awesome responsibility of running Holkham Hall and its estate in North Norfolk. On a stunning summer's day at his new Beach Café at Holkham's much-filmed beach, he spills the beans on 21st century responsibilities in 'New Tricks'. **Page 74**

SIR RICHARD FITZHERBERT of Tissington Hall, Derbyshire is one of a new breed of house owners who have embraced new technology & digital media. But the internet still can't protect him from Easter bunnies and 'much ado about nothing'... **Page 77**

Editor's choice
page 139

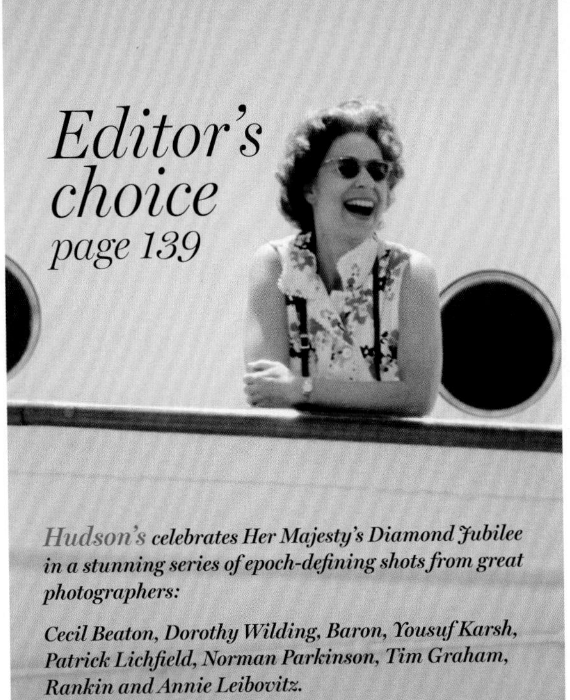

Hudson's celebrates Her Majesty's Diamond Jubilee in a stunning series of epoch-defining shots from great photographers:

Cecil Beaton, Dorothy Wilding, Baron, Yousuf Karsh, Patrick Lichfield, Norman Parkinson, Tim Graham, Rankin and Annie Leibovitz.

also in *Hudson's* 2012...

Hudson's was produced with the help of:
Group Managing Director - Ed Beale
Production Manager - Deborah Coulter
HHG Production - Claire Dollman and Anna Redding
HHG Design - Neil Pope, Jamieson Eley and Hanneke Lambert
Telesales Manager - Tracy Buckley
Sales Team - Matt Avery, Glen Bowdidge, Sam Harwood, Ben Skipper
Production - PDQ Digital Media; Printer - Wyndeham Press Group Ltd;
UK Trade Sales - Compass DSA; UK Distribution - NBN International.

JONATHAN WILD was once an RAF Squadron Leader seeing action in the Falklands and Bosnia. Now back to his first love of gardens, his northern tour touches upon Capability Brown, Gertrude Jekyll and the epic Alnwick Garden. **Page 86**

THE DUCHESS OF NORTHUMBERLAND has created perhaps the most talked-about 'new' heritage site in the UK with her spectacular and visionary Alnwick Garden. Although visited by millions, she explains why it's still such a personal project. **Page 90**

ROBERT INNES-SMITH spent a major part of his rich and varied career creating guidebooks to a vast number of stately homes. He wryly reflects on some of his more amusing aristocratic encounters. **Page 94**

LUCINDA LAMBTON represents all that is great about British (dare we say it) eccentricity and the arts. Compulsive viewing on TV, she started by snapping Bing Crosby and the rest is history. **Page 96**

RUTH GOODMAN and the Tudor Group take their 'hobby' very seriously indeed. Now a ubiquitous star of TV, Ruth explains what makes the Group tick as we follow in their foosteps at Haddon Hall. **Page 102**

LOYD GROSSMAN OBE is a man of many parts: raconteur, broadcaster, writer – and we hear he's very saucy too! As Chairman of the Churches Conservation Trust he urges us to treasure our parish churches. **Page 104**

THE DUKE AND DUCHESS OF ARGYLL live in the fairytale castle of Inveraray on the banks of Loch Fyne. Despite all the grandeur, they are remarkably down-to-earth, as Ruth Stokes discovers. **Page 116**

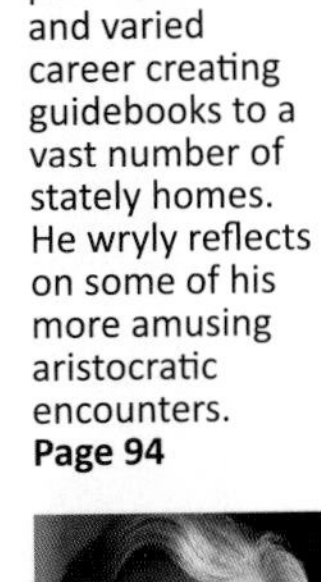

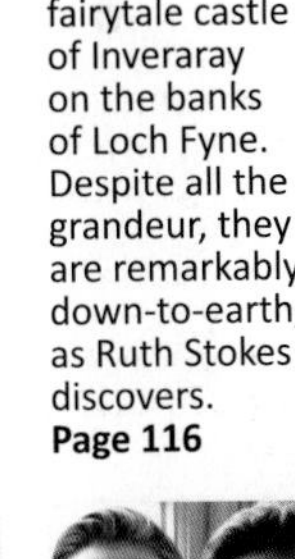

CLARE RUSSELL finds time to write best-selling recipe books when she is not acting as Lord Lieutenant of Banffshire, or running her Speyside castle, of Ballindalloch. *Hudson's* takes a visit to sample Clare's fabulous Cuisine. **Page 122**

ANGELIKA, DOWAGER COUNTESS CAWDOR has transformed the iconic castle of Shakespeare's 'Scottish Play', into an art house, both inside and in the gardens. Discover how in 'Cawdor Thou Art'. **Page 128**

JANE PRUDEN is a *Hudson's* writer and roving reporter. In 'Daddy Cool' she gets down and dirty with the irrepressible phenomenon of historic house music festivals. Jane has also given us her overview of the CLA Game Fair. **Page 132**

NICK McCANN trained at the Slade School of Fine Art and is a film-maker, photographer and painter. His love of birds takes him far and wide and his love of food keeps him in the kitchen. Nick is the Editor of *Hudson's*.

NIGEL GIBSON is *Hudson's* photographer. When the Editor asked him to pop along and visit his heritage heroine and fellow photographer, Lucinda Lambton, he was so excited he nearly left his lens cap on.

RUTH STOKES usually writes for the *Sunday Times Travel Magazine, The Guardian, Escape* and *Business Sense* among others. *Hudsons* is delighted Ruth has been working with us and we look forward to more collaborations.

NEIL POPE has edited consumer magazines – including *Angling Times, Today's Golfer* and *Garden News* – for over 20 years. Neil has helped the editorial team with the design and production of *Hudson's*.

Photographs:
Nigel Gibson

NORMAN HUDSON, visionary creator of the ***Hudson's*** Directory 25 years ago, returns to Broughton Castle. With the entertaining owner, Lord Saye and Sele by his side, he is interviewed by today's Editor, ***Nick McCann*** – keen to discover what inspired his big idea.

Norman's CONQUEST

NICK McCANN: Why is Broughton Castle so special to you Norman?
NORMAN HUDSON: It's one of the first places I worked 40 years ago – I cut my teeth here. It's very difficult to choose one house I like best, but there are a certain few from the early days that I do have a particular fondness for; Rockingham Castle in Leicestershire, Somerleyton Hall in Suffolk – and this one. Broughton was actually the first house to feature on the front of what has become *Hudson's*.

HISTORIC
HOUSE

NM: What was the spur behind your decision to create the directory in the first place?
NH: The number of visitors to historic houses was growing in the 1980s. The National Trust and the newly-formed English Heritage both had marketing expertise, and one or two private owners were also quite expert, but there were a vast number of privately-owned houses (more than the National Trust and English Heritage put together in fact) that weren't known about by either the public or the travel trade. So I set out to produce a manual incorporating all the wonderful places that didn't feature anywhere else. It was basically a bible for the travel trade.

NM: I imagine it was also very useful to film and television location managers?
NH: Yes, that was a fortunate by-product. I was working closely with George Howard at the time when *Brideshead Revisited* was being filmed at Castle Howard and we realised that most houses just didn't know how to deal with film people. In my Historic Houses Association capacity, I wrote a small guidance leaflet, >>

and later, *Hudson's* became the obvious starting point for location managers searching for suitable stately homes.

NM: The heritage industry has seen many changes since then. What would you say have been the greatest changes for historic houses since WWII?

NH: Well of course, after the War, a huge number were pulled down. Many had been occupied by the army, their domestic staff had disappeared, and senior family members had been killed in action so there was no direct descendant to inherit. Quite often dry rot had set in and they were in a terrible state. During one particular 18-month period in the early 1950s, on average, one country house was pulled down every four days. It was only later, in the 1970s, that people woke up to what a huge loss that was. When Sir Roy Strong put together a major exhibition at the V&A called 'The Destruction of the English Country House' in 1974, it was the first time the issue entered public consciousness. Another watershed came in 1976, when heritage properties were given special exemption from Capital Transfer Tax – but only on the condition that they opened their doors to the public.

NM: How do you see historic houses surviving and prospering in the present economic conditions – over the next five years, say?

NH: The industry has already been through a number of stages. Traditionally, visiting a stately home was something people did on Sundays. Then shops started opening seven days a week and there was much more competition for Sunday trade. Many properties introduced 'clip-on' attractions, such as adventure playgrounds and wildlife parks, before realising that potentially these could actually be damaging to the heritage they were trying to preserve. In recent years, competition from other tourist attractions and retail industries means we haven't seen an increase in day visitors at all. Where there has been growth, however, is in other areas – particularly in the use of houses as venues for functions and events. It's interesting to think that these great houses were originally designed as places of entertainment and that they are now going back to their roots, albeit on a commercial basis. The Marriage Act of 1995 made it possible for couples to get married in country houses, and for the last 15 years this has been a phenomenal growth area, to the extent where some have become what I call 'wedding factories'. They provide a great setting with a great sense of style.

NM: Here you are back at Broughton after 25 years – which part of the house would you say is your favourite?

NH: Definitely the Oak Room, for two reasons: it has a wonderful feel, with lots of light; and it also encapsulates what a good private owner does in creating a balance between the historic and the contemporary. Some new pieces of furniture have been commissioned by the Saye & Sele family, perhaps with the proceeds of filming that's taken place here, and this reflects their personal taste – something that I think makes private houses particularly special. There's so much variety here. The Star Chamber, for example, is an amazing room, with marvellous 18th century painted wallpaper, juxtaposed with a splendid late-20th century bed. Broughton isn't a museum – it's continuing to evolve, it's alive, it couldn't be more contemporary. The fact that it's in such marvellous condition today is because of a huge amount of personal effort by Lord Saye.

"I made a big mistake getting involved with those Roundheads, but let's just forget it!"

LORD SAYE

I think that if you're privileged to live in a house like this, then you've got to do it properly – it's no good fiddling around. When we put a new floor down we want it to last a few hundred years. The carpets in the three main rooms were all put down 35 years ago, and considering they've been walked on by 10,000 visitors a year, they've done pretty well. It's interesting that the Oak Room is Norman's favourite room – it's mine too. I always say, if there are such things as good rooms and bad rooms, this definitely has to qualify as a 'good' room. It's uplifting, with fantastic light and an elegant, restrained, 16th century ceiling which is neither too elaborate nor too grand – there's nothing to irritate. One of the paintings shows Charles II setting sail from Holland for the Restoration of the Monarchy in 1660. Broughton has significant Civil War connections. It was a Parliament House, against the King, but after the Restoration, Lord Saye was pardoned and served on Charles II's Privy Council. The painting is inscribed with the words, 'There is no pleasure in the memory of the past', which was probably Lord Saye's way of saying, 'I made a big mistake getting involved with those Roundheads, but let's just forget it!'

NM: Broughton has played host to many TV and film crews over the years – have they left any lasting legacies?

LS: Actually, some of the last internal building work was by a film company who wanted to disguise some rather ugly pipework. They only covered it with plywood, but it looked so much better than the exposed pipes, we've left it there. **>>**

NH: That reminds me of Chillingham Castle in Northumberland – an amazing place. There are two false fibreglass fireplaces there that were put in for filming purposes, and the owner, Sir Humphry Wakefield, decided to keep them because they looked so much better than the originals hidden behind. Mind you, you do come across some fairly horrific stories about film crews, too. In the early days, there weren't any proper contracts and they often wanted to take out the electric wiring without so much as a by-your-leave. But things have improved hugely since then.
LS: I remember Trevor Nunn directing Helena Bonham-Carter here in a film about Lady Jane Grey. In the action, she banged against the oak panelling and my wife was not best pleased!

NH: *The Morecambe and Wise Christmas Show* was filmed here one year, too. I came along to check all was going well and met them and their wives. Eric and Ernie were consummate professionals when they were working, but we had a great laugh. On another occasion, I came here when they were filming Henry Fielding's novel *Joseph Andrews*. One of the extras I knew socially.

NM: Lord Saye – how has Norman changed over years?
LS: If he's matured, then I'd say he's very well blended. And he hasn't got any taller – he's still what I call a sensible height!
NH: A friend of mine who is of a similarly modest stature always claims to be inordinately fond of his feet. He says they're the only part of his anatomy which are on the same level as everyone else's! >>

"Broughton isn't a museum – it's continuing to evolve, it's alive, it couldn't be more contemporary"

NM: What does the future hold for you personally?

NH: I've had such a special and privileged career. I've been extraordinarily fortunate to have seen so many great houses, to have been the recipient of so much hospitality, and to have got to know people I wouldn't have met in any other job. Now, in many ways I've got a whole new career in front of me. While I'm still retained as an advisor to the HHA, I'm also Chairman of a new charitable trust, the Country Houses Foundation, which has been set up to help finance the repair of country houses. At a time when English Heritage grants have diminished and the Lottery Fund's policy is still not to give money to private house owners, the Foundation can be of enormous use, especially in preserving ancillary buildings such as dovecotes, towers and obelisks. I'm entering a whole new era – it's rather fun. **>>**

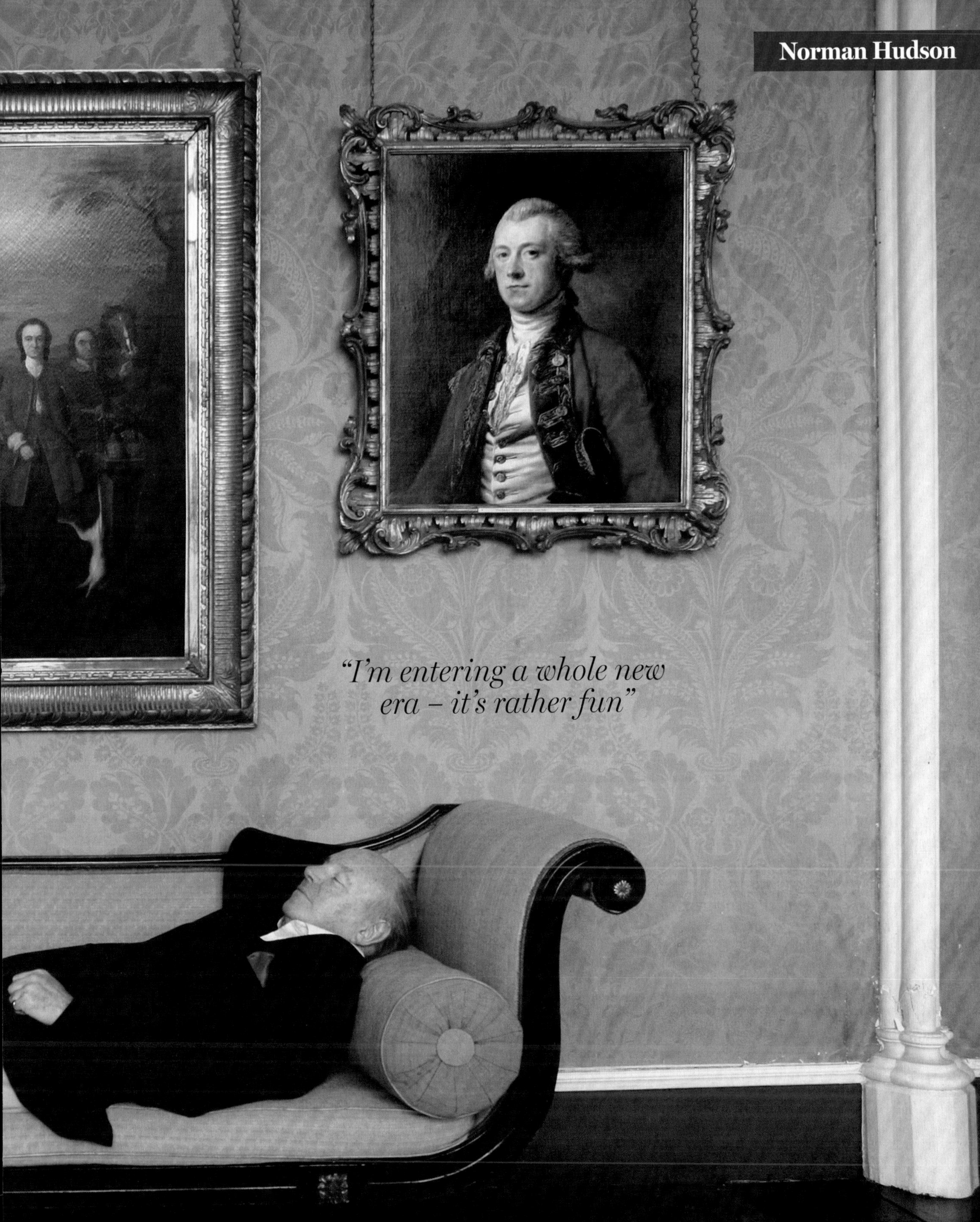

"I'm entering a whole new era – it's rather fun"

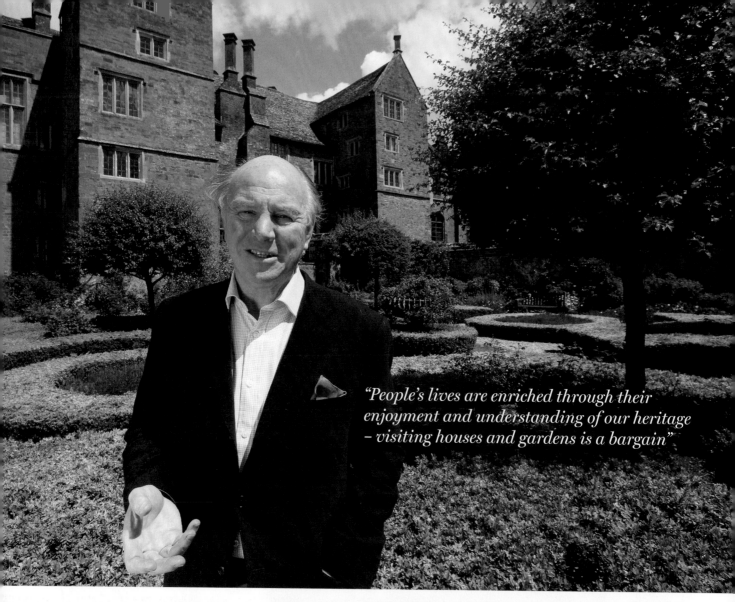

"People's lives are enriched through their enjoyment and understanding of our heritage – visiting houses and gardens is a bargain"

'Nowhere in the world are there so many historic country houses as in England, with an astonishing variety in their style and the richness of their collections, and of their parks and gardens. Of those that are open to the public, there are more that remain privately owned than those in the ownership of the National Trusts, English Heritage and their counterparts put together. They contribute widely to the national and local economy, providing for tourism, recreation and education. People's lives are enriched through their enjoyment and understanding of our heritage – and on a cost per hour of enjoyment basis, visiting houses and gardens is a bargain.'

NORMAN HUDSON OBE

FOR VISITOR INFORMATION ON BROUGHTON CASTLE TURN TO PAGE 203

The CLA (Countryside Landowners and Business Association) Game Fair is the world's leading country sports event, attracting over 140,000 visitors over three days. But it isn't just about shooting, fishing and ferreting. It is a family day out that offers the chance to learn from experts and have a go at different rural activities, from falconry to mountain boarding.

Game on

In 2012 the Game Fair returns to Belvoir Castle in Leicestershire, home to The Duke and Duchess of Rutland. The Duchess reveals what visitors can expect. 'It is one of those rare events where there is literally something for everyone: endless shopping, loads of sporting and rural craft demonstrations mixed with activities like quad-biking and a new craze to walk on water in an inflatable ball,' she says.

Despite its many varied attractions the Game Fair started out in 1958 as a two-day event for gamekeepers, shoot owners and shooting enthusiasts to get together and talk about... shooting. It was a typically genteel army-tented country show in the grounds of Stetchwork Park near Newmarket, put on for an estimated 1,000 visitors. A whopping 8,000, and their dogs, turned up: the corps d'elite noticeable in their Bentleys laden with giant picnics for family and friends. It was, and continues to be, a predominantly social occasion, underpinned with trade and gossip in a glorious stately-home setting. The CLA, former sponsors, took over the organisation and it grew into the polished business that today generates more than £15m within the showground and many more millions spent in different localities each year. >>

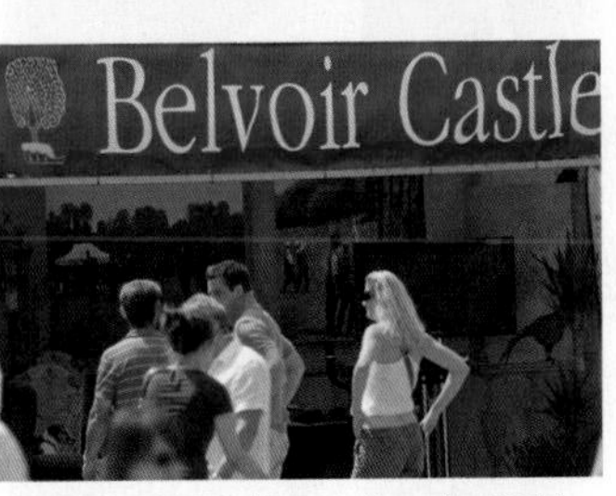

The Belvoir Castle stand at the 2011 CLA Game Fair at Blenheim Palace

Fair

The Duchess of Rutland in conference at the Game Fair

Photo: Georgina Pruden

'The changing venues showcase regional country sport and, since the successful initiative to support rural businesses in 2002, we are able to promote the many diverse enterprises from local landowners and businessmen,' explains Fiona Eastman at the CLA. The visitor demographic expanded in response and there is now more to do and see than ever.

Apart from the 900-plus shopping stands, craft tents and art and sculpture exhibitions, there is a multitude of themed sideshows: some of Chelsea Flower Show's Gold winning displays; the 'Active Countryside for All' zone where you can walk on water in a ball, try out the *Top Gear* simulator or have a crack at archery clays, laser combat or the bungee trampoline. The 'Door to Nature' section covers everything you need to know about woodland, ponds, bees, owls, otters, waterfowl, farming and wildlife. Sate your appetite with a smorgasbord of tastings and cooking demonstrations from regional food producers in the 'Totally Food Show'. Plus Express Eventing and a Qualifier for the Horse of the Year Show, acrobatic, dressage, side-saddle displays and the wonderful heavy horse and carriage events. And don't miss the 'Have-a-Go' area for falconry, 4x4, archery and airgun shooting to name but a few.

Every dog has its day, and never more so than at the Game Fair. The finely-trained canine athletes deployed as gundogs and the hearth-hugging family pooches are the real stars of the show. The Kennel Club is on site offering tips and healthcare checks for all breeds. You can talk to top breeders, many with examples of their progeny, and explore the complex lives of the terrier in 'The Terrier Pavilion'. Full of attitude and short on leg, these little characters, including many arcane breeds unfamiliar outside their rural communities – like the Sealyham, Plummer and Parsons Russells – make surprisingly good urban pets when deprived of their natural hunting ground and liberated from any narcissistic tendencies to control bunnies. For professionals, the international gundog championships vie for spectators with the amateur dog-handler scurries, and the dog agility course is a winner with every age group.

ATTWOOLLS

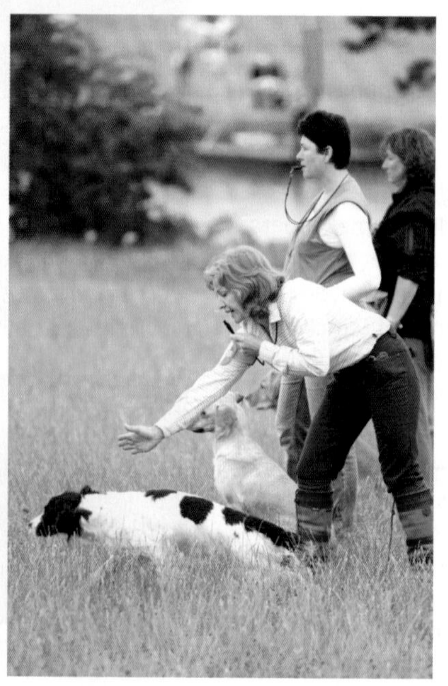

Primarily, of course, the fair is an unrivalled opportunity to see at first hand and learn more about

Hudson's Game Fair advice

- *Save money and buy your tickets in advance.*
- *Wear sensible shoes, there is a lot of walking over a 500-acre showground.*
- *Book a hotel or B&B, camping or caravan pitch on-site as early as possible if you want to stay locally.*
- *Beat the traffic and arrive early for a bacon butty. Gates open between 6.30am and 7am. The show starts at 9.30am.*
- *Plan your day, there is a lot to do and see.*
- *Take your dog, but use the dog-crèche if you need a break.*
- *Use the 'Shop and Drop' facility if you intend to buy heavy items early in the day.*
- *The 2012 CLA Game Fair takes place at Belvoir Castle, Grantham, Leicestershire NG32 1PE*
- *See the CLA Game Fair website: www.gamefair.co.uk*

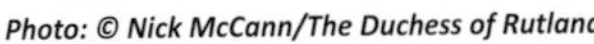

Photo: © Nick McCann/The Duchess of Rutland

country sports. The shooting exhibition is the largest in Europe with more displays and demonstrations than you can wave two barrels at. Fiona Eastman adds, 'We have the biggest gathering of gunmakers in the world at a public event. Visitors from all over the UK and abroad come to see the best and latest products on offer in "Gunmakers Row" packed with over 230 exhibitors.' Angling is a similar story. You can buy any rod, gun or item of kit and clothing, even a day's shooting or a week's fishing holiday; talk to the editor of your favourite shooting or fishing magazine and rub shoulders with some of the country's keenest shots and legendary fishermen.

It is impossible to experience the whole show in one day but you can stay in one of many very good local inns, hotels, bed and breakfasts or on the campsite. 'We are great staycationers,' says the Duchess of Rutland. 'My children and I love camping and we have all piled into a caravan on holidays in Wales, where I grew up – it is the best way to experience the beauty of your surroundings and in this case, beat the rush in the morning.' Staycation is a buzzword that would be as alien to the fair-goers of 1958 as a butler-served picnic from the back of a Bentley would be to the majority of us today. But the CLA Game Fair is an institution that continues to promote country sports and rural businesses to an increasingly wide audience and is enjoying an ever-wider appeal.

"We are great staycationers. My children and I love camping and we have all piled into a caravan on holidays in Wales, where I grew up – it is the best way to experience the beauty of your surroundings and in this case, beat the rush in the morning."

THE DUCHESS OF RUTLAND

Come and see the heritage you have helped save

ENGLISH HERITAGE

There are many fascinating places to visit which have recently been repaired with the help of grants from English Heritage. With over 1,300 to choose from, there's bound to be something near you and something to suit every taste. Some of them are opening their doors to the public for the first time.

We give grants for major repair projects on important heritage sites throughout England. The range is huge: houses from medieval to modern, forts and castles from the Romans to the Victorians, mills and mausoleums, follies and parks, and all sorts of places of worship. We also grant-aid essential professional work such as investigation, research and surveys to help plan repairs and future management more effectively. Alongside these grants for individual sites, we contribute to the costs of some public and charitable organisations working to care for the historic environment and to get more people involved. Last year, we spent a total of £34.8 million in grants.

It has always been a principle of English Heritage grant-giving that the public should be able to see the sites and buildings they have helped repair. The extent of public access varies from one property to another. Some are open throughout the year, some on certain days only and others by prior arrangement. Some open on Heritage Open Days as well. Full details of opening arrangements at grant-aided places are published on our website:
www.english-heritage.org.uk/daysout

Here you can find the grant-aided places with a database of over 1,300 different buildings, monuments, parks and gardens, searchable by location and type. Most of the properties are open free, but we give details of admission charges where they apply. There is also a brief description of each property and information on parking and access for people with disabilities. A selection of current examples is shown on the page opposite.

English Heritage is grateful to all those owners and custodians with whom we work; their commitment to keeping the nation's heritage in good repair and their support for these public access arrangements is vital.

The vast majority of this country's heritage is in the care of private individuals and voluntary groups. We are pleased to be able to help through grant-aid where we can, but we will only ever provide a fraction of the sums needed to pass on our historic environment to future generations. The private owners and voluntary groups who look after so many listed buildings, monuments and landscapes are today's custodians of tomorrow's heritage. Their contribution to the beauty and history of this country is vital.

We very much hope you enjoy the sites and properties you find, from the famous to the many lesser-known treasures - they are all worth a visit.

English Heritage
138-142 Holborn, London EC1N 2ST

Customer services:
Tel: +44 (0) 870 333 1181
Fax: +44 (0) 1793 414 926

Minicom text telephone for the deaf or hard of hearing: 0800 015 0516

Email: customers@english-heritage.org.uk
www.english-heritage.org.uk

The Belvedere

Powderham Castle, Kenton,
Devon EX6 8JQ

Gothic-style tower, built 1717 – 74, listed Grade.II*. Located on the Exe estuary in the deer park at Powderham Castle. Converted into two-storey accommodation between 1835 and 1839 and used as an estate cottage until the mid 20th century. It was gutted by two fires in the post-war era. English Heritage grant-aided the removal of vegetation and debris and repairs to perimeter walls.

www.powderham.co.uk

Grant Recipient: The Earl of Devon Estate

T: 01626 890243

E: castle@powderham.co.uk

Open: 1 April - 1 August: Sunday - Friday 11am - 4.30pm. Opening times are subject to variation. Access to the Belvedere Tower (exterior only) by paid admission to Powderham Castle.

Heritage Open Days: No

Parking: Ample parking available at foot of Powderham Castle. 10–15 minutes uphill walk from car park to the Tower.

Disabled access: Uphill walk to the Tower unsuitable for wheelchairs. WC for the disabled in the Castle. Guide dogs allowed.

Admission charge: Adult: £9.80, Child: £7.80 (4–16 years old), Senior: £8.80, Family: £27.80, Under 4s: Free (all charges include guided tour).

BRUNEL

Brunel Engine House

Railway Ave, Rotherhithe, Southwark,
London SE16 4LF

Scheduled monument. Designed and built by Isambard Kingdom Brunel and his father Sir Marc Brunel. Built in 1842, a year before the Thames Tunnel opened, and used to house the steam engines that drove the pumps that kept the tunnel dry. Today, it houses a permanent exhibition to highlight the dramatic story of the construction and subsequent history of the Thames Tunnel. English Heritage grant-aided survey work and repairs.

www.brunel-museum.org.uk/index.aspx

Grant Recipient: Trustees of the Brunel Museum

T: 0207 231 3314

E: info@brunel-museum.org.uk

Open: daily, 10am - 5pm. Closed Christmas Day, Boxing Day and New Years Day. Regular tours of Grand Entrance Hall (Brunel's shaft) on advertised days.

Heritage Open Days: Yes

Parking: On-street parking. One space for the disabled on cobbled drive.

Disabled access: Full. WC for the disabled. Guide dogs allowed.

Admission charge: Adult: £2.00, Concessions: £1.00, **Child:** Free, Art Fund Members: Free.

Bolton Percy Gatehouse

Gatehouse Lane, Bolton Percy,
North Yorkshire Y023 7AG

Grade II* listed 15th century gatehouse which originally formed the entrance to the village rectory. Today, the gatehouse provides holiday accommodation. English Heritage grant-aided the archaeological assessment of timbers, repairs to roof and walls and the replacement of the windows.

http://www.vivat-trust.org/properties.php

Grant Recipient: The Vivat Trust

Access contact: Bronwyn Neal

T: 0845 090 0194

E: enquiries@vivat-trust.org

Open: Access to the interior on Heritage Open Days 8 -11 September 10am - 4pm and by appointment between bookings.

Heritage Open Days: Yes

Parking: Off-road parking.

Disabled access: No wheelchair access to the building but the garden is wheelchair accessible. No WC for the disabled. Guide dogs allowed.

Admission charge: No

Victoria Baths

Hathersage Rd,
Manchester M13 0FE

Grade II* listed ornate municipal baths complex containing three swimming pools, Turkish and Russian Baths and Aeratone. Built 1903–06. Closed 1993. Features decorative stained glass windows and glazed interior tile work. English Heritage grant-aided two phases of repair.

www.victoriabaths.org.uk

Grant Recipient: The Manchester Victoria Baths Trust/Manchester City Council

Access contact: Gill Wright

T: 0161 224 2020

E: info@victoriabaths.org.uk

Open: 1 April – 31 October: every Wednesday afternoon for guided tours at 2pm; 1 April – mid November: first Sunday in each month 12 – 4pm. At other times by prior arrangement with the Manchester Victoria Bath Trust (tel: 0161 224 2020). Group visits welcome.

Heritage Open Days: Yes

Parking: 30 spaces.

Disabled access: Partial. Wheelchair access to ground floor. Most of the building can be seen from the ground floor. WC for the disabled. Guide dogs allowed.

Admission charge: Adult: £2.00/£2.50 (Open Days), £5.00/£5.50 (Wednesday Tours), Child: Free, Other: Group Tours (from £5.00). Free admission for Friends of Victoria Baths.

All opening times and admission charges correct at time of publication, please check before visiting.

ENGLISH HERITAGE

"Make sure the crew don't smoke, swear, tread mud into the carpet, put their feet on the chairs, or put film lamps too near the old paintings"

Location, Location, Location!

Britain's historic houses are some of the most sought after TV and film locations in the world. ***Ian Vasey***, Location Manager on period productions such as the BBC's ***North and South***, explains the fascination and shares the thrills and spills behind the scenes.

The courtyard of Knole in Kent, dressed as a market, during the filming of 'Burke & Hare' © NTPL/Megan Taylor © Burke & Hare Productions Ltd

Lady Mary Crawley (Michelle Dockery), steps from Downton Abbey (Highclere Castle), while the crew measure for focus © Nick Briggs

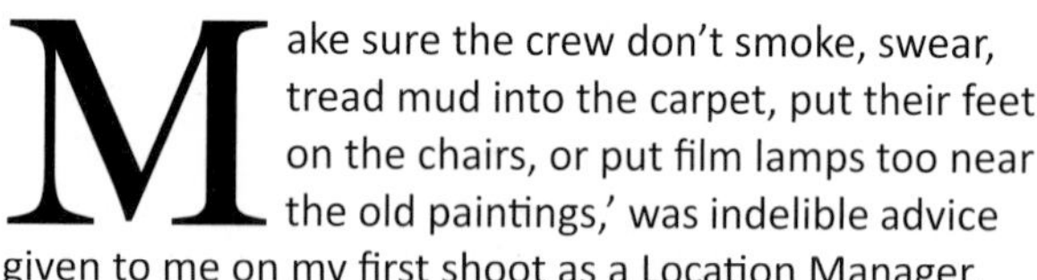

'Make sure the crew don't smoke, swear, tread mud into the carpet, put their feet on the chairs, or put film lamps too near the old paintings,' was indelible advice given to me on my first shoot as a Location Manager.

Trips to historic houses by production crews, as with any other outside organisation, involves a duty of care by the visitor. Haddon Hall in Derbyshire was no exception when it was used to shoot the feature film production of *Jane Eyre* in 2010 by BBC Films, Focus Features and Ruby Films. The medieval manor house, used for earlier adaptations by Franco Zefferelli in 1996, and in 2006 by the BBC TV version, has all the ghostly qualities featured in the novel that the director was trying to portray. It is even rumoured, but not proven, that Charlotte Bronte actually based Thornfield Hall on Haddon. Lord Edward Manners, owner of the great house recalls, however, 'Our House Manager, Janet Blackburn, had to delay filming one night. The props department was hoisting enormous chandeliers over beams and weighing them down in the Minstrels' Gallery, but the anchoring weights looked too heavy for the timbers.' Adding happily, 'Of course it all worked out in the end, we just worked together to minimise any risk to the fabric of the building.'

In the case of privately-owned houses, whether open to the public or not, a film or TV company needs to remember – they are entering someone's home – and be mindful of the disruption that filming entails.

Some feature film productions can bring a crew of 200-300 personnel, some television productions around 100, along with many vehicles, wardrobe and make-up trailers. Location Managers all know that however much you warn and prepare property owners, the

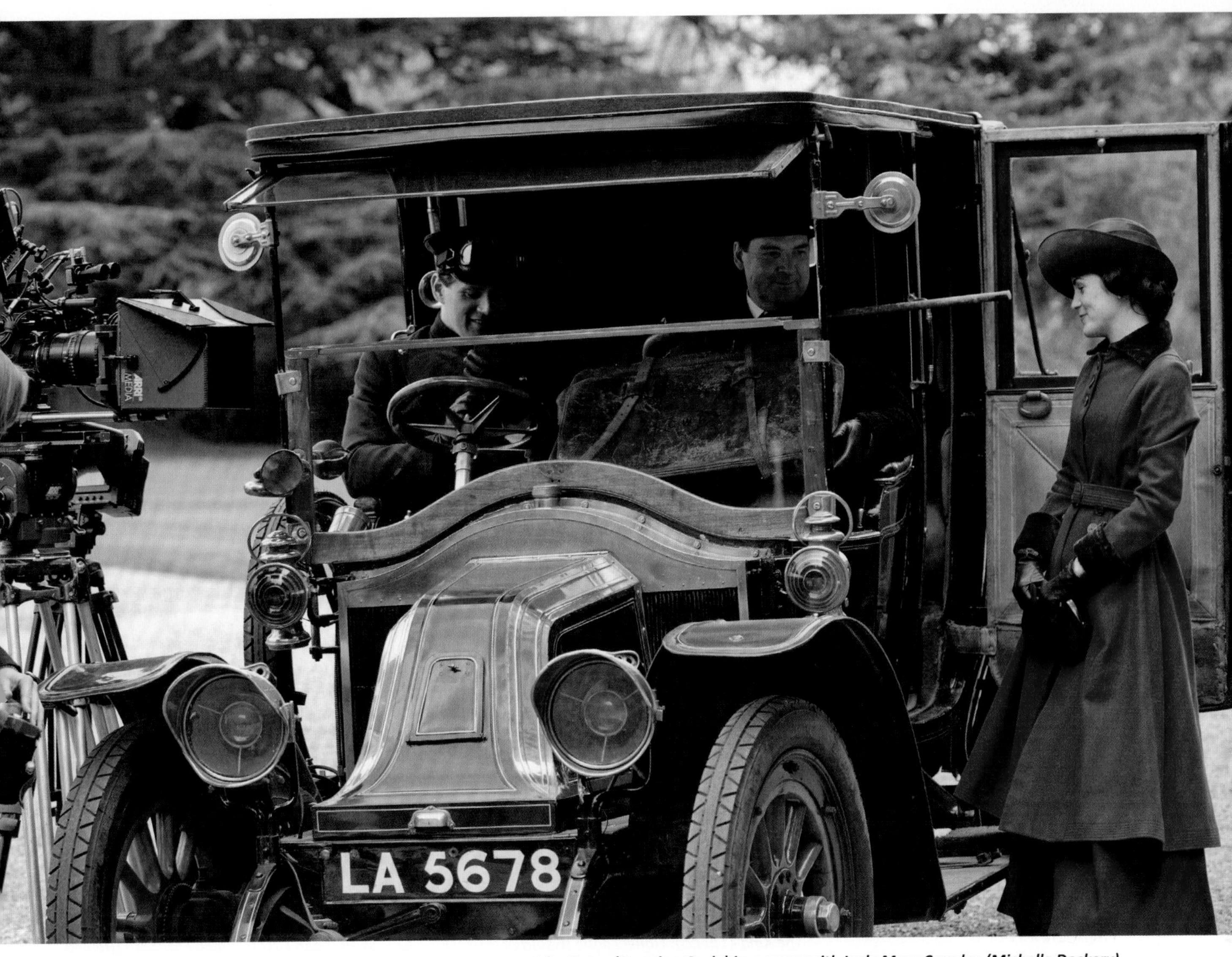
LA 5678

John Bates (Brendan Coyle) in a scene with Lady Mary Crawley (Michelle Dockery) and chauffeur, Tom Branson (Allen Leech) at Highclere Castle © Nick Briggs

arrival of the crew always comes as a surprise when they see it for the first time. Some owners are veterans and take it in their stride; some enjoy it, even on the first visit and some take time to adapt to the upheaval.

Low budget TV productions, even some major TV broadcasters, can on occasion turn up with a minimal crew of say 20 people, about three or four small vans and little or no facility vehicles. This delight for the location team can be short-lived however, when something like a mobile toilet trailer, usually present on larger shoots, hasn't been booked to save money. Location teams need to be alert for any bladder-challenged member of the crew and be ready to escort them to lavatory access, as a quick pee behind bushes is not acceptable.

What makes a production team pick a certain historic house above another? In the case of *Downton Abbey* set in 1912, made by Carnival Films for ITV, reasons for picking Highclere Castle, near Newbury in Hampshire were clear from the outset. Julian Fellowes (the Oscar winning writer) saw it, with its imposing gothic facade designed by Sir Charles Barry in 1842, as an architectural embodiment of all the displays of Victorian confidence. It is a distinctly dramatic backdrop to the series; different from the type of locations used for more genteel period dramas, which were often adapted from Victorian novels, rather than being an original work, as is *Downton Abbey*... 'Julian was also drawn to the fact that most of the required rooms could be used in the building,' says Gareth Neame, Executive Producer for Carnival Films, 'the rooms felt very intimate and you could travel from one to another without cutting to a studio set.' The 'below stairs' kitchen quarter however, had been modernised and was re-constructed in the **>>**

The King's Speech: Lionel Logue (Geoffrey Rush); King George VI (Colin Firth); Queen Elizabeth (Helena Bonham Carter). The King's Speech is now available on DVD and Blueray. Photo courtesy © Momentum Pictures

studios at Elstree. Another room, vital to the plot, was the servery, a utility area adjacent to many grand dining rooms but no longer in existence at Highclere, also had to be re-created as a set by the design team. This set, approximately the size of a large lift, was transported by lorry between Highclere in Newbury and the studios in London, so that scenes could be shot in it when there was time available in the filming schedule at either location. This would seem comical to the outsider, but is typical of the painstaking attention to detail under the pressure of tight shooting schedules. The set also became probably the most well travelled in television history!

All properties owned by the Royal family prohibit filming as a matter of course for any drama productions. A problem you may think for the British Oscar triumph of 2011, *The King's Speech*?

Visits to Royal premises by the production team, as members of the public, meant they recognised Knebworth House in Hertfordshire as a suitable double for interiors at Balmoral and Windsor Castle. In the words of Location Manager, Jamie Lengyel, the house just needed to be "tartan-ed up" for the occasion.

Knebworth's Grand Hall was used for David's party at Balmoral and the drawing room for its namesake at Windsor Castle where Queen Mary listens to Bertie's last speech. All straight-forward but the exterior shots, of the Balmoral approach road, had to be filmed in nearby Wendover Woods in between very real and heavy snowfalls during the winter of 2010. 'Shovelling snow from the drive, pushing cars and towing film trucks was only a part of the extra work during the booking,' explains Martha Lytton Cobbold, Knebworth's owner, whose home also appears in BBC 2's *The Hour*

The King's Speech: 'David' - Edward, Prince of Wales (Guy Pearce) pours Mrs Wallis Simpson (Eve Best) a glass of Champagne
Photo courtesy © Momentum Pictures

The Hangman played by comedian and musician, Bill Bailey, in 'Burke & Hare', directed by John Landis
© NTPL/Megan Taylor © Burke & Hare Productions Ltd

and Channel 4's, *Any Human Heart*. Adding, 'It was a brilliant experience working with the *King's Speech* location team. For all filming projects, our professional staff keep an open mind, tight control and very good communication skills to ensure that both parties meet their objectives and that the house and site are protected.'

National Trust properties have been hosting TV and film companies since 1960 when Cary Grant appeared in *The Grass is Greener* at Osterley Park. Many of their houses are uninhabited and there are literally hundreds of rooms that already look like film sets. But sometimes, finding space outside for all the paraphernalia can be a problem. Harvey Edgington from the NT tells me, 'The comedy thriller, *Burke & Hare* was filmed at Knole in Kent recently but there were so many tents and marquees in the grounds for all the extra actors, not to mention countless filthy pigs and cows, that it was a struggle to keep them out of shot.'

Hollywood in the home can have its drawbacks but they are countered by payments in the region of £5,000-£10,000 a day for the privilege for high-end Hollywood-backed feature films. TV productions pay considerably less but still a significant £1,000-£2,000, within the new climate of belt tightening by broadcasters. And it's not just the money that attracts houses to open their doors, visitor numbers increase enormously too. Antony House in Cornwall, used by Disney for *Alice in Wonderland* used to welcome up to 23,000 visitors a year but since the film's release in 2010 numbers rose to 100,000. It's all good news for the revenue and if you play your cards right, like Lady Carew-Pole who lives at the house with her husband, Sir Richard, you can feature as an extra too. 'It was terrific fun to be involved. I got to wear a pretty but rather tight crinoline with a boned corset from 5.30 in the morning to 6.30 at night. Nobody would recognise me in the film; I am a tiny blue blob in a great crowd during a tea party scene on the terrace.'

It seems that our historic houses and gardens will continue to secure lucrative contracts with TV and filmmakers. It's show-time not just for 90-odd minutes of fame and fortune on the silver screen but an opportunity to showcase the real star of the piece; the – location, location, location!

Knole's courtyard provides a convincing backdrop for the gallows scenes in 'Burke & Hare' *© NTPL/Megan Taylor © Burke & Hare Productions Ltd*

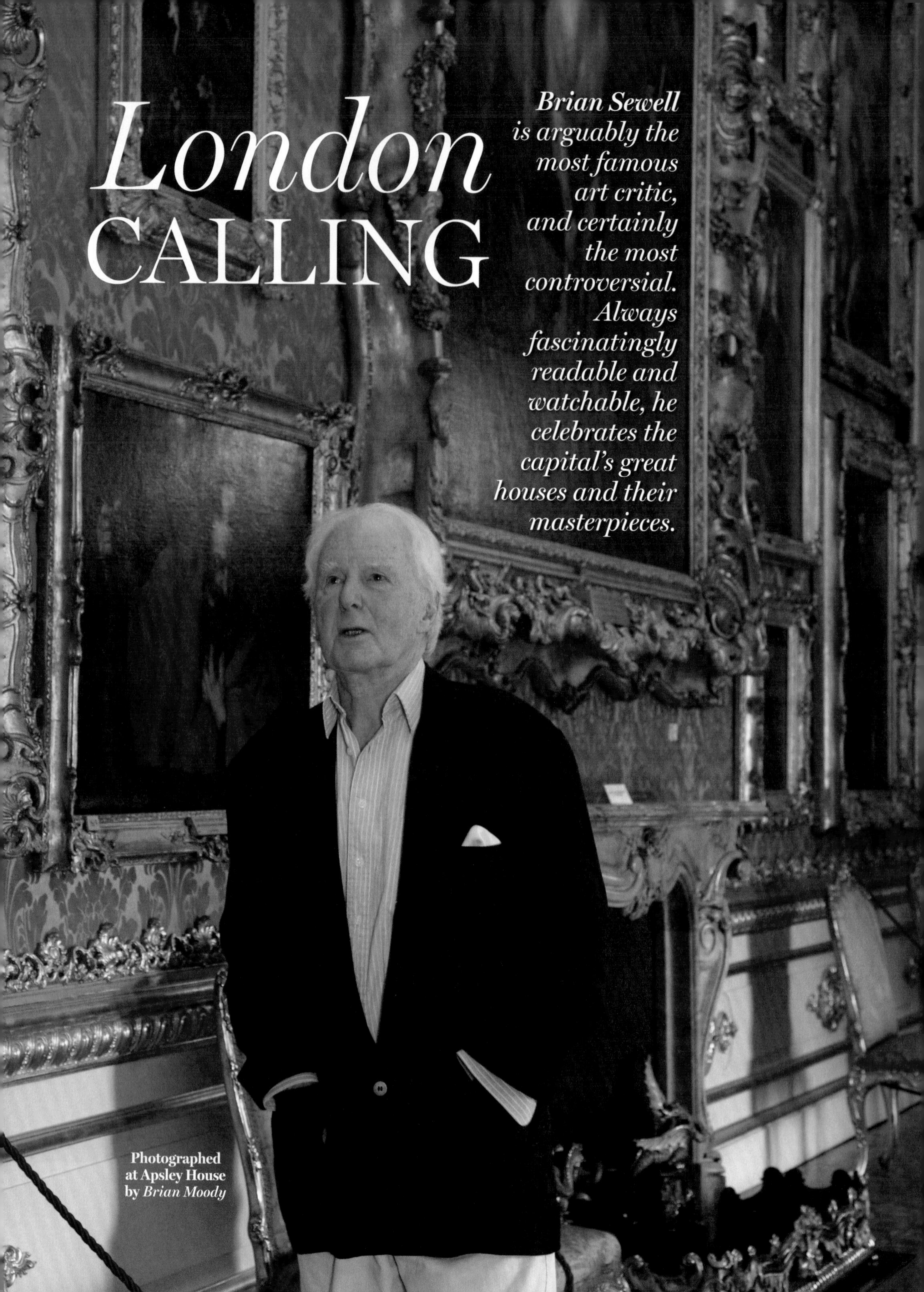

London CALLING

***Brian Sewell** is arguably the most famous art critic, and certainly the most controversial. Always fascinatingly readable and watchable, he celebrates the capital's great houses and their masterpieces.*

Photographed at Apsley House by ***Brian Moody***

Only in the wilds of central Wales and the far north of Scotland are those addicted to visiting the great houses of historic nabobs denied their easy fix. Such mansions, palaces and country seats, however, abound in every other region of the British Isles and even a few within the bounds of the great wen that is London, the congested metropolis that has swallowed a hundred villages and more in its unstoppable expansion. Of these communities the place-names and the churches commonly survive, but most decent houses with a patch of land, suddenly marooned by a sea of development, have been swept to oblivion by the tide of profit; only a few remain, like "the vast and trunkless legs" of Ozymandias to remind us of a grander past.

In Isleworth stands Syon House, once a monastery seized by Henry VIII in which his coffin burst as it lay overnight on the way from Westminster to Windsor, the exploded remains of his corpse consumed by dogs; here we see how the bold Percys, Dukes of Northumberland, displayed their temporal wealth and power. In nearby Osterley Park, the Childs, a banking family, so spendidly rebuilt a Tudor house that Horace Walpole, an exquisite critic, could in 1773, even before the work was completed, describe it as "the palace of palaces... all the Percys of Syon must die of envy." And in Hampstead, Kenwood House, a mansion remodelled in the 18th century to become "the finest country house in London," belonged to the first six Earls of Mansfield until the 1920s.

Though hushed by awe, in Osterley and, particularly, Syon, the visitor can still sense how things were done when they were new, sense the polite manners of the day, the customs and pursuits, sense the need for at least ten servants for each member of the family. These grandees had secretaries, librarians and curators of collections, their wives had companions and their children tutors and governesses, all of whom were neither quite "upstairs" nor "downstairs", but uncomfortably between, uncertain of their station; for lower servants there was no uncertainty, and as they scurried about with wood and coal, cutlery, crockery and food, made beds, swept and garnished living rooms and, below stairs and in the attics lived, made love and died – for these great houses were their homes too – there must always have been bustle and hushed noise everywhere. In Kenwood, however, it is easy to forget the footmen and the parlourmaids for it is now much more an art gallery than a house, with little but the splendid library to recall its original domestic purpose. As a gallery of great paintings it is astonishing, Gainsborough, Vermeer and Rembrandt among its heavyweights.

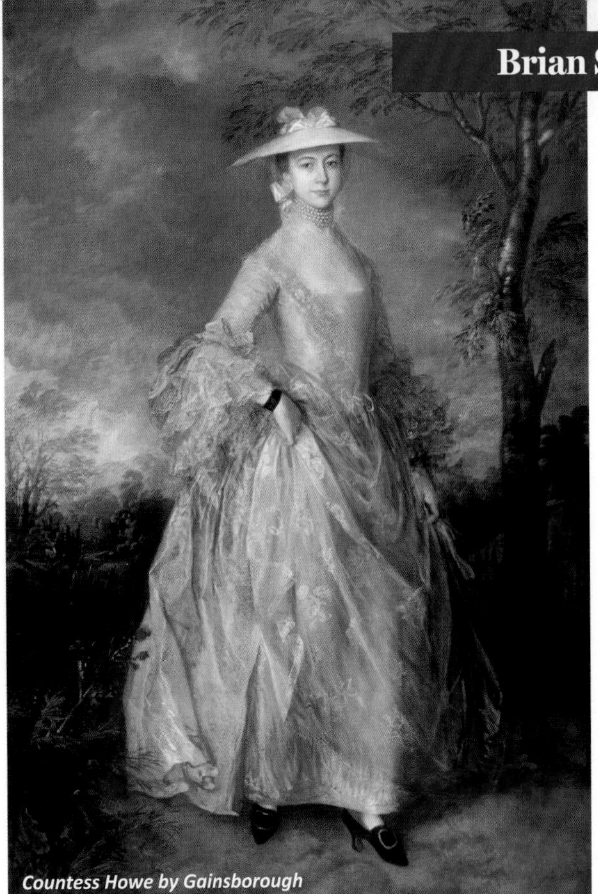

Countess Howe by Gainsborough

Collections images © English Heritage

The great Gainsborough is his erotically-charged Portrait of Countess Howe, reputedly his mistress (he 37, she 32), echoing the pose, palette and fleeting touch of Van Dyck, but with a suggestion of challenging hauteur in her demeanour and expression, while within the extravagant dress and its accoutrements, all painted with such extraordinary freedom and immediacy that hardly a stroke of paint below the face was not an impetuous adjustment, we have a revealing and sensual impression of her body. In enlightening contrast **>>**

Below: The Library at Kenwood House

Self Portrait by Rembrandt

Vermeer's Guitar Player, a late work, is pure mathematics, distilled order, exquisite imbalance, volume and void in counterpoint, the plucked note as frozen as the smile.

The Rembrandt is the great Self Portrait with two mysterious arcs described on the wall behind him: he confronts us, his gaze direct, the mouth set in silence; light falls heavily on his white cap, his brow and the sheen of sweat on his nose, and then fades in the crumple of his white shirt; these two patches of white paint frame and emphasise his face and give it dominance over the tonally retiring bulk of the stout body that supports it, brilliantly varied by the bold straight lines of brushes, mahlstick and rectangular palette all held in the left hand; the right, his painting hand, is wryly invisible.

Syon and Osterley are within ten miles of Hyde Park Corner, Kenwood within five, but one mansion sharing their grandeur and housing two hundred paintings (twice the number in Kenwood), stands on Hyde Park Corner itself – Apsley House, the Wellington Museum. How many of the wealthy staying amid the modern splendours of the Lanesborough Hotel on the south side of the Corner realise that across the road or through the underpass lies the genuine antique magnificence of the house in which lived the victor of Waterloo, Arthur Wellesley, first Duke of Wellington?

He bought it from his elder brother in 1816, the year after Waterloo, and later employed Benjamin Dean Wyatt (son of the more famous architect James Wyatt) to clad the whole house in Bath stone, add the picture gallery (known as the Waterloo Gallery) and make other extensive alterations, the eventual expenditure three times the estimate. He seems to have left most of the decisions on interior decoration and furnishings at first to Wyatt, with whom he quarrelled, and then to his friend Harriet Arbuthnot, for whom he cherished an amitié amoureuse without offending her husband, a close and confidential friend; but both she and Wyatt were appalled by his clinging obstinately to one element of his own choice – yellow damask on the walls of the picture gallery; "I can't bear the yellow silk," she wrote in her journal of March 1830. It is no longer yellow, but the conventional red of Georgian and Victorian taste.

The following century, in 1947 – just short of the centenary of his great ancestor's death in 1852 – the 7th Duke of Wellington presented Apsley House and its wonderful contents to the nation as a museum and memorial to the man who defeated Napoleon and brought about his exile far from Europe.

Here in his house stood his enemy

Wellington's old enemy, Napoleon, a naked giant 3.45 metres tall, in white marble from Carrara, has some reasonable claim to be the finest Neo-classical sculpture in Britain. Commissioned by Napoleon in 1803 and to be of the same scale as the Farnese Hercules, a much admired giant of Roman antiquity, it was finished within three years, but remained in Canova's studio until 1810. When it reached Paris in January 1811 Napoleon disliked it enough to forbid its exhibition to the public – it lacked, he thought, his natural gravity – and it was hidden in the cellars of the Louvre until, in 1816, the British Government, with wry humour, bought it as a gift for Wellington. What can he, precisely half its height, have thought of it? Here in his new house stood his enemy, not the little Corsican far shorter than himself, not the odious ignoble upstart who might, without Wellington's opposition, have been Emperor of all Europe, but a colossus made noble and sublime, broad of shoulder, ideally muscular of trunk and long of limb, the great head pensive, pondering abstractions of honour, virtue and gravitas. Holding a winged figure of Victory in his right hand, he seems to stride purposefully from a plinth tilted to exaggerate the energetic movement, about to turn and climb the curving flight of stairs behind him. **>>**

Inset above: Wellington by Sir Thomas Lawrence

"No other sculpture in the museum is one whit as challenging"

As Wellington himself climbed them, increasingly weary with age, they came almost nose to nose, and then, looking down, he saw the Roman curls, the heroic shoulders, and in the parted buttocks, the realism characteristic of Canova, enlivening the ideal. No other sculpture in the museum is one whit as challenging.

Upstairs, among his paintings, Wellington had convincing reminders that he had trounced his enemy, for among them are four masterpieces by Velazquez, together with others by Jan Brueghel, Correggio, Elsheimer, Murillo, Ribera and Rubens, that were victor's spoil, captured at the Battle of Vitoria in June 1813. This was the battle that at last, five years into the horrors of the Peninsular War, drove the French from Spain and took the British army into France in pursuit of forces led by Joseph Bonaparte, Napoleon's brother and usurper King of Spain. Joseph seems to have expected defeat, for he had some 165 paintings from the Spanish Royal Collection in his baggage, those on canvas cut from their stretchers to cram them in. Wellington attempted to return them to the restored Ferdinand VII, but he refused them on the grounds that they were Wellington's just and honourable booty. As there are several small portraits of Wellington in contemplative mood with his possessions, it is not unreasonable to imagine him brooding over Velazquez's Waterseller, a subject no doubt familiar to a man who had fought so long in Portugal and Spain. Velasquez was twenty or so when he painted it in Seville, his birthplace; when he moved to Madrid and the circle of the royal court, he took it with him as a demonstration of his youthful and provincial skills, his command of wrinkled character and smooth-skinned boy, of the reality of white linen crumpled in the laundering, bright white from drying in the sun, of the heavy stuff of a worn cloak, and of still life. Few painters by that time had lavished such scrupulous affection on kitchen earthenware, describing in its detail not only glaze and texture, but its very turning on the potter's wheel. Drops of condensation follow the trail of a pale glaze slopped by the potter, the narrow neck is stopped by a cork with an iron ring, and as the peasant gives the boy his precious glass, his other hand, as weathered as his face, steadies the great jar that echoes his own form. The bargain was struck with quiet solemnity, the water precious to both man and boy, the intense realism of the old man's troubled brow and the downcast gaze of the boy speaking of the grave symbolic purpose of the narrative.

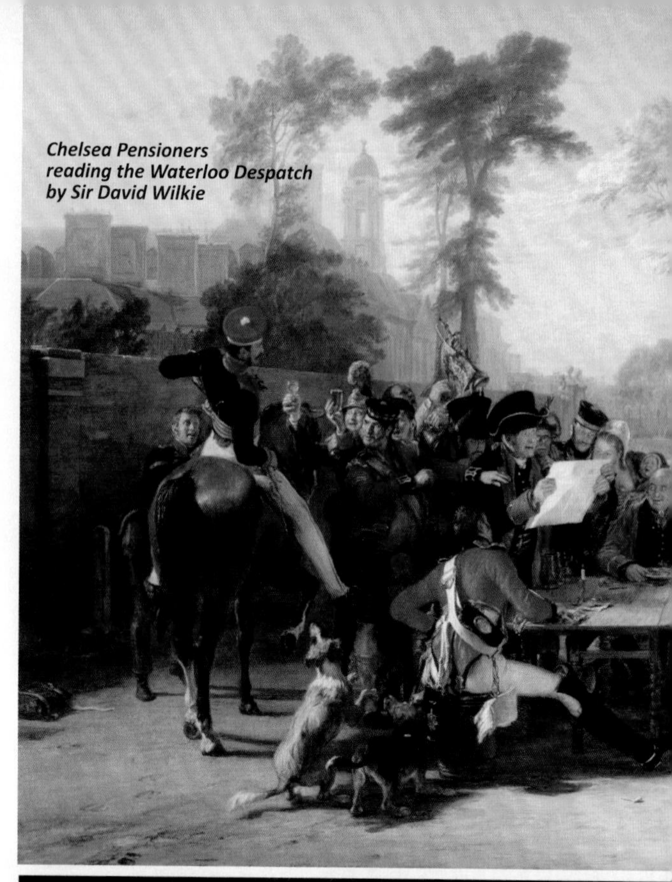

Chelsea Pensioners reading the Waterloo Despatch by Sir David Wilkie

The Waterseller by Velasquez

Two Men by Velasquez

Napoleon by Dabos

At a time when the restoration of oil paintings was an ill-informed and brutal process, this masterpiece and all the other booty paintings had not only been cut from their stretchers but deprived of their frames. Wellington seems, however, to have taken considerable care to employ responsible restorers and the Waterseller is, in spite of its vicissitudes, in good condition for its age. He also paid great attention to the replacement frames, finding and having enlarged, reduced or copied, frames that he thought both suitable for the paintings and coherent with his interior decoration. Most important, his booty pictures were not just trophies but the core of a much larger and more varied collection accumulated over subsequent decades, not only of old masters, principally 17th century Dutch, but of contemporary paintings, of which David Wilkie's Chelsea Pensioners reading the Waterloo Despatch, a commissioned work, is the most remarkable.

There can be no doubt that Wellington liked paintings for themselves and did not think of them as demonstrations of his taste and status, though there is no evidence of a scholarly bent in his collecting, nor was he ever, as Blake once put it, "connoisseured out of his senses." Whether, in his dotage, he could still see his pictures, crammed high and frame to frame, is another matter (he knew their order, but if interrupted in its recital, had always to return to the beginning); the present-day visitor, unused to such a hang in art galleries, may well not stoop to examine Elsheimer's Judith and Holofernes hanging low and shadowed, nor crane to see Velazquez's Two Young Men at a Table hanging high. This 19th century disposition gives us a sense of how things were almost two centuries ago, but it militates against the masterpiece – of which this collection contains many of great international status and inestimable worth.

The visitor to the Wellington Museum must work much harder than in most mansions open to the public, for it is set apart from these. It is essentially the house, not of a family, but of one great man, serving as his private retreat and his very public stage; it reflects and honours his achievements and is steeped in the politics and history of his day; with Canova's masterpiece it even honours his great enemy, Napoleon; and on its walls hang paintings worthy of the Prado and the Louvre, paintings that would wonderfully enrich the National Gallery. In this extraordinary combination of purposes and responsibilities it is unique.

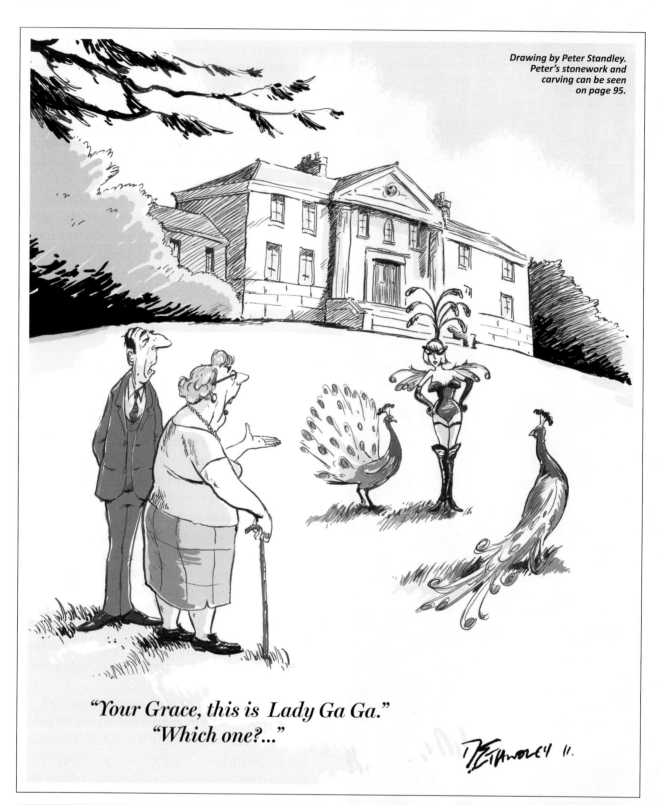

Drawing by Peter Standley. Peter's stonework and carving can be seen on page 95.

"Your Grace, this is Lady Ga Ga."
"Which one?..."

'my *favourite*'
by Jon Culverhouse

Collections Curator
Burghley House
www.burghley.co.uk

'One of my favourite pieces in the Collection at Burghley is a gorgeous gilt bronze-mounted George III commode made for the 9th Earl by Mayhew & Ince c.1770. I am particularly fond of it due to having discovered, many years ago in a dark and dirty store, its original leather case-cover. After a great deal of research to prove the link, the two were reunited.'

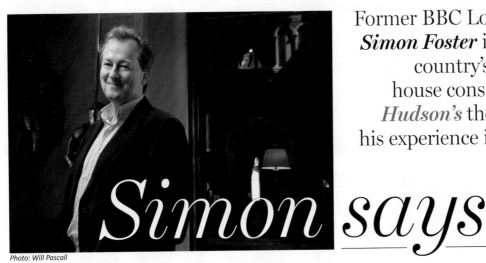

Photo: Will Pascall

Former BBC Location Manager, ***Simon Foster*** is now one of the country's leading historic house consultants. He gives ***Hudson's*** the benefit of his experience in the field.

Simon says

Ten years after the outbreak of Foot and Mouth disease and in addition to the devastating effect that the disease had on our farming industry, it is still seen as a turning point in the fortunes of the domestic tourism industry, particularly in the heritage sector. While historic houses across the length and breadth of the country remained closed in order to prevent the disease from spreading more widely, the general public found alternative leisure activities in the form of Sunday shopping at large out-of-town retail parks and garden centres.

Since then, heritage attractions have struggled to regain that market share and while some have been successful in building visitor numbers, many have seen a steady decline in footfall over the last ten years. There is no doubt that houses and gardens that have been successful in bucking the trend have been those that continue to take a degree of risk in terms of innovation and diversification.

It is widely acknowledged that it is no longer viable to open a historic house or garden and expect the attraction to survive on its own merits. Public expectations have evolved and customer service skills and facilities have become as important as the historic and aesthetic content of the attraction. However modest, adventure playgrounds, visitor reception and interpretation centres, cafés and restaurants, gift shops and good quality loos are now a necessity rather than a 'nice to have'.

Embracing diversity

Historic houses and gardens have also had to be creative by promoting events in their grounds to attract larger visitor numbers, particularly on bank holiday weekends and during the school holidays. Many heritage attractions have been successful in regaining market share among family visitors by offering not only child-friendly attractions and facilities, but also a competitively priced family ticket and a public events programme that appeals as much to children as it does to their parents. Blenheim Palace now boldly promotes a season ticket for the price of a single entry and by doing so has attracted a much larger and more diverse audience.

Heritage venues can provide a spectacular backdrop to large public park events such as country fairs, food festivals, classic car and caravan rallies, sporting events and outdoor concerts and festivals. Very often, the hosting of such events involves less risk and invasion of privacy for the landowner and the returns can be more lucrative (for the local area as well as the estate) than traditional day-visitor business. The Leeds Festival at Bramham, the V Festival at Weston Park, The Big Chill at Eastnor Castle, Sonisphere at Knebworth and Camp Bestival at Lulworth Castle are all examples of large successful music festivals in the grounds of historic houses.

Market forces

In tandem with efforts to re-bolster falling visitor numbers, the heritage sector has been highly successful in the weddings market and for many historic houses, income from weddings and receptions has become the backbone of the business. Whether owners allow hospitality inside the house or take the less risky option of providing a marquee on the lawn outside, this market has remained very strong through difficult times. Some historic house owners, however, are now responding to the challenging economic climate and offering more competitively priced alternative wedding venues, often in unusual tented structures and spaces, including woodlands and walled gardens.

Bamburgh Castle, Northumberland

Floors Castle, Scotland

Arley Hall, Cheshire

Friends of the HHA

Highclere Castle, Berkshire

Bodrhyddan, Wales

Chenies Manor House, Buckinghamshire

Heir-borne

Since the days of 17th century artists such as Kip and Knyff, aerial photography aristocrats ***Skyscan*** have revolutionised the way we look at Britain's heritage. Director, ***Brenda Marks***, comes down to earth and tells ***Hudson's*** what it's like looking down on the rest of us.

Skyscan first took off in 1984, when a custom-made, helium-filled, tethered balloon lifted a camera system above the ground to capture a series of low-level aerial photographs of Toddington Manor in the Cotswolds. The cameras were remotely controlled and the balloon-borne platform could lift them as high as 800 feet.

Our fascination with aerial views dates as far back as the 1700s, when Dutchmen Johannes Kip and Leonard Knyff used their draughtsmanship skills to produce highly-detailed engravings of country houses and estates, pictured from an overhead perspective. Working well before the Montgolfier brothers made their first balloon ascent in 1783, this represented a considerable feat of imagination. In pre-aircraft days, Victorian photographic pioneers Nadar and Spelterini also used balloon platforms to capture the landscape below, and in 1903 Julius Neubronner, an enterprising German amateur photographer, gave a literal meaning to 'birds-eye' views when he attached tiny cameras to pigeons in a successful experiment to trace their flights.

Such a birds-eye viewpoint shows both historic properties and archaeological sites to great advantage – buildings and gardens can be seen in much greater detail and the elevated angle allows the patterns of the landscape to stand out more clearly. **>>**

Toddington Manor taken in 1984 by Skyscan when owned by a private school. The house is now owned & being restored by the artist Damien Hirst to house his art collection

Inset: Engraving of Toddington Manor drawn by Leonard Knyff and engraved by Johannes Kip (1653-1722). Detail from Britannia Illustrata

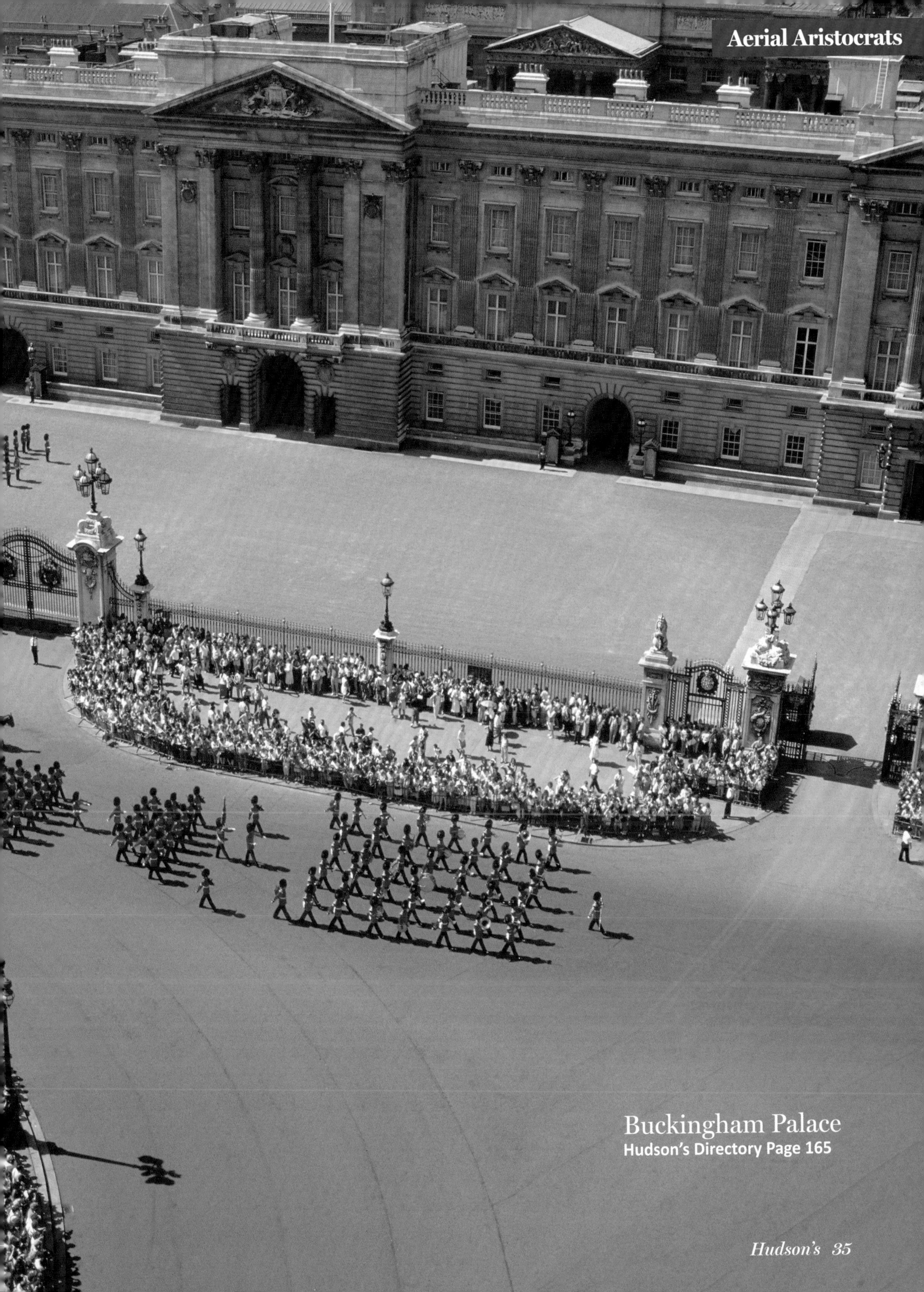

Buckingham Palace
Hudson's Directory Page 165

"Today's aerial photographers are fortunate to see the beauty below with their own eyes, and use modern technology and artistic skill to capture truly magic moments in which we can all share"

Kentwell Hall, Suffolk
Hudson's Directory Page 290

One of the first commissions undertaken by a youthful Skyscan was to photograph the lovely Tudor Rose Brick Maze then newly completed at Kentwell Hall in Suffolk; the intricate paths and patterns created a beautiful effect when captured by a camera hovering a hundred feet above.

In a career spanning over 25 years we have had many memorable moments. Work for a book on English Heritage properties found the Skyscan Land Rover (to which the balloon-borne camera platform is tethered) driving along a narrow stone pier at Tynemouth to photograph the Priory from the seaward side. Unfortunately this also meant a return journey reversing for 800 yards along a path only two feet wider than the vehicle and with a sheer drop to the sea on one side. On another occasion, our attempt to find that 'perfect' viewpoint at a remote Government establishment caused a similarly heart-stopping moment when a guard rushed up shouting, 'STOP immediately!' and demanded we reverse very carefully back along the same tracks. The Land Rover had just driven into a minefield!

One crisp winter day we made the difficult journey along snow-covered lanes to Stonehenge and were rewarded with a spectacular sunset which kept us on site far longer than we had anticipated. As the light died we found ourselves packing away equipment in total darkness in the middle of a deserted plain. An accident with a winch resulted in an emergency dash to Salisbury Hospital; the (minor) scars remain... but so does the beauty of those snowy, sunset photographs.

"Intricate paths and patterns create a beautiful effect when captured by a camera"

We have been fortunate to work at many beautiful locations. One project involved photographing over 80 historic estates from all over the UK for the book **>>**

Lochleven Castle, Perthshire
Owned and managed by HISTORIC SCOTAND, Lochleven Castle is reached by ferry from Kinross off the M90 and is open from April to September.

Uffington Cast
– White Hors
& Dragon Hil
Oxfordshir

Owned and managed b ENGLISH HERITAG The Uffington Castle White Horse & Drag Hill site is east Swindon accessible fro the M4 and is open a year 'any reasonab time in daylight hour

Tewkesbury Abbey, Gloucestershire

JULY 2007: The rivers of the Thames and Avon burst their banks causing widespread flooding to places such as Tewkesbury: the town's 12th century parish church, known as Tewkesbury Abbey, barely escapes inundation. The area around the church is protected from development by the Abbey Lawn Trust, originally funded by a benefactor from the United States.

Historic Family Homes and Gardens from the Air published by Hudson's. As well as the balloon camera, our photographers worked from aircraft and the result is a stunning book on sale in many of the estates. Technology continues to advance and in the last few years a new aerial platform has come to prominence. The camera is mounted upon a free-flying Unmanned Aerial Vehicle (UAV) fitted with a state-of-the-art global positioning system and remotely controlled by a radio link. Other systems use goggles worn by the photographer, which capture the scene in still pictures or in video and have produced some spectacular movie footage where the viewer feels they really are flying with the birds. Centuries ago Johannes Kip 'saw' these birds-eye views in his imagination and produced wonderfully detailed drawings of historic houses for us all to enjoy. Today's aerial photographers are fortunate to see the beauty below with their own eyes, and use modern technology and artistic skill to capture truly magic moments in which we can all share.

Deal Castle, Kent

Hudson's Directory Page 196

Chatsworth, Derbyshire

Hudson's Directory Page 297

*"It's often the **harshest conditions** that produce the **best pictures**. Our pilots and photographers are passionate about what they do and the subjects they portray: we like to think the results are clear to see"*
BRENDA MARKS, SKYSCAN DIRECTOR

Stonehenge, Wiltshire
Hudson's Directory Page 267

Skyscan's photographers use a variety of aerial platforms and work all over the world. Commissions are undertaken and they have a large stock photolibrary for use in books, magazines and marketing related publications. They are expert in the search and supply of historic air photos for evidence in property and legal investigations.

Further details can be found on their website: www.Skyscan.co.uk

The Unmanned Aerial Vehicle or 'Droidworx' in flight

Warwick Castle, Warwickshire

Hudson's Directory Page 332

Left: Broadcasting House completed in 1932, and (inset), 1933: the artist Eric Gill putting the finishing touches to the statue of Ariel, which gave rise to such controversy...

"Hello, good evening and welcome"

Robert Seatter is Head of BBC History, collaborating with programme makers, museums, cultural and educational partners, to bring the story of the BBC to life. Here he gives ***Hudson's*** a privileged insider's view of the historic buildings of the BBC and one or two new ones...

Right: Robert Seatter has worked for the BBC for 20 years, following careers in teaching, acting, publishing and journalism

BBC buildings form a unique part of our national psyche. They capture the disembodied voices we have heard for years on our radios, and contain the dreams and dramas of the TV screens that fill our everyday houses. In some strange way, we feel we know – own! – Broadcasting House in the centre of London or Television Centre tucked under the concrete Westway... But what are they really like? Let's take a look inside. **>>**

Top row: Television Centre under construction; the 'Doughnut'; Tom Baker and the Daleks. Bottom row: Designer, Graham Dawbarn's sketch for TV Centre; Fawlty Towers; Monty Python's Flying Circus; Top of The Pops and Television Centre. All photographs © BBC

Art Deco Splendour

Located at the top of elegant Regent Street, and a stone's throw from the shoppers' paradise of Oxford Street, is the Art Deco jewel of Broadcasting House. Designed by G Val Myer and built in 1932, Broadcasting House was the BBC's first purpose-built home for radio broadcasting in the UK.

Val Myer took his inspiration for the building from the skyscrapers of America. Initially he called it the 'top hat design', and with its accentuated front section bearing a clock tower and aerial mast, the building has often been compared to an ocean liner. It made an enormous impact when it opened, and the Architectural Review of 1932 described it as the 'new Tower of London'.

Artistic commissions adorn the building, as architects and artists of the day struggled to find a metaphor for the new magic of broadcasting. The most famous of these is Eric Gill's statue of Prospero and Ariel (from Shakespeare's last play, *The Tempest*; Ariel as the spirit of the air was felt to be an appropriate personification of the spirit of broadcasting) – you can see it just above the front entrance. The naked Ariel provoked outraged comments about the size of his genitalia. There were even questions in the House of Commons on 'the offence to public morals'. It is said Gill was ordered to adjust Ariel's dimensions to more decent proportions by the BBC's first Director-General, John Reith, a man of stern Scottish principle!

Out of this building came numerous broadcast 'firsts', as radio became the new passion and pastime of the 1930s, 40s and 50s, whether it were news, comedy, drama, music, children's or educational programmes. Many of these radio programmes have been running continuously for decades – take *Desert Island Discs*, rapidly approaching its 70th anniversary, or *Woman's Hour*, past its 60th.

The building is now being reinvented, with cutting-edge digital radio facilities and a magnificent new extension to house all of the BBC News teams. This will be completed in 2013, but you can visit the building now – to see the radio studios where your favourite programmes are made as well as the large performance theatre where comedy shows are recorded nearly every night.

The first purpose-built TV building

To the west of London is the other iconic BBC building, Television Centre, seen on our TV screens for over 50 years. Designed by Graham Dawbarn and built in 1960, this was the world's first purpose-built centre for television production. It has a highly distinctive shape (affectionately known in-house as the 'doughnut'), and the story of its creation is a beguiling one…

When Dawbarn first looked at the site, he was stuck for ideas and went to a local pub. He sat down, pulled out an old envelope then drew a question mark in the middle. How could he design a centre with eight studios, production galleries, dressing rooms, camera workshops, recording areas and offices to support them? It needed also to allow trucks onto the site with the sets, and areas for audiences and guests that were separate from the trucks. He looked at the question mark and in a flash of inspiration realised that it would make the perfect design!

The roll call of notable TV programmes that have been recorded here is never-ending. It includes legendary comedy shows, such as *Fawlty Towers* (voted the top TV programme ever in a recent BFI poll), *Morecambe & Wise*, *Monty Python's Flying Circus*, *Absolutely Fabulous*, *Only Fools and Horses*, *Blackadder*, *Little Britain* and *The Catherine Tate Show*. *Doctor Who* also landed his Tardis here, music fans gyrated to *Top of the Pops* for decades, and every major news story from the late 1960s onwards was co-ordinated via the newsroom at the heart of this busy building. In addition, the centre features the famous Blue Peter garden – loved by generations of child viewers, and many of *Blue Peter*'s famous pets are commemorated in the garden.

Top row: Blue Peter's Konnie Huq; Morecambe & Wise. Bottom row: Blackadder; Only Fools and Horses; The Catherine Tate Show

You can visit the building now, on one of its award-winning tours, where you get to see the studios in action and the stars' dressing rooms, plus a look into the world-famous newsroom and an exploration of the secrets of the weather presenter!

Like Broadcasting House, Television Centre also has its fair share of artistic commissions – at the centre of the 'doughnut' is the lofty statue of the sun god 'Helios' by T.B Huxley Jones, created to evoke the power of television, with its two further statues at the base of the sculpture symbolising 'sound' and 'vision'. When the building first opened, there used to be a fountain at this base. It was a limited success, however, as the sound of tinkling water made all the employees run to the loo, so it was quickly turned off!

New BBC Buildings

Broadcasting House and Television Centre are the two historical broadcast centres, which have a long-held fascination for listeners and viewers. But we are now building the broadcast centres of the future – just a few years ago, we opened BBC Scotland's brand new centre on the banks of the Clyde at Pacific Quay, Glasgow. Designed by leading architect David Chipperfield, it was the first ever digital broadcast centre in the UK. And in 2011, Media City in Salford Quays opened its doors – a new home to BBC Sport, Children's and Learning output. This is now the BBC's second biggest broadcast centre, and a clear expression of the BBC's ambition to reflect and enrich the whole of the UK. Come and visit!

To find out more about the history of the BBC – how radio and TV began, a timeline of broadcast innovations, its buildings and artworks, simply log on to ***bbc.co.uk/historyofthebbc***

There are many BBC buildings you can visit around the UK: to book a tour or see a BBC show, visit: ***bbc.co.uk/showsandtours***

Media City, Salford Quays – Photo: Peel Media

BBC BUILDINGS

- Built in 1932, Broadcasting House was the UK's first purpose-built broadcast centre. It is now Grade II* listed.
- Broadcasting House survived two major bomb attacks during WWII; the most serious of these was in October 1940 when the famously unflappable Bruce Belfrage continued to read the news as the ceiling collapsed above him.
- The new Broadcasting House will have an audience of 285 million worldwide.
- Television Centre was the world's first purpose-built TV building. It also housed the largest studio.
- It also features the famous Blue Peter garden, sadly vandalised on not one, but two occasions.
- Countless famous TV programmes have come from Television Centre, as well as record-breaking events: TV stars tapped their way around it, setting a new world record for the largest mass tap dance in history (*All Star Record Breakers*, 1977).
- Many BBC buildings had strange beginnings; Maida Vale, home of the BBC Symphony Orchestra, began its life as a roller skating rink!
- The BBC does not own all its buildings: Bush House, the iconic home of the World Service, actually belongs to a Japanese bank.

The fascinating history of Television Centre is told in this lavishly illustrated book written by Robert Seatter, and published by Hudsons Heritage Group. Available from the BBC

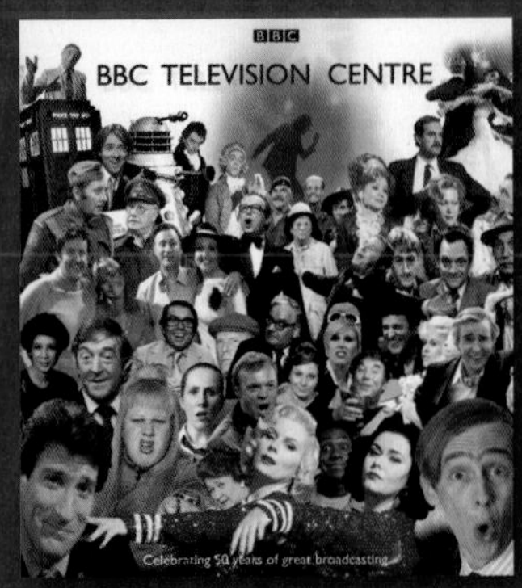
BBC
BBC TELEVISION CENTRE

Birds OF PRAY

Peregrine falcons were once to be seen only on remote sea cliffs, windswept estuaries in winter, or high up on moors and mountains. They now nest on many cathedrals and historic buildings.

Photographs: *Nick McCann*

THEY STOOP TO CONQUER – speeds of well over 200 mph have been recorded

MARK WARD, EDITOR, BIRDS MAGAZINE

RSPB

'Visitors to our historic buildings can now enjoy an added bonus: the chance to catch a glimpse of the fastest bird in the world, the peregrine. These high-speed hunters – they can 'stoop' at well over 200 mph – traditionally nested on cliffs, but they have returned to set up homes on a variety of high-rise, man-made accommodation in recent years. The RSPB's 'Date with Nature' events show peregrines to thousands of visitors every year at a variety of sites around the UK, including Chichester Cathedral and the Tate Modern. The RSPB has cameras, telescopes and viewing platforms at historic/iconic sites such as Lincoln Cathedral, Cardiff City Hall Clock Tower, Chichester Cathedral and Tate Modern.'

"There's now hardly an English county without a pair nesting on an artificial structure"

NICK BROWN, DERBY PEREGRINE PROJECT

'A pair of wild peregrine falcons arrived at Derby Cathedral around 2004/5, finding the tall tower to their liking. Derbyshire Wildlife Trust linked up with Derby Museum to fix a nest platform to the tower in 2006, as there was no suitable place the birds could nest. Within three weeks the female had laid her first clutch of eggs on the platform and she has reared broods every year since. In 2007, web cameras were set up and so far we have logged two million hits from over 70 countries. The birds have featured extensively on TV, and bird watchers and peregrine fans have been coming to Derby to visit the cathedral and its famous falcons ever since.'

To see the web cams and read the project blog, visit www.derby.gov.uk/peregrines

Work in progress

Lowther Castle, the derelict former home of the Lowther family, the Earls of Lonsdale, is set to become one of the UK's top visitor attractions. An £8.9 million re-development grant means the Cumbrian ruin, its massive stables and 130 acres will re-awaken from 70 years of abandonment. ***Jane Pruden*** talks to Andrew Mercer of the Lowther Castle and Gardens Trust.

This is big. Think 'Lost Gardens of Heligan' and the Eden Project. Imagine swathes of a huge, overgrown historic garden exploding with new and ordered life – year after year – under the castle's windowless gaze. It is a compelling renaissance. Visitors began arriving at the site near Penrith in Cumbria, in April 2011 to witness the start of one of the largest house and garden conservation programmes in Britain.

The ruined neo-Gothic castle, designed by Robert Smirke and completed in 1816 for the 1st Earl of Lonsdale, will be stabilised and enhanced, immortalising its romantic qualities and creating a dramatic focal point for the garden. It is expected to take a year to complete along with the adjacent two-storey stable block currently being converted into a visitor centre with shop and restaurant. Only the East Sculpture Gallery, the sole survivor of the building left with a roof, will profit from full restoration; its rare painted ceiling, by Francis Bernasconi, topping the bill of the Lowther Art Collection of silver and paintings.

The many layers of the garden's 400-year history, culminating with elaborate Edwardian additions, will resurface over several phases. 'By 2014 we should have all the infra-structure in place: the footpaths and roads plus 12 acres of lawns, four to five acres of borders and flowerbeds and some of the formal gardens,' explains, Andrew Mercer.

Dating back to the 17th century it was Viscount Lonsdale, inspired by the gardens at Versailles, who created his resplendent 130-acre garden (for an earlier house). It was riddled with walks, parterres and enormous flower borders; embellished with follies and temples. Its haunting imprint still inspires today. Landscape architect, Dominic Cole, who was instrumental in the Eden Project and was garden designer at Heligan, enthuses: 'Lowther has a quality of light and magnificence of setting that puts it into a league of its own.'

At the turn of the last century, the status of this enormously rich estate seemed secure for eternity, so what went wrong? Go back three generations to the notoriously flamboyant 5th Earl of Lonsdale, aka the 'Yellow Earl'. Here was an eccentric but popular man who simply shied from the responsibilities of securing Lowther's future in favour of having a good time.

As the second son his accountability was minimal and a hedonistic youth, albeit on a relatively tight allowance, was tolerated. Then, in 1882 his elder brother, the 4th Earl, died unexpectedly and he inherited the family's fortune, aged 25. He transcended, overnight, from poor relation to jackpot winner and he never stopped celebrating. Amongst his many joys, he loved yellow: his servants were dressed in yellow livery; his fleet of motorcars was yellow; he was a founder of the AA – hence the yellow logo; he had yellow dogs, and cream gardenias in his buttonhole. He loved football, hunting and racing and he instigated the Lonsdale Belt for boxing. He loved building, ornamenting Smirke's masterpiece for lavish entertainment and royal visits that included several from the Kaiser. He built new gate lodges, a five-mile long new drive, flattened 20 farms to expand the estate, remodelled the stables for an extra 50 horses and refaced the columns inside the castle with stone.

Then came the bombshell. It's New Year's Day, 1936 and news arrived. Due to his interminable spending, the catastrophic effects of the Depression and the ensuing fall in his annual income from £180,000 to £6,000, he was informed that he was, essentially, broke. Without further ado, his yellow Daimler pulled up at the porte-cochère and the 79-year-old 'Yellow Earl' and his wife, Gracie, were driven away. They never returned. Three years after his death, in 1947, the contents and architectural fittings were auctioned in the largest country house sale of the 20th century. At a time when many large country houses were bulldozed or opened to the public, his nephew, the 7th Earl, fighting crippling debts and unprecedented demands from the taxman, favoured demolition but was persuaded by the locals to keep the shell.

The ephemeral nature of a garden however, accelerates erosion. Strangled with overgrowth and reduced to a skeletal framework, only scant memories and photographs could flesh out the imagination. 'Much of what was left including the Japanese Garden, a Scented Garden and an Iris Garden, was trampled by the army in the Second World War to test a secret tank weapon. It was overplanted with forestry in the 50s and a vast chicken farm was built on the once immaculate lawns as part of a plan to restore the family's finances.'

"With an amazing team of people, all sharing the same vision, we now have the resources to begin what will be a long and exciting journey."

LORD MELVYN BRAGG
LOWTHER TRUST PATRON

But for the last five years, while the weeds and decay furthered their tenancy, extensive plans were developing to put Lowther back on the map. Finally, as a registered charity, the trustees were able to secure an £8.9m grant from the Northwest Development Agency and the European Regional Development Fund. Cumbrian-born, Lord Melvyn Bragg, the trust's Patron, agrees with Andrew, 'We believe Lowther can play its part in the economic and tourism development of Cumbria. With an amazing team of people, all sharing the same vision, we now have the resources to begin what will be a long and exciting journey.'

This is an ecological and heritage tourist attraction that will offer different appeal to different visitors as it grows over the forthcoming years. For now it is a rare opportunity to witness the expertise of craftsmen and women working on any number of building and gardening conservation projects. By 2013 the first phase will be complete, returning life to the Lowther family home once lost, but not forgotten.

Soane Ranger

Born in 1753, the youngest son of a bricklayer, Sir John Soane (central bust in photo), became one of England's greatest architects and collectors. On his death in 1837 his house, established as a museum, was left to the nation by an Act of Parliament, Soane stipulating that it be kept 'as nearly as possible in the state in which he shall leave it'.

Tim Knox (left), Director of London's hugely successful Soane Museum, talks to polymath and heritage enthusiast, *Geoffrey Bond* (right), about the challenges of running a fragile and precious central London museum. Together they discuss the progress of the major project, 'OPENING UP THE SOANE', a £7 million initiative to 'restore, refurbish and improve' the museum to ensure the future of this living monument to the extraordinary man who created it. Pictures by *Nigel Gibson* & *Linda Croose-Smith*.

Soane's prized statue of the 'Diana of Ephesus' – a much restored ancient Roman marble – in The Colonnade

Geoffrey Bond: How do you run the building commercially?

Tim Knox: The museum has to be free – Sir John Soane's Act of Parliament and will, both specify that – so we don't directly benefit no matter how many visitors we attract. What we can do though is improve what we sell in the shop and encourage people to make donations. Experience shows the most generous donors tend to be visitors from abroad. There are other ways we can help ourselves too, for example hiring the museum out for occasional dinners. They're limited to a maximum of 30 people and are quite 'high end', with prices starting at £5,000. Guests get to enjoy an incredible setting, and dine by candelight.

GB: You needed to raise £7m to fund your new project. How has that gone?

TK: We raised nearly all of it over a two year period and as of summer 2011, we were just short by £300,000. When you bear in mind the economic climate, that's quite an achievement. Credit must go to a number of extremely generous private donors and grant-making trusts. Plus I must thank all the smaller donors – the pennies all add up.

GB: If Sir John Soane returned today, would he recognise his house?

TK: Absolutely. He said that, as far as practicable, the house should be kept as it was in his lifetime. All the lower floors are exactly as Soane had them. What we're working towards in the second phase of our big project, is to reinstate exactly Soane's arrangements in the rest of the museum. Just a few months ago, we put the picture room back exactly to how it would have been in January 1837, the month he died. Very few collections can do that – usually the odd painting has been sold over the years – so it's an incredible opportunity. The hanging arrangements can seem slightly bizarre - for example, arguably the museum's most famous treasure, Hogarth's *A Rake's Progress*, is hung inside a great cupboard-like arrangement and the doors are only opened on request. It tells you more about Soane than if we had tried to rearrange things and hang the most famous pictures in a more easily accessible way.

GB: I understand you are working to make the entrance to the museum more visitor friendly?

TK: We're very keen to see that happen. The entrance to the museum is a bit of a problem – everyone has to enter through Soane's front door and narrow entrance hall. The plan is to take the cloakroom and visitor 'welcome' side of our operations out of the hall and put them next door in No 12. Visitors can then come into the museum and see the entrance hall as it was meant to be - as if they're visiting the house of an architect and gentleman collector of the early 19th century.

GB: Tell me about the genesis of the house...

TK: Soane originally lived next door. At that time most of his collections were housed in his country house, Pitzhanger Manor in Ealing. When he discovered that neither of his two sons had any ambitions to become an architect he gave up the manor and everything – the Hogarths, the Canalettos, Roman altars, Greek vases - all came tumbling back into the next-door house. Not surprisingly, there wasn't enough room. Soane initially persuaded his neighbours to give up their back garden so he could build a double-height dome area to display his artefacts and two years later, in 1812, he badgered them into moving as tenants into his house. He took control of their house, rebuilt it – and that's the Soane Museum you see today. It's an incredible architectural laboratory of his ideas. One rather charming little aside in the Soane story is Mrs Soane's dog – a small black and tan Manchester terrier called Fanny. She lived here for 17 years – far outliving Mrs Soane, who died after a couple of years' residence. Fanny became Soane's constant companion and when she died, he erected a mighty tomb for her remains, inscribed 'Alas, poor Fanny'. We still have the vets' bills in the archive. The real story here though (apart from remembering Soane as a great architect and considerable collector) is one of terrible family tragedy. He had two sons, John and George, and really wanted them to follow him into his profession – he dreamed of founding a dynasty to rival the Adams or Wyatts. Neither son was interested – instead they fell into bad habits and got into debt. George, the youngest, was particularly irksome. In 1815 he was arrested for debt and fraud and thrown into prison. Soane had helped him out many times before but refused this time. In response, George wrote a series of spiteful anonymous articles condemning his father, his works and his collection – for Soane it was devastating. Mrs Soane was ill at the time and on seeing the articles, she said George had dealt her death blow. She died weeks later. Soane never forgave George.

GB: Who owns the museum today... Who are the trustees?

TK: There are 13 trustees, as directed in Soane's will. These include representative trustees, one of which – Alderman Alison Gowman – is appointed by the Court of Aldermen of the City of London. The Royal Society of Arts, Royal Academy, the Royal Society and Society of Antiquities of London are also represented – all institutions Soane had admired and deemed worthy. Our Chairman is Simon Jervis, former Director of the Fitzwilliam Museum in Cambridge and my old boss at the National Trust. After Soane's death, there was a real danger the museum would be claimed by his son George and grandson Frederick. There were also determined attempts to overturn Soane's Act of Parliament and distribute the treasures to other institutions such as the British Museum. From the 1930s onwards, however, people began to realise what an amazing survival the museum was. Real success has come only comparatively recently. The museum reopened in 1947 after WWII and it was recognised that a Government grant was needed – it gives us just enough to pay for light, heat and staff salaries.

GB: What's a typical working day for you?

TK: There's no such thing really. It starts quite early and I often bring my dogs in – they spend their day in the office. Running the museum is quite a challenge, >>

DIRECTOR'S NOTES

A stained glass lantern. Soane loved coloured glass, including a fine collection of historic painted panels.

Plans to restore Soane's Model Room include the reinstatement of his celebrated model stand, bristling with architectural models.

Soane's Bedroom, another interior being reinstated by the current restoration project.

The Orgy, from William Hogarth's famous series *A Rake's Progress*, which hangs in the Picture Room.

The ancient Egyptian Sarcophagus of Seti I which reposes in the Crypt of the Museum.

Fanny, Mrs Soane's pet dog, by James Ward.

Additional pictures by courtesy of the Trustees of Sir John Soane's Museum

but a wonderful opportunity. Fundraising is a major focus for us here, and maintaining the museum and ensuring that the presentation of the house is up to scratch. We don't have labels and 'keep off' signs, and we keep the museum as dark and atmospheric as possible – although visitors can download a free podcast tour from our website (www.soane.org) to guide them around. People love exploring for themselves - I think they find it quite refreshing. We also have a busy research library.

GB: What are your plans for the future?
TK: Our current project 'Opening up the Soane' is due to be completed in 2014 and we're currently working on our plans beyond that. There are a number of historic reinstatements we want to do, plus general maintenance – the pine floorboards, for example, were never made to be walked on by 100,000 visitors. We're also planning to do much more via the website, including an online virtual tour, giving a genuine sense of the museum and its wonderful collections. The shop will also move to the house next door and we're planning a unique range of merchandise you can only get at the Soane, such as architectural models, replicas, and limited editions. The museum has 35 staff, including 18 warders (attendants) who are all paid, not volunteers. They are very well trained and informed and are extraordinary in their devotion and level of knowledge. They help to give the museum its hugely distinctive character.

GB: I've been interested in heritage all my life – you could say I'm a heritage enthusiast. Am I right to say that the Soane is probably one of the most idiosyncratic museums in the country?
TK: I would say so. It's unique in being the house of a great architect and collector, kept almost exactly as he had it. Soane acquired some truly remarkable things – masterpieces to grace any major museum – and they are displayed in a very idiosyncratic setting. It's a combination of order and wonderful disorder.

FOR VISITOR INFORMATION ON SIR JOHN SOANE'S MUSEUM TURN TO PAGE 169

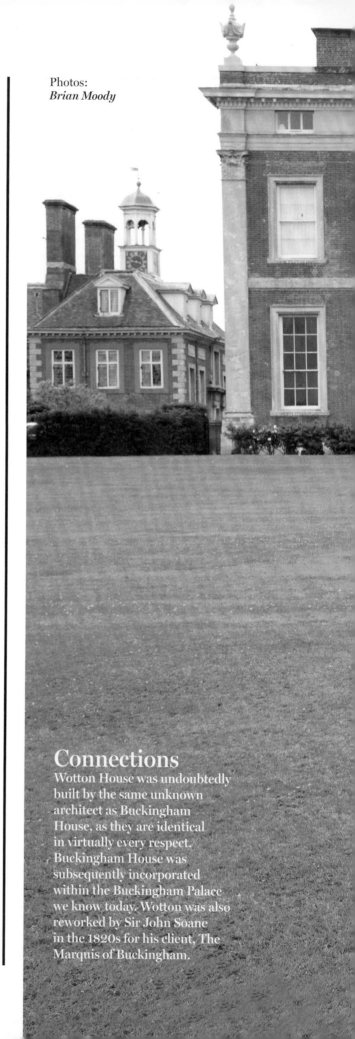

Photos:
Brian Moody

Connections

Wotton House was undoubtedly built by the same unknown architect as Buckingham House, as they are identical in virtually every respect. Buckingham House was subsequently incorporated within the Buckingham Palace we know today. Wotton was also reworked by Sir John Soane in the 1820s for his client, The Marquis of Buckingham.

House party

Writer, broadcaster and railway devotee, ***Michael Portillo***, let the train take the strain and took ***Hudson's*** on a journey of discovery to one of his favourite places; the little known gem of Wotton House in Buckinghamshire. Here he describes how, despite the British summer weather, it was a day to remember.

The great joy of Marylebone Station is the feeling of railway nostalgia it generates the moment you set foot in the place. The main ticket hall – one of the smallest in London – is beautifully preserved, and the entire station is covered with a glass roof, only recently restored to its full glory. The glass panels have been replaced, allowing light to pour into the station, and the supporting pillars have been painted a vibrant and uplifting red. The whole effect is magnificent.

I board the 08.27 Chiltern Railways service to Aylesbury Vale Parkway – a journey which takes me through familiar terrain, including Harrow-on-the-Hill, where I went to school, and Chorleywood, where my mother now lives. Arriving at my destination at 09.40, I am met by David Gladstone, the very charming owner – with his wife, April – of Wotton House. A retired diplomat, David is a direct descendant of the four-times Victorian Prime Minister, William Gladstone, and has kindly offered to drive me for the last few miles of my journey to his historic home in the village of Wotton Underwood.

My wife and I first discovered Wotton House in the late 1980s, when we were living in the village of Wingrave, between Aylesbury and Leighton Buzzard. The house is hidden as you approach, then you round the final bend in the drive and there it stands – so perfectly architecturally balanced and unspoilt by any other development, it takes your breath away.

We had been equally impressed by the very charming owner of the house, Elaine Brunner – a former actress and David Gladstone's mother-in-law – who gave us an unforgettable guided tour. So when almost 10 years later, the BBC contacted me to ask if I would contribute to a programme called *One Foot in the Past*,

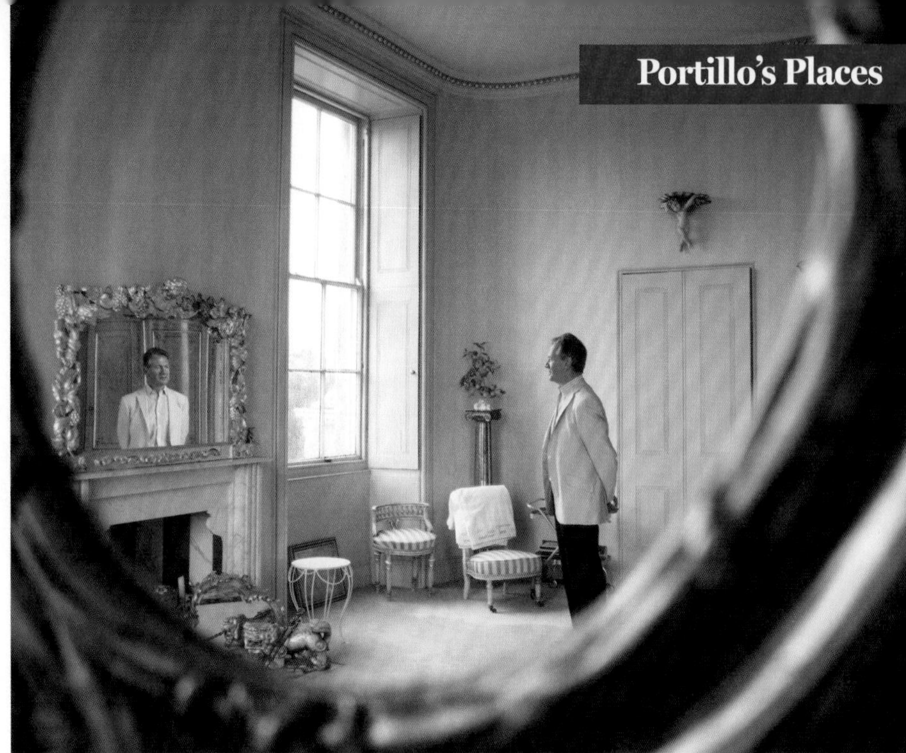

I immediately thought of Wotton. What they were after was a 10-minute film about a folly or an unusual house; what could be better than this beautiful historic property, reworked by the renowned architect, Sir John Soane (see previous feature), and now home to such a marvellous character?

Elaine and her husband, Patrick, had bought the house in the late 1950s, saving it from destruction literally days before it was due to meet the wrecker's ball. She told the story many times over the years – with ever-increasing embellishments, it has to be said!

However – as David and April tell me over a delightful lunch prepared in their small private kitchen – the basic facts are these.

In the late 1950s, country houses were disappearing at a rate of one a week or more. The county council was under great pressure to demolish Wotton and it was well-documented in the local newspapers of the time that many people felt it was time for it to go, making way for a much-needed new housing estate. Luckily, the council had insisted on hanging on until the last possible moment in the hope that someone would step in to rescue it.

Enter Elaine Brunner! In April 1957, the Brunners were living in a cottage near Beaconsfield and Elaine was taken to Wotton by a local antique dealer, who was keen for her to see it before it was demolished in just two weeks' time. Standing in front of the gates, she immediately knew she had to save it. **>>**

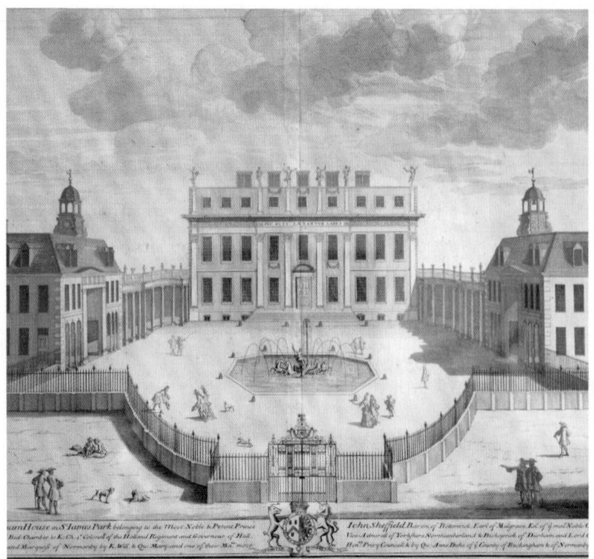

Buckingham House, identical in every respect to Wotton

Society actress, Elaine Brunner

As a former actress and society figure, Elaine knew many influential people – among them, Robin Feddon, then head of the National Trust. It was on his recommendation that the Brunners, having bought Wotton House at a price of £6,000, hired Donald Insall, a young conservation architect who was rapidly earning a very good reputation. Insall submitted a grant bid to the newly created Historic Buildings Council, and Wotton was awarded £40,000 – a figure calculated to be approximately 50 per cent of the cost of restoration.

The Brunners' instructions to Insall were to reinstate the interiors created by the architect, John Soane, in the 1820s. The original Wotton house had been built at the beginning of the 18th century and was almost identical in design to Buckingham House in London (above) – now integrated into Buckingham Palace. Tragically, in October 1820, the main house was gutted by a great fire, and all that survived intact were the two pavilions, linked to the house by low screen walls.

In the rebuild that followed, the external appearance of Wotton remained the same – although Soane did persuade his reluctant client, the Marquis of Buckingham, to let him reduce the overall height by eight to 10 feet. Soane claimed the fire had weakened the top storey irreparably, but this may just have been a convenient excuse for giving the William and Mary-style residence more 'modern' Georgian proportions.

Internally, Soane was given a relatively free hand, and thanks to Insall's 1950s restoration, we can still see the results today: a glorious sequence of interrelating spaces, including a central hall with the Saloon, main staircase and spine corridor opening off it – all cleverly designed as an Italian street scene.

The Saloon (which now serves as a concert hall) is one of three grand, interlinking rooms on the ground floor. Impressive double doors lead into the Eating Room at the north end and the Drawing Room to the south, giving a straight, uninterrupted view from one end of the house to the other. The hand of John Soane can be seen throughout, with a characteristic Greek key pattern on the Eating Room ceiling and a string of gilded beads in the corner – more of which have recently been discovered at the top of the house as a result of restoration work on the central Dome.

Donald Insall's initial restoration of Soane's interiors took four years in total – but to Elaine Brunner, Wotton was a lifelong project. Having saved the house from certain doom, all her time, energy – and much of her money – went into preserving it for future generations to enjoy. It is thanks to her passion and determination that the Wotton House we see today is almost exactly the way Soane left it. And with David and April Gladstone continuing to show the same dedication and commitment to conserving Elaine's legacy, Wotton couldn't be in safer hands.

FOR VISITOR INFORMATION ON WOTTON HOUSE TURN TO PAGE 175

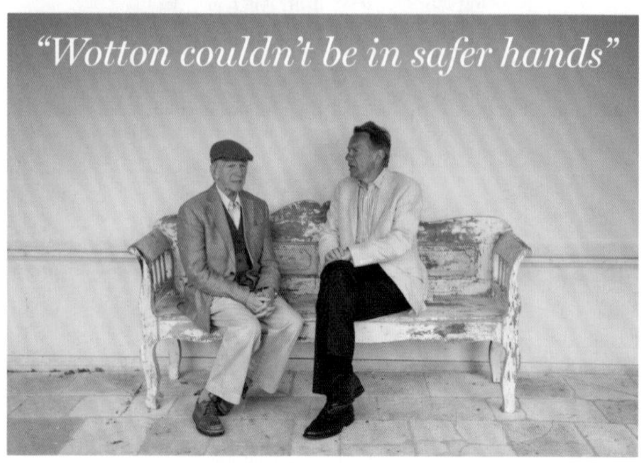
"Wotton couldn't be in safer hands"

Branching out

As the subject of my *One Foot in the Past* film for the BBC, Wotton formed the backdrop to my first-ever attempt to record a piece to camera. I must have had to do about five takes. Then suddenly, everything clicked into place and – in a classic *My Fair Lady* moment – I'd got it!

My TV career since has encompassed many different programmes, and I love the variety. The *Great Railway Journeys* series is going from strength to strength. Each one takes two days to film, in two-day stints. I have a great time: it's a topic I find incredibly interesting, and I love travelling by train and meeting members of the public – all sorts of unexpected things happen.

Great Railway Journeys came about through a senior executive at the production company, Talkback Thames, called Camilla Lewis, whose brother-in-law is an antiquarian bookseller. One day he turned up with a Bradshaws handbook from 1865, and she thought 'There's a series in that.' I'd already made a one-off railway programme for BBC2 – travelling through Spain and talking about my father's experiences during the Spanish Civil War – so they offered me the job!

Star quality

Elaine Brunner isn't the only thespian to have lived at Wotton House. The legendary actor, Sir John Gielgud, and his partner, Martin Hensler, owned the South Pavilion for many years, with Sir John famously keeping his Oscar (awarded in 1981 for his role as Dudley Moore's butler in *Arthur*) on the bathroom windowsill.

Gielgud died at South Pavilion, passing away peacefully in his drawing room armchair on 21 May 2000, at the age of 96. At his memorial service, held locally in Buckinghamshire, Sir Alec Guinness, Sir John Mills, Dame Maggie Smith and Lord Richard Attenborough were among those paying their respects.

Today, South Pavilion is again home to some high-profile residents, this time of the political persuasion, having been bought by former Prime Minister Tony Blair and his wife Cherie in 2008.

HUDSON'S
HERITAGE
Hudsonsheritage.com is now even better with the addition of many exciting new features...
• Fully searchable property listings featuring over 1,500 UK heritage properties open to the public
• Each property has its own page featuring beautiful images, opening times and specific news and events diary for every featured property
• Add your reviews of UK heritage attractions
• Share your favourites via Facebook and Twitter
• Ever-growing directory of local amenities to help you plan your days out
• Improved online bookstore, including downloadable e-book versions of our most popular titles
• Book and buy tickets online for heritage houses and UK events
• hudsonsheritage.com gets mobile with new iPhone and iPad apps
• All-new national heritage news section featuring audio and video
• Monthly newsletter including special offers for Hudson's members
Visit the all-new Hudsonsheritage.com today!

ENJOY GREAT DAYS OUT WITH HUDSON'S

USE THESE EXCLUSIVE HUDSON'S READER OFFER VOUCHERS TO CLAIM SPECIAL OFFERS AND DISCOUNTS AT A HOST OF BEAUTIFUL HERITAGE PROPERTIES AND ATTRACTIONS THROUGHOUT THE UK.

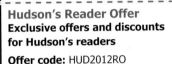

HUDSON'S

Hudson's Reader Offer
Exclusive offers and discounts for Hudson's readers

Offer code: HUD2012RO

Hudson's Heritage (a trading name of Heritage House Media Ltd) are not responsible for the details of special offers and discounts available.
All properties with the 'R' symbol have agreed to make such offers and discounts available to readers of Hudson's 2012 edition. Offers and discounts may be subject to change at any time. Hudson's Heritage and Heritage House Media accept no liability for issues arising from the use or attempted use of Reader Offer vouchers and all disputes should be addressed to the property concerned.

HUDSON'S

Hudson's Reader Offer
Exclusive offers and discounts for Hudson's readers

Offer code: HUD2012RO

Hudson's Heritage (a trading name of Heritage House Media Ltd) are not responsible for the details of special offers and discounts available.
All properties with the 'R' symbol have agreed to make such offers and discounts available to readers of Hudson's 2012 edition. Offers and discounts may be subject to change at any time. Hudson's Heritage and Heritage House Media accept no liability for issues arising from the use or attempted use of Reader Offer vouchers and all disputes should be addressed to the property concerned.

HUDSON'S

Hudson's Reader Offer
Exclusive offers and discounts for Hudson's readers

Offer code: HUD2012RO

Hudson's Heritage (a trading name of Heritage House Media Ltd) are not responsible for the details of special offers and discounts available.
All properties with the 'R' symbol have agreed to make such offers and discounts available to readers of Hudson's 2012 edition. Offers and discounts may be subject to change at any time. Hudson's Heritage and Heritage House Media accept no liability for issues arising from the use or attempted use of Reader Offer vouchers and all disputes should be addressed to the property concerned.

HUDSON'S

Hudson's Reader Offer
Exclusive offers and discounts for Hudson's readers

Offer code: HUD2012RO

Hudson's Heritage (a trading name of Heritage House Media Ltd) are not responsible for the details of special offers and discounts available.
All properties with the 'R' symbol have agreed to make such offers and discounts available to readers of Hudson's 2012 edition. Offers and discounts may be subject to change at any time. Hudson's Heritage and Heritage House Media accept no liability for issues arising from the use or attempted use of Reader Offer vouchers and all disputes should be addressed to the property concerned.

HUDSON'S

Hudson's Reader Offer
Exclusive offers and discounts for Hudson's readers

Offer code: HUD2012RO

Hudson's Heritage (a trading name of Heritage House Media Ltd) are not responsible for the details of special offers and discounts available.
All properties with the 'R' symbol have agreed to make such offers and discounts available to readers of Hudson's 2012 edition. Offers and discounts may be subject to change at any time. Hudson's Heritage and Heritage House Media accept no liability for issues arising from the use or attempted use of Reader Offer vouchers and all disputes should be addressed to the property concerned.

HUDSON'S

Hudson's Reader Offer
Exclusive offers and discounts for Hudson's readers

Offer code: HUD2012RO

Hudson's Heritage (a trading name of Heritage House Media Ltd) are not responsible for the details of special offers and discounts available.
All properties with the 'R' symbol have agreed to make such offers and discounts available to readers of Hudson's 2012 edition. Offers and discounts may be subject to change at any time. Hudson's Heritage and Heritage House Media accept no liability for issues arising from the use or attempted use of Reader Offer vouchers and all disputes should be addressed to the property concerned.

HUDSON'S

Hudson's Reader Offer
Exclusive offers and discounts for Hudson's readers

Offer code: HUD2012RO

Hudson's Heritage (a trading name of Heritage House Media Ltd) are not responsible for the details of special offers and discounts available.
All properties with the 'R' symbol have agreed to make such offers and discounts available to readers of Hudson's 2012 edition. Offers and discounts may be subject to change at any time. Hudson's Heritage and Heritage House Media accept no liability for issues arising from the use or attempted use of Reader Offer vouchers and all disputes should be addressed to the property concerned.

HUDSON'S

Hudson's Reader Offer
Exclusive offers and discounts for Hudson's readers

Offer code: HUD2012RO

Hudson's Heritage (a trading name of Heritage House Media Ltd) are not responsible for the details of special offers and discounts available.
All properties with the 'R' symbol have agreed to make such offers and discounts available to readers of Hudson's 2012 edition. Offers and discounts may be subject to change at any time. Hudson's Heritage and Heritage House Media accept no liability for issues arising from the use or attempted use of Reader Offer vouchers and all disputes should be addressed to the property concerned.

HUDSON'S

Hudson's Reader Offer
Exclusive offers and discounts for Hudson's readers

Offer code: HUD2012RO

Hudson's Heritage (a trading name of Heritage House Media Ltd) are not responsible for the details of special offers and discounts available.
All properties with the 'R' symbol have agreed to make such offers and discounts available to readers of Hudson's 2012 edition. Offers and discounts may be subject to change at any time. Hudson's Heritage and Heritage House Media accept no liability for issues arising from the use or attempted use of Reader Offer vouchers and all disputes should be addressed to the property concerned.

HUDSON'S

Hudson's Reader Offer
Exclusive offers and discounts for Hudson's readers

Offer code: HUD2012RO

Hudson's Heritage (a trading name of Heritage House Media Ltd) are not responsible for the details of special offers and discounts available.
All properties with the 'R' symbol have agreed to make such offers and discounts available to readers of Hudson's 2012 edition. Offers and discounts may be subject to change at any time. Hudson's Heritage and Heritage House Media accept no liability for issues arising from the use or attempted use of Reader Offer vouchers and all disputes should be addressed to the property concerned.

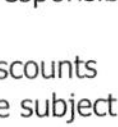

HUDSON'S

Hudson's Reader Offer
Exclusive offers and discounts for Hudson's readers

Offer code: HUD2012RO

Hudson's Heritage (a trading name of Heritage House Media Ltd) are not responsible for the details of special offers and discounts available.
All properties with the 'R' symbol have agreed to make such offers and discounts available to readers of Hudson's 2012 edition. Offers and discounts may be subject to change at any time. Hudson's Heritage and Heritage House Media accept no liability for issues arising from the use or attempted use of Reader Offer vouchers and all disputes should be addressed to the property concerned.

HUDSON'S

Hudson's Reader Offer
Exclusive offers and discounts for Hudson's readers

Offer code: HUD2012RO

Hudson's Heritage (a trading name of Heritage House Media Ltd) are not responsible for the details of special offers and discounts available.
All properties with the 'R' symbol have agreed to make such offers and discounts available to readers of Hudson's 2012 edition. Offers and discounts may be subject to change at any time. Hudson's Heritage and Heritage House Media accept no liability for issues arising from the use or attempted use of Reader Offer vouchers and all disputes should be addressed to the property concerned.

R

ENJOY GREAT DAYS OUT WITH HUDSON'S

USE THESE EXCLUSIVE HUDSON'S READER OFFER VOUCHERS TO CLAIM SPECIAL OFFERS AND DISCOUNTS AT A HOST OF BEAUTIFUL HERITAGE PROPERTIES AND ATTRACTIONS THROUGHOUT THE UK.

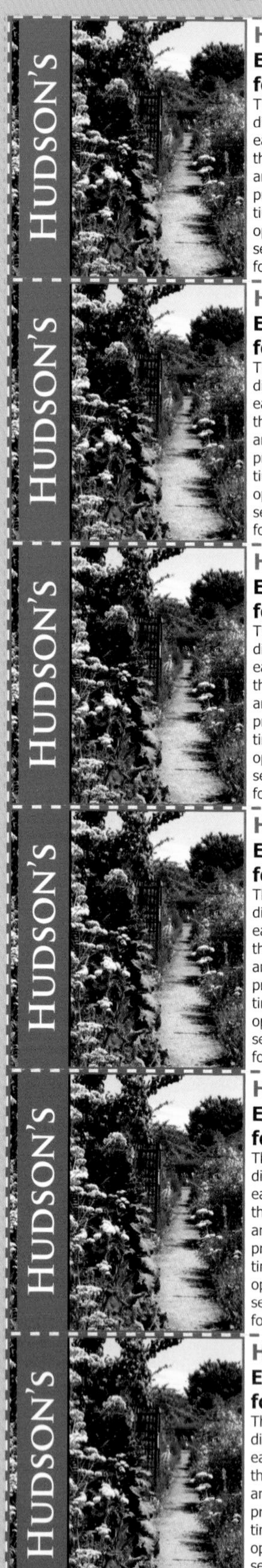
HUDSON'S

Hudson's Reader Offer

Exclusive offers and discounts for Hudson's readers

This voucher can be used to claim special offers and discounts at participating properties only. Properties are easily identified by the **'R'** symbol on their entries in the directory pages starting on page 151. Special offers and discounts will vary and are determined solely by the properties. Offers may only be available on specific days/ times and exclusions/conditions may apply. Please check opening times before visiting as these may vary. Please see the property pages on **www.hudsonsheritage.com** for further information or telephone the properties direct.

Hudson's Reader Offer

Exclusive offers and discounts for Hudson's readers

This voucher can be used to claim special offers and discounts at participating properties only. Properties are easily identified by the **'R'** symbol on their entries in the directory pages starting on page 151. Special offers and discounts will vary and are determined solely by the properties. Offers may only be available on specific days/ times and exclusions/conditions may apply. Please check opening times before visiting as these may vary. Please see the property pages on **www.hudsonsheritage.com** for further information or telephone the properties direct.

Hudson's Reader Offer

Exclusive offers and discounts for Hudson's readers

This voucher can be used to claim special offers and discounts at participating properties only. Properties are easily identified by the **'R'** symbol on their entries in the directory pages starting on page 151. Special offers and discounts will vary and are determined solely by the properties. Offers may only be available on specific days/ times and exclusions/conditions may apply. Please check opening times before visiting as these may vary. Please see the property pages on **www.hudsonsheritage.com** for further information or telephone the properties direct.

Hudson's Reader Offer

Exclusive offers and discounts for Hudson's readers

This voucher can be used to claim special offers and discounts at participating properties only. Properties are easily identified by the **'R'** symbol on their entries in the directory pages starting on page 151. Special offers and discounts will vary and are determined solely by the properties. Offers may only be available on specific days/ times and exclusions/conditions may apply. Please check opening times before visiting as these may vary. Please see the property pages on **www.hudsonsheritage.com** for further information or telephone the properties direct.

Hudson's Reader Offer

Exclusive offers and discounts for Hudson's readers

This voucher can be used to claim special offers and discounts at participating properties only. Properties are easily identified by the **'R'** symbol on their entries in the directory pages starting on page 151. Special offers and discounts will vary and are determined solely by the properties. Offers may only be available on specific days/ times and exclusions/conditions may apply. Please check opening times before visiting as these may vary. Please see the property pages on **www.hudsonsheritage.com** for further information or telephone the properties direct.

Hudson's Reader Offer

Exclusive offers and discounts for Hudson's readers

This voucher can be used to claim special offers and discounts at participating properties only. Properties are easily identified by the **'R'** symbol on their entries in the directory pages starting on page 151. Special offers and discounts will vary and are determined solely by the properties. Offers may only be available on specific days/ times and exclusions/conditions may apply. Please check opening times before visiting as these may vary. Please see the property pages on **www.hudsonsheritage.com** for further information or telephone the properties direct.

Hudson's Reader Offer

Exclusive offers and discounts for Hudson's readers

This voucher can be used to claim special offers and discounts at participating properties only. Properties are easily identified by the **'R'** symbol on their entries in the directory pages starting on page 151. Special offers and discounts will vary and are determined solely by the properties. Offers may only be available on specific days/ times and exclusions/conditions may apply. Please check opening times before visiting as these may vary. Please see the property pages on **www.hudsonsheritage.com** for further information or telephone the properties direct.

Hudson's Reader Offer

Exclusive offers and discounts for Hudson's readers

This voucher can be used to claim special offers and discounts at participating properties only. Properties are easily identified by the **'R'** symbol on their entries in the directory pages starting on page 151. Special offers and discounts will vary and are determined solely by the properties. Offers may only be available on specific days/ times and exclusions/conditions may apply. Please check opening times before visiting as these may vary. Please see the property pages on **www.hudsonsheritage.com** for further information or telephone the properties direct.

Hudson's Reader Offer

Exclusive offers and discounts for Hudson's readers

This voucher can be used to claim special offers and discounts at participating properties only. Properties are easily identified by the **'R'** symbol on their entries in the directory pages starting on page 151. Special offers and discounts will vary and are determined solely by the properties. Offers may only be available on specific days/ times and exclusions/conditions may apply. Please check opening times before visiting as these may vary. Please see the property pages on **www.hudsonsheritage.com** for further information or telephone the properties direct.

Hudson's Reader Offer

Exclusive offers and discounts for Hudson's readers

This voucher can be used to claim special offers and discounts at participating properties only. Properties are easily identified by the **'R'** symbol on their entries in the directory pages starting on page 151. Special offers and discounts will vary and are determined solely by the properties. Offers may only be available on specific days/ times and exclusions/conditions may apply. Please check opening times before visiting as these may vary. Please see the property pages on **www.hudsonsheritage.com** for further information or telephone the properties direct.

Hudson's Reader Offer

Exclusive offers and discounts for Hudson's readers

This voucher can be used to claim special offers and discounts at participating properties only. Properties are easily identified by the **'R'** symbol on their entries in the directory pages starting on page 151. Special offers and discounts will vary and are determined solely by the properties. Offers may only be available on specific days/ times and exclusions/conditions may apply. Please check opening times before visiting as these may vary. Please see the property pages on **www.hudsonsheritage.com** for further information or telephone the properties direct.

Hudson's Reader Offer

Exclusive offers and discounts for Hudson's readers

This voucher can be used to claim special offers and discounts at participating properties only. Properties are easily identified by the **'R'** symbol on their entries in the directory pages starting on page 151. Special offers and discounts will vary and are determined solely by the properties. Offers may only be available on specific days/ times and exclusions/conditions may apply. Please check opening times before visiting as these may vary. Please see the property pages on **www.hudsonsheritage.com** for further information or telephone the properties direct.

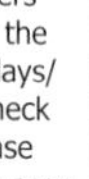

HISTORIC
TRUST
CHAPELS

The Historic Chapels Trust

Preserving and regenerating places of worship in England

The Historic Chapels Trust was established to take into ownership redundant chapels and other places of worship in England which are of outstanding architectural and historic interest – securing for public benefit their preservation, repair and regeneration. Below are 20 of the chapels in our care which you can visit on application to the keyholder. Farfield and Coanwood are, experimentally, left open.

Chapel	Telephone
Bethesda Methodist Chapel, Stoke-on-Trent	01782 856810
Biddlestone Chapel, Northumberland	01665 574420, 01669 630270, 01669 620230
Chantry Chapel, Thorndon Park, Essex	020 7481 0533
Coanwood Friends Meeting House, Northumberland	01434 321316
Cote Chapel, Oxfordshire	01993 851219
Farfield Friends Meeting House, West Yorkshire	01756 710587
The Dissenters' Chapel, Kensal Green Cemetery, London	020 7602 0173
Longworth Chapel, Bartestree, Herefordshire	01432 853200
Penrose Methodist Chapel, St Ervan, Cornwall	01841 540737
Salem Chapel, East Budleigh, Devon	01395 446189, 01395 445236
Shrine of Our Lady of Lourdes, Blackpool, Lancashire	01253 865770
St Benet's Chapel, Netherton, Merseyside	0151 520 2600
St George's German Lutheran Church, Tower Hamlets, London	020 7481 0533
Strict Baptist Chapel, Grittleton, Wiltshire	020 7481 0533
Todmorden Unitarian Church, West Yorkshire	01706 815407
Umberslade Baptist Church, Warwickshire	0121 704 2694
Wainsgate Baptist Church, West Yorkshire	01422 843315
Wallasey Unitarian Church, Merseyside	0151 639 9707
Walpole Old Chapel, Suffolk	01986 798308
Westgate Methodist Chapel, Co. Durham	020 7481 0533

Weddings can be arranged at certain chapels. For events, programmes and for further information please visit our website: **www.hct.org.uk** or telephone: 020 7481 0533

Historic Chapels Trust, St George's German Lutheran Church, 55 Alie Street, London E1 8EB
Tel: 020 7481 0533 **Fax:** 020 7488 3756 **E-mail:** chapels@hct.org.uk **Web:** www.hct.org.uk
Company No. 2778395 Registered Charity No. 1017321

Votive Shrine of Our Lady of Lourdes

Longworth Chapel

St George's German Lutheran Church

Bethesda Methodist Chapel

Biddlestone Chapel

Salem Chapel

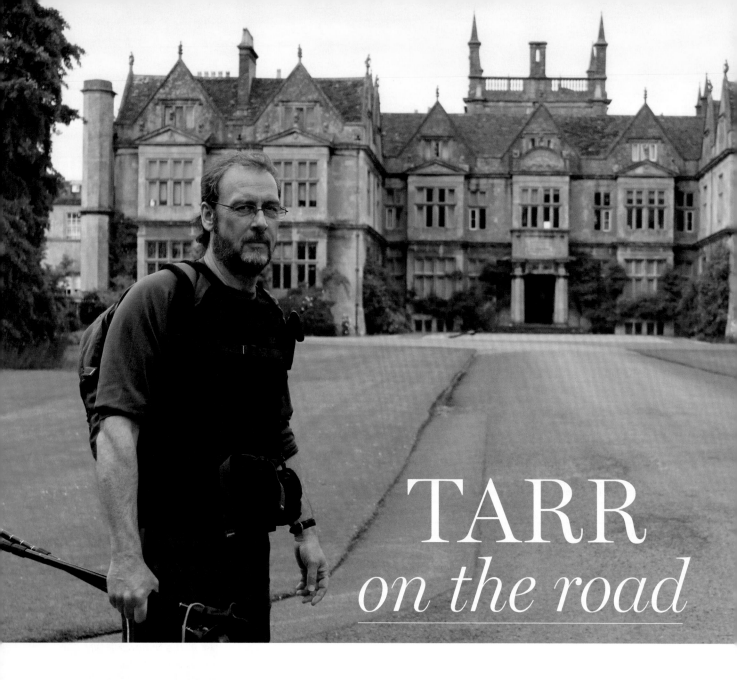

TARR *on the road*

Passionate walker and lifelong *National Trust* and *English Heritage* member, ***Derek Tarr***, samples Wiltshire's historic houses, snug stop-overs and mellow pubs. Discover England at its charming best...

Words: ***Derek Tarr***
Photos: ***Nicola Burford***

For many years I have been a member of both the National Trust and English Heritage and believe a subscription to these bodies is more than just a membership – it's an investment in the preservation of our historical treasures. Taking my long-time interest in all things heritage as my inspiration – along with the National Trust handbook, a map and my well-used copy of ***Hudson's*** of course – I scoured the country to find an area which was not only rich in historic houses but also looked like a good walk.

My eye fell upon Wiltshire, an area not particularly known for rambling routes but with much to offer. There are rolling hills, flood plains, thatched cottages, Cotswold stone and heritage sites in abundance.

Cottage flower stall in Lacock

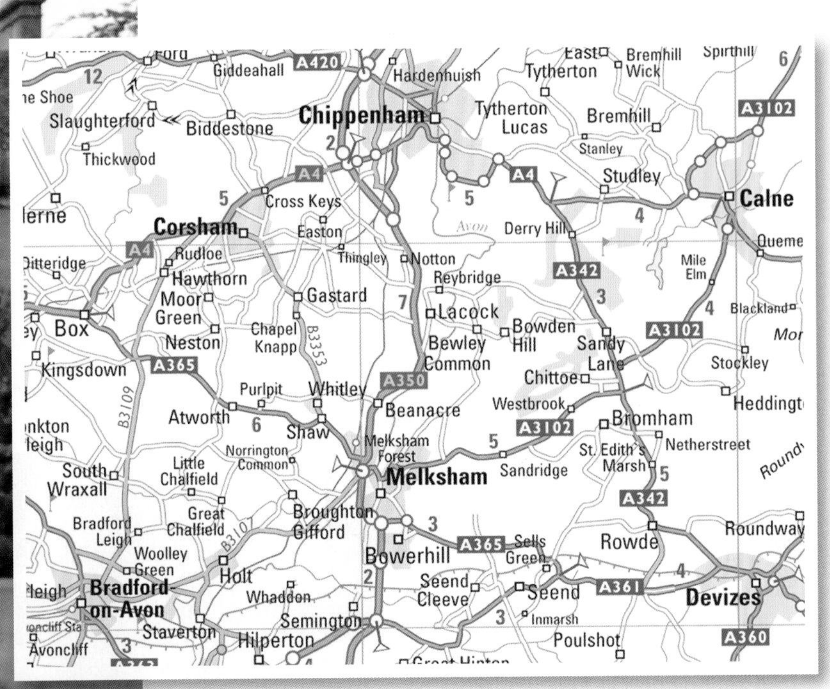
Giddeahall
A420
Hardenhuish
Tytherton
Bremhill
Wick
Spirthill
Slaughterford
Biddestone
Chippenham
Tytherton Lucas
Bremhill
A3102
Thickwood
Stanley
A4
Studley
Cross Keys
Calne
Corsham
Easton
Derry Hill
Rudloe
Thingley
Notton
Mile Elm
Hawthorn
Reybridge
A342
Moor Green
Gastard
Lacock
Box
Chapel Knapp
Bowden Hill
A3102
Neston
Bewley Common
Sandy Lane
Stockley
Kingsdown
A365
Chittoe
Purlpit
Whitley
A350
Atworth
Beanacre
Westbrook
Bromham
Heddington
Shaw
Melksham Forest
A3102
Norrington Common
Netherstreet
South Wraxall
Little Chalfield
St. Edith's Marsh
Melksham
Sandridge
A342
Great Chalfield
Broughton Gifford
Bradford Leigh
Roundway
Woolley Green
Bowerhill
A365
Sells Green
Rowde
Holt
Bradford-on-Avon
Seend Cleeve
Seend
A361
Devizes
Whaddon
Inmarsh
Semington
Staverton
Hilperton
Poulshot
A360
Avoncliff

© Crown Copyright

DEREK'S WALKS DAY BY DAY

Walk 1: Lacock to Rowde

Walk 2: Rowde to Whitely

Walk 3: Whitely to Corsham

Corsham Court

Avon
Derry Hill
Notton
Reybridge
A342
Mile Elm
Lacock
Bowden Hill
A3102
Bewley Common
Sandy Lane
Chittoe
Westbrook
A3102
Bromham
St. Edith's Marsh
Netherstreet
Sandridge
A342
A365
Sells
Rowde

Walk 1
LACOCK TO ROWDE
16.5 miles (plus detour to Sandy Lane – 3 miles)

My 40-mile route began in the beautiful village of Lacock, three miles south of Chippenham. Nestling on the River Avon, much of the village is owned and maintained by the National Trust and has changed little over the centuries. The original main road from London to Bristol once ran through Lacock, but after it was diverted to Chippenham the village became frozen in time. As a result it has been used on many occasions as a location for period productions such as the BBC's *Pride and Prejudice* and *Cranford*. After a pint in the comfortable Red Lion Inn and lunch in the nearby Stable Tea Rooms, I strolled towards the Abbey – the entrance to which houses a fascinating museum dedicated to the work of William Henry Fox Talbot and his development of photography. The Abbey itself has an air of mystery and I could see why it was chosen as a location for Hogwarts School in the *Harry Potter* films. Passing through the ancient cloisters, I came to the furnished rooms which were once the living quarters of Miss Matilda Gilchrist-Clark. She was the last member of the Talbot family to reside at the Abbey before handing it and the village to the National Trust in 1944. Lacock village has a wide variety of accommodation, with the charming 15th century 'At the Sign of the Angel' hotel of particular note. >>

National Trust
Shop
National Trust Shop

The National Trust Shop at Lacock

THE RED LION

The Red Lion, Lacock

'At the Sign of the Angel', Lacock

My route out of the village ran over the packhorse bridge by the ford. I crossed the River Avon at Reybridge, and continued over rolling countryside to Derry Hill, passing the old Wilts & Berks Canal. Since 1977, volunteers have been restoring this former canal with the aim of reopening the entire 52 miles from the Kennet and Avon Canal to Abingdon on the River Thames.

I entered the Bowood Estate through the imposing Golden Gate and followed a track and roadway through a wood before arriving at the house and gardens. The house, which is the family home of the Marquis and Marchioness of Lansdowne, dates back to the early 18th century. I was interested to find that Dr Joseph Priestley discovered oxygen gas here in 1774 while employed to teach the sons of the 1st Marquis. The Orangery, now a gallery, displays the Lansdowne collection of paintings, while outside, the beautiful Italianate terrace boasts magnificent clipped yews and imposing decorative stags.

Taking a public footpath through the estate I could see in the distance both The Cherhill White Horse reflecting the sunlight and the Lansdowne Monument standing proudly. I made a worthwhile detour to the village of Sandy Lane to see the many 'chocolate box' thatched cottages which border the main road and St Mary the Virgin & St Nicholas, a striking thatched timber church.

Leaving Bowood at Pillar Lodge on the east side, my walk headed south across fields to the village of Rowde. I booked in to The Vine Cottage bed and breakfast, which has excellent facilities for walkers and cyclists. There's even a sauna – a welcome luxury after a hard day's walk! My hosts, Mary and Ben, kindly booked me a table at the local pub, The George & Dragon, which had a welcoming atmosphere and a speciality menu featuring newly-caught fish from St Mawes in Cornwall.

St Mary the Virgin & St Nicholas, in the village of Sandy Lane

Bowood House

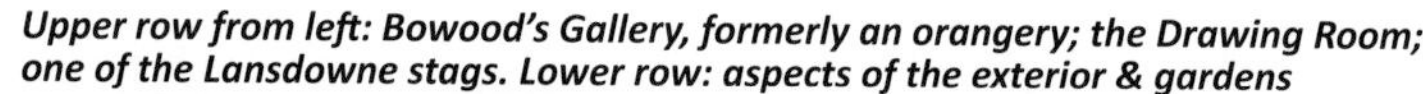

Upper row from left: Bowood's Gallery, formerly an orangery; the Drawing Room; one of the Lansdowne stags. Lower row: aspects of the exterior & gardens

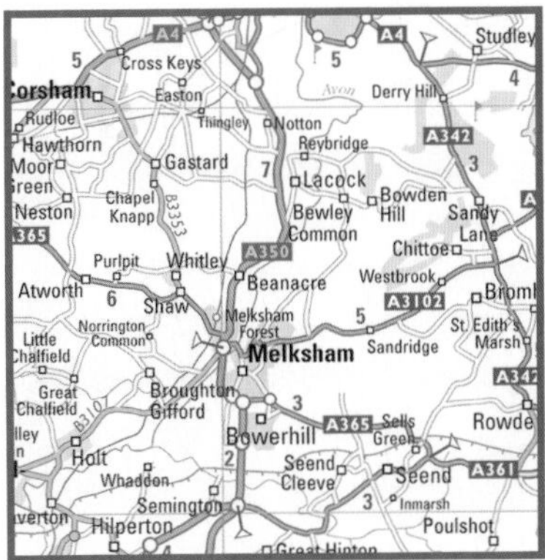
A4
Cross Keys
Corsham
Easton
Thingley
Notton
Avon
Derry Hill
Studley
Rudloe
Hawthorn
Moor Green
Gastard
Reybridge
A342
Lacock
Chapel Knapp
B3353
Neston
Bewley Common
Bowden Hill
Sandy Lane
A365
A350
Chittoe
Purlpit
Whitley
Beanacre
Westbrook
Atworth
Shaw
A3102
Melksham Forest
Norrington Common
St. Edith's Marsh
Little Chalfield
Melksham
Sandridge
Great Chalfield
Broughton Gifford
B3107
Bowerhill
A365
Sells Green
Rowde
Holt
Whaddon
Seend Cleeve
Seend
A361
Semington
Inmarsh
Hilperton
Poulshot

Walk 2

ROWDE TO WHITELY

13 miles

Poring over maps with Mary during breakfast, I decided on a short walk south from Rowde to the Kennet and Avon Canal and the remarkable Caen Hill Locks: a sequence of 16 locks 'stride' up a steep hill to Devizes – a feat of engineering that is a testament to the canal builders of the past. Designed by the engineer John Rennie, the locks opened in 1810 and have now been designated as a scheduled Ancient Monument. A walk westwards along the canal took me to Martinslade and a pleasant climb brought me to Seend, a lovely village with some impressive architecture, large houses and wonderful views, both north to Lacock and south toward Salisbury Plain. I returned to the canal and had a welcome coffee at the picturesque Barge Inn at Seend Cleeve before continuing through scenery of fields and farms, locks and swing bridges. The canal crossed the A350 on an impressive aqueduct before I reached Semington Bridge. I made my way over the fields to Whaddon before crossing back over the River Avon by way of an ancient packhorse bridge and reaching the beautiful Great Chalfield Manor via Broughton Gifford. This moated National Trust property, dating from the

The National Trust's property of Great Chalfield Manor has been voted among the six finest manor houses in England

Great Chalfield Manor & Gardens

Stained glass at Chalfield Manor's church

Welcome To The Barge Inn
Carrot & Coriander Soup with Rustic Bread £4.50
Homemade Cottage Pie with Vegetables £8.95
Gurnard Fillets with Mussels & Crayfish, Pomme Fondant & Wilted Spinach £11.50
Slow Roasted Belly of Pork with Mash, Dressed Green Beans, Black Pudding & a Hazelnut, Redcurrant & Balsamic Jus £13.95
Marinated Swordfish Steak with Chips & Salad £9.95
The specials board at Seend Cleeve's 'Barge

Caen Hill Locks

15th century, has been voted among the six finest manor houses in England and I could see why. The gardens, with their peaceful atmosphere and abundance of flowers, are beautiful, but what really caught my eye were the peacock blue delphiniums and the ancient black mulberry tree with its mighty limbs supported on poles.

House visits are by guided tours only. The Floyd family live here and as a result the house feels well loved. Inside there are many fascinating items including a medieval wall painting that is possibly the earliest known portrait of a 'commoner' Member of Parliament. In the 14th century church in the grounds, I was lucky enough to see fledgling swallows stretching their wings and flying around inside, mirroring the birds pictured in the colourful stained glass window. For Thomas Hardy lovers, the site is worth a visit as it was used for the mansion and farm in the 2008 BBC production of *Tess of the d'Urbervilles*.

That night I stopped at the Pear Tree Inn, Whitely, recently taken over by Marco Pierre White, where I took the opportunity to sample gulls' eggs, a delicacy I had never enjoyed before. **>>**

Corsham Court
HUDSON'S DIRECTORY PAGE 266

"A lasting memory is of the many colourful peacocks scattered around the estate. It is not unusual to meet one while shopping in Corsham High Street"

Walk 3
WHITELY TO CORSHAM
11 miles

The next morning I headed west towards South Wraxall, then turned north along the MacMillan Way – a long-distance path of 290 miles from Abbotsbury in Dorset to Boston in Lincolnshire that was developed to increase public awareness of the MacMillan Cancer Support charity. I reached the town of Box, with its famous railway tunnel built by Isambard Kingdom Brunel, before passing Real World Studios, a residential recording facility. Created by Peter Gabriel, a founder member of the rock group *Genesis*, the studios have been used by many musicians, including Robbie Williams, Stereophonics, Paul Simon and Kylie Minogue. Leaving Box, I followed alongside the captivating stream known as the By Brook. Call me an old romantic, but looking into the blue green water I am sure I caught a glimpse of John Everett Millais' 'Ophelia'. And as I walked through the tranquil countryside I felt at peace with not a soul in sight for miles.

At Weavern Farm I left the MacMillan Way and headed for the outskirts of Corsham, where I stopped at the Hare and Hounds, a pub serving food all day. Corsham is a busy modern town, but at its centre are a quaint high street and Corsham Court, an elegant house set in beautiful grounds and gardens designed by 'Capability' Brown and Humphry Repton. It has been privately owned by the Methuen family for eight generations. The important collection of art has been proudly displayed to the public for over 200 years and contains works by Van Dyck, Reynolds and Romney, with furniture by Thomas Chippendale. For me it was a portrait, 'Queen Elizabeth I in Old Age', painted by an unknown artist after her death, that I found particularly moving. Another lasting memory is of the many colourful peacocks scattered around the estate. It is not unusual to meet one while shopping in Corsham High Street.

The nearby Methuen Arms has excellent food and extremely comfortable bedrooms. It has recently come under the new ownership of Debbie and Martin Still and has been completely refurbished to a high standard. The food was superb and my favourite dish of tuna was cooked to perfection.

THE METHUEN ARMS

The Methuen Arms, Corsham – 'tuna cooked to perfection'

Corsham's picturesque Church Street

THE
GEORGE
INN
WADWORTH
The George, Lacock

THE
FLEMISH
WEAVER
The Flemish Weaver, Corsham

The By Brook near Box

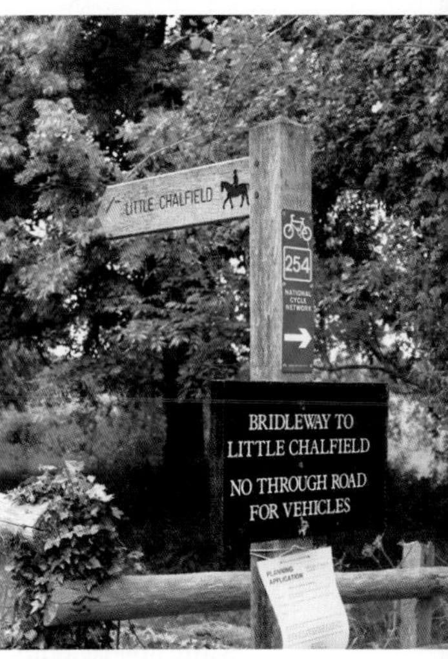
LITTLE CHALFIELD
254
BRIDLEWAY TO
LITTLE CHALFIELD
NO THROUGH ROAD
FOR VEHICLES

"The lovely folk of Wiltshire had been warm, welcoming and helpful, and the rolling countryside, great views and rich heritage had made my walk a delight. It may not have had the grandeur of the West Highland Way, or the drama of the South West Coastal path – or even the magnificent severity and bleakness of the Pennine Way – but it did have a charm all of its own."

If you would like to contact Derek Tarr about his walks please email him at:
tarrontheroad@yahoo.com

W.C.C.
PUBLIC
FOOTPATH
W.C.C.

St Brides Castle, Pembrokeshire

Enjoy the Best of Britain

with the Holiday Property Bond

In 1983 a group of investors saw the potential of a new ground breaking idea. If they each invested a few thousand pounds in a single fund, which was then used to buy top-quality holiday homes and securities, they could use these homes for their own holidays rent-free. And the more new investors that joined them, the more properties the fund could buy, both here in the UK and across Europe – giving every investor a growing choice of holiday homes and locations to enjoy.

It was the start of the Holiday Property Bond, a unique holiday property product which gives its investors rent-free holidays for the whole of their lives and their children's lives.

What's more, the idea certainly struck a chord with families who were looking for a higher standard of holiday accommodation. The number of investors (or 'Bondholders') has grown every year since HPB was founded and now totals over 40,000 families. Between them they enjoy the use of 1,325 properties – villas, apartments and cottages of an exceptionally high standard – 519 of which are here in the UK.

More holiday homes are built or purchased almost every year, increasing the choice of holiday properties and destinations, and as at 30th June 2011 the fund had net assets of over £250 million, with no borrowings.

A very British holiday

The Holiday Property Bond offers its investors a very British kind of holiday. Each of its 31 holiday locations offers space, peace and total relaxation, with each property full equipped and maintained in first-class condition by on-site staff. All HPB locations are in beautiful countryside or within easy reach of fine beaches.

The overseas properties are certainly impressive. Some, like Encosta Cabo Girao in Madeira and El Pueblito de Alfaix in southern Spain, are superb mini-resorts created exclusively for Bondholders

But what appeals to many Bondholders is the very large number of properties that HPB owns here in the UK. The 519 properties currently in HPB's UK portfolio are spread across 16 different locations. All of them are in stunningly beautiful places, and most are in designated National Parks or Areas of Outstanding Natural Beauty.

Britain's heritage restored

Many HPB properties are historic buildings, including stately homes and mansions, that have been lovingly restored and converted to holiday use. They include Tigh Mor Trossachs overlooking Loch Achray – a 19th century mansion – which was rescued from dereliction by HPB and magnificently restored.

In the village of Askrigg, HPB restored a number of historic buildings to create Lodge Yard, an award-winning development of cottages and apartments at the heart of the Yorkshire Dales National Park.

And in Cornwall, HPB restored Duloe Manor, a Queen Anne rectory built in the late 1690s, to provide holiday apartments and cottages exclusively for its Bondholders.

HPB's latest such venture is Merlewood a Grade II listed house originally built for the family of the poet Laurence Binyon, which has now been restored to its former glory. It is also superbly located, overlooking the resort of Grange-Over-Sands and Morecambe Bay.

Other magnificent HPB properties can be found in Anglesey, Devon, Dorset, the North Downs of Kent, the Lake District, Norfolk, the North York Moors, the Peak District, Pembrokeshire, Perthshire and the Shropshire Hills.

With properties of this calibre within easy reach, and so much to explore here in our own islands, it is no wonder that HPB's UK locations are proving so popular with Bondholders, whether for long family holidays or short breaks.

Your future holiday entitlements for life

Here in a nutshell is how HPB gives you rent-free holidays for life. You invest a few thousand pounds and in return you receive a number of Holiday Points each year, which you can exchange for holiday accommodation. How many Holiday Points you receive each year depends on the size of your investment – and the number is reassessed each year, to protect the level of your holiday entitlement.

There are no restrictions on when you can go on holiday, where, or what kind of holiday home you can book. And you won't pay a penny in rent for your holiday - just a no-profit user charge when you book your holiday to cover actual expenses

Just how HPB delivers these holiday benefits is summarised in 'How HPB works' opposite, together with the principal benefits and risks of an investment.

BEACH CAFÉ
Events
HOLKHAM
COUNTRY
FAIR !!
16-17 JULY 2011
BUY ADVANCE TICKETS
ONLINE
www.holkhamcountryfair.com

New TRICKS

Holkham Hall's vast estate and stunning coast is North Norfolk's jewel in the crown. Its dynamic owner, ***Viscount Tom Coke***, talks with *Hudson's* Editor, ***Nick McCann*** at the estate's new beach café.

The Holkham Estate has much to offer visitors, as a place both rich in natural beauty and deeply embedded in British culture. Over the years, its location on the Norfolk coast, its priceless artefacts and its appearance in a number of high-profile films and television shows have positioned Holkham as an attraction of considerable interest.

When it comes to maintaining visitor numbers, however, Holkham's current guardian is anything but complacent. Thomas, Viscount Coke is one of a new breed of young historic-property owners embracing modern business models and innovative ideas to maximise the potential of his estate.

The spot we meet at – a recently-opened café on the white-gold sand of Holkham Beach at Wells-next-the-Sea – is a perfect example of the way in which the Viscount is adapting the attraction for the modern-day visitor. The building used to be a brick outhouse fronted by white plastic seating and pub tables on concrete paving; under Lord Coke's guidance, it has been reborn with a fresh and welcoming feel. Inside, the building is painted white and pale blue, with wooden tables and terracotta flooring. Large skylights let in generous helpings of natural light and colourful marine pennants hangs from the ceiling. Outside, the building has been covered in barge boarding, decking has been laid and contemporary furniture installed

The café opened at Easter (2011) and the response was overwhelmingly positive. 'We are catering for the same market, but also attracting more people who wouldn't have thought of coming here before, says Tom. We haven't had a single complaint.

'I asked one of the girls who has worked here for years: 'Surely you must have had the occasional curmudgeon come in and say they preferred it the way it was before?' She said not one, and all the customers are coming back. I was chatting to two friends who go running on the beach and they said we do the best coffee in Wells.'

The estate team undertook plenty of research before embarking on the project, taking note of established beach cafés around the country to glean ideas and note examples of best practice. Careful attention to detail is the result – the Holkham café boasts local ingredients (the prawns are recommended), local art and photography on sale, and a wood-burning stove to keep the place warm in the winter.

Photos: ***Nigel Gibson***

BEACH CAFE

The new venture is one of a number of improvements the Viscount has initiated since taking control of the estate in 2006, intended to take advantage of, and improve, its current popularity. The beach, which is part of a nature reserve, plays no small part in this, attracting around 800,000 visitors annually and having just won Coast magazine's Best British Beach for the third year running. Tom makes good use of the beach to walk his Irish terrier, Jupiter, while those visiting in the summer time may be lucky enough to see the Household Cavalry riding their horses bareback in the water, using the four-mile stretch to let off steam whilst off duty. The beach's real claim to fame, though, is probably its role in the closing scene of the 1998 film, *Shakespeare in Love*, where Gwyneth Paltrow is seen cast ashore on a desert island.

"We are attracting more people who wouldn't have thought of coming here before"

Indeed, the full 25,000-acre estate has been a magnet for film makers for many years – myself included. I first discovered it back in 1992 when I was making *The Heart of Shelley*, a short film for Anglia Television that saw the beach become the site of the poet's cremation at Viarregio in northern Italy. More recently, Holkham Hall was used for *The Duchess*, featuring Keira Knightley and Ralph Fiennes, and *My Talks with Dean Spanley*, starring Peter O'Toole. This year, Tom also welcomed the BBC into his home, for a 90-minute special on the hall's extraordinary collection of Claude paintings.

Its attraction as a film set has not only provided an additional source of income and promotion, but has been an added incentive for the vigilant preservation of the hall and grounds. One of the outcomes of this is the honing of the estate's own maintenance and property development companies, involved in complex refurbishment projects in the hall and the essential repair of the estate cottages. >>

The need for longevity has also spawned a rather innovative venture, Holkham Linseed Paints. Lord Coke, it seems, has an eye for a good business opportunity. 'I was lucky enough to meet the principal conservation officer for Norfolk County Council, who introduced me to a Swedish family firm who were making linseed oil paint,' he explains. 'Its USP is that it's traditional, long-lasting, solvent-free and therefore healthy. We've just finished painting all the windows and doors in the hall – seven years' work. And we're slowly going around the estate.'

The paints are also supplied to external customers, with the company the sole UK distributor. Tom believes that linseed oil paint – which was widely used across Europe prior to the Second World War – is enjoying something of a revival. Crucially, it can protect the wood beneath an average of six to 10 years before it needs to be repainted.

The estate has 25 tenanted farms and, in addition to that, its enterprises have expanded to include a holiday park, several shops, a pub and an internationally-acclaimed hotel. Viscount Coke tells me the Pinewoods Holiday Park, a four-star caravan park behind the beach, has been particularly successful. For him, the key is in not only choosing suitable ventures but also in recognising the importance of the people who work there. 'It's no surprise to us that the holiday park has been successful,' he says. 'We entered into "Investors in People" four years ago and have just received the silver award – recognising, for instance, our very low staff turnover, the fact that everyone knows what they're doing, understand the business and that we have good systems in place.'

But he's not resting on his laurels just yet. He would like to see such standards extended across the whole estate,

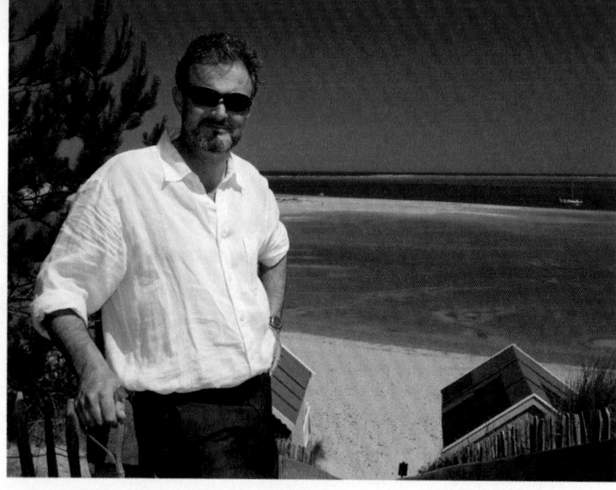

to more than 200 employees. 'My aim is to bring the rest of the estate into IIP throughout 2011 and 2012, with the result that we will have well-motivated staff who are confident of making their own decisions,' he explains.

Tom's long-term ambition is to pass the property on to the next generation in a better condition than he found it, (just as his father had done) and among possible plans for the future is a visitor centre for the nature reserve. He hopes that by combining the estate's natural beauty with some well thought-out improvements, the estate will become a leader in the industry.

'There are still a few tricks we can learn from successful estates such as Chatsworth,' he notes. 'But Norfolk retains its own unique charm and whatever we do, we do it to a high standard. Holkham is an iconic rural estate, and it is our aim to become the benchmark by which all other country estates measure themselves.'

FOR VISITOR INFORMATION ON HOLKHAM HALL TURN TO PAGE 284

"Holkham is an iconic rural estate, and it is our aim to become the benchmark by which all other country estates measure themselves" TOM, VISCOUNT COKE

TISSINGTON HALL

Baronet's BLOG

Sir Richard FitzHerbert is one of Derbyshire's most active and well-respected historic house owners. A much-followed *Tweeter*, he gives ***Hudson's*** his personal behind-the-scenes review of six months at his home and rural estate of Tissington Hall.

January

The year starts with snow... and more snow. Always the time to get the camera out to get some good shots for best-selling postcards. Having increased our troupe of dogs to five, it's difficult to keep them out of the frame, as they have more fun in the snow than we do. School closures mean the office is full not only with workers, but also their offspring playing computer games. Oh, for the thaw! At last, it does melt – and the billiard room roof reveals a hole that means new snooker cues and chalk are required for the next championships.

February

Planning in earnest now for the events we want to put on over the forthcoming year. We are persuaded to include two 'new for this year' events: an Easter Egg Hunt and a Teddy Bears' Picnic over our May Festival weekend. There is a mad rush to get images of teddy bears and Easter bunnies into our literature so we can distribute our leaflets in time. Over 60,000 arrive at the end of the month and, unlike neighbours Chatsworth and Haddon, who have their own dedicated vans to deliver to every B&B and guest house in the locality, the onus is on me to give that personal delivery touch. After 15 years, I now know every caravan site in the Peak District, most B&Bs and all of the bigger hotels! As I visit, I offer vouchers for free entry to Tissington Hall (all time-dated) but very few are taken up. Interesting.

March

Time to spring clean the house, as we prepare for early group visits. We are open throughout the year by appointment, and often the visitors at this time of year are the real 'cognoscenti' of country houses. One such group assembles in Derby for a three-day tour of all the major 'piles': from the National Trust-owned properties of Hardwick, Kedleston, Calke and Sudbury, to my fellow HHA members – Chatsworth, Haddon, Eyam, Casterne and Nottinghamshire's Holme Pierrepont (or HP, as we know it). By the time the group reaches us, I know they are showing 'country house fatigue', so I try to create a different impression, with dogs, cats, bats and lit fires in every room. My approach is of a practical nature, talking about everything from window cleaning (which costs us £600 twice a year) to the occasions when I am mistaken for the gardener! The group laughs and, I hope, will return home to talk about their joyful visit to Tissington. >>

Sir Richard and Tissington staff members face the local press for a charity fund-raising coffee morning

Photo courtesy of Ashbourne News Telegraph

April

We have been striving for over three years to obtain planning consent for a semi-permanent marquee in the arboretum to house our functions – mainly the weddings that we have hosted since 2003. The process has been long and arduous, culminating in a 'noise survey'. At a cost of £1500 (plus VAT), this revealed the startling news that there is NO noise in our quiet little village at midnight. Wow! We wait with bated breath and thankfully our application is passed 'under delegated powers', but with 18 conditions – one of which is that no food can be served outside of the marquee after 9pm. I think we may have to employ the 'canapé police' next summer!

May

Our well-dressing ceremony means we face the biggest week of our year, with over 35,000 visitors to be welcomed to our tiny village in the middle of Derbyshire. The well-dressing tradition dates back over many centuries, to the time when villagers praised the Lord for the life-giving properties of the water from the wells, which never dried up in times of drought or plague. We have six wells to decorate, or 'dress', which means six teams of 20, all striving to create marvellous mosaics with petals and natural substances, usually depicting a story from the Bible. Our week starts with the Service and Procession of the Blessing of the Wells on Ascension Day. St Mary's Church is packed with clergy and congregation, and the Hall is swamped with W.I. groups and historical societies combining the house and the wells in the same trip. Every available space in the village is set up with charity stands and stalls selling cakes, books and paintings by local artists. Some stallholders even camp out overnight! Numbers are good over the weekend, but a grumpy American provokes distaste among our guides as she explores the gardens and refuses to pay.

June

The start of the wedding season coincides with Ascot, and the garden is freshening up as the early-summer heat wave gives way to a damp early June. A deluge on the first Sunday of the month washes out the Murray tennis final at Queens, as well as a local fête, and we are thankful when it holds off for our main event of the month. The Rain or Shine Theatre Company has chosen a Wednesday night to perform its version of the Bard's Much Ado About Nothing. Although ticket sales seemed slow at first, our efforts to court publicity (I appeared as a 'Loudmouth' on BBC Radio Derby to promote it) bear results. The audience swells, and the cast duly arrives, needing a grass set and two electric hook-ups. Champagne corks are popping by the time Beatrice embraces Benedict for a third time, and the garden-giggles rebound around our 16th century courtyard auditorium.

Photo: *Nigel Gibson*

"I think we may have to employ the 'canapé police' next summer!"

SIR RICHARD & LADY FITZHERBERT

HUDSON^S ONLINE

The Website
hudsonsheritage.com

The APP

East Midlands
London Bridge railway arches awarded Grade II listing
Over 1,400 Heritage Attractions

HUDSON'S HERITAGE
EXPLORE BRITAIN'S
Historic Houses & Gardens
Attingham Park
Lulworth Castle & Park
HUDSON'S

For all the latest news about what's happening in Heritage throughout the UK visit www.hudsonsheritage.com.

In addition to property information you can now:

Find out what's on

Buy tickets online

Purchase your guidebooks before or after your visit

Access exclusive special offers

With our free App (available from the Apple App Store) Hudson's is more portable than ever before and visiting Britain's Brilliant Heritage is now even easier.

In addition to property information you can now:

Find attractions in your local vicinity

Receive special venue offers right to your phone

Access information on your favourite destinations

Soon available on Android and Blackberry

BRITAIN'S BRILLIANT HERITAGE BROUGHT TO LIFE

ENGLISH HERITAGE

The long view

A 20-year masterplan at Wrest Park is reviving one of England's most magnificent landscapes. This summer, the first phase can be enjoyed

WORDS **TOBY MUSGRAVE**

Wrest Park, which was home to the de Grey family from the Middle Ages until the early 20th century, is surrounded by gardens that deserve to be better known. Not only is the landscape one of great beauty and variety, it is also one of historic interest, offering a wealth of opportunity. Thankfully, English Heritage, which took ownership of 90 acres of the original estate in 2006, has recognised this and is undertaking a comprehensive restoration project. This has been made possible by the generous support of the Heritage Lottery Fund, J Paul Getty Jnr Charitable Trust and general donations from the public. The initial phase of a 20-year masterplan is due for completion by March 2013.

Already work is well advanced: in the walled kitchen garden, with its new visitor centre, café and two play areas; in the Conservatory and the house, in particular the newly dressed Countess's Sitting Room; and in the landscape beyond.

Walking these grounds, one is immediately struck by two things. First, there is such a diverse and interesting collection of statuary and garden buildings. Highlights of the latter include the recently restored Orangery from the mid-1830s, the Bowling Green House, possibly redesigned by Batty Langley in 1735, and Thomas Archer's baroque Pavilion, which, completed in 1711, sits gracefully yet imposingly at the south end of the Long Water.

Second, these structures and ornaments, while hugely enjoyable in their own right, play a central role in the ingenious layout, which is the fruit of a succession of inventive designers. For as one progresses along the newly uncovered and restored paths, surprise and mystery appears at every turn as eye-catching statues and buildings are artfully revealed and then hidden once again.

One of the most interesting aspects of the designed landscape at Wrest Park is that unlike so many other historic gardens where one garden incarnation has been laid on top of its predecessor, Wrest Park has expanded horizontally. Thus, over time, new elements have been incorporated around the edges of the original garden scheme that was largely commissioned in the early 18th century.

This makes for an absorbing walk through nearly 300 years of garden history and affords the opportunity to experience a rare example of an 18th-century transitional English landscape garden.

Survivors of this style, epitomised by the work of Charles Bridgeman (d1738) and Stephen Switzer (1682-1745), are rare because most of their work was covered up by successive designers.

'walk through nearly 300 years of garden history'

The present house (some of which can be explored by visitors) was designed and built between 1834 and 1839 by Thomas de Grey, 2nd Earl de Grey, an amateur architect. That he had an interest in the French style is obvious from the architecture of the house, which was based on designs for Parisian townhouses that he had seen in books. The Earl's decision to erect his new home some 300 metres or so north of its predecessor was a cunning bit of design for two reasons.

First, it provided the space to create his Parterre Garden on the terrace immediately below the house. The parterre de broderie (literally 'embroidery on the ground'), while a French innovation from the 17th century, was also an essential constituent of the prevailing 19th-century Italianate garden style. So Thomas's new garden was in vogue.

The new location also allowed Thomas to harmoniously integrate his new garden with the existing one – hence the linear evolution. In this, Thomas was fortunate for the earlier garden, often referred to as the Great Garden, was by now in a complementary form. By the time Rocque produced his 1737 engraving of Wrest Park, the Great Garden had been enlarged and modified, its form now echoing the 3rd Earl of Burlington's garden at Chiswick House and the early landscape style of Charles Bridgeman.

Yet, even as the wheel of garden fashion turned, succeeding generations respected the original layout – to the extent that the 'landscape improvements' made by Lancelot 'Capability' Brown between 1758 and 1760 were restricted to the periphery of the landscape.

Today, the urgent stabilisation work undertaken by English Heritage upon taking ownership in 2006 is complete, and emphasis has shifted to restoration. The project aims to conserve and restore the key elements of the garden – and in this English Heritage has been lucky because a wealth of archive material has survived. Family papers, plant lists and maps have been supplemented by archaeological surveys and digs, and a number of restorative works are now under way.

As of August 2011, visitors will arrive and park in the walled kitchen garden, within which will be the new visitor centre. A 74-seat café, with additional outdoor seating, sits alongside two play areas for young and older children. The planting here echoes the previous use of this space as a kitchen garden: the soft landscape of herbs and vegetables and the brick walls replanted with trained fruit trees. Many will be exact replantings because lead name tags from the fruit trees are still attached to the walls.

From here, visitors proceed along the Long Path – originally aligned on the Countess's Sitting Room so she could watch the gardeners at work – through the reinstated pear orchard and into the restored Italian Garden. With its formal design of geometric stone-edged beds filled with seasonal bedding plants and herbaceous perennials, this cheerful garden is the perfect scene-setter for the restored Conservatory and its collection of tender exotics.

Passing through the house and out to the rear, one is presented with the sweeping vista that takes in the Long Water and the distant Pavilion. Closer by, the parterres are due a spruce-up and will be flanked once again by 'platoons' of elm, which will frame the house when viewed from a distance. The cultivar is 'Lutece', which has so far proven resistant to Dutch Elm Disease. Lining the axial path leading from the house to the Long Water are adjacent rows of Portuguese laurels. Turning to the right (west) the formally patterned Rose Garden has been reinstated and together with the replanted long border makes a perfect link back to the Italian Garden.

Out and into the landscape, the restoration continues. The overgrown yew hedges around the Bowling Green have been removed and reinstated only at the corners as per an earlier design. And in the American Garden, paths were discovered by archaeologists under the soil, but not in exactly the same place as shown on the maps. So which to restore to? The decision was made to use the 'on the ground' evidence as this will provide an exact restoration of bed and path network. Work continues on the 'groves' either side of the Long Water, to redefine the network of allées, paths and open glades.

Much work has been done and much remains to be done. The dredging of the canals, for example, remains a mighty task for a later day. But the team at Wrest Park can and should be justly proud of their sterling achievements. Wrest Park, the sleeping beauty of the English landscape, is opening her eyes once more.

A great day out

To complement the revitalisation of the gardens, exciting new visitorfacilities have been built. Inside, you'll find a bright modern space with a traditional twist because the new café has been decorated with English Heritage historic paint donated by Little Greene Paint Company. There is plenty of space for children to explore, a new adventure play area and 'tracker packs' to help families discover more about Wrest Park in a fun way. Visitors can enjoy light refreshments in the new café, including delicious sandwiches and soups, made from locally sourced produce, and freshly baked cakes and snacks.

Grounds for celebration

There are plenty of things to see and do to make your trip to Wrest Park a memorable one

Beauty at every turn

The Chinese Temple and Chinese Bridge nestle among lush woodland *(right)*, echoing the look of the Chinese Pagoda at Kew Gardens.

Visitors who know little about Wrest Park will find plenty of illuminating interpretation in and around the property. You will find a simple introductory exhibition in the new visitor centre, three exciting exhibitions in the house itself and brand new displays in the Bowling Green House and the Pavilion. August 2011 saw the first phase of the restoration in place, the replanted gardens will bloom brighter and bolder as time goes on, as these artists' impressions reveal. All in all, it makes Wrest Park the perfect place for a memorable day out.

Email **customers@english-heritage.org.uk**
or visit **www.english-heritage.org.uk**

ENGLISH HERITAGE

A longer version of the article was originally published in ***Heritage Today*** *magazine, July 2011.*

The roses return

Until early 2011, the Rose Garden at Wrest Park was hidden under a blanket of turf. It has now been restored to the original design, as indicated in a photograph from a 1904 edition of Country Life magazine. Thanks to aerial photographs and topographical surveys, the gardening team has been able to determine an approximate layout of the now replanted rose beds.

Events for everyone

Even those for whom garden history is not an obvious attraction will find something to appeal at Wrest Park. Much is being done to provide an enriching and engaging visit foreveryone, and families, in particular, will find the new Wrest Park hard to resist. As well as the new visitor centre, café and children's play area, there are plenty of exciting events, too.

Take home something special

If you want a memento of your visit to Wrest Park, the new gift shop has a range of jewellery, scarves and gifts (some are pictured below) and there is an extensive range of plants for sale in the new plant centre.

WILD about Gardens

Jonathan
WILD
GARDENS
www.jonathanwildgardens.co.uk

Landscape gardener ***Jonathan Wild*** goes in search of Lancelot 'Capability' Brown's roots in Northumberland. He pays homage to Gertrude Jekyll at Holy Island and sees what Grand Design really means at the staggering Alnwick Garden.

Photos: *Nigel Gibson & Linda Croose Smith*

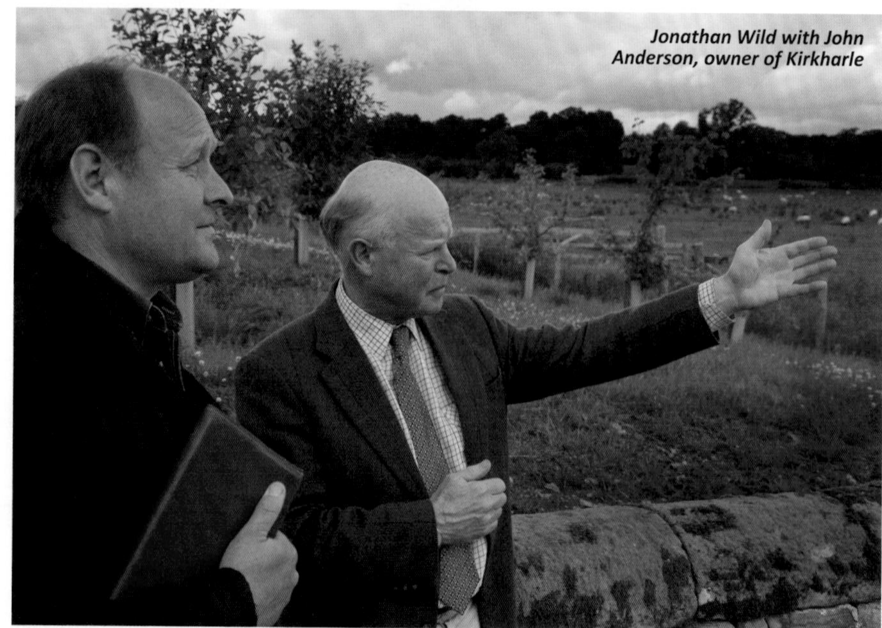
Jonathan Wild with John Anderson, owner of Kirkharle

John and Kitty Anderson with Brown's masterplan

KIRKHARLE
BROWN'S BIRTHPLACE

'Capability' Brown was born in Kirkharle in Northumberland in 1716 and went on to serve his gardening apprenticeship there, living and working on the estate until the age of 23.

The current owners, John and Kitty Anderson, have not only created a vibrant retail and cultural 'Courtyard' at Kirkharle but have also given life to Brown's unique vision for the otherwise unremarkable pasture land.

His plan is proudly displayed at the entrance to the new landscape, where sheep and cattle now share their grazing with the influx of wildlife that Brown's trademark serpentine lakes and wildflower meadows have brought.

As John proudly told me, 'Since the lakes were created 12 months ago we have seen 17 species of birds and an otter, so our next project is to try and make them feel more at home by creating an artificial holt. Our overall aim is to increase the biodiversity of the area as much as possible.'

Clearly this strategy is working, as we had to take care to avoid treading on newly metamorphosed frogs hopping all over the paths as well as a rich variety of wildflowers throughout the grassland – the result of carefully balanced

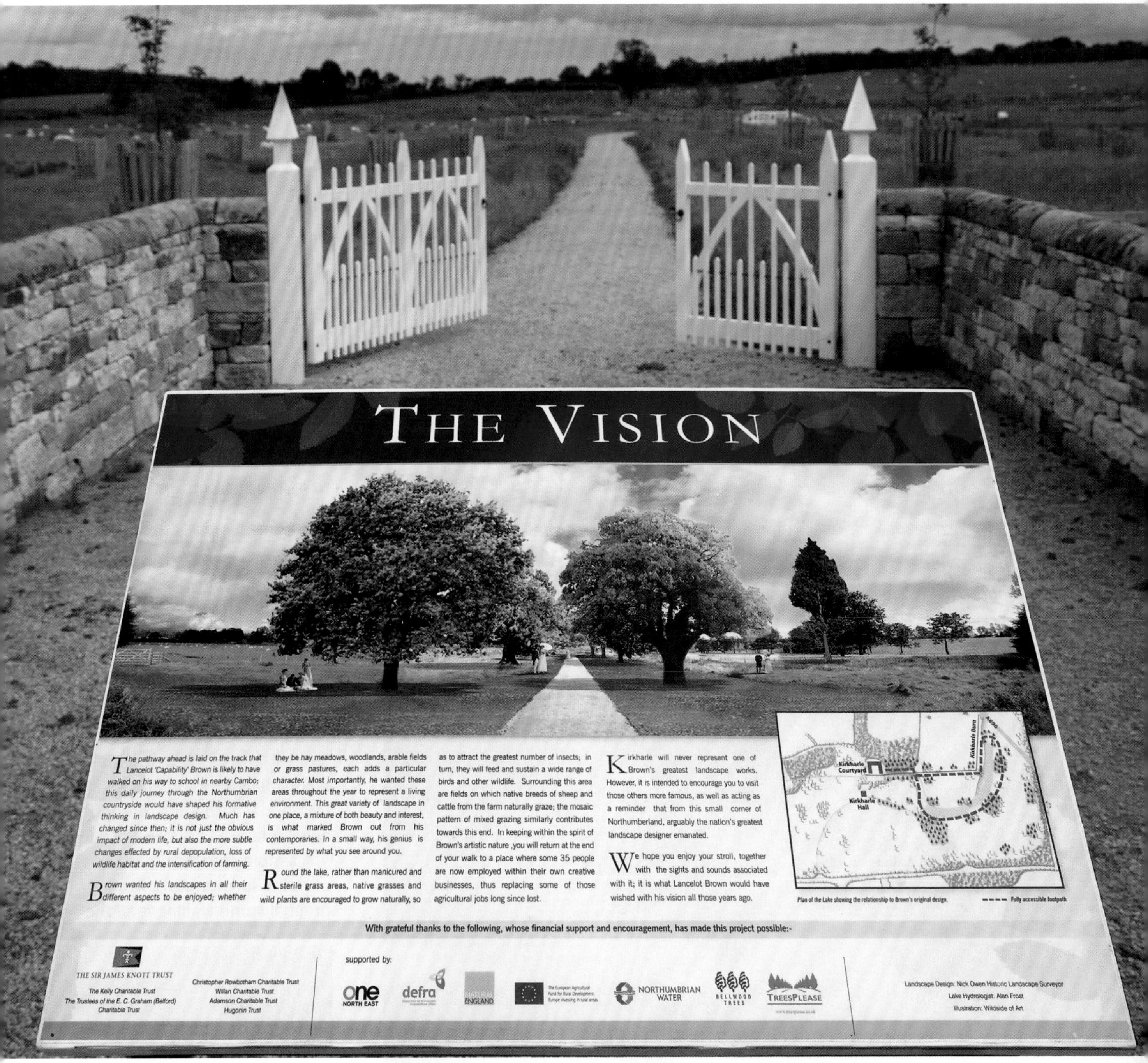

THE VISION
The pathway ahead is laid on the track that Lancelot 'Capability' Brown is likely to have walked on his way to school in nearby Cambo; this daily journey through the Northumbrian countryside would have shaped his formative thinking in landscape design. Much has changed since then; it is not just the obvious impact of modern life, but also the more subtle changes effected by rural depopulation, loss of wildlife habitat and the intensification of farming.
Brown wanted his landscapes in all their different aspects to be enjoyed; whether they be hay meadows, woodlands, arable fields or grass pastures, each adds a particular character. Most importantly, he wanted these areas throughout the year to represent a living environment. This great variety of landscape in one place, a mixture of both beauty and interest, is what marked Brown out from his contemporaries. In a small way, his genius is represented by what you see around you.
Round the lake, rather than manicured and sterile grass areas, native grasses and wild plants are encouraged to grow naturally, so as to attract the greatest number of insects; in turn, they will feed and sustain a wide range of birds and other wildlife. Surrounding this area are fields on which native breeds of sheep and cattle from the farm naturally graze; the mosaic pattern of mixed grazing similarly contributes towards this end. In keeping within the spirit of Brown's artistic nature ,you will return at the end of your walk to a place where some 35 people are now employed within their own creative businesses, thus replacing some of those agricultural jobs long since lost.
Kirkharle will never represent one of Brown's greatest landscape works. However, it is intended to encourage you to visit those others more famous, as well as acting as a reminder that from this small corner of Northumberland, arguably the nation's greatest landscape designer emanated.
We hope you enjoy your stroll, together with the sights and sounds associated with it; it is what Lancelot Brown would have wished with his vision all those years ago.
Kirkharle Courtyard
Kirkharle Hall
Kirkharle Burn
Plan of the Lake showing the relationship to Brown's original design.
Fully accessible footpath
With grateful thanks to the following, whose financial support and encouragement, has made this project possible:-
THE SIR JAMES KNOTT TRUST
The Kelly Charitable Trust
The Trustees of the E. C. Graham (Belford) Charitable Trust
Christopher Rowbotham Charitable Trust
Willan Charitable Trust
Adamson Charitable Trust
Hugonin Trust
supported by:
one NORTH EAST
defra
NATURAL ENGLAND
NORTHUMBRIAN WATER
BELLWOOD TREES
TREESPLEASE
Landscape Design: Nick Owen Historic Landscape Surveyor
Lake Hydrologist: Alan Frost
Illustration: Wildside of Art

seed mixes and a sensible interpretation of the original plans.

It is great testament to the hard work of John and Kitty that Kirkharle can finally boast another great Brown landscape to add to the Chatsworths and Blenheim Palaces of his later years – not to mention a new 'des res' for Northumberland's grateful otters! **>>**

Otter by Danny Green (rspb-images.com)

Capability Brown's KIRKHARLE LAKE & COURTYARD

If you are interested in visiting Kirkharle contact: John and Kitty Anderson, Kirkharle Courtyard, Kirkharle, Northumberland NE19 2PE

www.kirkharlecourtyard.net
enquiries@kirkharlecourtyard.net
Telephone: 01830 540362
Fax: 01830 540400

LINDISFARNE
SMALL IS BEAUTIFUL

'Capability' Brown's 18th century work was on a grand scale. Gertrude Jekyll's gardens were far more intimate. She was the leading Garden Designer of ***her*** era and designed this garden on Holy Island – an eighth-of-an-acre former veg plot – between 1906 - 1912. Tiny it may be, but the effect of a charming cottage garden set in open fields right by the sea is mesmeric.

Anyone one who has tried to recreate a 'cottage' effect with a good mix of annuals, perennials and edibles is well aware just how difficult it is to achieve. Luckily for the National Trust they have entrusted the care of Jekyll's garden to the very 'capable' hands of Philippa Hodkinson, who has virtually single-handedly made the garden 'honest' again – with original plants diligently sourced and traditional gardening methods adhered to.

A simple cruciform pattern of paths surrounded by the original stone walling is all the

Calendula Orange King provide a warm, sunny welcome

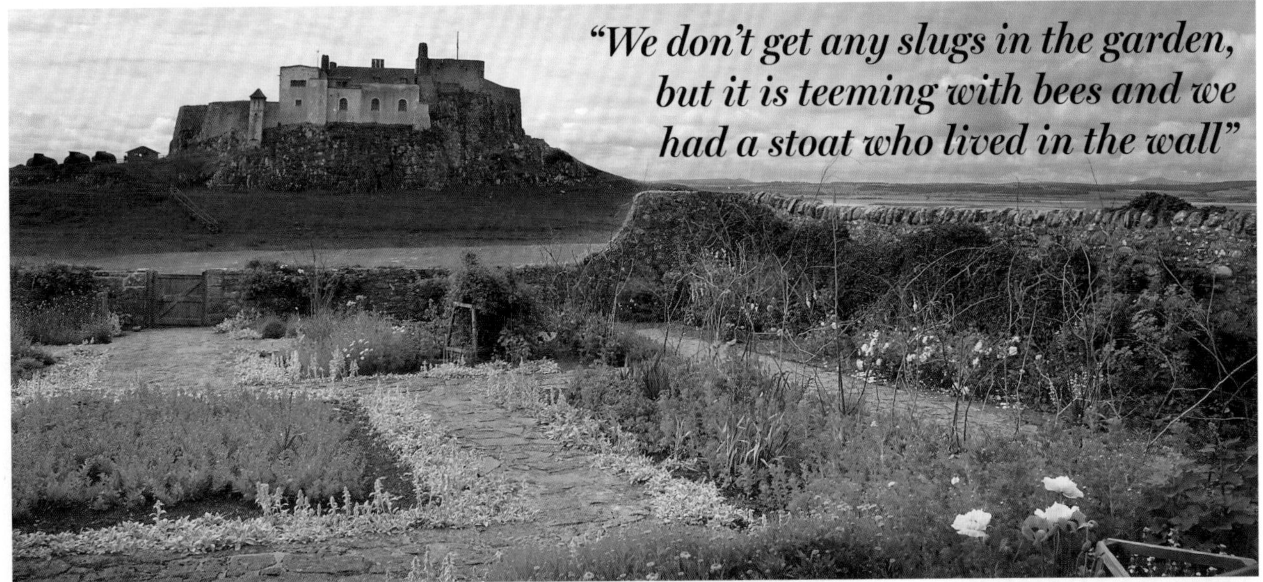
"We don't get any slugs in the garden, but it is teeming with bees and we had a stoat who lived in the wall"

Welcome to
Lindisfarne Castle
Gertrude Jekyll Garden

THE NATIONAL TRUST
This garden was designed by
GERTRUDE JEKYLL
Between 1906 -1912
Ticket for admission to castle and garden:
(Obtainable at castle entrance)
Garden admission if not visiting castle:
Donations welcome
THANK YOU FOR ENSURING THAT THE GATE IS
SECURELY FASTENED AT ALL TIMES TO PREVENT
THE SHEEP FROM DAMAGING THE PLANTS

'hard landscaping' necessary to frame the wonderful displays of godetias, marigolds, lambs tails and other familiar plants which as Philippa says, 'Would have had the wow factor in their day!'

As Philippa points out, the garden is not just there for the benefit of the 100,000 visitors it attracts every year – but also for the wildlife which also enjoys the facilities provided.

'We don't get any slugs in the garden, but it is teeming with bees and we even had a stoat who lived in the wall. This year the wagtails also nested and they like to keep me company as I work in the garden.' **>>**

FOR VISITOR INFORMATION ON LINDISFARNE CASTLE TURN TO PAGE 388

The Duchess of Northumberland
Photo: Margaret Whittaker

"My favourite part of Alnwick is the Ornamental Garden"

THE ALNWICK GARDEN

A DUCHESS'S DREAM

Alnwick Garden is arguably the most magnificent piece of modern landscaping in this country – and it would appear to be a big hit with the public, as well over half a million have visited annually since it opened in 2002.

Quite what 'Capability' Brown would have made of the very contemporary garden that has replaced his original design at Alnwick is hard to imagine. Resplendent with a very un-serpentine computer-operated water feature, tree house complex and bamboo labyrinth, it is very much the vision of the Duchess of Northumberland, who has been the driving force behind the garden's concept and design.

Heading up the gardening team of 11 staff is Trevor Jones.

'We recently under planted 360 cherry trees with over 600,000 'The Mistress' tulip bulbs – as chosen by the Duchess. Not a job for the faint hearted considering they have to be planted individually!' he says. Trevor is also rightly proud of the garden's family-friendly design. 'Our policy is to get children in to the gardens and wherever possible we let them pick any goodies such as strawberries. You won't see any "Keep Off" signs anywhere in the gardens – visitors can come and go as they like.' It is clear where his heart lies though: 'My favourite part of Alnwick is the Ornamental Garden – particularly the herbaceous plantings.'

Alnwick is still very much a work in progress and there are ambitious plans to extend the water cascade and provide synchronized fountains with light and sound plus another maze. Next time I must bring the kids!

FOR VISITOR INFORMATION ON THE ALNWICK GARDEN TURN TO PAGE 386

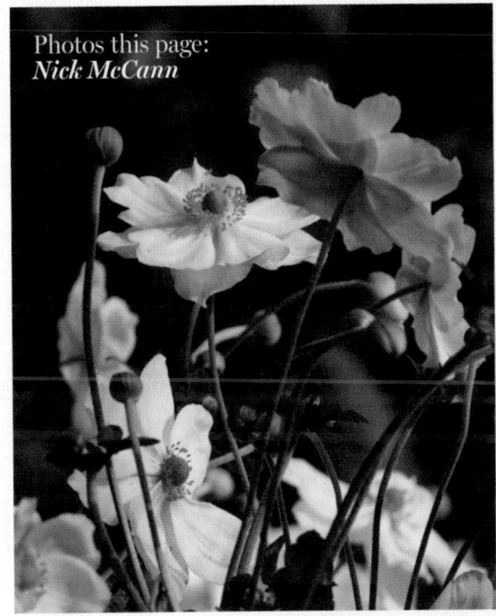

Photos this page: *Nick McCann*

'The Alnwick Garden was built to benefit the local community. To me, The Alnwick Garden is at its best when it is full of children running in and out of the water features being watched by rows of older people who enjoy seeing children play. Encouraging children to switch off their televisions was one of my key aims when working on the design and content of the garden. We run a large variety of charitable programmes for all ages and abilities which is the heartbeat of the garden. These programmes include teaching schools and school children to grow, nurture and cook fresh food, workshops for older people and children to help them learn to respect and understand each other better, drug awareness, gardeners, apprenticeships and internships, NVQ's in customer service training etc. Gardens and, in particular, how they are used, have the ability to alter lives for the better. That is where my interest in gardening lies.'

The Duchess of Northumberland

Robert Innes-Smith, for many years this country's foremost and most prolific producer of guidebooks, recalls with irreverence, some of his more memorable aristocratic encounters...

Guidebook maker

Robert is a talented writer, journalist, raconteur, mimic and joke-teller. In his years at English Life Publications & Pilgrim Press (now part of Hudson's Heritage Group) he produced an unequalled library of guidebooks to historic properties. When he retired in 1993 he was replaced by Hudson's Editor, Nick McCann, and the two became friends. Robert puts it like this: "Nick followed in my footsteps and stepped right in it."

The great levellers

When my children were young, I produced a guidebook for the late Duke of Hamilton's seat, Lennoxlove. Rather than have to trek all the way to Scotland to check the proofs, the Duke suggested I met him in the House of Lords bar to discuss it. I was able to park not far from Westminster (one could in those days) and walk to the Lords. After our business, the Duke asked me to give him a lift to where he was staying. When we got in the car I apologised for all the mess, blaming my children. 'Don't talk to me about kids and cars,' he said. 'It's all piss and biscuits!'

Private & confidential

In the great entrance hall at Rockingham Castle are two ancient iron-bound chests, one of which is said to have belonged to the ill-fated King John. The estate had previously belonged to the Culme-Seymour family and a friend of mine who knew old Lady Culme-Seymour had asked her what was in King John's chest (bearing in mind he died in 1216). She replied that she did not know and did not feel it was her right to pry! As far as I know, the chest still hasn't been opened to this day...

Perfect pitch

When, at the 10th Duke of Northumberland's invitation, I visited Alnwick Castle, I was met by Bill Hugonin, the charming agent there. 'The Duke does not normally see salesmen, but in your case he has made an exception,' he explained. 'Please let me do the talking and don't speak until you are spoken to.' His Grace was seated behind a huge desk with bookshelves behind. He did not greet me, or even look at me, and directed his questions at Bill, who then relayed them on. Taking exception to one of my suggestions, ('What does he want *that* in the guidebook for?' he asked Bill) he opened a huge tome and got down on his hands and knees to examine it. Rising slowly to resume his seat, he addressed me for the first time: 'You are quite right,' he said, and then personally showed me around the Castle. When I suggested including a certain 17th century portrait, he shook his head. 'I don't want *him* in the guidebook,' he said, 'he was a frightful s***!'

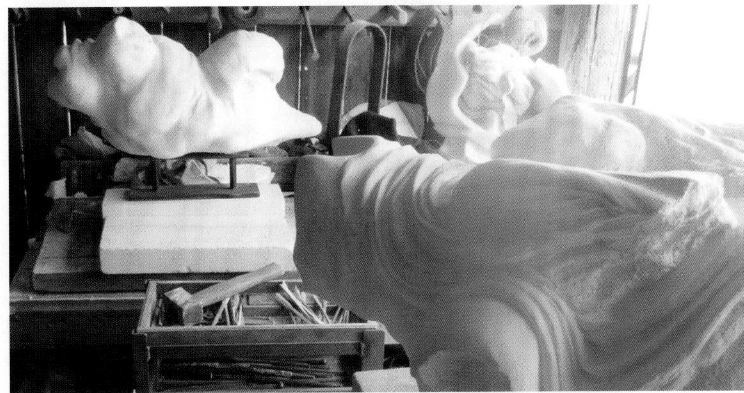

For more information on Peter and his work, visit: www.peterstandleydesign.com

Sculptor

Sculptor and garden designer, Peter Standley, is based in Southwell, Nottinghamshire, where he has a studio in the grounds of Norwood Park.

Peter discovered his love of working with stone in Athens, a city which he first visited as an art student, and where he then settled for five years. A frequent visitor to the Acropolis, he would watch the Greek masons at work and was fascinated by their restoration of a temple in Monastiraki using crisp white Pendelikon marble. Today, that juxtaposition of the ancient, decaying stone set against the background of a dry, arid landscape continues to influence and inspire his designs.

Peter then spent the following decade living in the mountains to the north of the city, where he learnt to cut, carve and build with stone, creating dry-stone walls from desert-coloured limestone and beautiful carvings from Greek marble.

On his return to the UK, he continued to sculpt and carve, while also branching out into garden design and stone interiors. In 2006, he exhibited at Sandringham House, Norfolk, where he was awarded a silver medal for his garden promoting British stone.

Peter's current portfolio includes decorative carving, restoration of stonework, and bespoke interior and exterior stonework, as well as garden design. He welcomes commissions (he also undertakes portraits in bronze) and is working on an exhibition of stone sculptures.

LUNCH *with Lucy*

Lucinda Lambton has been, and remains, an extraordinary advocate for British heritage, architecture, the quirky and the unusual. Beginning her career in the '60s as a photographer, she has gone on to write a positive library of fascinating and remarkable books, often illustrated with her own pictures. A complementary career in television as writer and broadcaster was inevitable and she has made over 55 films for the BBC and around 25 for ITV. On the day when her latest book, ***Places for Pigs – Animal Architecture and other Beastly Buildings,*** was published, ***Hudson's*** photographer, ***Nigel Gibson*** – something of a fan – was invited for lunch at her remarkable home: a day when the heaven's opened. Good job he managed to fix the wiring...

The cut-out figure was to promote 'Hurray For Today', a three-part ITV series on American Architecture. She's still a great fan of the country.

In amongst the myriad of decorations, the hallway walls are decorated with gilded stars rescued from an old circus in Liverpool

Lucinda Lambton greeted me warmly on the doorstep of her rural hideaway, tucked out of sight from the village road behind imposing green castellated gates.

Her career has taken many turns over the years – writer, presenter, photographer, raconteur, historian – and I was unsurprised to find that such a rich and varied life was reflected in the interior of her home.

The hallway walls were covered with architectural mouldings and rescued artefacts, and painted with colourful stage-set pictures of angels and saints in a style redolent of the Pre-Raphaelite Brotherhood or the arts and crafts movement. There were large display cabinets full to the brim with leather-bound books, death masks hanging above the doors, and the ceiling was a star chamber of dark blue decorated with gold, painted, five-point stars.

After chatting about the house and her wonderfully eclectic collection, Lucy headed into the kitchen to prepare lunch. Minutes later, her husband – Sir Peregrine Worsthorne, journalist and retired editor of *The Sunday Telegraph* – came rushing in from a trip to the village to say how heavy the rain was getting. No sooner had he delivered this news, the heavens opened – and I mean opened. It was a downpour of truly biblical proportions. The sound was cacophonous as it hit the roof and windows in what seemed a serious attempt to drown us all! Just as we thought it couldn't get any darker, there was a single, almighty clap **>>**

of theatrical rolling thunder, the house took a direct lightning strike, and all the lights and electricity were put out.

Having got over the initial shock, Lucy ran to the kitchen to rescue the fishcakes she had been cooking on the range – only to discover that the rear conservatory glass roof had become a waterfall and water was pouring straight into her dogs' beds. I offered to follow her around the house with my battery-powered LED lights and a hand-chain of bath towels was begun, from the upstairs airing cupboard to the kitchen, in an attempt to stem the flood.

Eventually, the rain abated and it took us a further ten minutes to locate the fuse boxes and restore power to a house which by now had taken on such a dark, brooding, Dickensian atmosphere, we could have been in a scene from a David Lean film.

With order and electricity duly restored – all with characteristically good humour on Lucy's part – we sat down to our lunch, which was served with a beautiful fresh green salad and the most delicious balsamic vinegar I had ever tasted.

"Considering I was a 17-year-old girl whom he'd never met, he rather improperly said, 'Don't mind if I do' – and in he came"

As we tucked in, we reflected on the morning's unexpectedly dramatic events and Lucy chatted to me at length about her early life.

One of her most exciting early memories, she revealed, is of the time when she was living in London with her parents and rather boldly invited the legendary crooner Bing Crosby to lunch:

'My mother was a fervent fan of Bing Crosby, so when I discovered he was standing outside our house, I invited him in for something to eat. Considering I was a 17-year-old girl whom he'd never met, he rather improperly said, "Don't mind if I do" – and in he came! My mother, who was about to have a baby at the time, was up a ladder, with her skirt sticking out and her knickers visible to all from below. I said, "Look who I have with me, it's your great hero," at which point she promptly fell off the ladder with shock. Bing had to catch her and she came down in his arms. The whole event was a great success and they spent all the afternoon together!'

Lucy was born and grew up in County Durham and it was there, rather than in London, that she undertook her first proper photographic assignment, working for what later became the Beamish Hall Open Air Museum. Curator and historian Frank Atkinson wished to record the life of the north-east's mining community before it vanished under the modern tide and invited anyone and everyone to get involved. Lucy answered the call and photographed the hundreds of donated artefacts: 'Everything from a row of pitman's teeth to a row of pitmen's cottages!' she recalled.

She went on to produce well over 50 television programmes over the years, including: *On The Throne – The History of the Lavatory*, *The Great North Road*, *A Cabinet of Curiosities* and *The Other House of Windsor*. *Sublime Suburbia*, her series of four films for ITV about the architectural and historic delights of London's suburbs, won the Regional Television award for the best documentary series of 2003. A further series of *Sublime Suburbia* in six parts, followed in 2004. Her numerous books include: *Temples of Convenience, a history of the lavatory*; *Beastly Buildings*, about architecture for animals; *Vanishing Victoriana; An Album of Curious Houses*; *Lucinda Lambton's A-Z of Britain*, a companion to her 26-part television series for the BBC; and her latest work – a further photographic investigation into aristocratic animal architecture, *Palaces for Pigs*.

'The most hopeful claim I could make,' she reflected over our dessert of strawberries and cream, 'is that I have recorded buildings and certain architectural elements that would otherwise never have been known about and that as a result, I've helped save them from demolition.' This is typically modest of someone who dislikes to use her inherited title "Lady" Lucinda Lambton. 'As a double blow I got it again through marrying Sir Peregrine,' she told me as I took my leave at the end what had been a fascinating and eventful visit – 'He did something to earn it!'

Lucy and her husband, Sir Peregrine Worsthorne

DASHERS

"Easy to prepare, easy to serve and easy to eat... It's the sort of food every host and hostess aspires to when entertaining. We need menus that can either be prepped well ahead or are no more than a quick 'assembly' job. In other words, well behaved dishes which are happy to sit around for a while and won't spoil whilst waiting. Here for Hudsons, are two suggestions to guarantee you stylish partying" ***Katie Dashwood***

Dishes with Dashers

COURGETTE & MINT SOUP

(Serves 4-6)

1 medium onion, peeled and finely diced
1 litre chicken or vegetable stock (I use a stock cube)
500-750g/ 1- 1 ½ lbs courgettes, topped and tailed and roughly sliced
200g /oz tub cream cheese
Seasoning
Handful fresh mint leaves, torn

Put the onion into a saucepan with the stock cube and add a little boiling water to cover. Cover the pan with a lid and cook the onion gently to soften, (7-10 mins) stirring from time and time and making sure there is enough liquid so that it doesn't 'catch' and burn. Next, add the courgettes and the rest of the water, replace the lid and cook for a further 12-15 minutes until the vegetables are done. Remove from the heat and add the cream cheese (I just spoon it into the mixture in dollops to break it up a bit) - whiz - either in a food processor or with an electric hand stick if you have one - until smooth, throwing in the mint leaves whilst the machine is running. Season to taste - remember that commercial stock cubes are quite salty so don't get too carried away! If too thick, thin down with cold water then cover and leave to cool. This is excellent served cold (in which case also chill the bowls in the fridge beforehand) or reheated. Garnish the top with of each one with a sprig of fresh mint.

MOROCCAN LAMB

(Serves 6)

The great thing about stews, casseroles and tagines is that they benefit from long, slow cooking and then improve with re-heating so you can do this one completely ahead of schedule (and freeze it if you like). It also works incredibly well with a cheaper cut of meat too - shanks, neck fillet/middle neck or shoulder are all fine. I've kept the fruit out of the tagine here and put it into the couscous instead but, if you like, some dried apricots, figs or dates would all go wonderfully well.

1 ½ - 2 kg/ 3 ½ - 4 lbs lamb – see above – cubed unless using shanks
4 tbsp olive oil
8 garlic cloves, crushed
4 onions, peeled and sliced
4 tsp root ginger, peeled and grated
1 ½ tsp coriander seeds, crushed
3 tsp ground cinnamon
1 cinnamon stick
Salt & Pepper
Good squirt tomato puree
400g tin tomatoes
2 - 3 strip of orange zest
Diced aubergine or butternut squash
4 - 5 tbsp honey
Handful each chopped mint and coriander leaves

Preheat the oven to 150 C. Heat half the oil in a casserole pan and when hot, sear the meat in batches for a few minutes on both sides until nicely coloured. Remove and set aside. Add the rest of the oil to the pan and cook the garlic, onions, ginger and spices until the onions are soft. Season generously with salt and pepper then add the lamb, tomato puree, tomatoes, orange zest, veggies and honey and cover and cook for at least 1 ½ hours in the oven.

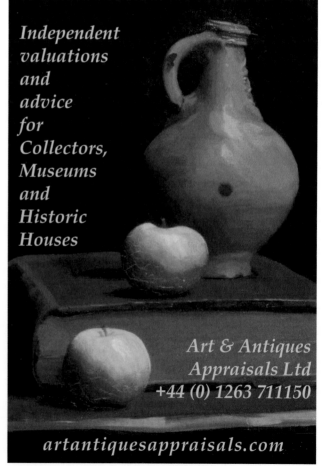

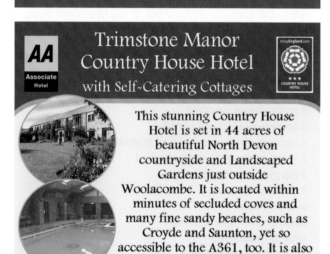

The Tudor Group is an extraordinary body of men, women and children who dedicate their spare time to re-enacting the lives of our Tudor forebears. Leader of the Group and television personality, ***Ruth Goodman***, talks to ***Hudson's*** at the stunning Haddon Hall in Derbyshire, where the Group appears regularly each year.

Photos: *Nigel Gibson & Linda Croose-Smith*

Costume DRAMA

& alter egos

The Tudor Group are a passionate bunch of people who meet to explore life in 16th century Britain, carrying out Tudor activities in Tudor places. At Haddon Hall in Derbyshire the food, cooking, etiquette, organisation and life of a large wealthy household forms the framework for recipes, personal hygiene, sword play and Elizabethan art It's a fantastic survival of a near-complete medieval/early-modern great house whose spaces cry out with echoes of a forgotten way of life. The layout, the wear patterns, the equipment and furnishings all complement the historical information revealed by documents, and by doing the right activities in the right spaces it all begins to make sense – the sounds and smells of the 1500s start to waft back. We feel it is a real privilege to be able to extend our understanding of history in this way and hope we can share both the fun and the insight we gain with all those who visit.

In contrast to the grandeur of Haddon, the Welsh National Museum of Folk Life is the setting for our investigations into the daily life and beliefs of a much humbler sort of community rooted in the Welsh countryside. Houses and a church relocated from different areas of Wales give us the opportunity to sleep on straw mat beds, to build fences and try to survive on the diet of the labouring classes as well as organise the sort of community activities in the church which formed the social glue of village life. The Weald and Downland Museum of West Sussex is another set of wonderful Tudor spaces that we are privileged to use in the traditional ways. Here, amongst other things, we have an opportunity to look into the commercial life of Tudor Britain with its shops and market square.

Everyone within the Tudor Group has their own specialisms and interests, from early drama to soap making, accountancy to blacksmithing. We come together to share these interests and recreate aspects of our Elizabethan heritage. No one can be an expert in everything and we enjoy hearing about each other's research and combining our skills to create the bigger picture. During the winter months we meet up to work on larger joint projects and try out new things. There are few things in life more fun than working together with likeminded people. We are a lucky bunch. For some of the members the pursuit of Tudor crafts has become a modern livelihood, supplying high-quality replica items to museums, theatre and film. Reviving lost arts, resurrecting old techniques and translating them into a living tradition carries a strong appeal for many of the Tudor group who between them can produce gilded leather jerkins, suits of armour, starched ruffs, bread, rush hats, beautifully bound books, knitted silk stockings, cutlery, beer, furniture, jewellery and much much more. Nor is it just about the finished products. The processes, tools, and the lives of people in the past who followed these trades and had these skills at their fingertips, are equally fascinating.

The Tudor group is a voluntary organisation involving people from many walks of life: archaeologists, historians, craftspeople, scientists – plus a host of members whose day jobs seem quite unrelated to history! Making clothes, workshops, research... there's plenty to keep them busy between Tudor events up and down the country. It's not so much a hobby as a passion.

The Tudor Group will be appearing at Haddon Hall in 2012. See Haddon's publicity and website for details

FOR VISITOR INFORMATION ON HADDON HALL TURN TO PAGE 298

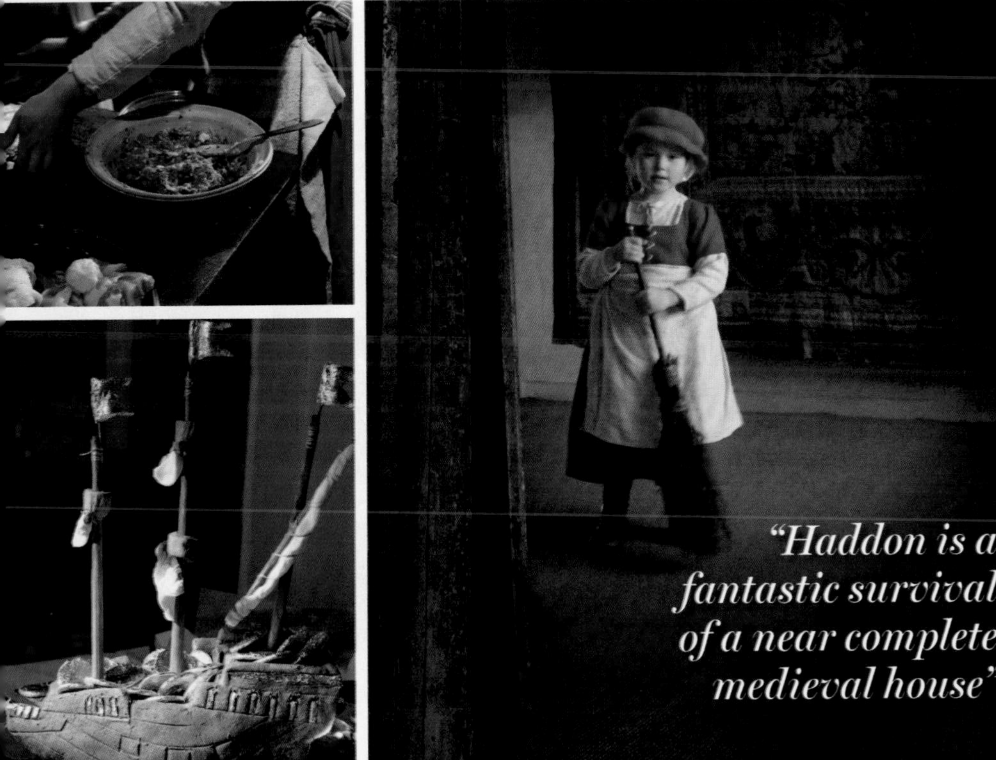

"Haddon is a fantastic survival of a near complete medieval house"

Chairman of the Churches Conservation Trust, the multi-talented and multi-faceted ***Loyd Grossman*** gives ***Hudson's*** his highly personal view on why this country's historic parish churches have so much to offer: as he says, 'something for everyone'.

BROAD *Church*

I grew up in New England where the picturesque formula of white clapboard meeting house (the New England term for a congregational church) and village green provided an instantly recognisible and inspirational heart for almost every village and small town. When I came to England as a student in the 1970s, I was delighted to discover that thousands of parish churches provided a similar spiritual and social anchor for urban neighbourhood and country village alike. In those days my local was Chelsea Old Church, one-time heart of the old manor of Chelsea, home in Tudor times to Sir Thomas More and in the 19th century to a dazzling group of artists and writers including James McNeill Whistler, Thomas Carlyle and Oscar Wilde. Bombed to ruination during the Blitz, Chelsea Old Church was painstakingly rebuilt after the war and as well as being the home of a lively parish remains a beautiful and fascinating précis of Chelsea's long and fascinating history. **>>**

THE QUEEN MOTHER

A needlework footstool for the Queen Mother

Photographed at Chelsea Old Church by ***Will Pascall***

England's parish churches – a staggering 12,000 of them are listed buildings due to their architectural merit – are an unrivalled epitome of over a thousand years of our history and culture. When you open the door to a historic church you are unhindered by glass cases, roped walkways or queues and you can enjoy heritage in a church in a way not possible anywhere else. In peace and quiet, often alone and free of admission charges you can wander round and discover for yourself the wonderful collections of art and sculpture, still in their original location, in England's parish churches. Saxon stonework, medieval wallpaintings and stained glass, Georgian furnishings or Victorian memorials, whatever you seek can be found in thousands of different and internationally important buildings across the land. No other heritage experience exists like this, in buildings still at the heart of communities and still in use for their original purpose.

The English landscape is defined by the towers and steeples of the parish church. They guide you to the treasures within, appearing through the trees as you approach. Maybe the bells will be ringing, creating a unique atmosphere and calling you along country lanes to tiny, unsigned villages or churches standing alone in a field where once there was a medieval town.

If the door is not already open you can collect the key next door and hear the stories of locals whose families have been associated with the church for generations. Maybe they will show you around, point out hidden features and tell you how the building has changed and grown over the centuries. You might get the chance to climb the steep spiral staircase to the top of the tower, past the clock and the bell chamber, to marvel at the view over surrounding countryside, or go down into the crypt where ancestors are buried or more treasures held. No two churches are the same but all are guaranteed to cause you to stop and think, soak up the centuries and learn a bit more about why these buildings are still important today.

It could be you are visiting a tiny, single-room Norman church almost unchanged since the day it was built. You will come across many, many churches which have been added to again and again over the centuries. Saxon origins, Norman arches, medieval arcades, Jacobean coats of arms and Georgian pews all in one harmonious building, each beautiful in their own right and glorious together, telling of England's rich architectural history and amazingly still there for you to touch, enjoy, even sit on. Or perhaps you'll find a stunning Victorian box of jewels, all of a piece and built by some great 19th century philanthropist using the best stonemasons, woodcarvers, glassmakers and artists of the time.

Left to right: St Andrew's, Winterborne Tompson; Shrewsbury St Mary's Jesse window; Goltho St George
Photographs: © The Churches Conservation Trust

The Churches Conservation Trust, of which I am privileged to be Chairman, is a national charity which looks after over 340 of the most beautiful and historically important of these parish churches, which are no longer in regular parish use. Our collection contains all of the above and more. Joining the Trust is a great way to come to know and understand historic parish churches.

At the Trust you'll find the tiny Winterborne Tomson St Andrew's in Dorset, alone in a farmyard and almost unchanged in 200 years. Contrast that with the grand town centre Shrewsbury St Mary with its internationally important Jesse window and St Bernard stained glass, and the clifftop splendour of Georgian Fylingdales St Stephen's on the North Yorkshire coast, with a dizzying triple-decker pulpit and fine furnishings inside and views across the sea from its sheep-grazed churchyard outside. If you want to understand more about a particular era you can plan a tour of Trust churches by architect, by era, style or contents. For example, I am especially fond of medieval wall paintings which are an often ghostly reminder of how colourful our pre-Reformation churches were. You can find these fragile survivors in unspoilt churches such as Inglesham St John the Baptist in Wiltshire, saved by William Morris from 'Victorianisation'. There is indeed so much to discover in churches all across the country like the magnificent and magnificently preserved alabaster monuments in Harewood All Saints near Leeds or the breathtaking Victorian grandeur of George Gilbert-Scott's All Souls Haley Hill Halifax. Follow in the footsteps of John Betjeman at the surprising Goltho St George in Lincolnshire which I recently visited for the first time. And children will be fascinated with tales of pirate graves in Skelton in Cleveland, peculiar corbals and gargoyles at medieval Edlington St Peter in Yorkshire or the feared Black Dog of Bungay in Suffolk.

This is just the very beginning of a trail of discovery which could fascinate you and your family for years to come. There is something for everyone and our historic churches are always open whatever the weather. All we ask is that you leave a donation to help us keep the roof on so that future generations can share the same pleasure and inspiration that we find. Please join us in our campaign to make sure our wonderful historic churches remain at the heart of communities all over England.

Using our website
www.visitchurches.org.uk
or leaflets and guides you can plan days out visiting churches alongside a country walk, lunch at the pub or a tour round the town or a stately home. Joining our membership keeps you in touch with events and teaches you about the specialist conservation work being carried out to keep these amazing buildings standing and open to the public every day of the year.

"There is something for everyone and our historic churches are always open whatever the weather. All we ask is that you leave a donation to help us keep the roof on so that future generations can share the same pleasure and inspiration that we find. Please join us in our campaign to make sure our wonderful historic churches remain at the heart of communities all over England."

The Churches Conservation Trust - Protecting 1000 years of history

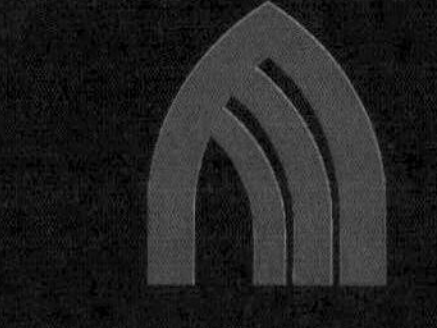

THE CHURCHES
CONSERVATION TRUST

www.visitchurches.org.uk

The Churches Conservation Trust, since being established 42 years ago, has saved over 340 unique and important buildings which now attract over two million visitors a year. Our churches range from tiny rural idylls to large urban buildings in disadvantaged areas and span a thousand years of history. All have been passed to the Trust by the Church Commissioners when their use as parish churches has come to an end.

The Trust has in the past relied on the Government and the Church Commissioners for its funding but it is clear the scale of the challenges the Trust now faces requires wider support. Not only is the number of churches being transferred to the Trust likely to increase but the cost of conservation will continue to rise.

It takes skilled craftsmanship to look after an old church. Many contain beautiful and fragile monuments from the past: tombs, painting, fittings and carvings, the conservation of which requires specialist skills. And it takes both vision and investment to make churches suitable for public use once more: often such buildings require money to be spent on heating and lighting, toilet facilities and disabled access.

In places such as ancient St Leonard-at-the-Hythe, Colchester, once the main church of a proud port, we have sensitive plans to convert the church as a venue for concerts, exhibitions, bringing the building back to life. Or All Saints, Cambridge, with rich stained glass windows and sumptuous wall paintings by some of the finest artists of the nineteenth century, all in desperate need of conservation. Or one of our favourite projects, the restoration and conversion of All Souls at Crompton, near Bolton, a magnificent church designed by Paley and Austin, which after many years of neglect will become a centre for the local predominately Asian community.

The Churches Conservation Trust relies heavily on donations and supporter membership. Last year, we welcomed over two million visitors to our churches. If each person donated just £2, this would enable us to keep our churches open, safe and watertight for you and future generations to enjoy. We very much hope that you will decide to support the Trust, and help it do even more to preserve our heritage of historic churches.

- You can make a donation online on The Churches Conservation Trust, www.visitchurches.org.uk which includes a gift aid declaration.
- Supporters who make a donation of £1000 or more are offered Patron membership. You can join this membership scheme online too, www.visitchurches.org.uk/joinus.
- You can make a card payment over the phone, by calling 020 72130673.
- Finally you can pay by cheque. Cheques must be made out to The Churches Conservation Trust

Using Gift Aid on all or part of your donation means that for every pound you donate, The Churches Conservation Trust can claim at least 25p from HM Revenue and Customs, at no additional cost to you, helping your donation do more.

Here are a few of our current projects that we are fundraising for:

- The tiny flint and stone chapel of St Andrews in Winterborne Tomson, Dorset was rescued from almost certain ruin in 1931 when Thomas Hardy manuscripts were sold to pay for repairs. The roof now needs to be recovered and bulging masonry repaired to maintain the structural integrity of the building at a cost of £49,000.
  A final £5,000 is needed for the project to begin.
- St Nicolas in Kings Lynn is the largest Chapel of Ease in the country. The magnificent 15th century door is in need of conservation due to damage from extreme weather conditions. The total cost of the project is £50,000; £10,000 is needed for the project to start in October.

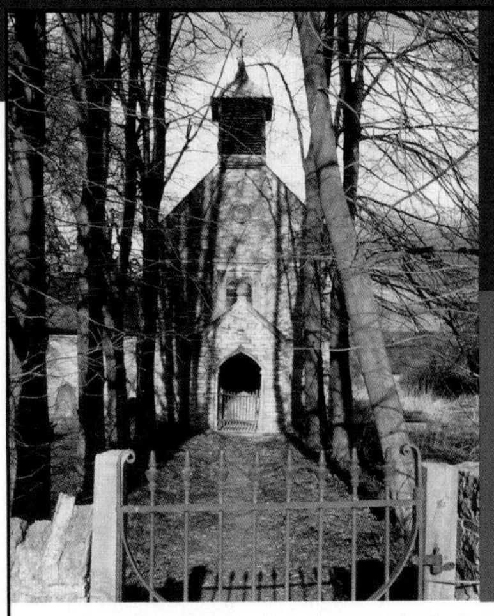

All Saints Church

Billesley
Stratford upon Avon
Warwickshire, B49 6NF

All Saints rises from a lovely wooded churchyard in the hamlet of Billesley near Stratford-upon-Avon. From its approach through an avenue of limes, it looks like a Georgian country church – but its origins go back 1,000 years. Tradition has it that William Shakespeare married Anne Hathaway here in 1582, and that his granddaughter's wedding also took place at Billesley. In 1692, Bernard Whalley rebuilt the church to create a fashionable classical addition to his Billesley estate. He installed a gallery for his staff complete with a butler's boxed seat. Whalley's own pew had a fine classical fireplace. His body lies, with his wife Lucy, in a sealed vault beneath the sanctuary floor.

Location: 4 miles west of Stratford-upon-Avon, off A46. Follow signs to Billesley and Billesley Manor Hotel. Nearest railway stations: Wilmcote (2.5 miles) and Stratford-upon-Avon (4 miles).

OS reference no: SP 148 568

Please call The Churches Conservation Trust on 020 7213 0660 (Monday - Friday, 9.00am - 5.00pm) for key holder information.

Holy Trinity Church, Privett, Hampshire

Merepond Lane, Privett, Alton, Hampshire, GU34 3PE

The spire of Holy Trinity soars high above the trees, visible for miles around in an idyllic corner of Hampshire. It is an extraordinary experience to find this lavishly decorated Medieval-style church with Italian marble mosaic floors in such a rural location. Built in 1876-78, the church was funded by William Nicholson - a local benefactor and gin distiller - and designed by Gothic architect Sir Arthur Blomfield, later responsible for the Royal College of Music. Blomfield used the best craftsmen of the day to produce the magnificent stonework, mosaics and stained glass. The walls are made from warm-toned Ham Hill stone with bands of Bath stone. Marble mosaic floors run across the church and are particularly colourful in the chancel.

Location: 5 miles west from Petersfield, off A272. Nearest railway station: Petersfield (4.7 miles). Bus route number 205 is 10-15 minutes walk away.

OS reference no: SU 677 270

Open: Open daily from 10.00am to 3.00pm

Please call The Churches Conservation Trust on 020 7213 0660 (Monday - Friday, 9.00am - 5.00pm) for key holder information.

Church of St Mary Magdelene,

Croome Park, Croome D'Abitot, Worcester, WR8 9DW

The original church at Croome was demolished by the 6th Earl of Coventry when he decided to replace his adjacent Jacobean house in the 1750s. His new house and park were designed and laid out by Capability Brown as was the church, set on a low hill nearby in Croome Park as an "eye catcher'. Built by some of the finest craftsmen in England, every detail has been considered, from pretty plaster mouldings to handsome carved pews - the church is a perfect fantasy of the period, with elegant Gothick windows and plasterwork, pulpit, communion rails, commandments and creed boards.

Location: 4m W of Pershore off A38 & A44; follow National Trust signs to Croome Park. The church is on the top of the hill overlooking the house and park. Parking at National Trust car park. Access to church via visitor centre. Nearest railway stations: Nearest railway station: Pershore (7 miles)

OS reference no: SO 886 450

Open: St Mary Magedelene is open when Croome Park is open. See the Croome Park website (National Trust) for detailed opening times.

Please call The Churches Conservation Trust on 020 7213 0660 (Monday - Friday, 9.00am - 5.00pm) for key holder information.

Church of St Thomas the Martyr

St Thomas Street,
Bristol, BS1 6QR

Located in Bristol' city centre, this handsome late 18th-century church was designed in 1789 by local architect and carver James Allen to replace a medieval church deemed unsafe for use. Allen retained the 15th-century west tower of the old church, intending it to be 'raised and modernised' in a Classical fashion, but the plan was never carried out and the church is an unusual - but pleasing - blend of both periods. There is a fine ring of eight bells; all cast by local founders from the 15th-yo the 19th-century. At the east end is a reredos of 1716 and at the west a gallery of 1728-32, both transferred from the previous church. On the north side of the chancel is a superb 18th-century organ case. Some of the other furnishings are 18th-century, but most date from the 1896 restoration by H Roumieu Gough. They are excellently designed and all contribute to one of the best interiors in Bristol.

Location: St Thomas Street, to south west of Bristol Bridge near intersection of Redcliff Street and Victoria Street. Public transport: Close to bus routes to city centre and bus station. Bus and coach terminus 1 mile. Nearest railway station: Bristol Temple Meads (0.25 mile). **OS reference no:** ST 591 727
Please call The Churches Conservation Trust on 020 7213 0660 (Monday - Friday, 9.00am - 5.00pm) for key holder information.

www.visitchurches.org.uk/hudsons or email: hhd@tcct.org.uk

THE CHURCHES CONSERVATION TRUST

All Saints' Church

Harewood Park,
Harewood, Leeds,
West Yorkshire,
LS17 9LG

Nestling in the grounds of Harewood House, All Saints' dates from the 15th century. It is remarkable for six pairs of effigies, dating from 1419 to 1510, commemorating the owners of Harewood and the nearby Gawthorpe estate. They are some of the greatest surviving examples of alabaster carving – virtually without rival in England – and offer a fascinating glimpse into the amour, robes, jewellery and headdresses of the day. The earliest depicts the fearless judge William Gascoigne in the robes of the Lord Chief Justice with a finely carved purse on one side and a dagger on the other, while his wife wears a square head-dress and rests her feet on a little dog. The church was restored in 1862-63 by Sir George Gilbert Scott, designer of St Pancras Station, the Albert Memorial and many churches.

Location: 7 miles north of Leeds off A61 in grounds of Harewood House; follow signs for Harewood House; once through ticket barrier, turn immediately right. Nearest railway station: Weeton (2.9 miles). **OS reference no:** SE 314 451
Please call The Churches Conservation Trust on 020 7213 0660 (Monday - Friday, 9.00am - 5.00pm) for key holder information.

Church of Christ the consoler

Newby Hall,
Skelton-cum-Newby,
Ripon, North Yorkshire,
HG4 5AE

With its colourful and vibrant interior, this Victorian church seems the very celebration of life, yet it stands as a testament to tragedy. It is a memorial to Frederick Vyner who, age 23, was captured and murdered by brigands in Greece in 1870. Standing inside the gates of the park, and surrounded by huge beech trees, the outside is impressive, with its lofty spire, pinnacles and fine rose window. The interior is wonderfully rich and colourful, with stained glass, fine marble and gilded mosaics filling the interior. Exquisite carvings on the corbels and on the organ case bring stone and wood to life, while in the rose window, Christ the Consoler presides.

Location: 4 miles south east of Ripon, off B6265; turn off A1 at Boroughbridge and follow B6265 to Ripon; turn left following brown signs to Newby Hall; go through main gateway, follow road towards the Hall. Church on right. Nearest railway stations: Knaresborough (6.5 miles). **OS reference no:** SE 360 679
Please call 0117 929 1766 before your visit to arrange. **Please call** The Churches Conservation Trust on 020 7213 0660 (Monday - Friday, 9.00am - 5.00pm) for key holder information.

St Martins Church

Allerton Park, Allerton
Mauleverer,
Knaresborough,
North Yorkshire,
HG5 0SE

Richard Arundell of Allerton Park, heir to the Mauleverers, remodelled St Martin's between 1745-46, adopting a neo-Norman style. It was designed in its parkland setting and the west front and central tower are impressive. Inside are a fine hammerbeam roof, pulpit, pews and benches, and a painting of Moses and Aaron over the chancel arch, as well as several timber Medieval effigies reputed to depict the Knights of Mauleverer, who were here for 600 years and founded the old church on this site.

Key facts: Due to the historic nature of our buildings, only a very small number of them have heating or running water meaning that they can be cold, and very rarely have toilet facilities. The lighting is usually operated via a 'push button' timer or a motion sensor. We do apologise for any inconvenience the lack of facilities may cause.

Location: 7 miles east of Harrogate, north of A59 and east of A1. Nearest railway stations: Cattal (2.5 miles), Hammerton (3.6 miles) and Knaresborough (4 miles). **OS reference no:** SE 416 579
Please call The Churches Conservation Trust on 020 7213 0660 (Monday - Friday, 9.00am - 5.00pm) for key holder information.

All Saints Church

Kedleston Hall,
Kedleston, Quarndon,
Derbyshire, DE22 5JH

All Saints' church is all that remains of the Medieval village of Kedleston, razed in 1759 by Sir Nathaniel Curzon to make way for the magnificent Kedleston Hall. The Curzon family has lived at Kedleston for 700 years and their stunning memorials fill the church. A dazzling marble tomb, with lifesize figures and watching angels, floats on a sea of green translucent quartz in its own little chapel with superb stained glass windows. Essentially 13th-century, with a classical east end, All Saints is filled with fine fittings including oak box pews, pulpit and communion rails. Its oldest feature is the Norman south doorway which has zigzag moulding and grotesque birds heads. Look out for the carving of the fiendish little cares of horseman and wild beasts that glare out at you just above the door!.

Location: The chapel is to the north of the centre of King's Lynn, close to the Saturday Market Place on St Ann's Street. Nearest railway station: King's Lynn (10 minutes walk). Bus station in Vancouver Centre by Sainsbury's (10 minute walk). **OS reference no:** TF 618 204 **Please call** The Churches Conservation Trust on 020 7213 0660 (Monday - Friday, 9.00am - 5.00pm) for key holder information.

St James' Church

Main Road, Cooling, Rochester, Kent, ME3 8DG

Charles Dickens used the churchyard of St James as his inspiration in the opening chapter of Great Expectations. The site, on the Hoo Peninsula with marshes stretching north to the Thames estuary, is dramatically desolate and bleak in winter, recalling the sinister opening scene in David Lean's 1946 film of the book. Inside, the church is light and spacious. There is a 500-year-old timber door that still swings on its ancient hinges , even though it now leads to a blocked north doorway! Another quirky feature is the 19th-century vestry – its walls are lined from top to bottom with thousands of cockle shells - the emblem of St James. The monuments in the church walls and floor include a slab with a brass effigy of Feyth Brook, who died in 1508 and was the wife of Lord Cobham, of nearby Cooling Castle.

Location: 6 miles north of Rochester off B2000. Nearest railway station: Higham (3.3 miles). Bus route number 133. **OS reference no: TQ 756 759**
Please call The Churches Conservation Trust on 020 7213 0660 (Monday - Friday, 9.00am - 5.00pm) for key holder information.

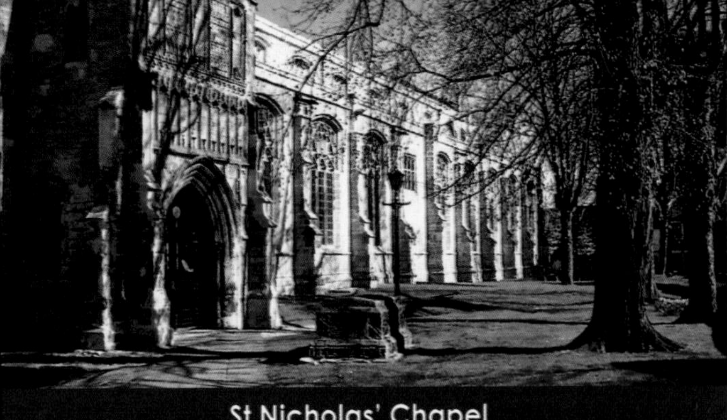

St Nicholas' Chapel

St Ann's Street, King's Lynn, Norfolk, PE30 1QS

From the tip of its 19th-century spire to its Norman foundations, everything about this town centre church is dazzling. Light floods from its magnificent windows into the interior. The vividly coloured picture panels to the east depict 32 scenes from the life of Jesus. Monuments from the 17th- and 18th-centuries, some with startlingly life-like painted figures, celebrate King's Lynn's seamen, merchants, mayors and shopkeepers and illustrate the town's long history as a busy commercial centre and port. Up in the 15th-century wooden roof, carved angels with outstretched wings sing and play musical instruments. At your feet is a fantastic collection of ledger stones including one dedicated to Robinson Cruso. The consistory court in the north-west corner of the chapel is a very rare survival.

Location: The chapel is to the north of the centre of King's Lynn, close to the Saturday Market Place on St Ann's Street. Nearest railway station: King's Lynn (10 minutes walk). Bus station in Vancouver Centre by Sainsbury's (10 minute walk). **OS reference no:** TF 618 204
Please call The Churches Conservation Trust on 020 7213 0660 (Monday - Friday, 9.00am - 5.00pm) for key holder information.

St Mary's Church

Church Street, Lower Higham, Rochester, Kent, ME3 7LS

St Mary's sits remote from Higham village in orchards on the edge of marshes running to the Thames. It is an unusual church with great charm and eccentricity. Its striped walls of ragstone and knapped flint and a near-symmetrical arrangement of two naves and two chancels are surmounted by a shingled spirelet. Originally Norman, it was remodelled and enlarged in the 14th-century, perhaps when a priory of Benedictine nuns was established nearby. There is some memorable woodwork including a 15th-century chancel screen in its original position, a 14th century pulpit and a particularly fine south door, treated like a four-light window with much delicate carving and some original ironwork. Restoration in 1863 provided most of the furnishings and the glass in the chancel windows.

Location: 4 miles north west of Rochester, off B2000. Nearest railway station: Higham (1 mile).

OS reference no: TQ 716 742

Please call The Churches Conservation Trust on 020 7213 0660 (Monday - Friday, 9.00am - 5.00pm) for key holder information.

Church of St Mary the Virgin

North Stoke, Arundel, West Sussex, BN18 9LS

The church is in the simple shape of a cross and remains virtually unaltered since Medieval times; its calm and peaceful atmosphere evokes centuries of prayer. Until recently, the church was known as North Stoke Church. But in 2007, archaeologists researching the church records in the archives at Kew, discovered a letter dated 1275 from a bishop to King Edward I, naming the church as St Mary. Traces of wall paintings dating from the 14th-century include flowers, leaves, and scrolls, showing that the church would have been a blaze of colour and decoration in the Middle Ages. Some very early and rare stained glass remains from the beginning of the 14th-century, including figures which may represent the Virgin Mary and King David. There is some intriguing stone carving, including a sheep's head above a recessed stone seat on the west wall, an appropriate symbol in sheep-rearing country - and a quaint little hand.

Location: 5 miles by road north of Arundel off B2139; signposted from Houghton Bridge. Nearest railway station: Nearest railway station: Amberley (1 mile).
OS reference no: TQ 019 108 **Please call** The Churches Conservation Trust on 020 7213 0660 (Monday - Friday, 9.00am - 5.00pm) for key holder information.

Pictures: Cadw, Welsh Government (Crown Copyright)

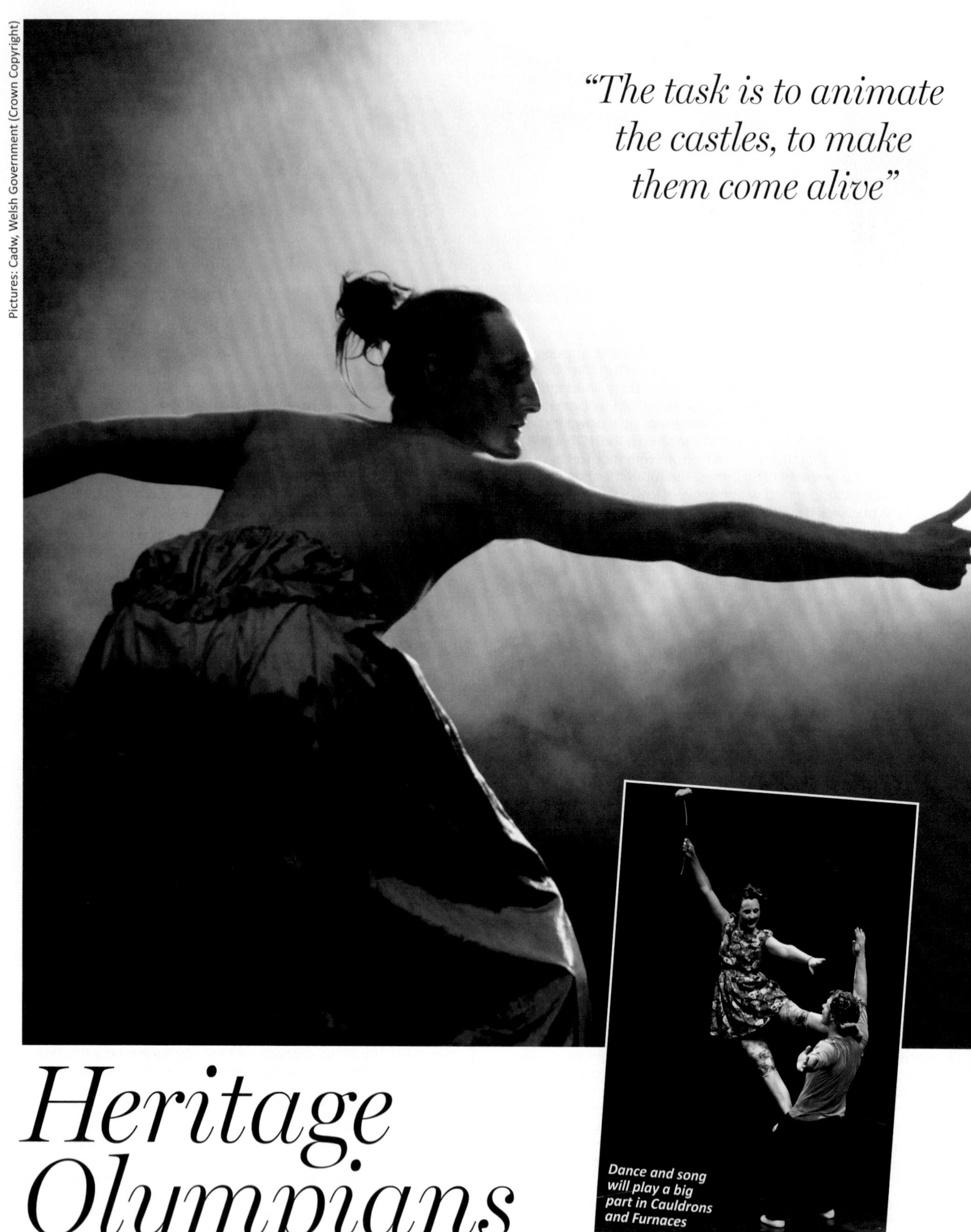

"The task is to animate the castles, to make them come alive"

Dance and song will play a big part in Cauldrons and Furnaces

Heritage Olympians

Wales's lasting legacy beyond 2012

Cadw

Llywodraeth Cymru
Welsh Government

Live performances at Caernarfon Castle

Dance, music and drama at Caerphilly Castle

Flashmobbing, rapping, graffiti artists and dramatic performances. Not your average day out at a Welsh historic monument? Think again! Cadw, is celebrating Wales's rich cultural diversity by bringing artistry and the creative talents of the nation's young people centre stage at eight of its heritage sites as part of Cauldrons and Furnaces in 2012.

The task is to animate the castles, to make them come alive. Visitors will discover the sites not through panels, exhibitions or guides, but through sounds, sights, images and even shadows. These sites are vessels – or cauldrons – which hold great stories.

Cauldrons and Furnaces is an exciting Cadw and Arts Council of Wales initiative – part funded by Legacy Trust UK – which forms part of the Cultural Olympiad, a UK wide programme of cultural events designed to mirror the celebrations leading up to London 2012.

At its heart Cauldrons and Furnaces tells extraordinary stories in extraordinary places.

A visitor who makes a journey around these eight iconic Cadw sites over the summer – Caernarfon Castle, Harlech Castle, Flint Castle, Denbigh Castle, St Davids Bishop's Palace, Laugharne Castle, Blaenavon Ironworks and Caerphilly Castle – will experience something of our small nation's rich and diverse cultural heritage from its mythic beginnings to modern times.

The journey starts, appropriately, with a pilgrimage departing from Llanthony Priory on 16 June. It follows the route of medieval pilgrims, kings, saints, madmen and pauper and arrives 22 days later in St Davids, Pembrokeshire.

At World Heritage Blaenavon Ironworks on Friday 29 & Saturday 30 June, Wales's metalworking heritage is celebrated in a project called Elemental and reinterpreted in twilight performances combining music, words, dance and drama.

Awen at Caerphilly Castle on Tuesday 11, Wednesday 12 and Thursday 13 July celebrates poetic inspiration through sculpture, film, dance, music and drama created by the people of Caerphilly County Borough.

In the north a different heritage experience is explored as Denbigh Castle's project Mantell celebrates the Bronze Age (Sunday 8 & Monday 9 July) and tells a heroic story (akin to Homer's Odyssey) inspired by the prehistoric riches of north-east Wales and, in particular, by the Mold gold cape.

Further north still the children of Flintshire have been on their own 3-year journey. Their work, Invasion, culminates in a historic pageant on Sunday 23 June at Flint Castle – a journey from mythic beginnings through to the Roman, Norman and English invasions.

Rappers, digital designers, composers, set designers, film makers, rock singers, actors and graffiti artists come together in Cipio'r Castell on Sunday 1 July at Caernarfon Castle for a startlingly original series of installations and live performances that mark the 'cofis' (the people of Caernarfon) inhabiting their castle.

The Harlech Music Festivals that ran in Harlech Castle every summer from 1867-1932 put Meirionydd on the map. Using the framework of the Harlech Pageant of 1922 the young people of south Gwynedd tell the story on Monday 16 and Tuesday 17 July of seven historic epochs through 21st-century eyes.

Cadw has a full calendar of events taking place across its sites throughout 2012 and together with Cauldrons and Furnaces the future's positively bubbling over with historic excitement.

The Harlech Music Festival

● **For further details go to www.cadw.wales.gov.uk**

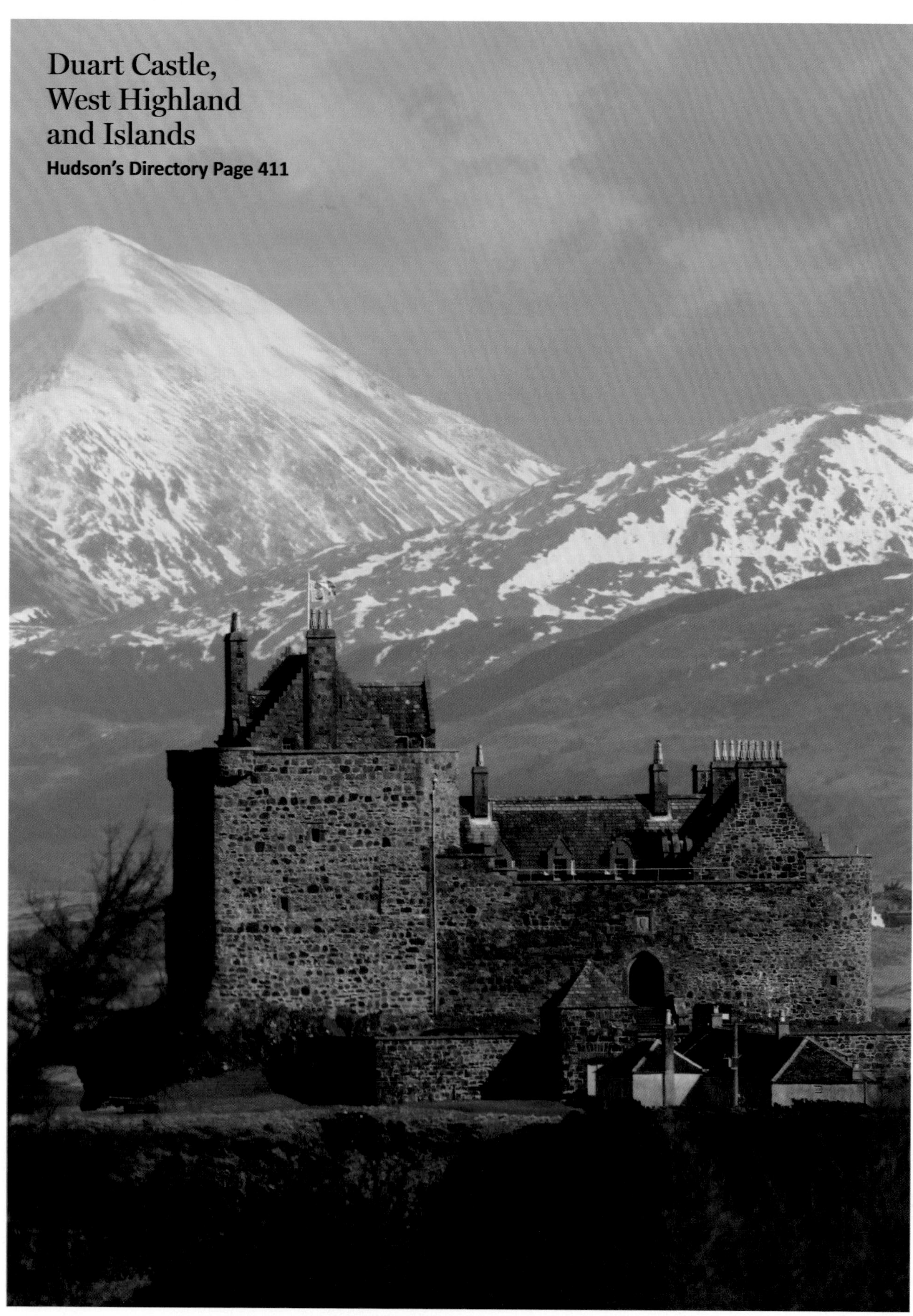

Duart Castle, West Highland and Islands

Hudson's Directory Page 411

The Sea Eagle's re-introduction into the Highlands over the last few decades, has been one of the great success stories of Scottish tourism, contributing many millions in revenue. These huge, awesome birds with an 8-foot wingspan can be seen - with patience and a little skill - from many historic sites throughout the country, such as Duart Castle (previous page), on the Isle of Mull, one of the birds' strongholds. They have also recently been re-introduced into Fifeshire.

Photos: Nick McCann

Hudson's Scotland

***FAMILY VALUES** – page 116*
At home with the Duke & Duchess of Argyll and family at their stunning home – Inveraray Castle

***CLARE'S CUISINE** – page 122*
Lady Laird of Ballindalloch Castle and cookery author on the best of Speyside's produce

***CAWDOR THOU ART** – page 128*
Art and style at 'Macbeth's' Cawdor Castle with the well-travelled Angelika, Dowager Countess

Inveraray Castle

FAMILY *Values*

DUKE

The first thing you notice about the ***Duke and Duchess of Argyll*** is how completely down-to-earth they seem. Despite their official titles and their grand home – Inverary Castle, Argyll – they have a knack of putting guests at ease.

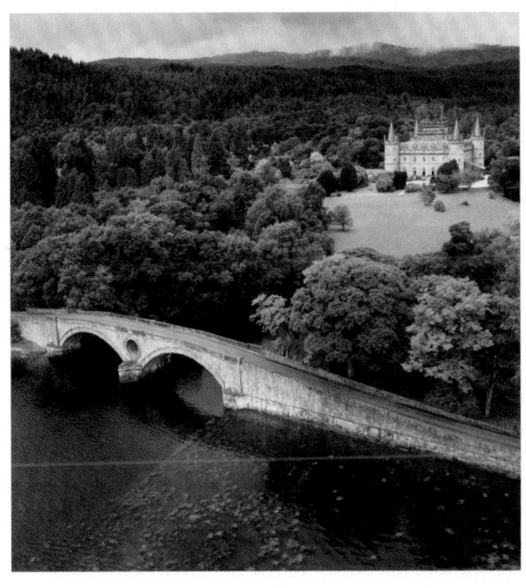

Words: *Ruth Stokes*
Pictures: *Nigel Gibson*

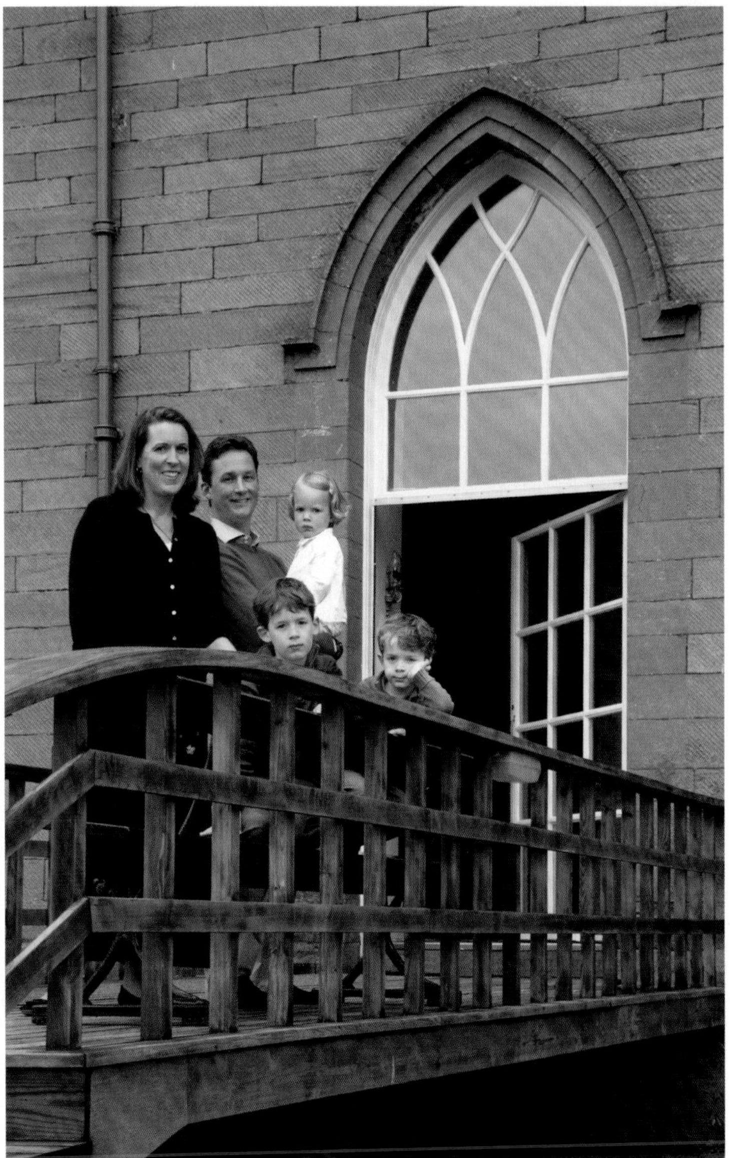

Contrary to what you might expect, it's not just that they dress comfortably and practically with little concern for show, but the warm and unassuming manner with which they greet people. The couple are so welcoming, in fact, that one recent visitor to the castle mistook the Duke for the head gardener. The Duke smiles at the memory. "I had to say: 'I can't take credit for that actually...' I think if people come to speak to me and I'm wearing chinos, trainers and a polo shirt, it somehow doesn't quite gel with what they expect." **>>**

"And if you get bits of Lego hurled at you, well...sorry! It comes with the territory"

It is this combination of grandeur and intimacy that makes Inverary Castle, which opens to the public from April to October, such a unique visitor experience. The castle is very much a family home, and the Duke and Duchess – also known as Torquhil and Eleanor – believe this helps to brings the place to life for their guests. Officially, half the property is open to the public and the other half is private, but in reality the two worlds cross over considerably.

"I think it's quite important to be hands-on," says Torquhil. "So I do spend a lot of time talking to people, meeting groups, signing guidebooks, smiling for photographs and talking to children. People seem to really appreciate it. A lot of heritage property houses are sort of museums, whereas we're a family house. If you hear the children screaming and shouting, that's part and parcel of the experience. And if you get bits of Lego hurled at you, well...sorry!" He laughs. "It comes with the territory."

The couple have three children – Archie, seven, Rory, five, and Charlotte, who is two-and-a-half – and although they admit it can occasionally be "a bit tricky" balancing parenting with the upkeep of a castle, the pair seem largely unfazed. "We're lucky because they're lovely children and they've got all that space," confides Eleanor, whose official role involves managing the on-site tea room and writing promotional material.

"When it's pouring with rain and dark in the winter, they've got an enormous great house to run around in. You can practically ride your tricycle around the armoury hall – although I'd advise against it..."

Having great halls at their disposal means the family must take care to preserve the artefacts they've inherited, and because of this they try to keep as much of the furniture as possible in situ. Behind the scenes, though, the castle has been adjusted and updated for the young family.

Torquhil and Eleanor took full control of the property 10 years ago and have since converted the top floor from what used to be servants' quarters into rooms for the children. They've installed 12 new bathrooms and 120 radiators, which they run on biofuel using wood from the forest on the 60,000-acre estate.

The family opened the gardens around the property for the first time last year, with the intention of making their public offering "bigger and better". The outdoor space hosts events such as highland games and a bluebell festival, but is also a great source of enjoyment to them all on a personal level. Torquhil is particularly passionate about the land, spending his free hours fishing, sporting, or even just admiring the azaleas, bluebells and daffodils. When the weather is nice, he and Eleanor can often be found picnicking with the children. >>

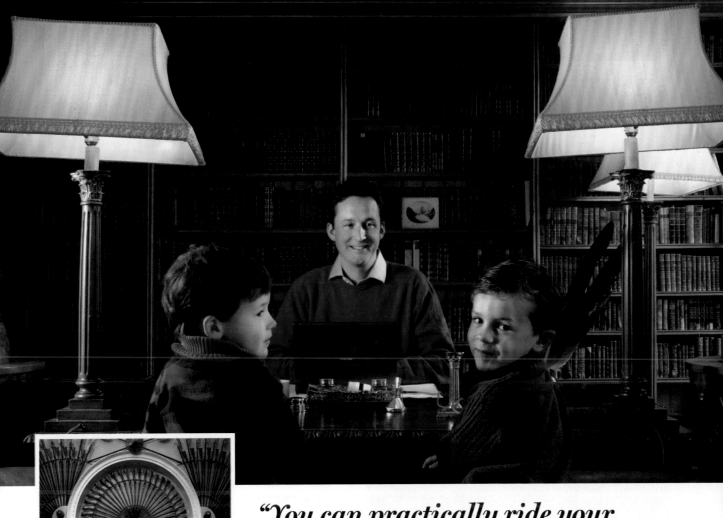

"You can practically ride your tricycle around the Armoury Hall although I'd advise against it..."

"It really is a fairytale castle"

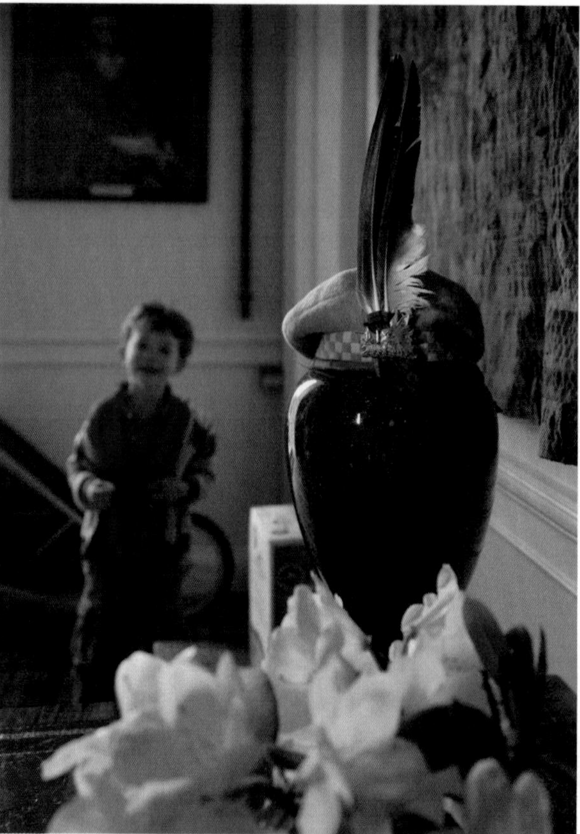

With the opening of the gardens for visitor use, Torquhil and Eleanor have blurred the lines between private and public space to a greater extent than any of their ancestors ever did. So do they ever feel the strain?

Eleanor admits that although it's something Torquhil is used to – he has lived at Inverary Castle all his life – she took a little bit of time to adjust. "I was totally surprised by it because I didn't grow up in that world at all," she says. "I found it very strange that you would be walking up the stairs and there would be someone smiling and waving at you."

Nevertheless, she now relishes the role, extolling the virtues of the castle as a combined tourist attraction and home. I get the impression that, really, she wouldn't want it any other way. "It really is a fairytale castle – right on the edge of Loch Fyne with the mountains behind," she says. "Our guides tell interesting stories about the things in the house and how they fit in with the family – rather than it being this museum of hushed whispers. I think people really enjoy visiting, and we're never bored!"

"Every day is a new challenge," confirms Torquhil. "Just making sure it's fun and warm and what people want to see. But we're very lucky, very privileged – and very willing to share the castle with other people."

FOR VISITOR INFORMATION ON INVERARY CASTLE TURN TO PAGE 410

"Every day is a new challenge, just making sure it's fun and warm and what people want to see. But we're very lucky, very privileged – and very willing to share the castle with other people"

Pictures: *John Paul Photography*

When she's not running her fabulous Ballindalloch Castle in Speyside, performing her duties as Lord Lieutenant of Banffshire, organising corporate events and shoots and appearing on television with the likes of *The Hairy Bikers, Monty Don* and others too numerous to mention - phew... ***Clare Russell*** somehow finds the time to be cookbook author. ***Hudson's*** is invited to Ballindalloch to taste the local produce in the mouth-watering recipes that have made her book ***"I Love Food"*** an extraordinary best-seller.

Clare's Cuisine

My great love of cooking began when I returned home to Ballindalloch in 1978. Inheriting a wonderful place is the easy part, hanging on to it is the difficult part. Hence I had to turn into 'cook and bottle-washer' at breakneck speed! "I Love Food" was derived from my many recipes, concocted over the years. It has been an unexpected success and it is now on its 14th print run. It has sold globally, from Presidents and Prime Ministers to many Royal households in Great Britain and Europe. "I Love Food 2" is now at the trying and testing stage. I hope you enjoy the recipes, both old and new... >>

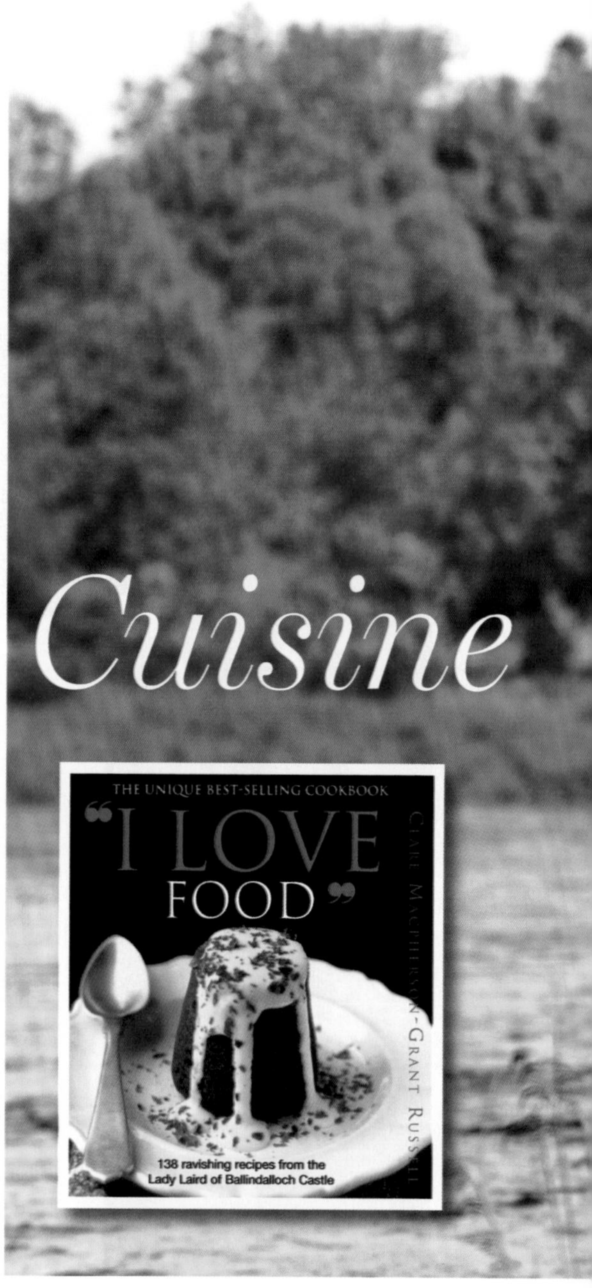
THE UNIQUE BEST-SELLING COOKBOOK
"I LOVE
FOOD"
CLARE MACPHERSON-GRANT RUSSELL
138 ravishing recipes from the
Lady Laird of Ballindalloch Castle

Ghillie Steve Brand shows Clare the intricacies of salmon flies and casting on the estate's part of the River Spey

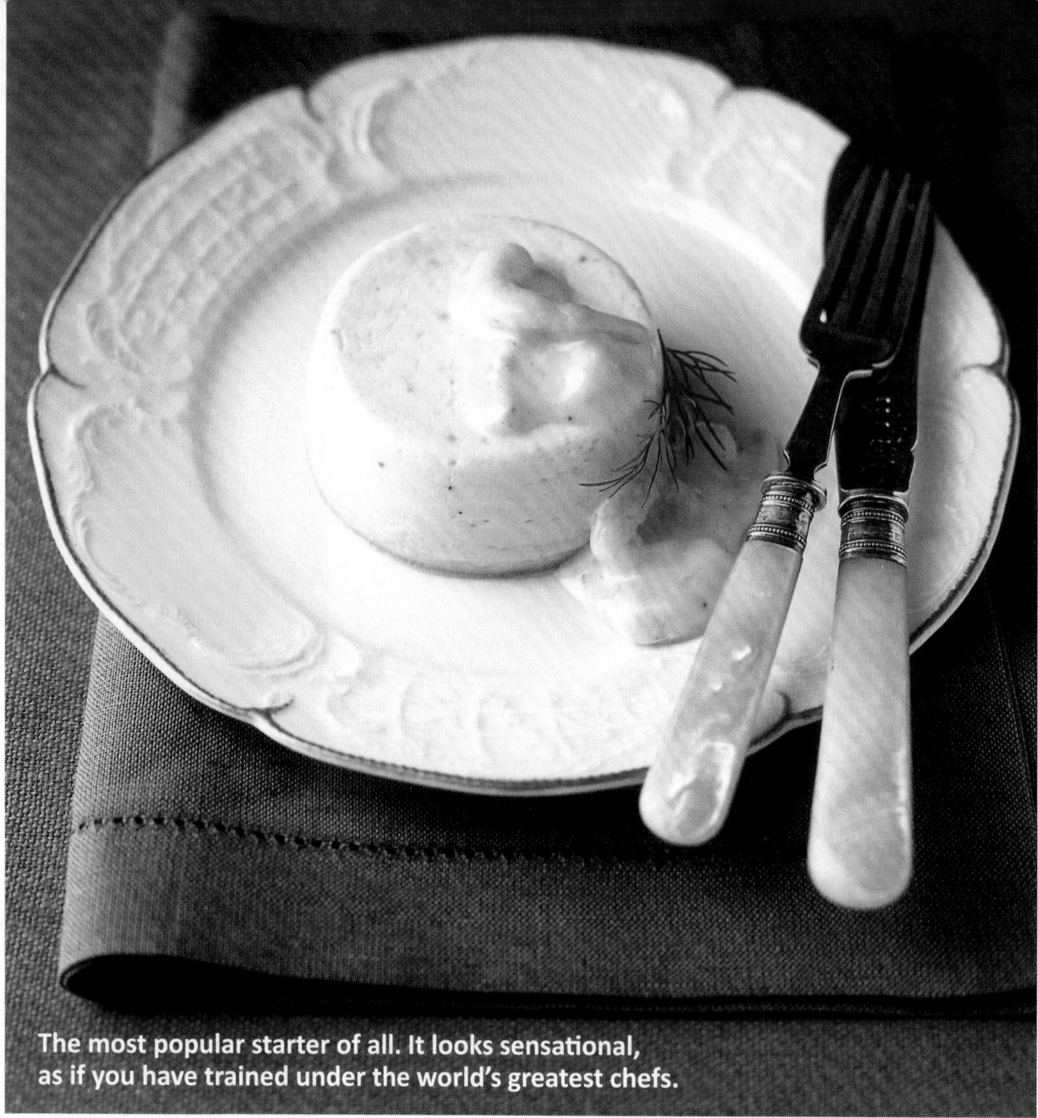

The most popular starter of all. It looks sensational, as if you have trained under the world's greatest chefs.

Fresh from the Spey

Smoked salmon mousselines with a prawn and hollandaise sauce

Mousselines
10oz (250g) smoked salmon
2 eggs, lightly beaten
Salt and pepper
Nutmeg
1½pt (300ml) double cream

Hollandaise
4 egg yolks
1 tbsp water
2 tbsp lemon juice
6oz (150g) melted butter
4oz (100g) large prawns
Salt and pepper

1 Skin and chop the smoked salmon. Liquidise with the salt, pepper and nutmeg. Blend in the beaten eggs and chill in the fridge for a few hours.

2 Place the smoked salmon mixture in a liquidiser with the cream, and process.

3 Butter 6 cocotte dishes and pour the processed mixture into them. Stand in a bain-marie (a baking tin half-filled with hot water) and bake at 180°C/350°F/Gas 4 for 30 minutes.

4 For the hollandaise, whisk the egg yolks, water and lemon juice in a bowl over hot water. Pour in the melted butter and whisk until thick. Add the prawns.

5 Turn out the mousselines and serve with the prawn hollandaise.

Cook's tip
If the hollandaise curdles, add an ice cube and whisk like mad!

Pride of place within the farming community of the estate goes to the Ballindalloch herd of Aberdeen Angus cattle, the oldest herd in the world in continuous existence, dating from the 1850s. Combined with local Cragganmore malt whisky sauce this is a real treat.

Highland excellence

Ballindalloch beef tournedos with a Cragganmore whisky cream sauce

2 Aberdeen Angus fillet steaks about 1 inch thick
2 rounds of fried bread
2oz (50g) butter
1 finely chopped onion
4oz (100g) sliced mushrooms
¼pt (150ml) cream
1 tbsp malt whisky (Cragganmore)
2 tsp chopped parsley
2oz (50g) fine pâté

1 Melt the butter in a pan and cook the steaks until done as desired.

2 Remove from the pan and keep warm.

3 Using the same pan fry off the onions and mushrooms in butter until soft.

4 Add whisky, cream, chopped parsley and seasoning and simmer for a few minutes.

5 Spread the warm fried bread rounds with pâté.

6 Place beef on bread rounds and serve the whisky sauce separately.

>>

At all our corporate parties, this is by far the most talked-about dessert. Simply sensational.

Dreamy and light as a feather

Scottish blackberry or raspberry & apple soufflé

6oz (150g) caster sugar
12oz (350g) blackberries plus 24 for the bottom of the soufflé
1 large cooking apple, peeled and finely diced
Zest and juice of 1 orange
3 egg whites
½pt double cream
Icing sugar for dusting

1 Cook the blackberries or raspberries, diced apple, zest and juice of the orange in a pan for 10 minutes until the apple is pulp.

2 Press through a sieve into a bowl. Stir in 2oz (50g) of caster sugar and cool.

3 Place a spoonful of fruit purée and 4 berries into the bottom of 6 ramekins (buttered and dusted with sugar). Set aside.

4 Whisk egg whites till very stiff. Gradually whisk in remaining sugar until glossy. Fold in remaining fruit purée and pour into ramekins.

5 Level the tops and run a knife around the edges of each dish.

6 Place on a hot baking tray (to make rise) and bake at 200°C/400°F/Gas 6 for about 10-15 minutes until risen and lightly brown. Dust tops with icing sugar and serve immediately with jug of double cream.

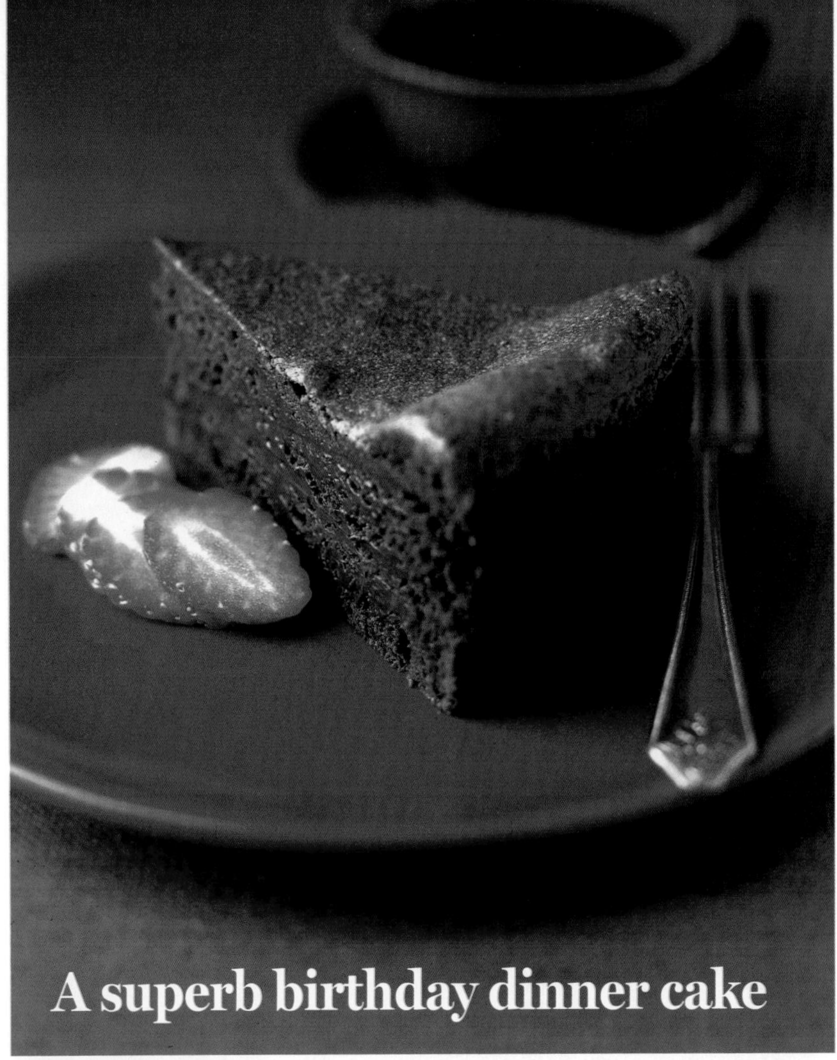

A superb birthday dinner cake

Chocolate mousseline cake

1lb (450g) good dark chocolate
8 large eggs, separated
8oz (225g) sugar
1 tbsp Drambuie
1 tbsp warm water
1pt (600ml) double cream
Strawberries for decoration

For the sponge base:
2oz plain flour
2 eggs
2oz caster sugar
2 tbsp cocoa powder
2oz melted butter

1 Make the sponge base first. Place eggs and sugar in a bowl over simmering water and whisk till light and fluffy. Sieve flour and cocoa and fold into the egg mixture.

2 Pour melted butter slowly into the sponge mixture, folding in gently with a large spatula. Place in a 10 inch (25 cm) greased and lined spring-loaded cake tin and bake at 180°C/350°F/Gas 4, for 10-15 mins till risen and springy to the touch. Cool.

3 Meanwhile, break chocolate into pieces and melt in a bowl over hot water. Set aside.

4 Place egg yolks and sugar in a bowl and whisk till light and fluffy. Stir in melted chocolate, then warm water and Drambuie.

5 Whisk egg whites in a bowl till soft peaks. Stir quarter of egg whites lightly into chocolate mixture and then add the rest carefully. Pour the mousse onto the sponge cake.

6 Bake at 180°C/350°F/Gas 4 for 15 minutes and take out of oven. Fridge for at least 2 hours. Remove from fridge 15 mins before serving. Cut into slices with a hot, wet knife and plate surrounded by a little double cream sprinkled with chocolate and a few sliced strawberries.

Ballindalloch Castle, Highlands

Hudson's Directory Page 418

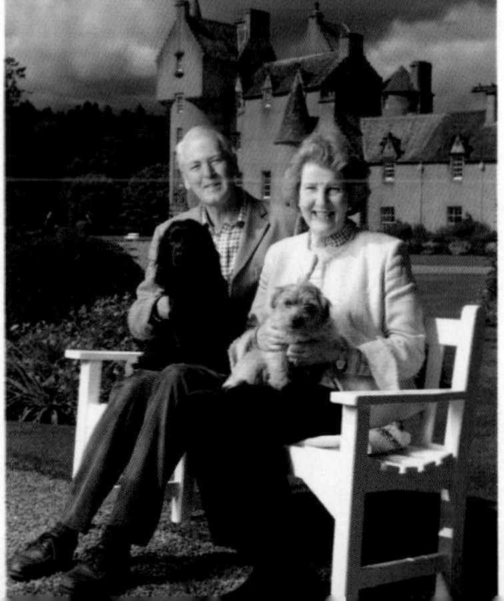

Clare and her husband Oliver and friends at their home, Ballindalloch Castle, Banffshire

Cawdor THOU ART

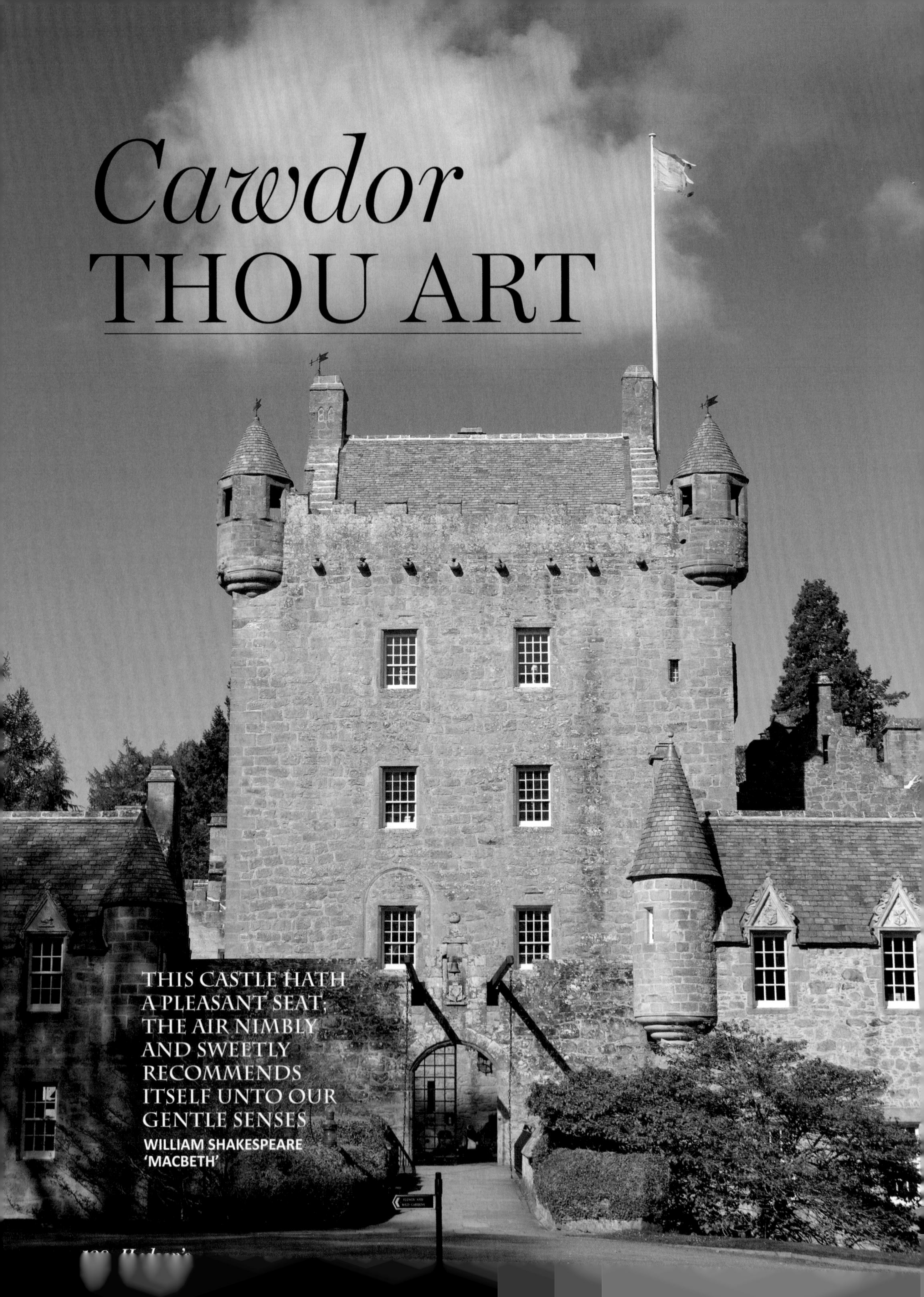

THIS CASTLE HATH A PLEASANT SEAT; THE AIR NIMBLY AND SWEETLY RECOMMENDS ITSELF UNTO OUR GENTLE SENSES

WILLIAM SHAKESPEARE 'MACBETH'

The connection between the Bard's 'Scottish Play' and Cawdor Castle - built long after the events in the play - is slight and can be controversial; the 5th Earl of Cawdor had his own view, "I wish the Bard had never written his damned play." Today, Cawdor represents the quintessential Scottish castle, but with stylish twists and turns, as ***Ruth Stokes*** discovered when she talked to its Chatelaine, ***Angelika Cawdor***, the present owner.

Words: *Ruth Stokes* Pictures: *John Paul Photography*

Cawdor Castle is a place of rich contrasts. Walk through its rooms and you'll find 17th century tapestries hung alongside modern art and traditional family portraits sharing corners with items from distant continents. In the castle grounds, there are three gardens: a 16th century walled garden, which incorporates the symbolic gardens, an 18th century flower garden and a 19th century wild garden. Contemporary sculptures, including a spherical slate fountain and a bronze 'Tree of Life', sit among the greenery.

This blend of styles is partly an accumulation of tastes from the many generations of the Cawdor family, but much of it is also down to the current owner, Angelika, Dowager Countess Cawdor. She is well-known for her sophistication, and her delicate management of the castle has preserved tradition while also allowing for some modern art additions.

When she talks about living at Cawdor, it's clear that the Countess sees the castle's upkeep as a priority. What drives her is a passion for the heritage of the property, which became her home in 1979 when she married the sixth earl, Hugh John Vaughn Cawdor, and where she has remained since his death in 1993.

"My husband loved Cawdor very much and was conscious of whatever was happening in the old castle. So I've taken it on after his death – and look after Cawdor as if it were an old relation," she says.

For her, it's the castle's patchwork of influences that makes it special. "The collections at Cawdor are eclectic and span many generations., and that continues because I've collected contemporary art for years," she explains. "I've found that the things I love seem to fit in perfectly well, and that there's no difficulty putting modern paintings next to antiques."

The modern artists and sculptors on show at Cawdor Castle include Henry Moore, Barry Flanagan, Xavier Corbero and Georges Jeanclos, Piper and Dali, among others. The Dowager Countess's love of art began at a young age and she was just a teenager when she started collecting old master drawings. Later she moved onto 19th century watercolours and for roughly the past 40 years her fascination has been contemporary art. >>

"I've found that the things I love seem to fit in perfectly well, and that there's no difficulty putting modern next to ancient."

Inevitably, her sense of style has been influenced to some extent by her life before Cawdor - a life that began in Bohemia, Czechoslovakia, took her to Africa for much of her childhood and then to Paris, where she fell in love, first with the city and later with the Earl.

"I was on my way to Cambridge University when I stopped in Paris for three months to learn French properly," she remembers. "And of course I never wanted to leave. So I stayed and had 20 wonderful years in Paris. And then I fell in love with a Scotsman and came here."

Since then, the Countess has continued to travel.

"I always bring something back," she says. "For people who have a keen eye, there are Tibetan prayer wheels or ancient Turkish harem shoes. If you look carefully you can find things from all over the world." She's also just commissioned two new sculptures, one from a Scottish artist and the other from an American artist. Both will appear in the grounds within the next few years, but for now the details are top secret.

Putting her own stamp on the castle has had one particularly welcome outcome – a homely atmosphere, often commented on by visitors. Ultimately, though, it's all about finding that perfect balance - and the Countess certainly doesn't take the responsibility lightly. "My role is that of a guardian," she says.

"I'm a link in a long chain that I hope will continue many many generations after me. I'm very aware of the character of the house and I try my best to be a strong link in that chain."

FOR VISITOR INFORMATION ON CAWDOR CASTLE TURN TO PAGE 416

"My role is that of a guardian. I'm a link in a long chain that I hope will continue many many generations after me"

Daddy Cool

Names like "Knebworth" are synonymous with the halycon days of the Stones and other great rock n' roll aristocrats. Many weekend music festivals – once the preserve of youth – have become popular with the over-40s; littering the mayhem with luxury campsites and gourmet food stands. *Jane Pruden* assesses the fallout and discovers robust family entertainment and a few bewildered offspring.

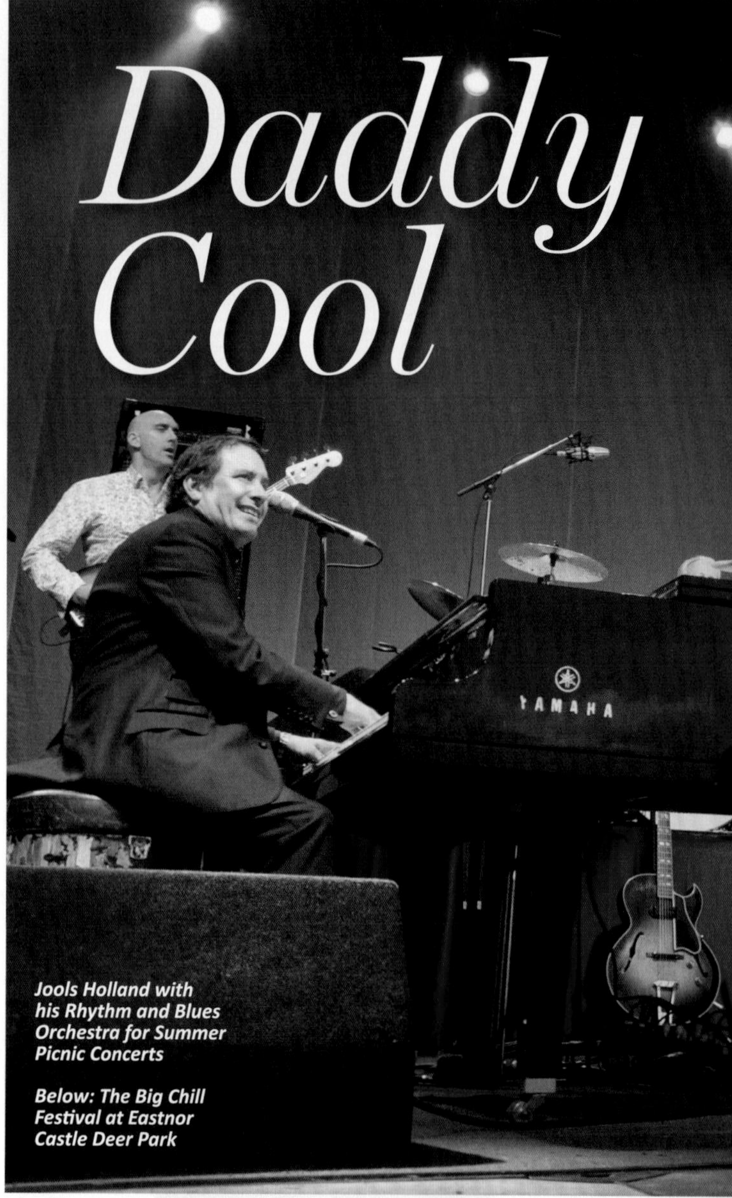

YAMAHA

Jools Holland with his Rhythm and Blues Orchestra for Summer Picnic Concerts

Below: The Big Chill Festival at Eastnor Castle Deer Park

Whether it's a mid-life crisis or the heady mix of live music and beautiful surroundings, hip parents are strutting their stuff, zoning-out and glamping in tipis. Festival-coolness, spawned from a Glastonbury breeding ground, has mutated, even the Prime Minister has been affected. Today's rock chick, like many of the stars, could be as close to collecting their pension as signing up for a student grant. 'It's a bit weird having mum and dad here,' mumbled one teenager at the Latitude Festival in Suffolk, 'but they bought my ticket and actually, I hardly see them.'

'For many families it's a great extended weekend with excellent entertainment,' says James Hervey-Bathurst. The father of five and occupier of The Big Chill venue, Eastnor Castle Deer Park in Herefordshire, adds, 'The Park is large but also intimate, because the hills and trees give it a relaxed atmosphere, and that appeals to all ages.'

If you want to lose your parents, you can quite easily; segregation is a natural process. You won't find an oldie in a screaming mosh pit as stages are designated for different music genres. It works both ways and avoids plummeting street-cred for the

under-21s too. But for regular cash handouts you may not see them at all.

The rest of Eastnor's 450-acre site, like many others, is divided into campsites, food areas, arts and entertainment arenas, a chill and therapy field and The Little Chill – special children's entertainment for the very small. Preparation for three or four nights camping is vital, although it's advice lost on a lads' tour. Erect tent: head for the bar. Food? We'll find something. Hygiene? No problem. End result: tired, stinking and half-starved: no tent, no money, no questions!

For older groupies help is at hand. There are family campsites with kids' areas, campervans and caravan parks or for shameless cheats, a ready-pitched and fully equipped tent. At a price, there are podpads, billed as 'quirky luxury with comfort and security' and 'your own little eco-friendly hobbit house, solidly built from weatherproof plywood and comes decorated – with solid floor, fitted carpet and shelving, a vanity mirror and a lock on the front door.' Or, 'treat yourself to the Yurtel experience with a real mattress, sumptuous duvet and white 400-count Egyptian cotton linen, bedside table, lamp, a vase of flowers and of course, the magical experience of sleeping in a yurt!' Waking up with your head buried in a goosedown pillow is all very middle-England but obviously no substitute for an en-suite.

Of course there are good basic facilities but one message is clear - if missing your bathroom is going to be an issue, get over it. There are must-haves and one opportunist website www.onestopfestival.com advertises the no-rinse body wash and shampoo, loo seat covers or, uh-hum, if the portaloo queue is too long, there is the 'TravelJohn' - a portable urinal for both sexes that turns the yellow stuff to jelly in a sealed container. Voicing these elementary sanitary concerns with my teenagers evokes a typically puerile reminder that I may have decamped to alien territory. 'Oh Mum, no one cares about all that stuff, just other people like you.' OK, but I'm going to add that for some people earplugs, support tights and Immodium aren't groovy but they have benefits. I'm on home ground with food and drink. >>

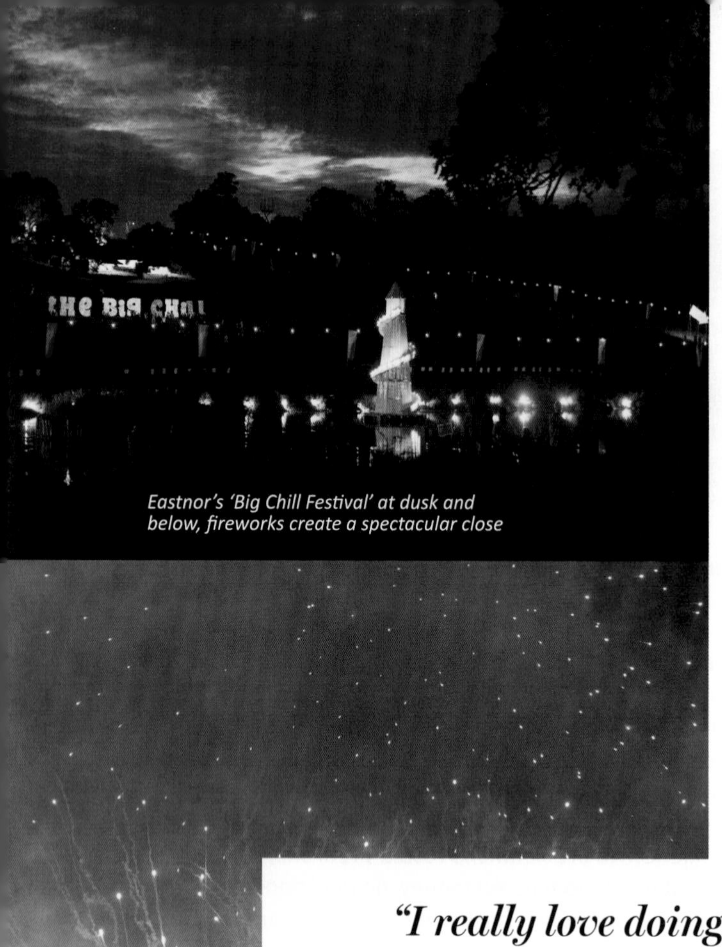

Eastnor's 'Big Chill Festival' at dusk and below, fireworks create a spectacular close

Like the audience it has become increasingly cosmopolitan. Expect to see Carluccio's next to the chippy, Nepalese curry, noodle, risotto, local produce and organic stands. At the unadulterated middle-age Rewind 80s festival, at Scone Palace in Scotland, you will also find plenty of Scottish cuisine and no shortage of haggis, Cullen Skink and Orcadian Oatmeal Soup from Scotland's Gourmet Kitchen.

Scone's chatelaine, Viscountess Stormont, tells me, 'The festival is a wonderful opportunity to showcase our local produce. One of our tenant famers, Jim Fairlie at Logiealmond plus Jamesfield Organic Centre and Thomas Thomson (Blairgowrie) Ltd will be among the top food producers coming together as 'Perthshire Farmers and Producers' to serve up the best of Perthshire to an expected crowd of 15,000 festival-goers.'

My money, for camping decadence, is on the cocktail bar and a very sophisticated riverside Bedouin tent on the banks of the Tay for relaxing in between Bananarama and Kid Creole and the Coconuts gigs.

"I really love doing them. We get out to different parts of the country on a really hot summer's evening and lift the spirits.We're literally running away with the fairies and playing amongst the trees" **JOOLS HOLLAND**

If however, you could be defeated by several nights in a field, the picnic concert is a perfect compromise. Jools Holland and his Big Band are pioneers of the stately home show circuit in this country. 'I really love doing them,' he says. 'We get out to different parts of the country on a really hot summer's evening and lift the spirits. The other thing is, if you're going somewhere amongst trees, that's always a nice element. Often I will refer to the trees, and pretend that they're talking to us. We are literally running away with the fairies and playing amongst the trees, which is great.'

Perhaps its too much excitement or mystical twilight, casting long shadows through the Repton and Brown landscapes, that stirs the blood. But for all the brouhaha, misspent youth has had a reprieve. Dad dancing with an air-guitar is not cool but do it anyway, just prepare for the kids to take your money and disown you.

YOUR FESTIVAL ESSENTIALS

www.onestopfestival.com

Podpads – **www.podpads.com**

Yurtels – **www.yurtel.co.uk**

The Big Chill at Eastnor Castle
www.bigchill.net

Latitude, Henham Park, Southwold
www.latitudefestival.co.uk

Rewind 80s at Scone Palace, Scotland
www.rewindfestival.com

Jools Holland at IML Concerts
www.imlconcerts.co.uk

English Heritage site concerts
www.picnicconcerts.com

FOR VISITOR INFORMATION ON EASTNOR CASTLE TURN TO PAGE 318

Visiting an airshow on a British summer's day is a great way to enjoy our heritage. Fresh air, fun for all the family and *what* phenomenal feelings

the Spirit of Great Britain

The 'Spirit of Great Britain' is the only flying Vulcan bomber in the world and has recently been successful in gaining a grant from the Heritage Lottery Fund to keep her flying. The bomber dates from the early 1950s and became famous for the bombing raids on Port Stanley Airfield at the outset of the Falklands conflict; the longest-ranged bombing raid in history at that time. A dedicated team of experts and enthusiasts keep this example flying today.

the Spirit of Great Britain

To gaze upwards at miraculous machines, leaves you with a very modern sense of awe. The experience also shows how good this country can be at making the very best. Whether it's the thunderous wail of a Vulcan, the unmistakeable whistle of a 'Spit's' Merlin engine, or the demonic air-splitting scream of an aptly-named Typhoon, it's very difficult not to feel *proud to be British.*

Photos: ***Nick McCann***

The Supermarine Spitfire is one of the iconic images of WWII. The aircraft held a special place in the hearts of the pilots that flew her during the Battle of Britain and is equally popular with the public today. A very beautiful aircraft in every sense, the Spitfire is the star attraction at any airshow.

Assembled in Warton, Lancashire, from parts manufactured across Europe, the Typhoon Eurofighter is the state-of-the-art in combat aircraft and can literally 'hang in the air' due to its computerised aeronautics. This particular aircraft had to fill in at short notice for an Italian example at Fairford in 2011, and as a result was fully armed. The delta wings borrow much from the heritage of the Vulcan and Concorde.

As traditional as strawberries and cream at Wimbledon and a glass of Pimms at Henley, the sight of the Red Arrows in the summer skies above Britain brings a lump to the throat and makes the hairs on the back of the neck start to tingle. So says *Hudson's* Editor, ***Nick McCann*** who photographed the red, white and blue spectacular at the Royal International Air Tattoo at RAF Fairford.

For the first time in 2011, when these pictures were taken, a woman flew as part of the famous nine – a case of the 'Red Baroness!' All the Arrows are front line pilots, well used to flying Tornados or Typhoons in conflict zones, as well as painting pictures above our historic houses and countryside. The sheer precision of the aerobatics is truly breathtaking - and not a little scary – as they perform their aerial balletics to awe-struck audiences up and down the land. When that red, white and blue smoke starts to appear, you can almost hear the National Anthem in your head, or at least 'The Dambusters March' – it's a singularly British emotional response.

If the Red Arrows are appearing near you, don't miss them. It is an unforgettable experience

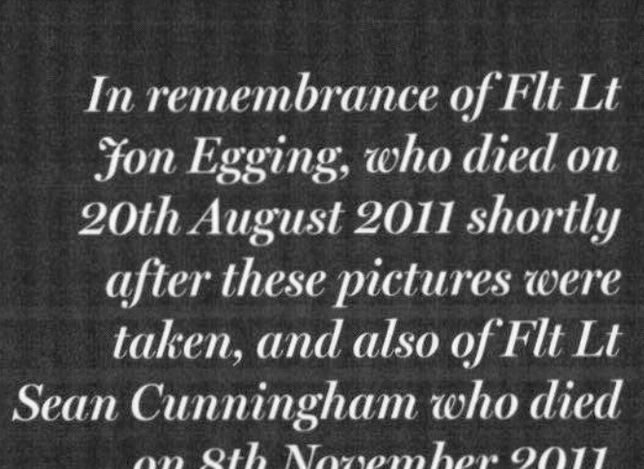

In remembrance of Flt Lt Jon Egging, who died on 20th August 2011 shortly after these pictures were taken, and also of Flt Lt Sean Cunningham who died on 8th November 2011.

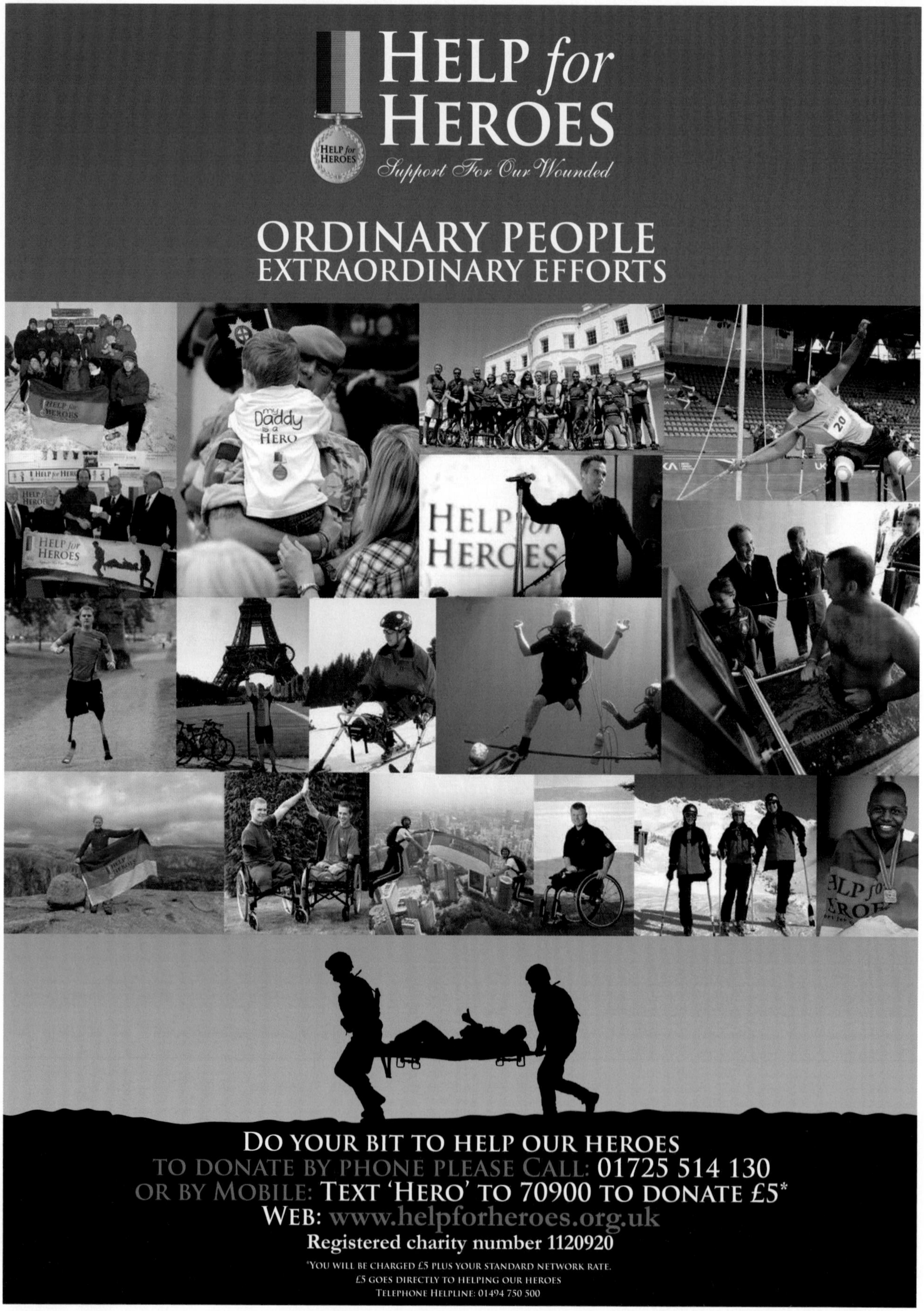

1942

16-year old Princess Elizabeth in her wartime WRVS uniform.

Cecil Beaton
© Victoria and Albert Museum, London

Happy & glorious

2012 marks the 60th anniversary of HM The Queen's ascension to the throne. In this Diamond Jubilee year, *Hudson's* presents a series of epoch defining portraits from some of the great photographers who have captured our Monarch throughout her remarkable life.

1946

Left:
A stylish post-war studio portrait of the Princess at 20.

Dorothy Wilding
© National Portrait Gallery

1953

Below left:
The newly-crowned Queen Elizabeth II.

Baron
© National Portrait Gallery

1966

Opposite:
The Queen's 40th birthday, wearing Mantle and Star of the Order of the Garter.

Photograph by Yousuf Karsh

July 1966: a moment England will never forget; the Queen presents Bobby Moore with the World Cup after victory over Germany at Wembley.

Evening Standard/Hulton Archive/ Getty Images

1972

On board Her Majesty's Yacht Britannia; and (right) holidaying with her corgis by the Garbh Allt burn on the Balmoral Castle estate.

Both from a series of photographs taken to mark the Queen and the Duke of Edinburgh's Silver Wedding Anniversary in 1972.

Photographs by Lichfield

1996

Below:
With South African President Nelson Mandela during his state visit to London.

Tom Stoddart
Tom Stoddart/Getty Images

1999

Bottom:
On a three-nation African tour with traditional dancers from the National Song and Dance group in Maputo.

Anna Zieminski
Anna Zieminski/AFP/Getty Images

1980

Opposite above:
Known as the 'Blue Trinity' portrait, this was taken to mark the Queen Mother's 80th birthday by much-loved photographer, Norman Parkinson.

© Norman Parkinson/ Sygma/Corbis

2001

Opposite below:
Trooping the Colour, with Prince Philip, Duke of Edinburgh, and Prince Charles, Prince of Wales, riding behind.

Tim Graham
Tim Graham/Getty Images

1997

The Brit Pop era

Shaking hands with Victoria Beckham (Posh Spice) at the Royal Command Performance.

Tim Graham
Tim Graham Picture Library/Getty Images

2002

Opposite:
Commissioned by the National Portrait Gallery to mark the Golden Jubilee.

Photograph by Rankin, Camera Press London

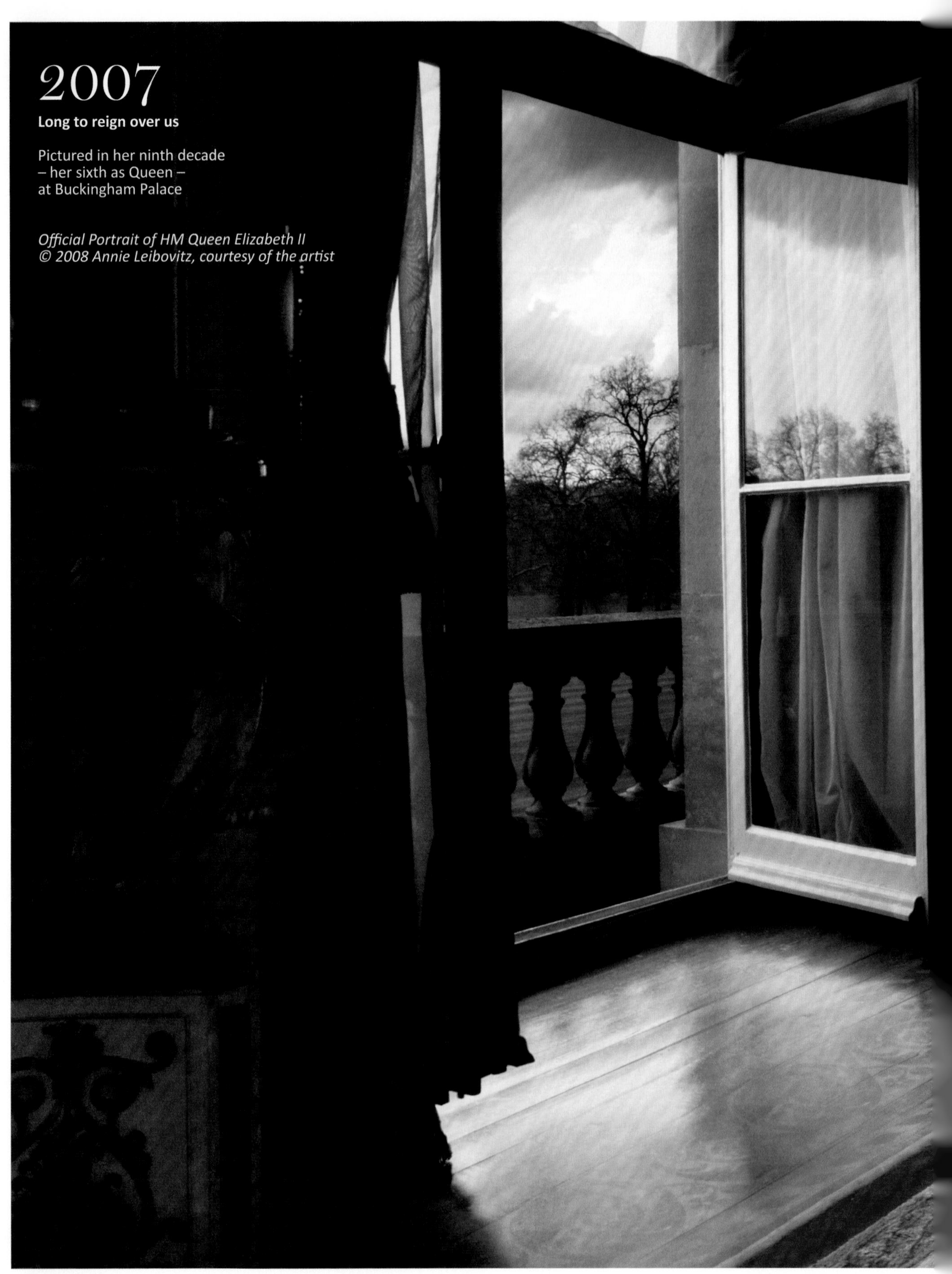

2007

Long to reign over us

Pictured in her ninth decade – her sixth as Queen – at Buckingham Palace

Official Portrait of HM Queen Elizabeth II © 2008 Annie Leibovitz, courtesy of the artist

Regional Directory

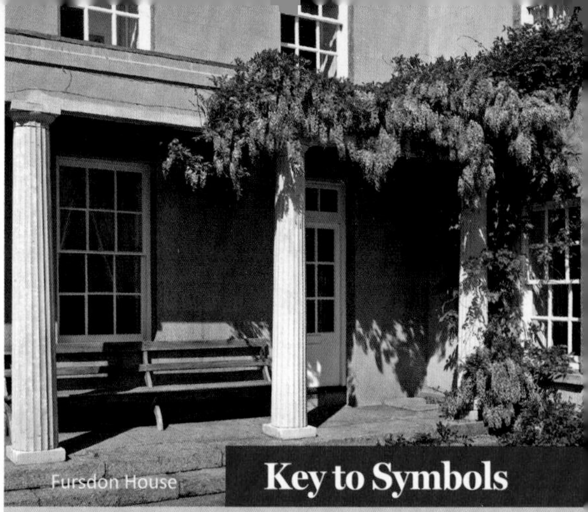

Fursdon House

Key to Symbols

- Information
- Shop
- Plant Sales
- Corporate Hospitality / Functions
- Suitability for the Disabled
- Refreshments / Cafe / Tearoom
- Restaurant
- Guided Tours
- Audio Tours
- Parking Available
- Education - School Visits
- Suitability for Dogs
- No Dogs
- Accommodation
- Civil Wedding Licence
- Open All Year
- Special Events
- Accept Euros
- R Special offers/discounts available to Hudson's readers
- Historic Houses Association Member, offering access under HHA Friends Scheme
- Property owned by National Trust.
- Property in the care of English Heritage
- Property owned by The National Trust for Scotland
- Property in the care of Historic Scotland
- Properties in the care of Cadw, the Welsh Government's historic environment service

Somerset House. The Edmond J. Safra Fountain Court
© Marcus Ginns

Palace of Westminster

London

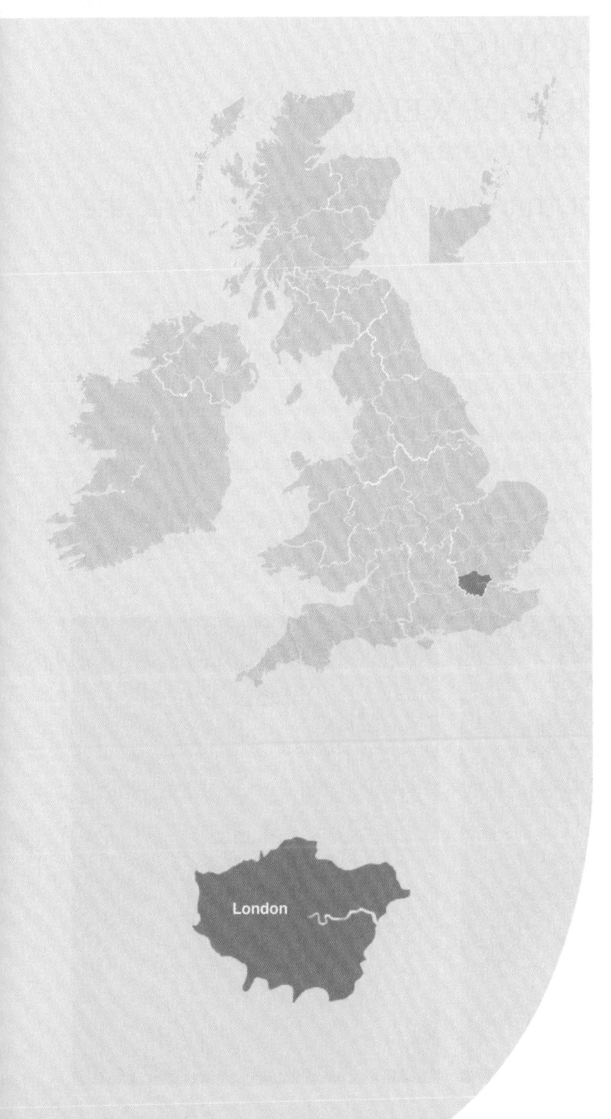
London

There is nowhere in the world quite like London, especially when it comes to must-see attractions. Central London is bursting with heritage sites including the majestic Somerset House, the historic Palace of Westminster, sumptuous Spencer House and regal Kensington Palace. There are smaller gems too like the Chelsea Physic Garden and the wonderfully eclectic 18 Stafford Terrace, former home of Punch cartoonist Edward Linley Sambourne. Venturing further afield in any direction reveals such treasures as leafy Hampstead's Kenwood House with its grand art collection, the fairytale Strawberry Hill at Twickenham, and the art deco elegance of Eltham Palace and Gardens.

VISITOR INFORMATION

Owner
English Heritage

Address
Apsley House
Hyde Park Corner
London W1J 7NT

Location
MAP 20:L8
OS Ref. TQ284 799
N. side of
Hyde Park Corner.
Underground:
Hyde Park Corner exit 1
Piccadilly Line.
Bus:
9, 22, 148.

Contact
House Manager
Tel: 020 7499 5676
E-mail: customers@english-heritage.org.uk

Opening Times
please visit www.english-heritage.org.uk for opening times and the the most up-to-date information.

Admission

Adult	£6.30
Child	£3.80
Child (under 5yrs)	Free
Conc.	£5.70

Joint ticket with Wellington Arch:

Adult	£7.90
Child	£4.70
Child (under 5yrs)	Free
Conc.	£7.10
Family	£20.50

Free for English Heritage members and for Overseas Visitor Pass holders.
Opening times and prices are valid until 31st March 2012.

Special events
There is an exciting events programme available throughout the year, for further details please contact the property or visit the website.

© English Heritage / Nigel Corrie

APSLEY HOUSE ⌗

THE HOME OF THE DUKES OF WELLINGTON

www.english-heritage.org.uk/apsleyhouse

Addresses don't come much grander than 'Number One London', the popular name for Apsley House.

Apsley House was originally designed and built by Robert Adam between 1771 and 1778 for Baron Apsley - from whom it takes its name. It passed to the Wellesley family in 1807, being first owned by Richard and then his younger brother Arthur Wellesley - the Duke of Wellington.

The Duke made Apsley House his London home after a dazzling military career culminating in his victory over Napoleon at Waterloo in 1815. Wellington enlarged the house adding the magnificent Waterloo Gallery by Benjamin Dean Wyatt which holds many of the masterpieces from the Duke's extensive painting collection. It has been the London home of the Dukes of Wellington ever since.

The seventh Duke gave the house and contents to the Nation in 1947, with apartments retained for the family. With its collections of outstanding paintings, porcelain, silver, sculpture, furniture, medals and memorabilia largely intact and the family still in residence, Apsley House is the last great aristocratic town house in London.

Apsley House is not only the last surviving great London town house open to the public, but also the only property managed by English Heritage in which the original owner's family still live.

KEY FACTS

- No photography in house.
- Partial.
- By arrangement.
- Free. English, French, Spanish & German.
- In Park Lane.

© English Heritage

© English Heritage

© English Heritage

CHISWICK HOUSE AND GARDENS ⌗

www.english-heritage.org.uk/chiswickhouse

Chiswick House is a glorious example of 18th century British architecture.

Chiswick House is internationally renowned as one of the first and finest English Palladian villas. Lord Burlington, who built the villa from 1725–1729, was inspired by the architecture and gardens of ancient Rome and this house is his masterpiece. His aim was to create a fit setting to show his friends his fine collection of art and his library. The opulent interior features gilded decoration, velvet walls and painted ceilings.

The important 18th century gardens surrounding Chiswick House have, at every turn, something to surprise and delight the visitor from the magnificent cedar trees to the beautiful Italianate gardens with their cascade, statues, temples, urns and obelisks. 2010 saw the culmination of a major project to restore the historic gardens to their former glory, including the Conservatory and its world famous camellia collection. Visitor facilities have also been improved and a new modern café, designed by award winning architects Caruso St John, offers a light airy space to enjoy a seasonal menu of freshly cooked dishes.

Chiswick House once acted both as a gallery for Lord Burlington's fine art collection and as a glamorous party venue where he could entertain friends, family and high society. With exclusive use, the lavishly gilded interiors today provide a stylish setting for civil wedding ceremonies and a sumptuous backdrop for corporate and private events.

KEY FACTS

- WCs. Filming, plays, photographic shoots.
- Private & corporate hospitality.
- Personal guided tours must be booked in advance.
- Free audio tours in English, French & German.
- Free if booked in advance. Tel: 020 7973 3485.

© English Heritage

© English Heritage

VISITOR INFORMATION

Owner
Chiswick House and Gardens Trust and English Heritage

Address
Chiswick House
Burlington Lane
London W4 2RP

Location
MAP 19:C8
OS Ref: TQ210 775
Burlington Lane
London W4.
Rail: 1/2 mile NE of Chiswick Station.
Underground: Turnham Green, 3/4 mile.
Bus: 190, E3.

Contact
House Manager
Tel: 020 8995 0508
E-mail: customers@english-heritage.org.uk

Venue Hire and Hospitality: Hospitality Co-ordinator
Tel: 020 8742 2762

Opening Times
please visit www.english-heritage.org.uk or www.chgt.org.uk for opening times and the most up-to-date information.

Admission

Adult	£5.50
Child (5–15yrs)	£3.30
Conc	£5.00
Family	£14.30.

Discount for groups (11+).

EH Members free.

Opening times and prices are valid until 31st March 2012.

Special events
There is an exciting events programme available throughout the year, for further details please contact the property or visit the website.

VISITOR INFORMATION

Owner
English Heritage

Address
Eltham Palace
Court Yard
Eltham
London SE9 5QE

Location
MAP 19:F8
OS Ref. TQ425 740

M25/J3, then A20 towards Eltham. The Palace is signposted from A20 and from Eltham High Street. A2 from Central London.

Rail: 30 mins from Victoria or London Bridge Stations to Eltham or Mottingham, then 15 mins walk.

Contact
Visits:
Administrator
Tel: 020 8294 2548
E-mail: customers@english-heritage.org.uk

Venue Hire and Hospitality:
Hospitality Manager
Tel: 020 8294 2577

Opening Times
Please visit www.english-heritage.org.uk for opening times and ring in advance for details.

English Heritage offers exclusive use of the Palace on Thu, Fri or Sat for daytime conferences, meetings and weddings and in the evenings for dinners, concerts and receptions.

Admission
House and Gardens:

Adult	£9.30
Child	£5.60
Conc	£8.40
Family (2+3)	£24.20

Gardens only:

Adult	£5.80
Child	£3.50
Conc.	£5.20

EH Members free. Group discount available.

Prices valid until 31st March 2012

Special events
There is an exciting events programme available throughout the year, for further details please contact the property or visit the website.

Conference/Function	
ROOM	Max Cap
Great Hall	300 standing 200 dining
Entrance Hall	100 seated
Drawing Room	120 standing 80 theatre-style
Dining Room	10 dining

© English Heritage

ELTHAM PALACE AND GARDENS ⌗

www.english-heritage.org.uk/eltham

Immerse yourself in 1930s Art Deco decadence at Eltham Palace.

The epitome of 1930s chic, Eltham Palace dramatically demonstrates the glamour and allure of the period.

Bathe in the light flooding from a spectacular glazed dome in the Entrance Hall as it highlights beautiful blackbean veneer and figurative marquetry. It is a tour de force only rivalled by the adjacent Dining Room – where an Art Deco aluminium-leafed ceiling is a perfect complement to the bird's-eye maple walls. Step into Virginia Courtauld's magnificent gold-leaf and onyx bathroom and throughout the house discover lacquered, 'ocean liner' style veneered walls and built-in furniture.

A Chinese sliding screen is all that separates chic Thirties Art Deco from the medieval Great Hall. Authentic interiors have been recreated by the finest contemporary craftsmen. Their appearance was painstakingly researched from archive photographs, documents and interviews with friends and relatives of the Courtaulds.

Outside you will find a delightful mixture of formal and informal gardens including a rose garden, pergola and loggia, all nestled around the extensive remains of the medieval palace.

A display celebrating the Royal Army Education Corps' (RAEC) post World War II illustrates a further chapter in the Palace's history.

As one of London's most sought-after wedding and party venues, the stylish art deco millionaire's mansion Eltham Palace and Gardens can now host celebrations for up to 420 people thanks to a new marquee site, licensed for drinks and dinner receptions, nestled within its tranquil 19-acre grounds.

KEY FACTS

- WCs. Filming, plays and photographic shoots.
- Exclusive private and corporate hospitality.
- WCs.
- Guided tours on request.
- Free. English, German & French.
- Coaches must book.

© English Heritage

© English Heritage

MYDDELTON HOUSE GARDENS

www.visitleevalley.org.uk

Delve into the enchanting eight acres of Myddelton House Gardens and discover the compelling story of Edward Augustus Bowles.

Mr Bowles was one of Britain's most famous self-taught gardeners, artists and expert botanists. He lived in Myddelton House from 1865 to 1954 and dedicated much of his life to transforming the gardens with his love of unusual and exotic plants.

The gardens boast an impressive range of flora and fauna to stimulate the senses each season. Explore the unusual plants of the Lunatic Asylum, newly restored Kitchen Garden, colourful Alpine Meadow and the extensive snowdrop collection which bring the gardens to life during February. The gardens are also home to a beautiful carp lake, a Victorian conservatory and a number of historical artefacts collected and treasured by Mr Bowles, including pieces from the original St Paul's Cathedral and the Enfield Market Cross. Don't miss the 109 year old Wisteria which turns a brilliant blue when it flowers during May.

In spring 2011 a newly restored Myddelton House Gardens was unveiled, following a two year Heritage Lottery funded project which renovated several areas of the gardens. In the new Visitor Centre, you can uncover the story of Mr Bowles. Look out for the two 280 year old lead ostriches that proudly guarded the Wisteria Bridge - the bridge spanned the original path of New River that once flowed through the gardens.

The Bowles Tea room offers a choice of hot and cold refreshments, selection of cakes or delicious cream teas.

KEY FACTS

 Suitable. WCs.

 By arrangement. Please ring 08456 770 600.

 Limited for coaches.

 Guide dogs only.

VISITOR INFORMATION

Owner
Lee Valley Regional Park Authority

Address
Bulls Cross
Enfield
Middlesex
EN2 9HG

Location
MAP 19:D4
OS Ref. TQ342 992.
1/4m W of A10 via Bullsmoor Lane 3/4m S M25/J25.
Rail: 15 minutes walk from Turkey Street station.

Contact
Tel: 08456 770 600
E-mail: info@leevalleypark.org.uk

Opening Times
The gardens are open every day (except Christmas,
May–September 9.30am–6pm,
October–April 9.30am–4.30pm.
Last admission 30 mins before closing.

Admission
Free admission.

Special events
The gardens hold a range of special events throughout the year, from Jazz in the Gardens to Behind the Scenes tours. Please visit the website for details.

VISITOR INFORMATION

Address
Spencer House
27 St James's Place
London SW1A 1NR

Location
MAP 20:L8
OS Ref. TQ293 803

Central London: off St James's Street, overlooking Green Park.

Underground: Green Park.

Contact
Jane Rick
Director
Tel: 020 7514 1958
Fax: 020 7409 2952
Recorded Info Line: 020 7499 8620
E-mail: tours@spencerhouse.co.uk

Opening Times
2012

Open on Sundays from: 22 January–15 July inclusive + 2 September–23 December inclusive. 10.30am-5.45pm.

Last tour 4.45pm. Regular tours throughout the day.

Maximum number on each tour is 20.

Monday mornings for pre-booked groups only. Group size: min 15–60.

Open for private and corporate hospitality except during January & August.

Admission
Adult: £12.00
Conc*: £10.00

*Students, Members of the V&A, Friends of the Royal Academy, Tate Members and senior citizens (only on production of valid identification), children under 16. No children under 10 admitted.

Prices include guided tour.

Garden
For updated information on opening dates for the restored 18th century garden view: www.spencerhouse.co.uk or telephone the recorded information line: 020 7499 8620.

Conference/Function		
ROOM	Size	Max Cap
Receptions		400
Lunches & Dinners		126
Board Meetings		40
Theatre-style Meetings		100

© Spencer House / Mark Fiennes

SPENCER HOUSE

www.spencerhouse.co.uk

London's most magnificent 18th century private palace.

Spencer House, built 1756–66 for the first Earl Spencer, an ancestor of Diana, Princess of Wales (1961–97), is London's finest surviving 18th century town house. The magnificent private palace has regained the full splendour of its late 18th century appearance, after a painstaking ten-year restoration programme.

Designed by John Vardy and James 'Athenian' Stuart, the nine State rooms are amongst the first neo-classical interiors in Europe. Vardy's Palm Room, with its spectacular screen of gilded palm trees and arched fronds, is a unique Palladian set-piece, while the elegant mural decorations of Stuart's Painted Room reflect the 18th century passion for classical Greece and Rome. Stuart's superb gilded furniture has been returned to its original location in the Painted Room by courtesy of the V&A and English Heritage. Visitors can also see a fine collection of 18th century paintings and furniture, specially assembled for the house, including five major Benjamin West paintings, graciously lent by Her Majesty The Queen.

The State Rooms are open to the public for viewing on Sundays. They are also available on a limited number of occasions each year for private and corporate entertaining during the rest of the week.

KEY FACTS

- No photography inside House or Garden.
- House only, ramps and lifts. WC.
- Obligatory. Comprehensive colour guidebook.
- None.
- Guide dogs only.

© Spencer House / Mark Fiennes

© Spencer House / Mark Fiennes

STRAWBERRY HILL ®

strawberryhillhouse.org.uk

A visit to the beautifully restored rooms of Strawberry Hill is a fairy-tale day out for all the family.

Strawberry Hill is Britain's finest example of Gothic Revival architecture and interior decoration. It began life in 1698 as a modest house, later transformed by Horace Walpole, the son of England's first Prime Minister.

Between 1747 and 1792 Walpole doubled its size, creating extraordinary rooms and adding towers and battlements in fulfilment of his dream. Strawberry Hill was a tourist site in its own day and has survived into ours, its rural surroundings gone, but its charm undiminished.

As they approach Strawberry Hill visitors will be met by the remarkable exterior, restored to its original 'wedding cake' appearance, lime washed in white. The castellated parapets and 3-metre high pinnacles create a dramatic and spiky silhouette. There are 25 show rooms on the ground and first floors, 20 of which have been fully restored to take the house back to the 1790s when Walpole had completed his creation.

In addition to extensive repairs to the roof, much work has been done to repair and conserve the fabric of the building employing the same structural design as the original. Of particular note is the huge collection of renaissance glass for which Strawberry Hill is famed.

Horace set up a private press, publishing historical texts and his own writings including a novel, The Castle of Otranto, considered to be the first piece of Gothic literature.

Following an £8.9 million restoration with the support of the Heritage Lottery Fund, the house is now open to the public as an extraordinary fairytale experience.

KEY FACTS

WCs.
Licensed.
By Arrangement.

Limited for cars. No coaches.
Guide dogs only.

VISITOR INFORMATION

Owner
Strawberry Hill Trust

Address
268 Waldegrave Road
Twickenham
London
TW1 4ST

Location
MAP 19:C8
OS Ref. TQ158 722
Off A310 between Twickenham and Teddington.
Bus: 33 Hammersmith - Fulwell or R68 Kingston - Kew.
Rail: Strawberry Hill (National Rail) 0.3 miles.
Underground: Richmond (District Line).

Contact
Nick Smith
Tel: 020 8744 1241
E-mail: nicholas.smith@strawberryhillhouse.org.uk

Opening Times
House:
April–October:
Monday, Tuesday & Wednesday, 2–4.20pm (last admisssion)
Saturday & Sunday 12–4.20pm (last admisson).
Cafe, museum, and temporary exhibitions (free admission):
Open as House from 11.30am
Garden: (free admisson)
Open year-round at all reasonable hours.
Shop:
30 minutes before house.

Admission

Adult	£8.00
Child	£5.00
Family	£20.00

(2 adults up to three children under 16)
Under 5 free admission.

VISITOR INFORMATION

Owner
The Duke of Northumberland

Address
Syon House
Syon Park
Brentford
TW8 8JF

Location
MAP 19:B8
OS Ref. TQ173 767
Between Brentford and Twickenham, off the A4, A310 in SW London.
Sat Nav: TW7 6AZ
Rail: Kew Bridge or Gunnersbury Underground then Bus 237 or 267.
Air: Heathrow 8m.

Contact
Estate Office
Tel: 020 8560 0882
Fax: 020 8568 0936
E-mail: info@syonpark.co.uk

Opening Times
Syon House
14 March–28 October, Wed, Thur, Sun & BHs, 11am–5pm (open Good Fri & Easter Sat). Other times by appointment for groups.
Gardens only
April–October, Sun–Thurs 10.30am–5pm, Fris & Sats 10.30–4pm, November–March, Sats & Suns, & New Year's day, 10.30am–4pm or dusk, whichever is earlier.
Last admissions House & Gardens 1 hr before closing.

Admission

House and Gardens	
Adult	£10.50
Child	£4.00
Conc.	£8.00
Family (2+2)	£22.00
Group bookings (15–50)	
Adult	£8.50
Conc.	£7.50
School Group	£2.00
Gardens & Great Conservatory	
Adult	£5.50
Child	£2.50
Conc.	£3.50
Family (2+2)	£11.00

Group bookings (15–50) Price on application (please telephone).
Syon House Ventures & The Lovaine Trust reserve the right to alter opening times.

Conference/Function

ROOM	Size	Max Cap
Great Hall	50'x30'	120
Great Conservatory	60'x40'	150
Room 3	35'x20'	60
Marquee		1000

SYON PARK

www.syonpark.co.uk

London home of the Duke of Northumberland with magnificent Robert Adam interiors, 40-acres of gardens, including the spectacular Great Conservatory.

Described by John Betjeman as the 'Grand Architectural Walk', Syon House and its 200-acre park is the London home of the Duke of Northumberland, whose family, the Percys, have lived here for 400 years. Originally the site of a late medieval monastery, excavated by Channel 4's Time Team, Syon Park has a fascinating history. Catherine Howard was imprisoned at Syon before her execution, Lady Jane Grey was offered the crown whilst staying at Syon, and the 9th Earl of Northumberland was imprisoned in the Tower of London for 15 years because of his association with the Gunpowder Plot. The present house has Tudor origins but contains some of Robert Adam's finest interiors, which were commissioned by the 1st Duke in the 1760s. The private apartments and State bedrooms are available to view.

The house can be hired for filming and photo shoots subject to availability. Within the 'Capability' Brown landscaped park are 40 acres of gardens which contain the spectacular Great Conservatory designed by Charles Fowler in the 1820s. The House and Great Conservatory are available for corporate and private hire. The Northumberland Room in Syon House is an excellent venue for conferences, meetings, lunches and dinners (max 60). The State Apartments make a sumptuous setting for dinners, concerts, receptions, launches and wedding ceremonies (max 120). Marquees can be erected on the lawn adjacent to the house for balls and corporate events. The Great Conservatory is available for summer parties, launches, filming, photoshoots and wedding receptions (max 150).

KEY FACTS

- No photography in house. Indoor adventure playground.
- Garden Centre.
- Partial. WCs.
- By arrangement.
- Guide dogs only.

© Tony Marshall

KEATS HOUSE

KEATS GROVE, HAMPSTEAD, LONDON NW3 2RR

www.cityoflondon.gov.uk/keatshousehampstead

This Grade I listed Regency house is where the poet John Keats lived from 1818 to 1820 with his friend Charles Brown. Here he wrote 'Ode to a Nightingale' and met and fell in love with Fanny Brawne. Suffering from tuberculosis, Keats left for Italy, where he died at the age of 25. Fanny wore his engagement ring until her death, and it is now displayed at the house. Their love story was immortalised in Jane Campion's film 'Bright Star', released in 2009. The museum runs regular poetry readings, talks and events suitable for families throughout the year.

Location: MAP 20:K3, OS Ref. TQ272 856. Hampstead, NW3. Nearest Underground: Belsize Park & Hampstead.

Owner: City of London **Contact:** The Manager

Tel: 020 7332 3868 **E-mail:** keatshouse@cityoflondon.gov.uk

Open: Keats House reopened in 2009 after the successful Magic Casements project funded by the Heritage Lottery Fund. Our opening hours are Easter–31 Oct: Tue–Sun, 1–5pm; 1 Nov–Easter: Fri–Sun, 1–5pm. School parties and pre-booked groups by arrangement. The house is also open on Bank Holiday Mondays.

Admission: Adults £5, Concessions £3, Children 16 and under are free. Tickets are valid for one year.

Key facts: WCs. None. Guide dogs only.

KENSINGTON PALACE

LONDON W8 4PX

www.kensington-palace.org.uk

Generations of royal Women have shaped this stylish palace. The birthplace and childhood home of Queen Victoria, the palace first became a royal residence for William and Mary in 1689. The famous Orangery was built in 1704 by Queen Anne, and George II's wife, Queen Caroline, another keen gardener, added further improvements. For 2012 it will celebrate 'Victoria Revealed'; and from 24.05.12 to 31.10.12 'Jubilee - a view from the crowd'.

Location: MAP 20:I8, OS Ref. TQ258 801. In Kensington Gardens.

Owner: Historic Royal Palaces **Tel:** 0844 482 7777

Venue Hire and Corporate Hospitality: 020 3166 6104

E-mail: groupsandtraveltrade@hrp.org.uk

Open: Nov–Feb: daily, 10am–6pm (last admission 5pm). Oct–Feb: daily, 10am–5pm (last admission 4pm). Closed 24–26 Dec. Closed for major re-presentation from 04.01.12 to 25.03.12

Admission: Telephone Information Line for admission prices: 0844 482 7777. Advance Ticket Sales: 0844 482 7799. Group bookings: 0844 482 7770. Quote Hudson's.

Key facts: No photography indoors. Partial. By arrangement. Nearby. Please book, 0844 482 7777.

© English Heritage

© English Heritage

KENWOOD HOUSE

KENWOOD HOUSE, HAMPSTEAD LANE, LONDON NW3 7JR

www.english-heritage.org.uk/kenwoodhouse

Kenwood, one of the treasures of London, is an idyllic country retreat close to the popular villages of Hampstead and Highgate. Kenwood is famous for the internationally important collection of paintings bequeathed to the nation by Edward Guinness, 1st Earl of Iveagh. Some of the world's finest artists are represented by works such as a Rembrandt Self Portrait, Vermeer's The Guitar Player; Mary, Countess Howe by Gainsborough and paintings by Turner, Reynolds and many others. Kenwood stands in 112 acres of landscaped grounds on the edge of Hampstead Heath, commanding a fine prospect towards central London.

Location: MAP 20:K1, OS Ref. TQ271 874. M1/J2. Signed off A1, on leaving A1 turn right at junction with Bishop's Ave, turn left into Hampstead Lane

Owner: English Heritage **Contact:** The House Manager

Tel: 020 8348 1286 **E-mail:** customers@english-heritage.org.uk

Open: Kenwood House will be closed for major works from April 2012 until Autumn 2013. This completed project will see one of London's best loved historic houses stunningly restored to it's former glory both inside and out, providing a greatly enhanced setting for it's internationally significant art collection.

Key facts: WCs. Concerts, exhibitions, filming. No photography in house. Exclusive private and corporate hospitality. Available on request (in English). Please call for details. West Lodge car park (Pay & Display) on Hampstead Lane. Parking for the disabled. Free when booked in advance on 020 7973 3485. Guide dogs only.

© National Maritime Museum

© National Maritime Museum

NATIONAL MARITIME MUSEUM, QUEEN'S HOUSE & ROYAL OBSERVATORY, GREENWICH

NATIONAL MARITIME MUSEUM, PARK ROW, GREENWICH, LONDON SE10 9NF

www.nmm.ac.uk

The National Maritime Museum details inspirational stories of exploration, discovery and endeavour from Britain's seafaring past as well as examining the continuing effects the oceans still have on the world today. The Queen's House, completed in around 1638 and designed by Inigo Jones, introduced England to the beauties of Palladian architecture. The Royal Observatory, Greenwich is the home of Greenwich Mean Time and the famous Prime Meridian of the World - 0° 0' 0". Built for the purpose of finding longitude at sea, Sir Christopher Wren's Royal Observatory is also a museum of time and astronomy.

Location: MAP 19:E7, OS Ref. TQ388 773. M25 (S) via A2. From M25 (N) M11, A12 and Blackwall Tunnel.

Owner: National Maritime Museum

E-mail: bookings@nmm.ac.uk / events@nmm.ac.uk

Open: Open daily, 10am–5pm. Last admission 30 minutes before closing. Late summer opening times apply. Visit nmm.ac.uk for further details. Closed 24–26 December.

Admission: Admission is free. Charges and age restrictions apply for planetarium shows, some special events and exhibitions. All information correct at time of print but may be subject to change.

Key facts: WCs. Obligatory. Limited for cars, no coaches. Guide dogs only.

© NTPL / Andrew Butler

OSTERLEY PARK AND HOUSE

JERSEY ROAD, ISLEWORTH, MIDDLESEX TW7 4RB

www.nationaltrust.org.uk/osterley

One of the last surviving country estates in London; Osterley is a spectacular mansion surrounded by gardens, park and farmland.

Created in the late 18th century by Robert Adam for the Child family to entertain and impress their friends and clients; this 'palace of palaces' remains as impressive today.

Explore the dazzling interior with handheld audio visual guides which bring the House to life in a completely new way. Outside, the gardens have been restored to their 18th century glory offering a delightful retreat from urban life, perfect for picnics and leisurely strolls.

Location: MAP 19:B7, OS Ref. TQ146 780. A4 between Hammersmith and Hounslow. Main gates at Thornbury and Jersey Road junction. SatNav: 'Jersey Road, TW7 4RB'

Owner: National Trust

Contact: Visitor Experience & Marketing Manager

Tel: 020 8232 5050

Fax: 020 8232 5080

E-mail: osterley@nationaltrust.org.uk

Open: House & Garden*: Wed–Sun & BH 11 Feb–4 Mar, 12–3.30pm (tours only). 7 Mar–28 Oct, 12–4.30pm. 1–16 Dec, Sat & Sun only, 12–3.30pm. *Garden open:11am–5pm.

Café & Shop**: 11 Feb–28 Oct, Wed–Sun, 11am–5pm. **Shop opens at 12noon 3 Nov–16 Dec, Wed–Sun, 12–4pm.

Admission: House and Garden*: Adult £9.65, Child £4.85, Family £24.15, Group (15+) £8.20. Garden: Adult £4.20, Child £2.10. Park: Free. Car Park: £3.50. Free to NT Members. *includes a voluntary 10% Gift Aid donation.

Key facts: No flash photography inside House. Partial. WCs. Licensed. By arrangement. Limited for coaches. Guide dogs only Please see website for event details.

PALACE OF WESTMINSTER

PARLIAMENT SQUARE, LONDON SW1A 0AA

www.parliament.uk/visiting/visiting-and-tours/

1000 Years of history which have shaped Britain can be discovered within one of the most iconic buildings in the world; the Houses of Parliament.

Insightful and entertaining guided tours last 75 minutes and follow the processional route taken by Her Majesty the Queen when she performs the State Opening of Parliament. Most of the buildings seen on the tour were built in the mid 19th century following a devastating fire, but the route also incorporates some of the earlier buildings, such as Westminster Hall, begun in 1097 by William Rufus, son of William the Conqueror.

Location: MAP 20:M8, OS Ref. TQ303 795. Central London, W bank of River Thames. 1km S of Trafalgar Square. Underground: Westminster.

Contact: Information Office

Tel: 0844 847 1672 / 0870 906 3773

Info: 020 7219 4272

Open: Guided tours run during Aug and Sept and on Sats throughout the year.

Admission: Adult: £15, Children: £6 (5-15 years), Family: £37, Conc: £10 (Students, Senior citizens (60+), Members of the Armed Forces).

Key facts: No photography. Partial. WCs. Licensed. Obligatory. None for cars. Limited for coaches.

© Matt Prince

© St Paul's Cathedral / Peter Smith

ST PAUL'S CATHEDRAL

ST PAUL'S CHURCHYARD, LONDON EC4M 8AD

www.stpauls.co.uk

St Paul's, with its world-famous Dome, is an iconic feature of the London skyline, but there is much more to Sir Christopher Wren's masterpiece than its impressive façade. A spiritual focus for the nation since its first service in 1697, many important events have taken place within its walls, from the State funerals of Lord Nelson, the Duke of Wellington and Sir Winston Churchill to the wedding of the Prince of Wales to Lady Diana Spencer and the Thanksgiving services for Her Majesty the Queen's Golden Jubilee and 80th Birthday. The results of the Cathedral's programme of cleaning and repair are breathtaking.
Location: MAP 20:N7, OS Ref. TQ321 812. Central London.

Owner: Dean & Chapter of St Paul's Cathedral
Contact: The Chapter House
Tel: 020 7246 8350 / 020 7236 4128 **Fax:** 020 7248 3104
E-mail: chapter@stpaulscathedral.org.uk
Open: Mon–Sat, 8.30am–4.30pm, last admission 4pm. Please see website or contact us for more details.
Admission: Please see website or contact us for more details.
Key facts: No photography, video or mobile phones. Licensed. None for cars, limited for coaches.

SOUTHSIDE HOUSE

3 WOODHAYES ROAD, WIMBLEDON, LONDON SW19 4RJ

www.southsidehouse.com

Described by connoisseurs as an unforgettable experience, Southside House provides an eccentric backdrop to the lives and loves of generations of the Pennington Mellor Munthe families. Maintained in traditional style, without major refurbishment, and crowded with family possessions of centuries, Southside offers a wealth of fascinating family stories. John Pennington-Mellor's daughter, Hilda, married Axel Munthe, the charismatic Swedish doctor and philanthropist. The preservation of the house was left to their youngest son who led a life of extraordinary adventure during the Second World War. Malcolm Munthe's surviving children continue to care for the property.
Location: MAP 20:D8, OS Ref. TQ234 706. On S side of Wimbledon Common (B281), opposite Crooked Billet Inn.
Owner: The Pennington-Mellor-Munthe Charity Trust

Contact: The Administrator
Tel: 020 8946 7643
E-mail: info@southsidehouse.com
Open: Easter Sat–26 Sept: Weds, Sats, Suns & BH Mons. Closed during Wimbledon fortnight last week in June/first week in July. Guided tours on the hour 2, 3 & 4pm. Other times throughout the year by arrangement with the Administrator for groups of 15 -24 @ £12.50 per head inc.
Admission: Adult £6, Child £3 (must be accompanied by an adult), Student conc. £4.50, Family £12.
Key facts: No Photography inside house. Obligatory. Dinners/lunches for up to 26 people, drinks parties for maximum 60. Concert programme.

TOWER OF LONDON

LONDON EC3N 4AB

www.tower-of-london.org.uk

These ancient stones reverberate with history, priceless jewels glint in, and pampered ravens strut the grounds. Despite a grim reputation, there are many more stories to be told about the Tower, and its intriguing cast of characters. From 2010, Henry VIII: 'Fit For A King' - journey back through his historic reign at this spectacular exhibition of his armour and weapons. Also 'Royal Beasts' an exciting new exhibition, recalling its role as a royal menagerie, and from April 2012 the fabulous Crown Jewels will be re-presented.

Location: MAP 20:P7, OS Ref. TQ336 806.

Owner: Historic Royal Palaces

Tel: 0844 482 7777 Venue Hire and Corporate Hospitality: 020 3166 6207

E-mail: groupsandtraveltrade@hrp.org.uk

Open: Summer: 1 Mar–31 Oct, Daily, Tues–Sat: 9am–6pm (last admission 5pm), Mons & Suns: 10am–6pm (last admission 5pm). Winter: 1 Nov–28 Feb, Tues–Sat: 9am–5pm, Mons & Suns: 10am–5pm (last admission 4pm). Closed 24–26 Dec and 1 Jan. Buildings close 30 minutes after last admission.

Admission: Telephone Information Line for admission prices: 0844 482 7777. Advance Ticket Sales: 0844 482 7799. Group bookings: 0844 482 7770. Quote Hudson's.

Key facts: No Photography in Jewel house. 020 3166 6311. Partial. WCs. Licensed. By arrangement. Yeoman Warder tours are free and leave front entrance every 1/2 hr. None for cars. Coach parking nearby. To book 0844 482 7777.

18 STAFFORD TERRACE

18 Stafford Terrace, London W8 7BH

www.rbkc.gov.uk/museums

From 1875, 18 Stafford Terrace was the home of Punch cartoonist Edward Linley Sambourne, his wife Marion, their two children and live-in servants. Originally decorated by the Sambournes in keeping with fashionable Aesthetic principles, the interiors evolved into wonderfully eclectic artistic statements within the confines of a typical middle-class home.

Location: MAP 20:I8, OS Ref. TQ252 794. Parallel to Kensington High St, between Phillimore Gardens & Argyll Rd.

Owner: The Royal Borough of Kensington & Chelsea **Contact:** Curatorial staff

Tel: 020 7602 3316 **Fax:** 020 7371 2467 **E-mail:** museums@rbkc.gov.uk

Open: Mid Sept–mid June. Visits are by guided tours only; Weds 11.15am, 2.15pm, Sats and Suns 11.15am, 1pm, 2.15pm, 3.30pm (weekend afternoon tours are costumed).

Admission: Adult £6, Concession £4, Child (under 18yrs) £1. Groups (12+): Min £96. Joint group (12+) guided tour with Leighton House Museum £14pp.

Key facts: No photography. Obligatory. Guide dogs only.

© Britainonview

BUCKINGHAM PALACE

London SW1A 1AA

www.royalcollection.org.uk

Buckingham Palace is the official London residence of Her Majesty The Queen and serves as both home and office. Its 19 State Rooms, which open for eight weeks a year, form the heart of the working palace. The garden walk offers superb views of the Garden Front of the Palace and lake. During August and September when The Queen makes her annual visit to Scotland, the Palace's nineteen state rooms are open to visitors.

Location: MAP 20:L8, OS Ref. TQ291 796. Underground: Green Park, Victoria, St James's Park.

Owner: Official Residence of Her Majesty The Queen

Contact: Ticket Sales & Information Office

Tel: 020 7766 7300

E-mail: bookinginfo@royalcollection.org.uk

Open: Please contact the information office or see our website.

Admission: Please contact the information office or see our website.

www.royalcollection.org.uk

CAPEL MANOR GARDENS

Bullsmoor Lane, Enfield EN1 4RQ

www.capelmanorgardens.co.uk

A beautiful 30 acre estate, first established in the late 13th century, Capel Manor provides a colourful & scented oasis surrounding a Georgian Manor House & Victorian Stables. Be inspired by prize winning themed, model & historical gardens including the latest additions the Old Manor House Garden (opened by her Majesty the Queen in June 2010) and the Family Friendly Garden (a 2010 Chelsea Flower Show Gold Medal Winner). Picnic by the lake or relax in the restaurant & finish with a visit to the gift shop. Free parking.
Location: MAP 19:E4, OS Ref. TQ344 997. Minutes from M25/J25. Tourist Board signs posted.
Owner: Capel Manor Charitable Organisation
Contact: Customer Services
Tel: 0845 6122 122
Fax: 01992 717 544
Open: Daily in summer: 10am–6pm. Last ticket 4pm, Gardens 5.30pm. Check for winter times.
Admission: Adult £5.50, Child £2.50, Conc. £4.50, Family £13.50. Charges alter for special show weekends and winter months.
Key facts: Grounds. WC. In grounds, on leads.

HAM HOUSE & GARDEN

Ham St, Richmond-Upon-Thames, Surrey TW10 7RS

www.nationaltrust.org.uk/hamhouse

One of a series of grand houses and palaces alongside the River Thames, Ham House and Garden is an unusually complete survival of the 17th century - a treasure trove waiting to be discovered. The gardens are a rare example of 17th century garden design.
Location: MAP 19:B8, OS Ref. TQ172 732. On S bank of the Thames, W of A307 at Petersham between Richmond and Kingston.
Owner: National Trust **Contact:** The Property Manager **Tel:** 020 8940 1950
Fax: 020 8439 8241 **E-mail:** hamhouse@nationaltrust.org.uk
Open: House: 20 Feb–8 Mar: Guided tours, Sat–Thur 12–4pm. 10 Mar–1 Nov, Sat–Thur: open 12pm, closing varies 4–5pm. Garden, Shop, Cafe: 1 Jan–19 Feb & 3–25 Nov, weekends 11am–3pm; 20 Feb–1 Nov: Sat–Thur open 11am, closing varies 4.30–6pm. Christmas event Dec.
Admission: House & Garden: 20 Feb–1 Nov Adult £10.90, Child £6.05, Family £27.90. Garden only: 1 Jan–19 Feb & 3–25 Nov Adult £1.85, Child £1.25, Family £4.90. 20 Feb–1 Nov and 1–16 Dec, Adult £3.65, Child £2.45, Family £9.75. *Gift Aid prices.
Key facts: Photography permitted in the House but no flash permitted. WCs. Licensed. Licensed. By arrangement. Limited for coaches. Guide dogs only.

FITZROY HOUSE

37 Fitzroy Street, Fitzrovia, London W1T 6DX

www.fitzroyhouse.org

Built in 1791, Fitzroy House was formerly inhabited by playwright George Bernard Shaw. Today it shows the life and work of L. Ron Hubbard, founder of Scientology, who worked there in the late 1950s. Steeped in 1950s memorabilia, the house displays a nostalgic collection of restored communications office equipment, complete with Adler typewriter, Grundig tape recorders, and Western Union Telefax.
Location: MAP 20:L6, OS Ref. TQ291 820. Underground: Warren St Underground.
Contact: Heritage Properties International
Contact: Sarah Eicker
Tel/Fax: 020 7255 2422
E-mail: info@fitzroyhouse.org
Open: All year. Guided tours of the house between 11am–5pm by appointment.
Admission: Free admission. Coach parties welcome, teas served.
Key facts: Morning Coffee and afternoon tea is served. Obligatory.

MARBLE HILL HOUSE

Richmond Road, Twickenham TW1 2NL

www.english-heritage.org.uk/marblehillhouse

This beautiful villa was built on the Thames in 1724–29 for Henrietta Howard, mistress of George II. It boasts an important collection of paintings and furniture, and is a must see for interior design enthusiasts. A recent installation recreates the Chinese wallpaper hung in the Dining Room in 1751.
Location: MAP 19:B8, OS Ref. TQ174 736. A305, 600yds E of Orleans House.
Owner: English Heritage
Contact: Visitor Operations Team
Tel: 020 8892 5115 **E-mail:** customers@english-heritage.org.uk
Open: Please see www.english-heritage.org.uk for opening times and the most up-to-date information.
Admission: Adult £5.30, Child £3.20, Conc. £4.80, Family £13.80. EH Members free. Group discount available. Opening times and prices are valid until 31st March 2012.
Key facts: Marble Hill House is available for corporate and private hire and is licensed for civil wedding ceremonies. On leads.

MUSEUM OF THE ORDER OF ST JOHN

St John's Gate, Clerkenwell, London EC1M 4DA

www.museumstjohn.org.uk

Tudor Gatehouse (built 1504), Priory Church and Norman Crypt. The remarkable history of the Knights Hospitaller is now revealed in new galleries showing our fine collections. Notable associations with Shakespeare, Hogarth, Dr Johnson, Dickens, David Garrick and many others. In Victorian times, St John Ambulance was founded here.

Location: MAP 20:N6, OS Ref. TQ317 821. St. John's Lane, Clerkenwell. Nearest Underground: Farringdon.

Owner: The Order of St John **Contact:** Pamela Willis

Tel: 020 7324 4005 **E-mail:** museum@nhq.sja.org.uk

Open: Mon–Sat 10am–5pm. See website for further details. Guided tours Tues, Fri & Sat at 11am & 2.30pm

Admission: Museum Galleries Free. Tours of the buildings: £5, OAP £4 (donation). Supported by the National Lottery through the Heritage Lottery Fund.

Key facts: WCs. Obligatory. Guide dogs only.

© NTPL / Geoffrey Frosh

SUTTON HOUSE

2 & 4 Homerton High Street, Hackney, London E9 6JQ

www.nationaltrust.org.uk/suttonhouse

A rare example of a Tudor red-brick house, built 1535 by Sir Ralph Sadleir, Principal Secretary of State for Henry VIII, with 18th century alterations and later additions. Restoration revealed 16th century detail, even in rooms of later periods. Notable features include original linenfold panelling and 17th century wall paintings.

Location: MAP 20:P3, OS Ref. TQ352 851. At the corner of Isabella Road and Homerton High St.

Owner: National Trust **Contact:** The Custodian

Tel: 020 8986 2264 **E-mail:** suttonhouse@nationaltrust.org.uk

Open: Historic Rooms: 23 Jul–29 Aug, Mon, Tues, Wed 10:30am–4.30pm. 2 Feb–14 Dec, Thurs & Fri 10:30am–4.30pm. 4 Feb–16 Dec, Sat & Sun 12–4.30pm

Admission: Adult £3, Child £1, Family £6.60. Group £2.70. Free to NT Members.

Key facts: Second-hand book shop. Ground floor only. WC. Obligatory.

© Jeff Knowles

SOMERSET HOUSE

Strand, London WC2R 1LA

www.somersethouse.org.uk

Somerset House is a spectacular neo-classical building in the heart of London. During summer 55 fountains dance in the courtyard, and in winter you can skate on London's favourite ice rink. Somerset House also hosts open-air concerts and films, contemporary art and design exhibitions, learning events and free guided tours.

Location: Map 20. OS Ref. TQ308 809. Sitting between the Strand and the River Thames. Entrances on Strand, Embankment and Waterloo Bridge.

Owner: Somerset House Trust **Contact:** Visitor Services Coordinator

Tel: 020 7845 8686 **Fax:** 020 7836 7613 **E-mail:** info@somersethouse.org.uk

Open: For opening times, please see website.

Admission: Embankment Galleries: Please see website for details. The Courtauld Gallery: adults £6, Conc. £4.50, full-time UK students/under 18s/ES40 holders free, Mondays 10am–2pm (excl. public holidays) free.

Key facts: WCs. Licensed. Licensed. By arrangement. On leads.

© English Heritage

WELLINGTON ARCH

Hyde Park Corner, London W1J 7JZ

www.english-heritage.org.uk/wellingtonarch

Set in the heart of Royal London, Wellington Arch is a landmark for Londoners and visitors alike. George IV originally commissioned this massive monument as a grand outer entrance to Buckingham Palace. Visit the balconies just below the spectacular bronze sculpture for glorious views over London.

Location: MAP 20:L8, OS Ref. TQ285 798. Hyde Park Corner Tube Station.

Owner: English Heritage **Contact:** Visitor Operations Team

Tel: 020 7930 2726 Venue Hire and Hospitality: 020 7973 3292

E-mail: customers@english-heritage.org.uk

Open: Please visit www.english-heritage.org.uk for opening times and the most up-to-date information.

Admission: Adult £3.90, Child £2.30, Conc. £3.50. Joint ticket with Apsley House: Adult £7.90, Child £4.70, Conc. £7.10. EH Members free. Opening times and prices are valid until 31st March 2012.

Key facts: Available for corporate and private hire. Mons for groups only.

© English Heritage

THE 'WERNHER COLLECTION' AT RANGER'S HOUSE ⌗

Chesterfield Walk, Blackheath, London SE10 8QX

www.english-heritage.org.uk/rangershouse

A truly hidden gem, in South East London's Greenwich Park, Ranger's House is home to the Wernher Collection - a sumptuous arrangement of glittering silver and jewels, paintings and porcelain. A wonderful day out for any art enthusiast, there are nearly 700 works on display.
Location: MAP 4:I2, OS Ref. TQ388 768. N of Shooters Hill Road.
Owner: English Heritage **Contact:** House Manager
Tel: 020 8853 0035 **E-mail:** customers@english-heritage.org.uk
Open: Please visit www.english-heritage.org.uk for opening times and the most up-to-date information.
Admission: Adult £6.30, Child £3.80, Conc. £5.70. EH Members free. Group discount available. Opening times and prices are valid until 31st March 2012.
Key facts: WC. No photography in the house. This property is available for corporate and private hire and licensed for civil wedding ceremonies.

WESLEY'S CHAPEL, JOHN WESLEY'S HOUSE & THE MUSEUM OF METHODISM

Wesley's Chapel, 49 City Road, London EC1Y 1AU

www.wesleyschapel.org.uk

Step back into 18th century London with a visit to this beautifully-preserved chapel, Wesley's Georgian townhouse and The Museum of Methodism. Discover how John Wesley lived, see his electrical machine and explore the wide-ranging fine art, furniture, metalwork and archive collections. Visit a hidden gem in the heart of London!
Contact: Tracey Smith - Office Manager, Christian Dettlaff - Curator
Tel: 020 7253 2262 **Fax:** 020 7608 3825
E-mail: museum@wesleyschapel.org.uk
Open: Mon–Sat, 10am–4pm. Sun, 12.30–1.45pm. Closed every Thur 12.45–1.30pm, Christmas Day & New Year, & public/bank holidays.
Admission: Admission is free but donations are gratefully received to help preserve this historic site and its collections. There is a charge for groups, please contact the Office Manager for information.
Key facts: Groups of 6+, including school parties, must book in advance through the Office Manager. Photography for private and study purposes allowed (except where indicated). Partial. WCs. By arrangement. Guide dogs only.

7 HAMMERSMITH TERRACE - HOME OF EMERY WALKER

7 Hammersmith Terrace, London W6 9TS

Emery Walker, friend and advisor to William Morris, lived in this riverside house for 30 years and it preserves the only authentic Arts and Crafts urban interior in Britain, with furniture, wallpapers, textiles and ceramics by Morris & Co, Philip Webb, William de Morgan, etc. Small, delightful garden.
Location: MAP 19:D7, OS Ref. TQ221 782. Between Chiswick Mall and South Black Lion Lane in Hammersmith, parallel with King Street.
Owner: The Emery WalkerTrust **Contact:** The Manager **Tel:** 020 8741 4104
E-mail: admin@emerywalker.org.uk **Website:** www.emerywalker.org.uk
Open: Apr–Sept: Guided tour. Please visit website for times, dates and booking arrangements. Admission strictly by pre-booked timed ticket.
Admission: Adult £10, Student £5. No children under 12yrs. Groups (max 8).
Key facts: No photography inside house. No WC. Refreshments available locally. Limited access to ground floor, no access to garden. Obligatory.

BANQUETING HOUSE

The Banqueting House, Horse Guards, Whitehall, London SW1 2ER

This revolutionary building, is the first in England to be designed in a Palladian style by Inigo Jones. The Banqueting House is most famous for one real life drama, the execution of Charles I.
Location: MAP 20:M8, OS Ref. TQ302 80.
Owner: Historic Royal Palaces
Tel: General Enquiries: 0844 482 7777 Enquiries: 020 3166 6150/6151
E-mail: groupsandtraveltrade@hrp.org.uk
Website: www.banqueting-house.org.uk
Open: All year, Mon–Sat, 10am–5pm. Last admission 4.30pm. Closed 24 Dec–1 Jan, Good Friday and other public holidays. NB. Liable to close at short notice for Government functions.
Admission: Enquiry line for admission prices: 0844 482 7777.
Key facts: Concerts. No photography inside. WCs. By arrangement. Video and audio guide. Limited.

BURGH HOUSE

New End Square, Hampstead, London NW3 1LT

Grade I listed building (1703) in the heart of Hampstead with original panelled rooms, "barley sugar" staircase banisters and music room. Hampstead Museum, permanent and changing exhibitions. Prize-winning terraced garden. Regular programme of concerts, art exhibitions, and events. Special facilities for schools visits. Rooms for hire. Wedding receptions and ceremonies.
Location: MAP 20:J2, OS Ref. TQ266 859. New End Square, E of Hampstead Underground station.
Owner: London Borough of Camden **Contact:** General Manager
Tel: 020 7431 0144 **Buttery:** 0207 794 2905 **Fax:** 020 7435 8817
E-mail: info@burghhouse.org.uk **Website:** www.burghhouse.org.uk
Open: Wed–Fri & Sun 12–5pm. Bank Hols 2–5pm. Closed Christmas fortnight. Groups by arrangement. Buttery: Wed–Fri 11am–5.30pm, Sat & Sun 9.30am–5.30pm. **Admission:** Free.
Key facts: Suitable. WCs. Licensed. Licensed. By arrangement. By arrangement. In grounds.

CHELSEA PHYSIC GARDEN

66 Royal Hospital Road, London SW3 4HS

Chelsea Physic Garden, founded in 1673, is London's oldest botanic garden and a unique living museum. Features include Europe's oldest pond rockery; pharmaceutical and perfumery beds; the Garden of World Medicine; a tropical plant greenhouse and over 5,000 different named plants. The Garden's renowned licensed cafe serves delicious homemade food.
Location: Map 20. OS Ref. TQ276 778. Underground stations Victoria or Sloane Square. **Owner:** Chelsea Physic Garden Company **Tel:** 020 7352 5646
Fax: 020 7376 3910 **E-mail:** enquiries@chelseaphysicgarden.co.uk
Website: www.chelseaphysicgarden.co.uk
Open: Apr–Oct: Suns & BHs 12–6pm. Tues, Weds, Thurs & Fris 12–5pm. Weds Openings Jul-Aug 12–10pm. Check website for Winter Openings.
Admission: Please see website for latest admission prices.
Key facts: No bicycles, ball games or wheeled toys. Max 2 Under 16s per adult. Under 16s must be accompanied by an adult. Suitable. WCs. Licensed. By arrangement. Guide dogs only.

Britain's Brilliant Heritage
Brought To Life
To find out more visit our website
www.hudsonsheritage.com
HUDSON'S HERITAGE

HONEYWOOD MUSEUM

Honeywood Walk, Carshalton SM5 3NX

Local history museum in a 17th century listed building next to the picturesque Carshalton Ponds, containing displays on the history of the house and local area, plus a changing programme of exhibitions and events on a wide range of subjects. Attractive garden at rear.

Location: MAP 19:D9, OS Ref. TQ279 646. On A232 approximately 4m W of Croydon.

Owner: London Borough of Sutton **Contact:** The Curator

Tel/Fax: 020 8770 4297 **E-mail:** lbshoneywood@btconnect.com

Website: www.sutton.gov.uk www.friendsofhoneywood.co.uk

Open: Wed–Fri, 11am–5pm. Sat, Suns & BH Mons, 10am–5pm. Closed for Heritage Lottery Funded refurbishment until late Spring 2012.

Key facts: Partial. WCs. By arrangement. Limited. Guide dogs only.

LITTLE HOLLAND HOUSE

40 Beeches Avenue, Carshalton SM5 3LW

The home of Frank Dickinson (1874–1961) who dreamt of a house which would follow the ideals of Morris and Ruskin. Dickinson designed, built and furnished the house himself from 1902 onwards. The Grade II* interior features handmade furniture, metalwork, carvings and paintings produced by Dickinson in the Arts and Crafts style.

Location: MAP 19:D9, OS Ref. TQ275 634. On B278 1m S of junction with A232.

Owner: London Borough of Sutton **Contact:** Ms V Murphy **Tel:** 020 8770 4781

Fax: 020 8770 4777 **E-mail:** valary.murphy@sutton.gov.uk

Website: www.sutton.gov.uk

Open: First Sun of each month & BH Suns & Mons (excluding Christmas & New Year), 1.30–5.30pm.

Admission: Free. Groups by arrangement, £5pp (includes talk and guided tour).

Key facts: No photography in house. Partial. By arrangement. Guide dogs only

THE NATIONAL ARMY MUSEUM

Royal Hospital Road, Chelsea, London SW3 4HT

Explore the impact behind Britain's Army and discover how Britain's military past has helped shape our present and future. 2012's major exhibition, War Horse: Fact & Fiction, follows Michael Morpurgo's novel and the National Theatre's production with touching real-life stories of warhorses and the men who depended on them.

Location: MAP 20:K10, TQ 27721 77911

Tel: 020 7730 0717 **E-mail:** info@nam.ac.uk **Website:** www.nam.ac.uk

Open: Daily 10am-5.30pm (except 24–26 December and 1 January).

Admission: Entry to the Museum is free, though some elements may carry a small admission charge.

Key facts: No photography. WCs. Licensed. By arrangement. Limited for cars & coaches. Guide dogs only.

PITZHANGER MANOR-HOUSE

Walpole Park, Mattock Lane, Ealing W5 5EQ

Pitzhanger Manor-House is a restored Georgian villa once owned and designed by the architect Sir John Soane in 1800. Rooms have been restored using Soane's highly individual ideas in design and decoration. The residence now also functions as a contemporary arts venue with a continually changing exhibitions programme.

Location: MAP 19:B7, OS Ref. TQ176 805. Ealing, London.

Owner: London Borough of Ealing **Contact:** Exhibition and Events Co-ordinator

Tel: 020 8567 1227 **Fax:** 020 8567 0595

E-mail: pmgallery&house@ealing.gov.uk

Website: www.ealing.gov.uk/pmgalleryandhouse

Open: All year: Tue–Fri, 1–5pm. Sat, 11am–5pm. Summer Sunday Openings, please ring for details. Closed Christmas, Easter, New Year and BHs.

Admission: Free.

Key facts: Partial. By arrangement.

SIR JOHN SOANE'S MUSEUM

13 Lincoln's Inn Fields, London WC2A 3BP

Built in 1812 by one of Britain's greatest architects, Sir John Soane, the Museum now contains his collection of classical antiquities, sculpture and an Egyptian Sarcophagus. The paintings include some by Canaletto, Turner and two series by William Hogarth, 'A Rake's Progress' and 'An Election'.

Location: MAP 20:M6, OS Ref. TQ308 816. E of Kingway, S of High Holborn.

Owner: Trustees of Sir John Soane's Museum **Contact:** Claire Lucky

Tel: 020 7405 2107 **Fax:** 020 7831 3957

E-mail: cjlucky@soane.org.uk **Website:** www.soane.org

Open: Tue–Sat, 10am–5pm. First Tue of the month 6–9pm, expect to queue. Groups must book. Last entry 30 mins before closing.

Admission: Free. Charge for 11am Saturday tour £5.

Key facts: Partial. Guide dogs only.

WESTMINSTER CATHEDRAL

Victoria, London SW1P 1QW

The Roman Catholic Cathedral of the Archbishop of Westminster. Spectacular building in the Byzantine style, designed by J F Bentley, opened in 1903, famous for its mosaics, marble and music. Bell Tower viewing gallery has spectacular views across London. New Exhibition displaying vestments, rare ecclesiastical objects and sacred relics.

Location: MAP 20:L9, OS Ref. TQ293 791. Off Victoria Street, between Victoria Station and Westminster Abbey.

Owner: Diocese of Westminster **Contact:** Revd Canon Christopher Tuckwell

Tel: 020 7798 9055 **Fax:** 020 7798 9090

Website: www.westminstercathedral.org.uk

Open: All year: 7am–7pm. Please telephone for times at Easter & Christmas.

Admission: Free. Tower lift/viewing gallery charge: Adult £5. Family (2+4) £11. Conc. £2.50. Exhibition prices as those for viewing gallery.

Key facts: Booking required. Worksheets & tours.

WHITEHALL

1 Malden Road, Cheam SM3 8QD

A Tudor timber-framed house, c1500, in the heart of Cheam Village. Displays on the history of the house and the people who lived here, Nonsuch Palace, Cheam School and Dr. Syntax (William Gilpin). Changing exhibitions and special events throughout the year. Attractive garden features medieval well. Homemade cakes in tearoom.

Location: MAP 19:C9, OS Ref. TQ242 638. Approx. 2m S of A3 on A2043 just N of junction with A232.

Owner: London Borough of Sutton **Contact:** The Curator **Tel:** 020 8643 1236

Fax: 020 8643 1236 **E-mail:** whitehallcheam@btconnect.com

Website: www.sutton.gov.uk

Open: Wed–Fri, 2–5pm; Sat 10am–5pm; Sun & BH Mons, 2–5pm. Tearoom closes 4.30pm.

Admission: Adult £1.60, Child (6–16yrs) 80p, under 5yrs Free. Groups by appt. Free admission to shop and tea room.

Key facts: Partial. By arrangement. Guide dogs only.

King's Chamber, Dover Castle
© English Heritage

Osborne House © English Heritage

South East

Bucks
Oxford-
shire
Berkshire
Surrey
Kent
Hampshire
West Sussex
East Sussex

Berkshire

Buckinghamshire

Hampshire

Kent

Oxfordshire

Surrey

Sussex

Isle of Wight

These eight counties contain a vast array of heritage properties, from Dover Castle high atop the famous White Cliffs, to the majestic Hampton Court Palace with its famous Maze and Osborne House on the Isle of Wight, Queen Victoria's lavish palace-by-the-sea. Smaller treasures such as the enchanting medieval St Mary's House in West Sussex and Monk's House, the small weather-boarded former home of Leonard and Virginia Woolf can also be uncovered in this region.

DORNEY COURT

Nr Windsor, Berkshire SL4 6QP

www.dorneycourt.co.uk

One of the finest Tudor Manor Houses in England - Country Life. Grade I listed and noted for its outstanding architectural and historical importance. Home of the Palmers since the 16th century. Highlights include the magnificent Great Hall, oak and lacquer furniture and artwork spanning the lifetime of the house.

Location: MAP 3:G2, OS Ref. SU926 791. 5 mins off M4/J7, 10mins from Windsor, 2m W of Eton.

Owner/Contact: Mrs Peregrine Palmer

Tel: 01628 604638 **E-mail:** palmer@dorneycourt.co.uk

Open: May–Jun, Mon–Fri inclusive. BH Suns and Mons in May. 1.30pm with last admissions at 4pm.

Admission: Adult: £8, Child (10yrs +) £5. OAP's: £7.50. Groups (10+): £7 when house is open to public. Private group rates at other times.

Key facts: Film & photographic shoots. No stiletto heels. Garden centre. Wedding receptions. Licensed. Licensed. Obligatory. Guide dogs only. €

© Britainonview / Pawel Libera

WINDSOR CASTLE

Windsor, Berkshire SL4 1NJ

www.royalcollection.org.uk

Windsor Castle, along with Buckingham Palace and the Palace of Holyroodhouse in Edinburgh, it is one of the official residences of Her Majesty The Queen. The magnificent State Rooms are furnished with some of the finest works of art from the Royal Collection.

Location: MAP 3:G2, OS Ref. SU969 770. M4/J6, M3/J3. 20m from central London.

Owner: Official Residence of Her Majesty The Queen

Contact: Ticket Sales & Information Office

Tel: 020 7766 7304

E-mail: bookinginfo@royalcollection.org.uk

Open: Contact information office.

Admission: Contact information office.

Key facts: Photography and filming (for private use only) are permitted in the Castle Precincts. Most public areas are accessible for wheelchair-users, including the State Apartments. Guided tours of the Castle Precincts are available at regular intervals throughout the day.

SHAW HOUSE

Church Road, Shaw, Newbury, Berkshire RG14 2DR

www.shawhouse.org.uk

Built in 1581 by Newbury clothier Thomas Dolman, this fine Elizabethan building was recently restored through a £6million project. The stories and characters from Shaw House's varied past are bought to life in the exhibition. Family friendly 'Wheelie-do' activities throughout the house. Exciting events programme.

Location: MAP 3:D2, OS Ref. SU 47573 68363. Near Newbury.

Owner: West Berkshire District Council

Tel: 01635 279279 **E-mail:** shawhouse@westberks.gov.uk

Open: 13–17 Feb: Mon–Fri, 10am–4pm. 11 Feb–26 Aug: Sat & Sun, 11am–4pm. 6 & 9 Apr, 7 May, 27 Aug: 11am–4pm. 6–8 Jun: Wed–Fri, 10am–4pm. 1–31 Aug: Wed–Fri, 10am–4pm. 8–9 Sept, 11am–4pm. 1–2 Dec, 11am–4pm.

Admission: Adult £3.75, Child £1.90, Conc. £3, Family Ticket £9.90. Discounts apply for West Berkshire Residents Card Holders.

Key facts: Partial. By arrangement. Limited.

ETON COLLEGE

Windsor, Berkshire SL4 6DW

Eton College, founded in 1440 by Henry VI, is one of the oldest schools in the country. The original and historic buildings of the Foundation are part of the heritage of the British Isles and visitors are invited to experience the beauty of the precinct, which includes the College Chapel.

Location: MAP 3:G2, OS Ref. SU967 779. Off M4/J5. Access from Windsor by footbridge only. Vehicle access from Slough 2m N.

Owner: Provost & Fellows **Contact:** Rebecca Hunkin

Tel: 01753 671177 **Fax:** 01753 671029

E-mail: r.hunkin@etoncollege.org.uk **Website:** www.etoncollege.com

Open: During school's holidays and Weds, Fris, Sats & Suns during term time between Mar–Oct. Please check with the Visits Office. Pre-booked groups welcome all year.

Admission: Guided tours only at 2pm & 3.15pm for interested individuals. Groups by appointment only. Rates vary according to tour type.

Key facts: Ground floor. WC. Limited. Guide dogs only.

Shaw House

CHENIES MANOR HOUSE

www.cheniesmanorhouse.co.uk

The Manor House is in the picturesque village of Chenies and lies in the beautiful Chiltern Hills.

The picturesque village of Chenies lies in the beautiful Chiltern Hills. The Manor House is approached by a gravel drive leading past the church. Home of the MacLeod Matthews family, this 15th and 16th century manor house with fortified tower is the original home of the Earls of Bedford, visited by Henry VIII and Elizabeth I. Elizabeth was a frequent visitor, first coming as an infant in 1534 and as Queen she visited on several occasions, once staying for six weeks. The Bedford Mausoleum is in the adjacent church. The house contains tapestries and furniture mainly of the 16th and 17th centuries, hiding places and a collection of antique dolls. Art exhibitions are held throughout the season in the restored 16th century pavilion. The Manor is surrounded by five acres of enchanting gardens which have been featured in many publications and on television. It is famed for the Spring display of tulips. From early June there is a succession of colour in the Tudor Sunken Garden, the White Garden, herbaceous borders and Fountain Court. The Physic Garden contains a wide selection of medicinal and culinary herbs. In the Parterre is an ancient oak and a complicated yew maze while the Kitchen Garden is in Victorian style with unusual vegetables and fruit. Attractive dried and fresh flower arrangements decorate the house. Winner of the Historic Houses Association and Christie's Garden of the Year Award, 2009.

KEY FACTS

Delicious home made teas in the Garden Room.

Obligatory.

VISITOR INFORMATION

Owner
Mrs E. MacLeod Matthews & Mr C. MacLeod Matthews

Address
Chenies
Buckinghamshire
WD3 6ER

Location
MAP 7:D12
OS Ref. TQ016 984

N of A404 between Amersham & Rickmansworth M25–Ext 18, 3m

Contact
Chenies Manor House
Tel: 01494 762888
E-mail: macleodmatthews@btinternet.com

Opening Times
4 April to end October 2012, Weds, Thurs and Bank Holiday Mondays 2–5pm (last entry to House 4.15pm).

Admission
House & Garden:

Adult	£6.50
Child	£4.00

Garden only:

Adult	£5.00
Child	£3.00

Groups (20+) by arrangement throughout the year.

Special Events
9 April
Easter Monday. House & Garden open 2–5pm.

The first mention of the distribution of eggs at Easter was at Chenies. Children's egg races, shop, plants for sale, homemade teas.

7 May
May Bank Holiday Monday. House & Garden open 2–5pm.

'Tulip Festival'. Bloms Tulips throughout the House and Gardens. Homemade teas, shop, plants for sale.

4 June
Spring Bank Holiday Monday. House & Garden open 2–5pm. 10am–5pm Carriage Driving Day (contact Shirley Higgins 01923 267919). Homemade teas, shop, plants for sale.

15 July
Sunday. Our 14th famous Plant & Garden Fair, 10am–5pm. 70 exhibitors from around the country. Gardens open 10am - 5pm. House open 2-5pm.

27 August
Summer Bank Holiday Monday. House & Garden open 2–5pm 'Dahlia Festival'. Large number of different varieties of dahlias.

24 & 25 October
Wed and Thurs. House & Garden open 2–5pm 'Spooks and Surprises'. Special scary tour of the house for children.

Come dressed for Spooks!

Homemade teas, shop.

VISITOR INFORMATION

Owner
Stowe House Preservation Trust

Address
Stowe House
Stowe
Buckingham
MK18 5EH

Location
OS Ref. SP666 366.

From London, M1 to Milton Keynes, 1 1/2 hrs or Banbury 1 1/4 hrs, 3m NW of Buckingham.

Bus: Buckingham 3m.

Rail: Milton Keynes 15m.

Air: Heathrow 50m.

Contact
Visitor Services Manager
Tel: 01280 818229
Fax: 01280 818186
E-mail: amcevoy@stowe.co.uk

Opening Times
House: Please check the website www.shpt.org or telephone 01280 818166 for information regarding opening times.

Admission
House (including optional tour)

Adults £4.75

National Trust Adults £4.10

Joint House and Gardens Tickets are available.

Open to private groups (15+ persons), all year round at discounted admission price. Please telephone 01280 818229 for further information or to pre-book.

Visit both Stowe House and National Trust Landscape Gardens.

Gardens

Opening times telephone 01280 822850 or visit www.nationaltrust.org.uk/stowegardens

STOWE HOUSE

www.shpt.org

Stowe owes its pre-eminence to the vision and wealth of two great owners.

From 1715 to 1749 Viscount Cobham, one of Marlborough's generals, continuously improved his estate, calling in the leading designers of the day to lay out the Gardens and commissioning leading architects – Vanburgh, Gibbs, Kent and Leoni – to decorate them with garden temples. From 1750 to 1779 Earl Temple, his nephew and heir, continued to expand and embellish both the House and Gardens. As the estate was expanded, and political and military intrigues followed, the family eventually fell into debt, resulting in two great sales – 1848 when all the contents were sold, and 1921 when the contents and the estate were sold off separately. The House is now part of a major public school (since 1923), and is owned by the Stowe House Preservation Trust (since 2000). Over the last four years, through the Trust, the House has undergone extensive restoration including three magnificent interiors – the Marble Saloon, the Large Library and the newly restored Egyptian Hall; funds continue to be raised to restore the remaining state rooms. Around the mansion is one of Britain's most magnificent and complete landscape gardens, taken over from Stowe School by the National Trust in 1989. The Gardens have since undergone a huge, and continuing, restoration programme, and, with the House restoration, Stowe is slowly being returned to its 18th century status as one of the most complete neo-classical estates in Europe.

KEY FACTS

- Indoor swimming pool, sports hall, tennis court, squash courts, astroturf, parkland, cricket pitches and golf course.
- International conferences, private functions, weddings, and prestige exhibitions. Catering on request.
- WCs.
- Obligatory. For parties of 15–60 at group rate. Tour time: house and garden 2.5–4.5 hrs, house only 1.5 hrs.
- Limited for coaches.
- On leads.
- Available.
- Civil Wedding Licence.
- House open to groups all year, tel for details.

Conference/Function

ROOM	Size	Max Cap
Roxburgh Hall		350
Music Room		100
Room 3		200
State Dining Rm		200

© NTPL / Matthew Antrobus

© NTPL / Andreas von Einsiedel

HUGHENDEN

HIGH WYCOMBE HP14 4LA

www.nationaltrust.org.uk/hughendenmanor

Amid rolling Chilterns countryside, discover the hideaway and colourful private life of Benjamin Disraeli, the most unlikely Victorian Prime Minister. Follow in his footsteps: stroll through his German forest, relax in his elegant garden and imagine dining with Queen Victoria in the atmospheric manor. Uncover the Second World War story of Operation Hillside, for which unconventional artists painted maps for bombing missions – including the famous Dambusters raid. Experience Sergeant Hadfield's wartime living room. Outdoors get tips for growing your own vegetables in our walled garden. Don't miss our ancient woodland, where you may spot red kites soaring overhead.

Location: MAP 3:F1, OS 165 Ref. SU866 955. 1½ m N of High Wycombe on the W side of the A4128.

Owner: National Trust **Contact:** The General Manager

Tel: 01494 755573 **Infoline:** 01494 755565

Fax: 01494 474284 **E-mail:** hughenden@nationaltrust.org.uk

Open: Garden, shop & restaurant: 11 Feb–16 Mar & 1 Nov–30 Dec, daily, 11am–4pm, 17 Mar–31 Oct, daily, 11am–5.30pm. House: 11 Feb–16 Mar & 1 Nov–30 Dec, daily, 11am–3pm, 17 Mar–31 Oct, daily, 12–5pm. Park: Open all year. Closed 24, 25 & 31 Dec.

Admission: House & Garden: Adult £8.50, Child £4.25, Family £21. Garden only: Adult £3.40, Child £2.30. Woodlands Free. Groups: Adult £7.20. Free to NT Members. Includes a voluntary 10% donation but visitors can choose to pay the standard prices.

Key facts: Partial. WCs. Licensed. By arrangement. For booked groups. Limited for cars. Guide dogs only.

ASCOTT

Wing, Leighton Buzzard, Buckinghamshire LU7 0PR

www.ascottestate.co.uk

Originally a half-timbered Jacobean farmhouse, Ascott was bought in 1876 by the de Rothschild family and considerably transformed and enlarged. It now houses an exceptional collection of fine paintings, Oriental porcelain and English and French furniture. The extensive gardens are a mixture of the formal and natural.

Location: MAP 7:D11, OS Ref. SP891 230. ½ m E of Wing, 2m SW of Leighton Buzzard, on A418.

Owner: National Trust **Contact:** Estate Manager

Tel: 01296 688242 **Fax:** 01296 681904 **E-mail:** info@ascottestate.co.uk

Open: House & Garden: 20 Mar–29 Apr: Tue–Sun, 2–6pm. 1 May–26 July: Tue–Thur, 2–6pm. 31 Jul–7 Sept: Tue–Sun, 2–6pm. Last admission 5pm. Open on Bank Holiday Mondays.

Admission: Adult £9.20, Child £4.60. Garden only: £4.60, Child £2.30. No reduction for groups. Groups must book prior to visit. NT members free, except NGS days, 7 May and 27 Aug.

Key facts: Wheelchairs available from the Entrance Kiosk. WCs. 220 metres. Limited for coaches.

WOTTON HOUSE

Wotton Underwood, Aylesbury, Buckinghamshire HP18 0SB

The Capability Brown Pleasure Grounds at Wotton, currently undergoing restoration, are related to the Stowe gardens, both belonging to the Grenville family when Brown laid out the Wotton grounds between 1750 and 1767. A series of man-made features on the 3 mile circuit include bridges, temples and statues.

Location: MAP 7:B11, OS Ref. 468576, 216168. Either A41 turn off Kingswood, or M40/J7 via Thame.

Owner: David Gladstone

Contact: David Gladstone

Tel: 01844 238363

Fax: 01844 238380

E-mail: david.gladstone@which.net

Open: 4 Apr–5 Sept: Weds only, 2–5pm. Also: 9 Apr, 28 May, 7 Jul, 4 Aug, 1 Sept: 2–5pm.

Admission: Adult £6, Child Free, Conc. £3. Groups (max 25).

Key facts: Obligatory. Limited parking for coaches. On leads.

COWPER & NEWTON MUSEUM

Home of Olney's Heritage, Orchard Side, Market Place, Olney MK46 4AJ

The home of 18th century poet William Cowper. Now contains furniture, paintings and personal belongings of Cowper and his ex-slave trader friend, Rev John Newton (author of "Amazing Grace"). Two beautiful gardens and Cowper's restored summerhouse. Important collection of lace, and local history displays, from dinosaur bones to WW2.

Location: MAP 7:D9, OS Ref. SP890 512. On A509, 6m N of Newport Pagnell, M1/J14.

Owner: Board of Trustees **Contact:** House Manager

Tel: 01234 711516 **E-mail:** cnmhousemanager@btconnect.com

Website: www.cowperandnewtonmuseum.org.uk

Open: 1 Mar–23 Dec: Tue–Sat & BH Mons, 10.30am–4.30pm. Closed Good Fri.

Admission: Adult £4, Conc. £3.25, Child (5–16) £1, Under 5's Free, Family £9, Groups (inc. introductory talk) £4.50, Guided Tour £5.50.

Key facts: Partial. WCs. By arrangement. Limited. Guide dogs only.

NETHER WINCHENDON HOUSE

Nether Winchendon, Nr Aylesbury, Buckinghamshire HP18 ODY

Medieval and Tudor Manor House with 18th century Strawberry Hill Gothick alterations. Early 16th century carved frieze and linenfold panelling. Home of Sir Francis Bernard, Bt. last Royal Governor of Massachussetts Province. Continuous family occupation since 1559. Fine furniture and family portraits. Garden (5 acres) with specimen trees.

Location: MAP 7:C11, OS Ref. SP734 121. North of A418, between Thame and Aylesbury.

Owner/Contact: Mr Robert Spencer Bernard

Tel: 01844 290101 **Fax:** 01844 290199

Website: www.netherwinchendonhouse.com www.timelessweddingvenues.com

Open: 24 Apr–25 May (not Sats) 4 Jun–27 Aug, 2.30–5.30pm. Tours only at quarter to each hour.

Admission: £8, concessions £5 (not w/ends or B/H's), HHA free (except when NGS). Groups by arrangement £10 (min £300, no concessions).

Key facts: Please tel in advance. By arrangement. Obligatory.

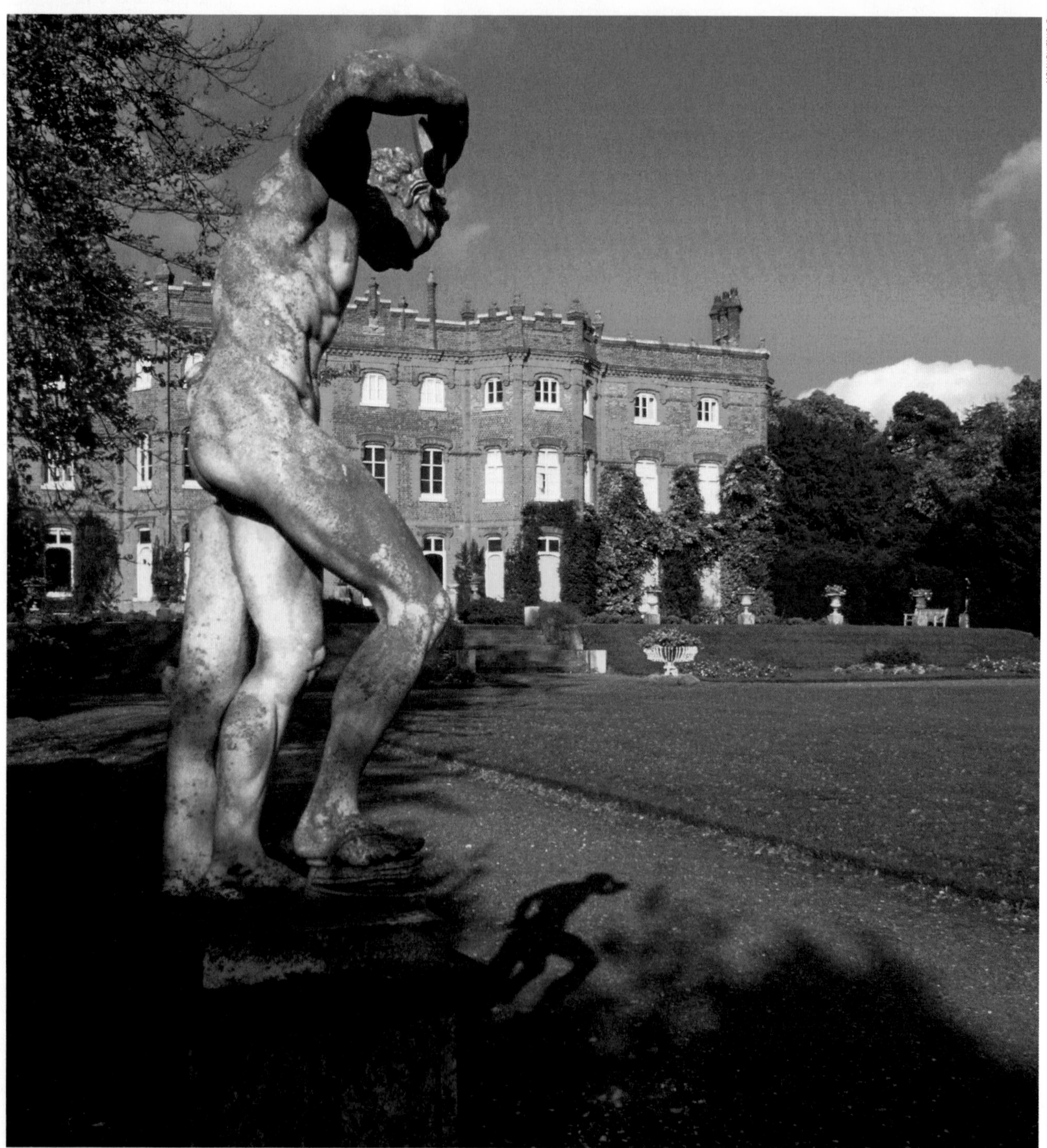

Garden to the rear of Hughenden Manor

BEAULIEU

www.beaulieu.co.uk

The Beaulieu Estate has been owned by the same family since 1538 and is still the private home of the Montagus.

Thomas Wriothesley, who later became the 1st Earl of Southampton, acquired the estate at the time of the Dissolution of the Monasteries when he was Lord Chancellor to Henry VIII.

Palace House, overlooking the Beaulieu River, was once the Great Gatehouse of Beaulieu Abbey with its monastic origins reflected in the fan vaulted ceilings of the 14th century Dining Hall and Lower Drawing Room. The rooms are decorated with furnishings, portraits and treasures collected by past and present generations of the family. Visitors can enjoy the fine gardens or take a riverside walk around the Monks' Mill Pond.

Beaulieu Abbey was founded in 1204 when King John gave the land to the Cistercians and although most of the buildings have now been destroyed, much of the beauty and interest remains. The former Monks' Refectory is now the local parish church and the Domus, which houses an exhibition and video presentation of monastic life, is home to beautiful wall hangings.

Beaulieu also houses the world famous National Motor Museum which traces the story of motoring from 1894 to the present day. 250 vehicles are on display including legendary world record breakers plus veteran, vintage and classic cars and motorcycles. New for 2012 is BOND IN MOTION, the world's largest display of official Bond vehicles with 50 vehicles to celebrate 50 years of the Bond franchise.

The modern Beaulieu is very much a family destination with many free and unlimited rides on a transportation theme to be enjoyed, including a mile long, high-level monorail and replica 1912 London open-topped bus.

When visiting Beaulieu arrangements can be made to view the Estate's vineyards. Visits can be arranged with Beaulieu Estate Office.

KEY FACTS

- Allow 3 hrs or more for visits. Last adm. 40 mins before closing. Helicopter landing point.
- Palace House Shop and Kitchen Shop plus Main Reception Shop.
- Disabled visitors may be dropped off outside Visitor Reception before parking. WC. Wheelchairs can be provided free of charge in Visitor Reception by prior booking.
- The Brabazon restaurant seats 250.
- Attendants on duty. Guided tours by prior arrangement for groups.
- 1,500 cars and 30 coaches. Coach drivers should sign in at Information Desk. Free admission for coach drivers plus voucher.
- Professional staff available to assist in planning of visits.
- In grounds, on leads only.

VISITOR INFORMATION

Owner
Lord Montagu

Address
Beaulieu
Hampshire SO42 7ZN

Location
MAP 3:C6
OS Ref. SU387 025

M27 to J2, A326, B3054 follow brown signs.

Bus: Local service within the New Forest.

Rail: Stations at Brockenhurst 7m away.

Contact
John Montagu Building
Tel: 01590 612345
Fax: 01590 612624
E-mail: info@beaulieu.co.uk

Opening Times
Summer
May–September
Daily, 10am–6pm.

Winter
October–April
Daily, 10am–5pm.
Closed Christmas Day.

Admission
All year
Individual rates upon application.
Groups (15+)
Rates upon application.

Special events
April 29
Boatjumble
May 19/20
Spring Autojumble
June 2/3
Steam Revival (TBC)
June 17
Custom and Hot Rod Festival (TBC)
July 15
Motorcycle Ride-In Day
September 8/9
International Autojumble
October 27
Fireworks Spectacular

All enquiries should be made to our Special Events Booking Office where advance tickets can be purchased. The contact telephone is 01590 612888.

Conference/Function

ROOM	Size	Max Cap
Brabazon (x3)	40' x 40'	85 (x3)
Domus	69' x 27'	150
Theatre		200
Palace House		60
Motor Museum		250

VISITOR INFORMATION

Owner
Hampshire County Council

Address
Castle Avenue
Winchester
Hampshire SO23 8PJ

Location
MAP 3:D4,
OS Ref. SU477 295.
Central Winchester. SE of Westgate archway. Tower Street car park is a 5 minute walk from the Great Hall.

Coach: There are two Coach set-down points at either end of the city. The drop off point at Sussex Street is a 5 minute walk from the Great Hall.

Rail: The Great Hall is a 10 minute walk from Winchester Station.

Contact
Custodian
Tel: 01962 846476
Email: the.great.hall @hants.gov.uk
Bookings: Online

Opening Times
Open all year round, 10am–5pm (except Christmas & Boxing day).

Admission
Donations towards the upkeep and running of the Great Hall are gratefully accepted. We suggest a donation of a minimum of £2 per head - or of £1 per head for group bookings.

THE GREAT HALL, ROUND TABLE & QUEEN ELEANOR'S GARDEN

www.hants.gov.uk/greathall

Built in the 13th century, the Great Hall is the only surviving part of Henry III's medieval castle.

The Great Hall has seen many characters from history within its walls, from Kings and Queens of England to judges and doomed prisoners. It is now one of Winchester's most visited attractions with people coming from near and far to walk in their footsteps.

Built in the 13th century, the Hall is the only surviving part of Henry III's medieval castle and was the centre of court and government life. During Henry's reign (1216-72) art, architecture and design became more refined and sophisticated and this trend was reflected in the Great Hall.

Following years of alterations and improvements, as well as a fire that destroyed the royal apartments, the Hall was eventually restored in the 1870s and was used last as a court between 1938 and 1974.

The Round Table, closely associated with the legend of King Arthur, has hung here for over 700 years. Although now known to have been constructed in the late 13th century, and painted in its present form for King Henry VIII, the table has for centuries been venerated by generations of tourists as the mysterious table of the 'Once and Future King' Arthur.

Another feature of the Great Hall is Queen Eleanor's Garden. In medieval times a garden offered pleasure, repose and refreshment to the senses as well as food and medicine. Queen Eleanor's Garden is an accurate example of such a garden and features include turf seats, bay hedges, a fountain, tunnel arbour and many beautiful herbs and flowers of the time.

KEY FACTS

- There is ramped access to the Great Hall. Visitors may ring for assistance at the entrance to the Hall and gift shop. There is seating for visitors in the Hall and Garden. Guide and Assistance dogs are welcome.
- Partial. WCs.
- By arrangement.
- Guide dogs only.

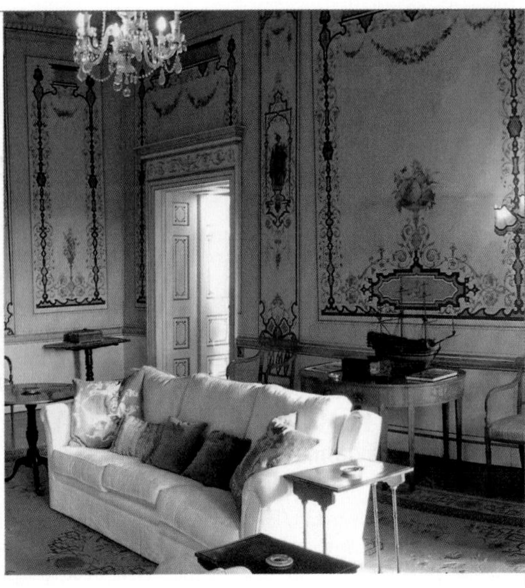

AVINGTON PARK

WINCHESTER, HAMPSHIRE SO21 1DB

www.avingtonpark.co.uk

Charles II and George IV both stayed here. It dates back to the 11th century, was enlarged in 1670 and now enjoys magnificent painted and gilded state rooms. The house and its parkland is perfect for seminars, exhibitions, weddings and private parties, as well as filming and photo shoots. The conservatories and the orangery make a delightful location for summer functions, whilst log fires offer a welcome during winter. All bookings at Avington are individually tailormade and only exclusive use is offered. Several rooms are licensed for Civil wedding ceremonies and a delightful apartment is available for short stays.

Location: MAP 3:D4, OS Ref. SU534 324. 4m NE of Winchester 1/2m S of B3047 in Itchen Abbas.
Owner/Contact: Mrs S L Bullen
Tel: 01962 779260 **E-mail:** enquiries@avingtonpark.co.uk
Open: May–Sept: Suns & BH Mons plus Mons in Aug, 2.30–5.30pm. Last tour 5pm. Other times by arrangement, coach parties welcome by appointment all year.
Admission: Adult £6, Child £3.
Key facts: Conferences. Partial. WC. Obligatory. In grounds, on leads. Guide dogs only in house.

ST AGATHA'S CHURCH

Market Way, Portsmouth PO1 4AD

A grand Italianate basilica of 1894 enriched with marble, granite and carved stone. The apse contains Britain's largest sgraffito mural, by Heywood Sumner c1901. Fine furnishings, untouched by Vatican II, by Randoll Blacking, Sir Ninian Comper, Sir Walter Tapper, Martin Travers, Norman Shaw and others.
Location: MAP 3:D3. OS ref. SU640 006. On route for Historic Ships. Near Cascades Centre car park.
Owner: St Agatha's Trust
Contact: Fr J Maunder
Tel: 02392 837050
Fax: 01329 230330
Open: All year, Sats, 10am–4pm. Suns, 10am–2pm (High Mass 11am). Jun–Aug, Weds, 10.30am–3pm. Other times by appointment – 01329 230330.
Admission: No charge.
Key facts: Available for hire – concerts, exhibitions & filming. Has featured in 'Casualty'. Partial. WCs. Obligatory, by arangement. Limited for coaches.

JANE AUSTEN'S HOUSE MUSEUM

Chawton, Alton, Hampshire GU34 1SD

www.jane-austens-house-museum.org.uk

17th century house where Jane Austen wrote or revised her six great novels. Contains many items associated with her and her family, documents and letters, first editions of the novels, pictures, portraits and furniture. Recreated Historic kitchen. Pleasant garden, suitable for picnics. Bakehouse with brick oven and wash tub, Jane's donkey carriage. Learning Centre.
Location: MAP 3:E4, OS Ref. SU708 376. Just S of A31, 1m SW of Alton, signposted Chawton.
Owner: Jane Austen Memorial Trust **Contact:** Ann Channon
Tel: 01420 83262 **E-mail:** enquiries@jahmusm.org.uk
Open: Jan/mid Feb: Sats & Suns, 10.30am–4.30pm. Mar–end May: daily, 10.30am–4.30pm. Jun–Aug: daily, 10am–5pm. Sept–end Dec: daily, 10.30am–4.30pm. Closed 25/26 Dec.
Admission: Fee charged.
Key facts: Bookshop. Ground floor & grounds. WC. Opposite house. Opposite house. Guide dogs only.

CHAWTON HOUSE LIBRARY

Chawton, Alton, Hampshire GU34 1SJ

www.chawtonhouse.org

Chawton House is a spectacular Elizabethan manor house which once belonged to Jane Austen's brother, Edward. It is now home to a unique collection of books written by women in English from 1600 to 1830 and a collection of fine portraits. There is a working rural estate and historic gardens.

Location: MAP 3:E4, OS Ref. SU709 370. Turn off left at A31/32 junction roundabout to Chawton and follow the brown tourist signs.

Owner: Chawton House Library (Charity)

Tel: 01420 541010

Fax: 01420 595900

E-mail: info@chawton.net

Open: Guided tours take place every Tue & Thur, Mar–Dec, & Tue only in Jan & Feb. The tours start at 2.30pm.

Admission: Admission is £6 for adults & £3 for children (5-15).

Key facts: No Photography. The Library is open free of charge to view or read the books in the collection,from 10am to 5pm weekdays, by prior appointment with Library staff. Partial. WCs. Obligatory. Limited for coaches. On leads.

GILBERT WHITE'S HOUSE & GARDEN & THE OATES COLLECTION

The Wakes, High Street, Selborne, Alton GU34 3JH

www.gilbertwhiteshouse.org.uk

Discover three fascinating stories of explorers of the Natural World… Gilbert White, 18th century naturalist. Explore his house and 25 acres of grounds. Captain Lawrence Oates, who travelled the epic journey to the South Pole in 1911-12 with Captain Scott. Frank Oates, 19th century explorer of Africa and the Americas.

Owner: Oates Memorial Trust **Contact:** Duty Manager

Tel: 01420 511275 **E-mail:** info@gilbertwhiteshouse.org.uk

Open: Open All Year - Please see our website for details

Admission: Adults £7.95*, Conc. £6.95*, Under 16 £2.50*, Under 5 Free, Family Ticket (2 adults + 3 children) £18.50*. *2011 PRICES

Key facts: No photography in house. Dogs on leads welcome in garden & grounds only. Partial. WCs. Licensed. Licensed. Obligatory, by arrangement. Limited for coaches. Guide dogs only.

EXBURY GARDENS & STEAM RAILWAY

Exbury, Southampton, Hampshire SO45 1AZ

www.exbury.co.uk

A spectacular 200-acre woodland garden showcasing the world-famous Rothschild Collection of rhododendrons, azaleas, camellias, rare trees and shrubs. Enchanting river walk, ponds and cascades. Daffodil Meadow, Rock, Heather and Bog Gardens and exotic plantings and herbaceous borders ensure year-round interest. A 1 1/4 mile steam railway is a great favourite with visitors of all ages. Licensed to host Civil Weddings and a beautiful reception venue for marquee and corporate events.

Location: MAP 3:D6, OS Ref. SU425 005. 20 mins Junction 2, M27 west. 11m SE of Totton (A35) via A326 & B3054 & minor road. In New Forest.

Owner: The Rothschild Family **Contact:** Estate Office

Tel: 023 8089 1203 **Fax:** 023 8089 9940

Open: 10 Mar–4 Nov 2012, 10am–5pm last admission. Gates close at 6pm or dusk if earlier.

Admission: (2011 prices) Adults £9; Seniors/Concessions £8.50; Children 3-15 £2; Children under 3 free; Family £21; Railway extra £3.50; Family Rail ticket extra £13.50. Chauffeur-driven buggy tours available £3.50 / £4. RHS members free Mar and Sept.

Key facts: Licensed. By arrangement. In grounds, on leads.

SIR HAROLD HILLIER GARDENS

Jermyns Lane, Ampfield, Romsey, Hampshire SO51 0QA

www.hilliergardens.org.uk

Open all year, Sir Harold Hillier Gardens, Romsey, offers 180 acres of beauty, inspiration and discovery. The internationally renowned Gardens feature a large variety of themed areas including woodlands, pond area and one of Europe's largest Winter Gardens. Stunning seasonal interest includes magnolias, azaleas and rhododendrons. Outstanding restaurant and tearooms.

Location: MAP 3:C5. OS Ref. SU381 235. From M3 London direction follow the M27 West. Exit Junction 3.

Owner: Hampshire County Council

Tel: 01794 369318

Fax: 01794 368027

E-mail: info@hilliergardens.org.uk

Open: 10am–6pm (summer) or 5pm (winter). Last entry one hour before closing. Closed only on 25 & 26 Dec.

Admission: Adults: £8.70, Concessions: £7.50, Children under 16 FREE. Groups: £6.95 per person (groups of 10+)

Key facts: Photography for commercial gain is via prior authorisation only. WCs. Licensed. Licensed. By arrangement. Guide dogs only.

HIGHCLERE CASTLE, GARDENS & EGYPTIAN EXHIBITION

Highclere Castle, Newbury, Berkshire RG20 9RN

www.highclerecastle.co.uk

This spectacular Victorian Castle is currently the setting for Downton Abbey. Visit the splendid State Rooms; explore the Egyptian Exhibition in the Castle Cellars, which recreates the discovery of Tutankhamun's tomb in 1922. Enjoy gardens inspired by Capability Brown including; Monk's Garden, Secret Garden and new Arboretum.

Location: OS Ref. SU445 587. M4/J13–A34 south. M3/J8–A303–A34 north.

Owner: Earl of Carnarvon **Contact:** The Castle Office **Tel:** 01635 253210

Fax: 01635 255315 **E-mail:** theoffice@highclerecastle.co.uk

Open: 1–15 Apr; 6,7,8 May; 3–7 Jun; 1 Jul–6 Sept, Sun–Thur. Information correct at time of publication.

Admission: Castle & Exhibition: Adult: £16, Child: £9.50, Conc. £14.50, Family: £44. Each element available separately; Group Rates available.

Key facts: Partial. WCs. Licensed. By arrangement. Guide dogs only.

HOUGHTON LODGE GARDENS

Stockbridge, Hampshire SO20 6LQ

www.houghtonlodge.co.uk

An 18th century Grade II* listed Gothic "Cottage Orné" idyllically set above the tranquil River Test. Peaceful formal and informal gardens with fine trees. Chalk Cob walls enclose traditional Kitchen Garden with espaliers, greenhouses, hydroponicum and orchid collection. 14 acres of picturesque countryside, meadow walks and 3 charming Alpacas.

Location: MAP 3:C4. OS Ref. SU344 332. 1½m S of Stockbridge (A30) on minor road to Houghton village.

Owner: Captain & Mrs Martin Busk **Contact:** Captain & Mrs Martin Busk

Tel: 01264 810502/912 **Fax:** 01264 810063

E-mail: info@houghtonlodge.co.uk

Open: 1 Mar–31 Oct, Thurs–Tue, 10am–5pm. Weds & House by appointment.

Admission: Adult £5. Additional £2.50 for meadow walk/alpacas. Children under 14 Free. Coach Tours and Groups welcome on any day by appointment – special rates if booked in advance.

Key facts: By arrangement. Hard standing for 2 coaches. On short leads.

© NT / Nick White

HINTON AMPNER

Bramdean, Alresford, Hampshire SO24 0LA

www.nationaltrust.org.uk

Best known for its fine garden, Hinton Ampner is an elegant country house with an outstanding collection of furniture, paintings and object d'art. House was remodelled after a fire in 1960. The garden is widely acknowledged as a masterpiece of 20th century design with formal and informal planting.

Location: MAP 3:E4, OS Ref. SU597 275. M3/J9 or A3 on A272, 1m W of Bramdean village.

Owner: National Trust **Contact:** The Property Manager

Tel: 01962 771305 **Fax:** 01962 793101

E-mail: hintonampner@nationaltrust.org.uk

Open: Garden, Shop & Tearoom: daily, 11 Feb–4 Nov, 10am–5pm; Sat–Wed, 5 Nov–28 Nov, 10am–5pm; 1-9 Dec, daily, 10am-4.30pm.
House: days as above, 11am-5pm; 1-9 Dec, 10.30am-4.30pm.

Admission: House & Garden: Adult £8.25, Child (5–16yrs) £4.10 Garden only: Adult £7, Child (5–16yrs) £3.50, Free to NT Members. *includes a voluntary 10% donation.

Key facts: WCs. Licensed. By arrangement. Limited for coaches. Guide dogs only.

KING JOHN'S HOUSE & HERITAGE CENTRE

Church Street, Romsey, Hampshire SO51 8BT

www.kingjohnshouse.org.uk

Three historic buildings on one site: Medieval King John's House, containing 14th century graffiti and rare bone floor, Tudor Cottage complete with traditional tea room and Victorian Heritage Centre with recreated shop and parlour. Beautiful period gardens, special events/exhibitions and children's activities. Gift shop and Tourist Information Centre. Receptions and private/corporate functions.

Location: MAP 3:C5, OS Ref. SU353 212. M27/J3. Opposite Romsey Abbey, next to Post Office.

Owner: King John's House & Tudor Cottage Trust Ltd **Contact:** Anne James

Tel: 01794 512200 **E-mail:** annerhc@aol.com

Open: Apr–Sept: Mon–Sat, 10am–4pm. Oct–Mar: Heritage Centre only. Limited opening on Sundays. Evenings also for pre-booked groups.

Admission: Adult £2.50, Child 50p, Conc. £2. Heritage Centre only: Adult £1.50, Child 50p, Conc. £1. Discounted group booking by appointment.

Key facts: Partial. By arrangement. Off Latimer St with direct access through King John's Garden. Guide dogs only.

© English Heritage

PORTCHESTER CASTLE

Portsmouth, Hampshire PO16 9QW

www.english-heritage.org.uk/portchestercastle

The rallying point of Henry V's expedition to Agincourt and the ruined palace of King Richard II. This grand castle has a history going back nearly 2,000 years and the most complete Roman walls in northern Europe. Exhibition telling the story of the castle and interactive audio tour.

Location: MAP 3:E6, OS196, Ref. SU625 046. On S side of Portchester off A27, M27/J11.

Owner: English Heritage

Contact: Visitor Operations Team

Tel/Fax: 02392 378291

E-mail: customers@english-heritage.org.uk

Open: Please visit www.english-heritage.org.uk for opening times and the most up-to-date information.

Admission: Adult £4.80, Child £2.90, Conc. £4.30. Family £12.50. 15% discount for groups (11+). EH Members Free. Opening times and prices are valid until 31st March 2012.

Key facts: WCs. Exhibition. On leads.

WINCHESTER CATHEDRAL

9 The Close, Winchester SO23 9LS

www.winchester-cathedral.org.uk

For over a thousand years, people have come to seek inspiration in this magnificent Cathedral. You'll find so much to discover: glorious church architecture and tiny crafted details, priceless treasures and great works of art, historic events and famous people. Major events include a Christmas Market and real ice rink.

Location: MAP 3:D4, OS Ref. SU483 293. Winchester city centre.

Owner: The Dean and Chapter

Tel: 01962 857200 (Monday to Friday)

Fax: 01962 857201

E-mail: visits@winchester-cathedral.org.uk

Open: Daily 9am–5pm (12.30–3pm Sunday), times may vary for services and special events. Please contact the Cathedral if making a special visit.

Admission: £10 annual pass, £6.50 adult, free to children under 16 with family. Concessions available for groups and seniors.

Key facts: Licensed.

© S.S.P.T.

STRATFIELD SAYE HOUSE

Stratfield Saye, Hampshire RG7 2BZ

www.stratfield-saye.co.uk

After the Duke of Wellington's victory against Napoleon at the Battle of Waterloo in 1815, the Duke chose Stratfield Saye as his country estate. The house contains many of the 1st Duke's possessions and is still occupied by his descendents being a family home rather than a museum.

Location: MAP 3:E2, OS Ref. SU700 615. Equidistant from Reading (M4/J11) & Basingstoke (M3/J6) 1½m W of the A33.

Owner: The Duke of Wellington

Contact: Estate Office

Tel: 01256 882694

Open: Thur 5–Mon 9 Apr. Thur 12 Jul–Mon 6 Aug.

Admission: Weekends: Adult £9.50, Child £5, OAP/Student £8.50. Weekdays: Adult £7, Child £4, OAP/Student £6. Groups by arrangement only.

Key facts: WC. Obligatory. Guide dogs only.

BROADLANDS

Romsey, Hampshire SO51 9ZD

Broadlands, the historic home of the late Earl Mountbatten of Burma, will open for visitors in June 2012. Please see website for details and our outdoor events programme.

Owner: Lord & Lady Brabourne

Tel: 01794 529750 **Website:** www.broadlandsestates.co.uk

WINCHESTER CITY MILL

Bridge Street, Winchester SO23 8EJ

Spanning the River Itchen and rebuilt in 1744 on an earlier medieval site, this corn mill has a chequered history. The machinery is completely restored making this building an unusual survivor of a working town mill. It has a delightful island garden and impressive mill races roaring through the building.

Location: MAP 3D:4, OS Ref. SU486 293. M3/J9 & 10. City Bridge near King Alfred's statue. 15 min walk from station.

Owner: National Trust **Contact:** Anne Aldridge **Tel:** 01962 870057

E-mail: winchestercitymill@nationaltrust.org.uk

Website: www.nationaltrust.org.uk/winchestercitymill

Open: 1 Jan–12 Feb, Fri–Mon, 11am–4pm. 13 Feb–30 Nov, Daily, 10am–5pm. 1–22 Dec, Daily, 10.30am–4pm.

Admission: Adults (£4.10*) £3.70 Children (£2.05*) £1.85 Family (£10.25*) £9.25 *Gift Aid Price.

Key facts: Obligatory. By arrangement. Nearby public car park. Guide dogs only.

BOUGHTON MONCHELSEA PLACE

www.boughtonplace.co.uk

Battlemented Manor House near Maidstone, with possibly the best view in Kent.

Boughton Monchelsea Place dates from the 16th century and is set within its own country estate of 74 hectares just outside Maidstone. This Grade 1 listed building has always been privately owned and is still lived in as a family home by the Kendricks.

From the lawns surrounding the property there are spectacular views over unspoilt Kent countryside, with our historic deer park in the foreground. At the rear of the house is a pretty courtyard herb garden with steps leading to the formal walled gardens and orchard, while an extensive range of Tudor barns and outbuildings surrounds the old stableyard behind. Next door is the medieval church of St Peter, with its rose garden and ancient lych gate.

Church tours are available by prior arrangement. Inside the manor house rooms vary in character from Tudor through to Georgian Gothic. There is a fine Jacobean oak staircase and several of the windows have interesting stained glass. Furnishings and paintings are mainly Victorian, with a few earlier pieces; the atmosphere is friendly and welcoming throughout.

The premises are licensed for civil marriage ceremonies although we do not offer evening receptions. We welcome location work, group visits and many types of corporate, private and public functions. All clients are guaranteed exclusive use of this prestigious venue.

KEY FACTS

 Unsuitable.

 Obligatory.

VISITOR INFORMATION

Owner
Mr and Mrs D Kendrick

Address
Church Hill
Boughton Monchelsea
Nr Maidstone
Kent
ME17 4BU

Location
MAP 4:L3
OS Ref. TQ772 499.
On B2163, 5m from M20/J8.
Rail: Maidstone or Marden (+ Taxi).

Contact
Mrs Marice Kendrick
Tel: 01622 743120
E-mail: mk@boughtonplace.co.uk

Opening Times
All year except 24 December–6 January.
Not open to individual visitors.
Group tours Tuesday to Thursday for groups of 15+, by prior arrangement only.
Private functions Monday–Friday, 9am–10pm.
8 hectare outdoor event site available for larger functions 8am–11.30pm seven days a week.

Admission
Gardens and guided house tour: £6.00 per person
min 15 persons, max 50.
Venue hire: POA

Special events
June 22–24 & July 6–8 2012
Open Air theatre 'As You Like It'
For tickets call Hazlitt Arts Centre, 01622 758611

VISITOR INFORMATION

Owner
The Denys Eyre Bower Bequest, Registered Charitable Trust

Address
Chiddingstone Castle
Nr Edenbridge
Kent TN8 7AD.

Location
MAP 19:G12
OS Ref. TQ497 452

10m from Tonbridge, Tunbridge Wells and Sevenoaks.
4m Edenbridge. Accessible from A21 and M25/J5.

London 35m.

Bus: Enquiries: Tunbridge Wells TIC 01892 515675.

Rail: Tonbridge, Tunbridge Wells, Edenbridge then taxi. Penshurst then 2m walk.

Air: Gatwick 15m.

Contact
Tel: 01892 870347
E-mail: events@chiddingstonecastle.org.uk

Opening Times
Sunday, Monday, Tuesday, Wednesday & Bank Holidays from Good Friday until Sunday 28 October (check the website for any unforeseen alterations to this).

Times: 11am–5pm.

Last entry to house 4:15pm.

Admission
Adults	£8.00
Children (5-13)	£4.00
Family	£21.50

(2 adults + 2 children or 1 adult + 3 children)

Free admision to Grounds and Tea Rooms.

Parking	£2.50

Victorian Tea Rooms and Gift Shop.

Special events
Throughout the year we run a series of family activity days linked to our collections, such as our Egyptian and Japanese Days (visit our website for more information). Llama trekking around the grounds is also available in the summer.

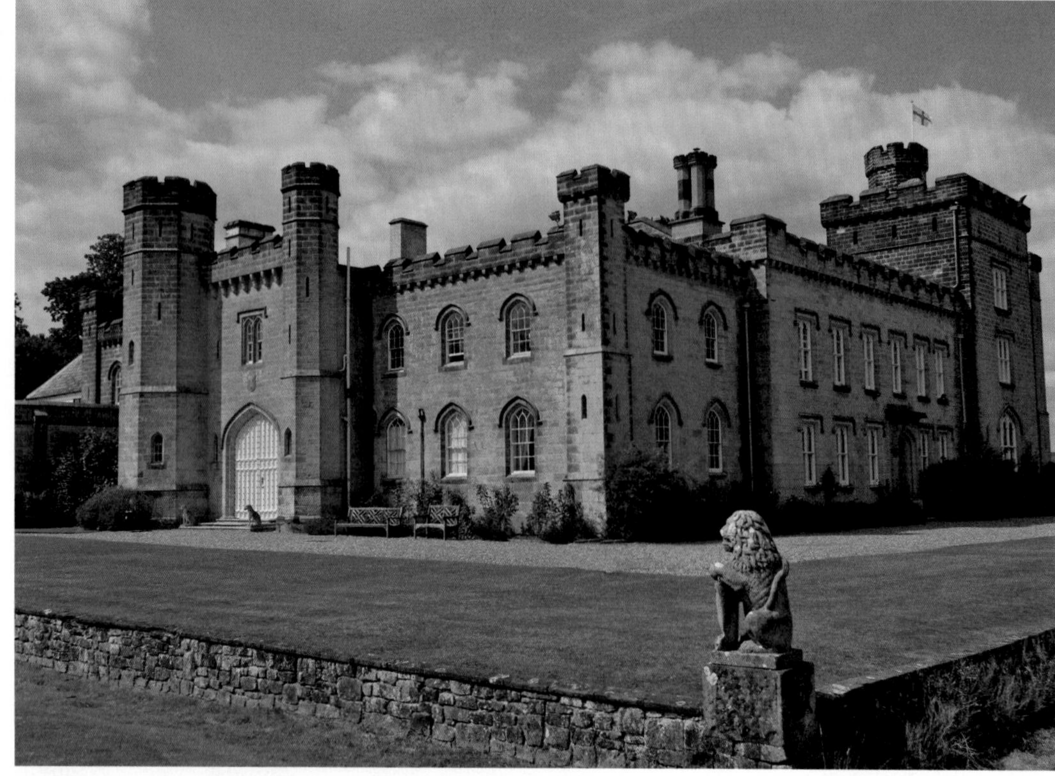

CHIDDINGSTONE CASTLE

www.chiddingstonecastle.org.uk

Chiddingstone Castle is a hidden gem in the Garden of England; a unique house with fascinating artefacts and beautiful grounds.

Situated in an historic village in the heart of the idyllic Kentish Weald, Chiddingstone Castle has Tudor origins and delightful Victorian rooms. Lying between Sevenoaks and Tunbridge Wells, it is conveniently located close to the M25 (Junction 5 – Sevenoaks or Junction 6 – Oxted). We welcome individuals, families and groups - guided tours are available. There is ample parking available and a beautifully restored Victorian Tea Rooms for delicious lunches and traditional cream teas.

Set in 35 acres of unspoilt grounds with a growing Japanese theme, including a lake, waterfall, rose garden and woodland, this attractive country house originates from the 1550s when High Street House, as the Castle was known, was home to the Streatfeild family. Several transformations have since taken place and the present building dates back to 1805 when Henry Streatfeild extended and remodelled his ancestral home in the "castle style" which was then fashionable. Rescued from creeping dereliction in 1955 by the gifted antiquary Denys Eyre Bower, the Castle became home to his amazing and varied collections. With a genius for discovering masterpieces before they had been recognised, he amassed a stunning collection of Japanese armour, swords and lacquer as well as Egyptian antiquities, Buddhist artefacts and Jacobean manuscripts and paintings. Today you can still enjoy Denys's eclectic collections as well as exhibitions devoted to both the Castle and local history.

Children are encouraged to have a hands-on, fun approach in relation to the Castle's collections in our special craft and activity rooms.

KEY FACTS

- Museum, weddings, business and private functions, scenic gardens and lake, picnics, fishing available.
- Well stocked gift shop.
- Available for special events. Licensed for Civil Ceremonies. Wedding receptions.
- WCs.
- Cream teas a speciality.
- By arrangement.
- We welcome visits from schools who wish to use the collections in connection with classroom work.
- In grounds on leads.

COBHAM HALL

www.cobhamhall.com

One of the finest and most important historic houses in Kent with landscaped gardens; ideal venue for events and lettings.

Cobham Hall, a beautiful red brick Elizabethan, Jacobean, Carolean style mansion, is set in 150 acres of historic Grade II listed landscaped gardens and parkland and described as "one of the largest, finest and most important houses in Kent".

The renowned Gilt Hall, originally created in the 17th century, features a magnificent gilded plaster ceiling and wall decorations and houses one of the only two remaining working historic 18th century Snetzler Organs. The former seat to the Earls of Darnley, Cobham Hall was used for recuperating Australian Servicemen during the First World War, and was home to the 'Ashes', a personal gift to the cricket playing 8th Earl in 1883.

The gardens were landscaped for the 4th Earl of Darnley by Humphry Repton and have recently been restored. They include a number of interesting architectural buildings and follies such as an Aviary, Pump House, an Ionic Temple, Repton's Seat built in memory of Humphry Repton by his sons, and a Gothic Dairy.

The naturalesque gardens are without doubt beautiful throughout the year, and especially during the Spring, when they are clothed with snowdrops, celandines, narcissi and daffodils, including many nationally rare varieties.

Cobham Hall is licensed for Civil Ceremonies and is an ideal venue for weddings, conferences, private functions and large or small corporate events.

The Hall is now an independent boarding and day school for girls, attracting girls from the UK and around the World.

KEY FACTS

- Weddings, Conferences, Corporate Events, Private Parties and Functions, Film Location, Residential Lets. Heated Swimming Pool, Tennis Courts, Activity Centre and Gym, Drama and Dance Studio, Music and Art Wing.
- In-house catering team.
- House tour - ground floor access only for w/chairs.
- Cream teas.
- House Tour time 1½ hrs.
- By Agreement
- Ample.
- Guide dogs only.
- Mainly dormitories plus shared rooms with some en suite.

VISITOR INFORMATION

Owner
Cobham Hall

Address
Cobham Hall
Cobham
Kent
DA12 3BL

Location
MAP 4:K2.
OS Ref. TQ683 689.

Situated adjacent to the A2/M2. 1/2m S of A2, 4m W of Strood, 8m E of M25/ J2 between Gravesend & Rochester. London 25m Rochester 5m Canterbury 30m.

Rail: Ebblesfleet 5.5m, Meopham 3m, Gravesend 5m, Taxi Ranks at all stations.

Air: Gatwick 1hr. Heathrow 1.5hrs, Stansted 1hr.

Contact
Enquiries
Tel: 01474 823371
Fax: 01474 825906
E-mail: enquiries@ cobhamhall.com

Opening Times
Please telephone to confirm or see website: www.cobhamhall.com.

Please note that mid-week opening times are restricted to pre-booked groups only. Pre-booked Parties (10+). The House is open on selected weekends.

House & Garden tours
House: 2–5pm. Last tour at 4pm.
Garden: Closes at 6pm.

Cream Teas available 2–5pm.

Admission
Adult £5.50
Conc. £4.50

Self-guided tour of gardens only £2.50

Historical/Conservation tour of Grounds (by arrangement)
Adult £6.00
Conc. £5.00

Special events
See website: www.cobhamhall.com

Conference/Function

ROOM	Size	Max Cap
Gilt Hall	41' x 34'	180
Wyatt Dining Room	49' x 23'	135
Oak Dining Room	24' x 23'	75
Activities Centre	119' x 106'	300

VISITOR INFORMATION

Owner
English Heritage

Address
Down House
Luxted Road
Downe
Kent BR6 7JT

Location
MAP 19:F9
OS Ref, TQ431 611
In Luxted Road, Downe, off A21 near Biggin Hill.
Rail: From London Victoria or Charing Cross.
Bus: Orpington (& Bus R8) or Bromley South (& Bus 146).
Bus R8 does not run on Sundays or BHs.

Contact
Visitor Operations Team
Tel: 01689 859119
Fax: 01689 862755
E-mail: customers@english-heritage.org.uk

Opening Times
Please visit www.english-heritage.org.uk for opening times and the most up-to-date information.

Admission

Adult	£9.90
Child	£5.90
Conc.	£8.90
Family	£25.70

EH Members Free.
Discount for groups (11+).
Opening times and prices are valid until 31st March 2012, after this date details are subject to change. Tour leader and coach driver have free entry. Tearoom and shop on site.

Special events
There is an exciting events programme available throughout the year, for further details please contact the property or visit the website.

© English Heritage

THE HOME OF CHARLES DARWIN ⌗

www.english-heritage.org.uk/darwin

Down House is a site of outstanding international significance, here the famous scientist Charles Darwin lived.

A visit to the Home of Charles Darwin, Down House, is a fascinating journey of discovery for all the family. It was here that Charles Darwin worked on his scientific theories and wrote his groundbreaking theory, On the Origin of Species by Means of Natural Selection. Down House was also Darwin's home for 40 years and his family's influence can be felt throughout, remaining much as it did when they lived here.

See the armchair in which Darwin wrote his groundbreaking theory of evolution and wander the family rooms on the ground floor. His study is much the same as it was in his lifetime and is filled with belongings that give you an intimate glimpse into both his studies and everyday life. On the first floor explore an exciting exhibition covering Darwin's life, his scientific work and the controversy it provoked. See manuscript pages from the Origin of the Species, Darwin's hat, microscope and notebooks, and a full scale replica of the cramped cabin he inhabited aboard HMS Beagle.

Outside, enjoy a stroll along the famous Sandwalk, then take time to explore the extensive gardens before sampling the delicious selection of home-made cakes in the tea room.

KEY FACTS

- WCs.
- Free.
- In grounds.

© English Heritage

© Richard Marsham

© English Heritage

DOVER CASTLE ⌗

www.english-heritage.org.uk/dovercastle

Spectacularly situated above the White Cliffs of Dover this magnificent castle has guarded our shores from invasion for 20 centuries.

Explore over 2,000 years of history at Dover Castle! Immerse yourself in the medieval world and royal court of King Henry II as you step inside the recently re-presented Great Tower. Meet the figures central to Henry II's royal court and on special days throughout the year interact with costumed characters as they bring to life the colour and opulence of medieval life. Also journey deep into the White Cliffs as you tour the maze of Secret Wartime Tunnels. Through sight, sound and smells, re-live the wartime drama of a wounded pilot fighting for his life. From June 2011, discover what life would have been during the dark and dramatic days of the Dunkirk evacuation with exciting new audio-visual experiences.

Above ground, enjoy magnificent views of the White Cliffs from Admiralty Lookout and explore the Fire Command Post, re-created as it would have appeared 90 years ago in the last days of the Great War. Also see a Roman Lighthouse and Anglo-Saxon church, as well as an intriguing network of medieval underground tunnels, fortifications and battlements.

Dover Castle was used as a film location for The Other Boleyn Girl starring Natalie Portman and Scarlett Johanssen and Zaffirelli's Hamlet amongst others.

KEY FACTS

- WCs. No flash photography within the Great Tower.
- Two.
- WCs.
- Licensed.
- Tour of tunnels: timed ticket system. Last tour 1 hr before closing.
- Ample.
- Free visits available for schools. Education centre. Pre-booking essential.
- On leads.

© English Heritage

© English Heritage

VISITOR INFORMATION

Owner
English Heritage

Address
Dover Castle
Dover
Kent CT16 1HU

Location
MAP 4:O4
OS Ref. TR325 419

Easy access from A2 and M20. Well signed from Dover centre and east side of Dover.
2 hrs from central London.

Rail: London St. Pancras Intl (fast train); London Victoria; London Charing Cross.

Bus: 0870 6082608.

Contact
Visitor Operations Team
Tel: 01304 211067
E-mail: customers@english-heritage.org.uk

Opening Times
Please visit www.english-heritage.org.uk for opening times and the most up-to-date information.

Admission

Adult	£16.00
Child	£9.60
Conc.	£14.40
Family	£41.60

EH Members Free.

Includes Secret Wartime Tunnels tour. Additional charges for members and non-members may apply on event days.

Groups: Discount for groups (11+). Free entry for tour leader and coach driver.

Prices are valid until 31st March 2012.

Special events
There is an exciting events programme available throughout the year, for further details please contact the property or visit the website.

VISITOR INFORMATION

Owner
Hever Castle Ltd

Address
Hever Castle
Hever
Edenbridge
Kent TN8 7NG

Location
MAP 19:G12
OS Ref. TQ476 450

Exit M25/J5 & J6 M23/ J10 30 miles from central London, 1 1/2m S of B2027 at Bough Beech, 3m SE of Edenbridge.

Rail: Hever Station 1m (no taxis), Edenbridge Town 3m (taxis).

Contact
Ann Watt
Infoline: 01732 865224
Fax: 01732 866796
E-mail: mail @HeverCastle.co.uk

Opening Times
Spring
13–19 February, April–October, daily, 10.30am–5pm.
Last exit 6pm.

Winter
March, November and December, please see website for details.

Admission
Individual

Adult	£14.50
Senior	£12.50
Child	£8.30
Family	£37.30
Gardens only	
Adult	£12.00
Senior	£10.50
Child	£7.80
Family	£31.80
Group	
Adult	£11.75
Senior	£10.75
Student	£9.50
Child	£6.50
Gardens only	
Adult	£9.75
Senior	£9.25
Student	£8.10
Child	£6.20

Groups (15+)
Available on request.
Pre-booked private guided tours are available before opening, during season.

Special events
Special Events throughout the year including 'Best of British Garden Festival' and Jousting Tournaments

Conference/Function

ROOM	Size	Max Cap
Dining Hall	35' x 20'	70
Breakfast Rm	22' x 15'	12
Sitting Rm	24' x 20'	20
Pavilion	96' x 40'	250
Moat Restaurant	25' x 60'	75

HEVER CASTLE & GARDENS

www.hevercastle.co.uk

Experience 700 years of colourful history and spectacular award-winning gardens at the childhood home of Anne Boleyn.

Hever Castle dates from 1270, when the gatehouse, outer walls and inner moat were first built. 200 years later the Boleyn family added the Tudor manor house constructed within the walls. This was the childhood home of Anne Boleyn, Henry VIII's second wife and mother of Elizabeth I. There are many Tudor artefacts including two Books of Hours signed and inscribed by Anne Boleyn. The Castle was later given to Henry VIII's fourth wife, Anne of Cleves.

In 1903, the estate was bought by the American millionaire William Waldorf Astor, who became a British subject and the first Lord Astor of Hever. He invested an immense amount of time, money and imagination in restoring the castle and grounds. Master craftsmen were employed and the castle was filled with a fine collection of paintings, furniture and tapestries. The Miniature Model Houses exhibition, a collection of 1/12 scale model houses, room views and gardens, depicts life in English Country Houses.

Gardens

Between 1904-1908, 125 acres of formal and natural gardens were laid out and planted; these have now matured into one of the most beautiful gardens in England. The unique four acre walled Italian Garden contains a magnificent collection of statuary. The glorious Edwardian Gardens include the Rose Garden, Tudor Garden, traditional yew maze and a 110 metre herbaceous border. There are several water features, a 38 acre lake with rowing boats, a water maze, lake walk, adventure playground, gift and garden shops and special events throughout the season.

KEY FACTS

- Filming, residential conferences, Corporate hospitality and Golf.
- Gift, garden & book.
- Weddings, receptions and private banqueting.
- Partial. WCs.
- Licensed.
- By Arrangement. Pre-booked tours in French, German, Dutch, Italian and Spanish (min 20).
- Free parking.
- English, French, German & Dutch.
- Private Residence.

© NT / John Miller

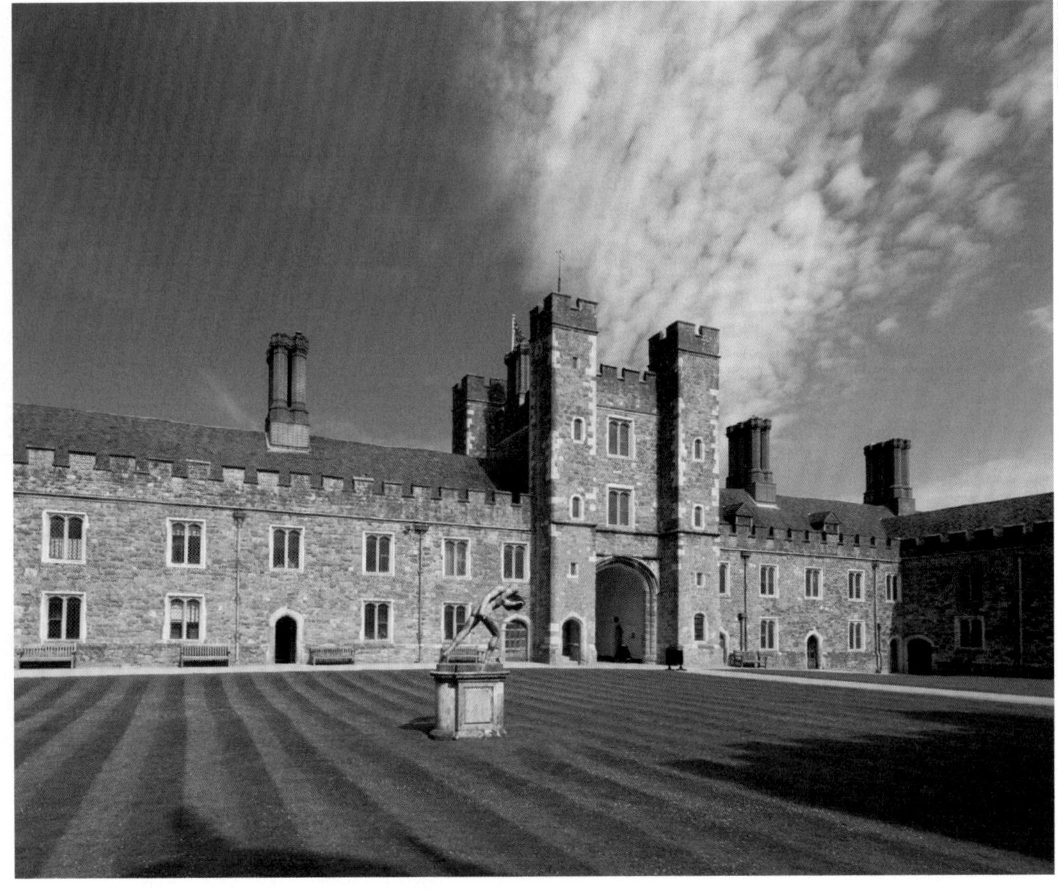

KNOLE

www.nationaltrust.org.uk/knole

The forgotten palace of England, leading the way in conservation

Knole, the forgotten palace of England, is one of our most important and complete historic houses. It covers four acres, is set in a thousand acres of medieval deer park, was once at the centre of court life and contains irreplaceable collections – yet it remains relatively unknown. To create Knole, a medieval manor house was rebuilt as an archiepiscopal palace, annexed as a Tudor royal residence, remodelled as a Stuart treasure house and filled with a glimmering collection of upholstered furniture from the royal palaces, hundreds of portraits and rich tapestries, bedding and silver ornaments. Painters represented include Lely, Mytens, Reynolds, Van Dyck and Vigée-Lebrun, while Knole also contains a set of early seventeenth-century tapestries by master weaver François Spiering. The house, now owned by the National Trust, is still a family home for the Sackville-Wests, and inspired Vita Sackville-West's *The Edwardians* and Virginia Woolf's *Orlando*, books which lovingly detail Knole and its collections, still on show as they have been for four centuries. Exhibitions in Knole's Orangery this year will include new x-ray photographs of objects from the collection, revealing their almost ethereal substance, works from Kent artists, plus a look at the curiosities of the house normally hidden from the public. Knole is making a name for itself with bold conservation experiments and new forms of interpretation, which will continue as the National Trust launches a major project this year to rebuild and conserve the show rooms and the collections inside them.

KEY FACTS

- Amateur outdoor photography welcomed.
- Full range of NT goods and souvenirs of Knole.
- Partial. WCs.
- Licensed.
- Guided tours for pre-booked groups, by arrangement. Short guides to the house available in French, Dutch & German.
- Limited coach parking available.
- Welcome. Contact Education Officer.
- Guide dogs only.
- Park open all year to pedestrians.

© NT / John Miller

© NT / John Miller

VISITOR INFORMATION

Owner
National Trust

Address
Knole
Sevenoaks
Kent TN15 0RP

Location
MAP 19:H10
OS Ref. TQ532 543

M25/J5 (for A21). 25m SE of London. Off A225 at S end of High Street, Sevenoaks, opposite St Nicholas Church. For satnav use TN13 1JA for the church, opposite park entrance.

Bus: Arriva 402 Tunbridge Wells–Bromley North.

Rail: 1/2hr from London Charing Cross to Sevenoaks.

Contact
Property Manager
Tel: 01732 462100
Info: 01732 450608
Fax: 01732 465528
E-mail: knole@nationaltrust.org.uk

Opening Times
House:
10 March–4 November, Wed–Sun, inc. Bank Holiday Mons, 12–4pm.

Tearoom:
7 January–26 February, Sat & Sun, 11am–4pm.

Shop, Tearoom, Visitor Centre & Orangery:
3–4 March, Sat & Sun, 11am–4pm.
10 March–1 April, Wed–Sun, inc Bank Holiday Mons, 10.30am–5pm.
3 April–30 September, Tues–Sun, inc Bank Holiday Mons, 10.30am–5pm.
3 October–4 November, Wed–Sun, inc Bank Holiday Mons, 10.30am–5pm.

Garden:
3 April–25 September, Tuesdays only, 11am–4pm.
Last admission to house and garden is 30 mins before closing.

Christmas Shop, Tearoom, Visitor Centre & Orangery:
7 November–23 December, Wed–Sun, 11am–4pm.

Park:
Deer park has pedestrian access all year round.

Admission
House	
Adult	£11.50*
Child	£5.75*
Family	£28.75*
Groups (pre-booked 15+)	
Adult	£9.75
Garden	
Adult	£5.00
Child	£2.50

NT members Free.
Parking £4.00 per car (free to members).

Park
Free to pedestrians

*includes a voluntary Gift Aid donation but visitors can choose to pay the standard prices displayed at the property and on the website.

Special events
Please telephone or visit website for details.

VISITOR INFORMATION

Owner
Viscount De L'Isle

Address
Penshurst
Nr Tonbridge
Kent TN11 8DG

Location
MAP 19:H12
OS Ref. TQ527 438

From London M25/J5 then A21 to Hildenborough, B2027 via Leigh; from Tunbridge Wells A26, B2176.

Bus: 231, 233 from Tunbridge Wells and Edenbridge.

Rail: Charing Cross/ Waterloo East– Hildenborough, Tonbridge or Tunbridge Wells; then bus or taxi.

Contact
Penshurst Place
Tel: 01892 870307
Fax: 01892 870866
E-mail: enquiries @penshurstplace.com

Opening Times
11 February–1 April: Saturdays & Sundays only, 10.30am–6pm or dusk if earlier.

2 April–4 November Daily, 10.30am–6pm.

House
Daily, 12 noon– last entry 4pm.

Grounds
Daily, 10.30am–6pm. Last entry 5pm.

Shop
Open all year.

Winter
Open to Groups by appointment only.

Admission
For 2012 individual prices see website for details.

2012 Group prices
(pre-booked 15+)
Freeflow

Adult	£8.00
Child	£5.00

House Tours

Adult	£10.00
Child	£5.50

Garden Tours
(pre-booked 15+)

Adult	£10.00
Child	£5.50

House & Garden Tours

Adult	£16.00
Child (5–16 yrs)	£10.00

*under 5s Free.

Special events
Weald of Kent Craft Show First May Bank Holiday and second weekend in September Friday–Sunday.

Glorious Gardens Week First week in June with official reopening of the Double Herbaceous Borders.

Conference/Function

ROOM	Size	Max Cap
Sunderland Room	45' x 18'	100
Baron's Hall	64' x 39'	250
Buttery	20' x 23'	50

© David Sellman / Penshurst Place

PENSHURST PLACE & GARDENS

www.penshurstplace.com

One of England's greatest family-owned historic houses with a history going back nearly seven centuries.

In some ways time has stood still at Penshurst; the great House is still very much a medieval building with improvements and additions made over the centuries but without any substantial rebuilding. Its highlight is undoubtedly the medieval Barons Hall, built in 1341, with its impressive 60ft-high chestnut-beamed roof. A marvellous mix of paintings, tapestries and furniture from the 15th, 16th and 17th centuries can be seen throughout the House, including the helm carried in the state funeral procession to St Paul's Cathedral for the Elizabethan courtier and poet, Sir Philip Sidney, in 1587. This is now the family crest.

Gardens

The Gardens, first laid out in the 14th century, have been developed over generations of the Sidney family, who first came to Penshurst in 1552. A twenty-year restoration and re-planting programme under-taken by the 1st Viscount De L'Isle has ensured that they retain their historic splendour. He is commemorated with an Arboretum, planted in 1991.

The gardens are divided by a mile of yew hedges into "rooms", each planted to give a succession of colour as the seasons change, with the completion of a major restoration project on the Victorian double Herbaceous border this year. There is also an Adventure Playground, Woodland Trail, Toy Museum and a Gift Shop which is open all year. A variety of events in the park and grounds take place throughout the season.

KEY FACTS

- Conference facilities. No photography in house.
- Conference and private banqueting facilities. Wedding ceremonies and receptions.
- Partial. Contact for details.
- Guided tours available by arrangement before the House opens to the public. Garden tours available 10.30am–4.30pm.
- Ample for cars and coaches.
- All year by appointment, discount rates, education room and teachers' packs.
- Guide dogs only.

POWELL-COTTON MUSEUM, QUEX HOUSE & GARDENS

www.quexpark.co.uk

Established in 1896 by Major Percy Horace Gordon Powell-Cotton (1866–1940) to house natural history specimens and cultural objects collected on expeditions to Asia and Africa.

Major Powell-Cotton was a pioneer in the use of the diorama to display mounted mammals in representations of their natural habitats. The Powell-Cotton Museum natural history dioramas are outstanding examples, unique to the UK, stunning for their size, quality and imagery. Today they still excite the imagination of young and old alike.

The world-class natural history and ethnographical collections at the Museum support the study, understanding and simple enjoyment of the zoological, cultural and ecological diversity of Africa and the Indian sub-continent.

The 15th-century Quex Estate was purchased by the financier John Powell in 1777 and the Regency-period Quex House was completed by his nephew in 1813. The house was remodelled and extended in the late 19th century. The beautiful gardens to be seen today were developed in Victorian times.

Group Visits can pre-book lunch and afternoon tea in the Hannah Dining Suite which also specialises in catering for all private and corporate events, from team building and seminars to parties and weddings.

Also on site at Quex Park: the Quex Falconry, Quex Craft Village, Jungle Jims Indoor and Outdoor family entertainment centre, The Secret Garden Centre, Quex Maize Maze (summer only) and Quex Barn Farmshop and Restaurant.

KEY FACTS

- Website available in French, German & Spanish.
- Gift Shop and Craft Village.
- Plants grown in Victorian Greenhouses available.
-
- Good Disabled Access.
- Light refreshments available, picnics permitted.
- Booking essential: 01843 844305
- Booking essential: 01843 842168.
- Free parking for coaches and cars.
- Workshops, School Visits and Tours.
- Enquiries: 01843 482004.
- Please see www.quexpark.co.uk for details.

VISITOR INFORMATION

Owner
Trustees of the Powell-Cotton Museum, Quex House & Gardens

Address
Quex Park
Birchington
Kent CT7 0BH

Location
MAP 4:N2
OS Ref. TR308 683
½m from Birchington Church via Park Lane.

Contact
Powell-Cotton Museum, Quex House & Gardens.
Tel: 01843 842168
E-mail: enquiries@quexmuseum.org

Opening Times
3 April–31 October 2012 (and February half term and Special Events).

The Museum & Gardens:
Tuesday–Sunday, 10am–5pm.

Quex House:
Tuesday–Sunday, 2–5pm.

Winter Season:
Closed.

The Museum is open to schools and groups throughout the year.

Admission

Museum, House & Gardens	
Adults	£7.00
Seniors & Children up to 16 years	£5.00
Students	£5.00
Family (2+3)	£20
Carers for Disabled	Free
Under 5	Free
Gardens only	
Adults	£2.00
Seniors & Children up to 16 years	£1.50
Students	£1.50
Carers for Disabled	Free
Under 5	Free
Groups of 20 or more	
Adults	£6.00
Seniors & Children up to 16 years	£4.50

General introductory talk £25. Full guided tour £60.

Groups of 20 or more (out of hours visits)	
Adults	£8.50
Seniors & Children up to 16 years	£6.50

Full guided tour £70. (groups of 40 or more will be split and charged accordingly).

Special events
Events program throughout the year including outdoor concerts with internationally renowned artists, country fairs, Victorian themed events, children's storytelling, outdoor theatre, craft fayres, firework displays and seasonal events.

Please see our website for details: www.quexpark.co.uk

VISITOR INFORMATION

Owner
John St A Warde Esq

Address
Squerryes Court
Westerham
Kent TN16 1SJ

Location
MAP 19:F11
OS Ref. TQ440 535
10 min from M25/J5 or 6 Off A25, 1/2m W from centre of Westerham
London 1–1 1/2 hrs.
Rail: Oxted Station 4m. Sevenoaks 6m.
Air: Gatwick, 30 mins.

Contact
Administrator
Mrs P A White
Tel: 01959 562345
Fax: 01959 565949
E-mail: enquiries@squerryes.co.uk

Opening Times
Summer
1 April–30 September, Wed, Sun & BH Mons, 12.30–5pm.
Last admission 4.30pm.
Grounds
11.30am–5pm
Last admission 4.30pm.
NB. Pre-booked groups welcome any day except Saturday.
Winter
October–31 March
Closed.

Admission
House & Garden

Adult	£7.50
Child (under 16yrs)	£4.00
Senior	£7.00
Family (2+2)	£16.00
Groups (20+ booked)	
Adult	£6.50
Child (under 16yrs)	£4.00

Wine Tasting Groups
(inc. House & Garden)

Adult	£9.50

New Exhibition
Edwardian Squerryes & Westerham
Please see website for details.

Garden only

Adult	£5.00
Child (under 16yrs)	£2.50
Senior	£4.50
Family (2+2)	£9.50
Groups (20+ booked)	
Adult	£4.50
Child (under 16yrs)	£3.00

Conference/Function

ROOM	Size	Max Cap
Hall	32' x 32'	70
Green Dining Room	20' x 25' 6"	50

SQUERRYES COURT

www.squerryes.co.uk

17th century manor house still lived in by the family, surrounded by magnificent gardens and parkland; close to historic Westerham.

Squerryes Court is a beautiful 17th century William and Mary manor house acquired by the Warde family in 1731. Visitors can enjoy the fine interior with the collection of Old Master paintings from the Italian, Dutch and 18th century English schools. The paintings, furniture, porcelain and tapestries were all collected or commissioned by the family in the 18th century.

The garden has interest throughout the seasons from the spring bulbs to the herbaceous borders flowering from June to September. Originally laid out in the formal style by the first Earl of Jersey in 1709, the Warde family have restored some of the formal garden using designs from the original plans. The lake and fine views add to the peaceful setting.

General Wolfe of Quebec, who lived in Westerham, was a friend of the family. A room in the house is devoted to him, and his portrait, sword and other items are on view. A Cenotaph in the garden was commissioned by the family to commemorate his victory at Quebec in 1759. The Tapestry Room has recently been redecorated with the kind support of Farrow & Ball.

New exhibition for 2012: "Squerryes in the First World War". The house became a convalescent home for wounded soldiers during the war. Memoribilia and period photographs will be on show in the house together with costumes from the period.
Please see website for details on conferences, private parties, marquee weddings and group visits.

KEY FACTS

- Suitable for conferences, product launches, filming, photography, outside events, garden parties. No photography in house. Picnics permitted by the lake.
- Small.
- Wedding receptions (marquee).
- Partial. WCs.
- Licenced.
- For pre-booked groups (max 55), small additional charge. Tour time 1 hr. Wine tasting groups by arrangement 45 mins–1 hr. Additional charge.
- Limited for coaches.
- On leads, in grounds.

© English Heritage

WALMER CASTLE AND GARDENS ⌗

www.english-heritage.org.uk/walmercastle

Walmer Castle was built during the reign of King Henry VIII and perches on the picturesque Kent coastline.

A Tudor fort transformed into an elegant stately home. The residence of the Lords Warden of the Cinque Ports, who have included HM The Queen Mother, Sir Winston Churchill and the Duke of Wellington.

Take the inclusive audio tour and see the Duke's rooms where he died over 150 years ago. Beautiful gardens including the Queen Mother's Garden, The Broadwalk with its famous yew tree hedge, Kitchen Garden and Moat Garden. Lunches and cream teas available in the delightful Lord Warden's tearooms.

The Garden Cottage, and its sister Greenhouse Apartment are situated within the walled kitchen garden, which has supplied the castle with fruit, vegetables and flowers for over 300 years.

KEY FACTS

- WCs.

© English Heritage

© English Heritage

VISITOR INFORMATION

Owner
English Heritage

Address
Deal
Kent
CT14 7LJ

Location
MAP 4:O3
OS Ref. TR378 501.
S of Walmer on A258, M20/J13 or M2 to Deal.

Contact
Visitor Operations Team
Tel: 01304 364288
Venue Hire and Hospitality: 01304 209889
E-mail: customers@english-heritage.org.uk

Opening Times
1 Apr–30 Sept: daily, 10am–6pm. 1–31 Oct: Wed–Sun, 10am–4pm. 1 Nov–28 Feb: Closed. 1–31 Mar: Wed–Sun, 10am–4pm. Closed 9–11 July when Lord Warden is in residence.

Admission

Adult	£7.00
Child	£3.50
Conc.	£6.00
Family	£17.50

Discount for groups (11+).

English Heritage members free.

Opening times and prices are valid until 31st March 2011, after this date details are subject to change please visit www.english-heritage.org.uk for the most up-to-date information.

Special events
There is an exciting events programme available throughout the year, for further details please contact the property or visit the website.

© NTPL / Rod Edwards

© NTPL / Jonathan Buckley

SISSINGHURST CASTLE

SISSINGHURST, CRANBROOK, KENT TN17 2AB

www.nationaltrust.org.uk/sissinghurst

Come and explore Sissinghurst Castle, one of the world's most celebrated gardens and a sensory paradise of colour, texture, beauty and perfume throughout the seasons. Vita Sackville-West, a Bloomsbury group member, and her husband Sir Harold Nicolson, a diplomat, author and politician, created the garden around the surviving parts of an Elizabethan mansion including the iconic viewing tower. The original design still exists today with a series of garden rooms, intimate in scale and romantic in atmosphere, providing outstanding design and colour all year. Highlights include the White Garden, Lime Walk, Tower with Vita's study and Cottage Garden.

Location: MAP 4:L4, OS Ref. TQ807 383. 2m NE of Cranbrook, 1m E of Sissinghurst village (A262). No. 5 Arriva bus from Staplehurst train station.

Owner: National Trust

Contact: The Administrator

Tel: 01580 710700 **Infoline:** 01580 710701

E-mail: sissinghurst@nationaltrust.org.uk

Open: 17 Mar–28 Oct: Garden, Shop and Restaurant open Mon, Tues, Fri, Sat, Sun 10.30am–5.30pm; Closed Wed/Thur. 29 Oct–22 Dec: Shop & Restaurant 11am–4pm. Vegetable Garden: 11 May–30 Sept, Mon, Tues, Fri, Sat, Sun, 10.30am–5.30pm. Late Night Opening until 8pm on: Fri 25 May, and every Fri throughout Jun.

***Admission:** Adult £11.50, Child £5.50, Family (2+3) £29, Groups £9.50. NT members free. *includes a voluntary donation but visitors can choose to pay the standard prices displayed at the property and on the website.

Key facts: WCs. Licensed. Ample, £2 per car (NT Members free). Please book coaches in advance. Guide dogs only in gardens, on leads in grounds.

© NTPL / John Millar

© NTPL / David Levenson

SMALLHYTHE PLACE

SMALLHYTHE, TENTERDEN, KENT TN30 7NG

www.nationaltrust.org.uk/smallhytheplace

Smallhythe Place is special. This half-timbered and rose clad 500 year old gem, has a peaceful intimacy in the house and pretty garden that enchants and sets it apart. Once home to the famous Victorian actress and personality Dame Ellen Terry, it contains her theatrical collection of national importance including rare costumes worn on stage with Sir Henry Irving. Visit the new display space with the restored iconic beetle wing dress, back after a 5 year absence, and worn by Ellen Terry in 1888 in the role of Lady Macbeth. Don't miss the Barn Theatre which has seen performances by many great stage names over the years and still hosts many productions today.

Location: MAP 4:L4, 2 miles S of Tenterden, on E side of the Rye Road (B2082). Coastal coaches 312 from Rye Station.

Owner: National Trust

Contact: The Administrator

Tel: 01580 762334

Open: 3 Mar–31 Oct, 11am–5pm. Open Mon, Tue, Wed, Sat & Sun. Closed Thur & Fri. Look out for our Christmas event over one weekend in December.

Admission: Adult £7.40, Child £4, Family £18, Groups £6.

Key facts: Partial. Licensed. By arrangement. Please book coaches in advance. Dogs allowed in gardens. Guide dogs only in the house.

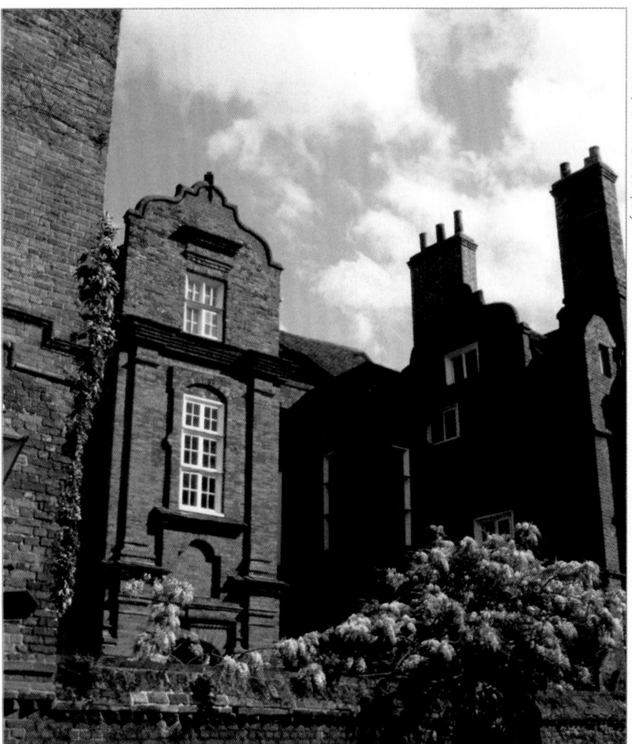

© David Winston, Period Piano Company

RESTORATION HOUSE

17–19 CROW LANE, ROCHESTER, KENT ME1 1RF

www.restorationhouse.co.uk

Unique survival of an ancient city mansion deriving its name from the stay of Charles II on the eve of The Restoration. Beautiful interiors with exceptional early paintwork related to decorative scheme 'run up' for Charles' visit. The house also inspired Dickens to situate 'Miss Havisham' here.
'Interiors of rare historical resonance and poetry', *Country Life.* Fine English furniture and pictures (Mytens, Kneller, Dahl, Reynolds and several Gainsboroughs). Charming interlinked walled gardens of ingenious plan in a classic English style. A private gem. 'There is no finer pre-Civil war town house in England than this' – Simon Jenkins, *The Times.*

Location: MAP 4:K2, OS Ref, TQ744 683. Historic centre of Rochester, off High Street, opposite the Vines Park.

Owner: R Tucker & J Wilmot **Contact:** Robert Tucker **Tel:** 01634 848520
Fax: 01634 880058
E-mail: robert.tucker@restorationhouse.co.uk
Open: 31 May–28 Sept, Thur & Fri, 10am–5pm. Sats 9 Jun & 14 Jul, 12–5pm.
Admission: Adult £6.50 (includes 32 page illustrated guidebook), Child £3.25, Conc £5.50. Booked group (8+) tours: £7.50pp.
Key facts: No stiletto heels. No photography in house. Garden by appointment. 1st, 2nd & 4th Thurs in month & other days by arrangement. By arrangement. None. Guide dogs only.

BELMONT HOUSE & GARDENS

Belmont Park, Throwley, Faversham ME13 0HH

www.belmont-house.org

Belmont is an elegant 18th century house with views over the rolling Kentish North Downs. Its hidden gardens range from a Pinetum complete with grotto, a walled ornamental garden, a walled kitchen garden with Victorian greenhouse leading to a yew-lined walk to the family pets' graveyard.
Location: MAP 4:M3, OS Ref. TQ986 564. 4 1/2m SSW of Faversham, off A251.
Owner: Harris (Belmont) Charity
Contact: administrator@belmont-house.org
Tel: 01795 890202 **Fax:** 01795 890042
E-mail: administrator@belmont-house.org
Open: 31 Mar–30 Sept. House: Sats, Suns & BH Mons. Tours, 2.15pm, 2.45pm, 3.30pm. Group tours weekdays by appointment. Pre-booked specialist clock tours last Sat of month, Apr–Sept. Gardens open all year.
Admission: House & Garden: Adult £8, Child (Under 12's free) £5, Conc. £7, Garden Only: Adult £5, Child (12-16yrs) £2.50, Conc. £4. Pre-booked Clock Tour (last Saturday of every month) £15.
Key facts: No photography in house. Partial. WC. Obligatory. Limited for coaches. In grounds, on leads.

© NTPL / Ian Shaw

CHARTWELL

Mapleton Road, Westerham, Kent TN16 1PS

www.nationaltrust.org.uk/chartwell

Chartwell was the much-loved Churchill family home and the place from which Sir Winston drew inspiration from 1924 until the end of his life. With its magnificent views over the Weald of Kent. The Mulberry Room at the restaurant can be booked for meetings, weddings, conferences, lunches and dinners.
Location: MAP 19:F11, OS Ref. TQ455 515. 2m S of Westerham, forking left off B2026.
Owner: National Trust **Contact:** Visitor Experience Manager
Tel: 01732 868381 **Fax:** 01732 868193 **E-mail:** chartwell@nationaltrust.org.uk
Open: House open from 10 Mar–28 Oct, Wed–Sun, 11am–5pm.
Garden, Exhibition, Studio, Shop and Restaurant open everyday from 10 Mar–31 Dec, times vary please call 01732 868381 for further details.
Admission: House, Garden, Studio: Adult £12.90, Child £6.50, Family £32.20. Garden, Studio only: Adult £6.50, Child £3.20, Family £16.10. Winter: Adult £6.50, Child £3.20, Family £16.10. Gift Aid prices.
Key facts: Conference, wedding and function facilities. Partial. WCs. Licensed. By arrangement. In grounds.

© English Heritage

DEAL CASTLE ⌑

Victoria Road, Deal, Kent CT14 7BA

www.english-heritage.org.uk/dealcastle

Crouching low and menacing, the huge, rounded bastions of this austere fort, built by Henry VIII, once carried 119 guns. A fascinating castle to explore, with long, dark passages, battlements and a huge basement. The interactive displays and exhibition give an interesting insight into the castle's history.

Location: MAP 4:O3, OS Ref. TR378 522. SE of Deal town centre.

Owner: English Heritage

Contact: Visitor Operations Team

Tel: 01304 372762 Venue hire and Hospitality: 01304 209889

E-mail: customers@english-heritage.org.uk

Open: Please visit www.english-heritage.org.uk for opening times and the most up-to-date information.

Admission: Adult £4.80, Child £2.90, Conc. £4.30. Family £12.50. EH Members free. Opening times and prices are valid until 31st March 2012.

Key facts: WCs. Coach parking on main road.

IGHTHAM MOTE

Ightham Mote, Mote Road, Sevenoaks, Kent TN15 0NT

www.nationaltrust.org.uk/ighthammote

Moated manor dating from 1320, reflecting seven centries of history, from the medieval Crypt to a 1960s Library. Owned by knights, courtiers to Henry VIII and society Victorians. Highlights include Great Hall, Drawing Room, Tudor painted ceiling, Grade 1 listed dog kennel and apartments of US donor.

Location: MAP 19:H11. OS Ref. TQ584 535. 6m E of Sevenoaks off A25. 2½m S of Ightham off A227.

Owner: National Trust **Contact:** Pamela Westaway

Tel: 01732 810378 **Fax:** 01732 811029

E-mail: ighthammote@nationaltrust.org.uk

Open: 10 Mar–4 Nov, daily except Tues & Wed, 11–5 (open Weds, Jun–Aug) 8 Nov–23 Dec, Thurs–Sun, 11–3 partial House & gardens, shop & restaurant.

Admission: Adult £11.50*, Child £5.75, Family £29

Groups 15 + Adult £9.75, Child £4.85. *includes voluntary donation visitors can pay standard prices displayed at property.

Key facts: No flash photography. Restaurant may not be fully open during private functions. Partial. WCs. Licensed. By arrangement. Guide dogs only.

EMMETTS GARDEN

Ide Hill, Sevenoaks, Kent TN14 6BA

www.nationaltrust.org.uk/emmetts

Influenced by William Robinson, this charming garden was laid out in the late 19th century and includes the highest treetop in Kent. Explore the rose and rock gardens, take in the spectacular views and enjoy the glorious shows of spring flowers and shrubs, followed by vibrant autumn colours.

Location: MAP 19:G11, OS Ref. TQ477 524. 11/2m N of Ide Hill off B2042. M25/J5, then 4m.

Owner: National Trust

Contact: Property Operations Manager

Tel: 01732 750367

Fax: 01732 750489

Info: 01732 751509

E-mail: emmetts@nationaltrust.org.uk

Open: 10 Mar–28 Oct, Sat–Wed, 10am–5pm. Open BH Mons and Good Friday.

Admission: Adult £6.90, Child £1.80, Family (2+3) £15.60. Group Adult £5.20.

Key facts: Partial, WCs. By arrangement. On leads.

LEEDS CASTLE

Leeds Castle, Maidstone, Kent ME17 1PL

www.leeds-castle.com

Set in 500 acres of beautiful parkland and gardens, Leeds Castle is the loveliest castle in the world and is also one of the Treasure Houses of England. The castle has a fine collection of paintings, tapestries and antiques and is also home to an unusual dog collar museum.

Location: MAP 4:L3, OS Ref. TQ835 533. From London to A20/M20/J8, 40m, 1 hr. 7m E of Maidstone, 1/4m S of A20.

Owner: Leeds Castle Foundation

Tel: 01622 765400

Fax: 01622 735616

E-mail: enquiries@leeds-castle.co.uk

Open: Please see website or contact us for up-to-date information.

Admission: Please see website or contact us for up-to-date information.

Key facts: Talks, conferences, weddings, team building, falconry, golf, croquet and helipad. Partial. WCs. Licensed. Licensed. Guides in rooms. Free parking. Guide dogs only. €

© English Heritage

LULLINGSTONE ROMAN VILLA

Lullingstone Lane, Eynsford, Kent DA4 0JA

www.english-heritage.org.uk/lullingstone

Recognised as a unique archaeological find, the villa has splendid mosaic floors and one of the earliest private Christian chapels. Step into the world of Roman Britain as a film and light show takes you back nearly 2,000 years. Marvel at the wall paintings and fascinating artefacts in the exhibition.

Location: MAP 19:G9, OS Ref. TQ529 651. ½m SW Eynsford toff A225, M25/J3. Flw A20 towards Brands Hach. 600yds N of Castle.

Owner: English Heritage **Contact:** Visitor Operations Team

Tel: 01322 863467 **E-mail:** customers@english-heritage.org.uk

Open: Please visit www.english-heritage.org.uk for opening times and the most up-to-date information.

Admission: Adult £5.90, Child £3.50, Conc £5.30, Family £14.80. EH Members Free. Group discount available. Opening times and prices are valid until 31st March 2012.

Key facts:

OLD SOAR MANOR

Plaxtol, Borough Green, Kent TN15 0QX

A solar chamber over a barrel-vaulted undercroft is all that remains of a late 13th century knight's dwelling of c1290 which stood until the 18th century.

Location: MAP 4:K3, OS Ref.TQ619 541. 1m E of Plaxtol.

Owner: National Trust

Contact: The Property Manager

Tel: 01732 810378

E-mail: oldsoarmanor@nationaltrust.org.uk

Open: 1 Apr–30 Sept: Sat–Thu, 10am–6pm. Daily except Fridays.

Admission: Free.

Key facts: Limited for cars, no coaches. €

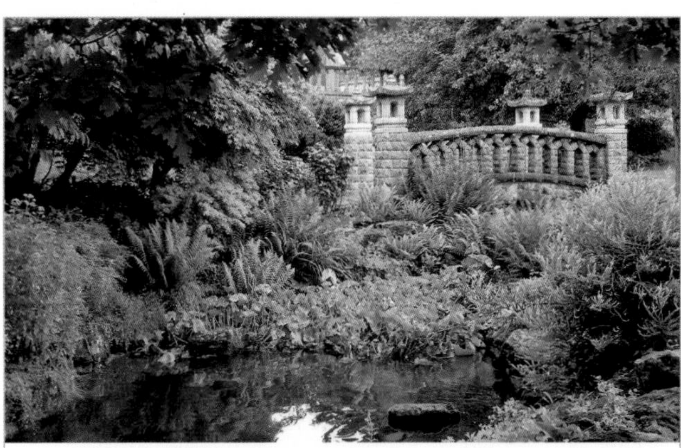

MOUNT EPHRAIM GARDENS

Hernhill, Faversham, Kent ME13 9TX

www.mountephraimgardens.co.uk

In these enchanting 10 acres of Edwardian gardens, terraces of fragrant roses lead to a small lake and woodland area. A new grass maze, Japanese-style rock garden, arboretum and many beautiful mature trees are other highlights. Peaceful, unspoilt atmosphere set in Kentish orchards.

Location: MAP 4:M3, OS Ref. TR065 598. In Hernhill village, 1m from end of M2. Signed from A2 & A299.

Owner: William Dawes & Family **Contact:** Lucy Dawes

Tel: 01227 751496

Fax: 01227 751011

E-mail: info@mountephraimgardens.co.uk

Open: Open Easter Sun–end Sept: Wed, Thu, Fri, Sat & Sun, 11am–5pm and BH Mons. Groups Mar–Oct by arrangement.

Admission: Adult £5, Child (4–16) £2.50. Groups (10+): £4.50

Key facts: Partial. WCs. Licensed. Licensed. By arrangement. On leads.

SCOTNEY CASTLE

Lamberhurst, Tunbridge Wells, Kent TN3 8JN

www.nationaltrust.org.uk/scotneycastle

Scotney Castle is simply one of the most stunning, picturesque gardens in England, with two celebrated former homes. You can enjoy discovering the rooms in the Victorian mansion or explore the ruins of the 14th century moated castle, which is the magnificent focal point of this truly romantic garden.

Location: MAP 4:K4, OS Ref. TQ688 353. Signed off A21 1m S of Lamberhurst.

Owner: National Trust **Contact:** Property Manager **Tel:** 01892 893868 **Fax:** 01892 890110 **E-mail:** scotneycastle@nationaltrust.org.uk

Open: House/Garden: 15 Feb–2 Nov, Wed–Sun, 11am–4pm; 3 Nov–23 Dec, Sat & Sun, 11am–2pm. Estate walks: All year, Mon–Sun. Open BH and Good Friday. Timed tickets for the house.

Admission: House & Garden: Adult £14, Child £7, Family £35. Garden only: Adult £9, Child £5.50, Family £25. NT members free. Includes a voluntary donation of at least 10% but visitors can choose to pay the standard prices.

Key facts: Wheelchairs available. No dogs in garden but welcome on leads on estate. Virtual tour of top floor for less able. Partial. WCs. Licensed. By arrangement. Limited for coaches.

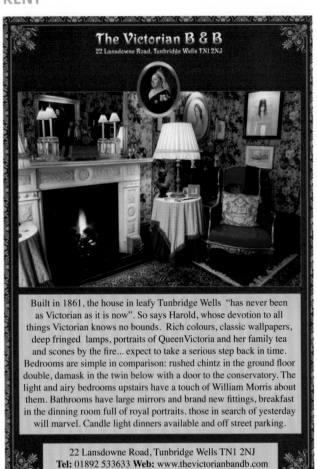

DODDINGTON PLACE GARDENS

Doddington, Nr Sittingbourne, Kent ME9 0BB

10 acres of landscaped gardens in an Area of Outstanding Natural Beauty.
Location: MAP 4:L3, OS Ref. TQ944 575. 4m N from A20 at Lenham or 5m SW from A2 at Ospringe, W Faversham.
Owner: Mr & Mrs Richard Oldfield
Contact: Mrs Richard Oldfield
Tel: 01795 886101
Website: www.doddingtonplacegardens.co.uk
Open: Easter Sun–end Sept: Suns 11am–5pm, BH Mons, 11am–5pm.
Admission: Adult £5, Child £1. Groups (10+) £4.50.
Key facts: Limited. On leads.

GOODNESTONE PARK GARDENS

Goodnestone Park, Nr Wingham, Canterbury, Kent CT3 1PL

The garden is approximately 14 acres. There is a woodland area with many fine trees, a large walled garden with a collection of old-fashioned roses, clematis and herbaceous plants, a new water feature has been installed in 2009. Jane Austen was a frequent visitor.
Location: MAP 4:N3, OS Ref. TR254 544. 8m Canterbury, 1½m E of B2046–A2 to Wingham Road, signposted from this road
Owner: Margaret, Lady FitzWalter **Contact:** Margaret, Lady FitzWalter
Tel/Fax: 01304 840107 **E-mail:** enquiries@goodnestoneparkgardens.co.uk
Website: www.goodnestoneparkgardens.co.uk
Open: Sun only 12noon–4pm from 19 Feb, Tues–Fri from 27 Mar–28 Sept 11am–5pm, Sun 12noon–5pm.Groups welcome any day with prior notice.
Admission: Adult £6, Child (6–16 yrs) £1, OAP £5.50, Family ticket (2+2) £13, Groups (20+) £5.50 out of opening hours £7.50.
Key facts: Suitable. WCs. Licensed. Partial, by arrangement.

CHILHAM CASTLE

Canterbury, Kent CT4 8DB

There has been a castle at the site of Chilham, on the edge of a wood, in the heart of Kent, for over eight centuries; perhaps thirteen or more. The house was built in 1616 on the site of the ancient castle and is now home to the Wheeler family.
Location: MAP 4:M3, OS Ref. TR065 525.
Owner: Stuart Wheeler
Tel: 01227 733100
E-mail: chilhamcastleinfo@gmail.com
Website: www.chilham-castle.co.uk
Open: Gardens: 2nd Tue every month in summer. House: Groups visits by appointment. (Visit website for up-to-date calendar of garden openings).
Admission: Please contact us by email or visit our website for further information.
Key facts: Partial. No coaches. On leads.

THE GRANGE

St Augustine's Road, Ramsgate, Kent CT11 9NY

Augustus Pugin built this house in 1843–4 to live in with his family. It was here that Pugin produced the designs for the interiors of the House of Lords and the Medieval Court but he reserved some of his finest and most characteristic flourishes for his own home.
Location: MAP 4:O2, OS Ref. TR3764
Owner/Contact: The Landmark Trust **Tel:** 01628 825925
E-mail: bookings@landmarktrust.org.uk **Website:** www.landmarktrust.org.uk
Open: Available for holidays. Parts are open to the public by appointment on Wednesday afternoons and 8 Open Days a year.
Admission: Free on Wednesday afternoons & Open Days and visits by appointment.
Key facts:

DANSON HOUSE

c/o Bexley Heritage Trust, Hall Place and Gardens, Bourne Road, Bexley, Kent DA5 1PQ

Completed in 1766, Danson was built for wealthy merchant Sir John Boyd. The house was designed to reflect its original purpose, that of a country house dedicated to entertainment. The sumptuous interior decoration tells stories that reveal the passion of Boyd for his wife and the love they shared.
Location: MAP 19:G8, OS Ref. TQ475 768. Signposted off the A2 and A221 Danson Park, Bexley, 5 minutes London-bound from M25 J/2.
Owner: Bexley Heritage Trust **Contact:** Miss Sarah Fosker
Tel: 020 8303 6699 **Fax:** 020 8304 6641
E-mail: info@dansonhouse.org.uk **Website:** www.dansonhouse.org.uk
Open: Please see website or contact us for up-to-date information.
Admission: Please see website or contact us for up-to-date information.
Key facts: Two. WCs. Licensed. By arrangement. Limited for coaches. For events and functions.

GROOMBRIDGE PLACE GARDENS

Groombridge Place, Groombridge, Tunbridge Wells, Kent TN3 9QG

Set in 200 acres, Groombridge features a series of magnificent, traditional walled gardens – set against the backdrop of a 17th century moated manor. Plus the ancient woodland of the "Enchanted Forest". Packed programme of special events throughout the year.
Location: MAP 4:J4, OS Ref. TQ534 375. Located on the B2110 just off the A264. 4m SW of Tunbridge Wells.
Owner: Groombridge Asset Management **Contact:** The Estate Office
Tel: 01892 861444 **Fax:** 01892 863996 **E-mail:** office@groombridge.co.uk
Website: www.groombridge.co.uk
Open: Apr–Oct, daily, 10am–5.30pm (or dusk if earlier). The house is not open to the public.
Admission: Please visit our website www.groombridge.co.uk for up to date admission prices. *Child under 3yrs Free.
Key facts: Film location. Wedding Ceremony Venue. Partial. WCs. By arrangement. Guide dogs only.

HALL PLACE

Hall Place & Gardens, Bourne Road, Bexley, Kent DA5 1PQ

A fine Grade I listed country house built in 1537 for Sir John Champneys, a wealthy merchant and former Lord Mayor of London. The house boasts a panelled Tudor Great Hall, minstrel's gallery, and various period rooms. The 17th century additions and improvements include a vaulted Long Gallery and splendid Great Chamber.
Location: MAP 19:G8, OS Ref. TQ502 743. On the A2 less than 5m from the M25/J2 (London bound).
Owner: Bexley Heritage Trust **Contact:** Mrs Janet Hearn-Gillham
Tel: 01322 526574 **Fax:** 01322 522921
E-mail: info@hallplace.org.uk **Website:** www.hallplace.org.uk
Open: Please see website or contact us for up-to-date information.
Admission: Free. Charge may apply on special event days. Prearranged guided tours (10+) available, please contact us for up-to-date prices.
Key facts: House, lift & WC. Licensed. By arrangement (10+). Guide dogs only.

HOLE PARK GARDENS

Rolvenden, Cranbrook, Kent TN17 4JA

A 15 acre garden with all year round interest, set in beautiful parkland with fine views. Trees, lawns and extensive yew hedges are a feature. Walled garden with mixed borders, pools and water garden. Natural garden with bulbs, azaleas, rhododendrons and flowering shrubs. Bluebell walk and autumn colours a speciality.
Location: MAP 4:L4, OS Ref. TQ830 325. 1m W of Rolvenden on B2086 Cranbrook road.
Owner: Edward Barham **Contact:** Edward Barham **Tel:** 01580 241344 / 241386
Fax: 01580 241882 **E-mail:** info@holepark.com **Website:** www.holepark.com
Open: 8 Apr–31 May. Daily. Open 11am–6pm. Jun–end Oct. Weds & Thurs. Oct 7, 14 & 21.
Admission: Adult £6, Child £1. Group visits with conducted tour of the gardens a speciality. Please contact us for details.
Key facts: WCs. Licensed. Licensed. By arrangement. Guide dogs only. €

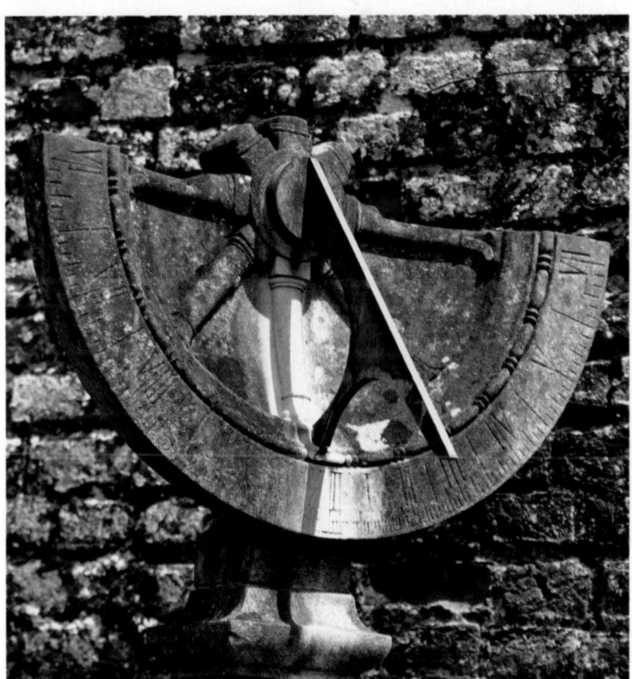
© Britainonview / David Sellman

Sundial at Penshurst Place

LULLINGSTONE CASTLE & WORLD GARDEN

Lullingstone, Eynsford, Kent DA4 0JA

Fine State rooms, family portraits and armour in beautiful grounds. The 15th century gatehouse was one of the first ever to be made of bricks. This is also the site for the World Garden of Plants and for Lullingstone's Parish Church of St Botolph.
Location: MAP 19:G9, OS Ref. TQ530 644. 1m S Eynsford W side of A225. 600yds S of Roman Villa.
Owner: Guy Hart Dyke Esq **Contact:** Guy Hart Dyke Esq **Tel:** 01322 862114
Fax: 01322 862115 **E-mail:** info@lullingstonecastle.co.uk
Website: www.lullingstonecastle.co.uk
Open: Apr–Sept: Fris, Sats, Suns & BHs 12 noon–5pm.
Admission: Adult £7, Child £4, OAP £6.50, Family £18; Groups (20+): £8 pp plus £40 for dedicated guide (Weds & Thurs).
Key facts: No interior photography. Wheelchairs available upon request. WCs. Teas/cakes available. Obligatory. By arrangement. Limited for coaches. School packs available. Guide dogs only.

NURSTEAD COURT

Nurstead Church Lane, Meopham, Nr Gravesend, Kent DA13 9AD

Nurstead Court is a Grade I listed manor house built in 1320 of timber-framed, crownposted construction, set in extensive gardens and parkland. The additional front part of the house was built in 1825. Licensed weddings are now held in the house with receptions and other functions in the garden marquee.
Location: MAP 4:K2. OS Ref. TQ642 685. Nurstead Church Lane is just off the A227 N of Meopham, 3m from Gravesend.
Owner: Mrs S Edmeades-Stearns **Contact:** Mrs S Edmeades-Stearns **Tel:** 01474 812368 **E-mail:** info@nursteadcourt.co.uk **Website:** www.nursteadcourt.co.uk
Open: Every Wed & Thur in Sept, Oct 5 and Oct 3 & 6, 2–5pm. All year round by arrangement.
Admission: Adult £5, Child £2.50, OAP/Student £4. Group (max 54): £4.
Key facts: Weddings & functions catered for. Licensed Obligatory, by arrangement. Limited for coaches. Guide dogs only.

QUEBEC HOUSE

Westerham, Kent TN16 1TD

Experience the intimacy of living in Quebec House, James Wolfe's boyhood home. Discover the glory of General Wolfe's greatest victory, explore the two sides of the conquest of Canada and reflect on the tragedy of General Wolfe's death. Enjoy the pretty garden, with new vegetable and herb beds.
Location: MAP 19:F10, OS Ref. TQ449 541. North side of A25, facing junction with B2026 Edenbridge road, M25 exit 5 or 6.
Owner: National Trust **Contact:** Property Operations Manager
Tel: 01732 868381 (Chartwell office) **E-mail:** quebechouse@nationaltrust.org.uk
Website: www.nationaltrust.org.uk/quebechouse
Open: 10 Mar–28 Oct: House; Wed–Sun, 1pm–5pm. Garden & Exhibition; Wed–Sun, 12pm–5pm. 10 Nov–23 Dec: House, Sat & Sun, 1pm–4pm.
Admission: Adult £5, Child £2, Family (2+3) £12. Group: Adult £4, child £1.50. Gift Aid.
Key facts: Partial. WCs. By arrangement. In grounds.

RIVERHILL HIMALAYAN GARDENS

Sevenoaks, Kent TN15 0RR

Historic hillside gardens, privately owned by the Rogers family since 1840. Extensive views across the Weald of Kent. Spectacular rhododendrons, azaleas and specimen trees. Bluebell Walk, Hedge Maze, Adventure Playground and Den Building Trail. Shop & Cafe serving light lunches, teas and coffee.
Location: MAP 4:J3, OS Ref. TQ541 522. 2m S of Sevenoaks on A225.
Owner: The Rogers Family
Contact: Mrs Rogers
Tel: 01732 459777
E-mail: sarah@riverhillgardens.co.uk
Website: www.riverhillgardens.co.uk
Open: 18 Mar–9 Sept 2012, Weds–Sun & Bank Holiday Mons, 10.30am–5pm
Admission: Adult £6.50, Child £4.50, Family £18.50, Seniors £5.90. Adult Pre-booked Groups (20+) House & Garden £9.80, Garden only £5.90
Key facts: Partial. By arrangement. Limited for coaches. Guide dogs only.

TONBRIDGE CASTLE

Castle Street, Tonbridge, Kent TN9 1BG

Standing in landscaped gardens overlooking the River Medway, Tonbridge Castle's mighty motte and bailey Gatehouse is among the finest in England. Experience the sights and sounds of the 13th century as we bring them to life with interactive displays, dramatic special effects and personal audio tour.

Location: MAP 19:H11, OS Ref. TQ588 466. 300 yds NW of the Medway Bridge at town centre.

Owner: Tonbridge & Malling Borough Council **Contact:** The Administrator

Tel: 01732 770929 **Website:** www.tonbridgecastle.org

Open: All year: Mon–Sat, 9am–4pm. Suns & BHs, 10.30am–4pm.

Admission: Gatehouse: Adult £6.80, Child/Conc. £3.90. Family £19.50 - max 2 adults. (2011 prices). Admission includes audio tour.

Key facts: No coaches.

WILLESBOROUGH WINDMILL

Mill Lane, Willesborough, Ashford, Kent TN24 0QG

Smock mill built in 1869, fully working. Civil Wedding Licence. Light refreshments available in Barn Cafe. Small souvenir shop.

Location: MAP 4:M4, OS Ref. TR031 421. Off A292 close to M20/J10. At E end of Ashford.

Tel: 01233 661866

E-mail: info@willesboroughwindmill.co.uk

Website: www.willesboroughwindmill.co.uk

Open: Apr–end Sept; Sats, Suns & BH Mons, also Weds in Jul & Aug, 2–5pm.

Admission: Adult £3, Conc. £1.50, Children (5-16yrs) £1.50, Family ticket £7.

Key facts:

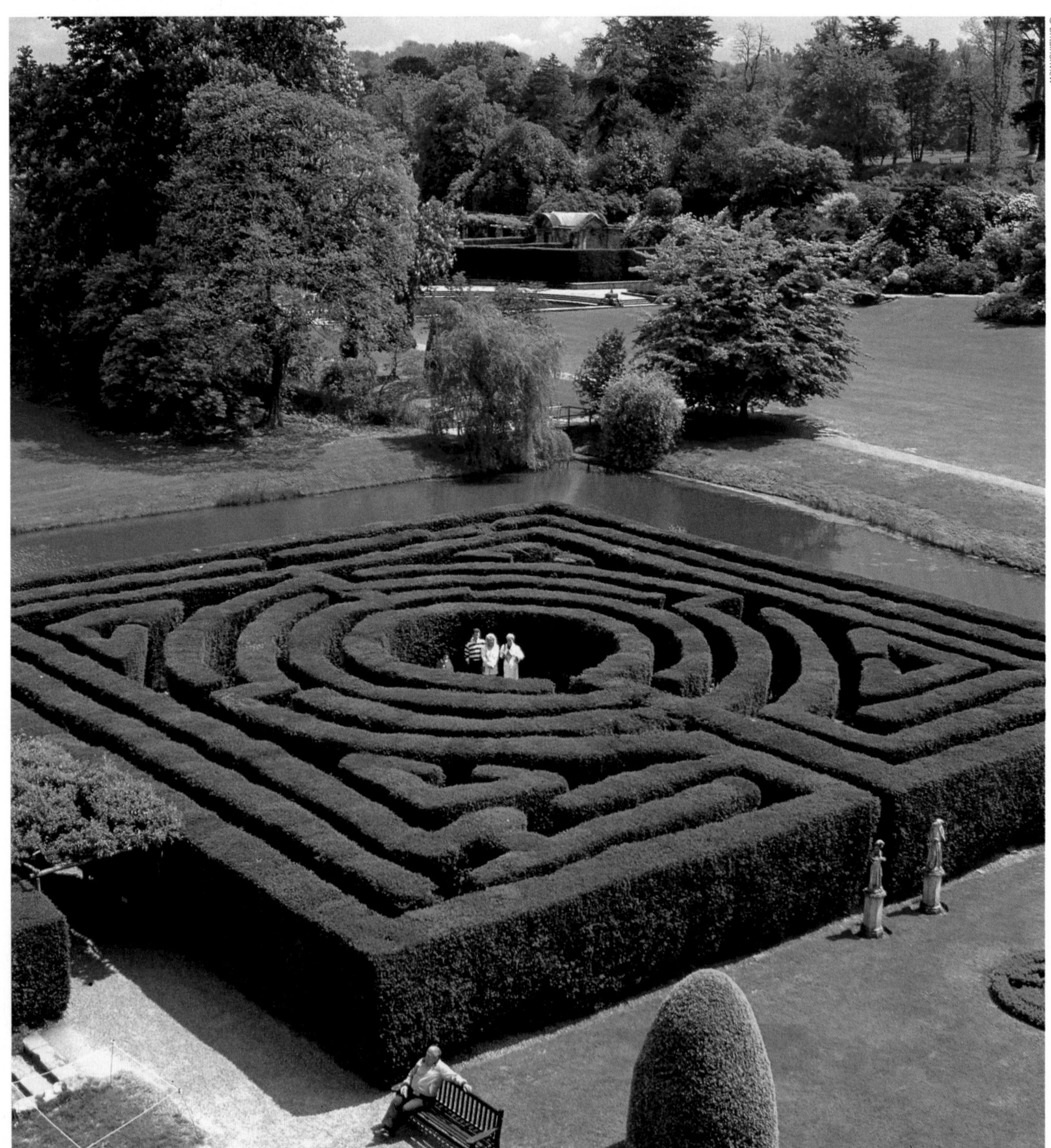

The maze at Hever Castle

ARDINGTON HOUSE

www.ardingtonhouse.com

VISITOR INFORMATION

Owner
The Baring Family

Address
Ardington House
Wantage
Oxfordshire
OX12 8QA

Location
MAP 3:D1
OS Ref. SU432 883
12m S of Oxford, 12m N of Newbury, 2½m E of Wantage.

Contact
Nigel Baring
Tel: 01235 821566
Fax: 01235 821151
E-mail: info@ardingtonhouse.com

Opening Times
6 August–14 September, 2012, Mon–Fri, 11–2pm and Bank Holiday Mondays.

Admission
House & Gardens

Adult	£5.00
Child	Free

Often described as Oxfords Baroque masterpiece, Ardington House, the private home of the Baring family, is an oasis of tranquility.

Just a few miles south of Oxford stands the tranquil and entirely beautiful Ardington House. Surrounded by manicured lawns, terraced gardens, peaceful paddocks, parkland and its own romantic temple on an island, this Baroque house is the private home of the Barings.

You will find it in the attractive village of Ardington, close to the Ridgeway on the edge of the Berkshire Downs. Built by the Strong brothers in 1720 with typical Georgian symmetry, the House is also famous for its Imperial Staircase. Leading from the Hall, the staircase is considered by experts to be one of the finest examples in Britain.

Away from the crowds and the hustle of the workplace Ardington House provides a private and secluded setting. The calm, exclusive use environment allows for weddings, offsite board meetings, conference and workshops utilising the stylish, splendid complimentary marquee, gardens and grounds. There is a heated outdoor swimming pool, tennis court, croquet lawn and trout river. Close by is the ancient Ridgeway Path, a popular place for walking.

Ardington House is licensed to hold Civil Wedding ceremonies. Poet Laureate Sir John Betjeman wrote of the homeliness and warmth of Ardington House, and the rooms have seen many special occasions and important visitors in the past with this tradition being continued.

The astonishing mixture of history, warmth and style you'll find at Ardington truly does place it in a class of its own.

KEY FACTS

- Weddings, Civil Ceremonies, Private Parties, Conferences, Films, Photography, Product Launches.
- Partial. WCs.
- Licensed.
- By members of the family.
- Free.
- Guide dogs only.

Conference/Function

ROOM	Size	Max Cap
Imperial Hall		80
Imperial Hall– U shape		30
Room 3		40
Oak Room– Theatre Style		40
Oak Room– U shape		20
Oak Room– Cabaret		30
Music Room– Theatre Style		40
Music Room– U shape		20
Music Room– Cabaret		30

VISITOR INFORMATION

Owner
The Duke of Marlborough

Address
Blenheim Palace
Woodstock
OX20 1PX

Location
MAP 7:A11
OS Ref. SP441 161
From London, M40, A44 (1½ hrs), 8m NW of Oxford. London 63m Birmingham 54m.
Bus: No.S3 from Oxford Station, Gloucester Green & Cornmarket.
Coach: From London (Victoria) to Oxford.
Rail: Oxford Station.
Air: Heathrow 60m. Birmingham 50m.

Contact
Operations Director
Tel: 01993 811091
Fax: 01993 810570
E-mail: operations@blenheimpalace.com

Opening Times
Sat 11 February–Sun 4 November 2012, Daily.
Wed 7 November–Sun 14 December 2012, Wed–Sun.

Palace
10.30am–5.30pm
(last admission 4.45pm).

Palace and Formal Gardens
10.00am–5.30pm
(last admission 4.45pm).

Park
9am–6pm or dusk during autumn and winter months.

Except Christmas Day, all areas to be vacated by 6pm.
Open daily except Mondays & Tuesdays from 7 November.
Main Season for Groups 15+ 11–19 February & 31 March–4 November 2012
Low Season for Groups 20 Feb–30 March & 7 November–14 December.

Admission
Palace, Garden & Park
11 Feb – 14 Dec

Adult	£20.00
Concessions	£15.50
Child*	£11.00
Family	£52.00

Park & Gardens

Adult	£11.50
Concessions	£8.50
Child*	£ 6.00
Family	£30.00

* (5-16 yrs)

Discounts on Group Bookings (15+) available by Contacting the Groups Coordinator on 01993 811091 email operations@blenheimpalace.com
Private tours by appointment only, prices on request

BLENHEIM PALACE

www.blenheimpalace.com

Blenheim Palace is home to the 11th Duke and Duchess of Marlborough and the birthplace of Sir Winston Churchill.

Surrounded by over 2,000 acres of 'Capability' Brown landscaped parkland and the great lake, the Palace was created a World Heritage Site in 1987.

Conceived in 1705 by Sir John Vanbrugh, Blenheim Palace is a masterpiece of English Baroque architecture steeped in inspirational history. Visit the room where Sir Winston Churchill was born before taking a guided tour of the gilded State Rooms graced with priceless portraits, exquisite porcelain and the magnificent tapestries which were commissioned by John Churchill, 1st Duke of Marlborough, charting his famous victory over the French during in the Wars of the Spanish Succession.

A permanent visitor experience 'Blenheim Palace: The Untold Story' is open inside the Palace bringing to life enticing tales of the last 300 years, seen through the eyes of the household staff. Visitors can delve deeper in to the lives of the illustrious Marlborough family in the information rooms with touch screens and audio/visual units.

The Palace is surrounded by award winning Formal Gardens including the tranquil Secret Garden, the majestic Water Terraces, the fragrant Rose Garden, the Grand Cascade and Lake. An audio garden tour is available to hire. The Pleasure Gardens can be reached by a miniature train, which includes the Marlborough Maze, the Butterfly House and Adventure Playground, making it a great area for young children.

KEY FACTS

- Filming, product launches, activity days. No photography inside the palace.
- Four shops.
- Corporate Hospitality includes weddings, receptions, dinners, meetings and corporate events.
- Suitable. WCs.
- Licensed.
- Licensed.
- Guided tours except Sundays, BHs and extremely busy days.
- Unlimited for cars and coaches.
- Sandford Award holder since 1982. Teacher pre-visits welcome.
- Guide dogs only.

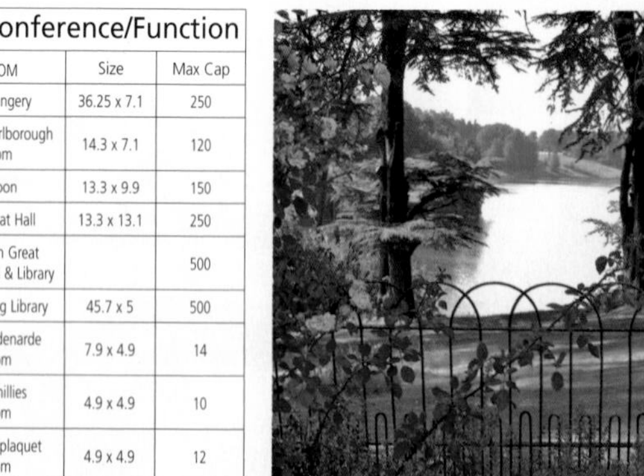

Conference/Function

ROOM	Size	Max Cap
Orangery	36.25 x 7.1	250
Marlborough Room	14.3 x 7.1	120
Saloon	13.3 x 9.9	150
Great Hall	13.3 x 13.1	250
with Great Hall & Library		500
Long Library	45.7 x 5	500
Oudenarde Room	7.9 x 4.9	14
Ramillies Room	4.9 x 4.9	10
Malplaquet Room	4.9 x 4.9	12
Spencer Churchill Room	10 x 8	70
Courtyard	19.4 x 10.7	180

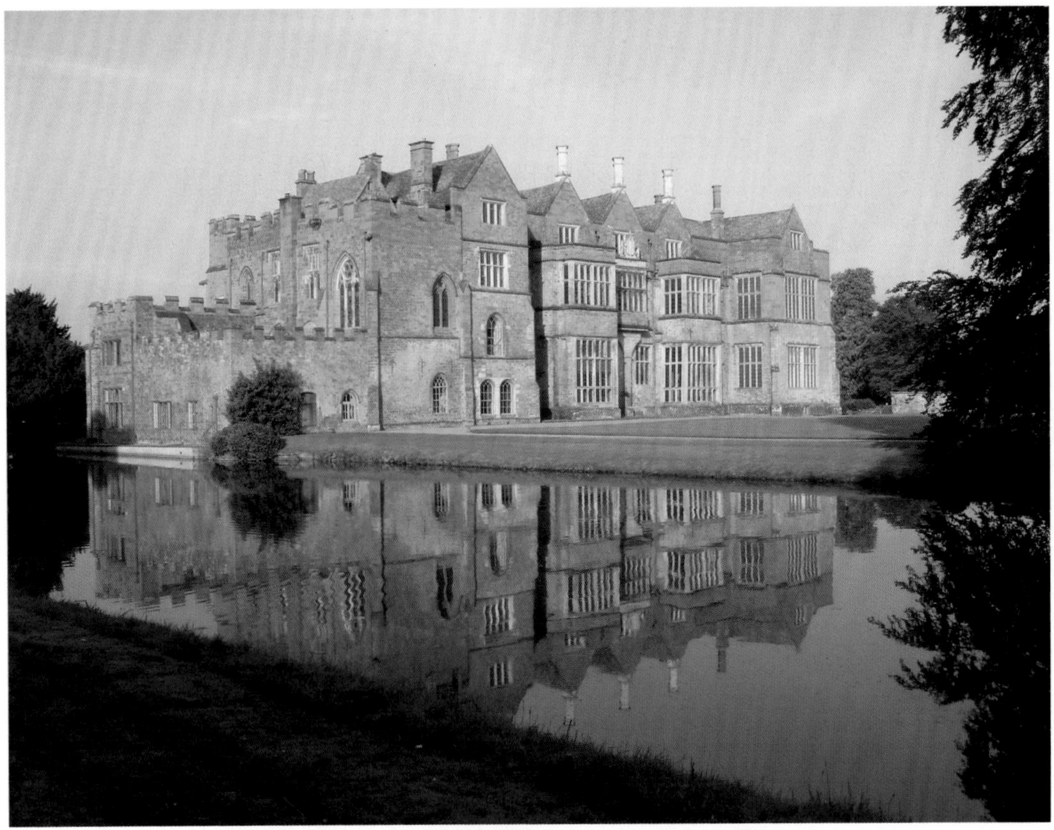

BROUGHTON CASTLE

www.broughtoncastle.com

"About the most beautiful castle in all England...for sheer loveliness of the combination of water, woods and picturesque buildings." Sir Charles Oman (1898).

Broughton Castle is essentially a family home lived in by Lord and Lady Saye & Sele and their family. The original medieval Manor House, of which much remains today, was built in about 1300 by Sir John de Broughton. It stands on an island site surrounded by a 3 acre moat. The Castle was greatly enlarged between 1550 and 1600, at which time it was embellished with magnificent plaster ceilings, splendid panelling and fine fireplaces. In the 17th century William, 8th Lord Saye & Sele, played a leading role in national affairs. He opposed Charles I's efforts to rule without Parliament and Broughton became a secret meeting place for the King's opponents. During the Civil War William raised a regiment and he and his four sons all fought at the nearby Battle of Edgehill. After the battle the Castle was besieged and captured. Arms and armour from the Civil War and other periods are displayed in the Great Hall. Visitors may also see the gatehouse, gardens and park together with the nearby 14th century Church of St Mary, in which there are many family tombs, memorials and hatchments.

Gardens

The garden area consists of mixed herbaceous and shrub borders containing many old roses. In addition, there is a formal walled garden with beds of roses surrounded by box hedging and lined by more mixed borders.

KEY FACTS

- Photography allowed in house.
-
- Partial.
- Teas on Open Days. Groups may book morning coffee, light lunches and afternoon teas.
- Available for booked groups.
- Limited.
-
- Guide dogs only in house. On leads in grounds.
- Open all year for groups.

VISITOR INFORMATION

Owner

Lord Saye & Sele

Address

Broughton Castle
Broughton
Nr Banbury
Oxfordshire OX15 5EB

Location

MAP 7:A10
OS Ref. SP418 382

Broughton Castle is 2½m SW of Banbury Cross on the B4035, Shipston-on-Stour – Banbury Road. Easily accessible from Stratford-on-Avon, Warwick, Oxford, Burford and the Cotswolds. M40/J11.

Rail: From London/ Birmingham to Banbury.

Contact

Manager, Mrs James
Tel: 01295 276070
E-mail: info@broughtoncastle.com

Opening Times

Summer

Easter Sun & Mon, 1 May–15 September Weds, Suns & BH Mons, 2–5pm.

Also Thurs in July and August, 2–5pm.

Last admission – 4.30pm.

Open all year on any day, at any time, for group bookings – by appointment only.

Admission

Adult	£8.00
Child (5–15yrs)	£4.00
OAP/Student	£7.00
Garden only	£4.00
Groups	
Adult	£8.00
OAP	£8.00
Child (5–10yrs)	£4.00
Child (11–15yrs)	£5.00
Garden only	£5.00

(There is a minimum charge for groups – please contact the manager for details.)

VISITOR INFORMATION

Owner
Mrs Francis Grant

Address
Kingston Bagpuize House
Abingdon
Oxfordshire OX13 5AX

Location
MAP 7:A12
OS Ref. SU408 981
In Kingston Bagpuize village, off A415 Abingdon to Witney road S of A415/A420 intersection. Abingdon 5m, Oxford 9m.

Contact
Virginia Grant
Visitor Enquiries:
01865 820259
E-mail: virginia@kbhadmin.com
Corporate and Wedding Enquiries:
see www.kingstonbagpuizehouse.com
Tel: 01865 820217
E-mail: info@kbhhospitality.com

Opening Times
Gardens Only (Snowdrops)
February, Sunday 5, 12, 19, 26, 2.00–5.00pm.
House & Gardens
March, Sunday 18 & Monday 19, 2.00–5.00pm.
April, Sunday 15 & Monday 16, 2.00–5.00pm.
13 May–3 July, Sunday, Monday & Tuesday, 2.00–5.00pm.
9–25 September, Sunday, Monday & Tuesday, 2.00–5.00pm.
(All visitors to the House enjoy a free flow system with last admission at 4.00pm).
This information may be subject to change, please visit website www.kingstonbagpuizehouse.com or call 01865 820259 to confirm.

Admission
House and Garden:

Adult	£7.50
Child (4–15)	£4.50
Family (2+3)	£20

Groups 20+ by appointment only
Gardens:

Adult	£5
Child (4–15)	£3

Season tickets available
Open days may be subject to change.
Please call 01865 820259 to confirm before travelling.

Special events
see website.

KINGSTON BAGPUIZE HOUSE

www.kingstonbagpuizehouse.com

A family home, this beautiful house is thought to have originally been built in the 1660s.

The home was remodelled for the Blandy family in the early 1700s in red brick with stone facings. There is French and English furniture in the elegant panelled rooms and the entrance hall is dominated by a handsome cantilevered staircase.

The house is surrounded by mature gardens and parkland notable for the important collection of rare cultivated plants and trees, planted to give year round interest. The display of snowdrops during February is followed by Magnolias and other spring shrubs & perennials in March and April, Wisteria, old garden and specie roses in May and June, herbaceous border and summer flowering trees in July and August, and autumn colour and rose hips in September. A raised terrace walk leads to an 18th century panelled pavilion which looks over the house and gardens. The view of main east front of the house is framed by Wellingtonia trees planted around 1860.

Following the recent restoration of the main gardens together with two adjacent copses the restoration of the walled garden and orchard, now in its 2nd year, continues and when complete will display the Silk Road Hybrid roses as The Mattock Rose Garden.

Licensed for civil ceremonies the new Temple in the woodland garden permits outdoor ceremonies in addition to those in the Drawing Room. The venue is also available for wedding receptions, special events, corporate functions, product launches and filming. There are facilities for small conferences.

KEY FACTS

- No photography in house on open days.
- WCs.
- Free flow for house opening, guided tours for groups only.
- Guide dogs only.

STONOR

www.stonor.com

Stonor – a story of continuity. The same family have lived here for 850 years and have always been Roman Catholics.

Stonor has been home to the Stonor family for over 850 years and is now home to The Lord and Lady Camoys. The history of the house inevitably contributes to the atmosphere, unpretentious yet grand. A façade of warm brick with Georgian windows conceals older buildings dating back to the 12th century and a 14th century Catholic Chapel sits on the south east corner. Stonor nestles in a fold of the beautiful wooded Chiltern Hills with breathtaking views of the park where Fallow deer have grazed since medieval times.

It contains many family portraits, old Master drawings and paintings, Renaissance bronzes and tapestries, along with rare furniture and a collection of modern ceramics.

St Edmund Campion sought refuge at Stonor during the Reformation and printed his famous pamphlet 'Ten Reasons', in secret, on a press installed in the roof space. A small exhibition celebrates his life and work.

Mass has been celebrated since medieval times in the Chapel. The stained glass windows were executed by Francis Eginton: installed in 1797. The Chapel decoration is that of the earliest Gothic Revival, begun in 1759, with additions in 1797. The Stations of the Cross were carved by Jozef Janas, a Polish prisoner of war in World War II and given to Stonor by Graham Greene in 1956.

The gardens offer outstanding views of the Park and valley and are especially beautiful in May and June, containing fine displays of daffodils, irises, peonies, lavenders and roses along with other herbaceous plants and shrubs.

KEY FACTS

- No photography in house. Dogs on leads in the park only.
-
-
- Partial.
-
- By arrangement, for 20–60.
- 100yds away.
-
- Guide dogs only.
-

VISITOR INFORMATION

Owner
Lord & Lady Camoys

Address
Stonor Park
Henley-On-Thames
Oxfordshire
RG9 6HF

Location
MAP 3:E1
OS Ref. SU743 893.
1 hr from London, M4/J8/9. A4130 to Henley-on-Thames. On B480 NW of Henley. A4130/B480 to Stonor.
Taxi: Henley on Thames 5m
Rail: Henley on Thames 5m, or Reading 9m
Air: Heathrow

Contact
Sue Gill
Tel: 01491 638587
E-mail: administrator@stonor.com

Opening Times
1 April–mid September: Sundays and BH Mondays. Also Wednesdays, July and August only.
Gardens
1–5.30pm
House, Tea Room & Giftshop
2–5.30pm Last Entry 4.30pm
Private Groups (20+): by arrangement Tuesday–Thursday, April–September.

Admission
House, Gardens and Chapel

Adults	£8.00
First Child (5–16)	£4.00

2 or more Children (5–16) Free, Under 5s Free

Gardens and Chapel

Adults	£4.00
First Child (5–16)	£2.00

2 or more Children (5–16) Free, Under 5s Free

Groups

Adults	£9.00
Child (5–16)	£4.50

Includes guided tour.

Special events
June 3
VW Owners' Rally.
August 24–27
Chilterns Craft Fair.

© NT / Paul Watson

© David Dixon

BUSCOT PARK

BUSCOT, FARINGDON, OXFORDSHIRE SN7 8BU

www.buscotpark.com

Family home of Lord Faringdon who cares for the property on behalf of the National Trust, together with the family art collection, the Faringdon Collection, displayed in the House. Consequently Buscot Park remains intimate and idiosyncratic and very much a family home, allowing each generation to refresh and enliven the property for the enjoyment of both family and visitors. The Collection contains old master paintings and contemporary works in various media, as well as fine furniture and decorative art. The Pleasure Grounds include the famous water garden designed by Harold Peto in 1904.

Location: OS Ref. SU239 973. Between Faringdon and Lechlade on A417.

Owner: National Trust (Administered on their behalf by Lord Faringdon)

Contact: The Estate Office

Tel: 01367 240932 **Fax:** 01367 241794 **E-mail:** estbuscot@aol.com

Open: House, Grounds and Tearoom: 1 Apr–30 Sept: Wed, Thu, Fri, 2–6pm (last entry to house 5pm). Also open BH's and the following weekends; 7/8, 21/22, Apr; 5/6, 12/13, 26/27 May; 9/10, 23/24 Jun; 14/15, 28/29 Jul; 11/12, 25/26 Aug; 8/9, 22/23 Sept. Grounds only: Mon & Tue, 2-6pm. Please note: The House, Grounds and Tearoom are closed for the Queen's Diamond Jubilee 2,3,4,5 June.

Admission: House & Grounds: Adult £8, Child £4. Grounds only: Adult £5, Child £2.50. NT members Free. Groups: Advance booking essential. Disabled visitors may book a single seater PMV in advance for use in the grounds.

Key facts: No photography in house. Regrettably Buscot House is unsuitable for any wheeled vehicle entry. Frail visitors may need help with the steep flight of 14 steps to the front door. Occasional plant sales. Partial. WCs. By arrangement. Ample for cars, 2 coach spaces. Guide dogs only.

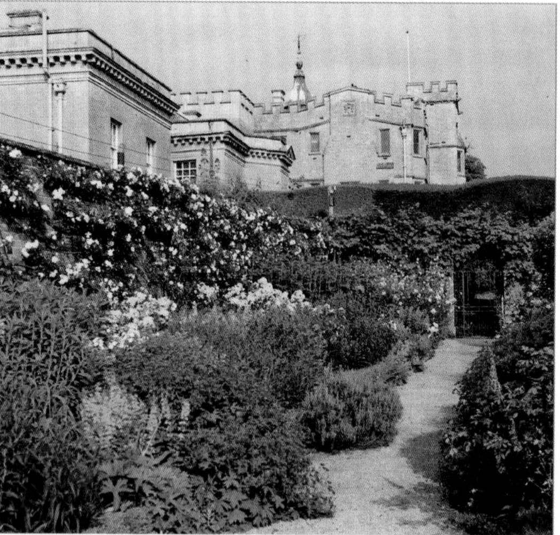

ROUSHAM HOUSE

NR STEEPLE ASTON, BICESTER, OXFORDSHIRE OX25 4QX

www.rousham.org

Rousham represents the first stage of English landscape design and remains almost as William Kent (1685–1748) left it. One of the few gardens of this date to have escaped alteration. Includes Venus' Vale, Townesend's Building, seven-arched Praeneste, the Temple of the Mill and a sham ruin known as the 'Eyecatcher'. The house was built in 1635 by Sir Robert Dormer. Dont miss the walled garden with their herbaceous borders, small parterre, pigeon house and espalier apple trees. A fine herd of Longhorn cattle are to be seen in the park. Rousham is uncommercial and unspoilt with no tea room and no shop. Bring a picnic, wear comfortable shoes and it is yours for the day. Excellent location for fashion, advertising, photography etc.

Location: MAP 7:A10, OS Ref. SP477 242. E of A4260, 12m N of Oxford, S of B4030, 7m W of Bicester.

Owner/Contact: Charles Cottrell-Dormer Esq

Tel: 01869 347110 07860 360407 **E-mail:** ccd@rousham.org

Open: Garden: All year: daily, 10am–4.30pm (last adm). House: Pre-booked groups, May–Sept. (Mon–Thur).

Admission: Garden: £5. No children under 15yrs.

Key facts: Partial. Rousham is an ideal Oxfordshire venue for wedding receptions, offering a site to pitch a marquee together with acres of landscape and formal gardens that can be used for photographs and pre-reception drinks. We have also held some car rallies, The Bentley, MG and Aston Martin owners clubs have all held rallies at Rousham. These events are held in the park, immediately next to the house. Open access to the house and garden can be arranged.

GREYS COURT

Rotherfield Greys, Henley-On-Thames Oxfordshire RG9 4PG

www.nationaltrust.org.uk

This enchanting and intimate family home in a sixteenth century mansion, is set amidst a patchwork of colourful walled gardens, courtyard buildings including a Tudor donkey wheel and medieval walls and towers. Beyond lies an estate and beech woodlands set in the rolling Chiltern Hills.

Location: MAP 3:E1 OS Ref. SU725 834. 3m W of Henley-on-Thames, E of B481.

Owner: National Trust **Contact:** The Property Operations Manager

Tel: 01494 755564 01491 628529 **E-mail:** greyscourt@nationaltrust.org.uk

Open: House: 21 Mar–28 Oct, Wed–Sun, 1–5pm. Garden, Shop & Tearoom: 21 Mar–28 Oct, Wed–Sun, 11am–5pm. 1 Dec-16 Dec, Sat-Sun, 1–4pm. House & Shop. Open BH Mons, closed Good Fri.

Admission: House & Garden: Adult £8.20, Child £5.40, Family £21.90. Garden Only: Adult £6, Child £3.20, Family £15.30. Groups must book in advance. Free to NT members. Includes a voluntary donation but visitors can choose to pay the standard prices displayed at the property and on the website.

Key facts: Partial. By arrangement. Limited for coaches.

MILTON MANOR HOUSE

Milton, Abingdon, Oxfordshire OX14 4EN

www.miltonmanorhouse.com

Dreamily beautiful mellow brick house, traditionally designed by Inigo Jones. Celebrated Gothick library and Catholic chapel. Lived in by the family; pleasant relaxed and informal atmosphere. Park with fine old trees, stables, walled garden and woodland walk. Picnickers welcome. Free Parking, refreshments and pony rides usually available.

Location: MAP 3:D1, OS Ref. SU485 924. Just off A34, village and house signposted, 9m S of Oxford, 15m N of Newbury. 3m from Abingdon and Didcot.

Owner: Anthony Mockler-Barrett Esq **Contact:** Alex Brakespear

Tel: 01235 831287 **Fax:** 01235 862321

Open: Easter Sun and BH Mon; Sun 6 May & BH Mon; Sun 20 May–Sun 3 Jun and Sun 19 Aug–Sun 2 Sept. Guided tours of house: 2pm, 3pm & 4pm. For weddings/events etc. please contact the Administrator. Groups by arrangement throughout the year.

Admission: House & Gardens: Adult £7.50, Child (under 14) £2.50. Garden & Grounds only: Adult £4, Child (under 14) £1.

Key facts: Grounds. Obligatory. Free. Guide dogs only.

MAPLEDURHAM HOUSE

Mapledurham, Reading RG4 7TR

www.mapledurham.co.uk

Late 16th century Elizabethan home of the Blount family. Original plaster ceilings, great oak staircase, fine collection of paintings and a private chapel in Strawberry Hill Gothick added in 1797. 15th century watermill fully restored producing flour, semolina and bran.

Location: MAP 3:E3, OS Ref. SU670 767. N of River Thames. 4m NW of Reading, 1½ m W of A4074.

Owner: The Mapledurham Trust

Contact: Mrs Lola Andrews

Tel: 0118 9723350

Fax: 0118 9724016

E-mail: enquiries@mapledurham.co.uk

Open: Easter–Sept: Sats, Suns & BHs, 2–5.30pm. Last admission 5pm. Midweek parties by arrangement only. Also Sunday afternoons in Oct.

Admission: Please call 01189 723350 for details. Mapledurham Trust reserves the right to alter or amend opening times or prices without prior notification.

Key facts: Partial.

MAPLEDURHAM WATERMILL

Mapledurham, Reading RG4 7TR

www.mapledurhamwatermill.co.uk

The last working watermill on the Thames still producing flour. It is a 600-year-old estate mill, powered by a wooden undershot waterwheel with parts of the original wooden structure still surviving inside the building. Sensitively repaired, visitors can see the milling process using French burr millstones.

Location: MAP 3:E3, OS Ref. SU670 767. N of River Thames. 4m NW of Reading, 1½ m W of A4074.

Owner: The Mapledurham Trust

Contact: Mrs Lola Andrews

Tel: 01189 723350

Fax: 01189 724016

E-mail: enquiries@mapledurham.co.uk

Open: Easter–Sept Sats & Suns B BH's 2–5.30pm. Midweek parties by arrangement only. Sun afternoons in Oct.

Admission: Please call 01189 723350 for details.

Key facts: Partial. WCs. By arrangement. In grounds.

26A EAST ST HELEN STREET

Abingdon, Oxfordshire

One of best preserved examples of a 15th century dwelling in the area. Originally a Merchant's Hall House with later alterations, features include a remarkable domestic wall painting, an early oak ceiling, traceried windows and fireplaces.

Location: MAP 7:A12, OS Ref. SU497 969.
Owner: Oxford Preservation Trust
Contact: Mrs Debbie Dance
Tel: 01865 242918
E-mail: info@oxfordpreservation.org.uk
Website: www.oxfordpreservation.org.uk
Open: By prior appointment.
Admission: Free.

DITCHLEY PARK

Enstone, Oxfordshire OX7 4ER

The most important house by James Gibbs, with magnificent interiors by William Kent and Henry Flitcroft. For three centuries the home of the Lee family, restored in the 1930s by Ronald and Nancy (Lancaster) Tree, it was frequently used at weekends by Sir Winston Churchill during World War II.

Location: MAP 7:A11, OS Ref. SP391 214. 2m NE from Charlbury. 13 miles NW of Oxford – 4 miles on from Woodstock (Blenheim Palace).
Owner: Ditchley Foundation
Contact: Brigadier Christopher Galloway
Tel: 01608 677346
Website: www.ditchley.co.uk
Open: Visits only by prior arrangement with the Bursar, weekdays preferred.
Admission: £7.50 per person (minimum charge £60).
Key facts:

WATERPERRY GARDENS

Waterperry, Nr Wheatley, Oxfordshire OX33 1JZ

Waterperry Gardens – eight acres of beautifully landscaped ornamental gardens, a quality plant centre housed in our walled garden, Gallery, Gift Barn, Garden Shop, Museum of Rural Life and Teashop offering home-baked lunches and some of the best cakes in the county! Groups and coach parties welcome by appointment.

Location: MAP 7:B12, OS Ref. SP610 068.
Tel: 01844 339226
Fax: 01844 339883
E-mail: office@waterperrygardens.co.uk
Website: www.waterperrygardens.co.uk
Open: All year except Christmas and New Year and from 19–22 Jul 2012. Low season 10am–5pm. High season 10am–5.30pm.
Admission: Jan–17 Feb Adults £4.30. 18 Feb–Oct Adults £6.30. Nov–Dec Adults £4.50. Children aged 16 and under free all year.
Key facts: WCs. Licensed. Licensed. By arrangement. Limited for coaches. Guide dogs only. (On leads.)

Britain's Brilliant Heritage
Brought To Life
To find out more visit our website
www.hudsonsheritage.com
HUDSONS
HERITAGE

Gardens at Rousham House

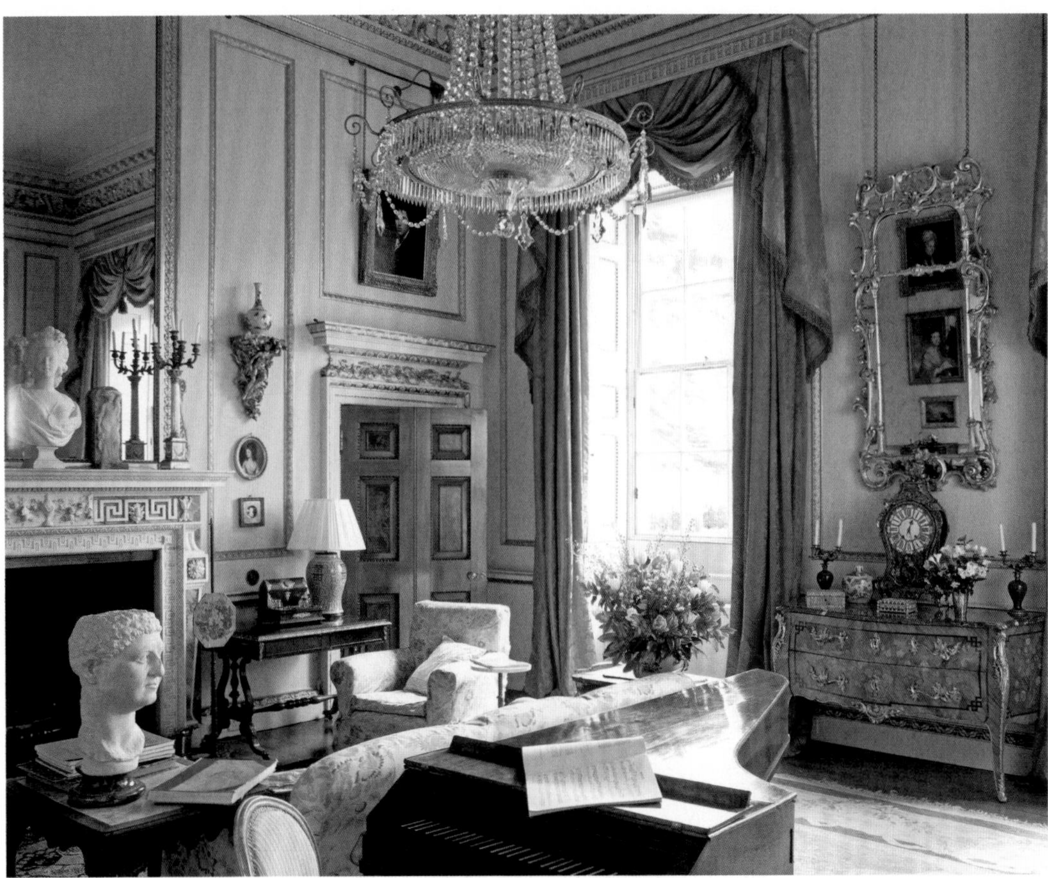

© NTPL / Bill Batten

CLANDON PARK & HATCHLANDS PARK

www.nationaltrust.org.uk/clandonpark

Clandon Park & Hatchlands Park, set amidst beautiful grounds, are two of England's most outstanding country houses.

Clandon Park & Hatchlands Park, built during the 18th century, are set amidst beautiful grounds. They are two of England's most outstanding country houses, only five minutes' drive apart.

Clandon Park is a Palladian Mansion, built c1730 for the Onslow family and notable for its magnificent Marble Hall. The Onslows have been active in political history, being the only family to have produced three Speakers of the House of Commons. The 4th Earl of Onslow transported Hinemihi, the Maori meeting house in Clandon's garden, from New Zealand as a reminder of his time as Governor in the 1890s. There is also an intimate sunken Dutch garden and a stunning bulb field. Displayed inside the house is a superb collection of 18th century furniture, textiles and porcelain.

Hatchlands Park was built in 1756 for Admiral Boscawen, hero of the Battle of Louisburg. The rooms are hung with the Cobbe Collection of Old Master paintings and portraits and also feature the Cobbe Collection of keyboard instruments, the world's largest group of early keyboard instruments owned or played by famous composers such as Purcell, JC Bach, Mozart, Liszt, Chopin, Mahler and Elgar. Hatchlands is set in a beautiful 430-acre Repton park, with a variety of way-marked walks offering vistas of open parkland and idyllic views. The woodlands are a haven for wildlife and there is a stunning Bluebell wood in May. There are frequent concerts based on the instruments in the collection (The Cobbe Collection Trust, 01483 211474, www.cobbecollection.co.uk).

KEY FACTS

- No Photography.
- For Clandon weddings and receptions tel: 01483 222502.
- Hatchlands Thur & Clandon – by arrangement.
- Limited for coaches.
- Guide dogs only.
- Clandon only.

© NTPL / John Miller

© NTPL / John Miller

VISITOR INFORMATION

Owner
National Trust

Address
Clandon Park & Hatchlands Park
East Clandon
Guildford
Surrey GU4 7RT

Location
MAP 19:A11

Clandon

OS Ref. TQ042 512.

At West Clandon on the A247, 3m E of Guildford

Rail: Clandon BR 1m.

Hatchlands

OS Ref. TQ063 516.

E of East Clandon on the A246 Guildford–Leatherhead road.

Rail: Clandon BR 2½m, Horsley 3m.

Contact
The Property Manager
Tel: 01483222482
Fax: 01483 223176
E-mail: hatchlands@nationaltrust.org.uk

Opening Times
Clandon – House

11 March–4 November Tues–Thur, Suns

November 11, 18 event days

30 July-27 August- open Mondays

Open BH Mons, Good Fri & Easter Sat 11am–5pm.

Clandon Garden

As house. 11am–5pm.

Surrey Infantry Museum

As house 11am–5pm.

Hatchlands – House

1 April–31 October Tue–Thur, Suns & BH Mon, Plus Fris in August.2–5.30pm.

Hatchlands Park Walks

1 April–31 October Daily 11am–6pm.

Admission

Clandon	
House/Grounds	£8.60
Child	£4.20
Family	£23.10
Pre-booked Groups Adult	£7.20
Hatchlands	
House/Grounds	£6
Child	£3.60
Family	£18.90
Park Walks only	£4.00
Child	£2.00
Pre-booked Groups Adult	£5.95
Combined ticket	
Adult	£12.20
Child	£6.10
Family	£35.10

*includes a voluntary donation but visitors can choose to pay the standard prices displayed at the property and on the website.

Conference/Function

ROOM	Size	Max Cap
Marble Hall Clandon Pk	40' x 40'	160 seated 200 standing

VISITOR INFORMATION

Owner
Trustees of the Titsey Foundation.

Address
Titsey
Oxted
Surrey RH8 0SD

Location
MAP 19:F10
OS Ref. TQ406 551

Contact
Information Line: 01273 715359
Events Organiser: 01273 715356
Fax: 01273 779783
E-mail: jo.dykes@struttandparker.com

Opening Times
Open season: 16 May–30 September 2012.

House and gardens open: 12.30–5pm every Wed & Sun. Also May & August bank holidays. Guided tours of the house at 1.30, 2.30 & 3.30pm.

Gardens only open: 12.30–5pm every Sat. Also Easter Mon.

No coaches on Wed, Sat & Sun please. Groups and coaches of 20 or more are welcome all year round on Mon, Tues, Thurs & Fri only, by prior arrangement via the events organiser on 01273 715356.

Admission

House and Garden	£7.00
Garden Only	£4.50
Children under 16	£1.00
Woodland walks and open 365 days.	Free

Pre-booked tours

House and garden inc. guide	£8.50 per person
Garden Only	£6.00 per person
Garden Guide	£50 per group

TITSEY PLACE

www.titsey.org

Dating from the 16th century, the Titsey Estate is one the largest surviving historic estates in Surrey.

Nestling under the North Downs, Titsey Place, with its stunning garden, lakes, woodland walks, walled kitchen garden and park offering panoramic views, enchants visitors. Enjoy the fine family portraits, furniture, a beautiful collection of porcelain and a marvellous set of four Canaletto pictures of Venice. After visiting the mansion house and grounds, why not relax in our tea room where light refreshments are available?

Titsey dates back to the mid 16th century, though the first impression now is of a comfortable early-19th century house in a picturesque park, under the North Downs which hereabout rise to over 800 feet. It is difficult to believe that this well-preserved stretch of country is barely twenty miles from the centre of London: only the M25 motorway intrudes into a landscape which otherwise has hardly changed in the last hundred years.

The estate was originally bought in 1534 by Sir John Gresham, of the famous London merchant dynasty, and descended in the early 19th century through the female line to the Leveson Gowers, a cadet branch of the family of the Dukes of Sutherland. The Leveson Gower family lived at Titsey until the death of Thomas Leveson Gower in 1992. House, garden and re-created kitchen garden are now opened to the public in the summer, and miles of well-marked woodland walks on the side of the North Downs are frequented by more than 20,000 visitors a year.

KEY FACTS

- Partial.
-
- Obligatory.
- Limited for coaches.
- Guide dogs only.

© HRP 2007

© HRP 2007

HAMPTON COURT PALACE

HAMPTON COURT PALACE, SURREY KT8 9AU

www.hrp.org.uk

Henry VIII is most associated with this majestic palace, that he extended and developed in grand style after acquiring it from Cardinal Wolsey in the 1520s. Plus the elegance and romance of the Baroque palace commissioned by William and Mary in the 17th century. The palace sits in 60 acres of gardens, including the famous Maze. The palace also has a new Tudor Court garden. Amongst the new for 2012 is the exhibition 'Wild, Beautiful and Damned' about beautiful women and glamour at Hampton Court; and from Summer a replica of Henry VIII's crown will be on display.

Location: MAP 19:B9, OS Ref. TQ155 686. From M25/J15 or M25/J12 or M25/J10.

Owner: Historic Royal Palaces **Tel:** 0844 482 7777

Venue Hire and Corporate Hospitality: 02031 666505

E-mail: groupsandtraveltrade@hrp.org.uk

Open: Mar–Oct: Daily, 10am–6pm (last admission 5.15pm). Nov–Feb: Daily, 10am–4.30pm (last admission 3.45pm). Closed 24–26 Dec.

Admission: Telephone Information Line for admission prices: 08444 827777. Advance Ticket Sales: 08444 827799. Group Bookings: 08444 827770, Quote Hudson's.

Key facts: Information Centre. No photography indoors. Partial. WCs. Licensed. By arrangement. Ample for cars, coach parking nearby. Rates on request 0844 482 7777. Guide dogs only.

POLESDEN LACEY

GREAT BOOKHAM, NR DORKING, SURREY RH5 6BD

www.nationaltrust.org.uk/polesdenlacey

This beautiful country estate was bought by Mrs Greville, a famous Edwardian hostess, in 1906 and re-modelled to be the perfect setting for her famous weekend parties where she entertained royalty, politicians and the best of Edwardian society. Marvel at her superb collection of fine paintings, porcelain and Fabergé as well as the lavishly decorated interior of the house. Wander through the landscaped formal gardens with their many hidden features, as well as the extensive grounds with stunning views of the Surrey Hills. The restaurant, coffee shop and gift shop are open daily, located outside the pay perimeter.

Location: MAP 19:B11, OS Ref. TQ136 522. 5m NW of Dorking, 2m S of Great Bookham, off A246.

Owner: National Trust **Tel:** 01372 452048 **Fax:** 01372 452023

E-mail: polesdenlacey@nationaltrust.org.uk

Open: House: 29 Feb–4 Nov: Wed–Sun, 11am–5pm (4pm from 31 Oct). 1–16 Dec: weekends, 11am–4pm. House tours (limited entry): Jan, Feb & Nov: weekends, 11am–3.30pm. Gardens, restaurant, shops: daily. 1 Jan–10 Feb: 10am–4pm; 11 Feb–28 Oct: 10am–5pm; 29 Oct–31 Dec: 10am–4pm. Closed 13 Mar, 24 & 25 Dec.

Admission: House & Grounds: Adults £12, Child £6, Family £30, Group £10.20. Grounds only: Adult £7.40, Child £3.70, Family £18.50, Group £6.30. Prices valid to Feb 2012, from Mar see website.

Key facts: WCs. Licensed. By arrangement. (Limited for coaches.) In grounds. Grounds only.

© NT / John Miller

CLAREMONT LANDSCAPE GARDEN

Portsmouth Road, Esher, Surrey KT10 9JG

www.nationaltrust.org.uk/claremont

One of the earliest surviving English landscape gardens, restored to its former glory. Begun by Sir John Vanbrugh and Charles Bridgeman before 1720, the garden was extended and naturalised by William Kent. 'Capability' Brown also made improvements. Features include a lake, island with pavilion, grotto, turf amphitheatre, viewpoints and avenues.

Location: MAP 19:B9, OS Ref. TQ128 632. On S edge of Esher, on E side of A307 (no access from Esher bypass).

Owner: National Trust

Contact: The Property Manager

Tel: 01372 467806

E-mail: claremont@nationaltrust.org.uk

Open: Open throughout the year. 1 Jan–12 Feb, 1 Nov–31 Dec: open Tues–Sun 10am–5pm or sunset if earlier. 13 Feb–31 Oct: daily: 10am–6pm. Closed 25 Dec.

Admission: Adult £7, Child £3.50. Family (2+2) £17.50 Groups (15+), £5.60. Coach groups must book; no coaches Sat, Sun, BH or during school holidays.

Key facts: WCs. Licensed. By arrangement. Limited for coaches. Guide dogs only. No dogs (Apr–Oct).

© Fred Holmes

PAINSHILL LANDSCAPE GARDEN

Portsmouth Road, Cobham, Surrey KT11 1JE

www.painshill.co.uk

Discover 158 acres of magnificent 18th century landscape garden with a 14 acre lake. Explore unusual follies, a unique crystal Grotto and enjoy spectacular views across Surrey. The landscape and plantings offer seasonal interest, and throughout the year you can enjoy entertaining events and talks.

Location: MAP 19:B10, OS Ref. TQ099 605. M25/J10/A3 to London. W of Cobham on A245. Signposted. **Owner:** Painshill Park Trust

Contact: Visitor Operations Team **Tel:** 01932 868113 **Fax:** 01932 868001

E-mail: info@painshill.co.uk education@painshill.co.uk

Open: All Year (Closed Christmas Day & Boxing Day). Mar–Oct 10.30am-6pm or Dusk if earlier (last entry 4.30pm). Nov–Feb 10.30am to 4pm or Dusk if earlier (last entry 3pm). **Admission:** Adult £6.60, Concessions £5.80, Child (5–16 yrs) £3.85, Family Ticket (2Adults & 4Children) £22, Under 5's & Disabled Carer: Free. Group rates available. **Key facts:** WCs. Film and photography location hire. Painshill Wine and Honey. Weddings, Private and Corporate. WCs. Accessible route. Free pre-booked wheelchair loan and guided buggy tours (Cap. Max 5). Licensed. Picnic area. Pre-book 10+ groups. English £2.50 pp. Free for disabled visitors. Free. Coaches must book. Pre-book via Education Dept. On short leads All year. Children's parties.

FARNHAM CASTLE

Farnham, Surrey GU9 0AG

Overlooking the picturesque town of Farnham the 12th century Castle, is one of the most important historical buildings in the South of England. The Castle consists of two parts: The Keep, a Scheduled Ancient Monument and The Bishop's Palace, a complex of Grade I and II listed buildings.

Location: MAP 3:F3, OS Ref. SU839 474. 1/2m N of Farnham town centre on A287.
Owner: Farnham Castle **Contact:** Jeff Toms
Tel: 01252 721194 **Fax:** 01252 711283
E-mail: info@farnhamcastle.com **Website:** www.farnhamcastle.com
Open: Bishop's Palace: Weds 2–4pm. Keep & Exhibition: 1 Feb–23 Dec, Mon–Fri 9am–5pm, Sat, Sun & Bank Holidays 10am–4pm.
Admission: Wednesday afternoon tours of the Bishop's Palace: Adults £3.50, Child/Conc £2.50, admission to Keep and Exhibition: free.
Key facts: Partial. WCs. Licensed. Licensed. Obligatory. Limited for coaches. Guide dogs only. Corporate events, private functions by arrangements including wedding receptions.

GODDARDS

Abinger Common, Dorking, Surrey RH5 6TH

Built by Sir Edwin Lutyens in 1898–1900 and enlarged by him in 1910. Garden by Gertrude Jekyll. Given to the Lutyens Trust in 1991 and now managed and maintained by the Landmark Trust. The whole house, apart from the library, is available for holidays.

Location: MAP 19:B12, OS Ref. TQ120 450.
Owner: The Lutyens Trust, leased to The Landmark Trust
Contact: The Landmark Trust
Tel: 01628 825925
E-mail: bookings@landmarktrust.org.uk
Website: www.landmarktrust.org.uk
Open: Available for holidays. Visits to parts of garden and house by prior appointment, Weds 2.30–5pm Easter to end Oct.
Admission: £4. Tickets available from Mrs Baker on 01306 730871, Mon–Fri, 9am & 6pm.
Key facts:

GREAT FOSTERS

Stroude Road, Egham, Surrey TW20 9UR

Set amongst 50 acres of stunning gardens and parkland Great Fosters is a fine example of Elizabethan architecture. Its past is evident in the mullioned windows, chimneys and brick finials, whilst the gardens include a Saxon moat, Japanese bridge, amphitheatre and knot garden designed by WH Romaine-Walker and Gilbert Jenkins.

Location: MAP 3:G2, OS Ref. TQ015 694. M25 J/13, follow signs to Egham and then brown historic signs for Great Fosters
Owner: The Sutcliffe family **Contact:** Amanda Dougans
Tel: 01784 433822 **Fax:** 01784 472455
E-mail: reception@greatfosters.co.uk **Website:** www.greatfosters.co.uk
Open: All year.
Admission: Free.
Key facts: WCs. Licensed. Licensed. Guide dogs only.

KEW GARDENS

Kew, Richmond, Surrey TW9 3AB

Kew Gardens is a World Heritage Site. It is a mixture of stunning vistas, magnificent glasshouses and beautiful landscapes beside the Thames. This once Royal residence represents nearly 250 years of historical gardens and today its 300 acres are home to over 40,000 types of plants from rainforest to desert.

Location: MAP 19:C7, OS Ref. TQ188 776. A307. Junc. A307 & A205 (1m Chiswick roundabout M4).
Contact: Visitor Information
Tel: 020 8332 5655 **Fax:** 020 8332 5610
E-mail: info@kew.org **Website:** www.kew.org
Open: All year: daily (except 24/25 Dec) from 9.30am. Closing time varies according to the season. Please telephone for further information.
Admission: Adults £13.90, Concessions £11.90, Child (under 17) Free. Discounts for groups (10+). School groups: Free.
Key facts: Licensed. Limited. Guide dogs only.

KEW PALACE, HISTORIC ROYAL PALACES

Kew Gardens, Kew, Richmond, Surrey TW9 3AB

Kew Palace and Queen Charlotte's Cottage. The most intimate of the five royal palaces, Kew was built as a private house but became a royal residence between 1728 and 1818. Both the palace and Queen Charlotte's cottage are most closely associated with King George III and his family.

Location: MAP 19:C7, OS Ref. TQ188 776.193. A307. Junc A307 & A205 (1m Chiswick roundabout M4).
Tel: Group Bookings 020 8332 5648 Visitor Information 0844 482 7777
E-mail: groupsandtraveltrade@hrp.org.uk
Website: www.hrp.org.uk
Open: 10 Apr–27 Sept: daily, 10am–5pm, Last admission 4.15pm.
Admission: By joint ticket purchased through Kew Gardens.
Key facts: WCs. Licensed. Licensed. By arrangement. Limited.

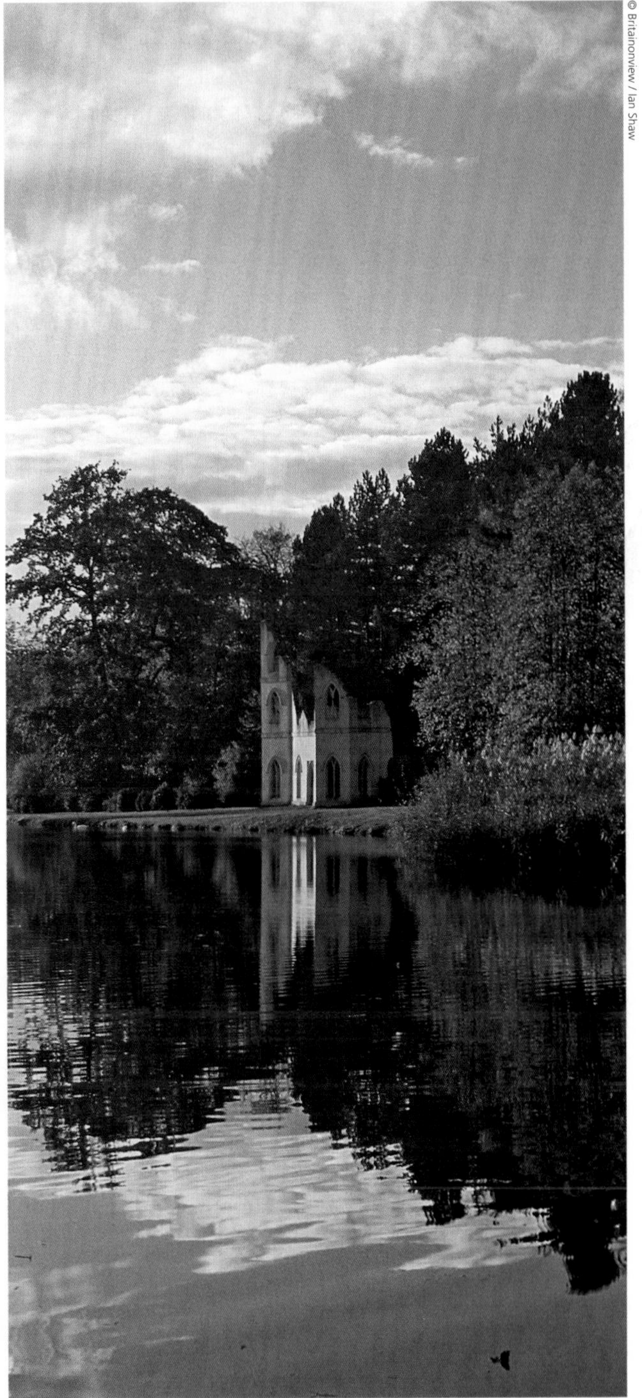

© Britainonview / Ian Shaw

Ruined Abbey by the lakeside in Painshill Park

VISITOR INFORMATION

Owner
English Heritage

Address
Battle
Sussex
TN33 0AD

Location
MAP 4:K5
OS Ref. TQ749 157
Top of Battle High Street. Turn off A2100 to Battle.

Contact
Visitor Operations Team
Tel: 01424 775705
E-mail: customers@english-heritage.org.uk

Opening Times
Please visit www.english-heritage.org.uk for opening times and the most up-to-date information.

Admission

Adult	£7.30
Child	£4.40
Conc	£6.60
Family	£19.00

English Heritage members Free.

Opening times and prices are valid until 31st March 2012.

Special events
Battle Abbey hosts the annual re-enactment of the Battle of Hastings, a spectacular sight to behold and unique experience not be missed.

There is an exciting events programme available throughout the year, for further details please contact the property or visit the website.

© English Heritage Photo Library

1066 BATTLE OF HASTINGS, ABBEY AND BATTLEFIELD ⌗

www.english-heritage.org.uk/1066

On 14 October 1066, Duke William of Normandy defeated King Harold of England at the battle of Hastings.

1066 is the year the Normans defeated the English at the Battle of Hastings. Visit the site of this momentous event and Battle Abbey, which was founded by William the Conqueror as penance for the bloodshed and as a memorial for the dead. Here, on the site of its high altar, you can stand at the very spot where King Harold of England fell.

An imaginative exhibition brings the background and impact of this renowned conflict to life, with interactive displays drawing a vivid picture from both English and Norman viewpoints. Listening points, graphic presentations, hands-on exhibits and touch-screen displays explore how life was on both sides of the battlefield. They also illustrate the impact this pivotal battle had on shaping English history.

Visit the monastic buildings which grew up around the battlefield as a result of its status as a symbol of Norman triumph. These include the impressive Great Gatehouse which is among the finest surviving monastic entrances in Britain.

The abbey museum explores the history of the abbey and includes artefacts found on site during excavations. Complete your visit with a cup of tea in the stylish café, which provides wonderful views of the historic gatehouse.

This single storey stone-built former gatehouse has been turned into a holiday cottage with something of a Hansel and Gretel feel about it, with partly leaded glass windows and an enclosed and secluded garden.

KEY FACTS

- WCs.
- Charge payable.
- On leads.

© English Heritage Photo Library

© English Heritage Photo Library

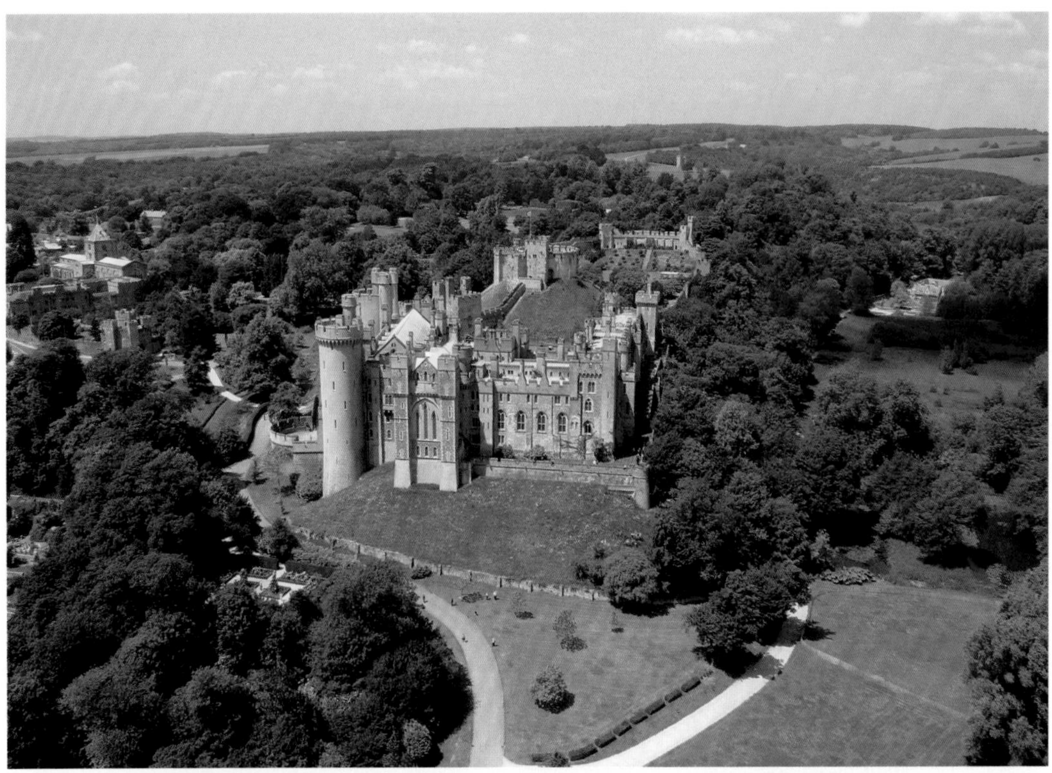

ARUNDEL CASTLE & GARDENS

www.arundelcastle.org

Ancient Castle, Stately Home & Gardens and The Collector Earl's Garden.

A thousand years of history is waiting to be discovered at Arundel Castle in West Sussex. Dating from the 11th century, the Castle is both ancient fortification and stately home of the Dukes of Norfolk and Earls of Arundel.

Set high on a hill, this magnificent castle commands stunning views across the River Arun and out to sea. Climb the Keep, explore the battlements, wander in the grounds and recently restored Victorian gardens and relax in the garden of the 14th century Fitzalan Chapel.

In the 17th century during the English Civil War the Castle suffered extensive damage. The process of structural restoration began in earnest in the 18th century and continued up until 1900. The Castle was one of the first private residences to have electricity and central heating and had its own fire engine.

Inside the Castle over 20 sumptuously furnished rooms may be visited including the breathtaking Barons' Hall with 16th century furniture; the Armoury with its fine collection of armour and weaponry, and the magnificent Gothic library entirely fitted out in carved Honduras mahogany. There are works of art by Van Dyck, Gainsborough, Canaletto and Mytens; tapestries; clocks; and personal possessions of Mary Queen of Scots including the gold rosary that she carried to her execution.

There are special event days throughout the season, including opera, Shakespeare, jousting, and medieval re-enactments.

Do not miss the magnificent Collector Earl's garden based on early 17th century classical designs.

KEY FACTS

- No photography or video recording inside the Castle.
- Distinctive and exclusive gifts.
- WCs.
- Licensed.
- Licensed.
- By prior arrangement. Tour time 1½–2 hrs. Tours available in various languages - please enquire.
- Ample car and coach parking in town car park. Free admission and refreshment voucher for coach driver.
- Norman Motte & Keep, Armoury & Victorian bedrooms. Special rates for schoolchildren (aged 5–16) and teachers.
- Guide dogs only.

VISITOR INFORMATION

Owner
Arundel Castle Trustees Ltd

Address
Arundel Castle
Arundel
West Sussex
BN18 9AB

Location
MAP 3:G6
OS Ref. TQ018 072
Central Arundel, N of A27 Brighton 40 mins, Worthing 15 mins, Chichester 15 mins. From London A3 or A24, 1.5 hrs. M25 motorway, 30m.
Bus: Bus stop 100 yds.
Rail: Station ½m.
Air: Gatwick 25m.

Contact
Bryan McDonald–
Castle Manager
Tel: 01903 882173
Fax: 01903 884581
E-mail: bryan.mcdonald@arundelcastle.org

Opening Times
31 March–4 November 2012 Tuesday–Sunday, Bank Holidays and Mondays in August.

Fitzalan Chapel, Gardens & Grounds, Gift Shop
10am–5pm

Castle Keep, Restaurant & Coffee Shop
10am–4.30pm

Main Castle Rooms
12 noon–5pm

Last entry 4pm

Admission
NB 2011 prices

Gold Plus
Castle Rooms & Bedrooms, Castle Keep, Fitzalan Chapel, The Collector Earl's Garden, Gardens & Grounds:

Adult	£16.00
Child (5-16)	£7.50
Conc.	£13.50
Family (2+3 max)	£39.00

Gold
Castle Rooms, Castle Keep, Fitzalan Chapel, The Collector Earl's Garden, Gardens & Grounds:

Adult	£14.00
Child	£7.50
Conc.	£11.50
Family (2+3 max)	£36.00

Silver
Castle Keep, Fitzalan Chapel, The Collector Earl's Garden, Gardens & Grounds:

Adult	£9.00
Child	£7.50

Bronze
Fitzalan Chapel, The Collector Earl's Garden, Gardens & Grounds:

All	£7.50

Group rates available. On special event days admission prices may vary. For further information visit our website, email or telephone.

VISITOR INFORMATION

Owner
The Goodwood Estate Co.Ltd. (Earl of March and Kinrara).

Address
Goodwood House
Goodwood
Chichester
West Sussex PO18 0PX

Location
MAP 3:F6
OS Ref. SU888 088

3½m NE of Chichester. A3 from London then A286 or A285. M27/A27 from Portsmouth or Brighton.

Taxi: From Chichester station (5 miles)

Rail: Chichester 3½m Arundel 9m.

Air: Heathrow 1½ hrs Gatwick ¾ hr

Contact
Assistant to the Curator
Tel: 01243 755048
01243 775537 (Weddings)
Recorded Info:
01243 755040
Fax: 01243 755005
E-mail: curator @goodwood.com or estatesalesofficeenquiries@ goodwood.com

Opening Times
Summer
25 March–15 October: Most Sundays and Mondays, 1–5pm, (last entry 4pm).

5–30 August: Sundays–Thursdays, 1–5pm.

Please check Recorded Info 01243 755040.

Connoisseurs' Days
2 May, 17 July, 4 September 2012.

Special tours for booked groups of 20+ only.

Closures
Closed for some special events and for two weekends between mid–June and mid–July for the Festival of Speed, and for one Sunday in September for the Revival Meeting.

Please ring Recorded Information on 01243 755040 to check these dates and occasional extra closures.

Admission
House

Adult	£9.50
Young Person (12–18yrs)	£4.00
Child (under 12yrs)	Free
Family	£22.00
Booked Groups (20–100)	
Open Day (am)	£11.00
Open Day (pm)	£9.00
Connoisseur	£11.00

Special events
Festival of Speed

Goodwood Revival

Glorious Goodwood Raceweek

Summer Exhibition *Royal Goodwood*

Please visit our website for up-to-date information. www.goodwood.com.

Conference/Function		
ROOM	Size	Max Cap
Ballroom	79' x 23'	180
6 other rooms available		

GOODWOOD HOUSE

www.goodwood.com

Goodwood House, ancestral home of The Dukes of Richmond and Gordon with magnificent art collection.

Goodwood is one of England's finest sporting estates. At its heart lies Goodwood House, the ancestral home of the Dukes of Richmond and Gordon, direct descendants of King Charles II. Today, it is lived in by the present Duke's son and heir, the Earl of March and Kinrara, with his wife and family. Their home is open to the public on at least 60 days a year.

The art collection includes a magnificent group of British paintings from the 17th and 18th centuries, such as the celebrated views of London by Canaletto and superb sporting scenes by George Stubbs. The rooms are filled with fine English and French furniture, Gobelins tapestries and Sèvres porcelain. Special works of art are regularly rotated and displayed and the books can be viewed by written application to the Curator (there is a special charge for these viewings).

The summer exhibition in 2012, entitled *Royal Goodwood*, will look at Goodwood's Royal heritage from Charles II to Her Majesty The Queen.

Goodwood is also renowned for its entertaining, enjoying a reputation for excellence. Goodwood's own organic farm provides food for the table in the various restaurants on the estate. With internationally renowned horseracing and motor sport events, the finest downland golf course in the UK, its own aerodrome and hotel, Goodwood offers an extraordinarily rich sporting experience.

KEY FACTS

- Conference and wedding facilities. No photography. Very well informed guides. Shell House optional extra on Connoisseurs' Days.
- WCs.
- Obligatory.
- Ample.
- Guide dogs only.
- Goodwood Hotel.
- Civil Wedding Licence. Telephone number for Weddings is 01243 775537 & email is estatesalesofficenquiries@goodwood.com.

GREAT DIXTER HOUSE & GARDENS

www.greatdixter.co.uk

A very special garden with a great deal of character, planted with flair, always something to see, whatever the season.

Great Dixter, built c1450, is the birthplace of the late Christopher Lloyd, gardening author. Its Great Hall is the largest medieval timberframed hall in the country, restored and enlarged for Christopher's father (1910–12). The house was largely designed by the architect, Sir Edwin Lutyens, who added a 16th century house (moved from elsewhere) knitting the buildings together as a family home. The house retains much of the collections of furniture and other items put together by the Lloyds early in the 20th century, with some notable modern additions by Christopher. The gardens feature a variety of topiary, ponds, wild meadow areas and the famous Long Border and Exotic Garden. Featured regularly in "Country Life" from 1963, Christopher was asked to contribute a series of weekly articles as a practical gardener – he never missed an issue in 42 years. There is a specialist nursery which offers an array of unusual plants of the highest quality, many of which can be seen in the fabric of the gardens. Light refreshments are available in the gift shop as well as tools, books and gifts. The whole estate is 57 acres which includes ancient woodlands, meadows and ponds which have been consistently managed on a traditional basis. Coppicing the woodlands, for example, has provided pea sticks for plant supports and timber for fencing and repairs to the buildings. There is a Friends programme available throughout the year. Friends enjoy invitations to events and educational courses as well as regular newsletters.

KEY FACTS

No photography in House.

Obligatory.

Limited for coaches.

Guide dogs only.

VISITOR INFORMATION

Owner

The Great Dixter Charitable Trust

Address

Northiam
Rye
East Sussex
TN31 6PH

Location

MAP 4:L5
OS Ref. TQ817 251
Signposted off the A28 in Northiam.

Contact

Perry Rodriguez
Tel: 01797 252878
Fax: 01797 252879
E-mail: office@greatdixter.co.uk

Opening Times

1 April–28 October:
Tue–Sun, House 2–5pm.
Garden 11am–5pm.

Specialist Nursery Opening times:

April–October: Mon–Fri, 9–5pm. Sat 9–5pm. Sun 10–5pm.

Nov–end of March: Mon–Fri 9–12.30pm, 1.30–4.30pm. Sat 9–12.30pm Sun closed.

Admission

House & Garden	£9.50
Child	£5.00
Garden only	£7.50
Child	£4.00

A GiftAid on admission scheme is in place.

Special Events

Study days on a wide range of subjects available. Please check the website for details.

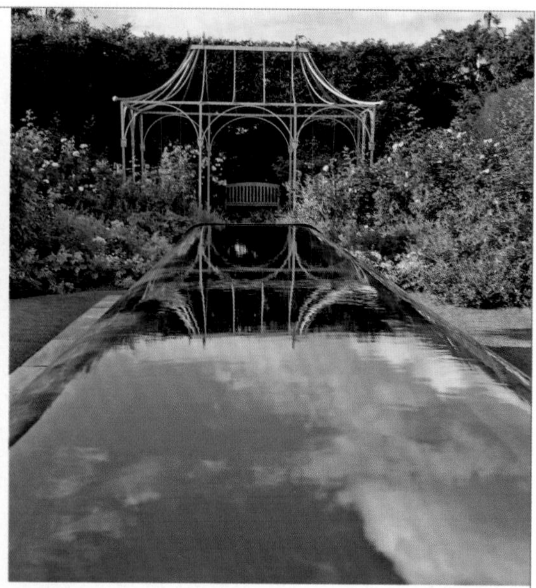

CLINTON LODGE GARDEN

FLETCHING, E SUSSEX TN22 3ST

Clinton Lodge is named after one of Wellington's generals at Waterloo. The simple lawn and parkland beyond the gate reflect the 18th century facade. Beyond are double blue and white herbaceous borders between yew and box hedges, a cloister walk swathed in white roses, clematis and geraniums, a Herb Garden where hedges of box envelop herbs, seats are of turf, paths of camomile.

A Pear Walk bursts with alliums or lilies, a Potager of flowers for cutting, old roses surround a magnificent water feature by William Pye, and much more. Private groups by appointment.

Location: MAP 4:I5, OS Ref. TQ428 238. In centre of village behind tall yew and holly hedge.
Owner/Contact: Lady Collum
Tel/Fax: 01825 722952
E-mail: garden@clintonlodge.com
Open: NGS Open Days: Sun 29 Apr, Sun 3, Mon 18 Jun & Mon 25 Jun, Mon 2 & Mon 30 Jul, Mon 6 Aug. Other days by appointment.
Admission: Entrance £5, Children free.
Key facts: WCs. Partial. By arrangement. Limited. Guide dogs only.

ST MARY'S HOUSE & GARDENS

BRAMBER, WEST SUSSEX BN44 3WE

www.stmarysbramber.co.uk

Features in Simon Jenkins' book 'England's Thousand Best Houses'. Enchanting medieval house. Fine panelled interiors, including unique Elizabethan 'Painted Room'. Interesting family memorabilia and rare Napoleonic collection. Traditional cottage-style tea room.
Five acres of grounds include formal gardens with amusing topiary, exceptional example of the prehistoric tree Ginkgo biloba and the Victorian 'Secret' Garden. Original fruit-wall and pineapple pits, Rural Museum, Jubilee Rose Garden, Terracotta Garden, woodland walk and unusual circular Poetry Garden.
In the heart of the South Downs National Park, St. Mary's is a house of fascination and mystery, with picturesque charm and atmosphere of friendliness and welcome.

Location: MAP 3:H6. OS Ref. TQ189 105. Bramber village off A283. From London 56m via M23/A23 or A24. Buses from Brighton, Shoreham and Worthing.
Owner: Mr Peter Thorogood MBE and Mr Roger Linton MBE
Tel: 01903 816205 **E-mail:** info@stmarysbramber.co.uk
Open: May–end Sept: Suns, Thurs & BH Mons, 2–6pm. Last entry 5pm. Groups at other times by arrangement.
Admission: House & Gardens: Adult £7.50, Conc. £7, Child £4. Groups (25+) £7.50 Gardens Only: Adults £4.50, Conc. £4, Child, £2, Groups £4.50.
Key facts: No photography in house. Partial. Obligatory for groups (max 60). Visit time 2½hrs. 30 cars, 2 coaches.

© NT / Nymans / Edward Shorthouse

© NT / Nymans / Edward Shorthouse

NYMANS

HANDCROSS, HAYWARDS HEATH, WEST SUSSEX RH17 6EB

www.nationaltrust.org.uk/nymans

In the late 1800s, an unusually creative family bought the Nymans estate in the picturesque High Weald. Inspired by the setting and the soil, the Messels created one of the great gardens, with experimental designs and new plants from around the world. Exploring further than the garden and house, you can go for a walk in the woods among avenues, wild flowers and lakes. The woods are delightful with lots to see, like the tallest tree in Sussex and the cascade waterfalls. Nymans is open all year so as to appreciate the garden's ever changing colours and scents.

Location: MAP 4:I4, OS Ref. SU187:TQ265 294. At Handcross on B2114, 12 miles south of Gatwick, just off London–Brighton M23.

Owner: National Trust **Contact:** Nymans

Tel: 01444 405250

E-mail: nymans@nationaltrust.org.uk

Open: Garden, woods, restaurant, shop & garden centre: 1 Jan–29 Feb, daily, 10am–4pm; 1 Mar–31 Oct, daily, 10am–5pm; 1 Nov–24 Dec, daily, 10am–4pm. House: 1 Mar–31 Oct: daily, 11am–3pm.

Admission: Adult £10 Child £5 Family £25 Family (1 adult) £15 Booked Groups (15+) Adult £8.50 Child £4.50

Free cup of tea or coffee in restaurant when arriving by green transport, including hybrid/electric cars.

Includes a voluntary donation but visitors can choose to pay the standard prices displayed at visitor reception and on the website.

Gift Aid admission prices shown.

Key facts: Suitable. WCs. Licensed. Licensed. By arrangement. Limited for coaches. Guide dogs only We have an all year round programme of events including family activities, summer open air theatre, horticultural workshops, compost demonstrations, bat walks and photography workshops.

PARHAM HOUSE & GARDENS

PARHAM PARK, STORRINGTON, NR PULBOROUGH, WEST SUSSEX RH20 4HS

www.parhaminsussex.co.uk

One of the top twenty in Simon Jenkins's book "England's Thousand Best Houses". Idyllically set in the heart of a 17th century deer park, below the South Downs, the house contains an important collection of needlework, paintings and furniture. The spectacular Long Gallery is the third longest in England. The award winning gardens include a four acre walled garden with stunning herbaceous borders. Parham has always been a much-loved family home. Now owned by a charitable trust, the house is lived in by Lady Emma Barnard, her husband James and their family.

Location: MAP 3:G5, OS Ref. TQ060 143. Midway between Pulborough & Storrington on A283. Equidistant from A24 & A29.

Owner: Parham Park Trust

Tel: 01903 742021

Fax: 01903 746557

E-mail: enquiries@parhaminsussex.co.uk

Open: Open Apr-Sept. Sundays in October. Please contact property for further details.

Admission: Please contact property for details.

Key facts: No photography in house. Licensed. By arrangement. In grounds, on leads.

© Marianne Majerus

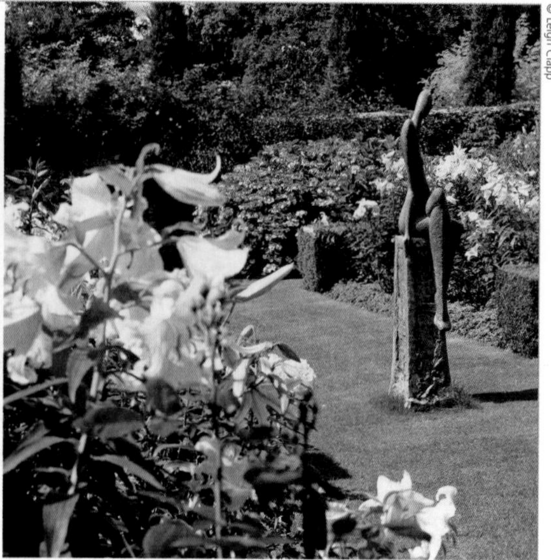
© Leigh Clapp

PASHLEY MANOR GARDENS

PASHLEY MANOR, TICEHURST, WADHURST, EAST SUSSEX TN5 7HE

www.pashleymanorgardens.com

Pashley offers a sumptuous blend of romantic landscaping, imaginative plantings, fine old trees, fountains and ponds.

Through April to May the fruit trees blossom, bluebells carpet the woodland, the wisteria is magnificent and there are thousands of tulips. June is fragrant with roses and lavender; July is perfumed with sweet peas and lilies and the Kitchen Garden is at its most bountiful. Summer bedding plants continue into August, then the herbaceous borders flourish.

Enjoy delicious homemade refreshments from the Garden Room Café with Terrace. Gift Shop; plant sales; exhibition of sculpture and botanical art; private parties and marquee wedding receptions.

Location: OS Ref. TQ707 291

Owner: Mr & Mrs James A Sellick **Tel:** 01580 200888 **Fax:** 01580 200102

E-mail: info@pashleymanorgardens.com

Open: 3 Apr–29 Sept: Tues, Weds, Thurs, Sat, Bank Holiday Mons and Special Event days, 11am–5pm. Oct: Garden only Mon–Fri,10am–3pm.

Admission: Adult £9, Children (6–16yrs) £5. Groups (15+) £8.50. Tulip Festival (no concessions) £9.50. Season Ticket £29.50. Coaches must book. Please telephone for details.

Key facts: Partial. WCs. Licensed By arrangement. Limited for Coaches. Guide dogs only.

© NT/Chris Roe

© NT/Lisa Barnard

SHEFFIELD PARK & GARDEN

SHEFFIELD PARK, EAST SUSSEX TN22 3QX

www.nationaltrust.org.uk/sheffieldpark

A magnificent landscaped garden and historic parkland, open all year to explore and discover. In the garden, four lakes mirror the beautiful planting and colour each season. Early spring bulbs, including snowdrops, daffodils and bluebells are followed in May/June, by an outstanding exhibition of colour when our rhododendrons and azaleas display their magnificent spring colour show.

Water lilies dress the lakes during the summer, whilst in the autumn the garden is transformed by the stunning autumn colour including Nyssa sylvatica, producing displays of gold, orange and crimson. The year ends with the chance to enjoy a beautiful crisp winter's walk.

Location: MAP 4:15. OS Ref. TQ415 240. Midway between East Grinstead and Lewes, 5m NW of Uckfield on E side of A275.

Owner: National Trust

Contact: Jo Hopkins, Visitor Services & Marketing Manager

Tel: 01825 790231 **Fax:** 01825 791264

E-mail: sheffieldpark@nationaltrust.org.uk

Open: Garden/Shop/Tearoom: Open all year (closed Christmas Day), please call 01825 790231 or log onto our website for details of times.

Parkland: Open all year, dawn to dusk.

Admission: For 2012 prices, please call 01825 790231 or log onto our website. Groups discount available (15+ prebooked)

NT, RHS Individual Members and Great British Heritage Pass holders Free.

Joint Ticket available with Bluebell Railway.

Key facts: Garden: Accessibility dogs only. Parkland: Dogs allowed under close control. Suitable. WCs. Licensed. Licensed. By arrangement. Limited for coaches. Guide dogs only. Event and activities programme throughout the year – please check our website.

© NTPL / Nadia MacKenzie

© NT / Chris Hill

STANDEN

EAST GRINSTEAD, WEST SUSSEX RH19 4NE

www.nationaltrust.org.uk/standen

Built in the 1890s for wealthy solicitor, James Beale, and his family, Standen has become an icon of the Arts & Crafts Movement with Morris & Co. interiors. The house is set for a 1920s weekend with visiting members of the Beale family. You can discover how they used Standen over a 24 hour period and enjoy the house and garden as they and their guests did.
You can buy your own piece of Arts and Crafts in our Shop which sells a range of Morris & Co. inspired gifts. Produce from our Kitchen Garden is used in our Restaurant.

Location: MAP 4:I4, OS Ref. TQ389 356. 2m S of East Grinstead, signposted from B2110.

Owner: National Trust **Contact:** The Property Manager

Tel: 01342 323029 **Fax:** 01342 316424 **E-mail:** standen@nationaltrust.org.uk

Open: 11–26 Feb; Sats & Suns, 11am–4.30pm (last entry to house 4pm). 29 Feb–4 Nov; Wed–Sun, 11am–5.30pm (last entry to house 4pm). Also Mons & Tues 28 Mar–15 Apr, 30 May–2 Sep, 24 Oct–4 Nov. 10 Nov–23 Dec; Sats & Suns, 11am–3pm (last entry to house 2.30pm).

Admission: House & Garden*: Adult £9.50, child £4.75, family £23.75. Pre-booked groups: £8.25 (minimum 15).
*Includes voluntary donation but visitors can choose to pay the standard prices displayed on the property and on the website.

Key facts: Suitable. WCS. Licensed. Licensed. Guide dogs only. Children's crafts every Monday during the school holidays, regular contemporary Arts & Crafts selling exhibitions, lecture lunches, Christmas lunches.

© NTPL / John Miller

ALFRISTON CLERGY HOUSE

The Tye, Alfriston, Polegate, East Sussex BN26 5TL

www.nationaltrust.org.uk/alfriston

Step back into the Middle Ages with a visit to this 14th century thatched Wealden 'Hall House' which in 1896 was the first to be acquired by the National Trust. Explore the delightful cottage garden and idyllic setting with stunning views across the meandering River Cuckmere. NT shop on site.

Location: MAP 4:J6, OS Ref. TQ521 029. 4m NE of Seaford, just E of B2108.

Owner: National Trust

Contact: The Property Manager

Tel: 01323 871961

E-mail: alfriston@nationaltrust.org.uk

Open: 25 Feb–4 Mar Sat & Sun, 11am–4pm; 10 Mar–4 Nov daily except Thur & Fri, 10.30am–5pm; (Open on Fri in August) 5 Nov–19 Dec daily except Thur & Fri 11am–4pm.

Admission: Adult £5, Child £2.55, Family (2+3) £12.50. Pre-booked groups (+15) £4.35.

Key facts: No WCs. By arrangement. Parking in village car parks. Guide dogs only.

© NTPL / John Miller

BATEMAN'S

Bateman's, Burwash, Etchingham, East Sussex TN19 7DS

www.nationaltrust.org.uk/batemans

Built in 1634 and home to Jungle Book author Rudyard Kipling for over 30 years, Bateman's lies in the richly wooded landscape of the Sussex Weald. Discover his book-lined study, Rolls Royce Phantom 1 and water-mill. Relax in the garden with its ornamental pond, formal lawns and meadow.

Location: MAP 4:K5, OS Ref. TQ671 238. 1/2m S of Burwash off A265.

Owner: National Trust

Contact: The Administrator

Tel: 01435 882302

Fax: 01435 882811

E-mail: batemans@nationaltrust.org.uk

Open: 9 Mar–28 Oct: Sat–Wed, Good Fri & BH Mons, 10am–5pm (House 11am).

Admission: House & Garden: Adult £9, Child £4.50, Family £22.60 (2+3). Groups £7.90.

Key facts: Partial. WCs. Limited for Coaches. Guide dogs only.

CHARLESTON

Charleston, Firle, Nr Lewes, East Sussex BN8 6L

www.charleston.org.uk

Charleston, with its unique interiors and beautiful walled garden, was the home of artists Vanessa Bell and Duncan Grant from 1916. They decorated the house, painting walls, doors and furniture and filling the rooms with their own paintings and works by artists they admired, such as Picasso, Derain and Sickert.

Location: MAP 4:J6. OS Ref. TQ490 069. 7m E of Lewes on A27 between Firle and Selmeston

Owner: The Charleston Trust

Tel: 01323 811626 **Fax:** 01323 811628

E-mail: info@charleston.org.uk

Open: Apr–Oct: Wed–Sat, guided tours only, 1pm (12pm in Jul & Aug), last entry 5pm, Sun & BH Mons, 1pm - last entry 4.30pm

Admission: House & Garden: Adult £9, Children £5, Themed tour £10, Garden only: Adults: £3, Children: £1.50, Open by arrangement for groups. Please check website for up to date information.

Key facts: Filming and photography by arrangement. Obligatory, except Sun and BH Mons.

COWDRAY

River Ground Stables, Midhurst, W Sussex GU29 9AL

www.cowdray.org.uk

As a major new attraction, Cowdray is one of the most important survivals of a Tudor nobleman's house. Set within the stunning landscape of Cowdray Park, the house was partially destroyed by fire in 1793. Explore the Tudor Kitchens, Buck Hall, Chapel, Gatehouse, Vaulted Storeroom and Cellars, Visitor Centre and Shop.

Location: MAP 3:F5, OS Ref. TQ891 216. E outskirts of Midhurst on A272.

Owner: Cowdray Heritage Trust

Contact: The Manager

Tel: 01730 810781

E-mail: info@cowdray.org.uk

Open: Mid Mar–end Oct Sun–Thurs. 10.30am-5pm last admission 4pm. Groups all year round by arrangement.

Admission: Check website for details.

Key facts: Partial. WCs. By arrangement. Nearby.

CHICHESTER CATHEDRAL

Chichester, W Sussex PO19 1RP

www.chichestercathedral.org.uk

In the heart of Chichester, this magnificent 900 year old Cathedral has treasures ranging from medieval stone carvings to world famous 20th century artworks. Open every day and all year with free entry. Free guided tours and special trails for children. Regular exhibitions, free weekly lunchtime concerts and a superb Cloisters Restaurant and Shop. A fascinating place to visit.

Location: MAP 3:F6, OS Ref. SU860 047. West Street, Chichester.

Contact: Visitor Services Officer **Tel:** 01243 782595 **Fax:** 01243 812499

E-mail: visitors@chichestercathedral.org.uk

Open: Summer: 7.15am–7.00pm, Winter: 7.15am–6.00pm. All are welcome. Choral Evensong daily (except Wed) during term time.

Admission: Free entry. Donations greatly appreciated.

Key facts: Private functions and conferences.

HAMMERWOOD PARK

East Grinstead, Sussex RH19 3QE

www.hammerwoodpark.com

The best kept secret in Sussex, "untouched by a corporate plan". Built by White House architect Latrobe in Greek Revival style in 1792, left derelict by Led Zeppelin, painstakingly restored by the Pinnegar family over the last 30 years and brought to life with guided tours, concerts and filming.

Location: MAP 4:J4, OS Ref. TQ442 390. 3.5 m E of East Grinstead on A264 to Tunbridge Wells, 1m W of Holtye.

Owner/Contact: David Pinnegar

Tel: 01342 850594

Fax: 01342 850864

E-mail: latrobe@mistral.co.uk

Open: 1 Jun–end Sept: Wed, Sat & BH Mon, 2–5pm. Guided tour starts 2.05pm. Private groups: Easter–Jun. Coaches strictly by appointment. Small groups any time throughout the year by appointment.

Admission: House & Park: Adult £6, Child £2. Private viewing by arrangement.

Key facts: Conferences. Obligatory. In grounds. B&B. €

HIGH BEECHES WOODLAND & WATER GARDEN

High Beeches Lane, Handcross, West Sussex RH17 6HQ

www.highbeeches.com

Explore 27 acres of magically beautiful, peaceful woodland and water gardens. Daffodils, bluebells, azaleas, naturalised gentians and glorious autumn colours. Rippling streams, enchanting vistas. Four acres of natural wildflower meadows. Marked trails. Recommended by Christopher Lloyd. Enjoy lunches and teas in the tearoom and tea lawn in restored Victorian farm building.

Location: MAP 4:I4, OS Ref. TQ275 308. S side of B2110. 1m NE of Handcross.

Owner: High Beeches Gardens Conservation Trust (Reg. Charity)

Contact: Sarah Bray **Tel:** 01444 400589 **Fax:** 01444 401543

E-mail: gardens@highbeeches.com

Open: 17 Mar–28 Oct: daily except Weds, 1–5pm (last adm. 4.30pm). Coaches/guided tours anytime, by appointment only.

Admission: Adult £6.50, Child (under 14yrs) Free. Concession for groups (20+). Guided tours for groups £10pp.

Key facts: Partial. WCs Tearoom fully accessible. Licensed. Licensed. By arrangement. Limited for coaches. Guide dogs only.

GARDENS AND GROUNDS OF HERSTMONCEUX CASTLE

Hailsham, E Sussex BN27 1RN

www.herstmonceux-castle.com

This breathtaking 15th century moated Castle is set within 500 acres of parkland and gardens (including Elizabethan Garden) and is ideal for picnics and woodland walks. At Herstmonceux there is something for all the family.

Location: MAP 4:K5, OS Ref. TQ646 104. 2m S of Herstmonceux village (A271) by minor road. 10m WNW of Bexhill.

Owner: Queen's University, Canada **Contact:** Caroline Harber

Tel: 01323 833816 **Fax:** 01323 834499

E-mail: c_harber@bisc.queensu.ac.uk

Open: 7 Apr–28 Oct: daily, 10am–6pm (last adm. one hour before closing). Closes 5pm from Oct.

Admission: Grounds & Gardens; Adults £6.00, Child under 15yrs & Students £3 (child under 5 Free), Conc. £4.95, Family £14. Group rates/bookings available.

Key facts: Visitor Centre. Partial. WCS. Licensed. Licensed. By arrangement. On leads.

© Peter Durant / arcblue.com

PALLANT HOUSE GALLERY

9 North Pallant, Chichester, West Sussex PO19 1TJ

www.pallant.org.uk

A Grade I-listed Queen Anne townhouse and landmark contemporary building holding one of the best collections of 20th century British art in the country. An extensive exhibition programme includes international exhibitions and print shows. There is also a critically acclaimed on-site restaurant with courtyard garden and first-class art bookshop.

Location: MAP 3:F6, OS Ref. SU861 047. City centre, SE of the Cross.

Owner: Pallant House Gallery Trust

Contact: Reception

Tel: 01243 774557

E-mail: info@pallant.org.uk

Open: Tue–Sat: 10am–5pm (Thur: 10am–8pm. Sun & BH Mons: 11am–5pm)

Admission: Adult £8.25 (£7.50 w/out Gift Aid); Child 6–15yrs £2.30, Students £4; Family £18.70 (£17 w/out Gift Aid); Groups £5.75 per person (advanced booking required); Unemployed/Friends/Under 5s Free.

Key facts: No photography. WCs. Licensed. Licensed. By arrangement. Guide dogs only.

© NTPL / Arnhel de Serra

PETWORTH HOUSE & PARK

Church Street, Petworth, West Sussex GU28 0AE

www.nationaltrust.org.uk/petworth

Explore this majestic mansion and beautiful landscaped deer park. Unlock the intriguing family history and marvel at the world famous painting collection. In contrast to the lavish House, venture 'below stairs' to the fascinating Servants' Quarters. On weekdays Lord and Lady Egremont kindly open private rooms for visitors to enjoy.

Location: OS Ref. SU976 218. In the centre of Petworth town (approach roads A272/A283/A285) Car park signposted.

Owner: National Trust **Contact:** The Administration Office

Tel: 01798 342207 **Fax:** 01798 342963

E-mail: petworth@nationaltrust.org.uk

Open: House & Restaurant 10 Mar–31 Oct, Sat–Wed 11am–5pm. Last admission 4.30pm. Café, Shop & Pleasure Grounds 10 Mar–31 Oct, Sat–Wed 10.30am–5pm (Grounds until 6pm). 7 Nov–23 Dec, Wed–Sun 10.30am–3.30pm.

Admission: House & Grounds Adult £12.10, Child (5–17yrs) £6.10, Child (under 5yrs) Free, Family (2+3) £30.10, Groups (pre-booked) Adult £10. Pleasure Grounds Adult £4.70, Child (5–17yrs) £2.40. Gift Aid prices.

Key facts: Events & Exhibitions throughout the year. Baby feeding and changing facilities Contact Retail & Catering Manager on 01798 345521. Partial. WCs. Licensed. Licensed. By arrangement with the Administration Office. Guide dogs only.

© NT / Raymond Woodham

UPPARK HOUSE AND GARDEN

South Harting, Petersfield GU31 5QR

www.nationaltrust.org.uk/uppark

Admire the Georgian grandeur of Uppark from its stunning hilltop location on the South Downs. Discover the fascinating world of Sir Harry Fetherstonhaugh, Lady Emma Hamilton and the dairymaid who married her master. See the famous doll's house, Victorian servants' quarters, picturesque garden and breathtaking views.

Location: MAP 3:F5, OS Ref 197 SU775 177. Between Petersfield & Chichester on B2146.

Owner: National Trust

Contact: The Administration Office

Tel: 01730 825415

Fax: 01730 825873

E-mail: uppark@nationaltrust.org.uk

Open: 18 Mar–1 Nov Sun–Thur. Garden, Shop & Restaurant 11am–5pm. House 11am–4.30pm (11am–12.30pm open for guided tours only, details on arrival). Suns 18 Nov–16 Dec. House, Garden, Shop & Restaurant 11am–3pm.

Admission: Adult £9.30, Child (5-17yrs) £4.70, Family (2+3) £23.10. Garden only: Adult £4.70, Child £2.40. Gift Aid prices.

Key facts: No photography in the house. WCs. Licensed. By arrangement. Guide dogs only.

STANSTED PARK

Stansted Park, Rowlands Castle, Hampshire PO9 6DX

www.stanstedpark.co.uk

Stansted Park, on the South Downs, is a beautiful Edwardian house with ancient private chapel, with spectacular views south over the Solent. The state rooms are furnished as if the 10th Earl of Bessborough was still at home, and the amazing servants' quarters are jam-packed with old-fashioned things to see.

Location: OS Ref. SU761 103. Follow brown heritage signs from A3(M) J2 Emsworth or A27 Havant.

Owner: Stansted Park Foundation **Contact:** House and Events Manager

Tel: 023 9241 2265 **Fax:** 023 9241 3773

E-mail: enquiry@stanstedpark.co.uk

Open: House: Apr–May: Sun & BHol 1–5pm (last adm.4pm). Jun–Sept: Sun–Wed 1–5pm (last adm. 4pm). Tea Room & Garden Centre: every day. Maze: Weekends and school holidays 11–4pm. Light Railway: Weds and weekends.

Admission: House & Chapel: Adult £7, Child (5–15yrs) £3.50, Conc. £6, Family (2+3) £18. Groups/educational visits by arrangement.

Key facts: Private & corporate hire Suitable. WCs. Licensed. By arrangement. By arrangement. Guide dogs only Grounds.

WEALD AND DOWNLAND OPEN AIR MUSEUM

Singleton, Chichester, West Sussex PO18 0EU

www.wealddown.co.uk

The Museum homes over 45 rescued historic buildings, reconstructed in beautiful parkland in the South Downs. Six historic houses include carefully researched period gardens, showcasing the plants, herbs and flowers grown by our ancestors. Enjoy the tranquillity of the Sussex downland, working Shire horses, cattle and traditional breed farm animals.

Location: MAP 3:F5, OS Ref. SZ128 875. Off A286 Chichester to Midhurst road at Singleton village.

Owner: Weald and Downland Open Air Museum Ltd

Contact: Henry Warner

Tel: 01243 811010 **E-mail:** operations@wealddown.co.uk

Open: 1 Jan–20 Feb, Wed, Sat and Sun only. From 21 Feb, open daily until 23 Dec, plus daily for 'A Sussex Christmas' 26 Dec–1 Jan.

Admission: Adult £10, Child £5, Over 60 £9, Family £27.

Key facts: Partial. WCs. By arrangement. On leads.

© Trevor Sims

WEST DEAN COLLEGE & GARDENS

West Dean, Chichester, West Sussex PO18 0RX

www.westdean.org.uk

Situated within the 6,400 acre West Dean Estate, West Dean College and Gardens is at the heart of the newly designated South Downs National Park. The Gardens are a showcase for variety in planting and excellence in presentation. Highlights include: the magnificent 90 metre-long Edwardian pergola; the Victorian walled kitchen garden and glasshouses; the Spring Garden with tranquil, winding rivers and intricate flint bridges; and picnic lawn. For breathtaking views of the Lavant Valley, enjoy the 2½ mile circular Parkland walk up to St Roche's arboretum.

Location: MAP 3:F5, OS Ref. SU863 128. SE of A286 Midhurst Road, 6m N of Chichester, 7m S of Midhurst.

Owner: The Edward James Foundation

Tel Gardens: 01243 818210 **Tel College:** 01243 811301

Fax: 01243 811342 **E-mail:** enquiries@westdean.org.uk

Open/Admission: For more information on Opening times and prices please see website www.westdean.org.uk.

Key facts: Licensed. By arrangement. Limited for coaches. Guide dogs only.

© NTPL / Stephen Robson

WOOLBEDING GARDENS

Midhurst, West Sussex GU29 9RR

www.nationaltrust.org.uk/woolbeding

Woolbeding is a modern garden masterpiece, with constantly evolving colour-themed garden rooms surrounding the house and magical woodland garden. View the glorious River Rother and the landscape garden, relax by the Chinese-style bridge and cascading waterfall. Booking essential; no onsite parking (apart from disabled)–local minibus service.

Location: MAP 3:F5, OS Ref. SU872227. No access by car, apart from disabled (booking essential).

Owner: National Trust **Contact:** The Administration Office

Tel: 01730 825415 **E-mail:** woolbedinggardens@nationaltrust.org.uk

Open: 12 Apr–28 Sept, 10.30am–4.30pm, Thurs and Fri only. All visits and local minibus must be booked on 01730 825415.

Admission: Adult £6.50, Child (5–17yrs) £3.20, Family (2+3) £19.40

Key facts: Gardens only, please book all visits and minibus service on 01730 825415. Partial. WCs.

ARUNDEL CATHEDRAL

Parsons Hill, Arundel, West Sussex BN18 9AY

French Gothic Cathedral, church of the RC Diocese of Arundel and Brighton built by Henry, 15th Duke of Norfolk and opened 1873.

Location: MAP 3:G6, OS Ref. TQ015 072. Above junction of A27 and A284.

Contact: Rev. Canon T. Madeley

Tel: 01903 882297

Fax: 01903 885335

E-mail: aruncath1@aol.com

Open: Summer: 9am–6pm. Winter: 9am–dusk. Mon, Tues, Wed, Fri, Sat: Mass 10am; Thurs: Mass 8.30am (at Convent of Poor Clares, Crossbush); Sat: Vigil Mass 6.15pm (at Convent of Poor Clares, Crossbush); Sun: Masses 9.30am and 11.15am. Shop open in the summer, Mon–Fri, 10am–4pm and after services and on special occasions and otherwise on request.

Admission: Free.

Key facts:

BORDE HILL GARDEN

Borde Hill Lane, Haywards Heath, West Sussex RH16 1XP

A truly spectacular garden in the rural Sussex countryside, which hosts some of the rarest and oldest trees and plants in Britain. Magical 'garden rooms', include the Azalea Ring, Rose and Italian Gardens. Fun for families to explore and picnic. Ideal for filming, photo shoots, weddings and corporate events.

Location: MAP 4:I5

Contact: Susan Lewis

Tel: 01444 450326

E-mail: info@bordehill.co.uk

Website: www.bordehill.co.uk

Open: 10 Mar–9 Sept & 20–28 Oct 2012 10am–6pm daily and weekends only between 10 Sept–19 Oct 10am–5pm.

Admission: Adults £8, Conc. £7.50, Group £7, Child £5. Season Tickets available see website www.bordehill.co.uk.

Key facts: WCs. Dogs allowed on leads.

DENMANS GARDEN

Denmans Lane, Fontwell, West Sussex BN18 0SU

A unique 20th century 4 acre garden designed for year round interest – through use of form, colour and texture – owned by John Brookes MBE, renowned garden designer and writer and Michael Neve. Beautiful plant centre, gift shop, garden shop and fully licensed multi award winning Garden Café.

Location: MAP 3:G6, OS197 Ref. SZ947 070. Off the A27 (westbound) between Chichester (6m) and Arundel (5m).

Owner: John Brookes MBE & Michael Neve **Contact:** Mrs Claudia Murphy

Tel: 01243 542808 **Fax:** 01243 544064

E-mail: denmans@denmans-garden.co.uk **Website:** www.denmans-garden.co.uk

Open: Daily all year round. Garden: 9am–5pm. Plant centre: 9am–5pm. Café: 10am–5pm. Please check website for winter opening times.

Admission: Adult £4.95, Child (4–16) £3.95, OAP £4.75, Pre-booked groups (15+) £4.50. 2010 prices – please telephone or check website for current prices.

Key facts: WC. Licensed. Licensed. Group menus on request. Guide dogs only.

Britain's Brilliant Heritage
Brought To Life
To find out more visit our website
www.hudsonsheritage.com
HUDSON'S
HERITAGE

MONK'S HOUSE

Rodmell, Lewes BN7 3HF

A small weather-boarded house and garden, the home of Leonard and Virginia Woolf until Leonard's death in 1969.

Location: MAP 4:I6, OS Ref. TQ421 064. 4 m E of Lewes, off former A275 in Rodmell village, near church.

Owner: National Trust

Contact: Property Office

Tel: 01273 474760 (Property Office).

Open: 4 Apr–28 Oct; Weds–Sun, 1–5.30pm (last admission 5pm). Open BH Monday's. Group by prior arrangement.

Admission: Adult £4.85, Child £2.45, Family £12.10, Groups £4.

WILMINGTON PRIORY

Wilmington, Nr Eastbourne, East Sussex BN26 5SW

Founded by the Benedictines in the 11th century, the surviving, much altered buildings date largely from the 14th century. Managed and maintained by the Landmark Trust, which lets buildings for self-catering holidays.

Location: MAP 3:F5, OS Ref. TQ543 042.

Owner: Leased to the Landmark Trust by Sussex Archaeological Society

Contact: The Landmark Trust **Tel:** 01628 825925

E-mail: bookings@landmarktrust.org.uk **Website:** www.landmarktrust.org.uk

Open: Available for holidays. Grounds, Ruins, Porch & Crypt: 30 days between Apr–Oct by appointment. Whole property on 8 of these days.

Admission: Free on Open Days and visits by appointment.

Key facts:

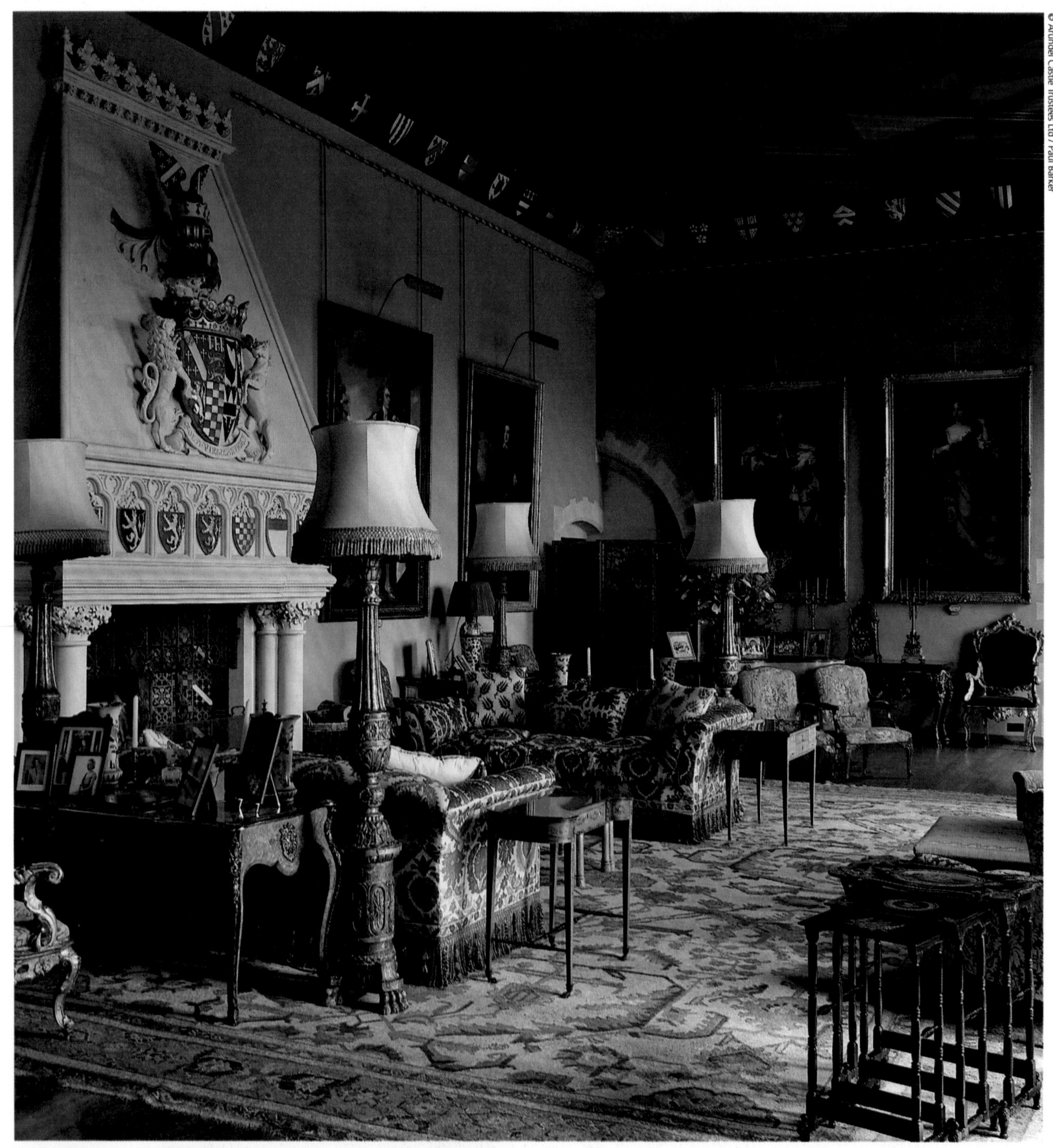

The Drawing Room, Arundel Castle

© English Heritage

VISITOR INFORMATION

Owner
English Heritage

Address
Newport
Isle Of Wight
PO30 1XY

Location
MAP 3:E7
OS196 Ref. SZ486 877.
Off the B3401, 1¼ miles SW of Newport.

Contact
Visitor Operations Team
Tel: 01983 522107
E-mail: customers@english-heritage.org.uk

Opening Times
1 April–30 September: daily, 10am–5pm.
1 October–31 March 2010: daily, 10am–4pm. Closed 24–26 Dec & 1 Jan.

Admission

Adult	£7.30
Child	£4.40
Conc.	£6.60
Family (2+3)	£19.00.

Discount for groups (11+).
EH Members Free.
Opening times and prices are valid until 31 March 2012, please visit www.english-heritage.org.uk for the most up-to-date information.

Special events
There is an exciting events programme available throughout the year, for further details please contact the property or visit the website.

CARISBROOKE CASTLE ⌗

www.english-heritage.org.uk/carisbrooke

See where King Charles I was imprisoned, climb the ramparts and keep and relax in the new Edwardian-style garden.

The island's royal fortress and prison of King Charles I before his execution in London in 1648. See the famous Carisbrooke donkeys treading the wheel in the Well House as donkeys would have done in the 18th century. Visit the on-site Carisbrooke Museum and take an invigorating battlements walk. Enjoy a fascinating presentation reflecting 800 years of colourful history at the castle, brought to life using dramatic film and interactive exhibits. Don't miss the new Edwardian-style Princess Beatrice Garden, designed by TV and radio gardening presenter Chris Beardshaw.

Carisbrook Castle has a second floor apartment in a prime position within the walls of this great castle. Guests have the freedom to enjoy the majority of the gardens and grounds of the castle 'out of hours'.

KEY FACTS

- WCs.
- Partial. WCs.
- Guide dogs only.
- Tel. for details.

© English Heritage

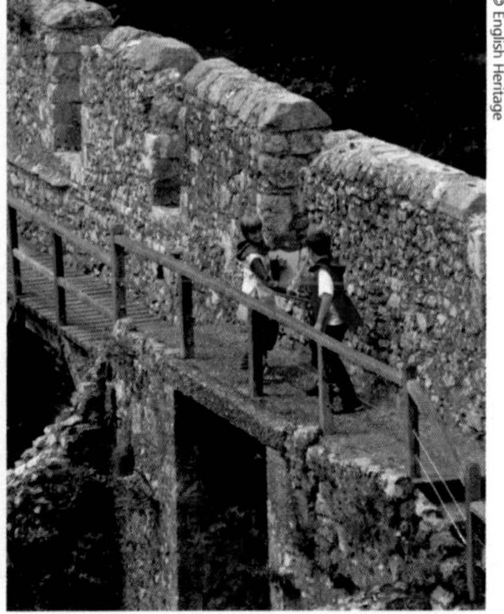

© English Heritage

VISITOR INFORMATION

Owner
English Heritage

Address
Osborne House
Royal Apartments
East Cowes
Isle of Wight
PO32 6JX

Location
MAP 3:D6
OS Ref. SZ516 948
1 mile SE of East Cowes.
Ferry: Isle of Wight ferry terminals.
Red Funnel, East Cowes $1^1/2$ miles
Tel: 02380 334010.
Wightlink, Fishbourne 4 miles
Tel: 0870 582 7744

Contact
The House Administrator
Tel: 01983 200022
Fax: 01983 281380
E-mail: customers@english-heritage.org.uk
Venue Hire and Hospitality:
Tel: 01983 203055

Opening Times
Please visit www.english-heritage.org.uk for opening times and the most up-to-date information.

Admission

Adult	£11.50
Child	£6.90
Conc.	£10.40
Family	£29.90.

EH members free.

Discount for groups (11+). Tour leader and driver have free entry.

Opening times and prices are valid until 31 March 2012, after this date details are subject to change please visit www.english-heritage.org.uk for the most up-to-date information.

Special events
There is an exciting events programme available throughout the year, for further details please contact the property or visit the website.

Conference/Function	
ROOM	Max Cap
Durbar Hall	standing 80 seated 50
Upper Terrace	standing 250
Walled Gardens	standing 100
Marquee	Large scale events possible

© English Heritage

OSBORNE HOUSE ⌗

www.english-heritage.org.uk/osborne

Queen Victoria and Prince Albert's family home. Glimpse into the private life of the royal family.

Osborne House was the peaceful, rural retreat of Queen Victoria, Prince Albert and their family; they spent some of their happiest times here.

Step inside and marvel at the richness of the State Apartments including the Durbar Room with its lavish Indian décor. The Queen died at the house in 1901 and many of the rooms have been preserved almost unaltered ever since. The nursery bedroom remains just as it was in the 1870s when Queen Victoria's first grandchildren came to stay. Children were a constant feature of life at Osborne (Victoria and Albert had nine). Don't miss the Swiss Cottage, a charming chalet in the grounds built for teaching the royal children domestic skills.

Enjoy the beautiful gardens with their stunning views over the Solent and the fruit and flower Victorian Walled Garden.

No other venue with the cachet of Osborne House - Queen Victoria's palace-by-the-sea - can offer both the superb coastal location and facilities for those who want to entertain on a grand scale in style.

KEY FACTS

- Available for corporate and private hire. Suitable for filming, concerts, drama. No photography in the house.
- Private and corporate hire.
- Wheelchairs available, access to house via ramp and first floor via lift. WC.
- Hot drinks, light snacks & waiter service lunches in the stunning terrace restaurant.
- Nov–Mar for pre-booked guided tours only. Tours allow visitors to see the Royal Apartments and private rooms.
- Ample.
- Visits free, please book. Education room.

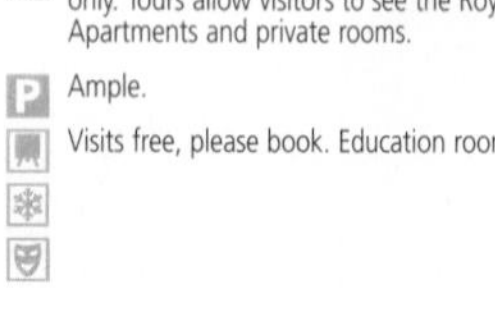

© English Heritage

© English Heritage

© English Heritage

APPULDURCOMBE HOUSE ⌗

Wroxall, Shanklin, Isle of Wight PO38 3EW

www.english-heritage.org.uk/appuldurcombehouse

The bleached shell of a fine 18th century Baroque style house standing in grounds landscaped by 'Capability' Brown. Once the grandest house on the Isle of Wight. An exhibition of photographs and prints depict the house and its history.

Location: MAP 3:D7, OS Ref. SZ543 800. 1/2mile W of Wroxall off B3327.

Owner: English Heritage

Contact: Mr & Mrs Owen

Tel: 01983 852484

E-mail: customers@english-heritage.org.uk

Open: Please visit www.english-heritage.org.uk for opening times and the most up-to-date information.

Admission: House: Adult £4, Child £2.75, Conc. £3.50, Family £13. EH members Free. Additional charge for the Falconry Centre. Opening times and prices are valid until 31 Mar 2012.

Key facts:

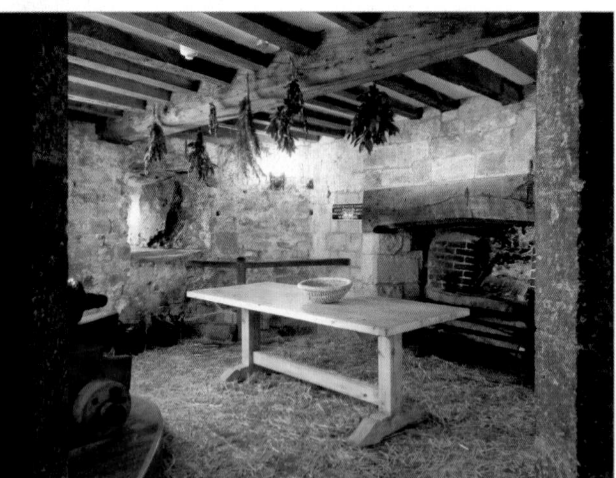

© English Heritage

YARMOUTH CASTLE ⌗

Quay Street, Yarmouth, Isle of Wight PO41 0PB

www.english-heritage.org.uk/yarmouthcastle

This last addition to Henry VIII's coastal defences was completed in 1547, unusually for its kind, square with a fine example of an angle bastion. Exhibition displays artefacts and an atmospheric recreation of how the rooms were used in the 16th century. Magnificent picnic spot, with views over the Solent.

Location: MAP 3:C7, OS Ref. SZ354 898. In Yarmouth adjacent to car ferry terminal.

Owner: English Heritage **Contact:** Visitor Operations Team

Tel: 01983 760678 **E-mail:** customers@english-heritage.org.uk

Open: Please visit www.english-heritage.org.uk for opening times and the most up-to-date information.

Admission: Adult £4, Child £2.40, Conc. £3.60. EH Members Free. Group discount available. Opening times and prices are valid until 31 Mar 2012.

Key facts:

NUNWELL HOUSE & GARDENS

Coach Lane, Brading, Isle Of Wight PO36 0JQ

Nunwell has been a family home for five centuries and reflects much architectural and Island history. King Charles I spent his last night of freedom here. Jacobean and Georgian wings. Finely furnished rooms. Lovely setting with Channel views and five acres of tranquil gardens. Family military collections.

Location: MAP 3:E7. OS Ref. SZ595 874. 1m NW of Brading. 3m S of Ryde signed off A3055.

Owner/Contact: Col J A Aylmer **Tel:** 01983 407240

Open: 23 Apr to 27 Jun: Mon to Wed, 1pm to 5pm. House tours: 2pm & 3.30pm. Groups by arrangement throughout the year.

Admission: Adult £5, Child (under 10yrs) £1, OAP/Student £4.50. Garden only £3. Charges may vary for groups outside advertised opening times.

Key facts: Obligatory. Guide dogs only.

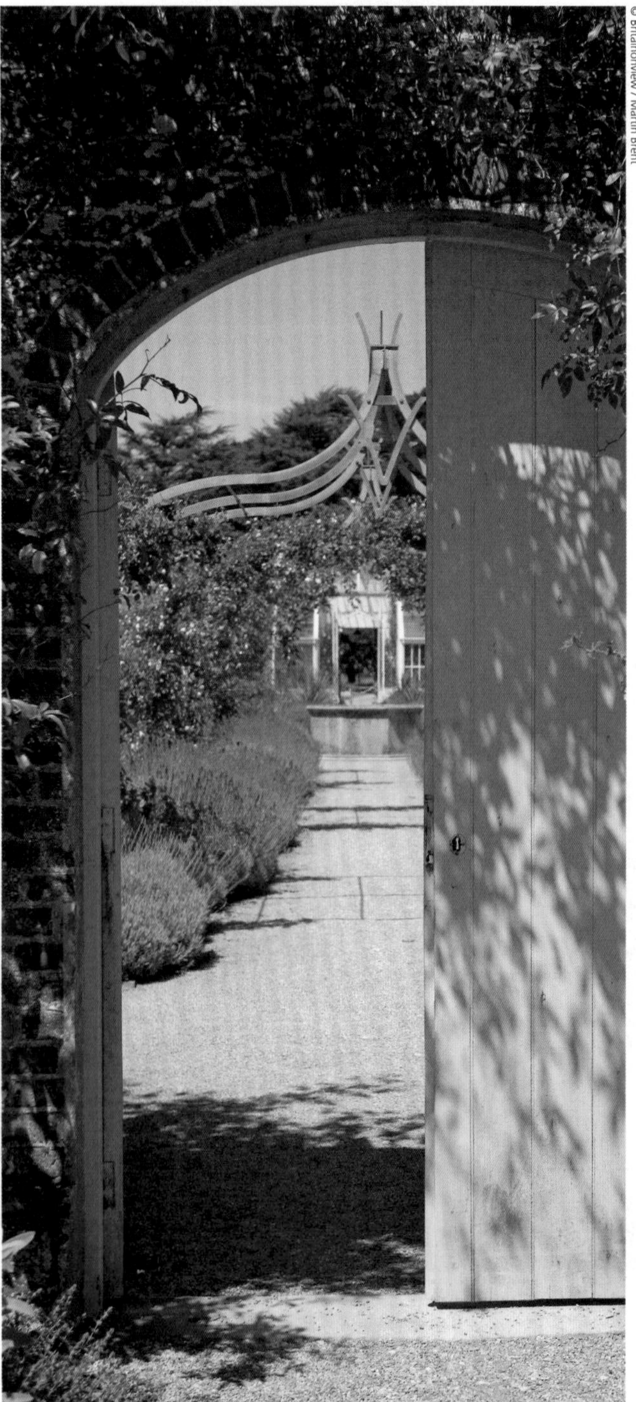

© Britainonview / Martin Brent

A view into the gardens of Osborne House

Plants blooming in a quiet corner of the Wall Garden at Great Dixter

Hartland Abbey

Sudeley Castle

South West

Glouces-
tershire
Wiltshire
Somerset
Devon
Dorset
Cornwall
Channel
Islands

Channel Islands

Cornwall

Devon

Dorset

Gloucestershire

Somerset

Wiltshire

Iconic St Michael's Mount hugs the stunning Cornwall coast. Sudeley Castle, the former home of Tudor Queen Katherine Parr, with its award-winning gardens and medieval ruins nestles in the Cotswolds. From fascinating Hartland Abbey on the North Devon Coast and Mapperton, a fine Jacobean country manor in Dorset, to the mysteries of Stonehenge and the exquisite Hestercombe Gardens in Somerset, the South West never fails to delight.

VISITOR INFORMATION

Owner
The Seigneur de Sausmarez

Address
Sausmarez Manor
Saint Martin
Guernsey
Channel Islands
GY4 6SG

Location
MAP 3:D10
2m S of St Peter Port, clearly signposted.

Contact
Peter de Sausmarez
Tel: 01481 235571 or 01481 235655
Fax: 01481 235572
E-mail: sausmarezmanor@cwgsy.net

Opening Times
The Grounds:
Easter–End Oct
Daily: 10am–5pm

Guided tours of House:
Easter–End Oct
Mon–Thurs:
10.30 & 11.30am
Additional 2pm tour during high season.

Admission
There is no overall charge for admission.

Sub Tropical Garden	£6.00
Sculpture Trail	£6.00
Short golf course	£6.00
Putting	£2.00
House Tour	£7.00
Ghost Tour: Including complimentary glass of wine	£10.00
Train Rides	£2.00

Discounts for Children, Students, OAPs & Organised Groups.

SAUSMAREZ MANOR

www.sausmarezmanor.co.uk www.artparks.co.uk

The home of the Seigneurs de Sausmarez since c1220 with a façade built at the bequest of the first Governor of New York.

An entertaining half day encompassing something to interest everyone. The family have been explorers, inventors, diplomats, prelates, generals, admirals, privateers, politicians and governors etc, most of whom left their mark on the house, garden or the furniture.

The sub-tropical woodland garden is crammed with such exotics as banana trees, tree ferns, ginger, 300 plus camellias, lilies, myriads of bamboos, as well as the more commonplace hydrangeas, hostas etc. The RHS recommends the gardens to its own members, as does 'The Good Garden Guide','1001 Gardens you must see before You Die' and the 'RHS Garden Finder'.

The sculpture in the art park with its 200 or so pieces by artists from a dozen countries is the most comprehensive in Britain and rated 5th in the Daily Telegraph's top ten. The Shortcourse is a testing 500m 9 hole par 3. The Copper, and Silversmith demonstrates his ancient skills and is the remaining craftsman making the traditional copper Guernsey Milk Can. The two lakes are a haven for ornamental wildfowl and some of the sculpture.

The community Farmers' and Plantsmen's Market is every Saturday morning, selling local Fish, Crab/Lobster, Guernsey Beef and Veal, Sark Lamb and Butter, fresh locally grown vegetables and plants, home made Cakes, Jams, Pasties, Pate, Pies, Vegetarian Delights as well as gifts, Handcrafts & Toys, Island made Jewellery and herbal remedies, Crystals and therapies.

KEY FACTS

Partial.

Guided tours of House Easter–Oct.

Guide dogs only.

Two holiday flats are available see www.cottageguide.co.uk

€

© English Heritage

PENDENNIS CASTLE

www.english-heritage.org.uk/pendennis

Pendennis Castle, Falmouth is one of the finest fortresses built by Henry VIII.

At the mouth of the River Fal estuary Pendennis and its neighbour, St Mawes, form the Cornish end of costal castles built by Henry VIII to counter threat of invasion from France and Spain. Thereafter Pendennis was frequently adapted to face new enemies over 400 years, right through to World War II.

Pendennis today stands as a landmark, with fine sea views and excellent site facilities including a hands-on discovery centre, exhibitions, a museum, guardhouse, shop and tearoom. It is also an excellent venue for special events throughout the year.

High on the steep ramparts with sweeping views over Falmouth Bay, stands the solid single storey holiday cottage in an enviable position. The second holiday cottage is set within the walls of Pendennis Castle and enjoys its own private, secluded garden. The historic town of Falmouth with shops, restaurants and cafés is within walking distance.

Set high upon the headland with panoramic views out to sea, Pendennis Castle is a spectacular location for memorable occasions. The impressive Cornish landmark combines a unique history with contemporary styling and modern facilities, offering a memorable setting for weddings, smart drinks receptions, exclusive dinners, conferences and meetings.

VISITOR INFORMATION

Owner
English Heritage

Address
Falmouth
Cornwall
TR11 4LP

Location
MAP 1:E10,
OS Ref. SW824 318.
On Pendennis Head.

Contact
Visitor Operations Team
Tel: 01326 316594
E-mail: pendennis.castle@english-heritage.org.uk
Venue and Hire Hospitality:
01326 310106

Opening Times
please visit www.english-heritage.org.uk for opening times and the most up-to-date information.

Admission

Adult	£6.30
Child	£3.80
Conc.	£5.70
Family	£16.40

Discount for groups (11+).

EH members Free.

Opening times and prices are valid until 31st March 2012.

Special events
There is an exciting events programme available throughout the year, for further details please contact the property or visit the website.

KEY FACTS

WC

Partial.

No coaches.

In grounds only.

0870 333 1187

€

© English Heritage

© English Heritage / Roger Dovey

VISITOR INFORMATION

■ Owner
English Heritage

■ Address
Tintagel
Cornwall
PL34 0HE

■ Location
MAP 1:F7, Landranger Sheet 200 Ref. SX048 891.
On Tintagel Head, ½m along uneven track from Tintagel.

■ Contact
Visitor Operations Team
Tel/Fax: 01840 770328
E-mail: tintagel.castle@english-heritage.org.uk

■ Opening Times
Please visit www.english-heritage.org.uk for opening times and the most up-to-date information.

■ Admission
Adult	£5.50
Child	£3.30
Conc.	£5.00
Family	£14.30

Discount for groups (11+).

EH members Free.

Prices are valid until 31st March 2012, after this date details are subject to change.

■ Special events
There is an exciting events programme available throughout the year, for further details please contact the property or visit the website.

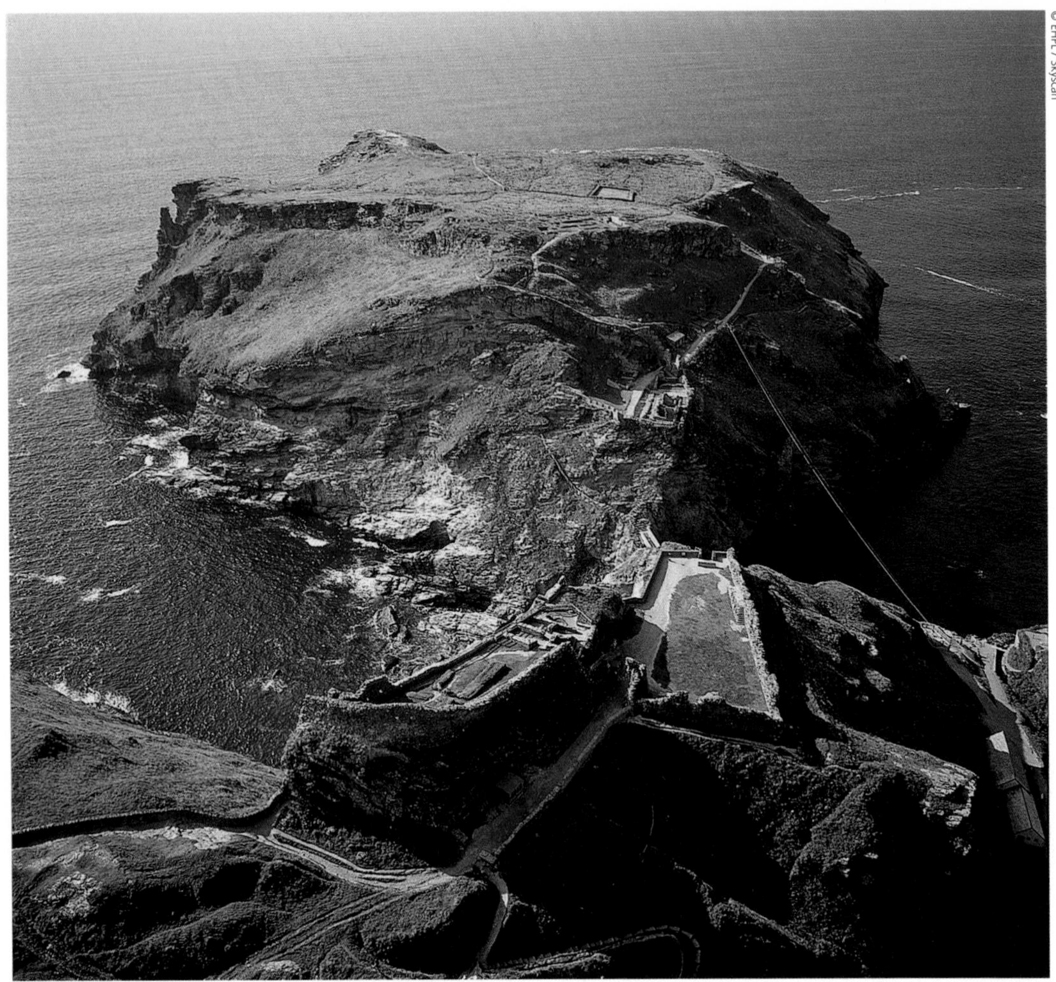

© EHPL / Skyscan

TINTAGEL CASTLE ⌗

www.english-heritage.org.uk/tintagel

Tintagel Castle is a magical day with its wonderful location, set high on the rugged North Cornwall coast.

Tintagel Castle is steeped in legend and mystery; said to be the birthplace of King Arthur, you can still visit the nearby Merlin's Cave. The castle also features in the tale of Tristan and Isolde.

Joined to the mainland by a narrow neck of land, Tintagel Island faces the full force of the Atlantic. On the mainland itself, the gaunt remains of the medieval castle represent only one phase in a long history of occupation.

The remains of the 13th century castle are breathtaking. Steep stone steps, stout walls and rugged windswept cliff edges encircle the Great Hall, where Richard Earl of Cornwall once feasted.

The site also offers a shop, visitor facilities and the cafe which is set above the beach, serves a delicious selection of hot and cold snacks and light meals all sourced from the finest local ingredients.

KEY FACTS

WC.

No vehicles. Parking (not EH) in village only.

On leads.

© English Heritage

© English Heritage

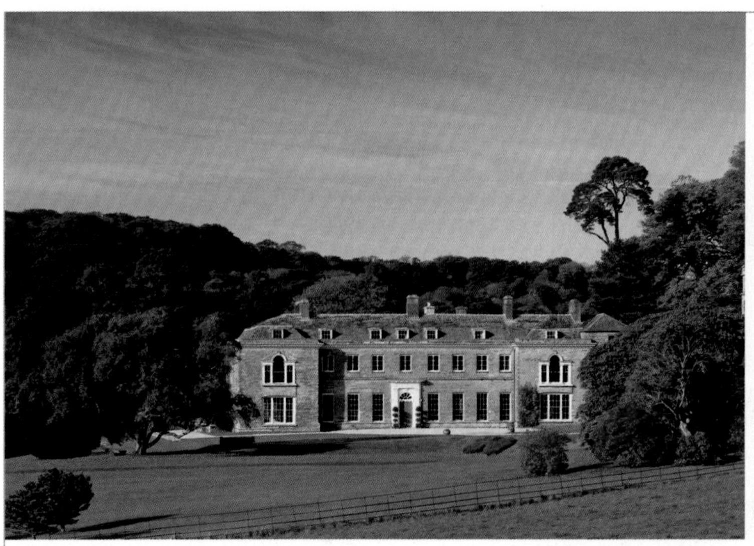

BOCONNOC

THE ESTATE OFFICE, BOCONNOC, LOSTWITHIEL, CORNWALL PL22 0RG

www.boconnoc.com

Bought with the famous Pitt Diamond in 1717 and home to three Prime Ministers, Boconnoc remains one of Cornwall's best kept secrets. Visitors can view architecture influenced by Sir John Soane, visit the Georgian Bath House and examine the conservation of the 18th century wall and ceiling paintings which line the double staircase. The superb parkland was first laid out by Thomas Pitt in the 18th century. The magnificent woodland garden, the site for the annual Cornwall Spring Flower Show, contains rhododendrons, azaleas, camellias and magnolias. Perfect for weddings, private and corporate events, filming, and there are residential and holiday houses to let.

Location: MAP 1:G8. OS Ref. 148 605. A38 from Plymouth, Liskeard or from Bodmin to Dobwalls, then A390 to East Taphouse and follow signs.

Owner: Anthony Fortescue Esq **Contact:** Veryan Barneby, Events Organiser

Tel: 01208 872507 **Fax:** 01208 873836 **E-mail:** info@boconnoc.com

Open: House & Garden: 6, 13, 20 & 27 May: Suns 2–5pm. Groups (15–255) by appointment all year.

Admission: House: £4, Garden: £4.50. Children under 12yrs Free.

Special Events: 31 Mar & 1 Apr: Cornwall Garden Society Spring Flower Show. 15 & 16 May: Spring Fair. 20 May: Dog Show. 20, 21 & 22 Jul: Boconnoc Steam Fair. 1 & 2 Oct: Michaelmas Fair. 20 Oct: Scratch Messiah.

Key facts: Conferences. Partial. Licensed. By arrangement. In grounds, on leads. 10 doubles (8 en suite). Church or Civil ceremony.

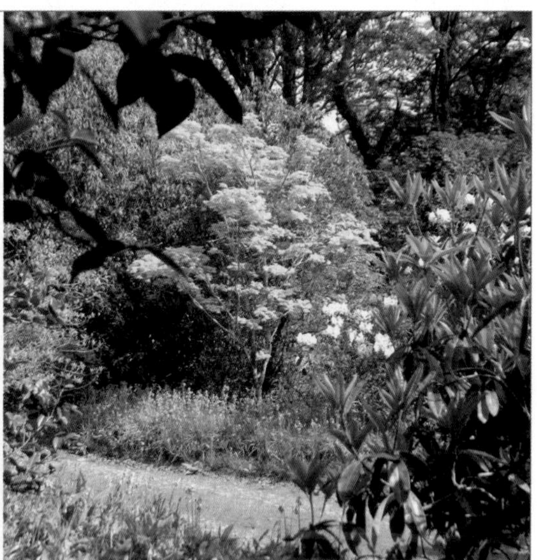

CAERHAYS CASTLE & GARDEN

CAERHAYS, GORRAN, ST AUSTELL, CORNWALL PL26 6LY

www.caerhays.co.uk

One of the very few Nash built castles still left standing – situated within approximately 60 acres of informal woodland gardens created by J C Williams, who sponsored plant hunting expeditions to China at the turn of the century. As well as guided tours of the house from March to June visitors will see some of the magnificent selection of plants brought back by the intrepid plant hunters of the early 1900s these include not only the collection of magnolias but a wide range of rhododendrons and the camellias which Caerhays and the Williams familly are associated with worldwide.

Location: OS Ref. SW972 415. S coast of Cornwall – between Mevagissey and Portloe. 9m SW of St Austell.

Owner: F J Williams Esq **Contact:** Lucinda Rimmington

Tel: 01872 501310 **Fax:** 01872 501870

E-mail: estateoffice@caerhays.co.uk

Open: House: 12 Mar–5 Jun: Mon–Fri only (including BHs), 12–4pm, booking recommended. Gardens; 13 Feb–5 Jun: daily (including BHs), 10am–5pm (last admission 4pm).

Admission: House: £7.50. Gardens; £7.50. House & Gardens; £12.00. Group tours: £8.50 by arrangement. Groups please contact Estate Office.

Key facts: No photography in house. Obligatory by arrangement. Limited for coaches.

PORT ELIOT HOUSE & GARDENS

ST. GERMANS, SALTASH, CORNWALL PL12 5ND

www.porteliot.co.uk

Port Eliot is an ancient, hidden gem, set in stunning fairytale grounds which nestle beside a secret estuary in South East Cornwall. It has the rare distinction of being a Grade I Listed house, park and gardens. This is due in part to the work of Sir John Soane, who worked his magic on the house and Humphrey Repton, who created the park and garden.

Explore the treasures in the house. Gaze at masterpieces by Reynolds and Van Dyck. Decipher the Lenkiewicz Round Room Riddle Mural. Still a family home, you will be beguiled by the warm atmosphere.

Location: MAP 1:H8, OS Ref. SX359 578. Situated in the village of St Germans on B3249 in South East Cornwall.

Owner: The Earl of St Germans **Contact:** Port Eliot Estate Office

Tel: 01503 230211 **Fax:** 01503 230112

E-mail: info@porteliot.co.uk

Open: 12 Mar–8 Jul (except 9 & 10 Jun). Open daily except Friday. Open 2–6pm. Last admission to the house at 5pm. Tea Room open 12.30–5.30pm.

Admission: House & Garden: *Adult £8, Children £4. Group (20+): Adult £7, *also visitors by public transport £7. Grounds only: Adult £5, Children £2.

Key facts: No photography. Suitable. WCs. By arrangement. Dogs allowed in grounds. Guide dogs in the house. In July, Port Eliot Festival 19–22 July 2012, is an annual celebration of words, music, imagination, laughter, exploration and above all–fun in one of the most beautiful and secret gardens in England. A Dog Festival in May each year.

PRIDEAUX PLACE

PADSTOW, CORNWALL PL28 8RP

www.prideauxplace.co.uk

Tucked away above the busy port of Padstow, the home of the Prideaux family for over 400 years, is surrounded by gardens and wooded grounds overlooking a deer park and the Camel estuary to the moors beyond. The house still retains its 'E' shape Elizabethan front and contains fine paintings and furniture. Now a major international film location, this family home is one of the brightest jewels in Cornwall's crown. The historic garden is undergoing major restoration work and offers some of the best views in the county. A cornucopia of Cornish history under one roof.

Location: MAP 1:E7, OS Ref. SW913 756. 5m from A39 Newquay/Wadebridge link road. Signposted by Historic House signs.

Owner/Contact: Peter Prideaux-Brune Esq

Tel: 01841 532411 **Fax:** 01841 532945 **E-mail:** office@prideauxplace.co.uk

Open: Easter Sun 8 Apr–Thur 12 Apr, Sun 13 May–Thur 11 Oct. Grounds & Tearoom: 12.30–5pm. House Tours: 1.30–4pm (last tour).

Admission: House & Grounds: Adult £8, Child £2. Grounds only: Adult £4, Child £1. Groups (15+) discounts apply.

Key facts: By arrangement. Partial. Ground floor & grounds. Fully licensed. Obligatory. By arrangement. On leads. By arrangement. Open Air Theatre, Open Air Concerts, Car Rallies, Art Exhibitions, Charity Events.

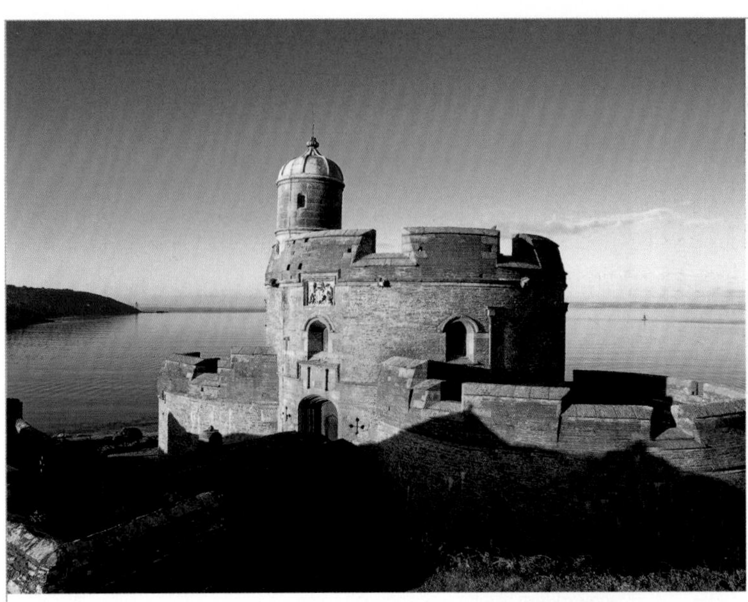

© English Heritage

© English Heritage

ST MAWES CASTLE

ST MAWES, CORNWALL TR2 5DE

www.english-heritage.org.uk/stmawes

St Mawes Castle is among the best-preserved of Henry VIII's coastal artillery fortresses, and the most elaborately decorated of them all. Situated on the edge of St Mawes village, this fine example of Tudor military architecture offers views over the little boat-filled harbour and the splendid surrounding coastline. Fort House holiday cottage has spectacular views over the sheltered Fal estuary and out towards the open sea. In addition to stunning rooms inside the Castle, we have now licensed the Lower Fort for outdoor civil wedding ceremonies. Set right at the water's edge making a stunning location for your outdoor ceremony.
Location: MAP 1:E10, OS204 Ref. SW842 328. W of St Mawes on A3078.

Owner: English Heritage **Contact:** Visitor Operations Team
Tel/Fax: 01326 270526 **Venue Hire and Hospitality:** 01326 310106
E-mail: stmawes.castle@english-heritage.org.uk
Open: please visit www.english-heritage.org.uk for opening times and the most up-to-date information.
Admission: Adult £4.30, Child £2.60, Conc. £3.90. 15% discount for groups (11+). EH members Free. Opening times and prices are valid until 31st March 2012.
Key facts: 01326 310106. Partial. Limited. Grounds only.

© NT / St Michael's Mount

© NT / St Michael's Mount

ST MICHAEL'S MOUNT

MARAZION, NR PENZANCE, CORNWALL TR17 0HT

www.stmichaelsmount.co.uk www.nationaltrust.org.uk

This beautiful island has become an icon for Cornwall and has magnificent views of Mount's Bay from its summit. There the church and castle, whose origins date from the 12th century, have at various times acted as a Benedictine priory, a place of pilgrimage, a fortress, a mansion house and now a magnet for visitors from all over the world. Following the Civil War, the island was acquired by the St Aubyn family who still live in the castle today.
Location: MAP 1:C10, OS Ref. SW515 300. 3 miles East of Penzance.
Owner: National Trust
Contact: Clare Sandry, St Aubyn Estates, West End, Marazion, Cornwall TR17 OEF
Tel: 01736 710507 (710265 tide information) **Fax:** 01736 719930
E-mail: mail@stmichaelsmount.co.uk
Open: Castle: 26 Mar–2 Nov, Sun–Fri, 10.30am–5pm (1 Jul–31 Aug, 10.30am–5.30pm). Last admission 45 mins before castle closing time.
Gardens: 16 Apr–29 June, Mon–Fri; 5 Jul–28 Sept, Thur & Fri, 10.30am–5pm (5.30pm Jul & Aug).
Admission: Castle Adult £7.50, Child (under 17) £3.75, Family £18.75, 1-Adult Family £11.25. Booked groups £6.50. Garden: Adult £3.50, Child £1.50. Combined Castle & Garden Tickets - Adult £9.25, Child £4.50, Family £23, 1-Adult Family £13.75. Groups £8.
Key facts: Parking on mainland (not NT). Dogs not permitted in the castle or gardens. For a full events calendar throughout the season, please check the website. Partial. WCs. Licensed. Licensed. By arrangement. Tel for details. On mainland, including coach parking (not NT.) Guide dogs only.

HEARTLANDS CORNWALL

Robinson's Shaft, Dudnance Lane, Pool, Redruth, Cornwall TR15 3QY

www.heartlandscornwall.com

Opening in Spring 2012, Heartlands Cornwall presents an exciting combination of heritage, gardens and culture. Set in 19 acres of stunning parkland, this World Heritage Site includes vibrant art galleries, breath-taking botanical gardens and water features, state-of-the art exhibitions exploring the history of Cornish mining and a large adventure playground.

Location: MAP1:D10, OS Ref. SW667 412. From A30, take exit signposted to Pool.

Owner: Heartlands Trust

Contact: Kate Turnbull, Marketing Manager

Tel: 01209 722327

E-mail: kate.turnbull@heartlandscornwall.com

Open: Due to open to the public in Spring 2012. Open every day of the year except Christmas Day.

Admission: Free.

Key facts: WCs. Licensed. Licensed. Obligatory. Limited for cars and coaches. On leads.

PENTILLIE CASTLE & ESTATE ®

Paynters Cross, St Mellion, Saltash, Cornwall PL12 6QD

www.pentillie.co.uk

Built by Sir James Tillie in the 17th century, historic Pentillie Castle is set within 2,000 acres of mature rolling woods and parkland overlooking the River Tamar. Now beautifully restored, the castle offers 5 star luxury accommodation and exclusive hire for weddings and corporate guests. Other activities available on request.

Location: MAP 1:H8, OS Ref. SX040 645. 7m West of Plymouth. Postcode: PL12 6QD.

Owner: Ted and Sarah Coryton **Contact:** Sammie Coryton

Tel: 01579 350044 **Fax:** 01579 212002 **E-mail:** contact@pentillie.co.uk

Open: Spring garden open days still to be confirmed at time of publication. Please visit www.pentillie.co.uk or telephone for more details. Private group tours and lunches available on request.

Admission: Gardens £6. House £3. Children under 12 free.

Key facts: Visit www.pentillie.co.uk for garden open days & event details. Partial. WCs. Licensed. Licensed. By arrangement. Limited for coaches. Guide dogs only. By appointment only.

PENCARROW

Bodmin, Cornwall PL30 3AG

www.pencarrow.co.uk

Owned, loved and lived in by the family. Georgian house and Grade II* listed gardens. Superb collection of portraits, furniture and porcelain. Marked walks through 50 acres of beautiful formal and woodland gardens, Victorian rockery, Italian garden, over 700 different varieties of rhododendrons, lake, Iron Age hill fort and icehouse.

Location: OS Ref. SX040 711. Between Bodmin and Wadebridge. 4m NW of Bodmin off A389 & B3266 at Washaway.

Owner: Molesworth-St Aubyn family **Contact:** Administrator

Tel: 01208 841369 **Fax:** 01208 841722 **E-mail:** info@pencarrow.co.uk

Open: House: 1 Apr–27 Sept 2012, Sun–Thur, 11am–4pm (guided tour only - last tour of the House at 3pm). Café & shop 11am–5pm. Gardens: 1 Mar–31 Oct, daily, 10am–5.30pm.

Admission: House & Garden: Adult £10.50, Conc. £9.50, Child (5-16 years) £5, Family ticket (2 adults & 2 children) £28. Grounds only: Adult £5.50, Conc. £5, Child (5-16 years) £2.50.

Key facts: Gift and plant shop, small children's play area, self-pick soft fruit. By arrangement. Suitable. WCs. Obligatory. In grounds.

© English Heritage

RESTORMEL CASTLE

Lostwithiel, Cornwall PL22 0EE

www.english-heritage.org.uk/restormel

Perched on a high mound, surrounded by a deep moat, the huge circular keep of this splendid Norman castle survives in remarkably good condition. It is still possible to make out Restormel's Keep Gate, Great Hall and even the kitchens and private rooms.

Location: MAP 1:F8, OS200 Ref. SX104 614. 1½m N of Lostwithiel off A390.

Owner: English Heritage

Contact: Visitor Operations Team

Tel: 01208 872687

E-mail: customers@english-heritage.org.uk

Open: Please visit www.english-heritage.org.uk for opening times and the most up-to-date information.

Admission: Adult £3.40, Child £2, Conc. £3.10. Discount for groups (11+). EH Members free. Opening times and prices are valid until 31st March 2012.

Key facts: WC.

Limited for coaches.

On leads.

Britain's Brilliant Heritage
Brought To Life
To find out more visit our website
www.hudsonsheritage.com
HUDSON'S
HERITAGE

GODOLPHIN BLOWINGHOUSE

Blowinghouse Cottage, Godolphin Cross, Breage, Helston, Cornwall TR13 9RE

The Blowinghouse dates from the 16th century and was built as part of the Godolphin family tin mining works. The tin ingots weighed in excess of three hundredweight and were stamped with a cat's head that was the Godophin Mine logo.

Location: MAP 1:D10, OS Ref. SW508 521, Situated in the Godolphin Woods- National Trust opposite entrance to the Godolphin Manor House.
Owner/Contact: Mr & Mrs B J Portch
Tel: 01736 763218
E-mail: brian.portch@ndirect.co.uk
Open: Sun, 5 Aug, 2012, 9.30am–4.30pm. Other times by appointment.
Admission: Free.
Key facts: WCs. Limited. No coaches.

BURNCOOSE NURSERIES & GARDEN

Gwennap, Redruth, Cornwall TR16 6BJ

The Nurseries are set in the 30 acre woodland gardens of Burncoose.

Location: MAP 1:D10, OS Ref. SW742 395. 2m SE Redruth on main A393 Redruth to Falmouth road.
Owner: C H Williams **Contact:** C H Williams **Tel:** 01209 860316
Fax: 01209 860011 **E-mail:** burncoose@eclipse.co.uk
Website: www.burncoose.co.uk
Open: Mon–Sat: 9am–5pm, Suns, 11am–5pm. Gardens and Tearooms open all year (except Christmas Day).
Admission: Nurseries: Free. **Gardens:** Adult/Conc. £3. Child Free. Group conducted tours: £2.50 by arrangement.
Key facts: WCs. Obligatory. By arrangement. Limited for coaches. On leads.

LAWRENCE HOUSE

9 Castle Street, Launceston, Cornwall PL15 8BA

Fine Georgian House, owned by the Trust, leased to Launceston Town Council, used as a "little jewel" of a museum and Mayor's Parlour.

Location: MAP 1:H7, OS Ref. SX330 848. Launceston.
Owner: National Trust
Contact: The Curator
Tel: 01566 773277
E-mail: lawrencehousemuseum@yahoo.co.uk
Website: www.lawrencehousemuseum.org
Open: Apr–Oct: Mon–Fri, 10.30am–4pm and occasional Sats. Other times by appointment. Open BHs.
Admission: Free, but donations welcomed.
Key facts: Partial. On leads.

FALMOUTH ART GALLERY

Municipal Art Gallery, The Moor, Falmouth TR11 2RT

Falmouth Art Gallery is an award winning gallery with one of the most important art collections in Cornwall. The permanent collection features major artists including Thomas Gainsborough, Edward Burne-Jones, Frank Brangwyn and Charles Napier Hemy. There is a changing programme of exhibitions/events throughout the year. Family and pet friendly.

Location: MAP 1:E10, OS Ref. SW800 693. On The Moor, in the upper floor of the Municipal Buildings above the Library.
Tel: 01326 313863
E-mail: info@falmouthartgallery.com
Website: www.falmouthartgallery.com
Open: Mon–Sat, 10am–5pm (including spring and summer bank holidays).
Admission: Free.
Key facts: Selection of prints, cards, art books and crafts. WC. Lift. Parking. Short stay on The Moor, Long Stay on Quarry Hill.

TREWITHEN

Grampound Road, Nr Truro, Cornwall TR2 4DD

Trewithen is an historic estate near Truro, Cornwall. Owned and lived in by the same family for 300 years, it is both private home and national treasure. The woodland gardens are outstanding with 24 champion trees and famously rare and highly prized plants. Tours of the house prove equally memorable.

Location: MAP 1:E9, OS Ref. SW914 524. Grampound Road, near Truro, Cornwall.
Owner: A M J Galsworthy **Contact:** The Estate Office
Tel: 01726 883647 **Fax:** 01726 882301 **E-mail:** info@trewithengardens.co.uk
Website: www.trewithengardens.co.uk
Open: House: Apr–Jul & Aug BH Monday. Garden: Mar–Sept. Please contact us or visit website for opening times.
Admission: Adult £7.50 Children under 12 Free. Combined entry and group rates. Please contact us or visit website for more information.
Key facts: No photography in house. WCs. By arrangement. On leads.

Caerhays Castle

VISITOR INFORMATION

Owner
The Hon. John Rous

Address
Clovelly
Nr Bideford
N Devon EX39 5TA

Location
MAP 1:H5
OS Ref. SS248 319

On A39 10 miles W of Bideford, 15 miles E of Bude. Turn off at 'Clovelly Cross' roundabout and follow signs to car park.

Air: Exeter & Plymouth Airport both 50 miles.

Rail: Barnstaple 19 miles.

Bus: from Bideford.

Contact
Visitor Centre
Tel: 01237 431781
Fax: 01237 431644
E-mail: visitorcentre@clovelly.co.uk

Opening Times
High season:
9am–6pm.

Low season:
10am–4.30pm.

Admission

Adult	£5.95
Child (7–16yrs)	£3.75
Child (under 7yrs)	Free
Family (2+2)	£15.90
Group Rates (20+)	
Adult	£4.95
Child	£3.50
Twin ticket rate for Clovelly and Hartland Abbey	£10.95.

The entrance fee covers parking, admission to the audio-visual film, Fisherman's Cottage, Kingsley Museum and contributes to the ongoing maintenance of the village, itself part of a private estate.

Prices correct at time of going to press.

Special events
Easter
Red Letter Days

May
Celebration of Ales & Ciders

July
Clovelly Maritime Festival
Woolsery Agricultural Show
Lundy Row

August
Lifeboat Day
Clovelly Gig Regatta

September
Lobster & Crab Feast

November
Clovelly Herring Festival

December
Christmas Lights

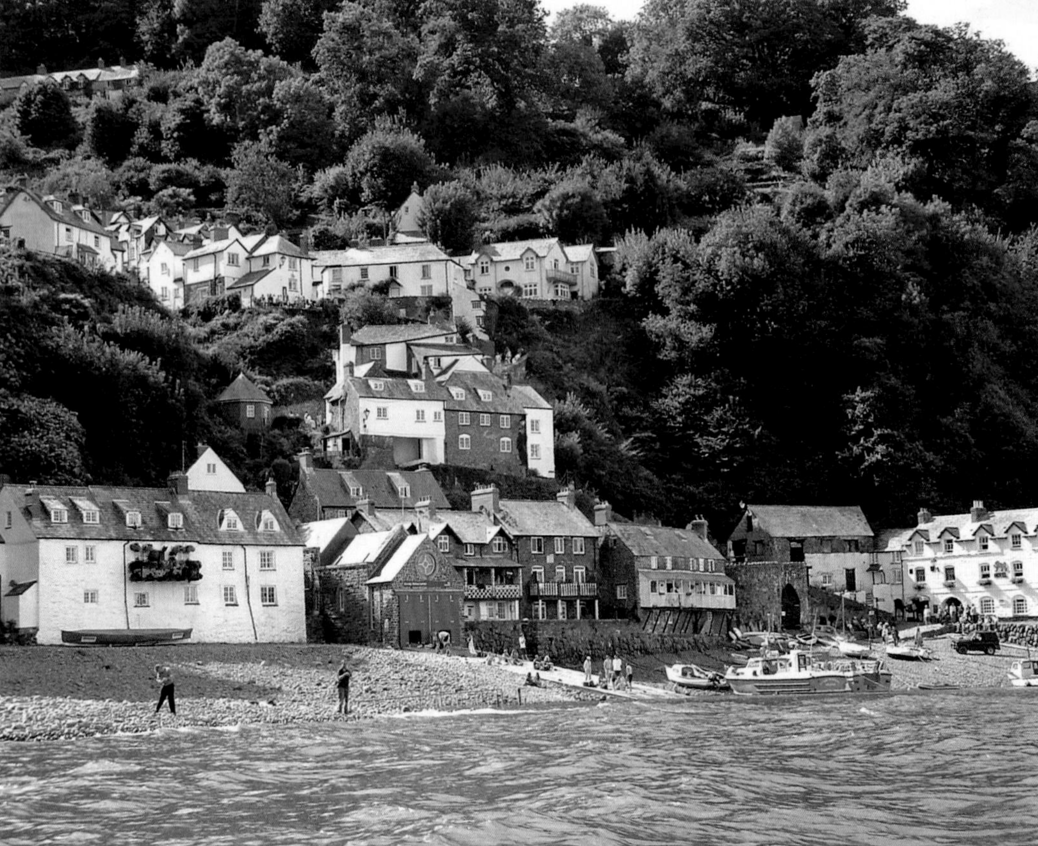

CLOVELLY

www.clovelly.co.uk

Most visitors consider Clovelly to be unique. Whatever your view, it is a world of difference not to be missed.

From Elizabethan days until today, Clovelly Village has been in private ownership, which has helped preserve its original atmosphere. The main traffic-free street, known as 'up-a-long' and 'down-a-long', tumbles its cobbled way down to the tiny harbour, which is protected by an ancient stone breakwater. It is a descent through flower-strewn cottages broken only by little passageways and winding lanes that lead off to offer the prospect of more picturesque treasures.

The New Inn, which is 400 years old, is halfway down the street, and another, the Red Lion, is right on the quayside. Both Inns have long histories and an atmosphere rarely found in the modern world. In 2012 it is planned to open a renovated Grade II listed building adjacent to the Red Lion to provide 7 new bedrooms and will be known as the Sail Loft.

In addition you'll find the Visitor Centre, a range of gift shops, a café and an audio-visual theatre in which visitors are treated to a history of the village. Just below is the Stable Yard with a pottery and silk workshop. There are beautiful coastal and woodland walks.

Access is restricted to pedestrians only via the Visitor Centre with a Land Rover taxi service for those unable to walk.

KEY FACTS

Rubber soled, low heel shoes are recommended.

Partial.

Licensed.

Licensed.

By arrangement.

On leads.

18 double, 1 single, all en suite.

Civil Wedding Licence

NEW INN

HARTLAND ABBEY

www.hartlandabbey.com

Hartland Abbey is a fascinating house straddling a narrow, wooded valley leading to an Atlantic cove, a short walk away.

Built in 1159 as an Augustinian monastery, at the Dissolution Henry VIII gifted the Abbey to the Keeper of his Wine Cellar whose descendants live here today. Visitors to Hartland Abbey can experience not only stunning architecture and interiors, fascinating collections, beautiful gardens and walks but the warmth and friendliness found only in a cherished family home. Close family connections to Poltimore House and Clovelly Court nearby are evident. BBC Antiques Roadshow was filmed here in 2011.

Amongst the impressive interiors spanning Mediaeval, Queen Anne, Georgian, Regency and Victorian periods you can see the three main Reception Rooms, the Alhambra Corridor by Sir George Gilbert Scott and the Gothic Library by Meadows with its fireplace by Batty Langley. Important paintings by artists including Reynolds and Gainsborough, furniture, porcelain, early photographs, a museum of documents from 1160 and changing displays of family memorabilia fascinate visitors.

Much of the 50 acres of gardens and walks had been lost since the First World War but since restoration began in 1996 once again beautiful paths wind through woodland gardens; the Bog Garden and Fernery, by Gertrude Jekyll, thrive again. In the three 18th century Walled Gardens climbers, herbaceous, tender perennials and vegetables delight; glasshouses protect stunning plants for display in the house.

Walk through carpets of primroses, historic daffodils, bluebells and wildflowers in spring to the newly restored Summerhouse in the woods, the Gazebo and Blackpool Mill with its beautiful beach and cottage, the film location for Jane Austen's 'Sense and Sensibility' and Rosamunde Pilcher's 'The Shell Seekers'. Donkeys, black sheep and peacocks roam. Children's Quiz. Five stunning wedding venues available. Holiday cottages to rent. The Hartland Abbey estate is on the SW Coastal Footpath in an Area of Outstanding Natural Beauty. Free parking. Gift Shop. 1 mile from Hartland Quay and St. Nectan's Church, the 'Cathedral of North Devon'.

KEY FACTS

Wedding receptions.

Partial. WC.

By arrangement.

In grounds, on leads.

VISITOR INFORMATION

Owner
Sir Hugh Stucley Bt

Address
Hartland Abbey
Nr. Bideford
North Devon
EX39 6DT

Location
MAP 1:G5
OS Ref. SS240 249
15m W of Bideford, 15m N of Bude off A39 between Hartland and Hartland Quay on B3248.

Contact
The Administrator
Tel: 01237 441264/234
01884 860225
Fax: 01237 441264
01884 861134
E-mail: ha_admin@btconnect.com

Opening Times
House
12 February, 18 March (11am–4pm). 1 April–20 May, Wed, Thur, Sun & BHs inc. Good Friday. 20 May–30 September Sun–Thurs, 2–5pm. Last adm. 4.30pm.

Gardens, Grounds & Beachwalk
12 February, 18 March (11am–4pm). 1 April–30 September, Daily except Sats, 11.00am–5pm.

Tea Room
Light lunches and cream teas 11.30am–5pm (House open days only).

Admission
House, Gardens, Grounds & Beachwalk

Adult	£10.00
OAP	£9.50
Child (5–15ys)	£4.00
Family (2+2)	£25.00

Gardens, Grounds & Beachwalk only

Adult & OAP	£5.50
Child (5–15ys)	£3.00
Family (2+2)	£14.00

Groups and coaches
Concessions to groups of 20+. Open to coaches at other dates and times. Booking essential.
Large car park adjacent to the house.

Special events
February
12 Snowdrop Sunday (11am–4pm)
March
18 Mothering Sunday and Daffodil Day. (11am–4pm)
April
22 and 29 Bluebell Sundays
(see website for further information on events).

POWDERHAM CASTLE

KENTON, NR EXETER, DEVON EX6 8JQ

www.powderham.co.uk

A splendid castle built in 1391 by Sir Philip Courtenay, remaining in the same family and now home to the 18th Earl of Devon. Set in a tranquil deer park alongside the Exe estuary, its stunning location offering glorious views. The Woodland Garden is delightful in the spring while the Rose Garden comes into bloom from June. Guided tours showcase the Castle's majestic rooms and stunning interiors, while fascinating stories bring its intriguing history to life. The tea room offers a selection of home cooked food. Gift shop, plant centre and extensive calendar of events create a wonderful day out.

Location: MAP 2:K7. OS Ref. SX965 832. 6m SW of Exeter, 4m S M5/J30. Access from A379 in Kenton village.

Owner: The Earl of Devon **Contact:** Mr Simon Fishwick – Estate Director

Tel: 01626 890243 **Fax:** 01626 890729

E-mail: castle@powderham.co.uk

Open: 1 Apr–30 Oct 2011: Sun–Fri, 11am–4.30pm/5.30pm in summer (Last guided tour 1hr before closing and 2.30pm on Fri). Available for private hire all year.

Admission: Adult £9.80, Child (4–16yrs) £7.80, Senior £8.80, Family: £27.80. Groups (15+) special rates available. (2011 prices)

Key facts: Available for private hire all year round. Partial. WCS. Licensed. Licensed. Obligatory. Included. 1hr. Free. Guide dogs only. Cooper Antiques Fair 2–4 Mar 2012. Wedding Show 24 & 25 Mar 2012.

CADHAY

Ottery St Mary, Devon EX11 1QT

www.cadhay.org.uk

Cadhay is approached by an avenue of lime-trees, and stands in an extensive garden, with herbaceous borders and yew hedges, with excellent views over the original medieval fish ponds. The main part of the house was built in about 1550 by John Haydon who had married the de Cadhay heiress. He retained the Great Hall of an earlier house, of which the fine timber roof (about 1420–1460) can be seen. An Elizabethan Long Gallery was added by John's successor at the end of the 16th century, thereby forming a unique courtyard with statues of Sovereigns on each side, described by Sir Simon Jenkins as one of the 'Treasures of Devon'.

Location: MAP 2:L6, OS Ref. SY090 962. 1m NW of Ottery St Mary. From W take A30 and exit at Pattesons Cross, follow signs for Fairmile and then Cadhay. From E, exit at the Iron Bridge and follow signs as above.

Owner: Mr R Thistlethwayte **Contact:** Jayne Covell **Tel:** 01404 813511

Open: May–Sept, Fris 2–5pm. Also: late May & Summer BH Sat–Sun–Mon. Last tour 4.15pm. **Admission:** Guided tours: Adult £7, Child £3. Gardens: Adults £3, Child £1. Parties of 15+ by prior arrangement. **Key facts:** Ground floor & grounds. Obligatory. Guide dogs only.

CASTLE HILL GARDENS

Castle Hill, Filleigh, Barnstaple, Devon EX32 0RQ

www.castlehilldevon.co.uk

Set in the rolling hills of Devon, Castle Hill Gardens provides a tranquil and beautiful setting. Stroll through the spectacular gardens, dotted with mystical temples, follies, statues and ponds. The path through the Woodland Gardens, filled with flowering shrubs, leads you down to the river and the magical Satyr's Temple.

Location: MAP 2:I14. OS Ref. SS661 362. A361, take B3226 to South Molton. Follow brown signs to Castle Hill.

Owner: Earl and Countess of Arran **Contact:** Clare Agertoft

Tel: 01598 760421 **Fax:** 01598 760457

E-mail: events@castlehill-devon.com

Open: Apr–Sept, 11am–5pm, except Sats, Refreshments available. Autumn walks daily Oct & Nov except Sats. Refreshments not available. Groups welcome by prior arrangement.

Admission: Adults £5, Senior Citizens £4.50, Children (5-15 years) £2.50. Groups (20+) £5.

Key facts: Partial. WCs. Licensed. By arrangement. On leads.

CULVER HOUSE

Longdown, Exeter, Devon EX6 7BD

www.culver.biz

Culver was built in 1836, but redesigned by the great Victorian architect, Alfred Waterhouse in a mock Tudor style.
The distinctive interior of the house makes it a favoured location for functions and featured in BBC1's 'Down to Earth'. The house has also been used by German and American film crews.

Location: MAP 2:J7. OS Ref. SX848 901. 5m W of Exeter on B3212.
Owner/Contact: Charles Eden Esq
Tel: 01392 8118851 **Fax:** 01392 811817
E-mail: info@culver.biz
Open: Not open to the public. Available for corporate hospitality.
Admission: Please telephone for booking details.
Key facts:

CUSTOM HOUSE

The Quay, Exeter EX2 4AN

The Custom House, located on Exeter's historic Quayside, was constructed from 1680–1682.
It is the earliest substantial brick building in Exeter and was used by HM Customs and Excise until 1989.
The building has an impressive sweeping staircase and spectacular ornamental plaster ceilings.

Location: MAP 2:K6, OS Ref. SX919 921. Exeter's historic Quayside.
Owner: Exeter City Council
Tel: 01392 265162
E-mail: estates@exeter.gov.uk
Open: 1 Apr–31 Oct: Guided tour programme, telephone 01392 265203.
Admission: Free.
Key facts: Obligatory.

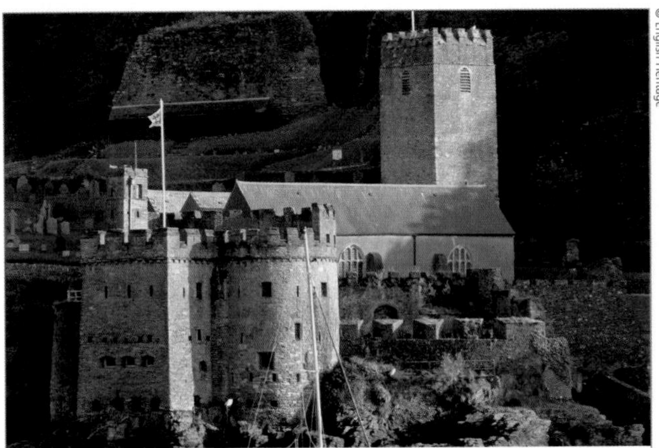

© English Heritage

DARTMOUTH CASTLE

Castle Road, Dartmouth, Devon TQ6 0JN

www.english-heritage.org.uk/dartmouth

One of the most picturesquely-sited forts in England, for six hundred years Dartmouth Castle has guarded the narrow entrance to the Dart Estuary and the busy, vibrant port of Dartmouth. A fascinating complex of defences dating back to 1388, today the castle is remarkably intact with excellent hands-on exhibitions.

Location: MAP 2:K9, OS202 Ref. SX887 503. 1m SE of Dartmouth off B3205, narrow approach road.
Owner: English Heritage **Contact:** Visitor Operations Team
Tel: 01803 833588 **Fax:** 01803 834445
E-mail: dartmouth.castle@english-heritage.org.uk
Open: Please visit www.english-heritage.org.uk for opening times and the most up-to-date information.
Admission: Adult £4.70, Child £2.80, Conc. £4.20. 15% discount for groups (11+). EH members Free. Opening times & prices are valid until 31st March 2012.
Key facts: WC (not EH). Limited (charged, not EH).

FURSDON HOUSE

Cadbury, Nr Thorverton, Exeter, Devon EX5 5JS

www.fursdon.co.uk

Fursdon House is at the heart of a small estate where the family has lived for 750 years. Set within a hilly and wooded landscape the gardens are attractive with walled and open areas. Family memorabilia with fine costume and textiles are displayed. Two private wings offer self catering accommodation.

Location: MAP 2:K6, OS Ref. SS922 046. Off A3072 between Bickleigh & Crediton, 9m N of Exeter signposted through Thorverton.
Owner: Mr E D Fursdon **Contact:** Mrs C Fursdon
Tel: 01392 860860 **Fax:** 01392 860126 **E-mail:** admin@fursdon.co.uk
Open: House: BH Mons except Christmas. Jun, Jul & Aug, Suns & Weds. Guided tours at 2.30 & 3.30pm. Garden: as house 2–5pm. Tea Room. Groups welcome by prior arrangement.
Admission: House and Garden: Adult £7, Child (10–16yrs) £4, Child (under 10yrs) Free. Garden only: £4.
Key facts: Conferences. No photography or video. Obligatory. Limited for coaches. Self-catering.

GREAT FULFORD

Dunsford, Nr Exeter, Devon EX6 7AJ

The ancient home of the Fulford family since circa 1190. Built round a courtyard it is mainly early Tudor. There is a superb panelled Great Hall and a marvellous 17th century Great Staircase. Other rooms in the 'gothic' taste by James Wyatt when the house was remodelled in 1805.

Location: MAP 2:J7, OS Ref. SX790 917. In the centre of Devon. 10 miles west of Exeter. South of the A30 between the villages of Cheriton Bishop and Dunsford.

Owner/Contact: Francis Fulford

Tel: 01647 24205 **Fax:** 01647 24401

E-mail: francis@greatfulford.co.uk

Open: All year by appointment only for parties or groups containing a minimum of 10 persons.

Admission: £7.50 per person.

Key facts: Obligatory.

© English Heritage

OKEHAMPTON CASTLE

Okehampton, Devon EX20 1JA

www.english-heritage.org.uk/okehampton

The ruins of the largest castle in Devon stand above a river surrounded by splendid woodland. There is still plenty to see, including the Norman motte and the jagged remains of the Keep. There is a picnic area and lovely woodland walks.

Location: MAP 2:I6, OS Ref. SX584 942. 1m SW of Okehampton town centre off A30 bypass.

Owner: English Heritage **Contact:** Visitor Operations Team

Tel: 01837 52844 **E-mail:** customers@english-heritage.org.uk

Open: Please visit www.english-heritage.org.uk for opening times and the most up-to-date information.

Admission: Adult £3.70, Child £2.20, Conc. £3.30. 15% discount for groups (11+). EH members Free. Opening times & prices are valid until 31st March 2012.

Key facts:

KNIGHTSHAYES

Bolham, Tiverton, Devon EX16 7RQ

www.nationaltrust.org.uk

One of the finest surviving Gothic Revival houses. A rare example of the work of the eccentric architect William Burges. Vast garden renowned for its rare trees, shrubs and seasonal colours. Fully productive organic kitchen garden.

Location: MAP 2:K5, OS Ref. SS960 151. 7 miles from M5 exit 27 A361. Switch off Sat Nav and follow signs.

Owner: National Trust

Contact: Alice Hodgson

Tel: 01884 254665

E-mail: knightshayes@nationaltrust.org.uk

Open: Daily early Mar–end Oct, 11am–5pm. House closed Fri. Limited winter opening. Please phone for details.

Admission: House & Garden: Adult £9.40, Child £4.70. Garden and Parkland: Adult £7.50, Child £3.80.

Key facts: No photography in the house.
WCs. Licensed.
By arrangement.
On leads in park.

© NTPL / Joe Cornish

SALTRAM

Plympton, Plymouth, Devon PL7 1UH

www.nationaltrust.org.uk

The house, with its magnificent decoration and original contents, was largely created between 1740-1820s by the Parker family. Featuring some of Robert Adam's finest rooms, exquisite plasterwork ceilings, Chinese wallpapers and an exceptional collection of paintings. The garden, contains an orangery, several follies, and beautiful shrubberies and imposing specimen trees.

Location: MAP 2:I9, OS Ref. SX520 557. From A38, City Centre/Plympton/ Kingsbridge exit, follow Plympton, right-hand lane, follow brown signs.

Owner: National Trust **Contact:** Administrator **Tel:** 01752 333500

Fax: 01752 336474 **E-mail:** saltram@nationaltrust.org.uk

Open: House: 11–19 Feb weekends only; 10 Mar–4 Nov daily except Fri, 12–4.30pm. Last admission 3.45pm. Garden, shop & restaurant: all year, daily, 11am–5pm (4pm Nov–Mar).

Admission: House & Garden: Adult £10.40, Child £5.10, Family £25.90, 1-Adult Family £15.60. Groups (15+): £8.50. Garden only: Tickets available. *GiftAid prices - standard prices displayed on website.

Key facts: Partial. WCs. By arrangements.
Limited for coaches. Guide dogs only in garden. Allowed in park.

SHILSTONE

Modbury, Devon PL21 0TW

www.shilstonedevon.co.uk

Shilstone is a Georgian house in the heart of the Devon countryside overlooking an important historical landscape. Recently restored, the house is now a private home and romantic wedding venue with beautiful elevations and exquisite detail that make it comfortable in its site, and timeless in its design.

Location: MAP 2:J9, OS Ref. SX674 536.
Owner: Sebastian and Lucy Fenwick
Contact: Katie Brydges
Tel: 01548 830888
E-mail: katie@shilstonedevon.co.uk
Open: Mon–Fri by appointment only.
Admission: £10 per person, minimum 4 people.
Key facts: Unsuitable. Obligatory. No coaches. Guide dogs only. €

UGBROOKE PARK

Chudleigh, Devon TQ13 0AD

www.ugbrooke.co.uk

Ugbrooke House: a hidden treasure set in a Devon combe. First mentioned in the Domesday Book, the house evolved and following Robert Adam's remodelling in the 1760s, resulted in the fine Georgian house of today, with magnificently restored interiors. Spectacular Capability Brown Parkland surrounds the house providing delightful lakeside walks.

Location: MAP 2:K7, OS Ref. SX 87714 78071. Just off the Exeter to Torbay A380, follow the brown tourist signs to Ugbrooke.
Owner: Lord Clifford of Chudleigh **Contact:** Mrs Meredith Harvey
Tel: 01626 852179 **Fax:** 01626 853322 **E-mail:** cliffordestate@btconnect.com
Open: Sun 8 Jul 2012–Thurs 27 Sept 2012. Open on Tue, Wed, Thur & Sun afternoons from 12.30pm.
Admission: Please contact Ugbrooke for details.
Key facts: Partial. WCs. Licensed. Obligatory. On leads.

TIVERTON CASTLE

Tiverton, Devon EX16 6RP

www.tivertoncastle.com

Part Grade I Listed, part Scheduled Ancient Monument, few buildings evoke such an immediate feeling of history. All ages of architecture from medieval to modern. Fun for children, try on Civil War armour; ghost stories, secret passages, beautiful walled gardens, including working kitchen garden. Interesting furniture, pictures. Comfortable holiday accommodation.

Location: MAP 2:K5, OS Ref. SS954 130. Just N of Tiverton town centre.
Owner: Mr and Mrs A K Gordon
Contact: Mrs A Gordon
Tel: 01884 253200 or 01884 255200
E-mail: info@tivertoncastle.com
Open: Easter–end Oct: Sun, Thur, BH Mon, 2.30–5.30pm. Last admission 5pm. Open to groups (12+) by prior arrangement at any time.
Admission: Adult £6, Child (7–16yrs) £2.50, Child under 7 Free. Garden only: £1.50.
Key facts: Partial. By arrangement. Limited for coaches. Guide dogs only. 4 Apartments, 2 Cottages.

DOWNES

Crediton, Devon EX17 3PL

Downes is a Palladian Mansion dating originally from 1692. The former home of General Sir Redvers Buller, the house contains a large number of items relating to his military campaigns. The property is now predominantly a family home with elegant rooms hung with family portraits, and a striking main staircase.

Location: MAP 2:K6, OS Ref. SX852 997. Approx a mile from Crediton town centre.
Owner: Trustees of the Downes Estate Settlement
Contact: Amanda Boulton
Tel: 01363 775142 **E-mail:** lucy.back@smithsgore.co.uk
Website: www.downesestate.co.uk
Open: Mons & Tues 09 Apr–10 Jul & Aug BH. Tours 2.15 & 3.30pm. Group bookings (15+) by prior appointment.
Admission: Adult £7, Child (5–16yrs) £3.50, Child (under 5yrs) Free. Groups (15+) £5.
Key facts: Partial. Obligatory Limited.

ESCOT GARDENS, MAZE & FOREST ADVENTURE

Escot Park, Ottery St Mary, Devon EX11 1LU

An idyllic setting for weddings, conferences & product launches. Park: Set within 220 acres of 'Capability' Brown parkland. Conservation activities within the park include water meadows restoration, studies on water voles and bats, resident beavers and even seahorses. Featuring a 4,000 beech-tree maze, wild boar, otters and birds of prey.

Location: MAP 2:L6, OS Ref. SY080 977 (gate). 9m E of Exeter on A30 at Fairmile.
Owner: Mr J-M Kennaway **Contact:** Lisa Benton
Tel: 01404 822188 **Fax:** 01404 822903 **E-mail:** escot@escot-devon.co.uk
Website: www.escot-devon.co.uk
Open: Gardens, Restaurant & Gift Shop: Winter: 10am–5pm. Summer: 10am–6pm.
Admission: Adult £8.50, Child £7, Child under 3yrs Free, Senior Citizens £7. Booked groups (10+).
Key facts: Maze, play barn and play areas. Partial. WCs. Licensed. Licensed. By arrangement. On leads.

MARWOOD HILL GARDEN

Marwood, Barnstaple, North Devon EX31 4EB

20 acre garden with 3 small lakes. Extensive collection of camellias, bog garden. National collection of astilbes. Trees and shrubs from around the world.

Location: MAP 2:I4, OS Ref. SS545 375. 4m N of Barnstaple. 1/2m W of B3230. Signs off A361 Barnstaple – Braunton Road.

Owner: Dr John Snowden

Contact: Mrs Patricia Stout

Tel: 01271 342528 **E-mail:** info@marwoodhillgarden.co.uk

Website: www.marwoodhillgarden.co.uk

Open: 1 Mar–31 Oct, daily, 10am–5pm.

Admission: Adult £5.50, Child 12–16 £2.50, Child under 12 Free. Pre-booked group of 10+ £5.

Key facts: 20 acres of stunning gardens set in a valley with lakes. Plant sales and Garden Tea Room open daily. Partial. WCs. By arrangement. On leads.

SAND

Sidbury, Sidmouth EX10 0QN

Sand is one of East Devon's hidden gems. The beautiful valley garden extends to 6 acres and is the setting for the lived-in Tudor house, the 15th century Hall House, and the 16th century Summer House. The family, under whose unbroken ownership the property has remained since 1560, provide guided house tours.

Location: MAP 2:L7, OS Ref. SY146 925. Well signed, 400 yards off A375 between Honiton and Sidmouth.

Contact: Mr & Mrs Huyshe-Shires **Tel:** 01395 597230

E-mail: info@SandSidbury.co.uk **Website:** www.SandSidbury.co.uk

Open: Suns & Mons in Jun & BH Suns & Mons. Other dates see website. Open 2–6pm. Groups by appointment.

Admission: House & Garden: Adult £7, Child/Student £1. Garden only: Adult £3, accompanied Child (under 16) Free.

Key facts: No photography in house. Partial. Obligatory. Limited for coaches. On leads.

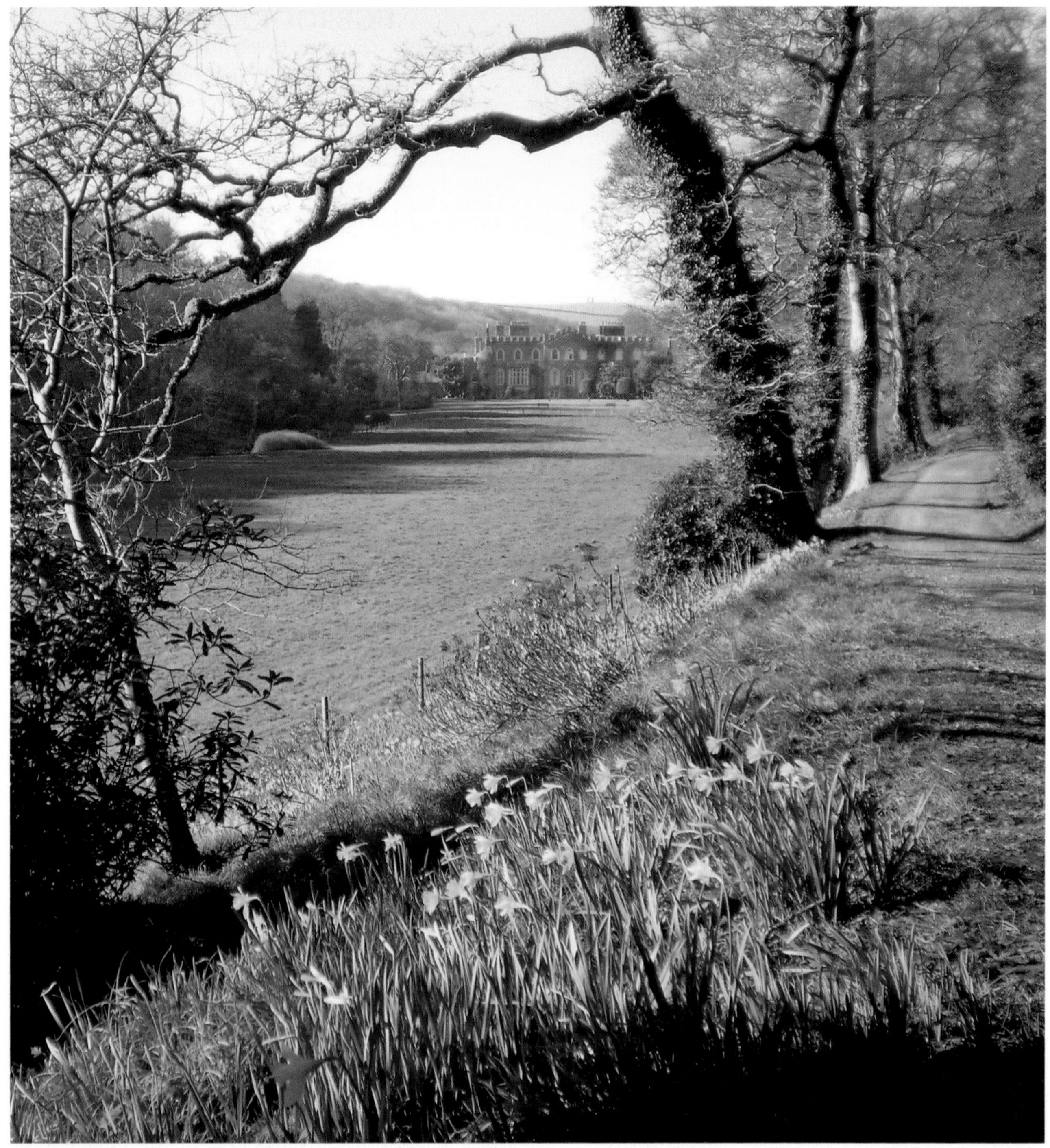

Hartland Abbey

ABBOTSBURY SUBTROPICAL GARDENS

www.abbotsbury-tourism.co.uk www.abbotsburyplantsales.co.uk

Established in 1765 by the first Countess of Ilchester. Developed since then into a 20-acre Grade I listed, magnificent woodland valley garden.

World famous for its camellia groves, magnolias, rhododendron and hydrangea collections. In summer it is awash with colour.

Since the restoration after the great storm of 1990 many new and exotic plants have been introduced. The garden is now a mixture of formal and informal, with charming walled garden and spectacular woodland valley views.

Facilities include a Colonial Restaurant for lunches, snacks and drinks, a plant centre and quality gift shop. Events such as Shakespeare and concerts are presented during the year. The floodlighting of the garden at the end of October should not be missed.

Voted "Our Favourite Garden" by readers of The Daily Telegraph.

"One of the finest gardens I have ever visited" Alan Titchmarsh BBC Gardeners World magazine.

KEY FACTS

Plants also for sale online.

Partial. WCs.
Licensed.

Licensed.
By arrangement.

Free.

In grounds, on leads.
Civil Wedding Licence

VISITOR INFORMATION

Owner
The Hon Mrs Townshend DL

Address
Abbotsbury
Weymouth
Dorset DT3 4LA

Location
MAP 2:N7
OS Ref. SY564 851
Off A35 nr Dorchester, on B3157 between Weymouth & Bridport.

Contact
Shop Manager
Tel: 01305 871387
E-mail: info@abbotsbury-tourism.co.uk

Opening Times
Mar–Nov: daily, 10am–6pm.

Winter: daily, 10am–4pm. (Closed Christmas and New Year.)

Last admission 1 hr before closing.

Admission

Adult	£10.50
Child	£7.50
OAP	£10.00

VISITOR INFORMATION

Owner
Mr & Mrs Julian Kennard

Address
Forde Abbey
Chard
Somerset TA20 4LU

Location
MAP 2:N6
OS Ref. ST358 041
Just off the B3167
4m SE of Chard.

Contact
Carolyn Clay
Tel: 01460 220231
E-mail: info@fordeabbey.co.uk

Opening Times
House
1st April–30 October
Tue–Fri, Sun & BH Mons
12 noon–4pm (last admission)
Gardens
Daily all year:
10am–4.30pm (last admission)

Admission
For current admission prices phone
01460 221290.

FORDE ABBEY & GARDENS

www.fordeabbey.co.uk

Once described as "...the most perfect monastery in England," Forde Abbey is a beacon of elegant antiquity, set within Dorset.

Forde Abbey is a treasure in an area already known for its outstanding beauty. More than 900 years of history are encapsulated in this elegant former Cistercian monastery and its 30 acres of award-winning gardens. In the peaceful solitude of its secluded position it is possible to imagine just how it looked to its previous owners: monks going about their daily round of work and prayer, prosperous parliamentary gentlemen discussing the Cavalier threat, gifted philosophers debating the imponderable, elegant Victorian ladies fanning themselves by the fireside and country gentlemen going about their work on the estate.

Set on the banks of the River Axe, this beautiful home contains many treasures including the Mortlake Tapestries, woven from cartoons painted for the Sistine Chapel by Raphael. The intricacy of their original design is matched by the story behind these particular tapestries involving Civil War, rebellion and loyalty rewarded.

The garden has been described by Alan Titchmarsh as "one of the greatest gardens of the West Country" and includes a mature arboretum, rockery, bog garden, working kitchen garden, sloping lawns and a cascade of lakes surrounding the Centenary Fountain, the highest powered fountain in England. The fruits of the garden and estate can be sampled in the Undercroft Tearoom with a wide selection of homemade lunches and cakes. A gift shop, plant centre and pottery exhibition add to the day.

KEY FACTS

Available for wedding receptions. No photography in house.

 Licensed.

Licensed.

By arrangement.

 On leads.

SHERBORNE CASTLE

NEW ROAD, SHERBORNE, DORSET DT9 5NR

www.sherbornecastle.com

Built by Sir Walter Raleigh in 1594, Sherborne Castle has been the home of the Digby family since 1617. Prince William of Orange was entertained here in 1688, and George III visited in 1789. Splendid interiors and collections of art, furniture and porcelain are on view in the Castle. Lancelot 'Capability' Brown created the 50 acre lake in 1753 and gave Sherborne the very latest in landscape gardening, with magnificent vistas of the surrounding parklands. Today, over 30 acres of beautiful lakeside gardens and grounds are open for public viewing. Refer to sherbornecastle.com/events for all special events.

Location: MAP 2:O5, OS Ref. ST649 164. 4m SE of Sherborne town centre. Follow brown signs from A30 or A352. ½m S of the Old Castle.

Owner: Mr & Mrs John Wingfield Digby **Contact:** The Custodians

Tel: 01935 812072 **Fax:** 01935 816727

E-mail: enquiries@sherbornecastle.com

Open: Castle, Gardens, Shop & Tearoom: 31 Mar–28 Oct 2012: daily except Mon & Fri (open BH Mons), 11am–4.30pm last admission. (On Sats, Castle interior from 2pm). Groups (15+) by arrangement during normal opening hours.

Admission: Castle & Gardens: Adult £10, Child (0–15yrs) Free (max 4 per adult), Senior £9.50. Apply for group discount prices.

Key facts: WCs. By arrangement. On leads. Spring Bulbs Weekend Sat 24 & Sun 25 Mar. Craft and Garden Fair Sat 5, Sun 6 and Mon 7 May. Country Fair Mon 4 Jun. Sunbeam Talbot Car Rally 1 Jul. Classics at the Castle Classic Car Show and Rally Sun 15 Jul. Sat 21 Jul Castle Concert.

ATHELHAMPTON HOUSE & GARDENS

Athelhampton, Dorchester, Dorset DT2 7LG

www.athelhampton.co.uk

An outstanding 15th century English Manor House with historic interiors and antique furnishings, set in stunning architectural grade 1 listed gardens. Excellent visitor facilities including restaurant, gift shop and cinema. Dogs welcome.

Location: MAP 2:P6, OS Ref. SY771 942. Off A35 (T) at Puddletown Northbrook junction, 5m E of Dorchester. Nearest rail station Dorchester.

Owner: Patrick Cooke Esq **Contact:** Owen Davies, Laura Dean or Rebecca Cox

Tel: 01305 848363 **E-mail:** enquiry@athelhampton.co.uk

Open: 1 Mar–31 Oct, Sun–Thur (Open Sun Nov–Feb), 10.30am–5pm/dusk. Last admission 4.30pm.

Admission: House & Gardens: Adult £12, Senior £10, Child £2, Disabled/ Student £7. Groups (12+) Adult £8 (£7 with pre-booked catering). See website for special offers and up-to-date admission charges.

Key facts: By arrangement. WCs. Licensed. Licensed. By arrangement.

HIGHCLIFFE CASTLE

Rothesay Drive, Highcliffe-On-Sea, Christchurch BH23 4LE

www.highcliffecastle.co.uk

Built in the 1830s in the Romantic/Picturesque style. Although no longer with it's rich interiors, the Castle now houses a Heritage Centre & Gift Shop providing a unique setting for exhibitions and events. Available for wedding receptions, banquets and corporate use. Cliff-top grounds. Access to Christchurch Coastal Path and beach.

Location: MAP 3:B6, OS Ref. SZ200 930. Off the A337 Lymington Road, between Christchurch and Highcliffe-on-Sea.

Owner: Christchurch Borough Council

Contact: David Hopkins

Tel: 01425 278807 **Fax:** 01425 280423

E-mail: enquiries@highcliffecastle.co.uk

Open: 1 Feb–23 Dec: daily, 11am–5pm. Last admission 4.30 (4pm Fri/Sat). Grounds: All year: daily from 7am. Limited access for coaches. Tearooms closed Christmas Day.

Admission: Adult £3, accompanied U16 free. Group (10+) rates available. Guided tours of unrestored areas: Adult £4. Grounds: Free *Prices correct at time of going to press.

Key facts: Wedding receptions. By arrangement. Limited. Parking charge. By arrangement.

MAPPERTON

Beaminster, Dorset DT8 3NR

www.mapperton.com

'The Nation's Finest Manor House'- Country Life. Jacobean manor, All Saints Church, stables and dovecote overlooking an Italianate garden, orangery, topiary and borders, descending to ponds and arboretum. A unique valley garden in an Area of Outstanding Natural Beauty with fine views of Dorset hills and woodlands.

Location: MAP 2:N6. OS Ref. SY503 997. 1m S of B3163, 2m NE of B3066, 2m SE Beaminster, 5m NE Bridport.

Owner/Contact: The Earl & Countess of Sandwich **Tel:** 01308 862645

Fax: 01308 861082 **E-mail:** office@mapperton.com

Open: House: 9 Jul–10 Aug (Mon-Fri) plus 4 Jun & 27 Aug, timed tours 2–4.30pm. Garden & Church: 1 Apr–31 Oct: daily (exc Sat) 11am–5pm. Café: Apr–Sept: daily (exc. Sat) 11am–5.00pm, 01308 863 348.

Admission: Gardens: Adult £5.00, Child (under 18yrs) £2.50, under 5yrs free. House: £4.50. Group tours by appointment. House and Gardens combined £9.00 for groups over 20.

Key facts: Partial. WCs. Licensed. By arrangement. Limited for coaches. Guide dogs only. Two charity plant fairs, one in Spring and one in the Autumn. Shakespeare in the garden in July.

LULWORTH CASTLE & PARK

East Lulworth, Wareham, Dorset BH20 5QS

www.lulworth.com

Stunning 17th century Castle & 18th century Chapel set in extensive parkland, with views to the Jurassic Coast. Built as a hunting lodge for Royalty, the Castle was destroyed by fire and has been externally restored and internally consolidated by English Heritage. The Castle holds informative displays & exhibitions on its history.

Location: MAP 3:A7. OS Ref. SY853 822. In E Lulworth off B3070, 3m NE of Lulworth Cove.

Owner: The Weld Estate **Tel:** 0845 4501054 **Fax:** 01929 400563

E-mail: enquiries@lulworth.com

Open: Castle & Park: All year, Sun–Fri. Opening dates & times may vary throughout the year, check website or call before visiting. Last admission to Castle is 1hr before closing.

Admission: Pay & Display parking £3, allowing access to Park walks, Play & Picnic areas. Admission applies for Castle & Chapel – Adult: £5, Child: £2 (4-15yrs). U4's free, EH & HHA members free.

Key facts: Concerts, corporate & private hire/events by arrangement. WCs. Obligatory, by arrangement. Guide dogs only. See website for details.

MINTERNE GARDENS

Minterne Magna, Nr Dorchester, Dorset DT2 7AU

www.minterne.co.uk

Landscaped in the manner of 'Capability' Brown, Minterne's unique garden has been described by Simon Jenkins as "a corner of paradise."
20 wild, woodland acres of magnolias, rhododendrons and azaleas providing new vistas at each turn, with small lakes, streams and cascades. Private House tours, dinners, corporate seminars, wedding and events.

Location: MAP 2:O6, OS Ref. ST660 042. On A352 Dorchester/Sherborne Rd, 2m N of Cerne Abbas.

Owner/Contact: The Hon Henry and Mrs Digby

Tel: 01300 341370

Fax: 01300 341747

E-mail: enquiries@minterne.co.uk

Open: 1 Mar–9 Nov: daily, 10am–6pm.

Admission: Adult £5, accompanied children under 12 free.

Key facts: Unsuitable.
By arrangement.
Free. Picnic tables in car park.
In grounds, on leads.

© English Heritage

PORTLAND CASTLE

Castletown, Portland, Weymouth, Dorset DT5 1AZ

www.english-heritage.org.uk/portland

Discover one of Henry VIII's finest coastal fortresses, perfectly preserved in a waterfront location overlooking Portland harbour. Explore the Tudor kitchen and gun platform, see the superb battlement views and enjoy lunch in the Captain's Tearoom. An audio tour, included with admission, brings the castle's long history to life.

Location: MAP 2:O7, OS Ref. SY684 743. Overlooking Portland harbour.
Owner: English Heritage **Contact:** Visitor Operations Staff
Tel: 01305 820539 **Fax:** 01305 860853
E-mail: customers@english-heritage.org.uk
Open: Please visit www.english-heritage.org.uk for opening times and the most up-to-date information.
Admission: Adult £4.30, Child £2.60, Conc. £3.90. Family £11.20. 15% discount for groups (11+). EH members Free. Opening times and prices are valid until 31st March 2012.
Key facts: Portland Castle is available for corporate and private hire and is licensed for civil wedding ceremonies. Partial. Limited for coaches. Guide dogs only.

WOLFETON HOUSE

Nr Dorchester, Dorset DT2 9QN

A fine medieval and Elizabethan manor house lying in the water-meadows near the confluence of the rivers Cerne and Frome. It was embellished around 1580 and has splendid plaster ceilings, fireplaces and panelling.
To be seen are the Great Hall, Stairs and Chamber, Parlour, Dining Room, Chapel and Cyder House.

Location: MAP 2:O6, OS Ref. SY678 921. 1½m from Dorchester on the A37 towards Yeovil. Indicated by Historic House signs.
Owner: Capt N T L L T Thimbleby
Contact: The Steward
Tel: 01305 263500
E-mail: kthimbleby.wolfeton@gmail.com
Open: Jun–end Sept: Mons, Weds & Thurs, 2–5pm. Groups by appointment throughout the year.
Admission: £6
Key facts: Catering for groups by prior arrangement.
By arrangement. By arrangement.
Limited for coaches.

© English Heritage

SHERBORNE OLD CASTLE

Castleton, Sherborne, Dorset DT9 3SA

www.english-heritage.org.uk/sherborne

The ruins of this early 12th century castle are a testament to the 16 days it took Cromwell to capture it during the Civil War, after which it was abandoned. A gatehouse, some graceful arcading and decorative windows survive.

Location: MAP 2:O5, OS Ref. ST647 167. ½m E of Sherborne off B3145. ½m N of the 'new' 1594 Castle.
Owner: English Heritage **Contact:** Visitor Operations Staff
Tel/Fax: 01935 812730 **E-mail:** customers@english-heritage.org.uk
Open: Please visit www.english-heritage.org.uk for opening times and the most up-to-date information.
Admission: Adult £3.40, Child £2, Conc. £3.10. 15% discount for groups of 11+. EH members Free. Opening times & prices are valid until 31st March 2012.
Key facts: Partial. Limited for coaches. Guide dogs only.

CHURCH OF OUR LADY & ST IGNATIUS

North Chideock, Bridport, Dorset DT6 6LF

Built by Charles Weld of Chideock Manor in 1872 in Italian Romanesque style, it is a gem of English Catholicism and the Shrine of the Dorset Martyrs. Early 19th century wall paintings in original barn-chapel (priest's sacristy) can be seen by arrangement. A museum of local history & village life displayed in adjoining cloister.

Location: MAP 2:N6, OS Ref. SY419 937. A35 to Chideock, turn into N Rd & ¼ mile on right.
Owner: The Weld Family Trust
Contact: Mrs G Martelli
Tel: 01308 488348
E-mail: amyasmartelli40@hotmail.com
Open: All year: 10am–4pm.
Admission: Donations welcome.
Key facts: Partial. Limited for coaches. Guide dogs only

CLAVELL TOWER

Kimmeridge, near Wareham, Dorset BH20 5PE

Built in 1830 by Reverend John Richards Clavell of Smedmore as an observatory and folly. Designed by Robert Vining with four storeys and a colonnade. Also known as the Tower of the Winds, it has a special place in literary history as it inspired both Thomas Hardy and PD James.

Location: MAP 2:A7, OS Ref. SY909 786.
Owner/Contact: The Landmark Trust
Tel: 01628 825925
E-mail: bookings@landmarktrust.org.uk
Website: www.landmarktrust.org.uk
Open: Available for holidays 2 people. Two Open Days a year. Other visits by appointment. Contact the Landmark Trust for details.
Admission: Free on Open Days and visits by appointment.
Key facts:

EDMONDSHAM HOUSE & GARDENS

Cranborne, Wimborne, Dorset BH21 5RE

Charming blend of Tudor and Georgian architecture with interesting contents. Organic walled garden, 6 acre garden with unusual trees and spring bulbs. 12th century church nearby.

Location: MAP 3:A5, SU062 116. Off B3081 between Cranborne and Verwood, NW from Ringwood 9m, Wimborne 9m.

Owner/Contact: Mrs Julia E Smith

Tel: 01725 517207

Open: House & Gardens: All BH Mons, Weds in Apr & Oct only, 2–5pm.

Gardens: Apr–Oct, Suns & Weds 2–5pm. Groups by arrangement (max 50).

Admission: House: Adult £5, Child £1 (under 5yrs Free). Garden only: Adult £2.50, Child 50p (under 5yrs Free).

Key facts: Partial. WCs. Only Weds Apr & Oct. Obligatory. Limited. Guide dogs only.

HIGHER MELCOMBE

Melcombe Bingham, Dorchester, Dorset DT2 7PB

Consists of the surviving wing of a 16th century house with its attached domestic chapel. A fine plaster ceiling and linenfold panelling. Conducted tours by owner.

Location: MAP 2:P6, OS Ref. ST749 024. 1km W of Melcombe Bingham.

Owner: Mr M C Woodhouse

Contact: Mr M C Woodhouse

Tel: 01258 880251

Website: www.highermelcombemanor.co.uk

Open: May–Sept by appointment.

Admission: Adult £2 (takings go to charity).

Key facts: Unsuitable. By written appointment only. Limited. Guide dogs only.

KINGSTON LACY

Kingston Lacy, Wimborne Minster, Dorset BH21 4EA

Kingston Lacy House lies at the heart of the 8,500 acre Bankes Estate. Opened to the public twenty five years ago, the 'secret estate' is still only slowly revealing itself. The 43 acres of formal gardens, many of them true to their Edwardian plantings, include the Fernery, Parterre and Sunk Gardens and the recently restored Japanese Gardens.

Location: MAP 3:A6, OS Ref. ST980 019. On B3082 – Blandford / Wimborne road, 1½m NW of Wimborne Minster.

Owner: National Trust **Contact:** The Property Manager

Tel: 01202 883402 **Fax:** 01202 882402

Website: www.nationaltrust.org.uk

Open: Please see website or contact us for up-to-date information.

Admission: Please see website or contact us for up-to-date information.

Key facts: Garden only. Licensed. By arrangement. On leads, in park.

SANDFORD ORCAS MANOR HOUSE

Sandford Orcas, Sherborne, Dorset DT9 4SB

Tudor manor house with gatehouse, fine panelling, furniture, pictures. Terraced gardens with topiary and herb garden. Personal conducted tour by owner.

Location: MAP 2:O5, OS Ref. ST623 210. 2½m N of Sherborne, Dorset 4m S of A303 at Sparkford. Entrance next to church.

Owner: Sir Mervyn Medlycott Bt **Contact:** Sir Mervyn Medlycott Bt

Tel: 01963 220206

Open: Easter Mon, 10am–5pm. May & Jul–Sept: Suns & Mons, 2–5pm.

Admission: Adults £5, Child £2.50. Groups (10+): Adult £4, Child £2.

Key facts: Unsuitable. Obligatory. Parking available. In grounds, on leads.

STOCK GAYLARD HOUSE

Stock Gaylard, Sturminster Newton, Dorset DT10 2BG

A Georgian house overlooking an ancient deer park with the parish church of St Barnabas in the garden. The grounds and principal rooms of the house are open to the public for 28 days a year.

Location: MAP 2:P5, OS Ref. ST722 130. 1 mile S of the junction of A357 and A3030 at Lydlinch Common.

Owner/Contact: Mrs J Langmead **Tel:** 01963 23215

E-mail: langmeadj@stockgaylard.com **Website:** www.stockgaylard.com

Open: 28 Apr–7 May: 22–30 Jun: 22–30 Sept: 2–5pm. Large parties by appointment. Access to the Park by arrangement.

Admission: Adult £5.

Key facts: Partial. Obligatory. In grounds, Guide dogs only.

Forde Abbey & Gardens

CHAVENAGE

www.chavenage.com

Elizabethan Manor Chavenage House, a TV/Film location is still a family home, offers unique experiences, with history, ghosts and more.

Chavenage is a wonderful Elizabethan house of mellow grey Cotswold stone and tiles which contains much of interest for the discerning visitor.

The approach aspect of Chavenage is virtually as it was left by Edward Stephens in 1576. Only two families have owned Chavenage; the present owners since 1891 and the Stephens family before them. A Colonel Nathaniel Stephens, MP for Gloucestershire during the Civil War was cursed for supporting Cromwell, giving rise to legends of weird happenings at Chavenage since that time.

There are many interesting rooms housing tapestries, fine furniture, pictures and relics of the Cromwellian period. Of particular note are the Main Hall, where a contemporary screen forms a minstrels' gallery and two tapestry rooms where it is said Cromwell was lodged.

Recently Chavenage has been used as a location for TV and film productions including a Hercule Poirot story The Mysterious Affair at Styles, episodes of The House of Elliot, Casualty and Cider with Rosie.

In 2005 Jeremy Musson visited in the BBC's The Curious House Guest. Chavenage has recently doubled as Candleford Manor in the BBC'S Lark Rise to Candleford. Scenes from the series Bonekickers and Tess of the D'Urbervilles were shot at Chavenage.

Chavenage is especially suitable for those wishing an intimate, personal tour, usually conducted by the owner or his family, or for groups wanting a change from large establishments. Meals for pre-arranged groups have proved hugely popular. It also provides a charming venue for wedding receptions, small conferences and other functions.

KEY FACTS

- Suitable for filming, photography, corporate entertainment, activity days, seminars, receptions and product launches.
- Occasional.
- Corporate entertaining. Private drinks parties, lunches, dinners, anniversary parties and wedding receptions.
- Suitable
- By owner. Large groups given a talk prior to viewing. Couriers/group leaders should arrange tour format prior to visit.
- Up to 100 cars. 2–3 coaches (by appointment). Coaches access from A46 (signposted) or from Tetbury via the B4014, enter the back gates for coach parking area.
- Chairs can be arranged for lecturing.

VISITOR INFORMATION

Owner
Mr David Lowsley- Williams

Address
Chavenage
Tetbury
Gloucestershire
GL8 8XP

Location
MAP. 3:A1
OS Ref. ST872 952.
Less than 20m from M4/J16/17 or 18. 13/4m NW of Tetbury between the B4014 & A4135. Signed from Tetbury. Less than 15m from M5/J13 or 14. Signed from A46 (Stroud–Bath road).
Taxi: Martin Cars 01666 503611.
Rail: Kemble Station 7m.
Air: Bristol 35m. Birmingham 70m. Grass airstrip on farm.

Contact
D Lowsley-Williams or Caroline Lowsley-Williams
Tel: 01666 502329
Fax: 01666 504696
E-mail: info@chavenage.com

Opening Times
Summer
May–September
Thur, Sun, 2–5pm. Last admission 4pm. Also Easter Sun, Mon & BH Mondays.
NB. Will open on any day and at other times by prior arrangement for groups.
Winter
October–March
By appointment only for groups.

Admission
Tours are inclusive in the following prices.
Summer
Adult £8.00
Child (5–16 yrs) £4.00
Winter
Groups only
(any date or time) Rates by arrangement.
Concessions:
By prior arrangement, concessions may be given to groups of 40+ and also to disabled and to exceptional cases.

Conference/Function

ROOM	Size	Max Cap
Ballroom	70' x 30'	120
Oak Room	25 'x 20'	30

VISITOR INFORMATION

■ Owner
Lady Ashcombe, Henry and Mollie Dent-Brocklehurst

■ Address
Winchcombe
Gloucestershire
GL54 5JD

■ Location
MAP 6:O10, OS Ref. SP032 277.
8m NE of Cheltenham, at Winchcombe off B4632. From Bristol or Birmingham M5/J9. Take A46 then B4077 towards Stow-on-the-Wold.
Bus: Castleways to Winchcombe.
Rail: Cheltenham Station 8m.
Air: Birmingham or Bristol 45m.

■ Contact
Kevin Jones
Tel: 01242 602308
Fax: 01242 602959
E-mail: enquiries@sudeley.org.uk

■ Opening Times
1 April–28 October 2012, daily, 10.30am–5pm.

■ Admission
Please refer to the website or call 01242 602308

■ Special events
Queen Katherine Parr; Quincentenary Celebrations takes place throughout 2012 at Sudeley Castle and within the neighbouring town of Winchcombe.

2012 sees a season of celebrations for the Tudor Queen's quincentenary; festivities include Tudor Fun Days, literary events and historical talks from respected authors and historians including Alison Weir and Dr. David Starkey.

Full details of the events and festivities can be found on the website.

Conference/Function

ROOM	Size	Max Cap
Chandos Hall		60
Banqueting Hall + Pavilion		100
Marquee		Unlimited
Long Room		80
Library		50

SUDELEY CASTLE & GARDENS

www.sudeleycastle.co.uk

Former home of Tudor Queen Katherine Parr: a Quincentenary Festival throughout 2012 with commentary by David Starkey. Award-winning gardens.

Award-winning gardens and medieval ruins surround Sudeley Castle, which nestles in the Cotswolds near the historic town of Winchcombe and has played host to many royal figures during its 1,000 year history. The Castle itself is the private home of Lady Ashcombe and her family. Their apartments are open for exclusive guided tours three days a week.

As part of Queen Katherine's quincentenary celebrations a new exhibition, featuring commentary from DAVID STARKEY, celebrates the life of this exceptional woman. Having survived Henry VIII, she married Thomas Seymour and lived at Sudeley along with the young Lady Jane Grey, only to die tragically after the birth of her daughter, Mary. Sudeley Castle is the only private residence where an English Queen lies buried: Katherine's tomb rests in St Mary's Church within the grounds. Her prayer book; her love letter to Thomas Seymour and a lock of her hair feature in the exhibition.

Sudeley's extensive gardens have been lovingly restored: nine individual designs reflect the Castle's fascinating past. The Queens Garden is amongst the finest rose gardens in England, sited on an original Tudor Parterre. An Herbal Healing Walk, introduced by Lady Ashcombe in 2011, echoes the traditional herb gardens used for culinary and medicinal purposes throughout Sudeley's fascinating history.

Sir Roddy Llewellyn is the most recent appointment to Sudeley's list of prestigious Garden Design Consultants.

The Pheasantry features a collection of rare birds and the children's play area boasts a giant wooden play fort and family picnic area.

KEY FACTS

- Connoisseur Tours of the private apartments Tue, Wed & Thur only.
- Corporate & private events, wedding receptions.
- Partial. WCs.
- 
- Licensed.
- By arrangement.
- Guide dogs only.

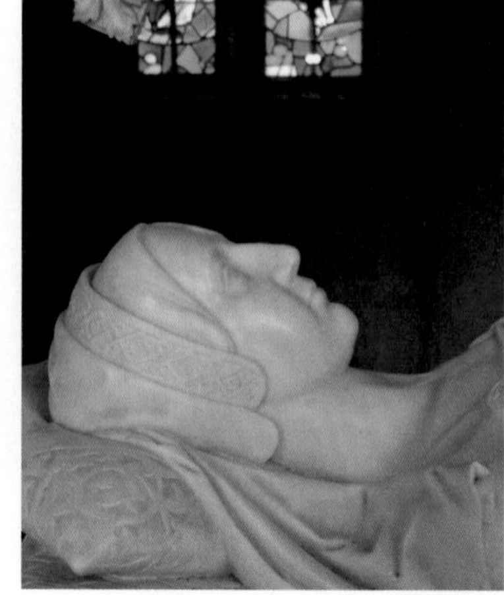

© Stephen Randall Photography

KELMSCOTT MANOR

KELMSCOTT, NR LECHLADE, GLOUCESTERSHIRE GL7 3HJ

www.kelmscottmanor.org.uk

"The loveliest haunt of ancient peace". Kelmscott Manor, a Grade I listed Tudor farmhouse adjacent to the River Thames, was William Morris' summer residence from 1871 until his death in 1896. Morris loved Kelmscott Manor, which seemed to him to have 'grown up out of the soil'. Its beautiful gardens with barns, dovecote, meadow and stream provided a constant source of inspiration. The house contains an outstanding collection of the possessions and work of Morris, his family and associates, including furniture, textiles, pictures, carpets and ceramics.

Location: MAP 6:P12, OS Ref. SU252 988. At SE end of the village, 2m due E of Lechlade, off the Lechlade–Faringdon Road.

Owner: Society of Antiquaries of London **Contact:** Jane Milne

Tel: 01367 252486 **Fax:** 01367 253754 **E-mail:** admin@kelmscottmanor.org.uk

Open: House and Garden Apr–Oct: Weds and Sats (closed Sat 14 Jul 2012), 11am–5pm (Ticket office opens 10.30am). Last admission to the house, 4.30pm. No advance bookings on public open days. House has limited capacity; timed ticket system operates.

Group visits Apr–Oct: Thurs. Must be booked in advance.

Admission: Adult £9, Child/Student £4.50. Garden only: £2.50. Carer accompanying disabled person Free.

Key facts: No photography in house. Partial. WCs. Licensed. Licensed. By arrangement. 10 mins walk. Limited for coaches. Guide dogs only. Please see the website.

RODMARTON MANOR

CIRENCESTER, GLOUCESTERSHIRE GL7 6PF

www.rodmarton-manor.co.uk

A Cotswold Arts and Crafts house, one of the last great country houses to be built in the traditional way and containing beautiful furniture, ironwork, china and needlework specially made for the house. The large garden complements the house and contains many areas of great beauty and character including the magnificent herbaceous borders, topiary, roses, rockery and kitchen garden. Available as a film location and for small functions.

Location: MAP 6:N12, OS Ref. ST943 977. Off A433 between Cirencester and Tetbury.

Owner: Mr Simon Biddulph **Contact:** John & Sarah Biddulph

Tel: 01285 841442

E-mail: jsb@irongate.uk.com

Open: House & Garden: Easter Mon, May–Sept; Weds, Sats & BHs, 2–5pm (Not guided tours). Garden (snowdrops): 5, 12, 16, 19 Feb: from 1.30pm. Guided tours of the house (approx. 1hr) may be booked for groups (15+) all year (min group charge £120). Groups (5+) may book guided or unguided tours of the garden at other times.

Admission: House & Garden: £8, Child (5–15yrs) £4. Garden only: £5, Child (5–15yrs) £1. Guided tour of Garden: Entry fee plus £40 per group.

Key facts: Colour guidebook & postcards on sale. Available for filming. No photography in house. WCs in garden. Garden & ground floor. Open days and groups by appointment. By arrangement. Guide dogs only.

STANWAY HOUSE & WATER GARDEN

STANWAY, CHELTENHAM, GLOS GL54 5PQ

www.stanwayfountain.co.uk

"As perfect and pretty a Cotswold manor house as anyone is likely to see" (Fodor's Great Britain 1998 guidebook). Stanway's beautiful architecture, furniture, parkland and village are complemented by the restored 18th century water garden and the magnificent fountain, 300 feet, making it the tallest garden and gravity fountain in the world. Teas available. Beer for sale. Wedding reception venue.

The Watermill in Church Stanway, now fully restored as a working flour mill, was recently re-opened by HRH The Prince of Wales. Its massive 24-foot overshot waterwheel, 8th largest waterwheel in England, drives traditional machinery, to produce stoneground Cotswold flour.

Location: MAP 6:O10, OS Ref. SP061 323. N of Winchcombe, just off B4077.

Owner: The Earl of Wemyss and March
Contact: Debbie Lewis
Tel: 01386 584528
Fax: 01386 584688
E-mail: stanwayhse@btconnect.com
Open: House & Garden: Jun–Aug: Tue & Thur, 2–5pm. Private tours by arrangement at other times.
Admission: Adult £7, Child £2, OAP £5. Garden only: Adult £4.50, Child £1.50, OAP £3.50.
Key facts: Film & photographic location. Wedding receptions. By arrangement. In grounds on leads.

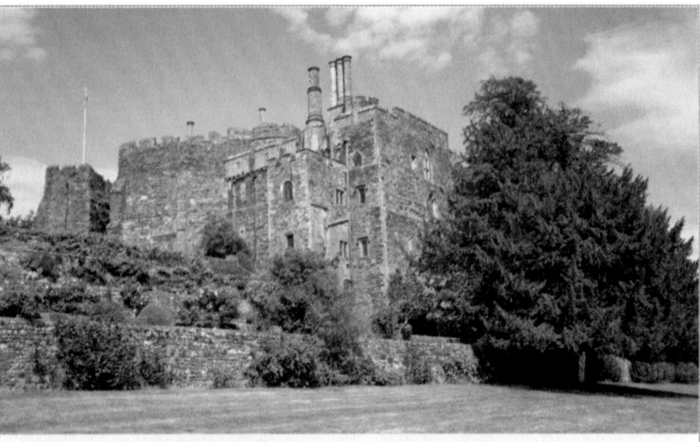

BERKELEY CASTLE

Berkeley, Gloucestershire GL13 9BQ

www.berkeley-castle.com

The Castle, once a Fortress, is now a comfortable family home. Visit the Norman Keep, the dungeon, Edward II's Cell, medieval kitchens, the Great Hall and the elegant State Apartments. Enjoy eight acres of gardens, Butterfly House and special events all year – a great day out for the family.

Location: MAP 6:M12, OS Ref. ST685 990. Midway between Bristol & Gloucester. Junction 13 or 14 of M5.
Owner: Mr R J G Berkeley **Contact:** The General Manager
Tel: 01453 810332 **Fax:** 01453 512995 **E-mail:** info@berkeley-castle.com
Open: Selected days from Sun 1 Apr–Sun 4 Nov 2012. Open Thurs, Suns & BHs. Also open Suns–Thurs during School Holidays; 11am–5.30pm.
Admission: Global Ticket: Adult £9.50, Child (5–16yrs) £5, Child (under 5s) Free, OAP £7.50, Family (2+2) £24, Groups (25+ pre-booked): Adult £9, Child (5–16yrs) £4, OAP £7.
Key facts: No photography inside. Wedding receptions and corporate. Partial. Licensed. Free. Max. 120 people. Tour time: 1.25 hours. Cars 150yds from Castle, 15 coaches 250yds away. Guide dogs only.

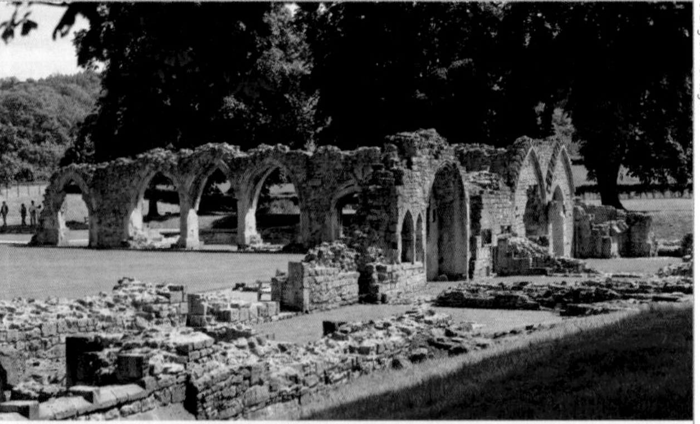

© English Heritage

HAILES ABBEY

Nr Winchcombe, Cheltenham, Gloucestershire GL54 5PB

www.english-heritage.org.uk/hailes

Seventeen cloister arches and extensive excavated remains in lovely surroundings of an abbey founded by Richard, Earl of Cornwall, in 1246. Let the audio tour bring this Cistercian Abbey to life and see sculptures, stonework and other site finds in the museum.

Location: MAP 6:O10, OS Ref. SP050 300. 2m NE of Winchcombe off B4632.
Owner: English Heritage & National Trust
Contact: Visitor Operations Staff
Tel/Fax: 01242 602398
E-mail: customers@english-heritage.org.uk
Open: Please visit www.english-heritage.org.uk for opening times and the most up-to-date information.
Admission: Adult £4.20, Child £2.50, Conc. £3.80. EH Members Free. Charge for audio tour (£1) and special events. Group discount available. Opening times and prices are valid until 31st March 2012.
Key facts: By arrangement. Limited for coaches. On leads.

PAINSWICK ROCOCO GARDEN

PAINSWICK, GLOUCESTERSHIRE GL6 6TH

www.rococogarden.org.uk

Unique 18th century garden restoration situated in a hidden 6 acre Cotswold combe. Charming contemporary buildings are juxtaposed with winding woodland walks and formal vistas. Famous for its early spring show of snowdrops. Anniversary maze.

Location: OS Ref. SO864 106. ½m NW of village Painswick on B4073.

Owner: Painswick Rococo Garden Trust **Contact:** P R Moir

Tel: 01452 813204 **Fax:** 01452 814888 **E-mail:** info@rococogarden.org.uk

Open: 10 Jan–31 Oct: daily 11am–5pm.

Admission: Adult £6.50, Child £3, OAP £5.50. Family (2+2) £16. Free introductory talk for pre-booked groups (20+).

Key facts: Partial. WCs. Licensed Licensed By arrangement On leads.

KIFTSGATE COURT GARDENS

Chipping Campden, Gloucestershire GL55 6LN

www.kiftsgate.co.uk

Magnificently situated garden on the edge of the Cotswold escarpment with views towards the Malvern Hills. Many unusual shrubs and plants including tree peonies, abutilons, specie and old-fashioned roses.

Winner HHA/Christie's Garden of the Year Award 2003.

Location: MAP 6:O9, OS Ref. SP173 430. 4m NE of Chipping Campden. 1/4 m W of Hidcote Garden.

Owner: Mr and Mrs J G Chambers

Contact: Mr J G Chambers

Tel/Fax: 01386 438777

E-mail: info@kiftsgate.co.uk

Open: May, Jun, Jul, Sat–Wed, 12 noon–6pm. Aug, Sat–Wed, 2pm–6pm. Apr & Sept, Sun, Mon & Wed, 2pm–6pm.

Admission: Adult: £7, Child £2.50. Groups (20+) £6.

Key facts: Partial. Limited for coaches. Guide dogs only.

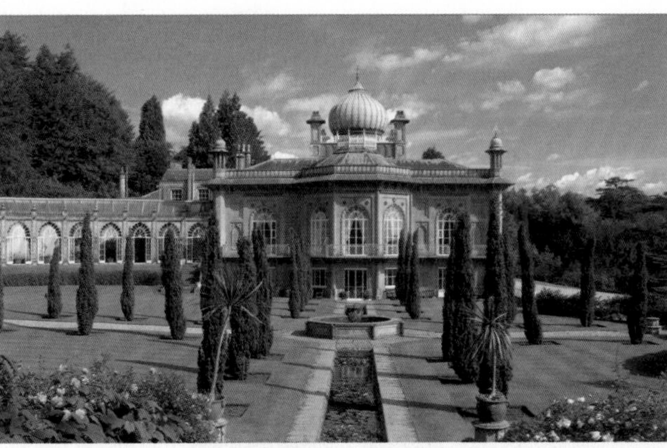

SEZINCOTE

Moreton-In-Marsh, Gloucestershire GL56 9AW

www.sezincote.co.uk

Exotic oriental water garden by Repton and Daniell. Large semi-circular orangery. House by S P Cockerell in Indian style was the inspiration for Brighton Pavilion.

Location: MAP 6:P10, OS Ref. SP183 324. 2 miles west of Moreton-in-Marsh on the A44 opposite entrance to Batsford Arboretum.

Contact: Dr E Peake

Tel: 01386 700444

E-mail: enquiries@sezincote.co.uk

Open: Garden: Thurs, Fris & BH Mons, 2–6pm except Dec. House: As above May–Sept. Teas in Orangery when house open.

Admission: House: Adult £10 (guided tour). Garden: Adult £5, Child £1.50 (under 5yrs Free).

Key facts: For full information for disabled visitors please email enquiries@sezincote.co.uk. Café. Obligatory. Guide dogs only. Weddings. Groups welcomed weekdays, please contact for details. Please see our website for up-to-date events and special openings.

TYTHE BARN

Tanhouse Farm, Churchend, Frampton-on-Severn, Gloucestershire GL2 7EH

Tythe Barn Grade II* c1650 recently restored in conjunction with English Heritage. Barn incorporating cow shed, the exceptional length and width of the timber framed structure upon a low stone plinth with box framing and undaubed wattle panels marks it out from other contemporary farm buildings.

Location: MAP 6:M12, OS Ref. SP014 206. Southern end of Frampton-on-Severn, close to church.

Owner: Michael Williams

Contact: Michael Williams

Tel: 01452 741072

E-mail: cottages@tanhouse-farm.co.uk

Open: By arrangement all year 10am–4pm.

Admission: Free.

Key facts: Partial. Obligatory. By arrangement. Limited. None for coaches.

WHITTINGTON COURT

Cheltenham, Gloucestershire GL54 4HF

Elizabethan and Jacobean manor house in a green setting, with a mediaeval church adjacent and tithe barn and stables. Excellent collections of glass and ceramics from the Roman period to the 20th century, and an interesting range of fabrics, fossils & furniture, with family possessions & block-printed fabrics in attic.

Location: MAP 6:N11, OS Ref. SP014 206. 4m E of Cheltenham on N side of A40.

Owner: Mr & Mrs Jack Stringer

Contact: Mrs J Stringer

Tel: 01242 820556

Fax: 01242 820218

Open: 7 Apr–22 Apr & 11–27 Aug: 2–5pm.

Admission: Adult £5, Child £1, OAP £4.

Key facts:

Britain's Brilliant Heritage
Brought To Life
To find out more visit our website
www.hudsonsheritage.com
HUDSONS
HERITAGE

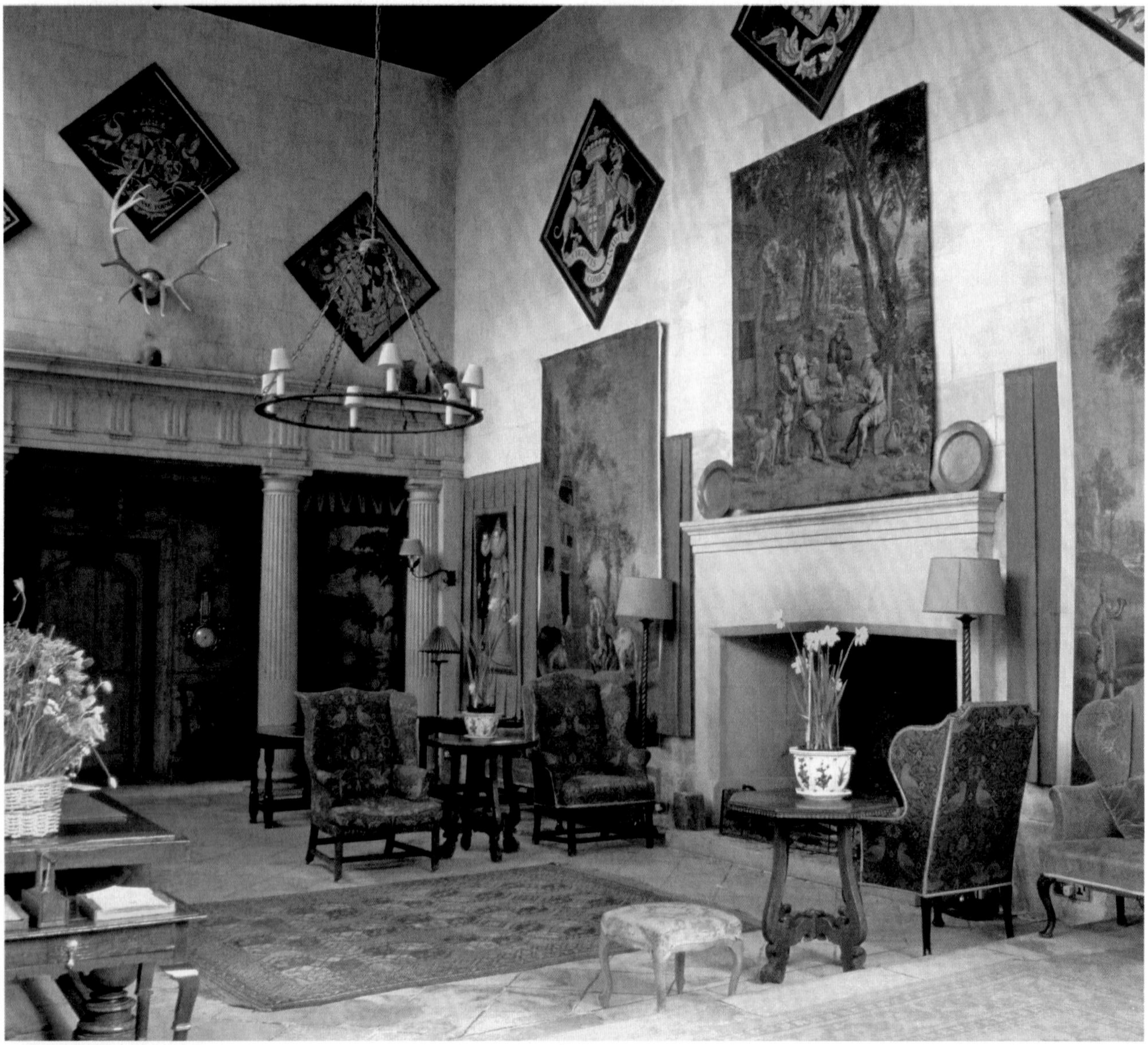

Stanway House

STOBERRY HOUSE

STOBERRY PARK, WELLS, SOMERSET BA5 3LD

www.stoberry-park.co.uk

Set within 26 acres of parkland, with breathtaking views over Wells and the Vale of Avalon, this 6 acre family garden planted sympathetically within its landscape provides a stunning combination of vistas accented with wild life ponds, water features, sculpture, 1 1/2 acre walled garden, sunken garden, gazebo, potager, lime walk. Colour and interest in every season; spring bulbs, irises, roses, acer glade, salvias. The garden has seats strategically placed to take advantage of the outstanding views and as darkness falls the walled garden is lit so guests can enjoy the visual difference and contrast of light and shadow on the plants and sculptures – it is like painting with light.

Location: MAP 2:O4. OS Ref. ST553 914. Situated within walking distance of Wells. From Bristol / Bath enter Wells on the A39; take the first left turn into College Road; then immediately left into Stoberry Park.

Owner: Frances and Tim Meeres Young

Contact: Frances Meeres Young

Tel: 01749 672906

E-mail: stay@stoberry-park.co.uk

Open: Open by appointment; guided tours can be arranged on Tues, Weds & Thurs. Wedding receptions; corporate functions by arrangement; special events: we will have several different sculpture exhibitions during the year - see website www.stoberry-park.co.uk for details.

Admission: Adult £5; children under 12 free; champagne luxury teas: £25; special cream teas £10.

Key facts: Licensed. Ample. All rooms en suite.

COTHAY MANOR & GARDENS

Greenham, Wellington, Somerset TA21 0JR

www.cothaymanor.co.uk

Twelve acres of magical, romantic gardens surround what is reputedly the most perfect example of a small classic medieval manor. Many garden 'rooms' sit off a 200yd yew walk. Features: a bog garden with azaleas, primuli and bog plants; fine trees; a cottage garden; courtyards; river walk. A plantsman's paradise.

Location: MAP 2:L5, OS Ref. ST085 212. M5(W) J27/A38 (Wellington)/M5 (N) J26/A38 (Wellington)/4miles (both directions) Brown signs off A38 'Greenham'/Fingerposts to Cothay/in lanes always left.

Owner: Mr & Mrs Alastair Robb **Contact:** The Administrator

Tel: 01823 672283 **E-mail:** cothaymanor@btinternet.com

Open: Apr (1st Sun) until end Sept: Tue/Wed/Thu/Sun & BHs, 11am–5pm, last entry 4.30pm. Sunday House Tours (general public, no children) at 11.45am & 2.15pm. Groups (20+) by appointment on most days throughout the year.

Admission: Adults: £7; Children (2–12yrs) £3. Guided House Tour £6.50 (requires garden admission). Season Tickets available. Discounts for Groups (20+) visiting both House and Garden. Cash and cheques only.

Key facts: No photography in house. WCs. Guide dogs only.

© English Heritage

FARLEIGH HUNGERFORD CASTLE

Farleigh Hungerford, Bath, Somerset BA2 7RS

www.english-heritage.org.uk/farleighhungerford

Extensive ruins of a 14th century castle with a splendid chapel containing rare medieval wall paintings, stained glass and the fine tomb of Sir Thomas Hungerford, builder of the castle. Displays in the Priest's House and a complimentary audio tour tell of the castle's sinister past.

Location: MAP 2:P3, OS173, ST801 577. In Farleigh Hungerford 3 1/2m W of Trowbridge on A366. 9 miles SE of Bath.

Owner: English Heritage

Contact: Visitor Operations Staff

Tel/Fax: 01225 754026

E-mail: customers@english-heritage.org.uk

Open: Please visit www.english-heritage.org.uk for opening times and the most up-to-date information.

Admission: Adult £4, Child £2.40, Conc. £3.60. 15% discount for groups of 11+. EH Members free. Opening times & prices are valid until 31st March 2012.

Key facts: Partial.
By arrangement.
Limited for coaches.

FLEET AIR ARM MUSEUM

RNAS Yeovilton, Ilchester, Somerset BA22 8HT

www.fleetairarm.com

As much an 'attraction' as it is a 'museum', the Fleet Air Arm Museum is where Museum meets theatre. Go on-board Concorde and 'fly' by helicopter flight to the aircraft carrier HMS ARK ROYAL. Experience the thrills and sounds of a working flight deck and see a nuclear bomb.

Location: MAP 2:O5. Situated in South Somerset close to the junction of A303 and A37. 7 miles North of Yeovil.

Tel: 01935 840565

Fax: 01935 842631

E-mail: marketing@fleetairarm.com

Open: Apr–Oct, daily, from 10am. Nov–Mar, Wed–Sun, from 10am. Closed Dec 24/25/26.

Admission: Adult £13, Child £9, Family (2 adults & 3 Children) £38, Concessions £11.

Key facts: WCs. Licensed. Licensed. By arrangement. Guide dogs only.

Islington House
Wrinkle Mead

HESTERCOMBE GARDENS

Cheddon Fitzpaine, Taunton, Somerset TA2 8LG

www.hestercombe.com

Exquisite Georgian landscape garden designed by Coplestone Warre Bampfylde, Victorian terrace/shrubbery, and Edwardian Lutyens/Jekyll formal gardens together make up fifty acres of woodland walks, temples, terraces, pergolas, lakes and cascades. Licensed Restaurant/Coffee Shop & Courtyard. Conference and wedding venue, Shop/Plant Centre. Beautifully restored 17th century watermill, seasonal Mill Tea Garden.

Location: MAP 2:M5, OS Ref. ST241 287. 4m NE from Taunton, 1m NW of Cheddon Fitzpaine.

Owner: Hestercombe Gardens Trust **Contact:** The Administration Office

Tel: 01823 413923 **Fax:** 01823 413747 **E-mail:** info@hestercombe.com

Open: All year: daily, 10am–6pm (last admission 5pm). Groups & coach parties by arrangement.

Admission: Adult: £9.50, Conc. £8.80, Children: £3.60, Family Saver £23.40 (2 adults and up to 4 children). Guided Tours: £60 for professional tour guide. Groups very welcome by pre-booking.

Key facts: No picnics in the gardens - only in designated picnic area. Partial. WC. WCs. Licensed. Licensed. By arrangement. Ample parking for general visitors and coaches.

KILVER COURT GARDENS

Kilver Street, Shepton Mallet, Somerset BA4 5NF

www.kilvercourt.com

Stunning gardens created in the 1880s with further additions by Chelsea gold medallist George Whitelegg for the Showering family of Babycham fame (and where the drink was first invented). In the 1990s fashion brand Mulberry were based here. Don't miss the Designer Emporium, Farm and Gift Shop and Harlequin Cafe.

Location: MAP 2:O4, OS Ref. ST 626 436. Just off A37 in Shepton Mallet.

Owner: Mr Roger Saul

Contact: The General Manager

Tel: 01749 340410

Fax: 01749 340420

E-mail: info@kilvercourt.com

Open: Open Daily

Admission: Adult £5, Concession £4.50, Child £2.50.

Key facts: Partial. WCs.
Licensed. Licensed.
By arrangement. Limited for coaches.
Guide dogs only
A range of special events are held all year. Visit our website for details.

MAUNSEL HOUSE

North Newton, Nr Taunton, Somerset TA7 0BU

www.maunselhouse.co.uk

Maunsel House is a magnificent 13th century Manor set in 100 acres of stunning parkland at the heart of a sprawling 2,000 acre Estate comprising of lakes, orchards, Somerset wetlands, walnut groves, cottages and ancient barns. Available for luxury weddings, house hire, celebration parties, conferences, film shoots and photo shoots.

Location: MAP 2:M4. OS Ref. ST302 303. Bridgwater 4m, Bristol 20m, Taunton 7m, M5/J24, A38 to North Petherton.
Owner: Sir Benjamin Slade Bt **Contact:** The Events Team **Tel:** 01278 661076
Fax: 01278 661074 **E-mail:** info@maunselhouse.co.uk
Open: Office hours are: Mon–Fri, 9am–5pm.
Pre-booked viewings only. Coaches & groups welcome by appointment. Caravan rally field available.
Admission: Price on application.
Key facts: Functions. WCs. Obligatory.

© English Heritage

MUCHELNEY ABBEY

Muchelney, Langport, Somerset TA10 0DQ

www.english-heritage.org.uk/muchelney

Well-preserved ruins of the cloisters, with windows carved in golden stone, and abbot's lodging of the Benedictine abbey, which survived by being used as a farmhouse after the Dissolution. Tactile displays and interactive video illustrate monastic life.

Location: MAP 2:N5, OS193 Ref. ST428 248. In Muchelney 2m S of Langport.
Owner: English Heritage **Contact:** Visitor Operations Staff
Tel: 01458 250664 **Fax:** 01458 253842
E-mail: customers@english-heritage.org.uk
Open: Please visit www.english-heritage.org.uk for opening times and the most up-to-date information.
Admission: Adult £4.20, Child £2.50, Conc. £3.80. 15% discount for groups (11+). EH Members free. Opening times & prices are valid until 31st March 2012.
Key facts: Partial. By arrangement. In grounds.

BARRINGTON COURT

Barrington, Ilminster, Somerset TA19 0NQ

The enchanting formal garden, influenced by Gertrude Jekyll, is laid out in a series of walled rooms, including the White Garden, the Rose and Iris Garden and the Lily Garden. The working Kitchen Garden has espaliered apple, pear and plum trees trained along high stone walls.

Location: MAP 2:N5, OS Ref. ST395 181. In Barrington village, 5m NE of Ilminster, on B3168.
Owner: National Trust
Contact: Visitor Services Manager
Tel: 01460 241938
Info: 01460 242614
E-mail: barringtoncourt@nationaltrust.org.uk
Website: www.nationaltrust.org.uk
Open: Please see website or contact us for up-to-date information.
Admission: Please see website or contact us for up-to-date information.
Key facts: Grounds. WC. Licensed.

DODINGTON HALL

Nr Nether Stowey, Bridgwater, Somerset TA5 1LF

Small Tudor manor house on the lower slopes of the Quantocks. Great Hall with oak roof. Semi-formal garden with roses and shrubs.

Location: MAP 2:L4. OS Ref. ST172 405. 1/2m from A39, 11m W of Bridgwater, 7m E of Williton.
Owner: Lady Gass
Contact: P Quinn (occupier)
Tel: 01278 741400
Open: 3–13 June, 2–5pm.
Admission: Donations to Dodington Church.
Key facts: No inside photography. Limited. No coach parking. Guide dogs only.

FAIRFIELD

Stogursey, Bridgwater, Somerset TA5 1PU

Elizabethan and medieval house. Occupied by the same family (Acland-Hoods and their ancestors) for over 800 years. Woodland garden. Views of Quantocks and the sea. House described in Simon Jenkins' book 'England's Thousand Best Houses'. Garden open for NGS and charities on dates advertised in Spring.

Location: MAP 2:L4. OS Ref. ST187 430. 11m W Bridgwater, 8m E Williton. From A39 Bridgwater/Minehead turn North. House 1m W Stogursey.
Owner: Lady Acland-Hood Gass
Contact: Fairfield Estate
Tel: 01278 732251
Open: Easter Mon 9 Apr; 11 Apr–25 May, 6–15 Jun Wed, Thurs, Fri. Guided house tours at 2.30 & 3.30pm.
Admission: £5 in aid of Stogursey Church. Advisable to contact to confirm dates.
Key facts: No inside photography. Obligatory. No coach parking. Guide dogs only.

KENTSFORD

Washford, Watchet, Somerset TA23 0JD

Location: MAP 2:L4, OS Ref. ST058 426.
Owner: Wyndham Estate **Contact:** Mr R Dibble **Tel:** 01984 631307
Open: House open only by written appointment with Mr R Dibble. Gardens: 6 Mar–28 Aug: Tues & BHs. **Admission:** House: £3, Gardens: Free.
Key facts: Gardens only. Limited. In grounds, on leads.

GLASTONBURY ABBEY

Abbey Gatehouse, Magdalene Street, Glastonbury BA6 9EL

"Unique", "Peaceful", "Such atmosphere", "A hidden gem". Come and discover this wonderful place for yourself. From March to October hear, from our enactors, how the monks used to live and some of the history of this once great Abbey. See website for events. Outdoor Summer Café.

Location: MAP 2:N4, OS Ref. ST499 388. 50 yds from Market Cross, in centre of Glastonbury. M5/J23, then A39.
Owner: Glastonbury Abbey Estate
Contact: Francis Thyer
Tel: 01458 832267 **Fax:** 01458 836117
E-mail: info@glastonburyabbey.com
Website: www.glastonburyabbey.com
Open: Jan, Feb, Dec: 9am–4pm. Mar, Apr, May: 9am–6pm. Jun, Jul, Aug 9am–9pm Sept, Oct, Nov 9am–5pm. Last entry 30min prior to closing.
Admission: Adult £6, Child (5-15 yrs) £4, Conc. £5, Family (2+2) £16.
Key facts: Summer only.

MILTON LODGE GARDENS

Old Bristol Road, Wells, Somerset BA5 3AQ

Charming, mature, Grade II listed terraced garden (designed 1909) with stunning views of Wells Cathedral and the Vale of Avalon. Replanned 1962 with mixed shrubs, herbaceous plants, old fashioned roses and ground cover; numerous climbers; old established yew hedges. Fine trees in garden and in 7 acre arboretum across Old Bristol Road.

Location: MAP 2:O3, OS Ref. ST549 470. ½m N of Wells from A39. Free car park first gate on left.
Owner/Contact: S Tudway Quilter Esq
Tel: 01749 672168
Website: www.miltonlodgegardens.co.uk
Open: Garden & Arboretum: Easter–end Oct: Tues, Weds, Suns & BHs, 2–5pm. Parties & coaches by prior arrangement.
Admission: Adult £5, Children under 14 Free.
Key facts: Unsuitable.

ORCHARD WYNDHAM

Williton, Taunton, Somerset TA4 4HH

English manor house. Family home for 700 years encapsulating continuous building and alteration from the 14th to the 20th century.

Location: MAP 2:L4, OS Ref. ST072 400. 1m from A39 at Williton.
Owner: Wyndham Estate
Contact: Wyndham Estate Office
Tel: 01984 632309
Open: Telephone for details.
Admission: Telephone for details.
Key facts: Obligatory & pre-booked. Limited. No coach parking. In grounds, on leads.

ROBIN HOOD'S HUT

Halswell, Goathurst, Somerset TA5 2EW

An 18th century garden building with two faces. One side is a rustic cottage, with thatched roof, the other an elegant pavilion complete with umbrello. In the 1740s, Charles Kemeys Tynte began to transform the landscape around Halswell House into one of the finest Georgian gardens in the south west.

Location: MAP 2:M4, OS Ref. ST255 333.
Owner/Contact: The Landmark Trust
Tel: 01628 825925
E-mail: bookings@landmarktrust.org.uk
Website: www.landmarktrust.org.uk
Open: Available for holidays. Other visits by appointment. Please contact the Landmark Trust for details.
Admission: Free on Open Days and visits by appointment.
Key facts:

WOODLANDS CASTLE

Ruishton, Taunton, Somerset TA3 5LU

Woodlands Castle is a beautiful period house in 12 acres of private grounds situated on Junction 25 of the M5. Woodlands is available for private functions from weddings and conferences to barbecues, birthdays and wakes. Ample free parking. Accommodation within walking distance.

Location: MAP 2:M5, OS Ref. ST258 248.
Owner: Sir Benjamin Slade
Contact: Gemma Halliwell
Tel: 01823 444955
Fax: 01823 444019
E-mail: info@woodlandscastle.co.uk
Website: www.woodlandscastle.co.uk
Open: All year to private bookings only.
Admission: No admission.
Key facts: Partial. Licensed. Licensed. By arrangement. Ample for cars. Limited for coaches. In grounds.

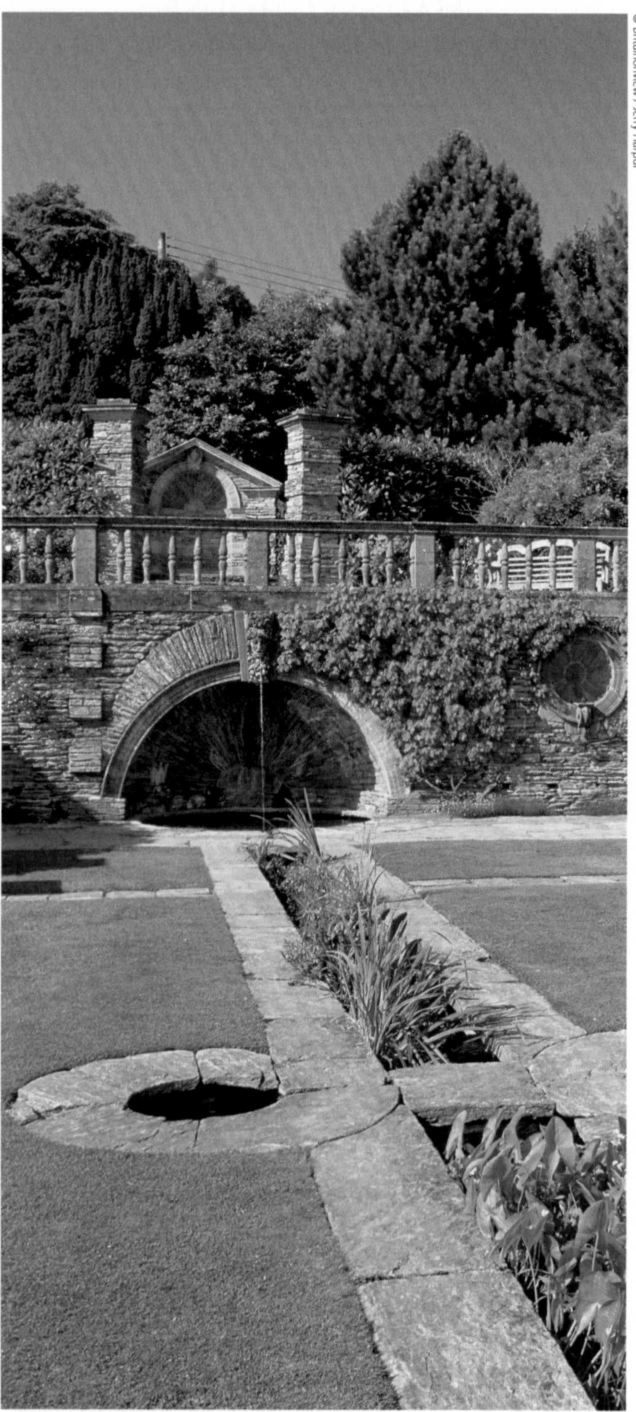

Hestercombe Gardens

THE ABBEY HOUSE GARDENS

www.abbeyhousegardens.co.uk

With 1300 years of history, an English King, 2 Saints and now one of the Great Gardens of the World.

Where the Cotswolds meets the West Country, featured on many TV programmes this truly spectacular 5 acre garden beside the 12th century Abbey Church in the centre of Medieval Malmesbury and straddling the River Avon has brought praise from around the world.

Words used to describe it range from Unique, Unforgettable, Magical, Paradise, Heaven on Earth, through to 'This garden alone made my visit to the UK worthwhile,' 'The loveliest truly English garden on the planet,' 'A real national treasure for the future' and from Alan Titchmarsh 'The WOW factor is here in abundance!'

Featuring formal knot gardens, spring bulbs, tulips (quarter of a million), hostas, laburnum tunnel, colonnade walk, roses (largest collection in the UK), japanese maples, fruit trees, double herbaceous borders, irises, alstroemerias, herb garden, monastic fish ponds. Woodland and riverside walks with wildlife from water voles, the occassional otter, goldcrests, long tailed tits, tree creepers, kingfishers, woodpeckers to sparrowhawks, buzzards and swans.

The spirit of the place shines through and could be the best garden visit you ever make.

KEY FACTS

- Guided tours by the owner available for booked groups and evening visits available for groups at additional cost. See abbeyhousegardens.co.uk for details.
- Various plants and climbers.
- WCs.
- Tea room serving light lunches.
- By arrangement.
- Town's long stay car park adjacent to gardens.
- Guide dogs only.
- Licenced for Weddings.
- Open Air Events.

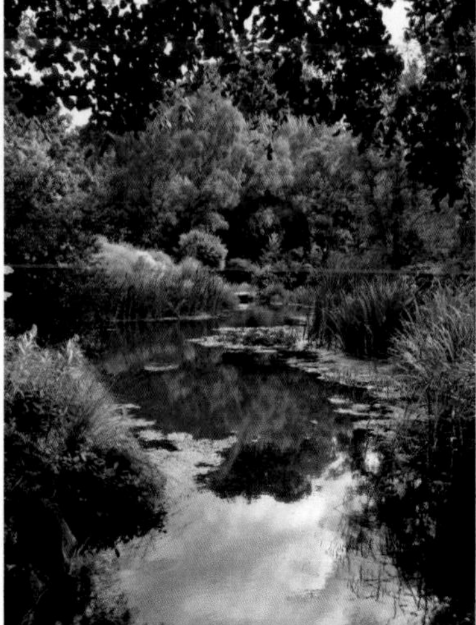

VISITOR INFORMATION

Owner
Ian & Barbara Pollard

Address
Market Cross
Malmesbury
Wiltshire SN16 9AS

Location
MAP 3:A1
OS Ref. ST933 187
Head to the centre of Malmesbury adjoining the Abbey. From South J17 of the M4. From North J11a M5.

Contact
Tel: 01666 822212 or 01666 827650
E-mail: info@abbeyhousegardens.co.uk

Opening Times
March 21–October 31, 11am–5.30pm daily, Last admission 4.45pm.

Admission

Adults	£9.00
Concessions	£8.50
Family (2+2)	£22.00
Children 5–15	£4.00
Groups (10 +)	£7.50

Annual Season Tickets available from £35

Special events
Clothes Optional days one day per month May to September.

Weddings
Capacity information:
Library 100
Hall 50
Belvedere 130
Bower House 6 + 100

The Flowering Calendar
at Abbey House Gardens. There is always masses of colour but these are some of the highlights.

March
Crocus, Narcissi, Hellebore, Hyacinth, Camellia.

April
Tulips, Primula, Fritillaries, Acers, Cherry blossom.

May
Laburnum, Wisteria, Rhododendron, Azaleas, Peonys, Apple blossom, Alliums.

June
Roses, Knifophia, Geraniums, Delphiniums, Poppies, Clematis.

July
Roses, Lillies, Alstromeria, Astilbes, Hostas, Lavendar, Hydrangea.

August
Roses, Alstromeria, Salvia, Gladioli, Phlox.

September
Roses, Salvia.

October
Michaelmas Daisies, Anemones, Salvias fruit, Acers.

CORSHAM COURT

CORSHAM, WILTSHIRE SN13 0BZ

www.corsham-court.co.uk

Corsham Court, a splendid Elizabethan house dating from 1582, was acquired in 1745 to display Sir Paul Methuen's celebrated collection of 16th and 17th century Old Master paintings. This internationally renowned collection includes important works by Van Dyck, Carlo Dolci, Filippo Lippi, Salvator Rosa, Reynolds and Romney.

Capability Brown was employed during the 1760's to enlarge the house, creating the magnificent Picture Gallery and suite of State Rooms. These rooms still retain their original silk wall-hangings and furniture designed by Chippendale, Johnson, Cobb and the Adam brothers.

Surrounding the Court are the delightful gardens and parkland which were initially designed by Brown and later completed by Humphry Repton. The gardens are particularly admired for the collection of magnolias, specimen trees and spring bulbs.

Location: MAP 3:A2, OS Ref. ST874 706. Car: Signposted from the A4, approx 4m W of Chippenham. Bus: Bath to Chippenham. Rail: Chippenham Station 6m.

Owner: J Methuen-Campbell Esq **Contact:** The Curator

Tel/Fax: 01249 712214 / 701610 **E-mail:** staterooms@corsham-court.co.uk

Open: Spring / Summer: 20 Mar–30 Sept. Daily, except Mons & Fris but including Bank Holidays 2–5.30pm. Last admission 5pm. Winter: 1 Oct–19 Mar (closed Dec).Weekends only 2–4.30pm. Last admission 4pm. NB: Open throughout the year by appointment for groups. For further details and special viewings of the the collection, see our website.

Admission: House & Garden: Adult £7, Child (5–15yrs) £3, OAP £6. Groups (includes guided tour) Adult £6. Garden only: Adult £2.50, Child (5–15yrs) £1.50, OAP £2.

Key facts: No photography in house. WCs. Max 45. If requested the owner may meet the group. Bookings for morning tours are preferred. Tour time 1hr. 120 yards from the house. Coaches may park in Church Square. Coach parties must book in advance. No camper vans, no caravans. Available: rate negotiable. A guide will be provided.

© English Heritage

© English Heritage

OLD SARUM

CASTLE ROAD, SALISBURY, WILTSHIRE SP1 3SD

www.english-heritage.org.uk/oldsarum

High above the Salisbury Plain stands the mighty hill fort of Old Sarum, the former site of the city of Salisbury. The Romans, Saxons and Normans have all left their mark on this site. Discover where the Norman cathedral once stood, and enjoy magnificent views over the surrounding countryside.

Location: MAP 3:B4, OS184, SU138 327. 2m N of Salisbury off A345.

Owner: English Heritage

Contact: Visitor Operations Team

Tel: 01722 335398

E-mail: customers@english-heritage.org.uk

Open: Please visit www.english-heritage.org.uk for opening times and the most up-to-date information.

Admission: Adult £3.70, Child £2.20, Conc. £3.30. 15% discount for groups (11+). EH Members Free. Opening times & prices are valid until 31st March 2012.

Key facts: WCs. Partial. By arrangement. Limited for coaches. On leads.

© English Heritage

© English Heritage

STONEHENGE

AMESBURY, WILTSHIRE SP4 7DE

www.english-heritage.org.uk/stonehenge

The great and ancient stone circle of Stonehenge is unique; an exceptional survival from a prehistoric culture now lost to us. The monument evolved between 3,000BC and 1,600BC and is aligned with the rising and setting of the sun at the solstices, but its exact purpose remains a mystery. To this day Stonehenge endures as a source of inspiration and fascination and, for many, a place of worship and celebration. Discover the history and legends which surround this awe-inspiring site with a complimentary audio tour available in 10 languages (subject to availability).

Location: MAP 3:B4, OS Ref. SU122 422. 2m W of Amesbury on junction of A303 and A344 / A360.

Owner: English Heritage

Tel: 0870 3331181 (Customer Services)

E-mail: customers@english-heritage.org.uk

Open: Please visit www.english-heritage.org.uk for opening times and the most up-to-date information.

Admission: Adult £7.50, Child £4.50, Conc £6.80, Family (2+3) £19.50. Groups (11+) 10% discount. NT/EH Members Free. Opening times and prices are valid until 31st March 2012.

Key facts: Guide dogs only.

WILTON HOUSE

WILTON, SALISBURY SP2 0BJ

www.wiltonhouse.com

Wilton House has been the Earl of Pembroke's ancestral home for 460 years. Inigo Jones and John Webb rebuilt the house in the Palladian style after the 1647 fire whilst further alterations were made by James Wyatt from 1801. Recipient of the 2010 HHA/Sotheby's Restoration Award, the chief architectural features are the 17th century state apartments (Single and Double Cube rooms), and the 19th century cloisters. The House contains one of the finest art collections in Europe and is set in magnificent landscaped parkland featuring the Palladian Bridge. A large adventure playground provides hours of fun for younger visitors.

Location: MAP 3:B4, OS Ref. SU099 311. 3m W of Salisbury along the A36.

Owner: The Earl of Pembroke **Contact:** The Estate Office

Tel: 01722 746714 **Fax:** 01722 744447

E-mail: tourism@wiltonhouse.com

Open: Summer: House: 6–9 Apr inclusive, 5 May–2 Sept, Sun–Thur plus BH Sats, 11.30am–4.30pm, last admission 3.45pm. Grounds: 1–15 Apr, 5 May–16 Sept, daily, 11am–5pm. Winter: Open for bespoke tours by prior arrangement.

Admission: House & Grounds*: Adult £14, Child (5–15) £7.50, Concession £11.25, Family £34. *includes admission to Dining & South Ante Rooms when open. Grounds: Adult £5.50, Child (5–15) £4, Concession £5, Family £16.50. Group Admission: Adult £12, Child £6, Concession £9.50. Guided Tour £6.

Key facts: Film location, fashion shows, product launches, equestrian events, garden parties, antiques fairs, concerts, vehicle rallies. No photography in house. French, German, Spanish, Italian, Japanese and Dutch information. WCs. Licensed. Licensed. By arrangement. £6. Tours in French, German and Spanish. 200 cars and 12 coaches. Free coach parking. Group rates (min 15), drivers' meal voucher. National Curriculum KS1/2. Free preparatory visit for teachers. Sandford Award Winner 2002 & 2008. Guide dogs only.

© Skyscan. Taken from the book 'Historic Family Homes & Gardens from the Air'.

HAMPTWORTH LODGE

Hamptworth, Landford, Salisbury, Wiltshire SP5 2EA

www.hamptworthestate.co.uk

Jacobean style manor house standing in mature deciduous woodland within the northern perimeter of the New Forest National Park. Grade II* with period furniture. The Great Hall has an unusual roof truss construction. There is a collection of prentice pieces and the Moffatt collection of contemporary copies of Tudor furniture. One room has late 17th century leather wall coverings. Henry Willis organ. Available for Receptions, Weddings and Corporate Events.

Location: MAP 3:C5, OS Ref. SU227 195. 10m SE of Salisbury on road linking Downton on A338. (Salisbury to Ringwood road) to Landford on A36 (Salisbury to Southampton road).

Contact: N D Anderson Esq **Tel:** 01794 390700 **Fax:** 01794 390644

E-mail: enquiries@hamptworthestate.co.uk

Open: House and Garden: 19–23 Mar, 10–14 Apr, 4–11 May (closed 6 May), 11–15 Jun, 30 July–3 Aug. 2.15pm–last admission 4.15pm. Private Groups and coaches only by prior arrangement on an agreed date.

Admission: Adult £8, Child (under 5yrs) Free.

Key facts: Ground floor & grounds. Obligatory.

© NTPL / Peter Cook

MOMPESSON HOUSE

Cathedral Close, Salisbury, Wiltshire SP1 2EL

www.nationaltrust.org.uk

Elegant, spacious house in the Cathedral Close, built 1701. Featured in award-winning film Sense and Sensibility. Magnificent plasterwork and fine oak staircase. Good period furniture and the Turnbull collection of 18th century drinking glasses. The delightful walled garden has a pergola and traditional herbaceous borders. Garden Tea Room serves light refreshments.

Location: MAP 3:B4, OS Ref. SU142 297. On N side of Choristers' Green in Cathedral Close, near High Street Gate. Rail: Salisbury Station 1/2 mile.

Owner: National Trust **Contact:** The Property Manager

Tel: 01722 335659 **Infoline:** 01722 420980

Fax: 01722 321559

E-mail: mompessonhouse@nationaltrust.org.uk

Open: 10 Mar–4 Nov: Sat–Wed, 11am–5pm. Last admission 4.30pm. Open Good Fri.

***Admission:** Adult £5.90, Child £2.95, Family (2+3) £14.70, Groups £4.90. Garden only: £1. Tearoom vouchers when arriving by public transport. *includes voluntary donation, visitors can choose to pay the standard prices.

Key facts: WCs. By arrangement. Guide dogs only.

LYDIARD PARK

Lydiard Tregoze, Swindon, Wiltshire SN5 3PA

www.lydiardpark.org.uk

Lydiard Park is the ancestral home of the Viscounts Bolingbroke. The Palladian house contains original family furnishings and portraits, exceptional plasterwork and rare 17th century window. The Georgian ornamental Walled Garden has beautiful seasonal displays of flowers and unique garden features. Exceptional monuments, including the Golden Cavalier, in the church.

Location: MAP 3:B1. OS Ref. SU104 848. 4m W of Swindon, 1½m N of M4/J16.

Owner: Swindon Borough Council **Contact:** Lydiard Park Manager

Tel: 01793 770401 **Fax:** 01793 770968

E-mail: lydiardpark@swindon.gov.uk

Open: House & Walled Garden: Tues–Sun, 11am–5pm (4pm Nov–Feb). Grounds: all day, closing at dusk. Victorian Christmas decorations in December.

Admission: House & Walled Garden: Adult £4.50, Senior Citizen £4, Child £2.25* Pre- booked groups: Adult £4, Senior Citizen £3.50*

*May change April 2012

Key facts: No photography in house. WCs. By arrangement. Limited for coaches. In grounds.

© English Heritage

OLD WARDOUR CASTLE

Nr Tisbury, Wiltshire SP3 6RR

www.english-heritage.org.uk/oldwardour

In a picture-book setting, the unusual hexagonal ruins of this 14th century castle stand on the edge of a beautiful lake, surrounded by landscaped grounds which include an elaborate rockwork grotto.

Location: MAP 3:A5, OS184, ST939 263. Off A30 2m SW of Tisbury.

Owner: English Heritage

Contact: Visitor Operations Team

Tel/Fax: 01747 870487

E-mail: customers@english-heritage.org.uk

Open: Please visit www.english-heritage.org.uk for opening times and the most up-to-date information.

Admission: Adult £4, Child £2.40, Conc. £3.60. 15% discount for groups (11+). EH Members Free. Opening times & prices are valid until 31st March 2012.

Key facts: WCs.

Partial.

Limited for coaches.

On leads.

THE PETO GARDEN AT IFORD MANOR

Bradford-on-Avon, Wiltshire BA15 2BA

www.ifordmanor.co.uk

Unique Grade-1 Italian-style garden set on a romantic hillside above the River Frome. Designed by Edwardian architect Harold Peto, who lived at Iford from 1899–1933, the garden features terraces, colonnades, cloisters, casita, statuary, evergreen planting and magnificent rural views. Winner of the 1998 HHA/Christie's *Garden of the Year* Award.

Location: MAP 2:P3, OS Ref. ST800 589. 7m SE of Bath via A36, signposted Iford. 1 1/2m SW of Bradford-on-Avon via B3109.

Owner/Contact: Mrs E A J Cartwright-Hignett

Tel: 01225 863146 **Fax:** 01225 862364 **E-mail:** info@ifordmanor.co.uk

Open: Apr–Sept: Tue–Thur, Sats, Suns & BH Mons, 2–5pm. Oct: Suns only, 2–5pm. Tearoom at weekends May–Sept. Children under 10yrs preferred weekdays only for safety reasons.

Admission: Adult £5, Conc. £4.50. Groups (10+) welcome outside normal opening hours, by arrangement only, £5.

Key facts: No professional photography without permission. Partial. WCs. Limited for coaches. On leads.

TWIGS COMMUNITY GARDENS

c/o Manor Garden Centre, Cheney Manor, Swindon, Wilts SN2 2QJ

www.richmondfellowship.org.uk/twigs

TWIGS is a delightful 2 acre community garden full of surprises. Features include; 7 individual display gardens, ornamental pond, plant nursery, iron age roundhouse, artwork, fitness trail, a separate 1 acre organic allotment site, Swindon Bee keepers and the Haven-overflowing with wildflowers. As featured on www.greatbritishgardens.co.uk.

Location: MAP 3:B1. OS Ref. SU134 588. Free parking.

Owner: Richmond Fellowship **Contact:** Alan Holland

Tel: 01793 523294 **E-mail:** twigs@richmondfellowship.org.uk

Open: Mon, Weds & Fris (Not BHs), all year, 10am–3.30pm. Open Sun 22 Apr & Sun 24 Jun, 11am–4pm.

Admission: Adults £2, Conc. £1.50, OAPs £1.50, Children free. Groups by prior appointment.

Key facts: Well behaved dogs on leads, Children must be supervised at all times. Partial. WCs. By arrangement. Limited for coaches. On leads.

LONGLEAT

Longleat, Warminster, Wiltshire BA12 7NW

Set within 900 acres of 'Capability' Brown landscaped parkland, Longleat House is regarded as one of the best examples of high Elizabethan architecture in Britain and widely acknowledged as one of the most beautiful stately homes open to the public. The Murals, created by Lord Bath, are unique to Longleat.

Location: MAP 2:P4, OS Ref. ST809 430. Just off the A36 between Bath–Salisbury (A362 Warminster–Frome). 2hrs from London following M3, A303, A36, A362 or M4/J18, A46, A36.

Owner: Marquess of Bath

Tel: 01985 844400 **Fax:** 01985 844885 **E-mail:** enquiries@longleat.co.uk

Website: www.longleat.co.uk

Open: Daily Feb–Oct. Please contact us or see www.longleat.co.uk for up-to-date information on opening times.

Admission: Please contact us or see www.longleat.co.uk for prices.

Key facts: Service Dogs only.

NEWHOUSE

Redlynch, Salisbury, Wiltshire SP5 2NX

A brick, Jacobean 'Trinity' House, c1609, with two Georgian wings and a basically Georgian interior. Home of the Eyre family since 1633.

Location: MAP 3:B5, Landranger sheet 184. SU218 214. 9m S of Salisbury between A36 & A338.

Owner: George & June Jeffreys

Contact: Mrs Jeffreys

Tel: 01725 510055

Open: 1 Mar–10 Apr, Mon–Fri & 27 Aug: 2–5pm.

Admission: Adult £5, Child £3, Conc. £5. Groups (15+): Adult £4, Child £3, Conc. £4.

Key facts: No photography in house, except at weddings. Partial. By arrangement. Limited for coaches. On leads.

NORRINGTON MANOR

Alvediston, Salisbury, Wiltshire SP5 5LL

Built in 1377 it has been altered and added to in every century since, with the exception of the 18th century. Only the hall and the 'undercroft' remain of the original. It is currently a family home and the Sykes are only the third family to own it.

Location: MAP 3:A5, OS Ref. ST966 237. Signposted to N of Berwick St John and Alvediston road (half way between the two villages).

Owner/Contact: Mr & Mrs J Sykes

Tel: 01722 780 259

Open: By appointment in writing.

Admission: A donation to the local churches is asked for.

Key facts: Unsuitable. Obligatory, by arrangement. Limited for cars, none for coaches.

STOURHEAD

Stourton, Nr Warminster BA12 6QD

'A living work of art' is how a magazine described Stourhead when it first opened in the 1740s. Explore the world-famous landscape garden, experience the Grand Tour in the Palladian mansion and enjoy fresh air with a walk in the woods or on the chalkdowns.

Location: MAP 2:P4, OS Ref. ST780 340. At Stourton off the B3092, 3m NW of A303 (Mere), 8m S of A361 (Frome).

Owner: National Trust **Contact:** The Estate Office

Tel: 01747 841152 **Fax:** 01747 842005

E-mail: stourhead@nationaltrust.org.uk

Website: www.nationaltrust.org.uk

Open/Admission: Please call us for opening times and admission prices.

Key facts: Suitable. WCs. Licensed. Licensed. Group tours, by arrangement. Limited for coaches. On leads. Please contact us or visit the website for details of our full events programme.

Audley End

Framlingham Castle

East of England

Bedfordshire

Cambridgeshire

Essex

Hertfordshire

Norfolk

Suffolk

Norfolk is home to many fine country estates including Holkham Hall, a breathtaking Palladian mansion with an award-winning beach and national nature reserve, and the Queen's retreat at Sandringham. Cambridge University Botanic Garden, opened in 1846, showcases over 8000 plant species from around the globe and Audley End in Essex is one of England's finest country houses. In Suffolk, visitors can experience life throughout the ages at Framlingham's magnificent 12th century castle and The Natural History Museum at Tring provides a fascinating window to the past in the Hertfordshire countryside.

VISITOR INFORMATION

Owner
The Duke and Duchess of Bedford & The Trustees of the Bedford Estates

Address
Woburn Abbey
Woburn
Bedfordshire MK17 9WA

Location
MAP 7:D10
OS Ref. SP965 325

On A4012, midway between M1/J13, 3m, J14, 6m and the A5 (turn off at Hockliffe). London approx. 1hr by road (43m).

Rail: London Euston to Leighton Buzzard, Bletchley/Milton Keynes. Kings Cross Thameslink to Flitwick.

Air: Luton 14m. Heathrow 39m.

Contact
Tel: 01525 290333
Fax: 01525 290271
E-mail: admissions@woburn.co.uk

Opening Times
Woburn Abbey
Please telephone or visit our website for details.

Gardens & Deer Park
All year: Daily (except 24–26 December).

Antiques Centre
All year: Daily (except 24–26 December).

Admission
Please telephone or visit our website for details.

Group rates available.

Special events
The Woburn Abbey Garden Show

Outdoor theatre performances

Gardening School Days

Study Days

Maze open Bank Holidays

Jubilee celebrations

Conference/Function

ROOM	Size	Max Cap
Sculpture Gallery	128' x 24'	300 250 (sit-down)
Lantern Rm	44' x 21'	60
Long Harness Room	35' x 21'	80

WOBURN ABBEY

www.woburn.co.uk/abbey

Visit the home of Afternoon Tea, enjoy priceless treasures, uncover fascinating stories, stroll beautiful gardens and browse the antiques centre.

Set in a 3,000 acre deer park with nine free roaming species of deer, Woburn Abbey has been the home of the Russell Family for nearly 400 years, and is now home to the 15th Duke of Bedford and his family.

Admired as one of the world's finest private art collections, there are over 250 pieces, including paintings by Cuyp, Gainsborough, Reynolds, Van Dyck, Queen Victoria and Richard Stone. The Abbey also houses the largest private collection of Venetian views painted by Canaletto in one room (pictured below).

The tour of the Abbey covers three floors, including the vaults, with 18th century furniture, gold and silver collections, a wide range of porcelain and many family keepsakes treasured by the Russell family throughout the centuries on display. The English tradition of Afternoon Tea is said to have originated in the late 1830s with Duchess Anna Maria, wife of the 7th Duke, who entertained her friends in the Blue Drawing Room.

There are 30 acres of gardens to enjoy, from sweeping lawns and flower beds to woodland glades and ponds. Watch ongoing historical restoration projects unfold, follow the Information Trail, complete the children's quiz and download gardeners' podcasts to learn even more.

2012 will see a number of events throughout the year, including craft fairs, open air theatre performances, contemporary sculpture exhibitions and the annual Woburn Abbey Garden Show.

KEY FACTS

- Suitable for fashion shows, product launches and company 'days out'. Use of parkland and garden. No photography in House.
- Conferences, exhibitions, banqueting, luncheons, dinners.
- Unsuitable.
- Licensed.
- Licensed.
- By arrangement, max groups of 8. Tours in French, German & Italian available. Guide book and audio guide available (additional charge).
- Please telephone for details.
- Guide dogs only in gardens.

© English Heritage

WREST PARK ⌗

www.english-heritage.org.uk/wrest

Wrest park boasts one of the most magnificent gardens in England yet one of the least well known.

Unseen and unknown for decades, the 'Sleeping Beauty' of English gardens wakes from its slumbers after a revitalisation project. Wrest Park boasts a new visitor centre in its Walled Garden - complete with introductory exhibition, shop, children's play area and café.

Wrest Park is unique in allowing visitors to see the evolution of garden styles over the 18th and 19th centuries. The De Grey family, owners from the middle ages until the early 20th century, commissioned famous designers over 250 years. Whereas in other gardens previous designs were lost in the pursuit of new gardening vogues, each generation at Wrest Park respected the vision of their predecessors.

In July 2011 Wrest Park will reopen with extended opening times and a greater programme of events. Improved access will lead visitors to the newly-restored Italian and Rose gardens and the amazing classical and Baroque garden buildings. They include the 18th century Pavilion by Thomas Archer, focal point of the extensive grounds at the end of a long stretch of water. Other buildings include a French-style Orangery and the 18th century Bowling Green House.

Inside the mansion, inspired by 18th century Parisian architecture, exciting new exhibitions tell the story of the estate, its evolution and its personalities. Selected rooms can be viewed, including the restored Countess' Sitting Room, shown as it would have been in the mid-19th century.

Wrest Park is a striking venue for wedding receptions, corporate functions and evening entertainment. We are also newly licensed to host civil wedding ceremonies.

KEY FACTS

- WCs. Picnickers welcome. Buggies available. Please note no photography or stiletto heels in the house.
- On leads.

© English Heritage

© English Heritage

VISITOR INFORMATION

Owner
English Heritage

Address
Silsoe
Luton
Bedfordshire
MK45 4HS

Location
MAP 7:E10
OS Ref 153. TL093 356

3/4m E of Silsoe off A6, 10m S of Bedford.

Contact
Visitor Operations Team
Tel: 01525 860152
E-mail: customers@english-heritage.org.uk

Opening Times
please see www.english-heritage.org.uk for opening times and the most up-to-date information. The house may be closed if an event is booked. The gardens may also close early. Please call to check.

Admission

Adult	£5.50
Child	£2.80
Conc.	£4.70
Family	£13.80

Group discounts.
EH members Free.

Opening times and prices are valid until 31st March 2012.

Special events
There is an exciting events programme available throughout the year, for further details please contact the property or visit the website.

BUNYAN MEETING

JOHN BUNYAN MUSEUM AND BUNYAN MEETING

Mill Street, Bedford, Bedfordshire MK40 3EU

www.bunyanmeeting.co.uk

Experience the life and times of the famous 17th century preacher, pastor and author of 'The Pilgrim's Progress'. Discover Bunyan's most celebrated work in over 200 languages and many of his personal possessions. Explore the Church, with its magnificent bronze entrance doors and 20th century stained glass windows.

Location: MAP 7:E9. OS Ref. TL051 234. Bedford is near the A6 and A421 and 20 minutes from the M1.

Contact: Nicola Sherhod (Curator) **Tel:** 01234 270303

E-mail: curator@bunyanmeeting.co.uk

Open: Museum open Mar–End of Oct, Tue–Sat, 11am–4pm (last entry 3.45pm). Closed Good Friday. Church open all year Tue–Fri, 10.15am–3.45pm. Sat 10.15am–1pm.

Admission: Free. Groups (10+) and school parties by prior arrangement throughout the year. Donations welcome.

Key facts: WCs. By arrangement. No cars, limited for coaches. Guide dogs only.

SWISS GARDEN

Old Warden Park, Bedfordshire

www.shuttleworth.org

The Swiss Garden is a late Regency garden created in the 1820's and is an outstanding example of the Swiss picturesque. The Swiss Cottage provides the main element for this unusual atmospheric garden. Interesting things to see are a grotto and fernery, a thatched tree shelter and an Indian Kiosk.

Location: MAP 7:E9, OS Ref. TL150 447. 1$^1/_2$m W of Biggleswade A1 roundabout, signposted from A1 and A600.

Contact: The Shuttleworth Trust

Tel: 01767 627927

Open: Mar–Oct: 9.30am–5pm; Nov–Feb: 9.30am–4pm. Closed Christmas week.

Admission: Adult £5, Child Free, Conc. £4. Special rates for groups, tours & private hire.

Key facts: Catering. Refreshments adjacent.

MOGGERHANGER PARK

Park Road, Moggerhanger, Bedfordshire MK44 3RW

Award Winning Georgian Grade I listed Country House designed by Sir John Soane, recently restored, in 33 acres of Humphry Repton designed parkland and woodland. Moggerhanger House has 3 executive conference suites and 2 function rooms, making an ideal venue for conferences, promotions, corporate entertainment, family functions and weddings. **Location:** MAP 7:E9 OS Ref. TL048 475. On A603, 3m from A1 at Sandy, 6m from Bedford.

Owner: Moggerhanger House Preservation Trust **Contact:** Mrs Tracy Purser

Tel: 01767 641007 **Fax:** 01767 641515

E-mail: enquiries@moggerhangerpark.com **Website:** www.moggerhangerpark.com

Open: House Tours: See website or telephone for current information. Grounds, Tearooms & Visitors Centre: Open all year.

Admission: Please telephone 01767 641007.

Key facts: No photography. No smoking. Suitable. WCs. Licensed. Licensed. By arrangement. Limited for coaches. On leads.

QUEEN ANNE'S SUMMERHOUSE

Shuttleworth, Old Warden, Bedfordshire SG18 9DU

The outstanding brickwork of this foursquare folly makes it likely to date from the early 18th century. Surrounded by the flora and fauna of a woodland, this is a magical spot. The Landmark Trust, a building preservation charity, undertook the major restoration of the building.

Location: MAP 7:E10, OS Ref. TL144436.

Owner/Contact: The Landmark Trust

Tel: 01628 825925

E-mail: bookings@landmarktrust.org.uk

Website: www.landmarktrust.org.uk

Open: Available for holidays. Six Open Days a year and visits by appointment. Contact the Landmark Trust for details.

Admission: Free on Open Days and visits by appointment.

Key facts:

TURVEY HOUSE

Turvey, Bedfordshire MK43 8EL

A neo-classical house set in picturesque parkland bordering the River Great Ouse. The principal rooms contain a fine collection of 18th and 19th century English and Continental furniture, pictures, porcelain, objets d'art and books. Walled Garden.

Location: MAP 7:D9, OS Ref. SP939528. Between Bedford and Northampton on A428.

Owner: The Hanbury Family **Contact:** Daniel Hanbury

Tel/Fax: 01234 881244 **E-mail:** danielhanbury@hotmail.com

Open: 24 Mar. 7, 21 & 28 Apr. 7, 8, 10, 12, 22 & 24 May.
4, 5, 7, 9, 19, 21 & 23 Jun. 3, 5, 7, 17, 19, 21 & 31 Jul. 2, 4, 25 & 27 Aug, 2–5pm. Last Admission 4.30pm.

Admission: Adult £6, Child £3.

Key facts: No photography in house. Obligatory. Ample for cars, none for coaches.

© Property of Woburn Abbey

Chinese Dairy, Woburn Abbey Gardens, June 2011.

© NT / Richard Todd

© Brian & Nina Chapple

ANGLESEY ABBEY, GARDENS & LODE MILL

QUY ROAD, LODE, CAMBRIDGESHIRE CB25 9EJ

www.nationaltrust.org.uk/angleseyabbey

A passion for tradition and style inspired one man to transform a run-down country house and desolate landscape. Step into his elegant home and encounter the luxuries enjoyed by guests. Experience the warmth and comfort and be amazed at rare and fabulous objects. Lord Fairhaven was a generous host, delighting in entertaining guests and a life occupied with horse racing and shooting. The 114 acre garden, with its working watermill, wildlife discovery area and statuary offers inspiration and planting for all seasons. Explore the borders, meadow and avenues bursting with vibrant colour, delicious scent and the simple pleasures of nature.

Location: MAP 7:G8, OS Ref. TL533 622. 6m NE of Cambridge on B1102, signs from A14 jct35.

Owner: National Trust **Contact:** Administrator

Tel: 01223 810080 **Fax:** 01223 810088

E-mail: angleseyabbey@nationaltrust.org.uk

Open: House: 14 Mar–28 Oct, Wed–Sun, 11am–5pm; House (guided tours only): 12 Mar–23 Oct, Mon & Tues, 12–3pm; 5 Nov–31 Dec, Mon–Sun, 12–3pm; Garden, Restaurant, Shop & Plant Centre: open all year, 7 days a week, 10.30am–5.30pm (4.30pm in winter). House open in full on BHs. Property closed 24–26 December.

***Admission:** House, Garden & Mill: Adult £11, Child £5.50, Family £27.50. Groups: Adult £9.35, child £4.65. *includes a voluntary Gift Aid donation of at least 10% which will be put towards the restoration and upkeep of this property.

Key facts: Suitable. WCs. Licensed. By arrangement. Guide dogs only. From garden study mornings to live theatre, children's fun days and wildlife watchings, there are events to suit everyone all year round.

©Nigel Luckhurst

CAMBRIDGE UNIVERSITY BOTANIC GARDEN

1 BROOKSIDE, CAMBRIDGE CB2 1JE

www.botanic.cam.ac.uk

The Cambridge University Botanic Garden was opened in 1846 by John Henslow, mentor to Charles Darwin, and today showcases over 8000 plant species from around the globe, including nine National Plant Collections and the best arboretum in the region.

Landscape highlights include the Winter Garden, the richly-fragranced Scented Garden, the buzzing Bee Borders and the unique Systematic Beds. The Glasshouse displays range from architectural cactus to flamboyant, tropical rainforests.

Opening daily at 10am, the Cambridge University Botanic Garden is an inspiration year-round, and an exciting introduction to the natural world for families (children can borrow the free Young Explorer backpacks).

Location: MAP 7:G9, OS Ref. TL453 573. 3/4 m S of Cambridge city centre, some pay & display parking along Trumpington Road.

Owner: University of Cambridge

Contact: Enquiries Desk

Tel: 01223 336265

Fax: 01223 336278

E-mail: enquiries@botanic.cam.ac.uk

Open: Apr–Sept, daily, 10am–6pm; closes 5pm in Feb, Mar & Oct, and 4pm from Nov–Jan. Closed over Christmas and New Year, please telephone for details.

Admission: From 1 Mar 2012: Gift aid admission £4.95, Standard admission £4.50, Concession Gift Aid £4.35, Concession £3.95. Groups must pre-book with at least one week's notice.

Key facts: WCs. By arrangement. Street/Pay & Display. Schools and leisure groups must book. Guide dogs only.

© NT / Fisheye Images

WIMPOLE ESTATE

ARRINGTON, ROYSTON, CAMBRIDGESHIRE SG8 0BW

www.nationaltrust.org.uk www.wimpole.org

A unique working estate still guided by the seasons, an impressive mansion at its heart with beautiful interiors by Gibbs, Flitcroft and Soane. Uncover the stories of the people who have shaped Wimpole; soak up the atmosphere; take in the spectacular views and find your own special place. Stroll through the Pleasure Grounds to the Walled Garden, bursting with seasonal produce and glorious herbaceous borders. At Home Farm contrast the traditional farmyard with the noisy modern piggery and cattle sheds. Ask our Stockman about our rare breeds and learn more about your food and our farming.

Location: MAP 7:F9, OS154. TL336 510. 8m SW of Cambridge (A603), 6m N of Royston (A1198). Rail: Shepreth 5ml. Royston with a taxi rank 8ml.

Owner: National Trust **Contact:** Estate Office

Tel: 01223 206000 **Fax:** 01223 207838

E-mail: wimpolehall@nationaltrust.org.uk

Open: Hall: 11 Feb–4 Nov, Sat–Thur, 11am–5pm. Garden, Restaurant, Shop: 1 Jan–8 Feb, Sat–Wed, 11am–4pm. 11 Feb–4 Nov, Daily, 10.30am–5pm. 5 Nov–24 Dec, 11am–4pm, Sat–Wed, 11am–4pm. Home Farm: 1 Jan–5 Feb Sat/Sun, 11am–4pm. 11 Feb–4 Nov, Daily, 10.30am–5pm. 10 Nov–23 Dec, 11am–4pm, Sat–Sun. Park: Daily, Dawn-dusk.

Admission: Hall: Adult £10.30, Child £5.80. Joint ticket with Home Farm: Adult £15.50, Child £8.40, Family £40.70. Garden: £4.30.
Farm & Garden: Adult £8.40, Child (3yrs & over) £5.80, Family £26.20.
Discount for NT members. For Standard prices check the website.

Key facts: Partial. WCs. Licensed. By arrangement. Guide dogs only.

ISLAND HALL

Godmanchester, Cambridgeshire PE29 2BA

www.islandhall.com

An important mid 18th century mansion of great charm, owned and restored by an award-winning interior designer. This family home has lovely Georgian rooms, with fine period detail, and interesting possessions relating to the owners' ancestors since their first occupation of the house in 1800. A tranquil riverside setting with formal gardens and ornamental island forming part of the grounds in an area of Best Landscape. Octavia Hill wrote "This is the loveliest, dearest old house, I never was in such a one before."

Location: MAP 7:F8, OS Ref. TL244 706. Centre of Godmanchester, Post Street next to free car park. 1m S of Huntingdon, 15m NW of Cambridge A14.

Owner: Mr Christopher & Lady Linda Vane Percy **Contact:** Mr C Vane Percy

Tel: (Groups) 01480 459676 (Individuals via Invitation to View) 01206 573948

E-mail: cvp@cvpdesigns.com

Open: Groups by arrangement: All year round. Individuals via Invitation to View.

Admission: Groups: (40+) £6.50. (30+) £7. (20+) £7.50. Under 20 persons min charge £150 per group.

Key facts: See website for more details. Home made teas.

THE MANOR, HEMINGFORD GREY

Huntingdon, Cambridgeshire PE28 9BN

www.greenknowe.co.uk

Built about 1130 and one of the oldest continuously inhabited houses in Britain. Made famous as 'Green Knowe' by the author Lucy Boston. Her patchwork collection is also shown. Four acre garden, laid out by Lucy Boston, surrounded by moat, with topiary, old roses, award winning irises and herbaceous borders.

Location: MAP 7:F8, OS Ref. TL290 706. A14, 3m SE of Huntingdon. 12m NW of Cambridge. Access via small gate on riverside.

Owner: Mrs D S Boston **Contact:** Diana Boston **Tel:** 01480 463134

E-mail: diana_boston@hotmail.com

Open: House: All year (except May), to individuals or groups by prior arrangement. May guided tours daily at 2pm (booking advisable). Garden: All year, daily, 11am–5pm (4pm in winter).

Admission: House & Garden: Adult £7, Child £2, OAP £5.50 Family £18. Garden only: See website.

Key facts: No photography in house. Partial. Obligatory. Cars: Disabled only. Coaches: Nearby.

© NTPL / Andreas von Einsiedel

PECKOVER HOUSE & GARDEN

North Brink, Wisbech, Cambridgeshire PE13 1JR

wwww.nationaltrust.org.uk

Peckover House is an oasis hidden away in an urban environment. A classic Georgian merchant's townhouse, it was lived in by the Peckover family for 150 years and reflects their Quaker lifestyle. The gardens are outstanding - two acres of sensory delight, complete with orangery, summer houses, croquet lawn.
Location: MAP 7:G6, OS Ref. TF458 097. On N bank of River Nene, in Wisbech B1441.
Owner: National Trust **Contact:** The Property Secretary **Tel:** 01945 583463
Fax: 01945 587904 **E-mail:** peckover@nationaltrust.org.uk
Open: House: 10 Mar–4 Nov, Sat–Wed 1–5pm.
Garden: As house, plus 11 Feb–4 Mar, Sat & Sun 12–4pm. Please call for details of special holiday opening.
Admission: Adult £7, Child £3.50, Family £17.50. Groups discount (min 15 people) - book in advance with Property Secretary.
Key facts: No photography in House. PMV available for loan in grounds. Free garden tours most days. Partial. WCs. Licensed. By arrangement. Signposted. Guide dogs only.

PETERBOROUGH CATHEDRAL

Cathedral Office, Minster Precincts, Peterborough PE1 1XS

www.peterborough-cathedral.org.uk

Magnificent Norman Architecture, a unique 13th century Nave ceiling and the burial place of Katharine of Aragon make a visit to the Cathedral an unforgettable experience. You can also take a guided tour - please call for tour times. Musical concerts held throughout the year: please check our website for details. Rooms also available to hire for meetings and private functions.
Location: MAP 7:E6, OS Ref. TL194 986. 4m E of A1, in City Centre.
Contact: Amber Homer-Wooff
Tel: 01733 355300
Fax: 01733 355316
E-mail: amber.homer-wooff@peterborough-cathedral.org.uk
Open: All year apart from Boxing Day: Mon–Fri, 9am–6.30pm (restricted access after 5.30pm because of Evensong). Sat, 9am–5pm. Sun: services from 7.30am; visitors: 12 noon–5pm.
Admission: No fixed charge – donations are requested.
Key facts: Visitors' Centre. By arrangement. None. Guide dogs only. See website for details.

DOCWRA'S MANOR GARDEN

Shepreth, Royston, Hertfordshire SG8 6PS
Extensive garden with choice plants for all year interest within the old farm walls.
Location: MAP 7:F9. OS Ref. TL393 479. In Shepreth via A10 from Royston to Cambridge.
Owner: Mrs Faith Raven
Contact: Peter Rocket
Tel: 01763 261473
Website: www.docwrasmanorgarden.co.uk
Open: All year: Weds & Fris, 10am–4pm & 1st Sun in month Feb-Nov: 2–4.30pm.
Admission: £4
Key facts: Suitable. WCs. By arrangement. Limited for coaches. Guide dogs only.

ELTON HALL

Nr Peterborough PE8 6SH
Historic family house for 400 years. The property houses a very good collection of Old Masters and English 18th and 19th century pictures. One of the best libraries in private hands. Stunningly restored gardens with finely clipped topiary, new Flower Garden, Millennium Orangery and Box Walk.
Location: MAP 7:E7, OS Ref. TL091 930. Close to A1 in the village of Elton, off A605 Peterborough – Oundle Road.
Owner: Sir William Proby Bt, CBE **Contact:** The Administrator
Tel: 01832 280468 **Fax:** 01832 280584 **E-mail:** office@eltonhall.com
Website: www.eltonhall.com
Open: Jun BH (Sun 3 & Mon 4); Jun & Jul: Wed, Thur. Aug: Wed, Thur, Sun & BH Mon, 2–5pm. Private groups by arrangement Apr–Sept.
Admission: House & Garden: Adult £9, Conc. £8. Garden only: Adult £6.50, Conc. £6. Accompanied child under 16 Free.
Key facts: No photography in house. Garden suitable. Obligatory. Guide dogs in gardens only.

KIMBOLTON CASTLE

Kimbolton, Huntingdon, Cambridgeshire PE28 0EA
Vanbrugh and Hawksmoor's 18th century adaptation of 13th century fortified house. Katharine of Aragon's last residence. Tudor remains still visible. Courtyard by Henry Bell of King's Lynn. Outstanding Pellegrini murals. Gatehouse by Robert Adam. Home of Earls and Dukes of Manchester, 1615–1950. Family portraits in State Rooms. Now Kimbolton School.
Location: MAP 7:E8, OS Ref. TL101 676. 7m NW of St Neots on B645.
Owner: Governors of Kimbolton School **Contact:** Mrs N Butler
Tel: 01480 860505 **Fax:** 01480 861763
Website: www.kimbolton.cambs.sch.uk/thecastle
Open: 4 Mar & 4 Nov, 1–4pm.
Admission: Adult £5, Child £2.50, OAP £4. Groups by arrangement throughout the year, including evenings, special rates apply.
Key facts: Unsuitable. By arrangement.
Parking for coaches limited. On leads. In grounds only.

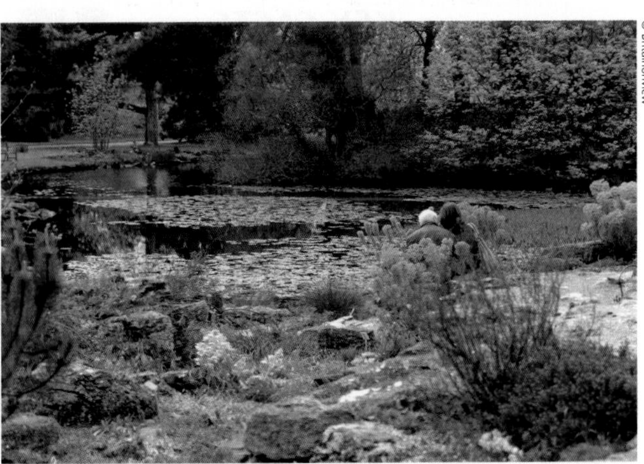

© Britainonview

Cambridge University Botanic Garden

VISITOR INFORMATION

■ Owner
English Heritage

■ Address
Audley End House
Audley End
Saffron Walden
Essex CB11 4JF

■ Location
MAP 7:G10
OS Ref. TL525 382
1m W of Saffron Walden on B1383, M11/J8 & J10.
Rail: Audley End 1¼ m.

■ Contact
Visitor Operations Team
Tel: 01799 522842
Fax: 01799 521276
E-mail: customers@english-heritage.org.uk

■ Opening Times
Please visit www.english-heritage.org.uk for opening times and the latest information.

■ Admission
Full Estate:

Adult	£12.50
Child (5–15yrs)	£7.50
Child (under 5yrs)	Free
Conc	£11.30
Family (2+3)	£32.50.

Stables, Service Wing and Gardens:

Adult	£8.70
Child (5–15yrs)	£5.20
Child (under 5yrs)	Free
Conc	£7.80
Family (2+3)	£22.60

Discount for groups (11+).

EH Members free.

Opening times and prices are valid until 31 March 2012.

■ Special events
There is an exciting events programme available throughout the year, for further details please contact the property or visit the website.

© English Heritage

AUDLEY END ⌗

www.english-heritage.org.uk/audleyend

One of England's finest country houses, Audley End is also a mansion with a difference. Enjoy a great day out.

The stable yard which opened in spring 2010 means visitors can now enjoy a day out with a difference, as the daily routine of a Victorian stable yard is brought to life. Complete with resident horses and a costumed groom, the stables experience includes an exhibition where you can find out about the workers who lived on the estate in the 1880s, the tack house and the Audley End fire engine. There is also a children's play area and café which are ideal for family visitors.

Every great house needed an army of servants and the restored Victorian Service Wing shows a world "below stairs" that was never intended to be seen. Immerse yourself in the past as you visit the kitchen, scullery, pantry and laundries with film projections, introductory wall displays and even original food from the era.

The cook, Mrs Crocombe, and her staff can regularly be seen trying out new recipes and going about their chores.

Audley End House is itself a magnificent house, built to entertain royalty. Among the highlights is a stunning art collection including works by Masters Holbein, Lely and Canaletto. Its pastoral parkland is designed by "Capability" Brown and there is an impressive formal garden to discover. Don't miss the working Organic Kitchen Garden with its glasshouses and vinery growing original Victorian varieties of fruit and vegetables.

Audley End also boasts Cambridge Lodge a two storey detached holiday cottage. The sitting room enjoys magnificent views of the grounds of Audley End House.

KEY FACTS

- Open air concerts and other events. WCs.
- Service Yard and Coach House Shops.
-
- Partial.
-
- By arrangement for groups.
- Coaches to book in advance. Free entry for coach drivers and tour guides.
- School visits free if booked in advance. Contact the Administrator or tel 01223 582700 for bookings.
- On leads only.

© English Heritage

© English Heritage

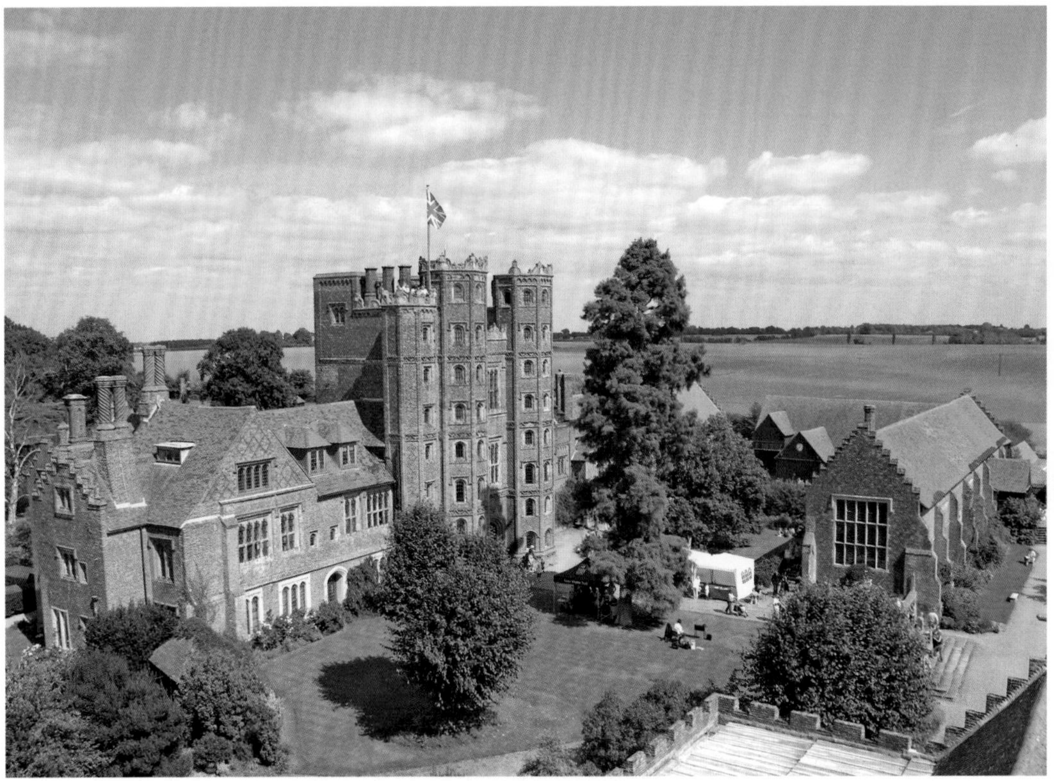

LAYER MARNEY TOWER

www.layermarneytower.co.uk

Layer Marney Tower, the tallest Tudor Gatehouse in the country.

Layer Marney Tower is a wonderful Tudor building of soft red brick and buff coloured terracotta, set within delightful gardens and parkland. In many respects the apotheosis of the Tudor gatehouse, Layer Marney Tower soars over the surrounding countryside offering spectacular views to those who climb to the top.

Built in the reign of Henry VIII by Henry, 1st Lord Marney, Layer Marney Tower is the tallest Tudor gatehouse in Great Britain and was intended to surpass Cardinal Wolsey's rival work at Hampton Court. Henry Marney died in 1523 before his ambition was realized and the death of son John two years later brought an end to the building work.

By then the gatehouse and principal range were completed, as well as the stable block, outbuildings and the parish church. Layer Marney Tower has some of the finest terracotta work in the country, probably executed by Flemish craftsmen trained by Italian masters.

Visitors may now wander through the recently restored tower rooms and up to the viewing platform on the roof. The new lavatory block is a delight, worth a visit in its own right. There are fine outbuildings, including the Long Gallery and the medieval barn. The gardens follow a relatively formal Edwardian layout; herbaceous borders, broad paths and plentiful roses that flourish in the heavy Essex clay.

One of the country's most desirable wedding venues, Layer Marney Tower is also used for corporate functions. Special events are arranged throughout the year ranging from Lantern Tours to Kite Festivals.

KEY FACTS

No photography inside the house. Suitable for functions. Park and woodland for sports, corporate events, open air concerts, team building, balloon festivals and helicopter landing. Film location. Wedding ceremonies and receptions.

Partial. WC.

Licensed.

Tea room.

By arrangement – about 1½ hrs.

Cars & Coaches.

On a lead.

Self catering cottage. Glamping.

By appointment for groups and special events.

VISITOR INFORMATION

Owner

Mr Nicholas Charrington

Address

Layer Marney Tower
Nr Colchester
Essex
CO5 9US

Location

MAP 8:J11
TL929 175
7m SW of Colchester, signed off B1022.

Contact

Mr Nicholas Charrington
Tel: 01206 330784
E-mail: info@layermarneytower.co.uk

Opening Times

12noon–5pm:

April, May, June and September, Weds & Suns.

July & August, Sun–Thurs.

Admission

Adults	£6.00
Children (3–15)	£4.00
Family ticket	£18.00

Group visits and guided tours throughout the year, by arrangement.

Guided tours £10.00 per person, minimum charge for a group–£200.00

Group visits £5.00 person, minimum group size 20.

Special events

See website www.layermarneytower.co.uk for details.

BRENTWOOD CATHEDRAL

BRENTWOOD CATHEDRAL

INGRAVE ROAD, BRENTWOOD, ESSEX CM15 8AT

The new (1991) Roman Catholic classical Cathedral Church of St Mary and St Helen incorporates part of the original Victorian church. Designed by classical architect Quinlan Terry with roundels by Raphael Maklouf. Architecturally, the inspiration is early Italian Renaissance crossed with the English Baroque of Christopher Wren. The north elevation consists of nine bays divided by Doric pilasters. This is broken by a half-circular portico. The Kentish ragstone walls have a rustic look, which contrasts with the smooth Portland stone of the capitals and column bases. Inside is an arcade of Tuscan arches with central altar with the lantern above.

Location: MAP 4:J1. OS Ref. TQ596 938. A12 & M25/J28. Centre of Brentwood, opposite Brentwood School.
Owner: Diocese of Brentwood
Tel: 01277 232266
E-mail: bishop@dioceseofbrentwood.org
Open: All year, daily.
Admission: Free.
Key facts: Suitable. Limited. None for coaches.

© Peter Gamble

COPPED HALL

Crown Hill, Epping, Essex CM16 5HS

www.coppedhalltrust.org.uk

Mid 18th century Palladian mansion under restoration. Situated on ridge overlooking landscaped park. Ancillary buildings including stables and racquets court. Former elaborate gardens being rescued from abandonment. Large 18th century walled garden – adjacent to site of 16th century mansion where *'A Midsummer Night's Dream'* was first performed. Ideal film location.
Location: MAP 7:G12, OS Ref. TL433 016. 4m SW of Epping, N of M25.
Owner: The Copped Hall Trust
Contact: Alan Cox
Tel: 020 7267 1679
E-mail: coxalan1@aol.com
Open: Ticketed events and special open days. See website for dates. By appointment only for groups (20+).
Admission: Open Days £5. Guided Tour Days £7. Gardens Only £3.50.
Key facts: Partial.
In grounds, on leads.
Concerts, plays and study days.

HYLANDS HOUSE & ESTATE

Hylands Park, London Road, Chelmsford CM2 8WQ

www.chelmsford.gov.uk/hylands

Hylands House is a beautiful Grade II* listed building, set in 574 acres of historic landscaped parkland. Built c1730, the original House was a Queen Anne style mansion. Subsequent owners modernised and enlarged the property. The Stables Visitor Centre, incorporates a Gift Shop, Café, Artist Studios and a Second-hand Bookshop.
Location: MAP 7:H12, OS Ref. TL681 054. 2m SW of Chelmsford. Signposted on A414 from J15 of A12, near Chelmsford.
Owner: Chelmsford Borough Council **Contact:** Ceri Lowen
Tel: 01245 605500 **Fax:** 01245 605510 **E-mail:** hylands@chelmsford.gov.uk
Open: House: Suns & Mons, 10am–5pm Apr–Sept, Sun only 10am–4pm Oct–Mar, Closed 25 Dec. Stables Visitor Centre and Park: Daily. Guided Tours, Talks and Walks are available by arrangement.
Admission: House: Adult £3.80, Conc. £2.80, accompanied children under 16's Free. Visitor Stables Centre and Park: Free.
Key facts: Visitor Centre. Daily. By arrangement.
By arrangement. In grounds. Guide dogs only in house.

INGATESTONE HALL

Hall Lane, Ingatestone, Essex CM4 9NR

www.ingatestonehall.com

16th century mansion, with 11 acres of grounds (formal garden and wild walk), built by Sir William Petre, Secretary of State to four Tudor monarchs, which has remained in his family ever since. Furniture, portraits and memorabilia accumulated over the centuries – and two Priests' hiding places.

Location: MAP 7:H12, OS Ref. TQ654 986. Off A12 between Brentwood & Chelmsford.

Owner: The Lord Petre **Contact:** The Administrator

Tel: 01277 353010 **Fax:** 01245 248979

E-mail: house@ingatestonehall.co.uk

Open: 8 Apr–30 Sept: Wed, Suns & BH Mons (not Weds in Jun), 12noon–5pm.

Admission: Adult £6, Child £2.50 (under 5yrs Free), Conc. £5. (Groups of 20+ booked in advance: Adult £5, Child £1.50, Conc. £4.)

Key facts: No photography in house. Partial, WCs. By arrangement. Guide dogs only.

THE MUNNINGS COLLECTION

Castle House, Castle Hill, Dedham, Essex CO7 6AZ

www.siralfredmunnings.co.uk

Castle House, standing in spacious grounds, was the home of Sir Alfred PPRA and Lady Munnings. The house is part Tudor and Georgian and contains works by the artist representing his whole career. Visitors may also view his original studio where his working materials are displayed.

Location: MAP 8:K10, OS Ref. TM060 328. Approximately 3/4m from the village centre on the corner of East Lane.

Owner: Castle House Trust

Contact: The Administrator

Tel: 01206 322127

E-mail: info@siralfredmunnings.co.uk

Open: 1 Apr–31 Oct. Wed, Thur, Sat, Sun & BH Mon 2-5pm. All information correct at time of going to press.

Admission: Adult £5, Child £1, Conc. £4

Key facts: Partial. WCs. On leads.

MARKS HALL ARBORETUM & GARDEN

Coggeshall, Essex CO6 1TG

www.markshall.org.uk

Marks Hall Gardens and Arboretum provides a great day out for the whole family. Wonderful woodland walks, a delightful children-friendly walled garden, lovely lakes and trees and amazing plants from around the world. We even have a Visitor Centre for refreshments and a shop for retail therapy too.

Location: MAP 8:I11. OS Ref. TL840 642. Follow brown tourism signs from A120.

Owner: The Marks Hall Estate **Contact:** Graham Game

Tel: 01376 563796 **Fax:** 01376 563132 **E-mail:** enquiries@markshall.org.uk

Open: Apr-Oct: Tue-Sun, 10.30am-5pm. Winter: Weekends inc. Fri, 10.30am until dusk.

Admission: Adults £4, Children (age 6-16) £1, Concessions £3.50, Family (2 adults and up to 4 children) £8.

Key facts: WCs. By arrangement. Limited for coaches. No dogs in Arboretum. Dogs permitted on Woodland Walks.

HARWICH REDOUBT FORT

Main Road, Harwich, Essex

180ft diameter circular fort built in 1808 to defend the port against Napoleonic invasion. Being restored by Harwich Society and part is a museum. Eleven guns on battlements.

Location: MAP 8:K10, OS Ref. TM262 322. Rear of 29 Main Road. CO12 3LT.

Owner: The Harwich Society

Contact: Mr A Rutter

Tel/Fax: 01255 503429

E-mail: info@harwich-society.co.uk

Website: www.harwich-society.co.uk

Open: 1 May–31 Aug: daily, 10am–4pm. Sept–Apr: Suns only, 10am–4pm. Groups by appointment at any time.

Admission: Adult £2, Child Free (no unaccompanied children).

Key facts: €

PAYCOCKE'S

West Street, Coggeshall, Colchester, Essex C06 1NS

Marvel at the stunning woodcarving and elaborate panelling inside this merchant's house. Built around 1500 for Thomas Paycocke, the house is a grand example of the wealth generated by the cloth trade in the 16th century. Outside, there is a beautiful and tranquil cottage garden.

Location: MAP 8:I11, OS Ref. TL848 225. Signposted off A120.

Owner: National Trust

Contact: The Custodian

Tel: 01376 561305

Website: www.nationaltrust.org.uk

Open: Mar–Oct. Please call or check website for up to date details.

Admission: Adult £3.60, Child £1.80. Groups (10+) by prior arrangement. Please call or check website for up to date details.

Key facts: No WC, nearest one at Coggeshall Grange Barn. By arrangement. NT's at the Coggeshall Grange Barn. Guide dogs only.

KNEBWORTH HOUSE

KNEBWORTH HOUSE, KNEBWORTH, HERTFORDSHIRE SG3 6PY

www.knebworthhouse.com

Home of the Lytton family since 1490, and still a lived-in family house. Transformed in early Victorian times by Edward Bulwer-Lytton, the author, poet, dramatist and statesman, into the unique high gothic fantasy house of today, complete with turrets, griffins and gargoyles. 25 acres of formal gardens, simplified by Lutyens, including pollarded lime avenues, formal rose garden, maze, Gertrude Jekyll herb garden, the walled kitchen garden and the wilderness walk which includes a dinosaur trail with 72 life-size dinosaurs. 250 acres of parkland, with herds of red and sika deer, includes children's giant adventure playground and miniature railway.

Location: MAP 7:E11, OS Ref. TL230 224. Direct access off the A1(M) J7 Stevenage, SG1 2AX, 28m N of London, 15m N of M25/J23.

Owner: The Hon Henry Lytton Cobbold **Contact:** The Estate Office

Tel: 01438 812661 **Fax:** 01438 811908

E-mail: info@knebworthhouse.com

Open: Open daily 31 Mar–15 Apr, 2–10 Jun, 30 Jun–2 Sept (closed 5–10 July. For up to date information on closed days visit www.knebworthhouse.com) Weekend and bank holidays: 24–25 Mar, 21 Apr–27 May, 16–24 Jun, 8–30 Sept; Park, Playground & Gardens: 11am–5pm; House & British Raj Exhibition: 12–5pm (last tour 4pm).

Admission: Including House: Adults: £10.50, Child*/Conc: £10, Family Ticket (4): £37, Groups (20+) Adult: £9.50, Child*/Conc: £9. Excluding House: All persons: £8, Family Ticket (4): £28, Groups (20+) All persons: £7. *4-16yrs, under 4s free.

Key facts: Suitable for conferences and banquets, product launches, weddings, commercial photography, filming, exhibitions, garden shows, concerts and festivals. Obligatory. National Curriculum based school activity days. In grounds. Licensed Knebworth House, Garden Gazebo & Manor Barn.

HATFIELD HOUSE

Hatfield, Hertfordshire AL9 5NQ

www.hatfield-house.co.uk

Hatfield House is ideal for a day's visit – there is so much to do! Visit the fine Jacobean House, home to Lord & Lady Salisbury. Delightful garden and country park. Traditional breed farm and adventure play area. Exclusive shopping and restaurant. Regular events. Entrance opp station - London 20 minutes.

Location: MAP 7:F11, OS Ref. TL 237 084. 21m N of London, M25/ J23 7m, A1(M)/J4, 2m.

Owner: The 7th Marquess of Salisbury **Contact:** Director – Visitors & Events

Tel: 01707 287010 **Fax:** 01707 287033 **E-mail:** visitors@hatfield-house.co.uk

Open: 7 Apr–30 Sept 2012. House: Wed–Sun & BH 12–5pm (last admission 4pm). Garden, Park, Farm, Shops, Restaurant: Tues–Sun & BH's 10am–5.30pm (or dusk).

Admission: W.Garden, sculpture exhibition & park: Adult £9.50, Senior £8.50, Conc: £5. House £6 extra. East garden (weds only) £4 person extra.

Key facts: No photography in house. Tel 01707 262055. Banquets held in the Old Palace. WCs. Parking next to house. Lift. Tel: 01707 262030. Group tours available by prior arrangement. Ample. Hardstanding for coaches. In park only, on leads. €

© NHM

NATURAL HISTORY MUSEUM AT TRING

The Walter Rothschild Building, Akeman Street, Tring, Hertfordshire HP23 6AP

www.nhm.ac.uk/tring

Built in 1889 to house the private natural history collection of Walter Rothschild, the Natural History Museum at Tring is a fascinating Noah's ark in the Hertfordshire countryside.

Enjoy its authentic Victorian atmosphere alongside modern facilities and services.

Location: MAP 7:D11. OS Ref. SP923 851.

Tel: 020 7942 6171

Fax: 020 7942 6150

Open: Mon–Sat 10am–5pm, Sun 2pm–5pm. The Museum is open every day except 24–26 Dec.

Admission: Free. Admission to the Natural History Museum at Tring is free for everyone. Children under eight years old must be accompanied by an adult.

Key facts:

BENINGTON LORDSHIP GARDENS

Stevenage, Hertfordshire SG2 7BS

7 acre garden overlooking lakes in a timeless setting. Features include Norman keep and moat, Queen Anne manor house, James Pulham folly, formal rose garden, renowned herbaceous borders, walled vegetable garden, grass tennis court and verandah. Spectacular display of snowdrops in February. All location work welcome.

Location: MAP 7:F11, OS Ref. TL296 236. In village of Benington next to the church. 4m E of Stevenage.

Owner/Contact: Mr & Mrs R R A Bott **Tel:** 01438 869668 **Fax:** 01438 869622

E-mail: garden@beningtonlordship.co.uk **Website:** www.beningtonlordship.co.uk

Open: Snowdrops 4–26 Feb, daily, 12–4pm. Easter & May BH Mons, 12–5pm. Floral Festival 23 & 24 Jun, 12–5pm. Chilli Festival 26 & 27 Aug 10–5pm (adm £7.50).

Admission: Adult £5, conc £4, Child under 12 free.

Key facts: February. Partial. By arrangement. Limited.

GORHAMBURY

St Albans, Hertfordshire AL3 6AH

Late 18th century house by Sir Robert Taylor. Family portraits from 15th–21st centuries.

Location: MAP 7:E11, OS Ref. TL114 078. 2m W of St Albans. Access via private drive off A4147 at St Albans.

Owner: The Earl of Verulam

Contact: The Administrator

Tel: 01727 854051

Fax: 01727 843675

Open: May–Sept: Thurs, 2–5pm (last entry 4pm).

Admission: House & Gardens; Adult £8, Senior £7, Disabled, Carer, Child £5 including guided tour. Special groups by arrangement (Thurs preferred).

Key facts: No photography. Partial. Obligatory.

Hatfield House

VISITOR INFORMATION

Owner
Trustees of the Holkham Estate. Home of the Coke family.

Address
Holkham Estate Office
Wells-next-the-Sea
Norfolk NR23 1AB

Location
MAP 8:I4
OS Ref. TF885 428

From London 120m
Norwich 35m
King's Lynn 30m.

Bus: On the King's Lynn to Cromer Coasthopper route.

Coach: Access via the South Gates only.

Rail: Norwich Station 35m. King's Lynn Station 30m.

Air: Norwich Airport 32m.

Contact
Marketing Manager
Laurane Herrieven

Tel: 01328 710227
Fax: 01328 711707
E-mail: enquiries@holkham.co.uk

Opening Times
Hall:
1 April–31 October, 12–4pm, Sunday, Monday & Thursday.

Bygones Museum, History of Farming Exhibition, Stables Café, Gift Shop and Walled Gardens:
1 April–31 October. 10am–5pm, every day.

NB: The Libraries, Chapel & Strangers' Wing form part of the private accommodation and are open at the family's discretion.

Admission
Hall, Museum & Walled Gardens:

Adult	£12.00
Child (5-16yrs)	£6.00
Family (2 adults & up to 3 children)	£30.00

Museum & Walled Gardens:

Adult	£7.00
Child (5-16yrs)	£3.50
Family (2 adults & up to 3 children)	£17.50

Groups:
(20+) 10% discount, group organiser free entry, coach driver's refreshment voucher.

Private Guided Tours:
Minimum 12 people, price per person £20.00

History of Farming:
Free

Cycle Hire:
For rates and availability visit www.cyclenorfolk.co.uk

Special Events
Full events programme throughout the year. Grounds for shows, weddings, product launches, rallies and filming.

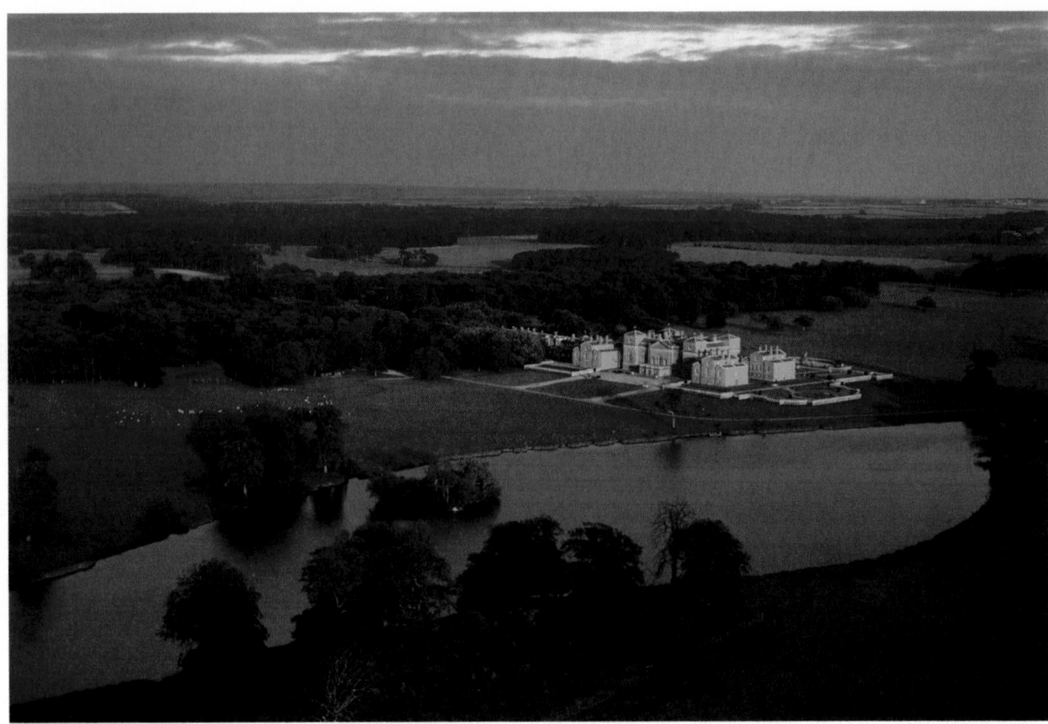

HOLKHAM HALL

www.holkham.co.uk

A breathtaking Palladian mansion with an outstanding art collection, panoramic landscapes and the best beach in England.

At the heart of a thriving 25,000 acre estate on the north Norfolk coast, this elegant 18th century Palladian style mansion, based on designs by William Kent, was built by Thomas Coke 1st Earl of Leicester and is home to his descendants.

The Marble Hall is a spectacular introduction to this imposing house, with its 50ft pressed plaster dome ceiling and walls of English alabaster, not marble as its name implies. Stairs lead to magnificent state rooms displaying superb collections of ancient statuary, original furniture, tapestries and paintings by Rubens, Van Dyck, Claude, Gaspar Poussin and Gainsborough.

The original stables, brew and malt houses, laundry and a building that once housed the huge machines generating electricity, are now home to a fascinating museum displaying 20th century agricultural and domestic appliances, steam engines and vintage cars, as well as a gift shop offering souvenirs and crafts made by skilled local artisans and a café where you can enjoy delicious homemade produce.

Surrounded by parkland there are opportunities to discover the wildlife and landscape with cycle hire and nature trails. A visit to the vast 18th century walled gardens to see the restoration project, now in its third year, to sensitively restore the gardens to their former glory, is a must.

At the north entrance to the park in Holkham village are the Holkham Estate businesses; The Victoria Hotel and Rose Garden Café. Directly opposite is the award-winning Holkham beach and national nature reserve, renowned for its golden sands and panoramic vista.

KEY FACTS

- Photography allowed in hall. Our stair climbing machine in the hall offers unrestricted access for most manually operated wheelchairs. Elsewhere, full disabled access.
- Gift shop in the park.
- In gift shop and at walled gardens.
- Hall & grounds.
- WCs.
- Licensed.
- Licensed.
- Private guided tours by arrangement.
- Ample. Parking charge.
- Hall, Bygones Museum, Farming Exhibition, Walled Gardens, Nature Trail. Key stages 1 & 2.
- Guide dogs only.
- Victoria Hotel and Globe Inn.
- Weddings and Civil Partnerships.
- Theatre productions and concerts.

HOUGHTON HALL

HOUGHTON, KING'S LYNN, NORFOLK PE31 6UE

www.houghtonhall.com

Houghton Hall one of the finest examples of Palladian architecture in England. Built in the 18th century by Sir Robert Walpole, Britain's first prime minister. Original designs by James Gibbs & Colen Campbell, interior decoration by William Kent. The House has been restored to its former grandeur, containing many of its original furnishings. Award-winning 5-acre walled garden divided into 'rooms'. Stunning 120 yard double-sided herbaceous borders, formal rose garden with over 150 varieties, mixed kitchen garden, fountains and statues. Unique Model Soldier Collection, over 20,000 models arranged in various battle formations. Contemporary Sculptures in the Gardens.

Location: MAP 8:I5, OS Ref. TF792 287. 13m E of King's Lynn, 10m W of Fakenham 1½m N of A148.

Owner: The Marquess of Cholmondeley **Contact:** Susan Cleaver

Tel: 01485 528569 **Fax:** 01485 528167 **E-mail:** info@houghtonhall.com

Open: Open Easter Sun 8 Apr–27 Sept. Weds, Thurs, Suns & BH Mons. Park, Walled Garden, Soldier Museum, Restaurant & Gift Shop: 11.30am–5.30pm. (last admission 5pm) House: 1.30–5pm. (last admission 4.30pm).

Admission: 2011 Prices: Adult £8.80, Child (5–16) £3.50, Family (2+2) £22. Everything but the House: Adult £6, Child £2.50, Family (2+2) £15. Group (20+) discounts available, please tel for details.

Key facts: WCs. Licensed. Licensed. By arrangement. On leads.

© NTPL / Nick Daly

© NTPL / Bill Batten

OXBURGH HALL

OXBOROUGH, KING'S LYNN, NORFOLK PE33 9PS

www.nationaltrust.org.uk

No-one ever forgets their first sight of Oxburgh. A romantic moated manor house, it was built by the Bedingfeld family in the 15th century and they have lived here ever since. Inside, the family's Catholic history is revealed, complete with a secret priest's hole which you can crawl inside. See the astonishing needlework by Mary, Queen of Scots, and the private chapel, built with reclaimed materials. Outside, you can enjoy the panoramic views from the Gatehouse roof and follow the woodcarving trails in the gardens and woodlands. The late winter drifts of snowdrops and aconites are not to be missed.

Location: MAP 8:16. OS Ref. TF742 012. At Oxborough, 7m SW of Swaffham on S side of Stoke Ferry road.

Owner: National Trust **Contact:** The Property Secretary **Tel:** 01366 328258 **Fax:** 01366 328066 **E-mail:** oxburghhall@nationaltrust.org.uk

Open: House: 25 Feb–31 Oct, 11am–5pm (closes 4pm in Feb, Mar & Oct). Daily in Easter holidays, Whitsun week, throughout Aug and Oct half-term. Garden: As House plus 7 Jan–19 Feb and 3 Nov–23 Dec 11am–4pm weekends only.

Admission: House & Garden: Adult £8.60, Child £4.30, Family £21.50. Garden only: Adult £4.50, Child £2.25, Family £11.25. Groups discount (min 15) - must book in advance with the Property Secretary.

Key facts: Admission to house may be by timed tours only at certain times in the season. No picnics or dogs allowed in Garden; no photography in House. Free garden tours daily. Souvenir guides, gift shop, second-hand bookshop. Partial. WCs. Licensed. By arrangement. Limited for coaches. Guide dogs only. Events throughout the year, including Christmas. Ask for leaflet.

© English Heritage

CASTLE ACRE PRIORY

Stocks Green, Castle Acre, King's Lynn, Norfolk PE32 2XD

www.english-heritage.org.uk/castleacrepriory

Explore the romantic ruins of this 12th century Cluniac priory, set in the picturesque village of Castle Acre. The impressive Norman façade, splendid prior's lodgings and chapel, and delightful recreated medieval herb garden should not be missed.

Location: MAP 8:I5, OS Ref. TF814 148. 1/4m W of village of Castle Acre, 5m N of Swaffham.

Owner: English Heritage

Contact: Visitor Operations Team

Tel: 01760 755394

E-mail: customers@english-heritage.org.uk

Open: Please see www.english-heritage.org.uk for opening times and the most up-to-date information.

Admission: Adult £5.60, Child £3.40, Conc. £5.00. Family £14.60. Group discount available. Opening times and prices are valid until 31st March 2012.

Key facts: Picnickers welcome. Partial. Limited for coaches. On leads.

© NTPL / Rupert Truman

FELBRIGG HALL

Felbrigg, Norwich, Norfolk NR11 8PR

www.nationaltrust.org.uk

One of the finest 17th century country houses in East Anglia complete with its original 18th century furniture. The Walled Garden features a series of pottager gardens and a working dovecote. The Park has way-marked walks and is well known for its magnificent and aged trees.

Location: MAP 8:K4, OS Ref. OS133, TG193 394. Nr Felbrigg village, 2m SW of Cromer, entrance off B1436, signposted from A148 and A140.

Owner: National Trust **Contact:** The Property Manager

Tel: 01263 837444 **Fax:** 01263 837032 **E-mail:** felbrigg@nationaltrust.org.uk

Open: House: 3 Mar–4 Nov: Sat–Weds, 11am–5pm. Open daily in Aug (Open Good Fri.) Gardens, Catering & Gift Shop: 3 Mar–4 Nov, daily (open Good Fri), 11am–5pm.

Admission: House & Garden: Adult £9.70, Child £4.60, Family £24. Garden only: Adult £4.60, Child £2. Includes a voluntary donation but visitors can choose to pay the standard prices.

Key facts: Indoor photography permitted without the use of flash. 01263 837040. 01263 838237. Partial. WCs. Licensed. Licensed. By arrangement. Limited for coaches. Guide dogs only.

CASTLE RISING CASTLE

King's Lynn, Norfolk PE31 6AH

www.castlerising.co.uk

Possibly the finest mid-12th century Keep in England: it was built as a grand and elaborate palace. It was home to Queen Isabella, grandmother of the Black Prince.

Still in good condition, the Keep is surrounded by massive ramparts up to 120 feet high. Picnic area, adjacent tearoom. Audio tour.

Location: OS Ref. TF666 246. Located 4m NE of King's Lynn off A149.

Owner: Lord Howard

Contact: The Custodian

Tel: 01553 631330

Fax: 01553 631724

Open: 1 Apr–1 Nov: daily, 10am–6pm (closes at dusk if earlier in Oct). 2 Nov–31 Mar: Wed–Sun, 10am–4pm. Closed 24–26 Dec.

Admission: Adult £4, Child £2.50, Conc. £3.30, Family £12.
15% discount for groups (11+). Opening times and prices are subject to change.

Key facts: Picnic area. Suitable.

MANNINGTON GARDENS & COUNTRYSIDE

Mannington Hall, Norwich NR11 7BB

www.manningtongardens.co.uk

The gardens around this medieval moated manor house feature a wide variety of plants, trees and shrubs in many different settings. Throughout the gardens are thousands of roses especially classic varieties. The Heritage Rose and 20th century Rose Gardens have roses in areas with designs reflecting their date of origin from the 15th century to the present day.

Location: MAP 8:K5, OS Ref. TG144 320. Signposted from Saxthorpe crossroads on the Norwich–Holt road B1149. 1 1/2m W of Wolterton Hall.

Owner: The Lord & Lady Walpole **Contact:** Lady Walpole

Tel: 01263 584175 **Fax:** 01263 761214

Open: Gardens: May–Sept: Suns 12–5pm. Jun–Aug: Wed–Fri, 11am–5pm, and at other times by prior appointment. Walks: daily from 9am. Medieval Hall open by appointment. Grounds & Park open all year.

Admission: Adult £6, Child (under 16yrs) Free, Conc. £5.
Groups by arrangement.

Key facts: Grounds. WCs. Licensed. By arrangement. £2 car park fee (walkers only). In park only. Park. €

RAVENINGHAM GARDENS

Raveningham, Norwich, Norfolk NR14 6NS

www.raveningham.com

Superb herbaceous borders, 18th century walled kitchen garden, Victorian glasshouse, herb garden, Edwardian rose garden, contemporary sculptures, 14th century church and much more.

Location: MAP 8:L7, OS Ref. TM399 965. Between Norwich & Lowestoft off A146 then B1136.

Owner: Sir Nicholas Bacon Bt

Contact: Diane Hoffman

Tel: 01508 548152

Fax: 01508 548958

E-mail: diane@raveningham.com

Open: Easter–Aug BH: Thur, 11am–4pm. BH Suns & Mons, 2–5pm. Snowdrops, Agapanthus, Rose and Vegetable weekends - see website.

Admission: Adult £4, Child (under 16yrs) Free, OAP £3.50 Groups by prior arrangement.

Key facts:

WOLTERTON PARK

Norwich, Norfolk NR11 7LY

www.manningtongardens.co.uk

18th century Hall. Portrait collection annual exhibitions. Historic park with lake.

Location: MAP 8:K5, OS Ref. TG164 317. Situated near Erpingham village, signposted from Norwich–Cromer Rd A140.

Owner: The Lord and Lady Walpole

Contact: The Lady Walpole

Tel: 01263 584175/768444

Fax: 01263 761214

E-mail: admin@walpoleestate.co.uk

Open: Park: daily from 9am. Hall: 29 Apr–28 Oct: Fridays, 2–5pm (last entry 4pm) by appointment and various events.

Admission: £6. £2 car park fee only for walkers. (Groups by application: from £5.)

Key facts: Small. Partial. WC. In park, on leads. Park. €

Holkham Hall

BLICKLING HALL

Blickling, Norwich, Norfolk NR11 6NF

Built in the early 17th century and one of England's great Jacobean houses. Blickling is famed for its spectacular long gallery, superb library and fine collections of furniture, pictures and tapestries.

Location: MAP 8:K5, OS133 Ref. TG178 286. 1½m NW of Aylsham on B1354. Signposted off A140 Norwich (15m) to Cromer.

Owner: National Trust

Contact: The General Manager

Tel: 01263 738030

Fax: 01263 738035

E-mail: blickling@nationaltrust.org.uk

Website: www.nationaltrust.org.uk

Open: Please see website or contact us for up-to-date information.

Admission: Please see website or contact us for up-to-date information.

Key facts:

CAISTER CASTLE CAR COLLECTION

Caister-On-Sea, Great Yarmouth, Norfolk NR30 5SN

Large collection of historic motor vehicles from 1893 to recent. Moated Castle built by Sir John Falstaff in 1432. Car park free.

Location: MAP 8:M6. OS Ref. TG502 122. Take A1064 out of Caister-on-sea towards Filby, turn left at the end of the dual carriageway.

Owner: Mr J Hill

Contact: Mr J Hill

Tel: 01572 787649

Open: Mid May–End Sept: Sun–Fri (closed Sats), 10am–4.30pm.

Admission: Contact property for details.

Key facts: No photography. Partial. WCs.

CLIFTON HOUSE

Queen Street, King's Lynn PE30 1HT

Magnificent grade-one listed merchant's house being restored as a family home. Features include 13th century tiled floors and a 14th century vaulted undercroft. Remodelled interiors date from 1500 to 1740. The spectacular Elizabethan tower contains original wall paintings.

Location: MAP 7:H5, OS Ref. TF615 198.

Owner/Contact: Anna Keay & Simon Thurley

E-mail: anna@kingstaithe.com

Website: www.cliftonhouse.org.uk

Open: Sat 21 & Sat 28 Jul 2012, 12–4pm. Pre-booked guided tours throughout the year. See www.cliftonhouse.org.uk for details.

Admission: Adult admission on open days: £3.50.

Key facts: Partial. By arrangement. Guide dogs only.

KIMBERLEY HALL

Wymondham, Norfolk NR18 0RT

Magnificent Queen Anne house built in 1712 by William Talman for Sir John Wodehouse, an ancestor of P G Wodehouse. Towers added after 1754 and wings connected to the main block by curved colonnades in 1835. Internal embellishments in 1770s include some very fine plasterwork by John Sanderson and a 'flying' spiral staircase beneath a coffered dome. The park, with its picturesque lake, ancient oak trees and walled gardens was laid out in 1762 by 'Capability' Brown.

Location: MAP 8:K6, OS Ref. TG091 048. 10m SW of Norwich, 3m from A11.

Owner/Contact: R Buxton **Tel:** 01603 759447 **Fax:** 01603 758244

E-mail: events@kimberleyhall.co.uk **Website:** www.kimberleyhall.co.uk

Open: House & Park not open to the public. Grounds, certain rooms and refurbished function space are available for corporate hospitality and weddings (licensed for Civil ceremonies and partnerships). Six Indian tipis equipped with beds, bedding and fires within walled garden available for hire.

Admission: Please telephone for details.

Key facts:

NORWICH CATHEDRAL

12 The Close, Norwich NR1 4DH

A fine example of Romanesque architecture featuring the world's largest collection of medieval roof bosses, England's second tallest spire and largest cloister. Visitors encounter a true learning experience in the recently completed Hostry – the Visitors and Education Centre which houses a classroom, conference facilities and a digital interpretative exhibition space.

Location: MAP 8:K6, OS Ref. TG 235 087. South side of Norwich City Centre. A11 from London.

Contact: Susan Brown

Tel: 01603 218300 **Fax:** 01603 766032

E-mail: reception@cathedral.org.uk **Website:** www.norwichcathedral.org.uk

Open: Mon–Sat 7.30am–6.30pm, Sun 11.45am–3.30pm.

Admission: Suggested donation: Adult £5, Conc £4, Family £12. Group rates available.

Key facts: Partial. WCs. Licensed. Licensed. By arrangement. Limited. No coaches. Guide dogs only.

SANDRINGHAM

The Estate Office, Sandringham, Norfolk PE35 6EN

Sandringham House, the Norfolk retreat of Her Majesty The Queen, is set in 60 acres of beautiful gardens. The main ground floor rooms used by The Royal Family, still maintained in the Edwardian style, are open to the public, as well as the fascinating Museum and the charming parish church.

Location: MAP 7:H5, OS Ref. TF695 287 8m NE of King's Lynn on B1440 off A148.

Owner: H M The Queen **Contact:** The Public Enterprises Manager **Tel:** 01485 545408 **Fax:** 01485 541571 **E-mail:** visits@sandringhamestate.co.uk

Website: www.sandringhamestate.co.uk

Open: 1 Apr–late Jul & early Aug–4 Nov.

Admission: House, Museum & Gardens, Adult £11.50, Child £6, Conc. £9.50. Museum & Gardens, Adult £8, Child £4.50, Conc. £7.

Key facts: No photography in house. Plant Centre. Visitor Centre only. WCs. Licensed. Licensed. By arrangement. Private evening tours. Ample. Guide dogs only.

WALSINGHAM ABBEY GROUNDS & SHIREHALL MUSEUM

Common Place, Little Walsingham, Norfolk NR22 6BP

Walsingham Abbey is at the heart of Little Walsingham, famous for pilgrimage since the 11th century. Spectacular 18 acres of naturalised snowdrops in February, ruins of the medieval Augustinian Priory, tranquil gardens, woodland and river walks. Entrance through Shirehall Museum, with original Georgian Courtroom and displays on Walsingham's fascinating history.

Location: MAP 8:J4, OS Ref. TF934 367. B1105 N from Fakenham–5m.

Owner: Walsingham Estate Company **Contact:** Jackie Seals

Tel: 01328 820510 or 01328 824432 **Fax:** 01328 820098

E-mail: museum@walsinghamabbey.com **Website:** www.walsinghamabbey.com

Open: Daily during snowdrop season (February) 10am–4pm. March: weekends only, 11am-4pm. 1 Apr–28 Oct: daily, 11am–4pm. By appointment outside these times.

Admission: Adult £4, child 6-16 £2.50.

Key facts: No commercial photography. Partial. By arrangement. On leads.

Houghton Hall

FRAMLINGHAM CASTLE

FRAMLINGHAM, SUFFOLK IP13 9BP

www.english-heritage.org.uk/framlingham

Framlingham is a magnificent 12th century castle. From the continuous curtain wall linking 13 towers, there are excellent panoramic views of the town and the charming reed-fringed Mere. Visitors can experience life at Framlingham Castle through the ages with our introductory exhibition, themed trails and variety of indoor and outdoor games. Entry also includes access to the Lanman Trust's Museum of local history.

Location: MAP 8:L8, OS Ref. TM287 637. In Framlingham on B1116. NE of town centre.

Owner: English Heritage **Contact:** Visitor Operations Team

Tel: 01728 724189 **E-mail:** customers@english-heritage.org.uk

Open: Please see www.english-heritage.org.uk for opening times and the most up-to-date information. The property may close early if an event is booked, please ring in advance for details.

Admission: Adult £6.30. Child £3.80, Children under 5 Free. Conc. £5.70, Family £16.40. EH Members/OVP Free. Group discount available. Opening times and prices are valid until 31st March 2012.

Key facts: Picnickers welcome. Partial. WCs. Limited for coaches. On leads.

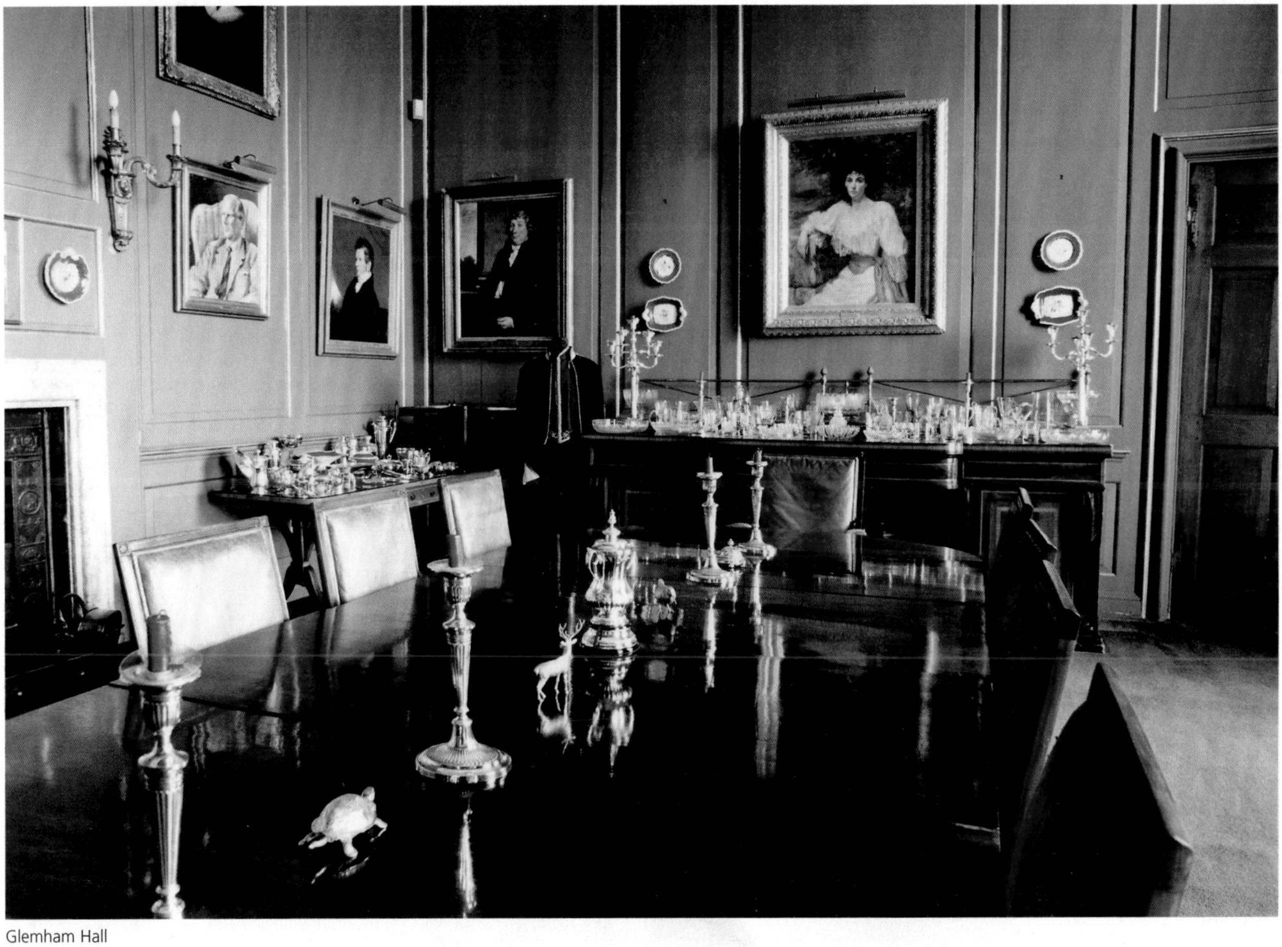

Glemham Hall

KENTWELL HALL & GARDENS

LONG MELFORD, SUFFOLK CO10 9BA

www.kentwell.co.uk

A beautiful mellow redbrick Tudor Mansion, surrounded by a broad moat, with rare service building of c1500. Interior 'improved' by Thomas Hopper in 1820s. Still a lived-in family home.

Restoration – Famed for long-time, long term, ongoing works in House & Gardens.

Gardens – Over 30 years' endeavour has resulted in gardens which are a joy in all seasons. Moats, massed spring bulbs, mature trees, delightful walled garden, with potager, herbs and ancient espaliered fruit trees. Much topiary from massive ancient yews to the unique 'Pied Piper' story.

Re-Creations – renowned for the award-winning Re-Creations of Tudor Life. Also occasional Re-Creations of WW2 Life and now too of a Dickensian Christmas in December. Re-Creations take place on selected weekends from April to December.

Corporate – House and upgraded 2500 sq ft Function Room for conferences, dinners, banquets of all sizes and Corporate Activity Days of originality.

Schools – Perhaps the biggest, most original and stimulating educational programme in the region enjoyed by about 20,000 schoolchildren each year.

Filming – Much used for medieval and Tudor periods for its wide range of perfectly equipped locations inside and out and access to Kentwell's 700 Tudors as extras.

Scaresville – Award-winning Scariest Halloween Event 15–31 October.

Location: MAP 8:I9, OS Ref. TL864 479. Off the A134. 4m N of Sudbury.
Owner: Patrick Phillips Esq QC **Contact:** The Estate Office
Tel: 01787 310207 **Fax:** 01787 379318 **E-mail:** info@kentwell.co.uk
Open: For full details see our website or call for Opening Leaflet.
Admission: Charges apply according to the Event (if any) on. Call for details.
Key facts: No photography in house. Conferences, dinners, Tudor feasts for groups of 40 or more. Car rallies. Home-made food. Including themed ceremonies. Open-air theatre, opera and concert season Jul–Aug.

GAINSBOROUGH'S HOUSE

46 Gainsborough St, Sudbury, Suffolk CO10 2EU

www.gainsborough.org

Gainsborough's House is the birthplace museum of Thomas Gainsborough RA (1727–1788) and displays an outstanding collection of his paintings, drawings and prints. A varied programme of temporary exhibitions is also shown throughout the year. The historic house dates back to the 16th century and has an attractive walled garden.
Location: MAP 8:I10. OS Ref. TL872 413. 46 Gainsborough St, Sudbury town centre.
Owner: Gainsborough's House Society **Contact:** Rosemary Woodward
Tel: 01787 372958 **Fax:** 01787 376991 **E-mail:** mail@gainsborough.org
Open: All year: Mon–Sat, 10am–5pm. Closed: Suns, Good Fri and Christmas to New Year.
Admission: Please telephone 01787 372958 for details of admission charges.
Key facts: No photography in the House. Suitable. WCs. By arrangement. Guide dogs only.

GLEMHAM HALL

Little Glemham, Woodbridge, Suffolk IP13 0BT

www.glemhamhall.co.uk

Built around 1560, the Hall remained in the Glemham family until 1700 when passed to the Norths (Earls of Guilford). Dudley North's wife Catherine was daughter of Elihu Yale, founder of the American University. The Cobbolds acquired the Hall in 1923. Old English: Gleam(happy) + ham(village) + Parva(small) hence Little Glemham.
Location: MAP 8:L9. OS Ref. TM212 GR347 592. Heritage signs off A12 between Woodbridge & Saxmundham.
Owner: Philip & Raewyn Hope-Cobbold
Contact: Joanne Rasmussen-Events Manager
Tel: 01728 746704 **E-mail:** events@glemhamhall.co.uk
Open: Various months/days/times throughout the year (see website).
Admission: Adult £15, Child under 13 Free, Groups min 10 max 30.
Key facts: Partial. WC. By arrangement.

HELMINGHAM HALL GARDENS

Helmingham, Suffolk IP14 6EF

www.helmingham.com

Grade 1 listed gardens, redesigned by Lady Tollemache in a 400 acre deer park surrounding a moated Tudor Hall. Visitors are enchanted by the stunning herbaceous borders, the walled kitchen garden, herb, knot, rose and wild gardens. Coach bookings warmly welcomed. There are a variety of events throughout the season.

Location: MAP 8:K9, OS Ref. TM190 578. B1077, 9m N of Ipswich, 5m S of Debenham.

Owner: The Lord & Lady Tollemache

Contact: Events Office

Tel: 01473 890799

Fax: 01473 890776

E-mail: events@helmingham.com

Open: Gardens only 1 May–16 Sept 2012 (12–5pm Tuesdays, Wednesdays, Thursdays, Sundays).

Admission: Adults £6, Child (5–15yrs) £3. Groups (30+) £5

Key facts: WCs. Licensed. By arrangement. Pre-booking required. On leads.

LAVENHAM: THE GUILDHALL OF CORPUS CHRISTI

The Market Place, Lavenham, Sudbury CO10 9QZ

www.nationaltrust.org.uk

With its numerous timber-framed houses and magnificent church, a visit to picturesque Lavenham is a step back in time. The 16th century Guildhall is the ideal place to begin with its exhibitions on the woollen cloth industry, agriculture and local history bringing to life the fascinating stories behind this remarkable village.

Location: MAP 8:J9, OS155, TL915 942. 6m NNE of Sudbury. Village centre. A1141 & B1071.

Owner: National Trust **Contact:** Jane Gosling

Tel: 01787 247646 **E-mail:** lavenhamguildhall@nationaltrust.org.uk

Open: 3–25 Mar, Wed–Sun, 11am–4pm; 26 Mar–31 Oct, daily, 11am–5pm; 3–25 Nov, Sat & Sun, 11am–4pm. Parts of the building may be closed occasionally for community use.

Admission: Adult £4.75, Child £2, Family £11.50, Groups: Adult £3.95, Child £1.50. School parties by arrangement.

Key facts: By arrangement.

ICKWORTH HOUSE, PARKLAND, WOODLAND & GARDENS

Horringer, Bury St Edmunds, Suffolk IP29 5QE

www.nationaltrust.org.uk/ickworth

Built as a magnificent 18th century showcase for the 4th Earl of Bristol's collections of Georgian silver, Regency furniture, Old Masters and family portraits - the House's grand Rotunda dominates the landscape. In the newly restored servant's basement, discover what happened below stairs. Explore the landscaped parkland and formal gardens.

Location: MAP 8:I9, OS155 Ref. TL816 611. In Horringer, 3m SW of Bury St Edmunds on W side of A143.

Owner: National Trust **Contact:** Property Administrator

Tel: 01284 735270 **Fax:** 01284 735153 **E-mail:** ickworth@nationaltrust.org.uk

Open: House: 2 Mar–4 Nov, Fri–Tue, 11am–5pm. Parkland & Gardens: Daily 8am–8pm. West Wing Shop & Restaurant: Daily 11am–4pm. All BHs except Christmas Day (25 Dec). *Limited catering available 24 & 26 Dec 2012.

Admission: Gift Aid Admission (standard admission prices in brackets) House, Park & Gardens £11.50 (£10.40), Child £5.50 (£5), Family £28.50 (£25.80). For other prices visit www.nationaltrust.org.uk/ickworth.

Key facts: Licensed. Obligatory. Limited for coaches. In grounds. €

MELFORD HALL

Long Melford, Sudbury, Suffolk CO10 9AA

www.nationaltrust.org.uk/melfordhall

For over two centuries Melford Hall has been the much loved family home of the Hyde Parkers. The interior charts their changing tastes and fashions and the stories about visits by Beatrix Potter and family life at Melford show that a home is far more than just bricks and mortar.

Location: MAP 8:I9, OS Ref. TL867 462. In Long Melford off A134, 14m S of Bury St Edmunds, 3m N of Sudbury.

Owner: National Trust

Contact: The Property Administrator

Tel: 01787 379228

E-mail: melford@nationaltrust.org.uk

Open: Apr & Oct Sats & Suns only; May–Sept, Wed–Sun. Also open on Bank Holiday Mons. All 1.30–5pm.

Admission: Please call 01787 379228 for details of current admission prices. National Trust Members: Free.

Key facts: No flash photography in house. WCs. Limited parking for coaches. Guide dogs only.

ORFORD CASTLE

Orford, Woodbridge, Suffolk IP12 2ND

www.english-heritage.org.uk/orford

It has a warren of passageways and chambers to be explored, with a winding staircase right to the top where you can enjoy spectacular views of Orford Ness.

Location: MAP 8:M9, OS169, TM419 499. In Orford on B1084, 20m NE of Ipswich.

Owner: English Heritage

Contact: Visitor Operations Team

Tel: 01394 450472

E-mail: customers@english-heritage.org.uk

Open: Please visit www.english-heritage.org.uk for opening times and the most up-to-date information.

Admission: Adult £5.60, Child £3.40, Conc. £5, Family £14.60.
EH Members OVP Free. Group discount available.
Opening times and prices are valid until 31st March 2012.

Key facts:

SOMERLEYTON HALL & GARDENS

Somerleyton, Lowestoft, Suffolk NR32 5QQ

www.somerleyton.co.uk

Originally Jacobean the Hall was extensively re-modelled in 1844, guided tours of the state rooms are available on all open days. 12 acres of fabulous landscaped gardens include the famous yew hedge maze, 300ft pergola, Vulliamy tower clock, Paxton glasshouses, formal and arboreal gardens, wintergarden tearooms and giftshop.

Location: MAP 8:M8, OS Ref. TM493 977. 5m NW of Lowestoft on B1074, 7m SW of Great Yarmouth off A143.

Owner: Hon Hugh Crossley **Contact:** Carolyn Ashton **Tel:** 08712 224244 (office) **Fax:** 01502 732143 **E-mail:** carolyn.ashton@somerleyton.co.uk

Open/Admission: Please visit www.somerleyton.co.uk or call the estate office on 01502 734901 for 2012 opening dates and admission prices.

Key facts: No photography in house. Receptions/functions/ conferences/weddings. Suitable. WCs. Obligatory. Guide dogs only.

OTLEY HALL

Otley, Ipswich, Suffolk IP6 9PA

www.otleyhall.co.uk

Stunning medieval Moated Hall (Grade I) frequently described as "one of England's loveliest houses". Noted for its richly carved beams, superb linenfold panelling and 16th century wall paintings. The unique 10-acre gardens include historically accurate Tudor re-creations and were voted among the top 10 gardens to visit in Great Britain.

Location: MAP 8:K9, OS Ref. TM207 563. 7m N of Ipswich, off the B1079.

Owner: Dr Ian & Mrs Catherine Beaumont

Contact: Louise Rutterford

Tel: 01473 890264

Fax: 01473 890803

E-mail: enquiries@otleyhall.co.uk

Open: BH Suns, 1–5pm (6 May, 3 Jun & 26 Aug) Dates to be confirmed. Afternoon teas available. Groups and individuals welcome all year by appointment for private guided tours.

Admission: BHs: Adult £6, Child £3.

Key facts: Partial. Licensed. By arrangement.

SUTTON HOO

Woodbridge, Suffolk IP12 3DJ

www.nationaltrust.org.uk/suttonhoo

Home to one of the world's greatest archaeological discoveries. Walk around the ancient mounds and discover the incredible story of the royal Anglo-Saxon ship burial. Enjoy beautiful period interiors of Mrs Pretty's Country House. Site includes exhibition hall, café, shop, site walks. Special events all year.

Location: MAP 8:L9, OS Ref. TM288 487. Off B1083 Woodbridge to Bawdsey road. Follow signs from A12. Train 1/2m Melton.

Owner: National Trust **Contact:** The Property Manager

Tel: 01394 389700 **Fax:** 01394 389702

E-mail: suttonhoo@nationaltrust.org.uk

Open: Jan–5 Feb, 25 Feb–1 Apr, 10 Nov–23 Dec: Weekends 11am–4pm Half Terms: Daily 11am–4pm Apr–Oct: Daily 10.30am–5pm 27–31 Dec: Daily 11am–4pm Estate: All year 9am–6pm except Thurs Nov–Jan.

Admission: NT members free. Adult £7.50, Child £3.90. Family £18.90. Voluntary donation included, standard prices available at the property and on the website. Discount if arriving by cycle or on foot.

Key facts: Suitable. WCs. Licensed. Licensed. By arrangement. Limited for coaches.

WYKEN HALL GARDENS

Stanton, Bury St Edmunds, Suffolk IP31 2DW

www.wykenvineyards.co.uk

Wyken is an Elizabethan manor house surrounded by a romantic, plantlovers' garden with maze, knot and herb garden and rose garden featuring old roses. A walk through ancient woodlands leads to award-winning Wyken Vineyards. The 16th century barn houses the Vineyard Restaurant featured in Michelin and Good Food Guides, and the Leaping Hare Country Store, described in *Country Living* as 'a model of what a shop should be.'

Location: MAP 8:J8, OS Ref. TL963 717. 9m NE of Bury St. Edmunds 1m E of A143. Follow brown tourist signs to Wyken Vineyards from Ixworth.

Owner: Sir Kenneth & Lady Carlisle **Contact:** Mr Graham Uney

Tel: 01359 250287 **Fax:** 01359 253821

Open: 6 Jan–24 Dec: daily, 10am–6pm. Garden: 1 Apr–1 Oct: daily except Sat, 2–6pm. Open for dinner from 7pm Fri & Sat (advisable to book).

Admission: Gardens: Adult £4, Child (under 16yrs) Free, Conc. £3.50. Groups by appointment.

Key facts: WC. No dogs in garden.

FRESTON TOWER

Nr Ipswich, Suffolk IP9 1AD

An Elizabethan six-storey tower overlooking the estuary of the River Orwell. The tower was built in 1578 by a wealthy Ipswich merchant called Thomas Gooding, perhaps to celebrate the recent grant of his coat of arms. Freston Tower is cared for by The Landmark Trust.

Location: MAP 8:K9, OS Ref. TM177 397.

Owner/Contact: The Landmark Trust

Tel: 01628 825925

E-mail: bookings@landmarktrust.org.uk

Website: www.landmarktrust.org.uk

Open: Available for holidays for up to 4 people. Open Days on 8 days a year. Other visits by appointment.

Admission: Free on Open Days and visits by appointment.

Key facts: €

HAUGHLEY PARK

Stowmarket, Suffolk IP14 3JY

Grade 1 listed red-brick manor house of 1620 set in gardens, park and woodland. Original five-gabled east front, north wing rebuilt in Georgian style, 1820. Varied six acre gardens including walled kitchen garden. Way-marked woodland walks. 17th century barn bookable for Weddings, Meetings etc.

Location: MAP 8:J8, OS Ref. TM005 618. Signed from J47a and J49 on A14.

Owner: Mr & Mrs Robert Williams

Contact: Barn Office

Tel: 01359 240701

Website: www.haughleyparkbarn.co.uk

Open: Garden only: May–Sept: Tues, 2–5.30pm. For Bluebell Sunday dates, see website.

Admission: Garden: £3. Child under 16 Free.

Key facts: Picnics allowed. Bluebell Sun. WCs. By arrangement. Limited for coaches. On leads.

ST EDMUNDSBURY CATHEDRAL

Angel Hill, Bury St Edmunds, Suffolk IP33 1LS

The striking Millennium Tower, completed on 2005, is the crowning glory of St Edmundsbury Cathedral. Further enhanced with the stunning vaulted ceiling in 2010, the 150ft Lantern Tower, along with new chapels, cloisters and North Transept, completes nearly fifty years of development in a style never likely to be repeated.

Location: MAP 8:I8, OS Ref. TL857 642. Bury St Edmunds town centre.

Owner: The Church of England

Contact: Sarah Friswell

Tel: 01284 748720

Fax: 01284 768655

E-mail: cathedral@stedscathedral.org

Website: www.stedscathedral.co.uk

Open: All year: daily 8.30am–6pm.

Admission: Donation invited.

Key facts:

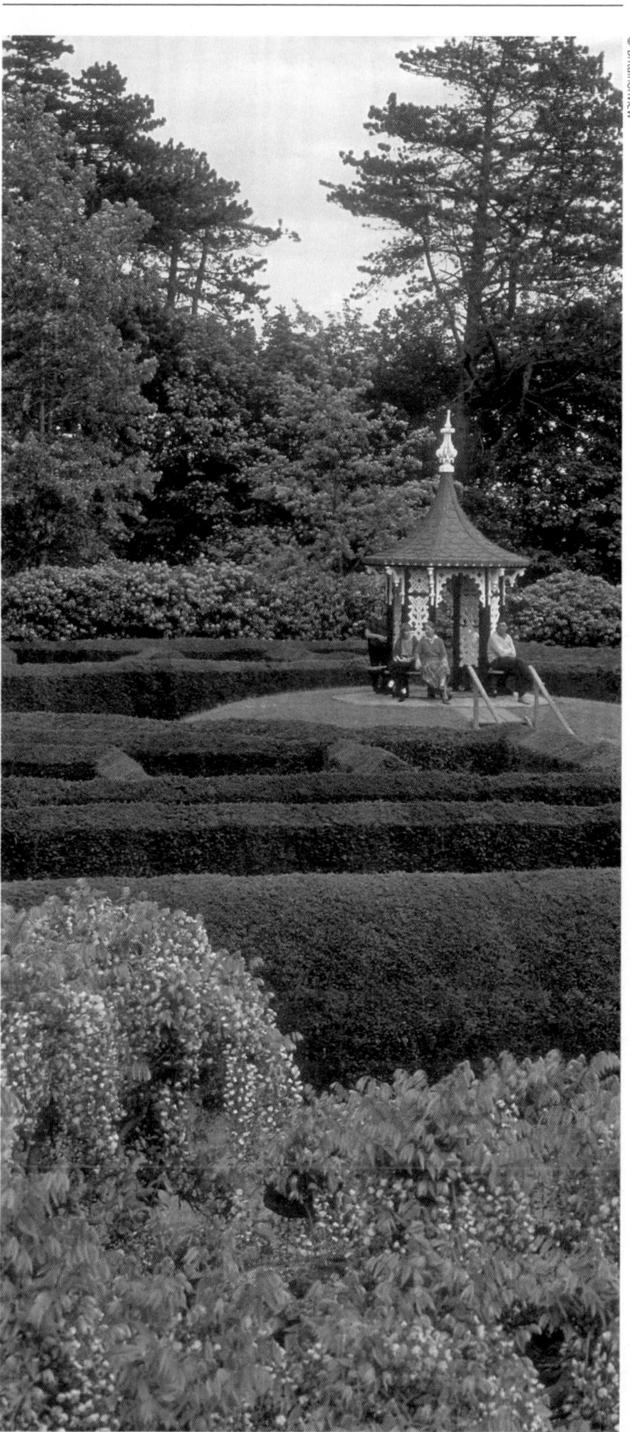

Somerleyton Hall and maze, Somerleyton, Suffolk, England

Wootton Hall, Althorp House
© Althorp

Burghley House

East Midlands

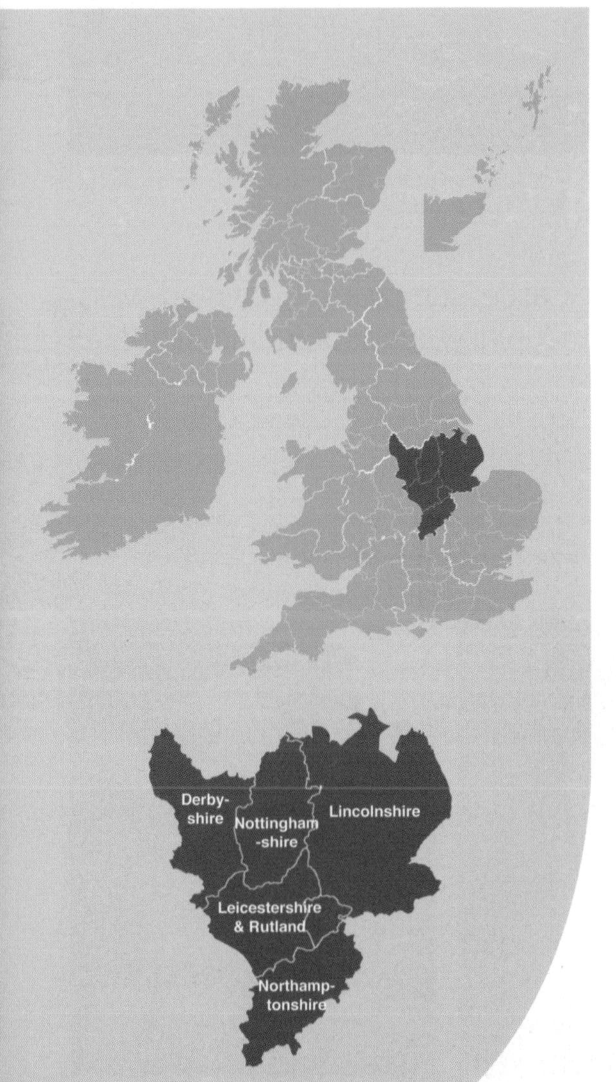
Derby-
shire
Nottingham
-shire
Lincolnshire
Leicestershire
& Rutland
Northamp-
tonshire

Derbyshire

Leicestershire & Rutland

Lincolnshire

Northamptonshire

Nottinghamshire

Grand country houses abound in the East Midlands. Chatsworth is one of the country's greatest Treasure Houses while the imposing 16th century Burghley House is set in a 300-acre deer park landscaped by 'Capability' Brown. Peveril Castle, with breathtaking views of the Peak District, is one of the earliest Norman castles to be built in England and in Lincoln, the magnificent 'Cathedral on the hill' is Lincolnshire's most distinguishing landmark. Other finds in this relatively compact region include the romantic 400 year old Easton Walled Garden and 17th century Woolsthorpe Manor, birthplace of Sir Isaac Newton.

VISITOR INFORMATION

Owner
English Heritage

Address
Castle Street
Bolsover
Derbyshire S44 6PR

Location
MAP 7:A2
OS120, SK471 707.
Signposted from M1/J29A, 6m from Mansfield. In Bolsover 6m E of Chesterfield on A632.

Contact
Visitor Operations Team
Tel: 01246 822844
E-mail: customers@english-heritage.org.uk

Opening Times
Please visit www.english-heritage.org.uk for opening times and the most up-to-date information. Part of the castle may close if an event is booked. To confirm please call: 01246 822844

Admission

Adult	£7.80
Child	£4.70
Conc.	£7.00
Family	£20.30

Discount for groups (11+).

EH members Free.

Opening times and prices are valid until 31st March 2012, after this date details are subject to change please visit www.english-heritage.org.uk for the most up-to-date information.

Special events
There is an exciting events programme available throughout the year, for further details please contact the property or visit the website.

© English Heritage / Jonathan Bailey

BOLSOVER CASTLE ⌗

www.english-heritage.org.uk/bolsover

There's a fairytale quality to Bolsover Castle; sumptuously painted walls, intricately carved fireplaces and the magnificent indoor Riding School.

An enchanting and romantic spectacle, situated high on a wooded hilltop dominating the surrounding landscape. Built on the site of a Norman castle, this is largely an early 17th century mansion. The 'Little Castle', houses intricate carvings, panelling and wall painting. See the restored interiors of the Little Castle including the only remaining copies of Titian's Caesar Paintings, and the Venus Fountain and statuary. There is also an impressive 17th century indoor Riding House built by the Duke of Newcastle. Interesting interpretation facilities include Audio/Visual and scale model of Little Castle.

Bolsover Castle is available for Civil weddings, receptions and corporate hospitality, including three indoor and two outdoor areas licensed for civil wedding ceremonies.

KEY FACTS

Picnickers welcome.

© English Heritage

© English Heritage

CHATSWORTH

www.chatsworth.org

The home of the Duke and Duchess of Devonshire is one of the country's greatest Treasure Houses.

The house is renowned for the quality of its art, landscape and hospitality. Home of the Cavendish family since the 1550s, it has evolved through the centuries to reflect the tastes, passions and interests of succeeding generations. Today Chatsworth contains works of art that span 4000 years, from ancient Roman and Egyptian sculpture, and masterpieces by Rembrandt, Reynold and Veronese, to work by outstanding modern artists, including Lucian Freud, Edmund de Waal, Sean Scully and David Nash.

The garden is famous for its rich history, historic and modern waterworks and sculptures, the Victorian rock garden and the maze. Younger visitors also enjoy the farmyard and adventure playground and the 1000 acre park is open every day.

2012 reveals the restored exterior of the south and west fronts of the house, with the sandstone cleaned and window frames and finials re-gilded in 24 carat gold. In the New Gallery, we open with an exhibition of modern British masterpieces from Frank and Cherryl Cohen's art collection, and in the garden an exhibition of sculpture by Sir Anthony Caro, both ending in June. From June, some treasures from our collection of old master drawings will be displayed for the first time at Chatsworth, with works by Rembrandt, Leonardo Da Vinci and Van Dyck.

Our events programme includes Spring Blooms, International Horse Trials, Country Fair, 'Florabundance', and a visual celebration of Christmas in the house, themed on pantomimes.

KEY FACTS

- 5 gift shops and Farm shop.
- Available for conferences and private functions. Contact Catering.
- WCs.
- Licensed.
- Licensed.
- Small charge for daily tours. Groups pre-book.
- Handheld and audio guides available to hire in English.
- Cars 100 yds, Coaches drop off at house.
- Guided tours, packs, and self guiding materials. Free preliminary visit.
- On leads.
- Holiday cottages.

© David Vintiner

VISITOR INFORMATION

Owner
Trustees of the Chatsworth Settlement. Home of the Devonshire family

Address
Chatsworth
Bakewell
Derbyshire DE45 1PP

Location
MAP 6:P2
OS Ref. SK260 703

From London 3 hrs M1/J29, signposted via Chesterfield.

3m E of Bakewell, off B6012, 10m W of Chesterfield.

Rail: Chesterfield Station, 11m.

Bus: Chesterfield – Baslow, 1 1/2m.

Contact
The Booking Office
Tel: 01246 565300
Fax: 01246 583536
E-mail: visit@chatsworth.org

Opening Times
House, garden and farmyard open daily, from mid March to 23 December. The park is open every day and the shopping and food areas open from 9 January 2012.

Admission
The admission prices for the house, garden and farmyard are listed on our website at www.chatsworth.org. Discounted day tickets can be purchased online.

Conference/Function

ROOM	Size	Max Cap
Hartington Rm		80
Burlington Rm		80
Racing Rm		22

VISITOR INFORMATION

Owner
Lord Edward Manners

Address
Estate Office
Haddon Hall
Bakewell
Derbyshire DE45 1LA

Location
MAP 6:P2
OS Ref. SK234 663
From London 3 hrs
Sheffield 1/2 hr
Manchester 1 hr
Haddon is on the E side of A6 1 1/2m S of Bakewell. M1/J29.
Rail: Chesterfield Station, 12m.
Bus: Chesterfield Bakewell.

Contact
Janet Blackburn
Tel: 01629 812855
Fax: 01629 814379
E-mail: info@haddonhall.co.uk

Opening Times
31 March–30 April, Saturday, Sunday & Monday.
Easter 6–10 April.
May–September, open daily (except for 30 June & 1 July).
October, Saturday, Sunday & Monday.
Opening times: 12 noon–5 pm (last admission 4 pm).
Christmas 5–19 December opening times: 10.30am–4 pm (last admission 3.30 pm).

Admission

Summer	
Adult	£9.50
Child (5–15yrs)	£5.50
Conc	£8.50
Family (2+3)	£27.50
Regular Visitor Pass	£18.00
Groups (15+)	
Adult	£8.50
Child (5–15yrs)	£4.50
Conc	£7.50
Parking	£1.50

Due to age and nature of Haddon, there are many uneven floors and steps within the house and gardens and this should be borne in mind when visiting. Please telephone in advance for further information and to hear about the assistance we can give.

Special events
Regular programme of special events - check website for details.

HADDON HALL

www.haddonhall.co.uk

Haddon Hall sits on a rocky outcrop above the River Wye near the market town of Bakewell, looking much as it would have done in Tudor Times.

There has been a dwelling here since the 11th century but the house we see today dates mainly from the late 14th century with major additions in the following 200 years and some alterations in the early 17th century including the creation of the Long Gallery. William the Conqueror's illegitimate son Peverel, and his descendants, held Haddon for 100 years before it passed to the Vernon family. In the late 16th century the estate passed through marriage to the Manners family, in whose possession it has remained ever since. When the Dukedom of Rutland was conferred on the Manners family in 1703 they moved to Belvoir Castle, and Haddon was left deserted for 200 years. This was Haddon's saving grace as the Hall thus escaped the major architectural changes of the 18th and 19th centuries ready for the great restoration at the beginning of the 20th century by the 9th Duke of Rutland. Henry VIII's elder brother Arthur, who was a frequent guest of the Vernons, would be quite familiar with the house as it stands today. Haddon Hall is a popular location for film and television productions. Recent ones include 'Pride and Prejudice', and both the BBC dramatization of 'Jane Eyre' and the 2011 feature film 'Jane Eyre' in which Haddon Hall doubled as Mr Rochester's Thornfield.

Gardens

Magnificent terraced gardens, adorned with roses, clematis and beautiful herbaceous borders, provide colour and scent throughout the summer. Fountain Terrace recently re-designed by award winning garden designer, Arne Maynard.

KEY FACTS

- Haddon Hall is ideal as a film location due to its authentic and genuine architecture requiring little alteration. Suitable locations are also available on the Estate.
-
-
- Unsuitable, WCs.
-
- Licensed.
- Special tours £11.50pp for groups of 15, 7 days' notice.
- Ample. 450 yds from house. £1.50 per car.
- Tours of the house bring alive Haddon Hall of old. Costume room also available, very popular!
- Guide dogs only.
-

© NTPL / Oliver Benn

© NTPL / Dennis Gilbert

KEDLESTON HALL

KEDLESTON HALL, DERBY DE22 5JH

www.nationaltrust.org.uk/kedleston

Kedleston was built between 1759 and 1765 for the Curzon family and boasts the most complete and least altered sequence of Robert Adam interiors in England, with magnificent State rooms retaining much of their great collections of paintings and furniture. The Adam influence can be seen across the 18th century pleasure grounds and park. The Eastern Museum houses a remarkable collection, collected by Lord Curzon when he was Viceroy of India (1899–1905). Kedleston has a year wide programme of events and can be used for corporate events and civil weddings. Please call or visit the website for details.

Location: MAP 6:P4, OS Ref. SK312 403. 5 miles NW of Derby, signposted from the roundabout where the A38 crosses A52 Derby ring road.

Owner: National Trust **Contact:** Victoria Flanagan

Tel: 01332 842191 **Fax:** 01332 844059

E-mail: kedlestonhall@nationaltrust.org.uk

Open: House & Grounds: 18 Feb–28 Oct, Sat–Wed, 12noon–4.15pm, Open Good Friday. Park & Grounds: 10am–6pm daily. Park: 29 Oct–22 Feb, daily, 10am–4pm, with occasional day closures. Restaurant & Shop: 18 Feb–28 Oct, Sat–Wed, 11am–5pm. 29 Oct–17 Feb, Sat/Sun 11am–3pm.

Admission: Hall (Gift Aid): Adult £9.90, Child £4.90, Family £24.80. Garden & Park (Gift Aid): Adult £4.40, Child £2.20, Family £11.10. Groups Hall: Adult £7.60, Child £3.95. Groups Park & Garden: Adult £3.70, Child £1.80. Winter charge £1 per adult & 50p per child.

Key facts: We welcome photography, but for the enjoyment of all our visitors, we ask visitors not to use tripods or flash. Also available as a filming location. Partial. WCs. Licensed. Licensed. Must be booked in advance. Limited for coaches. Guide dogs only.

RENISHAW HALL AND GARDENS

RENISHAW, NR SHEFFIELD, DERBYSHIRE S21 3WB

www.renishaw-hall.co.uk

Renishaw Hall and Gardens have been home to the Sitwell family for over 400 years. Its present owner, Alexandra, welcomes you.

Renishaw is set in eight acres of Italianate gardens featuring marble statues and yew hedges alongside herbaceous borders and ornamental ponds. Mature woodlands and lakes offer wonderful walks. The stables house the Sitwell Museum and Gallery, the Gallery Café offering homemade food and the shop stocked with gifts including Renishaw's own white and sparkling wines.

The Hall is available for hire as a film location, weddings and is open for guided tours. Booking essential.

Location: MAP 7:A2, OS Ref. SK435 786. On A6135 3m from M1/J30, equidistant from Sheffield and Chesterfield.

Owner: Mrs Hayward

Contact: The Operations Manager

Tel: 01246 432310 **Fax:** 01246 430760

E-mail: enquiries@renishaw-hall.co.uk

Open: 2012 Season: 30 Mar–30 Sept. Open in Dec for Christmas. Gardens open Wed–Sun & BH Mons,10.30am–4.30pm. Hall open to public when prebooking on guided tours on Fris 12.30 or 2.30pm. Hall Tours are available for private groups by appointment on Weds, Thurs & Fris.

Admission: *2011 prices held* Gardens, museum and gallery: Adults £6, Concessions £5, Children £3, under 5s free. Parking £1. Season Tickets available. HHA /RHS members free to gardens. Guided garden, hall and vineyard tours £6. Full event programme runs throughout season.

Key facts: Gallery Cafe, Gift Shop, museum and exhibition plus WC facilities are available during garden opening. Partial. WCs. Licensed. Licensed. By arrangement. On leads.

CATTON HALL

Catton, Walton-On-Trent, South Derbyshire DE12 8LN

www.catton-hall.com

Catton, built in 1745, has been in the hands of the same family since 1405 and is still lived in by the Neilsons as their private home. This gives the house a unique, relaxed and friendly atmosphere, with its spacious reception rooms, luxurious bedrooms and delicious food and wine. Catton is centrally located for residential or non-residential business meetings/seminars, product launches and team-building activities, as well as for accommodation for those visiting Birmingham, the NEC, the Belfry – or just for a weekend celebration of family and friends. The acres of parkland alongside the River Trent are ideal for all types of corporate and public events.

Location: Between Lichfield & Burton-on-Trent (8m from each). Birmingham NEC 20m. **Owner/Contact:** Robin & Katie Neilson

Tel: 01283 716311 **E-mail:** r.neilson@catton-hall.com

Open: By prior arrangement all year, for corporate hospitality, shooting parties, or private groups. Tours of the house every Monday in August and all Bank Holiday Mondays.

Key facts: Conference facilities. By arrangement. By arrangement for groups. 4 x four posters, 5 twin, all en-suite.

© English Heritage

HARDWICK OLD HALL

Doe Lea, Nr Chesterfield, Derbyshire S44 5QJ

www.english-heritage.org.uk/hardwickoldhall

This large ruined house, finished in 1591, still displays Bess of Hardwick's innovative planning and interesting decorative plasterwork. Graphic panels focus on the rich interiors Bess created. The views from the top floor over the country park and 'New' Hall are spectacular.

Location: MAP 7:A3, OS120, SK463 638. 7$^1/_2$m NW of Mansfield, 9$^1/_2$m SE of Chesterfield, off A6175, from M1/J29.

Owner: National Trust, managed by English Heritage

Contact: Visitor Operations Team

Tel: 01246 850431

E-mail: customers@english-heritage.org.uk

Open: Please see www.english-heritage.org.uk for opening times and the most up-to-date information.

Admission: Adult £4.80, Child £2.90, Conc. £4.30, Family £12.50. 15% discount for groups (11+). EH members Free. Opening times and prices are valid until 31st March 2012.

Key facts: Picnickers welcome. WC. Free with admission.

© Robert Kerr, Blank Canvas Photography

EYAM HALL

Eyam, Hope Valley, Derbyshire S32 5QW

www.eyamhall.co.uk

This beautiful, unspoilt Jacobean manor house was built by the Wright family in 1671 and is still their much loved family home. The guided tour includes portraits, tapestries, costumes and family possessions. The walled garden is included in the tour. A working craft centre and licensed restaurant are on site.

Location: MAP 6:P2, OS Ref. SK216 765. Car: Approx 10m from Sheffield and Chesterfield, Eyam Hall is in the centre of the village. Bus: 65 from Sheffield, 66 from Chesterfield. Rail: to Grindleford.

Owner: Mr R H V Wright

Contact: Mrs N Wright

Tel: 01433 631976

E-mail: nicolawright@eyamhall.co.uk

Open: House & Garden: Easter Sun–7 May & 22 Jul–30 Aug, Wed, Thurs, Sun & BH Mon, 12noon–4pm. Craft Centre: All year except Jan, Tues–Sun.

Admission: House & Garden: Adult £7.50, Child £4, Conc. £6.50. Group discounts.

Key facts: Craft Centre, Free. Suitable. WCs. Licensed. Licensed. Obligatory. Free. Limited for coaches. In grounds.

MELBOURNE HALL & GARDENS

Melbourne, Derbyshire DE73 8EN

www.melbournehall.com

This beautiful house of history, in its picturesque poolside setting, was once the home of Victorian Prime Minister William Lamb. The fine gardens, in the French formal style, contain Robert Bakewell's intricate wrought iron arbour and a fascinating yew tunnel. Upstairs rooms available to view by appointment.

Location: MAP 7:A5, OS Ref. SK389 249. 8m S of Derby. From London, exit M1/J24.

Owner: Lord & Lady Ralph Kerr **Contact:** Mrs Gill Weston

Tel: 01332 862502 **Fax:** 01332 862263

E-mail: melbhall@globalnet.co.uk

Open: Hall: Aug only (not first 3 Mons) 2–5pm. Last admission 4.15pm. **Gardens:** 1 Apr–30 Sept: Weds, Sats, Suns, BH Mons, 1.30–5.30pm. Additional open days possible in August.

Admission: Hall: Adult £4, Child £3, OAP £3.50. **Gardens:** Adult £4.50, Child/OAP £3.50. **Hall & Gardens:** Adult £6.50, Child £4.50, OAP £5.50

Key facts: Crafts. No photography in house. Partial. WCs. Obligatory in house Tue–Sat. Limited. No Coach Parking Guide dogs only

© English Heritage

PEVERIL CASTLE ⌗

Market Place, Castleton, Hope Valley S33 8WQ

www.english-heritage.org.uk/peveril

This is one of the earliest Norman castles to be built in England. The Castle walkway opens up new areas and breathtaking views of the Peak District. The Visitor Centre has displays which tell the story of Peveril as the focal point of the Royal Forest of the Peak.

Location: MAP 6:O2, OS110, SK150 827. S side of Castleton, 15m W of Sheffield on A6187.

Owner: English Heritage

Contact: Visitor Operations Team

Tel: 01433 620613

E-mail: customers@english-heritage.org.uk

Open: Please visit www.english-heritage.org.uk for opening times and the most up-to-date information.

Admission: Adult £4.30, Child £2.60, Conc. £3.90, Family £11.20. 15% discount for groups (11+). EH members Free. Opening times and prices are valid until 31st March 2012.

Key facts: Picnickers welcome. WCs.

TISSINGTON HALL

Ashbourne, Derbyshire DE6 1RA

www.tissingtonhall.co.uk

Tissington Hall stands at the centre of it's estate, built in 1609 by Francis FitzHerbert it still remains in the family. The Hall is open on published days. Private group tours, functions and weddings are welcome all year-round, all of which can enjoy the fabulous gardens and 5 acre arboretum.

Location: MAP 6:P3, OS Ref. SK175 524. 4m N of Ashbourne off A515 towards Buxton.

Owner: Sir Richard FitzHerbert Bt **Contact:** Victoria Moore

Tel: 01335 352200 **E-mail:** events@tissingtonhall.co.uk

Open: 9–13 Apr, 12–3pm. 21–25 May, 12–3pm. 4–5 Jun, 12–3pm. 23 Jul–23 Aug. Open Mon–Thur 12–3pm. Mon 27 Aug 12–3pm. Prior arranged Group Visits welcome throughout the year.

Admission: Hall & Gardens: Adult £9, Child (10–16yrs) £4, Conc. £8. Gardens only: Adult £4, Child £2, Conc. £4. Group Visits welcome throughout the year at prior arrangement.

Key facts: No photography in house. Licensed. Obligatory. Limited. Guide dogs only

HARDWICK ESTATE

Doe Lea, Chesterfield, Derbyshire S44 5QJ

One of the most splendid houses in England. Built by Bess of Hardwick in the 1590's, and unaltered, yet huge windows and high ceilings make it feel modern. Rich tapestries, plaster friezes and alabaster fireplaces colour the rooms. Stainsby Mill is a 19th century water-powered corn mill in working order.

Location: MAP 7:A3, OS120, SK456 651. 7½m NW of Mansfield, 9½m SE of Chesterfield.

Owner: National Trust **Contact:** Support Service Assistant

Tel: 01246 850430 **Fax:** 01246 858424

Shop/Restaurant: 01246 858409

E-mail: hardwickhall@nationaltrust.org.uk

Website: www.nationaltrust.org.uk/hardwick

Open: Please see website or contact us for up-to-date information.

Admission: Please see website or contact us for up-to-date information.

Key facts: Partial. WCs. Licensed. By arrangement. Limited for coaches. Guide dogs only.

© Britainonview

Haddon Hall

STANFORD HALL

LUTTERWORTH, LEICESTERSHIRE LE17 6DH

www.stanfordhall.co.uk

Stanford has been the home of the Cave family, ancestors of the present owner, since 1430. In the 1690s, Sir Roger Cave commissioned the Smiths of Warwick to pull down the old Manor House and build the present Hall. Throughout the house are portraits of the family and examples of furniture and objects which they collected over the centuries. There is also a collection of Royal Stuart portraits. The Hall and Stables are set in an attractive Park on the banks of Shakespeare's Avon. There is a walled Rose Garden and an early ha-ha.

Location: MAP 7:B7. OS Ref. SP587 793. M1/J18 6m,M1/J19 (from/to the N only) 2m, M6 exit/access at A14/M1(N)J 2m, A14 2m. Follow Historic House signs.

Owner: Mr & Mrs N Fothergill **Contact:** Sarah Maughan **Tel:** 01788 860250 **Fax:** 01788 860870 **E-mail:** s.maughan@stanfordhall.co.uk

Open: Special two week Easter opening – Sun 1–Sun 15 Apr 2012. Other open days in conjunction with park events. Please see our website or telephone for details. House open any day or evening (except Sats) for pre-booked groups.

Admission: House & Grounds: Adult £6, Child (5–15yrs) £2.50. Private Group Tours (20+): Adult £6.50, Child (5–15yrs) £2.50. Grounds only: Adult £3.50 Child (5–15yrs) £1.50. Special admission prices may apply on event days.

Key facts: Craft centre (most Suns). Corporate days, clay pigeon shoots, filming, photography, small conferences, accommodation. Parkland, helicopter landing area, lecture room, Stables cafe. Caravan site. Lunches, dinners & wedding receptions. Partial. WCs. Tour time: 3/4 hr in groups of approx 25. 1,000 cars and 6–8 coaches. Free meals for coach drivers, coach parking on gravel in front of house. On leads. Accommodation available.

© English Heritage

ASHBY DE LA ZOUCH CASTLE ⌗

South Street, Ashby de la Zouch, Leicestershire LE65 1BR

www.english-heritage.org.uk/ashbydelazouchcastle

The impressive ruins of this late medieval castle are dominated by a magnificent tower, over 80 feet high, which was split in two during the Civil War. Panoramic views. Explore the tunnel linking the kitchens to the Hastings Tower. New interpretation and audio tour.

Location: MAP 7:A7, OS128, SK363 167. In Ashby de la Zouch, 12m S of Derby on A511. SE of town centre.

Owner: English Heritage **Contact:** Visitor Operations Team

Tel: 01530 413343 **E-mail:** customers@english-heritage.org.uk

Open: Please visit www.english-heritage.org.uk for opening times and the most up-to-date information.

Admission: Adult £4.30, Child £2.60, Conc. £3.90, Family £11.20. 15% discount for groups (11+). EH Members free. Opening times and prices are valid until 31st March 2012.

Key facts: Picnickers welcome. WC. Free with admission. Restricted.

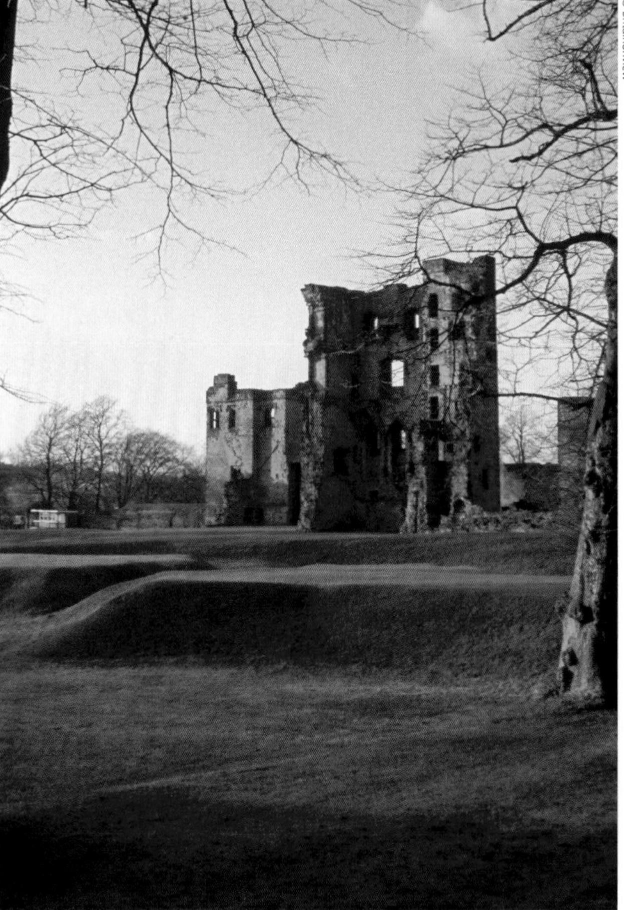
© Britainonview

Ashby De La Zouch Castle

VISITOR INFORMATION

■ Owner
Burghley House Preservation Trust Ltd

■ Address
House Manager
Stamford
Lincolnshire
PE9 3JY

■ Location
MAP 7:E7
OS Ref. TF048 062

Burghley House is 1m SE of Stamford. From London, A1 2hrs.

Visitors entrance is on B1443.

Rail: London – Peterborough 1hr (GNER). Stamford Station 12 mins, regular service from Peterborough.

Taxi: Direct Line: 01780 481481.

■ Contact
The House Manager
Tel: 01780 752451
Fax: 01780 480125
E-mail: burghley@burghley.co.uk

■ Opening Times
Summer
House & Gardens
17 March–28 October (closed 30 August-2 September):
Open Daily (House closed on Fridays), 11am–5pm, (last admission 4.30pm).

■ Admission*
House & Gardens

Adult	£13.80
Child (3–15yrs)	£7.00
Conc.	£12.50
Family	£36.50

Groups (20+)

Adult	£11.00
School (up to 15yrs)	£6.30

Gardens of Surprise only

Adult	£8.00
Child (3–15yrs)	£5.30
Conc.	£6.80
Family	£26.00

*Includes a voluntary Gift Aid donation but visitors can choose to pay the standard prices displayed on our website.

■ Special events
The Burghley Horse Trials 30th August - 2nd September

Conference/Function		
ROOM	Size	Max Cap
Great Hall	70' x 30'	160
Orangery	100' x 20'	120

BURGHLEY HOUSE

www.burghley.co.uk

Burghley House, home of the Cecil family for over 400 years is one of England's Greatest Elizabethan Houses.

Burghley was built between 1555 and 1587 by William Cecil, later Lord Burghley, principal adviser and Lord High Treasurer to Queen Elizabeth. During the 17th and 18th centuries, the House was transformed by John 5th Earl of Exeter and Brownlow, the 9th Earl; travelling to the cultural centres of Europe and employing many of the foremost craftsmen of their day. Burghley contains one of the largest private collections of Italian art, unique examples of Chinese and Japanese porcelain and superb items of 18th century furniture. Principal artists and craftsmen of the period are to be found at Burghley: Antonio Verrio, Grinling Gibbons and Louis Laguerre all made major contributions to the beautiful interiors.

Park and Gardens

The house is set in a 300-acre deer park landscaped by 'Capability' Brown. A lake was created by him and delightful avenues of mature trees feature largely in his design. The park is home to a large herd of Fallow deer, established in the 16th century. The Garden of Surprises is a modern oasis of flowing water and fountains, statues, and obelisks. The contemporary Sculpture was reclaimed from 'Capability' Brown's lost lower gardens in 1994 and is dedicated to exhibiting innovative sculptures. The private gardens around the house are open in April for the display of spring bulbs.

KEY FACTS

- Suitable for a variety of events, large park, golf course, helicopter landing area, cricket pitch. No photography in house.
- WCs.
- Licensed.
- Licensed.
- By arrangement.
- Ample. Free refreshments for coach drivers.
- Welcome. Guide provided.
- Guide dogs only.
- Civil Wedding Licence.

AYSCOUGHFEE HALL MUSEUM & GARDENS

Churchgate, Spalding, Lincolnshire PE11 2RA

www.ayscoughfee.org

Ayscoughfee Hall, a magnificent Grade II* listed building, was built in the 1450s. The Hall is set in extensive landscaped grounds which include, amongst other features, a memorial designed by Edwin Lutyens. The Museum features the history of the Hall, the people who lived there, and the surrounding Fens.

Location: MAP 7:F5, OS Ref. TF249 223. E bank of the River Welland, 5 mins walk from Spalding town centre.

Owner: South Holland District Council

Contact: Museum Officer

Tel: 01775 764555

E-mail: museum@sholland.gov.uk

Open: House: 10.30am–4pm Wed–Sun throughout the year (we are also open on BH Mons). Gardens: 8am until dusk Mon–Sat, 10am until dusk Sun.

Admission: Free.

Key facts: Photography allowed throughout the Hall, apart from the Geest Gallery art exhibitions. WCs. By arrangement. Guide dogs only.

© Country Life Picture Library

GRIMSTHORPE CASTLE, PARK & GARDENS

Grimsthorpe, Bourne, Lincolnshire PE10 0LZ

www.grimsthorpe.co.uk

Building styles from 13th century. North Front is Vanbrugh's last major work. State Rooms and picture galleries including tapestries, furniture and paintings. 3,000 acre park with lakes, ancient woods, cycle trail, hire shop. Extensive gardens. Groups can explore the park in their own coach by booking a one-hour, escorted park tour.

Location: MAP 7:D5. OS Ref. TF040 230. 4m NW of Bourne on A151, 8m E of Colsterworth Junction of A1. **Owner:** Grimsthorpe and Drummond Castle Trust Ltd. A Charity Registered in England & Wales (507478) and in Scotland (SCO39364). **Contact:** Ray Biggs **Tel:** 01778 591205 **Fax:** 01778 591259 **E-mail:** ray@grimsthorpe.co.uk **Open:** Castle: Apr & May: Suns, Thurs & BH Mons. Jun–Sept: Sun–Thur. 1–5pm (last admission 4pm). Park & Gardens: As Castle, 11am–6pm (last admission 5pm). Groups: Apr–Sept: by arrangement. **Admission:** Castle, Park & Garden: Adult £10, Child £4, Conc. £9, Family (2+3) £24. Park & Gardens: Adult £5, Child £2, Conc. £4, Family (2+3) £12. Group rates on application. **Key facts:** No photography in house. Conferences (up to 40), inc catering. Partial. WCs. Obligatory except Suns. Ample On leads.

DODDINGTON HALL & GARDENS

Lincoln LN6 4RU

www.doddingtonhall.com

Romantic Smythson house standing today as it was built in 1595. Still a family home. Georgian interior with fascinating collection of porcelain, paintings and textiles. Five acres of wild and walled formal gardens boast pageant of colour from earliest spring until autumn. Award-winning Farm Shop, Cafe & Restaurant.

Location: MAP 7:D2, OS Ref. SK900 710. 5m W of Lincoln on the B1190, signposted off the A46.

Owner: Mr & Mrs J J C Birch **Contact:** The Estate Office

Tel: 01522 812510 **Fax:** 01522 848294 **E-mail:** info@doddingtonhall.com

Open: Gardens only: 12 Feb–1 Apr & Oct: Suns only 11am–4pm. House & Gardens: 8 Apr–30 Sep, Wed, Sun & BH Mon 1–5pm (Gardens open 11am).

Admission: Gardens only: Adult £5, Child £2.75. House & Gardens: Adult £9.50, Child £4.75. U4 free. Family & Season Tickets available. Group visits (private guided tours for 20+) £9.50 per head.

Key facts: No photography in Hall. No stilettos. WCs. Licensed. Licensed. By arrangement. Free. Limited for coaches. Guide dogs only.

Ayscoughfee Hall

LINCOLN CATHEDRAL

Lincoln LN2 1PZ

www.lincolncathedral.com

Welcome to the Cathedral on the hill! Lincolnshire's most distinguishing landmark visible from 25 miles away, even more stunning close up both by day and night. "The very first time I entered Lincoln Cathedral I remember I just stood, gazing in awesome wonder. I was overwhelmed by the sheer space before me and that was before I could begin to struggle to imagine how these men, my ancestors, could have built it over eight hundred years ago." Phil Hamlyn Williams – Chief Executive.

Location: MAP 7:D2, OS Ref. SK978 718. At the centre of Uphill, Lincoln.
Contact: Communications Office **Tel:** 01522 561600 **Fax:** 01522 561634
Open: All year: Jun–Aug, 7.15am–8pm. Sept–May, 7.15am–6pm. Sun closing 6pm in Summer, 5pm in Winter.
Admission: £6, Child (5–16yrs) £1, Child (under 5s) Free, Conc. £4.75, No charge for services. Contact Communications for any restrictions / special events.
Key facts: Twitter @LincsCathedral Facebook.com/Lincoln.Cathedral Guide dogs only.

© English Heritage

LINCOLN MEDIEVAL BISHOPS' PALACE

Minster Yard, Lincoln LN2 1PU

www.english-heritage.org.uk/lincolnmedievalbishopspalace

Constructed in the late 12th century, the medieval bishops' palace was once one of the most important buildings in England. Built on hillside terraces, it has views of the cathedral and the Roman, medieval and modern city. See a virtual tour of the Palace and explore the grounds.

Location: MAP 7:D2, OS121 Ref. SK981 717. S side of Lincoln Cathedral, in Lincoln.
Owner: English Heritage **Contact:** Visitor Operations Team
Tel/Fax: 01522 527468 **E-mail:** customers@english-heritage.org.uk
Open: Please visit www.english-heritage.org.uk for opening times and the most up-to-date information.
Admission: Adult £4.40, Child £2.60, Conc. £4, Family £11.40. EH Members free. Opening times and prices are valid until 31st March 2012.
Key facts: Picnickers welcome.

© NT / S Crow

TATTERSHALL CASTLE

Sleaford Road, Tattershall, Lincolnshire LN4 4LR

www.nationaltrust.org.uk/tattershall

A vast fortified tower built c1440 for Ralph Cromwell, Lord Treasurer of England. The Castle is a national example of an early brick building, with a tower rising 130ft, rescued from dereliction and restored by Lord Curzon 1911–14. Explore all 6 floors, from basements to the battlements.

Location: MAP 7:E3, OS122 Ref. TF209 575. On S side of A153, 12m NE of Sleaford, 10m SW of Horncastle.
Owner: National Trust **Contact:** Visitor Services Manager
Tel: 01526 342543 **Fax:** 01526 348826
E-mail: tattershallcastle@nationaltrust.org.uk
Open: 12 Mar–4 Nov, 5 days a week, 11am–5pm, closed Thurs & Fri. 10 Nov–16 Dec, weekends only, 11am–4pm.
***Admission:** Adult £6, Child £3, Family £15. Group discounts. *includes Gift Aid voluntary donation but visitors can choose to pay the standard prices displayed at the property and on the website.
Key facts: Free audio guide available. Shop serves light refreshments. Family friendly. Biker friendly. Picnic in the grounds. Partial. WCs. Free. Limited for coaches. Guide dogs only.

© NTPL / Nick Meers

WOOLSTHORPE MANOR

Water Lane, Woolsthorpe by Colsterworth, Grantham NG33 5PD

www.nationaltrust.org.uk/woolsthorpemanor

Isaac Newton, scientist, Master of the Royal Mint and President of the Royal Society, was born in this modest 17th century manor house in 1642 and developed his theories about light and gravity here. Visit the apple tree, explore his ideas in the Science Discovery Centre, see the short film.

Location: MAP 7:D5, OS Ref. SK924 244. 7m S of Grantham, 0.5 m NW of Colsterworth, 1m W of A1.
Owner: National Trust **Contact:** The Visitor Services Manager
Tel: 01476 862820 **Fax:** 01476 862826
E-mail: woolsthorpemanor@nationaltrust.org.uk
Open: House & Grounds: 2–11 Mar, Fri, Sat, Sun, 11am–5pm; 14 Mar–28 Oct, Wed–Sun, 11am–5pm; Open BH Mons and Good Fri 11am–5pm.
Admission: Adult £6.65*, Child £3.35*, Family £16.65*, reduction for groups which must book in advance. *includes voluntary donation; visitors may pay standard prices displayed at the property and on the website.
Key facts: Partial. WCs. By arrangement. Limited for coaches. Guide dogs only.

AUBOURN HALL

Lincoln LN5 9DZ

Almost 5 acres of lawns and floral borders surround this homely Jacobean manor house. The Rose and Prairie Gardens are new favorites and the Turf maze, Dell Garden and Stumpery all add to the fascination of this much loved family home. Guided tours available throughout the season. Weddings also welcomed.

Location: MAP 7:D3, OS Ref. SK928 628. 6m SW of Lincoln. 2m SE of A46.

Owner: Mr & Mrs Christopher Nevile

Contact: Andrew Widd, Head Gardener.

Tel: 01522 788224 **Fax:** 01522 788199

E-mail: estate.office@aubournhall.co.uk

Website: www.aubournhall.co.uk

Open: Garden: Open for Events, Groups and Garden visits from May–Sept. Please contact the property for details.

Admission: Adults £4. Children free.

Key facts: Partial. WCs. By arrangement. Limited for coaches. Guide dogs only.

BELTON HOUSE

Grantham, Lincolnshire NG32 2LS

The perfect English country house, set in its own extensive deer park, Belton was designed to impress. Built in the late 17th century by 'Young' Sir John Brownlow. Opulent décor, stunning silverware, wonderful woodcarvings, imposing paintings – including many old masters – and personal mementos convey wealth, but also a family atmosphere.

Location: MAP 7:D4, OS Ref. SK929 395. 3m NE of Grantham on A607, Signed off the A1.

Owner: National Trust **Contact:** Support Services Team

Tel: 01476 566116 **Fax:** 01476 542980

E-mail: belton@nationaltrust.org.uk

Website: www.nationaltrust.org.uk/belton

Open: Please see website or contact us for up-to-date information.

Admission: Please see website or contact us for up-to-date information.

Key facts: Adventure playground. Partial. Licensed. Civil Wedding License.

© Britainonview

Lincoln Cathedral floodlit.

EASTON WALLED GARDENS

Easton Walled Gardens, Easton, Grantham, Lincolnshire NG33 5AP

In 1901 President Franklin Roosevelt described these gardens as a 'Dream of Nirvana … almost too good to be true'. Abandoned for 50 years these romantic 400 year old gardens are celebrating 10 years of revival and include: snowdrops, Roses, Sweet Peas, cut flower, cottage and vegetable gardens and meadows.

Location: MAP 7:D5, OS Ref. SK938 274. 1m from A1 (between Stamford and Grantham) North of Colsterworth, onto B6403 and follow signs.

Owner: Sir Fred & Lady Cholmeley **Contact:** Mary Mckinlay **Tel:** 01476 530063

Fax: 01476 530063 **E-mail:** info@eastonwalledgardens.co.uk

Website: www.eastonwalledgardens.co.uk

Open: 18–26 Feb daily for snowdrops: 11am–4pm; Wed, Thurs, Fri, Suns & BH Mons. March–Oct. Sweet Pea Week 1–8 July daily. For events and extended opening times please see website.

Admission: Please check website.

Key facts: Groups can book out of hours if wished. Partial. WCs. By arrangement. Guide dogs only.

FULBECK MANOR

Fulbeck, Grantham, Lincolnshire NG32 3JN

Built c1580. 400 years of Fane family portraits. Open by written appointment. Guided tours by owner approximately 11/4 hours. Tearooms at Craft Centre, 100 yards, for light lunches and teas.

Location: MAP 7:D3. OS Ref. SK947 505. 11m N of Grantham. 15m S of Lincoln on A607. Brown signs to Craft Centre & Tearooms and Stables.

Owner/Contact: Mr Julian Francis Fane

Tel: 01400 272231

Fax: 01400 273545

E-mail: fane@fulbeck.co.uk

Open: By written appointment.

Admission: Adult £6. Groups (10+) £5.

Key facts: No photography. Partial. WCs. Obligatory. Ample for cars. Limited for coaches. Guide dogs only.

LEADENHAM HOUSE

Leadenham House, Lincolnshire LN5 0PU

Late eighteenth century house in park setting.

Location: MAP 7:D3. OS Ref. SK949 518. Entrance on A17 Leadenham bypass (between Newark and Sleaford).

Owner: Mr P Reeve

Contact: Mr and Mrs P Reeve

Tel: 01400 273256

Fax: 01400 272237

E-mail: leadenhamhouse@googlemail.com

Open: 2–5, 11&12, 16–20 & 30 Apr, 1–4, 14–18, 21–25 May, Spring & Aug BHs. All 2–5pm.

Admission: £5. Please ring door bell. Groups by prior arrangement only.

Key facts: No photography. Partial. Obligatory. Limited for cars & coaches. Guide dogs only.

MARSTON HALL

Marston, Grantham NG32 2HQ

The ancient home of the Thorold family. The building contains Norman, Plantaganet, Tudor and Georgian elements through to the modern day. Marston Hall is undergoing continuous restoration some of it which may be disruptive. Please telephone in advance of intended visits.

Location: MAP 7:D4, OS Ref. SK893 437, 5m N of Grantham and about 1m E of A1.

Owner/Contact: J R Thorold

Tel: 07812 356237

Fax: 0208 7892857

E-mail: johnthorold@aol.com

Open: 25, 26, 27 & 28 Feb. 10, 11, 12 & 13 Mar. 6, 7, 8, 9 & 10 Apr. 5, 6, 7, 19, 20 & 21 May. 4, 5, 23, 24 & 25 Jun. 25, 26, 27 & 28 Aug.

Admission: Adult £4, Child £1.50. Groups must book.

Key facts: No photography.

VISITOR INFORMATION

■ Owner
The Rt Hon The 9th Earl Spencer

■ Address
Northampton
NN7 4HQ

■ Location
MAP 7:C9
OS Ref. SP682 652.

From the M1/J16, 7m J18, 10m. Situated on A428 Northampton – Rugby. London on average 85 mins away.

Rail: 5m from Northampton station. 14m from Rugby station.

■ Contact
Althorp
Tel: 01604 770107
Fax: 01604 770042
E-mail: mail@althorp.com

■ Opening Times
Summer:
July and August, daily, 11am–5pm. (excluding 31 August.) Last admission 4pm.

Winter:
Closed.

■ Admission
House & Grounds:
Contact for admission prices and group rates. Carers accompanying visitors with disabilities are admitted free. Please check website for up to date information.

ALTHORP

www.althorp.com

Explore this classic English stately home which also houses a fascinating collection of art, furniture and ceramics.

The history of Althorp is the history of a family. The Spencer's have lived and died here for over five centuries and nineteen generations. Since the death of Diana, Princess of Wales, Althorp has become known across the world, but before that tragic event, connoisseurs had heard of this most classic of English stately homes on account of the magnificence of its contents and the beauty of its setting. Althorp contains a fascinating variety of pictures, furniture and ceramics, a result of one family's uninterrupted occupancy for over 500 years. Enjoy the work of Van Dyck, Rubens, Gainsborough and Reynolds in one of Europe's finest private collections of the decorative arts. Next to the mansion at Althorp lies the honey-coloured stable block, a truly breathtaking building which at one time accommodated up to 100 horses and 40 grooms. The stables are now the setting for the Exhibition celebrating the life of Diana, Princess of Wales. All visitors are invited to view the House, Exhibition and Grounds as well as the Round Oval where Diana, Princess of Wales is laid to rest. The House and grounds are available for weddings, private hire, events and specialist set location filming.

KEY FACTS

- No indoor photography with still or video cameras.
-
-
- WCs.
-
- By arrangement.
- Audio tour narrated by Lord Spencer.
- Limited for coaches.
- Guide dogs only.
-
-

DEENE PARK

www.deenepark.com

Home of the Brudenell family since 1514, this sixteenth century house incorporates a medieval manor with important Georgian additions.

Seat of the 7th Earl of Cardigan who led the charge of the Light Brigade at Balaklava in 1854, today the house is the home of Mr. Edmund and the Hon. Mrs. Brudenell and the rooms on show are regularly used by their family and friends. It has grown in size as generations have made their own mark through the years, providing the visitor with an interesting yet complementary mixture of styles. There is a considerable collection of family portraits and possessions, including memorabilia from the Crimean War.

The gardens are mainly to the south and west of the house and include long borders, old-fashioned roses and specimen trees. Close to the house there is a parterre designed by David Hicks in the 1990s. The topiary teapots, inspired by the finial on the Millenium obelisk, form a fine feature as they mature.

Open parkland lies across water from the terraced gardens providing enchanting vistas in many directions. The more energetic visitor can discover these during a rewarding walk in the tranquil surroundings. As well as the flora, there is also a diversity of bird life ranging from red kites to kingfishers and black swans to little grebes. On public open days home-made scones and cakes are available in the Old Kitchen and souvenirs can be found in the Courtyard Gift Shop. Group visits are available at anytime by prior arrangement, with booked lunches and suppers available.

KEY FACTS

- Suitable for events, filming and lectures. No photography in house.
- Including buffets, lunches and dinners.
- Partial. Visitors may alight at the entrance, access to ground floor and garden.
- Special rates for groups, bookings can be made in advance, menus on request.
- By arrangement.
- Available for group visits by arrangement (approx 90 mins).
- Unlimited for cars, space for 3 coaches 10 yds from house.
- In car park only.
- Residential conference facilities by arrangement.

VISITOR INFORMATION

Owner
E Brudenell Esq

Address
Deene Park
Corby
Northamptonshire
NN17 3EW

Location
MAP 7:D7
OS Ref. SP950 929

6m NE of Corby off A43. From London via M1/J15 then A43, or via A1, A14, A43–2 hrs. From Birmingham via M6, A14, A43, 90 mins.

Rail: Corby Station 10 mins and Kettering Station 20 mins.

Contact
The Administrator
Tel: 01780 450278
Fax: 01780 450282
E-mail: admin@deenepark.com

Opening Times
Open Easter Sun & Mon, Suns and BH Mons from May to end August & Weds in May & 5 September 2–5pm.

Last admission 4pm.

Refreshments available in the Old Kitchen.

Open at other times by arrangement for groups.

Admission
Public Open Days

House & Gardens

Adult	£8.50
Child (10–14yrs)	£4.50
Conc.	£7.50

Gardens only

Adult	£6.00
Child (10–14yrs)	£3.00

Groups (20+) by arrangement:

Weekdays, Sundays & BHs	£7.50 (Min £150)
Saturdays	£8.50 (Min £170)

Child up to 10yrs free with an accompanying adult.

Special events
12 & 19 February
Snowdrop Sundays
(Gardens Only), 11am–4pm

1 April
Daffodil Day
(Gardens Only), 11am–4pm

6 June
Head Gardener's Tour with Supper
Booking Essential, 6pm

For more information about these and other events please visit our website.

Conference/Function

ROOM	Size	Max Cap
Great Hall		150
Tapestry Rm		75
East Room		18

COTTESBROOKE HALL & GARDENS

COTTESBROOKE, NORTHAMPTONSHIRE NN6 8PF

www.cottesbrookehall.co.uk

Dating from 1702 the Hall's beauty is matched by the magnificence of the gardens and the excellence of the picture, furniture and porcelain collections. The Woolavington collection of sporting pictures is possibly the finest of its type in Europe and includes paintings by Stubbs, Ben Marshall and artists renowned for works of this genre. Portraits, bronzes, 18th century English and French furniture and fine porcelain are among the treasures.

The formal gardens are continually being updated and developed by influential designers. The Wild Gardens, a short walk across the Park, are planted along the course of a stream.

Location: MAP 7:B8, OS Ref. SP711 739. 10m N of Northampton near Creaton on A5199 (formerly A50). Signed from Junction 1 on the A14.

Owner: Mr & Mrs A R Macdonald-Buchanan

Contact: The Administrator

Tel: 01604 505808

Fax: 01604 505619

E-mail: enquiries@cottesbrooke.co.uk

Open: May–end of Sept. May & Jun: Wed & Thur, 2–5.30pm. Jul–Sept: Thur, 2–5.30pm. Open BH Mons (May–Sept), 2–5.30pm. The first open day is Wed 2 May 2012.

Admission: House & Gardens: Adult £8, Child £4, Conc £7.
Gardens only: Adult £5.50, Child £3, Conc £5. RHS members receive free access to gardens. Group & private bookings by arrangement.

Key facts: No large bags or photography in house. Filming & outside events. Partial. WCs. Hall guided tours obligatory. Guide dogs only. The Cottesbrooke Hall Plant Fair is held from Friday 22nd June to Sunday 24th June, 2012.

HOLDENBY

HOLDENBY, NORTHAMPTON NN6 8DJ

www.holdenby.com

Once the largest private house in England and subsequently the palace of James I and prison of Charlies I, Holdenby has a special atmosphere all of its own.
It's suite of elegant state rooms overlooking the Grade I listed gardens and rolling countryside make it a magnificent venue for corporate events, dinners and meetings, as well as an ideal location for filming. Couples continue to choose Holdenby as an enchanting venue for weddings creating a truly memorable day.

With the falconry centre based at Holdenby visitors can arrange to visit the centre and arrange for displays of the impressive birds.

Location: MAP 7:B8, OS Ref. SP693 681. M1/J15a. 7m NW of Northampton off A428 & A5199.

Owner: James Lowther

Contact: Gilly Wrathall, Commercial Manager

Tel: 01604 770074 **Fax:** 01604 770962

E-mail: gilly@holdenby.com

Open: Gardens open: Apr–Sept; Suns & Bank Holiday Mons; 1–5pm.

Admission: Adult £5, Child £3.50, Conc. £4.50, Family (2+3) £15; Different prices on event days. Groups must book.

Key facts: Children's play area. Obligatory, by arrangement. Limited for coaches. 6 times Sandford Award Winner. On leads.

KELMARSH HALL AND GARDENS

KELMARSH, NORTHAMPTON NN6 9LY

www.kelmarsh.com

Built in the Palladian style to a James Gibbs design, 18th century Kelmarsh Hall is set in beautiful gardens with views over the surrounding parkland.
The former home of society decorator, Nancy Lancaster, Kelmarsh still reflects the essence of her panache and flair. Within the Hall is the Croome Exhibition, showcasing furniture and paintings on loan from Croome Court in Worcestershire. The award-winning gardens include a formal terrace, horse chestnut avenues, rose gardens and the historic walled kitchen garden.
Kelmarsh Hall, gardens and parkland can be hired exclusively for weddings, corporate events and private parties.

Location: MAP 7:C8, OS Ref. SP736 795. 1/3 m N of A14–A508 jct 2. Rail & Bus: Mkt Harborough.

Owner: The Kelmarsh Trust **Tel:** 01604 686543 **E-mail:** enquiries@kelmarsh.com

Open: House and gardens open Apr 8 & 9 2012, May 6 & 7, then Thurs, May 10 until Sept 27. Gardens open Tues, Weds, Thurs, Suns & BH Mons & Tues, 11am–5pm. House open Thurs & BH Suns, Mons & Tues, from 2–5pm.

Admission: House or Croome tour: Adults £6, Child £4, Conc. £5.50
Gardens; Adults £5, Child £3.50, Conc. £4.50,
Garden season tickets are available.

Key facts: WCs. Licensed. Obligatory. We welcome visits from schools. On leads. Snowdrop weekends: Sat 11 & Sun 12 Feb 2012. Sat 18 & Sun 19 Feb 2012. Hardy Plant Fair: May 6 & 7. English Heritage's Festival of History: Jul 14 & 15 €

© English Heritage

© English Heritage

KIRBY HALL

DEENE, CORBY, NORTHAMPTONSHIRE NN17 3EN

www.english-heritage.org.uk/kirbyhall

Kirby Hall is one of England's greatest Elizabethan and 17th century Houses. The partial ruins contain exceptional decoration, full of renaissance detail. The Great Hall and state rooms remain in tact, restored to authentic 17th and 18th century style decor. The 'cutwork' gardens boast beautiful statues, seating and topiary. Kirby Hall was used as one of the locations for the filming of the recent film version of Jane Austen's Mansfield Park. Peacock Cottage is hidden away through an avenue of chestnut trees. Ideal for two couples, this well-equipped cottage is a perfect place for BBQs and picnics.

Location: MAP 7:D7 OS Ref. SP926 927. On unclassified road off A43, Corby to Stamford road, 4m NE of Corby. 2m W of Deene Park.

Owner: The Earl of Winchilsea & Nottingham (Managed by English Heritage)

Contact: Visitor Operations Team **Tel:** 01536 203230

E-mail: customers@english-heritage.org.uk

Open: Please visit www.english-heritage.org.uk for opening times and the most up-to-date information.

Admission: Adult £5.60, Child £3.40, Conc. £5, Family £14.60. 15% discount for groups (11+). EH Members Free. Opening times and prices are valid until 31st March 2012.

Key facts: Picnickers welcome. WC. Free with admission.

LAMPORT HALL & GARDENS

LAMPORT HALL, NORTHAMPTONSHIRE NN6 9HD

www.lamporthall.co.uk

The facade is by John Webb and the Smiths of Warwick. The Hall contains an outstanding collection of furniture, books and paintings, including portraits by Van Dyck, Kneller, Lely and other important works of art, many from a Grand Tour in the 17th century. The gardens owe much to the 10th Baronet who created the famous rockery and made a small Italian garden. Other features include a 17th century cockpit and an 18th century box bower. The 2 acre walled garden houses one of the largest cutting gardens in England including tall, unusual plants sourced from Piet Oudolf's Dutch nursery.

Location: MAP 7:C8, OS Ref. SP759 745. Entrance on A508. Midway between Northampton and Market Harborough, 3m S of A14 J2.

Owner: Lamport Hall Trust **Contact:** Executive Director

Tel: 01604 686272 **Fax:** 01604 686224 **E-mail:** admin@lamporthall.co.uk

Open: Easter Sun–14 Oct, guided house tours at 2.15 and 3pm. Wed & Thurs and non guided tours BH Suns/Mons + Oct 13 & 14. Guided garden tours 1st Wed of the month & BH Mons at 2.05pm and 3.30pm. Private tours at other times by arrangement. Please check website for up-to-date opening times and prices.

Admission: House & Garden: Adult £8, Senior £7.50, Child (11–18) £3, Gardens Only: Adult £4.50, Senior £4, Child (11–18) £2. Private groups: House & gardens £8, Gardens only: £4.50 minimum charge £250 House and Gardens, £100 Gardens only.

Key facts: No photography in house. Available for filming. Partial. WCs. Licensed. Obligatory other than Fair Days. Limited for coaches. Guide dogs only Groups only.

ROCKINGHAM CASTLE

ROCKINGHAM, MARKET HARBOROUGH, LEICESTERSHIRE LE16 8TH

www.rockinghamcastle.com

Rockingham Castle stands on the edge of an escarpment giving dramatic views over five counties and the Welland Valley below. Built by William the Conqueror, the Castle was a royal residence for 450 years. In the 16th century Henry VIII granted it to Edward Watson and for 450 years it has remained a family home. The predominantly Tudor building, within Norman walls, has architecture, furniture and works of art from practically every century. Surrounding the Castle are 18 acres of gardens following the foot print of the medieval castle. The 400 year old "Elephant Hedge" bisects the formal terraced gardens.

Location: MAP 7:D7, OS Ref. SP867 913. 1m N of Corby on A6003. 9m E of Market Harborough. 14m SW of Stamford on A427.

Owner: James Saunders Watson

Contact: Andrew Norman, Operations Manager

Tel: 01536 770240 **Fax:** 01536 771692

E-mail: estateoffice@rockinghamcastle.com

Open: 8 Apr–end May, Suns & BH Mons, Jun–30 Sept, Tues (except 5 Jun), Suns & BH Mons. Grounds open at 12 noon, Castle opens at 1pm. Last entry 4.30pm.

Admission: House & Grounds: Adult £9, Seniors £8, Child (5–16yrs) £5, Family (2+2) £23. Grounds: Adult/Child £5 (Not event days). Groups (20+ visitors): Adult (open days) £8, Adult (tour) £10, Child (5–16yrs) £4.75. Schools (20+ visitors): Adult £8, Child £4.75.

Key facts: No photography in Castle. Partial. WCs. Licensed. Licensed. By arrangement. Limited for coaches. On leads.

CANONS ASHBY

Canons Ashby, Daventry, Northamptonshire NN11 3SD

www.nationaltrust.org.uk/canonsashby

Home of the Dryden family since the 16th century, this Elizabethan manor house was built c1550. Elizabethan wall paintings and outstanding Jacobean plasterwork are of particular interest. A formal garden includes terraces, walls and gate piers of 1710. There is also a medieval priory church and a 70 acre park.

Location: MAP 7:B9, OS Ref. SP577 506. Access from M40/J11, or M1/J16. Signposted from A5, 3m S of Weedon crossroads.

Owner: National Trust **Contact:** The Property Manager

Tel: 01327 861900 **E-mail:** canonsashby@nationaltrust.org.uk

Open: Feb–Dec weekends, 17 Mar–31 Oct, Sat–Wed, Fri also in Jun, Jul and Aug. Guided House Tours before 1pm, free flow visiting 1–5pm.

Admission: Free to NT members. Adult £8.70, Child £4.35. Garden only £3.60/£2.05.

Key facts: No flash photography. No high heeled shoes. Very limited. WCs. By arrangement. Limited for coaches. Guide dogs only.

COTON MANOR GARDEN

Nr Guilsborough, Northamptonshire NN6 8RQ

www.cotonmanor.co.uk

Traditional English garden laid out on different levels surrounding a 17th century stone manor house. Many herbaceous borders, with extensive range of plants, old yew and holly hedges, rose garden, water garden and fine lawns set in 10 acres. Also wild flower meadow and bluebell wood.

Location: MAP 7:B8, OS Ref. SP675 716. 9m NW of Northampton, between A5199 (formerly A50) and A428.

Owner: Ian & Susie Pasley-Tyler

Contact: Sarah Ball

Tel: 01604 740219

Fax: 01604 740838

E-mail: pasleytyler@cotonmanor.co.uk

Open: 3 Apr–29 Sept: Tue–Sat & BH weekends; also Suns Apr–May: 12 noon–5.30pm.

Admission: Adult £6, Child £2, Conc. £5.50. Groups: £5.

Key facts: Partial. Licensed. Licensed. By arrangement.

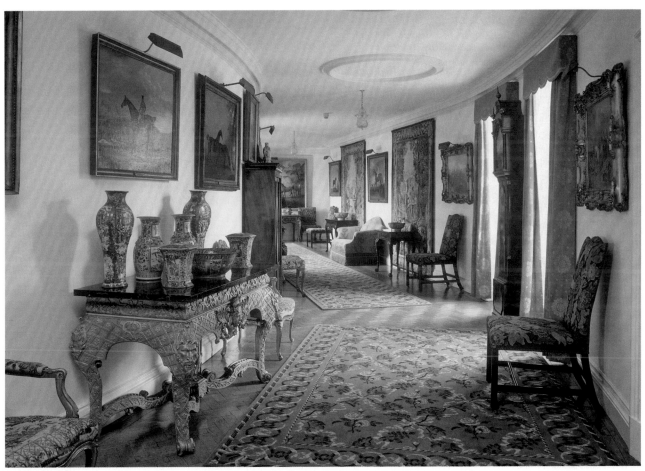

Cottesbrooke Hall

78 DERNGATE: THE CHARLES RENNIE MACKINTOSH HOUSE & GALLERIES

82 Derngate, Northampton NN1 1UH

Winner Enjoy England Gold Award for Best Small Visitor Attraction 2009. 78 Derngate was remodelled by the world-famous architect and designer, Charles Rennie Mackintosh, in his iconic modernist style. Free entry to the Gallery Upstairs, restaurant, shop and contemporary craft. Truely is a must-see venue.

Location: MAP 7:C9, OS Ref. SP759 603. In the heart of Northampton close to The Royal & Derngate Theatres.

Owner: 78 Derngate Northampton Trust **Contact:** House Manager

Tel: 01604 603407 **E-mail:** info@78derngate.org.uk

Website: www.78derngate.org.uk

Open: 1 Feb–16 Dec 2012, Tues–Sun & BH Mons: 10am–5pm. Group and school bookings are also available.

Admission: Adult £6.50, Concession £6, Family (2+2) £17, Groups (15+) £5.50.

Key facts: No indoor photography Partial. WCs. Licensed. Licensed. By arrangement. Guide dogs only.

CASTLE ASHBY GARDENS

Castle Ashby, Northampton NN7 1LQ

Castle Ashby House is the ancestral home of the 7th Marquis of Northampton. The house is set amidst a 10,000 acre working estate with an extensive 25 acres of gardens which are open to the public 365 days a year.

A children's playground with a wide selection of rare breed animals can also be found within the gardens and now include a tea room, plant centre and gift shop.

Location: MAP 7:D9. OS Ref. SP862 592. Castle Ashby is situated off the A428 between Northampton and Bedford, and is also accessible from the A45.

Contact: Mark Brooks–Head Gardener / Peter Cox–Assistant Head Gardener

Tel: 01604 695200 **E-mail:** markbrooks@castleashby.co.uk

Website: www.castleashbygardens.co.uk

Open: 1 Apr–30 Sept, 10am–5.30pm. 1 Oct–31 Mar, 10am–4.30pm.

Admission: Adults: £5, OAP/children over 10 £4.50, Family £16, and children under 10 free.

Key facts: Disabled Access. Guide tours available. Booking required. Length of visit: 2–3 hours.

HADDONSTONE SHOW GARDENS

The Forge House, Church Lane, East Haddon, Northampton NN6 8DB

See Haddonstone's classic garden ornaments in the beautiful setting of the walled manor gardens including: planters, fountains, statuary, birdbaths, sundials and balustrading–even an orangery and other landscape follies. As featured on BBC Gardeners' World. New features include a statue walk, contemporary garden and wildflower meadow. Gastro pub nearby.

Location: MAP 7:B8, OS Ref. SP667 682. 7m NW of Northampton off A428. Signposted.

Tel: 01604 770711 **Fax:** 01604 770027 **E-mail:** info@haddonstone.co.uk

Website: www.haddonstone.com

Open: Mon–Fri, 9am–5.30pm. Closed weekends, BHs & Christmas period. Check press or website for details of NGS weekend openings.

Admission: Free. Groups by appointment only. Not suitable for coach parties.

Key facts: No photography without permission. Suitable. By arrangement. Limited, no coaches. Guide dogs only. Weekend opening for National Garden Scheme. See press or website for details.

LYVEDEN NEW BIELD

Nr Oundle, Northamptonshire PE8 5AT

An incomplete Elizabethan garden house and moated garden. Begun in 1595 by Sir Thomas Tresham to symbolise his Catholic faith, Lyveden remains virtually unaltered since work stopped when Tresham died in 1605. Fascinating Elizabethan architectural detail; remains of one of the oldest garden layouts; set amongst beautiful open countryside.

Location: MAP 7:D7, OS141, SP983 853. 4m SW of Oundle via A427. 3m E of Brigstock, off Harley Way.

Owner: National Trust **Contact:** Operations Manager **Tel:** 01832 205358

E-mail: lyveden@nationaltrust.org.uk **Website:** www.nationaltrust.org.uk/lyveden

Open: House & Garden: 31 Jan–30 Nov, Sat & Sun, 11am–4pm, 1 Mar–31 Oct, Wed–Sun, 10.30am–5pm. Jun–Sept, daily 10.30am–5pm.

Admission: Adult £5, Child Free. *Includes a voluntary donation. Visitors can choose to pay the standard prices displayed at the property.

Key facts: Partial. By arrangement. Limited for coaches. On leads.

SOUTHWICK HALL

Nr Oundle, Peterborough PE8 5BL

A family home since 1300, retaining medieval building dating from 1300, with Tudor rebuilding and 18th century additions. Exhibitions: Archives changing each year, Victorian and Edwardian Life, collections of agricultural and carpentry tools and local archaeological finds.

Location: MAP 7:E7, OS Ref. TL022 921. 3m N of Oundle, 4m E of Bulwick.

Owner: Christopher Capron

Contact: G Bucknill

Tel: 01832 274064

E-mail: southwickhall@hotmail.co.uk

Website: www.southwickhall.co.uk

Open: BH Suns & Mons: 8/9 Apr; 6/7 May; 3/4 Jun; 26/27 Aug; 9 Sept under HOD scheme; all 2–5pm; last admission 4.30pm.

Admission: House & Grounds: Adult £7, Child £3.50

Key facts: Partial By arrangement

STOKE PARK PAVILIONS

Stoke Bruerne, Towcester, Northamptonshire NN12 7RZ

The two Pavilions, dated c1630 and attributed to Inigo Jones, formed part of the first Palladian country house built in England by Sir Francis Crane. The central block, to which the Pavilions were linked by quadrant colonnades, was destroyed by fire in 1886. The grounds include extensive gardens and overlooks former parkland, now being restored.

Location: MAP 7:C10, OS Ref. SP740 488. 7m S of Northampton.

Owner/Contact: A S Chancellor Esq

Tel: 01604 862329 or 07768 230325

Open: Aug: daily, 3–6pm. Other times by appointment only.

Admission: Adult £3, Child £1.50.

Key facts: Grounds. Limited. In grounds, on leads.

WAKEFIELD LODGE

Potterspury, Northamptonshire NN12 7QX

Georgian hunting lodge with deer park.

Location: MAP 7:C10, OS Ref. SP739 425. 4m S of Towcester on A5. Take signs to farm shop for directions.

Owner/Contact: Mrs J Richmond-Watson

Tel: 01327 811395

Fax: 01327 811051

Open: House: 18 Apr–31 May: Mon–Fri (closed BHs), 12 noon–4pm. Appointments by telephone. Access walk open Apr & May.

Admission: £5

Key facts: No photography. Obligatory. Guide dogs only.

WESTON HALL

Towcester, Northamptonshire NN12 8PU

This is a small Northamptonshire manor house with an interesting collection much of which is associated with the literary Sitwell family.

Location: MAP 7:B10, OS Ref. SP592 469, five miles west of Towcester.

Owner: Mrs Sitwell

Contact: Mrs Sitwell

Tel: 01295 768212

E-mail: susanna.sitwell@uwclub.net

Open: Throughout the year by prior written appointment. Heritage Open Days 12–13 Sept.

Admission: £8. No charge on Heritage Open Days.

Key facts: No photography. Obligatory. Limited. On leads.

© NT / Clumber Park / Judith Unell

CLUMBER PARK

Clumber Park, Worksop, Nottinghamshire S80 3AZ

www.nationaltrust.org.uk/clumberpark

Once the country estate of the Dukes of Newcastle, today Clumber offers freedom to discover a haven for wildlife within glimpses of its grand past – from the 'cathedral in miniature' and pleasure ground to the Walled Kitchen Garden where you can experience sights, scents and a taste of the past.

Location: MAP 7:B2, OS120 Ref SK625 745. 4.5m SE of Worksop, 6½m SW of Retford, just off A1/A57 via A614. 11m from M1/J30.

Owner: National Trust **Contact:** Visitor Enquiries Point

Tel: 01909 544917 **Fax:** 01909 500721

E-mail: clumberpark@nationaltrust.org.uk

Open: Parkland and visitor facilities (Cafe, Shop, Plant Sales, Cycle Hire Centre, Discovery Centre) Barkers Restaurant: Weds–Sun, throughout the year. Walled Kitchen Garden: 17 Mar–28 Oct, daily. See website or contact property for details. **Admission:** Vehicle £5.70. Walled Kitchen Garden: Adults £3, children free. NT members free. **Key facts:** WCs, level or ramped access. Licensed. Special interest tours, available for an additional fee. Separate coach parking. Must be on leads in Walled Kitchen Garden, Pleasure Grounds and grazing areas.

HODSOCK PRIORY GARDENS

Blyth, Nr Worksop, Blyth S81 0TY

Celebrating 21 years of Snowdrops at Hodsock. Roam around our Historic Gardens and Woods from 4 Feb–4 Mar 2012 as we welcome the first glimpse of spring. Short Breaks from £95 in our award-winning 5* B&B - an overnight stay for two and afternoon tea in our café bar.

Location: MAP 7:B1, OS Ref. SK612 853. W of B6045 Worksop/Blyth road, 1m SW of Blyth, less than 2m from A1.

Owner: Sir Andrew & Lady Buchanan

Contact: George Buchanan

Tel: 01909 591204

Website: www.snowdrops.co.uk

Open: 4 Feb–4 Mar 2012, 10am–4pm.

Admission: Adult £5, accompanied Child (6–16yrs) £1.

Key facts: Heritage shop.

PAPPLEWICK HALL

Papplewick, Nottinghamshire NG15 8FE

A beautiful classic Georgian house, built of Mansfield stone, set in parkland, with woodland garden laid out in the 18th century. The house is notable for its very fine plasterwork, and elegant staircase. Grade I listed.

Location: MAP 7:B3, OS Ref. SK548 518. Half way between Nottingham & Mansfield, 3m E of M1/J27. A608 & A611 towards Hucknall. Then A6011 to Papplewick and B683 N for ½m

Owner: Mr & Mrs J R Godwin-Austen

Tel: 0115 9632623

E-mail: mail@papplewickhall.co.uk

Website: www.papplewickhall.co.uk

Open: 1st, 3rd & 5th Wed in each month 2–5pm, and by appointment.

Admission: Adult £5. Groups (10+): £4.

Key facts: No photography. Obligatory. Limited for coaches. In grounds, on leads.

© NTPL / David Noton

Allium heads and herbaceous geranium in the border of the walled kitchen garden at Clumber Park, Nottinghamshire.

Upton Cressett

Warwick Castle

Heart of England

Herefordshire

Shropshire

Staffordshire

Warwickshire

West Midlands

Worcestershire

Stafford-
shire
Shropshire
West Midlands
Worcester-
shire
Warwick-
shire
Herefordshire

Visit old favourites like Warwick Castle where elegant rooms, special events and battle re-enactments bring over 1000 years of history to life. Upton Cressett Hall is a romantic Elizabethan manor set in unspoilt Shropshire countryside, while the 12 acre Dorothy Clive Garden in Staffordshire is a delight for the discerning garden visitor. Take an exciting step back into Birmingham's industrial past by visiting the last remaining courtyard of Back to Back houses, or take a tour of Little Malvern Court, a 15th century former Benedictine Monastery with a fascinating collection of religious vestments and relics.

VISITOR INFORMATION

Owner
Mr J Hervey-Bathurst

Address
Eastnor Castle
Nr Ledbury
Herefordshire HR8 1RL

Location
MAP 6:M10
OS Ref. SO735 368

2m SE of Ledbury on the A438 Tewkesbury road. Alternatively M50/J2 & from Ledbury take the A449/A438.

Tewkesbury 20 mins, Malvern 20 mins, Gloucester 25 mins, Hereford 25 mins, Worcester 30 mins, Cheltenham 30 mins, B'ham 1 hr, London 2¼ hrs.

Taxi: Richard James 07836 777196.

Contact
Castle Office
Tel: 01531 633160
Fax: 01531 631776
E-mail: enquiries@eastnorcastle.com

Opening Times
Easter Weekend: Fri 6, Sat 7, Sun 8 & BH Mon 9 April.

May/June Bank Holiday Weekends: Sun 6, Mon 7 & Sun 3, Mon 4, Tues 5 June. Every Sunday from 10 June–30 September.

Sun–Thurs from 15 July–30 August.

Admission

Castle & Grounds	
Adult	£9.00
Seniors	£8.00
Child (3-15yrs)	£6.00
Family (2+3)	£24.00
Grounds only	
Adult	£6.00
Seniors	£5.00
Child (3-15yrs)	£4.00
Family (2+3)	£16.00
Groups (20+)	
Guided	£11.00
Non-Guided	£7.50
Schools	£6.50
Groups (40+)	
Guided	£10.50
Non-Guided	£7.25

Privilege Pass
Valid for 1 year and includes all Castle special events (apart from theatre productions)

Adult	£24.00
Child (3–15yrs)	£15.00
OAP	£21.00
Family (2+3)	£63.00

Special events
See website for further details and to pre-book discounted tickets on-line.

Conference/Function

ROOM	Size	Max Cap
Great Hall	16 x 8m	150
Dining Rm	11 x 7m	80
Gothic Rm	11 x 7m	80
Octagon Rm	9 x 9m	50

EASTNOR CASTLE

www.eastnorcastle.com

A magnificent Georgian Castle dramatically situated in the foothills of the Malverns, surrounded by a beautiful lake and arboretum.

In the style of a medieval Welsh-border fortress, Eastnor Castle was built in the early 19th century by John First Earl Somers and is a good example of the great Norman and Gothic revival in architecture of that time. The Castle is dramatically situated in a 5000 acre estate in the Malvern Hills and remains the family home of the Hervey-Bathursts, his direct descendants.

This fairytale home is as dramatic inside as it is outside. A vast, 60' high Hall leads to a series of State Rooms including a Gothic Drawing Room designed by Pugin, with its original furniture, and a Library in the style of the Italian Renaissance, with views across the Lake. The Hervey-Bathursts have lovingly restored the interiors and many of the Castle's treasures which have been buried away in the cellars and attics since the Second World War – early Italian Fine Art, medieval armour, 17th century Venetian furniture, Flemish tapestries and paintings by Van Dyck, Reynolds, Romney and Watts and early photographs by Julia Margaret Cameron.

Gardens

Castellated terraces descend to a 21 acre lake with a restored lakeside walk. The arboretum holds a famous collection of mature specimen trees. There are spectacular views of the Malvern Hills across a 300 acre deer park, once part of a mediaeval chase and now designated a Site of Special Scientific Interest. The gardens also have a knight's maze, tree trail, children's adventure playground and junior assault course.

Exclusive use for weddings, private and corporate events.

KEY FACTS

- Corporate events – off-road driving, team building, private dinners, exclusive hire, public events.
- Gift shop open on public open days, also on-line shop.
- Product launches, TV and feature films, concerts and charities.
- Wheelchair stairclimber to main state rooms.
- Licensed.
- By arrangement, Mons & Tues all year, outside normal opening hours.
- Ample 10–200 yds from Castle. Coaches phone in advance to arrange parking & catering. Tearoom voucher for drivers.
- Guides available.
- On leads.
- Exclusive use accommodation.
- Exclusive use for weddings.

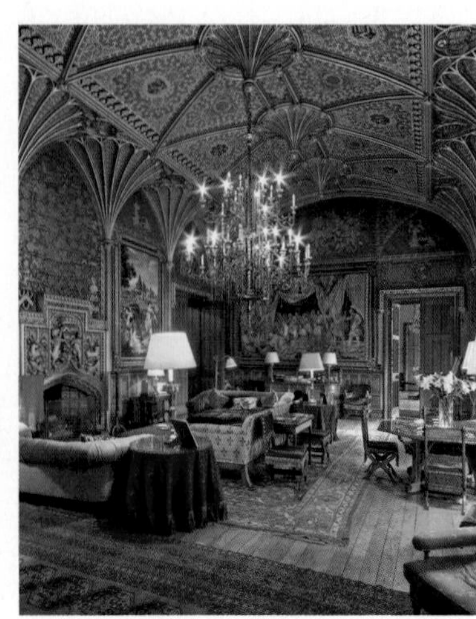

© English Heritage

© English Heritage

GOODRICH CASTLE ⌗

ROSS-ON-WYE HR9 6HY

www.english-heritage.org.uk/goodrich

The castle was begun in the 11th century by the English thegn Godric who gave the castle its name. Dramatically set on a rocky outcrop with stunning views over the Wye Valley, Goodrich Castle gives a fascinating insight into life in a medieval castle boasting one of the most complete sets of medieval domestic buildings surviving in any English castle. Climb to the battlements for wonderful views and learn about the murder holes built into the castle walls. Finally, relax in our delightful castle café, and take in the views of the beautiful surroundings.

Location: MAP 6:L11, OS162 Ref. SO577 200. 5m S of Ross-on-Wye, off A40.

Owner: English Heritage **Contact:** Visitor Operations Team

Tel: 01600 890538 **E-mail:** customers@english-heritage.org.uk

Open: Please visit www.english-heritage.org.uk for opening times and the most up-to-date information.

Admission: Adult £5.80, Child £3.50, Conc. £5.20, Family £15.10. Discount for groups (11+). EH Members Free. Opening times and prices are valid until 31 Mar 2012.

Key facts: WC. Guidebooks. Hazardous. Ovp. £2 parking, refundable upon admission. Family learning resources available. On leads.

HELLENS

MUCH MARCLE, LEDBURY, HEREFORDSHIRE HR8 2LY

Built as a monastery and then a stone fortress in 1292 by Mortimer, Earl of March, with Tudor, Jacobean and Stuart additions and lived in ever since by descendants of the original builder. Visited by the Black Prince, Bloody Mary and the 'family ghost'. Paintings, relics and heirlooms from the Civil War and possessions of the Audleys, Walwyns and Whartons as well as Anne Boleyn. Beautiful 17th century woodwork carved by the 'King's Carpenter', John Abel. These historical stories incorporated into guided tours, revealing the loves and lives of those who lived and died here. Goods and chattels virtually unchanged.

Location: MAP 6:M10, OS Ref. SO661 332. Off A449 at Much Marcle. Ledbury 4m, Ross-on-Wye 4m.

Owner: Pennington-Mellor-Munthe Charity Trust

Contact: The Administrator **Tel:** 01531 660504

Open: 8 Apr–30 Sept: Wed, Thur, Sun & BH Mons. Guided tours only at 2pm, 3pm & 4pm. Other times by arrangement with the Administrator.

Admission: Adult £6, Child £3, Concession £4.50, Family £12.

Key facts: No photography inside house. Obligatory.

HERGEST CROFT GARDENS

Kington, Herefordshire HR5 3EG

www.hergest.co.uk

Garden for all seasons; from bulbs to spectacular autumn colour includes spring and summer borders, roses, azaleas and an old-fashioned kitchen garden growing unusual vegetables. Brightly coloured rhododendrons 30ft high grow in Park Wood. Over 60 champion trees set in 70 acres of spectacular countryside of the Welsh Marches.

Location: OS Ref. SO281 565. Follow brown tourist signs along A44 to Rhayader.

Owner: E J Banks **Contact:** Mrs Melanie Lloyd **Tel:** 01544 230160

Fax: 01544 232031 **E-mail:** gardens@hergest.co.uk

Open: March: Sats & Suns. 1 Apr–31 Oct: daily, 12 noon–5.30pm. Season tickets and groups by arrangement throughout the year.

Admission: Adult £6, Child (under 16yrs) Free. Pre-booked groups (20+) £5. Season ticket £25.

Key facts: Rare plants. Partial. WCs. By arrangement. Guide dogs only. Flower Fair, Mon 7 May 10.30am–5pm Plant Fair, Sun 14 Oct 10.30am–4.30pm Contact website for other events.

KINNERSLEY CASTLE

Kinnersley, Herefordshire HR3 6QF

www.kinnersleycastle.co.uk

Marches castle renovated around 1580. Still a family home; many interesting owners with unusual connections. Fine plasterwork solar ceiling. Organic gardens with specimen trees including one of Britain's largest gingkos.

Location: MAP 6:K9, OS Ref. SO3460 4950. A4112 Leominster to Brecon road, castle drive behind Kinnersley village sign on left.

Owner: Katherina Garratt-Adams

Contact: Katherina Garratt-Adams

Tel: 01544 327407

E-mail: katherina@kinnersleycastle.co.uk

Open: Contact local Tourist Information Office or check Kinnersley Castle website.

Admission: Adult £5.50. Child £2. Concs. & Groups over 8: £4.50.

Key facts: No indoor photography. Coach parties by arrangement throughout year. Unsuitable. Obligatory.

BERRINGTON HALL

Berrington Hall, Nr Leominster, Herefordshire HR6 0DW

Austere exterior belies the lavishness of the interior.

Location: MAP 6:L8, OS Ref. OS137 SP510 637. 3m N of Leominster, 7m S of Ludlow on W side of A49.

Owner: National Trust **Contact:** The Property Manager

Tel: 01568 615721 **Fax:** 01568 613263

HEREFORD CATHEDRAL

Mappa Mundi and Chained Library Exhibition. Hereford HR1 2NG

The newly restored Cathedral Close preserves the elegance of a place of worship used since Saxon times. Art and architecture from Norman times to the present day including the medieval shrine of St Thomas, Mappa Mundi (the spectacular medieval map of the world) and historic Chained Library.

Location: MAP 6:L10, OS Ref. SO510 398. Hereford city centre on A49.

Contact: The Visits Manager **Tel:** 01432 374202 **Fax:** 01432 374220

E-mail: visits@herefordcathedral.org **Website:** www.herefordcathedral.org

Open: Cathedral: Daily, 7.30am–Evensong. Exhibition: Easter–Oct: Mon–Sat, 10am–4.30pm. Nov–Easter: Mon–Sat, 10am–3.30pm. Sundays subject to change, please telephone to check before you visit.

Admission: Admission for Mappa Mundi Exhibition: Adult £6, Cons £5, Family £14, Small Family £10, Child under 5yrs Free.

Key facts:

LANGSTONE COURT

Llangarron, Ross on Wye, Herefordshire HR9 6NR

Mostly late 17th century house with older parts. Interesting staircases, panelling and ceilings. **Location:** MAP 6:L11, OS Ref. SO534 221. Ross on Wye 5m, Llangarron 1m. **Owner/Contact:** R M C Jones Esq **Tel:** 01989 770254

Open: 20 May–31 Aug: Wed & Thur, 11am–2.30pm, also spring & summer BHs.

Admission: Free.

OLD SUFTON

Mordiford, Hereford HR1 4EJ

A 16th century manor house which was altered and remodelled in the 18th and 19th centuries and again in this century. The original home of the Hereford family (see Sufton Court) who have held the manor since the 12th century.

Location: MAP 6:L10, OS Ref. SO575 384. Mordiford, off B4224 Mordiford–Dormington road.

Owner: Trustees of Sufton Heritage Trust **Contact:** Mr & Mrs J N Hereford

Tel: 01432 870268 / 01432 850328 **Fax:** 01432 850381

E-mail: jameshereford@waitrose.com

Open: By written appointment to Sufton Court or by fax or email.

Admission: Adult £5, Child 50p.

Key facts: Partial. Obligatory. Small school groups. No special facilities.

SUFTON COURT

Mordiford, Hereford HR1 4LU

Sufton Court is a small Palladian mansion house. Built in 1788 by James Wyatt for James Hereford. The park was laid out by Humphry Repton whose 'red book' still survives. The house stands above the rivers Wye and Lugg giving impressive views towards the mountains of Wales.

Location: MAP 6:L10, OS Ref. SO574 379. Mordiford, off B4224 on Mordiford–Dormington road.

Owner: J N Hereford **Contact:** Mr & Mrs J N Hereford

Tel: 01432 870268 / 01432 850328 **Fax:** 01432 850381

E-mail: jameshereford@waitrose.com

Open: 15–28 May & 14–27 Aug: 2–5pm. Guided tours: 2, 3 & 4pm.

Admission: Adult £5, Child 50p.

Key facts: Obligatory. Only small coaches. Small school groups. No special facilities. In grounds, on leads.

UPTON CRESSETT HALL

www.uptoncressetthall.co.uk

Moated, romantic Elizabethan manor with 14th century Great Hall and turreted gatehouse set in unspoilt Shropshire countryside near market towns of Bridgnorth and Ludlow.

Located next to a fine Norman church, Upton Cressett's gatehouse, featuring original oak spiral staircase and rare 16th century ornamental plasterwork, has been likened to the Sissinghurst Tower. The property was admired by Pevsner and is included in Simon Jenkins' Best Houses of Britain who described it as an 'Elizabethan gem'. Country Life describes Upton Cressett as 'a splendid example of the English manor house at its most evocative'.

The Hall, the oldest dated brick manor in Shropshire, was the historic home of the Cressett family before Bill Cash MP and his family began living there in 1971. The young king Edward V stayed in 1483 from Ludlow on his way to the Tower. In the Civil War, Sir Francis Cressett was Treasurer to Charles I and Prince Rupert stayed in the gatehouse, as did Margaret Thatcher in the 20th century. The gatehouse has a secret tunnel and is also home to the Upton Cressett Foundation.

The Hall has fine 16th century furniture and portraits as well as modern art. Of special interest is the restored Great Hall dining room with a unique Tudor hand-painted ceiling, and main newel stair reminiscent of Knole, completed by the artist Adam Dant, winner of the Jerwood Prize. His unique series of murals and work in the Elizabethan garden have been acclaimed by Country Life as 'remarkable' and 'daring'. The extensive gardens are being transformed in a project led by the celebrated gardener and writer Dr Katherine Swift.

The spectacular gatehouse, one of the country's most romantic and luxuriously appointed hideaways, is also available for private let, being perfect for mini-breaks and honeymoons. The manor and grounds are available for weddings, receptions, events, concerts and filming. The property can accommodate groups (such as corporate retreats or art tours) of up to sixteen people in a unique, secluded and inspirational historic atmosphere.

KEY FACTS

No photography in the house.

Corporate retreats and events, including full dining facilities in the great hall dining room for up to 24.
Receptions for up to 200 can be hosted in luxury marquees in the moated garden or the Gatehouse lawn.

Tea room on all daily open days and pre-booked lunches for groups of over ten.

Ample.

On leads.

Single & en suites.

€

VISITOR INFORMATION

Owner
William Cash

Address
Upton Cressett Hall
Bridgnorth
Shropshire WV16 6UH

Location
MAP 6:M7
OS Ref. OS506 592

Birmingham 35 miles.
Ludlow 17 miles.
Three miles west of Bridgnorth off A458 towards Shrewsbury. Nearest village is Morville. See website for map.

Rail: Wolverhampton (1 hr 40 mins from Euston, trains at 23 minutes past every hour).

Taxi: (Brambles, 01746 767076).

Contact
The Administrator
Tel: (Office) 01746 714616
E-mail: enquiries@uptoncressett.co.uk

Opening Times
1 April–30 September, Sunday (2–5pm), Wednesday and Thursday and all BH Mondays (11.30am–5pm).

Last entry all days 4.30pm.

Tearoom (including home-made cakes and sandwiches) open from 12–4.30pm. There is also a farm shop and gift shop.

The historic 12th century church of St Michael, Upton Cressett, (www.visitchurches.org.uk), with rare medieval frescos, is adjacent to the manor.

Admission
Hall, gardens and guided house tour:

Adult:	£6.50
Child (0-5 years):	free
Child (5-16):	£3.50
Senior: (65 & over):	£5.00

*gatehouse is normally open but please check website.

Gardens only:

Adult:	£4.00
Child (5-16):	£2.00
Senior:	£3.50

Special events
Tours:
Owner led tours (including specialist history tours by Bill Cash) are available all year for groups (over 15) with tea and cake served in the Great Hall dining room.

Exhibition:
Permanent exhibition featuring the work of Adam Dant, archive photography from the restoration of Upton Cressett (1971-2011) and history of Cressett family.

Concerts, literary talks and open air theatre:
Please check website for all special events.

Banqueting and private events:
VIP lunches, dinners, banquets and other events (weddings, corporate away days etc) are available in the Hall or in a marquee on the Gatehouse Lawn or Moat Lawn.

VISITOR INFORMATION

Owner
The Weston Park Foundation

Address
Weston Park
Weston-under-Lizard
Nr Shifnal
Shropshire TF11 8LE

Location
MAP 6:N6
OS Ref. SJ808 107

Birmingham 40 mins. Manchester 1 hr. Motorway access M6/J12 or M54/J3 and via the M6 Toll road J11A. House situated on A5 at Weston-under-Lizard.

Rail: Nearest Railway Stations: Wolverhampton, Stafford or Telford.

Air: Birmingham, West Midlands, Manchester.

Contact
Kate Thomas
Tel: 01952 852100
Fax: 01952 850430
E-mail: enquiries@weston-park.com

Opening Times
Open daily from Saturday 26 May–Sunday 2 September.

Except 15–22 August. House is closed on Saturdays.

Admission
Park & Gardens

Adult	£5.00
Child (3–14yrs)	£3.00
Family (2+3 or 1+4)	£22.00
OAP	£4.50
House admission	+£3.00

Groups (Parks & Gardens)

Adult	£4.00
Child (3–14yrs)	£3.00
OAP	£4.00
House admission	+£2.00

Granary Farm Shop & Art Gallery
Free entry and open all year round.

Granary Grill, Bar & Restaurant
Open daily, all year round, for lunch and dinner.

Prices are correct at the time of going to print.

Conference/Function

ROOM	Size	Max Cap
Dining Room	52' x 23'	90
Orangery	56'1" x 22'4"	120
Music Room	55' x 17'	60
The Hayloft	32' x 22'	40
Doncaster	49' x 18'7"	80

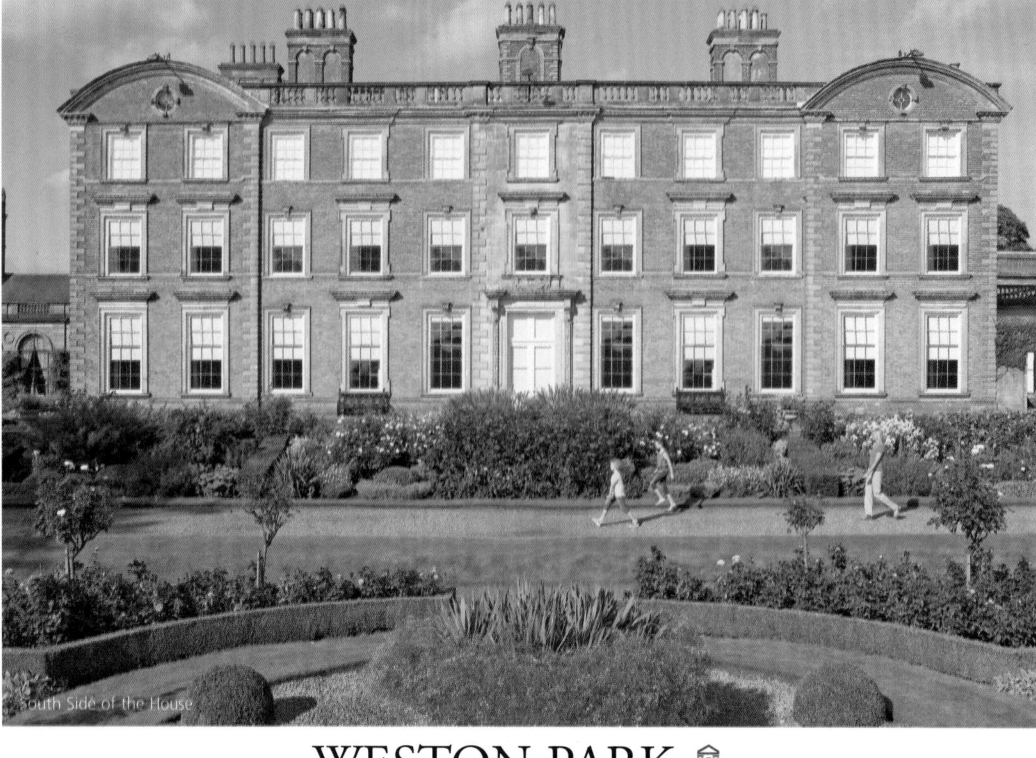
South Side of the House

WESTON PARK

www.weston-park.com

Weston Park is a magnificent Stately Home and Parkland situated on the Shropshire/Staffordshire border.

The former home of the Earls of Bradford, the park is now held in trust for the nation by the Weston Park Foundation.

Built in 1671 by Lady Elizabeth Wilbraham, this warm and welcoming house boasts internationally important paintings, including work by Van Dyck, Gainsborough and Stubbs, furniture and objets d'art, providing continued interest and enjoyment for all its visitors.

Step outside to enjoy the 1,000 acres of glorious Parkland, take one of a variety of woodland and wildlife walks, all landscaped by the legendary 'Capability' Brown in the 18th century.

Relax in the Stables Coffee Bar with coffee, sandwiches and homemade cake. With the exciting Woodland Adventure Playground, Orchard and Deer Park, as well as the Miniature Railway, there is so much for children to do.

The Granary Farm Shop stocks the best in locally produced food and drink and the Art Gallery stages a series of exciting changing exhibitions throughout the year.

The Granary Grill, Bar & Restaurant sizzles up lunch and dinner seven days a week and is open all year round.

The House can be hired on an exclusive use basis for corporate hospitality, meetings, weddings and private parties.

KEY FACTS

- Interior photography by prior arrangement only.
- Gift Shop.
- Full event organisation service. Residential parties, special dinners, wedding receptions.
- House and part of the grounds. WCs.
- Licensed.
- The Stables provides light snacks. Licensed. Granary Grill, Bar & Restaurant.
- By arrangement.
- Ample free parking.
- Award-winning educational programme available during all academic terms. Private themed visits aligned with both National Curriculum and QCA targets.
- In grounds, on leads.
- Weston Park offers 28 delightful bedrooms with bathrooms (25 doubles & 3 singles) 17 en suite.

Entrance Hall

Granary Grill, Bar & Restaurant

© NTPL / Matthew Antrobus

© NTPL / David Levenson

ATTINGHAM PARK

ATCHAM, SHREWSBURY, SHROPSHIRE SY4 4TP

www.nationaltrust.org.uk/attinghampark

Attingham, former home of the Berwicks', reflects the Regency splendour of England with richly furnished rooms and is surrounded by beautiful parkland with walled garden and deer park. But physical structures are only part of the story - Attingham has been the setting for romantic love and despair, accumulated fortunes, followed by flamboyant overspending, bankruptcy and desertion. Now stunning developments in the mansion and walled garden are part of the Attingham Re-discovered project of conservation and restoration. Highlights include the atmospheric evening banquet in the Dining Room, the delicate feminine Boudoir and the rich, opulent textiles of the masculine Octagon-Room.

Location: MAP 6:L6, OS Ref. 127 SJ837 083. 4m SE of Shrewsbury on N side of B4380 in Atcham village.

Owner: National Trust **Contact:** The Property Administrator

Tel: 01743 708170 / 162 **Fax:** 01743 708155 **Infoline:** 01743 708123

E-mail: attingham@nationaltrust.org.uk

Open: Mansion: 10 Mar–4 Nov: Daily 11am–12.30pm, guided tours only, 12.30–5.30pm free flow. Last admission 4.30pm. Weekend Winter Tours: 7 Jan–4 Mar & 10–25 Nov, Sat & Sun 11am–2pm. Mansion Christmas opening: 8 & 9 & 15–23 Dec, 11am–4pm. Last admission 3.30pm. Park, Walled Garden and Café: Open daily except Christmas Day from 9am.

Admission: NT Members and under 5s free. House & Grounds: Adult £9.90, Child £5.80, Family £22. Park & Walled Garden: Adult £4.50, Child £2.40, Family £11.40. Groups discount: 15%, Includes voluntary Gift Aid donation, execpt for group prices.

Key facts: Attingham Re-discovered conservation and restoration programme. Range of walks. Produce for sale when in season. High-tea in the mansion's Lady B's. No unaccompanied children. Includes plants grown by volunteers. WCs. Licensed. Available from 11am. Can be booked upon arrival. Private Guided Tours must be prebooked. Large range of guided and selfguide educational tours. Pre-booking essential. In grounds.

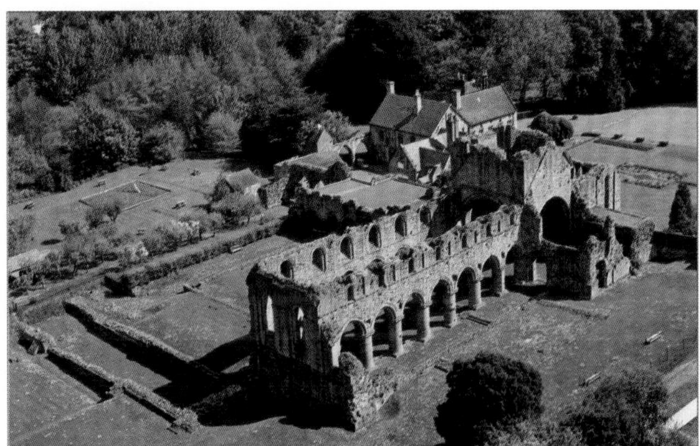

BUILDWAS ABBEY

Iron Bridge, Telford, Shropshire TF8 7BW

www.english-heritage.org.uk/buildwas

Extensive remains of a Cistercian abbey built in 1135, set beside the River Severn against a backdrop of wooded grounds. The remains include the church which is almost complete except for the roof.

Location: MAP 6:M6, OS127, SJ643 043. On S bank of River Severn on A4169, 2m W of Ironbridge.

Owner: English Heritage

Contact: Visitor Operations Team

Tel: 01952 433274

E-mail: customers@english-heritage.org.uk

Open: Please visit www.english-heritage.org.uk for opening times and the most up-to-date information.

Admission: Adult £3.40, Child £2, Conc. £3.10. EH Members free. Group discount available. Opening times and prices are valid until 31 Mar 2012.

Key facts: Guidebooks. Hazardous. Ovp.

On leads.

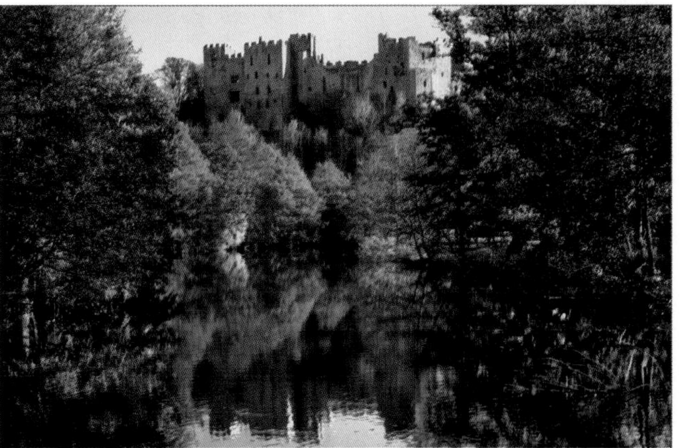

LUDLOW CASTLE

Castle Square, Ludlow, Shropshire SY8 1AY

www.ludlowcastle.com

This magnificent ruin, extended over the centuries to a fortified Royal Palace and seat of the government. Privately owned by the Earls of Powis since 1811. Castle Tea Rooms serve fresh foods. The Beacon Rooms are available for Civil weddings. Three self-catering holiday apartments - ideal for staying in Ludlow.

Location: MAP 6:L8, OS Ref. SO509 745. Shrewsbury 28m, Hereford 26m. A49 centre of Ludlow.

Owner: The Earl of Powis & The Trustees of the Powis Estates

Contact: Helen J Duce (Custodian)

Tel: 01584 873355 / 874465 **E-mail:** info@ludlowcastle.com

Open: Jan & Dec: Sat & Sun, 10am–4pm, Feb–Mar & Oct–Nov: daily, 10am–4pm. Apr–Sept: daily, 10am–5pm (7pm Aug). Daily 26 Dec–1 Jan. Last adm. 30mins before closing. Closed Christmas Day.

Admission: Adult £5, Child £2.50, Conc. £4.50, Family £13.50. 10% reduction for groups (10+).

Key facts: Partial. WCs. Licensed. By arrangement. None. Guide dogs only. Rated 4*-5* enjoyEngland.com

MAWLEY HALL

Cleobury Mortimer DY14 8PN

www.mawley.com

Built in 1730 and attributed to Francis Smith of Warwick, Mawley is set in 18th century landscaped parkland with extensive gardens and walks down to the River Rea. Magnificent plasterwork and a fine collection of English and Continental furniture and porcelain.

Location: MAP 6:L8, OS137, SO688 753. 1m N of Cleobury Mortimer on the A4117 and 7m W of Bewdley.

Owner: R Galliers-Pratt Esq

Contact: Mrs R Sharp

Tel: 0208 298 0429

Fax: 0208 303 0717

E-mail: rsharp@mawley.com

Open: 16 Apr–19 Jul: Mons & Thurs, 3–5pm and throughout the year by appointment.

Admission: £10.

Key facts: By arrangement.

STOKESAY COURT

Onibury, Craven Arms, Shropshire SY7 9BD

www.stokesaycourt.com

Unspoilt and secluded, Stokesay Court is an imposing late Victorian mansion with Jacobean style façade, magnificent interiors and extensive grounds containing a grotto, woodland and interconnected pools. Set deep in the beautiful rolling green landscape of South Shropshire near Ludlow, the house and grounds featured as the Tallis Estate in the award winning film 'Atonement'.

Location: MAP 6:K7, SO444 786. A49 Between Ludlow and Craven Arms.

Owner/Contact: Ms Caroline Magnus **Tel:** 01584 856238

E-mail: info@stokesaycourt.com

Open: Guided tours Apr–Oct for booked groups (20+). Groups (up to 60) can be accommodated. Tours for individuals take place on dates advertised on website. Booking essential. Tours are usually taken by the owner.

Admission: Adult £15pp to include light refreshments (full catering service available on request).

Key facts: No stilettos. No photography in house. Partial. WCs. Obligatory. Guide dogs only. €

© English Heritage

STOKESAY CASTLE

Nr Craven Arms, Shropshire SY7 9AH

www.english-heritage.org.uk/stokesaycastle

Nestling in a green valley in the heart of Shropshire, Stokesay is England's most delightful fortified medieval manor. This beautiful house dates to the 11th century with a great hall that has remained unaltered since 1291. An audio tour will help to bring the history of the castle to life.

Location: MAP 6:K7, OS148, SO446 787. 7m NW of Ludlow off A49.

Owner: English Heritage **Contact:** Visitor Operations Team

Tel: 01588 672544 **E-mail:** customers@english-heritage.org.uk

Open: Please visit www.english-heritage.org.uk for opening times and the most up-to-date information.

Admission: Adult £5.80, Child £3.50, Conc. £5.20, Family £15.10. 15% discount for groups (11+). EH Members free. Opening times and prices are valid until 31 Mar 2012.

Key facts: Guidebooks. Hazardous. Ovp. Family learning resources available.

© English Heritage

WENLOCK PRIORY

Much Wenlock, Shropshire TF13 6HS

www.english-heritage.org.uk/wenlockpriory

The remains of this medieval monastery are set on the edge of beautiful Much Wenlock. The priory's grandeur can be traced in the ruins of its 13th century church, ornate Norman chapter house and rare monk's wash house. These majestic ruins are set in green lawns and topiary.

Location: MAP 6:L6, OS127, SJ625 001. In Much Wenlock.

Owner: English Heritage **Contact:** Visitor Operations Team

Tel: 01952 727466

E-mail: customers@english-heritage.org.uk

Open: Please visit www.english-heritage.org.uk for opening times and the most up-to-date information.

Admission: Adult £4, Child £2.40, Conc. £3.60. EH Members free. Group discount available. Opening times and prices are valid until 31 Mar 2012.

Key facts: WC. Baby changing facilities. Gardens. Guidebooks. Ovp. On leads.

© English Heritage

WROXETER ROMAN CITY

Wroxeter, Shrewsbury, Shropshire SY5 6PH

www.english-heritage.org.uk/wroxeter

The part-excavated centre of the fourth largest city in Roman Britain, originally home to some 6,000 men and several hundred houses. Impressive remains of the 2nd century municipal baths. There is a site museum in which many finds are displayed, including those from work by Birmingham Field Archaeological Unit.
Location: MAP 6:L6, OS126, SJ565 087. At Wroxeter, 5m E of Shrewsbury, on B4380.
Owner: English Heritage **Contact:** Visitor Operations Team
Tel: 01743 761330 Email: customers@english-heritage.org.uk
Open: Please visit www.english-heritage.org.uk for opening times and the most up-to-date information.
Admission: Adult £4.80, Child £2.90, Conc. £4.30, Family £12.50. EH Members free. Group discount available. Opening times and prices are valid until 31 Mar 2012.
Key facts: WC. Museum. Hazard. Ovp. On leads.

COMBERMERE ABBEY

Whitchurch, Shropshire SY13 4AJ

Combermere Abbey, its large mere and 1000 acre park began as a Cistercian monastery, remodelled as a Tudor manor house and in 1820 as a Gothic house. Group tours include the restored Walled Gardens, The Glasshouse and Fruit Tree Maze. Excellent accommodation is available on the Estate.
Location: MAP 6:L4, OS Ref. SJ599 434. 5m E of Whitchurch, off A530.
Owner: Mrs S Callander Beckett **Contact:** Administrator **Tel:** 01948 662880
Fax: 01948 871604 **E-mail:** estate@combermereabbey.co.uk
Website: www.combermereabbey.co.uk
Open: 20 Mar-24 May: Tues/Weds/Thurs only for tours, 12 noon/2pm/4pm. Advance bookings necessary. Group visits (20–60) by arrangement.
Admission: On open days: Adult £5.50, Child (under 16yrs) £3.50. Group tours: £10.50 per person inclusive of refreshments.
Key facts: No photography inside the house. By arrangement. Parking for coaches limited. Guide dogs only. For groups. Annual Bluebell Walk & Open Gardens - Sun Apr 22 2012. 1–4.30pm.

COUND HALL

Cound, Shropshire SY5 6AH

Queen Anne red brick Hall. **Location:** MAP 6:L6, OS Ref. SJ560 053.
Owner: Mr & Mrs D R Waller **Contact:** Mrs J Stephens **Tel:** 01743 761721
Fax: 01743 761722 **Open:** Mon 13–Fri 17 Aug 2012, 10am–4pm.
Admission: Adult £4.50, Child £2.30, Conc. £3.40, Family £11.30.
Key facts: No photography. Limited.

DUDMASTON ESTATE

Quatt, Bridgnorth, Shropshire WV15 6QN

Covers 3500 acres with Dudmaston Hall and gardens.
Location: MAP 6:M7, OS Ref. SO748 888. 4m SE of Bridgnorth on A442.
Owner: National Trust **Contact:** The House & Visitor Services Manager
Tel: 01746 780866 **Fax:** 01746 780744

HODNET HALL GARDENS

Hodnet, Market Drayton, Shropshire TF9 3NN

The 60+ acres are renowned as amongst the finest in the country. Forest trees provide a wonderful backdrop for formal gardens planted to give delight during every season, with extensive woodland walks amongst wild flowers and unusual flowering shrubs along the banks of a chain of ornamental pools.
Location: MAP 6:L5, OS Ref. SJ613 286. 12m NE of Shrewsbury on A53; M6/J15, M54/J3.
Owner: Mr and the Hon Mrs Heber-Percy **Contact:** Secretary **Tel:** 01630 685786
Fax: 01630 685853 **E-mail:** secretary@heber-percy.freeserve.co.uk
Website: www.hodnethallgardens.org
Open: Apr 8, 9, 22 & 29. May 6, 7, 16, 20 & 27. Jun 3, 4, 17 & 24. Jul 4, 22 & 25. Aug 15, 26 & 27. Sept 9 & 19.
Admission: Adult £5. Children £2.50.
Key facts: Groups of 25+ at other times by appointment. Partial, WCs. Educational package linked to Key Stages 1 & 2 of National Curriculum. On leads.

LONGNER HALL

Uffington, Shrewsbury, Shropshire SY4 4TG

Designed by John Nash in 1803, Longner Hall is a Tudor Gothic style house set in a park landscaped by Humphry Repton. The home of one family for over 700 years. Longner's principal rooms are adorned with plaster fan vaulting and stained glass.
Location: MAP 6:L6, OS Ref. SJ529 110. 4m SE of Shrewsbury on Uffington road, 1/4m off B4380, Atcham.
Owner: Mr R L Burton **Contact:** Mrs R L Burton **Tel:** 01743 709215
Open: Apr–Sept: Tues & BH Mons, 2–5pm. Tours at 2pm & 3.30pm. Groups at any time by arrangement.
Admission: Adult £5, Child/OAP £3.
Key facts: No photography in house. Partial. Obligatory. Limited for coaches. By arrangement. Guide dogs only.

SHIPTON HALL

Much Wenlock, Shropshire TF13 6JZ

Built in 1587 the house remained in the Mytton family for 300 years. Georgian additions by Thomas Pritchard include elegant rococco interior decorations, also Tudor and Jacobean panelling. Family home. Visitors are welcome to explore the garden, dovecote and parish church dating back to Saxon times.
Location: MAP 6:L7, OS Ref. SO563 918. 7m SW of Much Wenlock on B4378. 10m W of Bridgnorth.
Owner: Mr J N R Bishop **Contact:** Mrs M J Bishop
Tel: 01746 785225 **E-mail:** mjanebishop@hotmail.co.uk
Open: Easter–end Sept: Thurs, 2.30–5.30pm. BH Suns/Mons, 2.30–5.30pm. Groups 20+ any time of day/year by prior arrangement.
Admission: Adult £5, Child (under 14yrs) £2.50. 10% Discount for groups (20+).
Key facts: Unsuitable. By arrangement for groups (20+). Obligatory. Guide dogs only.

THE WHITE HOUSE

Aston Munslow, Shropshire SY7 9ER

Dating back to the 13th century, with Tudor and Jacobean rooms, with wide oak floorboards and a jumble of pleasing windows.
Location: MAP 6:L7, OS Ref. SO510867.
Owner: The Landmark Trust
Contact: The Landmark Trust
Tel: 01628 825925
E-mail: bookings@landmarktrust.org.uk
Website: www.landmarktrust.org.uk
Open: Available for holidays up to 8 people. Other visits by appointment only.
Admission: Free on visits by appointment.
Key facts:

CHILLINGTON HALL

CODSALL WOOD, WOLVERHAMPTON, STAFFORDSHIRE WV8 1RE

www.chillingtonhall.co.uk

Home of the Giffards since 1178. Third house on the site. The present house was built during the 18th century, firstly by the architect Francis Smith of Warwick adding the South Wing to the Tudor House in 1724 and then completed by John Soane in 1786 replacing the Tudor House in its entirety. Parkland laid out by 'Capability' Brown in the 1760s with additional work by James Paine and possibly Robert Woods. Chillington was the winner of the HHA/Sotheby's Restoration Award 2009 for work done on Soane's magnificent Saloon. Brown's great showpiece The Pool with its follies can be seen by those who want more than a stroll in the garden.

Location: MAP 6:N6. OS Ref. SJ864 067. 2m S of Brewood off A449. 4m NW of M54/J2.

Owner/Contact: Mr & Mrs J W Giffard

Tel: 01902 850236

E-mail: info@chillingtonhall.co.uk

Open: House: Mon–Thur, 9 Apr–24 May, 2–5pm. Last entry 4pm. Grounds: As House. Parties by prior arrangement.

Admission: Adult £6, Child £3. Grounds only: half price.

Key facts: Available for corporate hospitality, meetings, weddings and other celebrations and photoshoots. The 18th century Stableblock and Model Farm have undergone substantial renovation and will shortly be available as a meeting room / educational facility, suitable for filming as well. WCs. Obligatory. Limited for coaches. In grounds. €

THE DOROTHY CLIVE GARDEN

WILLOUGHBRIDGE, MARKET DRAYTON, SHROPSHIRE TF9 4EU

www.dorothyclivegarden.co.uk

Stephen Lacey noted in The Garden under the title of 'The Season Starts Here' (RHS, March 2009); 'This 4.8ha (12 acre) hillside garden displays an extensive and discerningly chosen collection of perennials and bulbs around handsome scree and waterfall features. Highlights include the Quarry Garden's rhododendron and azalea collection'. The garden is quite simply a treasure trove for the plant enthusiast and a delightful discovery for the discerning garden visitor. Glorious framed views to the surrounding countryside punctuate the garden at regular intervals; whilst a network of criss-crossing paths provide for a stimulating and inspiring walk.

Location: MAP 6:M4, OS Ref. SJ753 400. A51, 2m S of Woore, 3m from Bridgemere.

Owner: The Willoughbridge Garden Trust

Contact: Administrator

Tel: 01630 647237 **E-mail:** info@dorothyclivegarden.co.uk

Open: Sat 31 Mar–Sun 30 Sept 2012, every day. 10am–5.30pm (last admissions at 4.30pm).

Admission: Adult £6.30, OAP £5.30, 5 and over £1, Pre-booked groups (20+) £5 per person.

Special Events: Plant Hunters' Fair. August Bank Holiday 2012. This event will feature approximately 20 highly acclaimed nurseries including Chelsea and RHS Medal Winners. Visitors can enjoy the delights of the garden and tea room throughout the day. 10am–5pm. All enquiries 01630 647237 or email info@dorothyclivegarden.co.uk. There is a special admission price for Plant Hunters' Fair and Garden. The special fundraising event in aid of The Dorothy Clive Garden will help our core mission of providing a beautiful place of rest and recreation for the public.

Key facts: Dogs on leads welcome. Wheelchairs available free of charge. WCs. By arrangement. On leads.

BOSCOBEL HOUSE & THE ROYAL OAK

Bishop's Wood, Brewood, Staffordshire ST19 9AR

www.english-heritage.org.uk/boscobel

This 17th century hunting lodge played a vital part in Charles II's escape from the Roundheads. See a descendant of the Royal Oak and 'priest-hole' in the attic, which both sheltered the fugitive future King from Cromwell's troops in 1651. Then explore Boscobel's more recent past as a Victorian farm.

Location: MAP 6:N6, OS127, SJ838 082. On unclassified road between A41 & A5. 8m NW of Wolverhampton.
Owner: English Heritage **Contact:** Visitor Operations Team
Tel: 01902 850244
E-mail: customers@english-heritage.org.uk
Open: Please visit www.english-heritage.org.uk for opening times and the most up-to-date information.
Admission: Adult £5.80, Child £3.50, Conc. £5.20, Family £15.10. EH Members free. Opening times and prices are valid until 31 Mar 2012.
Key facts: Exhibition. Guidebooks. Pinic Area. Hazardous. Ovp.

© Phil Evans

MOSELEY OLD HALL

Fordhouses, Wolverhampton WV10 7HY

www.nationaltrust.org.uk/moseleyoldhall

Elizabethan timber-framed house encased in brick in 1870 with original interiors. Charles II hid here after the Battle of Worcester. Guided tours. 17th century style garden with formal box parterre, only 17th century plants are grown. The property is a Sandford Education Award Winner.

Location: MAP 6:N6, OS Ref. SJ932 044. 4m N of Wolverhampton between A449 and 460.
Owner: National Trust **Contact:** House & Visitor Services Manager
Tel: 01902 782808 **E-mail:** moseleyoldhall@nationaltrust.org.uk
Open: 3 Mar–1 Jul & 12 Sep–31 Oct: Sats, Suns & Weds;
2 Jul–9 Sep: Sats–Weds; 3 Nov–16 Dec: Sats & Suns. 12–5; BH Mon 11–5
Admission: Adult £6.90, Child £3.45, Family £17.25. Groups (15+) £6pp
Private visits outside normal open times £8.50 (min 20). NT members free with valid membership card during normal opening times.
Key facts: Partial. WCs. By arrangement. No coaches. In grounds.

THE HEATH HOUSE

Tean, Stoke-On-Trent, Staffordshire ST10 4HA

www.theheathhouse.co.uk

Set in rolling parkland with fine formal gardens, Heath House is an early Victorian mansion built 1836-1840 in the Tudor style for John Burton Philips. The original collection of paintings and chattels remains intact. The house recently featured in Channel 4's 'Country House Rescue.'

Location: MAP 6:O4, OS Ref. SK030 392. A522 off A50 at Uttoxeter 5m W, at Lower Tean turn right.
Owner: Mr John Philips **Contact:** Mr Ben Philips
Tel: 01538 723944 or 01386 792110
E-mail: ben.philips@theheathhouse.co.uk
Open: Easter Weekend (Fri–Mon), BH Mons and May Sun–Thurs inc 2.30–5pm. Tours begin at 2.30. Teas by prior arrangement £3.50. Please telephone in advance.
Admission: £6.50. No Conc. No reductions for groups.
Key facts: Photography allowed. WCs. Obligatory.

WHITMORE HALL

Whitmore, Newcastle-Under-Lyme ST5 5HW

Grade I 1676 manor house of considerable historical and architectural interest dating back to a much earlier period. For 900 years the seat of the Cavenagh-Mainwaring's, direct descendants of the original Norman owners. Good family portraits from 1624. Beautiful home park and lake including outstanding, rare Elizabethan stable block.

Location: MAP 6:M4, OS Ref. SJ811 413. On A53 Newcastle–Market Drayton Road, 3m from M6/J15.
Owner: Mr Guy Cavenagh-Mainwaring
Contact: Mr Guy Cavenagh-Mainwaring
Tel: 01782 680478
Fax: 01782 680906
Open: 1 May–31 Aug: Tues, Weds, 2–5pm (last tour 4.30pm).
Admission: Adult £5, Child 50p.
Key facts: Ground floor & grounds. Afternoon teas for booked groups (15+), May–Aug. Obligatory.

CASTERNE HALL

Ilam, Nr Ashbourne, Derbyshire DE6 2BA

Panelled manor house in own grounds in stunning Peak District location. A seat of the Hurt family for 500 years. Georgian front, 17th century and medieval rear. Finalist in 'Country Life' magazine's 'England's Favourite House' competition. Featured in 5 films including Sherlock Holmes and Hercule Poirot.

Location: MAP 6:O3, OS Ref. SK123 523. Take first turning on left N of village and continue past 'Casterne Farms only' sign.

Owner: Charles Hurt

Contact: Charles Hurt

Tel: 01335 310489

E-mail: mail@casterne.co.uk

Website: www.casterne.co.uk

Open: 25 Jun–1 Aug: weekdays only for tour at 2pm only.

Admission: £6.

Key facts: Partial. Obligatory. Limited for coaches. Guide dogs only. €

ERASMUS DARWIN HOUSE

Beacon Street, Lichfield, Staffordshire WS13 7AD

Grandfather of Charles Darwin and a founder member of the Lunar Society, Erasmus Darwin (1731–1802) was a leading doctor, scientist, inventor and poet. This elegant Georgian house was his home and contains an exhibition of his life, theories and inventions. There is also an 18th century herb garden.

Location: MAP 6:P5, OS Ref. SK115 098. Situated at the West end of Lichfield Cathedral Close.

Owner: Erasmus Darwin Foundation **Contact:** Alison Wallis

Tel: 01543 306260 **Fax:** 01543 306261

E-mail: enquiries@erasmusdarwin.org

Website: www.erasmusdarwin.org

Open: Apr–Oct, Tues–Sun, 11am–5pm. Nov–Mar, Thur–Sun, 12–4.30pm. Check website or phone for details.

Admission: Adult £3, Conc. £2, Child £1.

Key facts: Suitable. WCs. By arrangement. Disabled only. Guide dogs only.

The Trentham Estate

© The Trentham Estate

THE TRENTHAM ESTATE

Stone Road, Trentham, Staffordshire ST4 8AX

Winners of the 2010 European Award for Historic Garden Restoration. Enjoy Trentham Gardens where vast perennial plantings by renowned garden designers and Chelsea gold-medal winners Tom Stuart-Smith and Piet Oudolf, present breath-taking vistas throughout the seasons. Enjoy the lake, woodlands and the country's first barefoot walk. There's something for everyone at Trentham.

Location: MAP 6:N4, OS Ref. SJ864 408, SAT NAV: ST4 8JG. 5 minute drive M6/J15. 45 minutes from Birmingham & Manchester.

Owner: St Modwen Properties **Group Booking contact:** Jackie Grice

Tel: 01782 646646 **Fax:** 01782 644536 **E-mail:** enquiry@trentham.co.uk

Website: www.trentham.co.uk

Open: Please see website or contact us for up-to-date information.

Admission: Please see website or contact us for up-to-date information.

Key facts: Wheelchair loan available. Licensed. By arrangement. Free. On leads.

ARBURY HALL

www.arburyestate.co.uk

Arbury Hall, original Elizabethan mansion house, Gothicised in the 18th century surrounded by stunning gardens and parkland.

Arbury Hall has been the seat of the Newdegate family for over 450 years and is the ancestral home of Viscount Daventry. This Tudor/Elizabethan House was Gothicised by Sir Roger Newdegate in the 18th century and is regarded as the 'Gothic Gem' of the Midlands. The principal rooms, with their soaring fan vaulted ceilings and plunging pendants and filigree tracery, stand as a most breathtaking and complete example of early Gothic Revival architecture and provide a unique and fascinating venue for corporate entertaining, product launches, fashion shoots and activity days. Exclusive use of this historic Hall, its gardens and parkland is offered to clients. The Hall stands in the middle of beautiful parkland with landscaped gardens of rolling lawns, lakes and winding wooded walks. Spring flowers are profuse and in June rhododendrons, azaleas and giant wisteria provide a beautiful environment for the visitor. George Eliot, the novelist, was born on the estate and Arbury Hall and Sir Roger Newdegate were immortalised in her book 'Scenes of Clerical Life'.

KEY FACTS

Corporate hospitality, film location, small conferences, product launches and promotions, marquee functions, let day shooting. No cameras or video recorders indoors.

Exclusive lunches and dinners for corporate parties in dining room, max. 50, buffets 80.

WCs.

Obligatory. Tour time: 50min.

200 cars and 3 coaches 250 yards from house. Follow tourist signs. Approach map available for coach drivers.

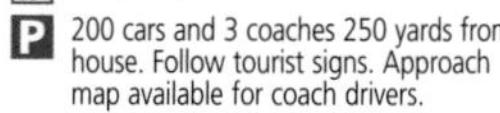

Welcome, must book. School room available.

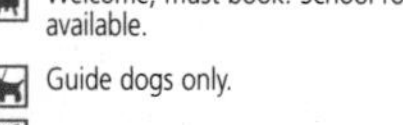

Guide dogs only.

VISITOR INFORMATION

Owner
The Viscount Daventry

Address
Arbury Hall
Nuneaton
Warwickshire CV10 7PT

Location
MAP 7:A7
OS Ref. SP335 893.

London, M1, M6/J3 (A444 to Nuneaton), 2m SW of Nuneaton. 1m W of A444. Nuneaton 5 mins. Birmingham City Centre 20 mins. London 2 hrs, Coventry 20 mins.

Bus/Coach: Nuneaton Station 3m.

Air: Birmingham International 17m.

Contact
Events Secretary
Tel: 024 7638 2804
Fax: 024 7664 1147
E-mail: info@arburyestate.co.uk

Opening Times
Hall & Gardens open on BH weekends only (Sun & Mon) Easter - August.

Admission
Hall & Gardens

Adult	£7.50
Child (up to 14 yrs)	£4.50
Family (2+2)	£19.00

Gardens Only

Adult	£5.50
Child (up to 14 yrs.)	£4.00

Groups/Parties (25+) By arrangement.

Hall Tours

Guided tours of the Hall on Bank Holidays and Private Groups

Tours last approx 50 minutes

Wheelchair access to Hall

Gravel pathways around gardens

Conference/Function

ROOM	Size	Max Cap
Dining Room	35' x 28'	120
Saloon	35' x 30'	70
Room 3	48' x 11'	40
Stables Tearooms	31' x 18'	80

VISITOR INFORMATION

■ Owner
English Heritage

■ Address
Kenilworth
Warwickshire
CV8 1NE

■ Location
MAP 6:P8
OS140, SP278 723
In Kenilworth off A46, W end of town.

■ Contact
Visitor Operations Team
Tel: 01926 852 078
E-mail: customers @english-heritage.org.uk

■ Opening Times
Please visit www.english-heritage.org.uk for opening times and the most up-to-date information.

■ Admission

Adult	£8.00
Child	£4.80
Conc.	£7.20
Family	£20.80

Discount for groups (11+).

EH Members Free.

Opening times and prices are valid until 31st March 2012, after this date details are subject to change please visit www.english-heritage.org.uk for the most up-to-date information.

■ Special events
There is an exciting events programme available throughout the year, for further details please contact the property or visit the website.

© English Heritage Photo Library

KENILWORTH CASTLE ⌗ & ELIZABETHAN GARDEN

www.english-heritage.org.uk/kenilworth

Robert Dudley created this ornate palace to impress his beloved Queen in 1575.

A vast medieval fortress which became an Elizabethan palace, Kenilworth Castle is one of Britain's largest and most impressive historic sites. Spanning more than five centuries, Kenilworth's varied buildings and architectural styles reflect its long connection with successive English monarchs. Geoffrey de Clinton, Henry I's treasurer, began the massive Norman keep at the core of the fortress in the 1120s, and subsequent monarchs and noblemen all left their mark on the romantic ruin.

Kenilworth's greatest period of fame was during the Elizabethan era as the home of Robert Dudley, the great love of Queen Elizabeth I. Dudley created an ornate palace at Kenilworth to impress his beloved queen, which included a spectacular garden. Due to extensive redevelopments to the site, this magnificent garden has been authentically re-created and is now astounding visitors once more.

As part of the multi-million pound English Heritage investment in Kenilworth Castle, Leicester's Gatehouse is displayed with the chambers on its lower floors re-created as they might have appeared when the gatehouse was last inhabited in the 1930s. The top floor houses an exhibition that tells the story of Elizabeth's relationship with Dudley, and her four visits to Kenilworth.

No visit to the castle is complete without a visit to the castle tearoom, housed in the impressively timbered Tudor stables. The stables also feature a fascinating interactive display on the castle's history.

The Gatehouse has been restored by English Heritage and is now available to hire for weddings and receptions.

KEY FACTS

- WC. Guidebooks. Hazard. Ovp. Picnic area.
- Exhibition. Family learning resources available.
- On leads.

© English Heritage Photo Library

© English Heritage Photo Library

Shakespeare's Birthplace

THE SHAKESPEARE HOUSES

www.shakespeare.org.uk

Five beautifully preserved Tudor houses and gardens telling the complete Shakespeare story and all directly linked with William Shakespeare and his family.

Shakespeare's Birthplace
This is where it all began, where William Shakespeare was born and spent the first years of his life. Begin your journey with the Life, Love & Legacy exhibition before discovering the Tudor town house that was the Shakespeare family home and glove making business. It's a special place that everyone should see at least once in their lifetime.

Mary Arden's Farm - A Real Working Tudor Farm
Visit the childhood home of Shakespeare's mother and see the farm's history brought to life. Step back into the 1570s and encounter the authentic sights, sounds and smells of a working farm in Shakespeare's day. Our Tudor costumed residents will invite you to get involved and help with the day-to-day running of the farm and try out traditional rural skills.

Anne Hathaway's Cottage – The Most Romantic Shakespeare House
Discover and fall in love with this beautiful English thatched cottage and family home of Shakespeare's wife. Stroll through and admire the award winning cottage garden which overflows with old-fashioned plants, orchards and traditional vegetables.

Hall's Croft – The Jacobean Doctor's House
Explore the elegant house with its lavish rooms once owned by Shakespeare's daughter Susanna and her wealthy physician husband Dr John Hall.
Examine the fascinating collection of apothecary's equipment and books. Relax in the tranquil gardens and savour the fragrant herb beds, like those used by Dr John Hall in his remedies.

Nash's House & New Place – Where the Shakespeare Story Ended
Take in the period splendour of Nash's House and visit the archaeological excavations of New Place, Shakespeare's final home. Enjoy the exquisite horticultural designs of the Elizabethan Knot Garden and picnic in the Great Garden.

KEY FACTS

- City Sightseeing bus tour connecting town houses with Anne Hathaway's Cottage and Mary Arden's Farm. No photography inside houses.
- Gifts available at all five houses.
- Plants for sale at Anne Hathaway's Cottage, Mary Arden's Farm, Hall's Croft.
- Available, tel for details. Partial. WCs.
- Mary Arden's Farm.
- Hall's Croft.
- By special arrangement.
- Free coach terminal for groups drop off and pick up at Birthplace. Max stay 30 mins. Parking at Anne Hathaway's Cottage and Mary Arden's Farm.
- Available for all houses. For information 01789 201804.
- Guide dogs only.
- Please check our website for further details.

Mary Arden's Farm

Anne Hathaway's Cottage

VISITOR INFORMATION

Owner
The Shakespeare Birthplace Trust

Address
Henley Street
Stratford-upon-Avon
CV37 6QW

Location
MAP 6:P9
OS Refs:
Birthplace – SP201 552
New Place – SP201 548
Hall's Croft – SP200 546
Hathaway's – SP185 547
Arden's – SP166 582

Rail: Direct service from London (Marylebone)

2 hrs from London
45 mins from Birmingham by car.

4m from M40/J15 and well signed from all approaches.

Contact
The Shakespeare Birthplace Trust
Tel: 01789 204016 (General enquiries)
Tel: 01789 201806/201836 (Group Visits)
Fax: 01789 263138
E-mail: info@shakespeare.org.uk
groups@shakespeare.org.uk

Opening Times
The Shakespeare Houses are open daily throughout the year except Christmas Day and Boxing Day.

1 November–31 March: Last entry 4pm.

Feb Half-Term (19–27), 1 April–31 October: Last entry 5pm.

July & August: Last entry 6pm at Shakespeare's Birthplace only.

Please note that Mary Arden's Farm is open from 19 March–31 October 2012.

Admission
Tickets to the Shakespeare Houses are valid for a full year, with unlimited entry. So for the price of one ticket, you can enjoy days out at the Shakespeare Houses all year round –for free!

Visit the website for further details.

VISITOR INFORMATION

Address
Warwick Castle
Warwick CV34 4QU

Location
MAP 6:P8
OS Ref. SP284 648
2m from M40/J15.
Birmingham 35 mins,
Leeds 2 hrs 5 mins,
London 1 hr 30 mins.
Vehicle entrance from A429 ½ m SW of town centre.

Rail: Intercity from London Euston to Coventry. Direct service from Marylebone & Paddington to Warwick.

Contact
Tel: 0870 442 2000
Fax: 0870 442 2394
E-mail: customer.information@warwick-castle.com

Opening Times
All year, daily, except 25 December.
10am–6pm
(closes 5pm during October–March).

Admission
Prices vary – see website for details.
www.warwick-castle.com

WARWICK CASTLE

www.warwick-castle.com

Experience a totally electrifying day out at Britain's Ultimate Castle.

We will immerse you in over 1000 years of jaw-dropping history, come rain or shine, where ancient myths and spell-binding tales will set your imagination alight. Meet history face to face, be prepared to participate fully in Castle life from battles and gore to romance and chivalry.

Your journey begins on the East Front with the iconic Guy's and Caesar's towers before you enter the Castle through the mighty Barbican and experience the preparations for battle at first hand in Kingmaker and Dream of Battle.

Later, marvel at the splendour of the Great Hall and State Rooms fully restored to their 17th century elegance and home to the Castle's most prized artefacts. Witness a state banquet fit for the Queen in the State Dining Room before accepting your invitation from the Countess of Warwick herself in Secrets and Scandals.

We invite brave souls to delve into the most blood curdling parts of Warwick's history in the Castle Dungeon where live actors and special effects transport guests back to the Castle's darkest times!

Warwick Castle is also home to Merlin: The Dragon Tower – the World's first attraction linked to the hit BBC show Merlin.

Explore the gardens surrounding the Castle and discover the Peacock Garden, Victorian Rose garden and the Pageant Field, 'Capability' Brown's very first solo commission. Don't miss the River Island home to Warwick's very own trebuchet.

Throughout the year spectacular events and expert demonstrations, from archery to jousting and battle re-enactments, bring the castle to life.

KEY FACTS

- Corporate events, receptions, Feasts, Dungeon's After Dark and Highwayman's Suppers. Guide books in English, French, German, Japanese and Spanish. Ghosts & Ghouls evenings.
- Three shops.
- Partial
- For groups (pre-booked). Guides in most rooms.
- Group rates apply. To qualify for group rates please call 0870 442 2371. Education packs available.

Conference/Function

ROOM	Size	Max Cap
Great Hall	61' x 34'	130
State Dining Room	40' x 25'	30
Undercroft	46' x 26'	120
Coach House	44' x 19'	80
Marquees		2000

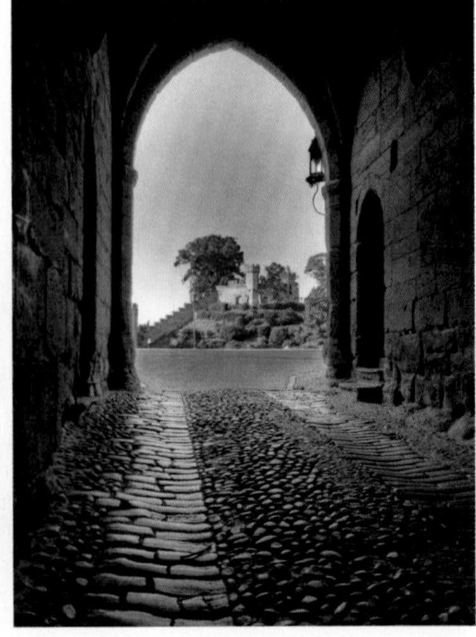

LORD LEYCESTER HOSPITAL

HIGH STREET, WARWICK CV34 4BH

www.lordleycester.com

This magnificent range of 14th and 15th century half-timbered buildings was adapted into almshouses by Robert Dudley, Earl of Leycester, in 1571. The Hospital still provides homes for ex-Servicemen and their wives. The Guildhall, Great Hall, chantry Chapel, Brethren's Kitchen and galleried Courtyard are still in everyday use. The regimental museum of the Queen's Own Hussars is housed here. The historic Master's Garden was featured in BBC TV's Gardener's World, and the Hospital buildings in many productions including, most recently, "Dr Who" and David Dimbleby's "How We Built Britain".

Location: MAP 6:P8, OS Ref. 280 648. 1m N of M40/J15 on the A429 in town centre. Rail: 10 minutes walk from Warwick station.

Owner: The Governors
Contact: The Master
Tel: 01926 491422
Open: All year: Tue–Sun & BHs (except Good Fri & 25 Dec), 10am–5pm (4pm in winter). Garden: Apr–Sept: 10am–4.30pm.
Admission: Adult £4.90, Child £3.90, Conc. £4.40. Garden only £2. 5% discount for adult groups (20+).
Key facts: Partial. WCs. By arrangement. Limited for cars. No coaches. Guide dogs only.

COMPTON VERNEY

Compton Verney, Warwickshire CV35 9HZ

www.comptonverney.org.uk

Set within a Grade I listed mansion remodelled by Robert Adam in the 1760s, Compton Verney offers a unique art gallery experience. Relax and explore the 120 acres of 'Capability' Brown landscaped parkland, discover a collection of internationally significant art, enjoy free tours and a programme of popular events.

Location: MAP 7:A9, OS Ref. SP312 529. 9m E of Stratford-upon-Avon, 10 mins from M40/J12, on B4086 between Wellesbourne and Kineton. Rail: Nearest station is Banbury or Leamington Spa. Air: Nearest airport Birmingham International.

Owner: Compton Verney House Trust **Contact:** Ticketing Desk
Tel: 01926 645500 **Fax:** 01926 645501
E-mail: info@comptonverney.org.uk
Open: Open from 31 Mar 2012, Tues–Sun & BH Mons, 11am–5pm. Last entry to Gallery 4.30pm. Groups welcome, please book in advance.
Admission: Please call for details. Group discounts are available.
Key facts: No photography in the Gallery. WCs. Licensed. Licensed. By arrangement. Ample. Guide dogs only.

© Coughton Court

COUGHTON COURT GARDENS

Alcester, Warwickshire B49 5JA

www.coughtoncourt.co.uk

Heralded by the RHS as one of the finest gardens in Britain, the beautiful 25 acres of grounds include a walled garden, lake, riverside walk and bog garden, colour themed gardens, daffodils and orchards and fruit gardens. The Rose Labyrinth, designed by daughter Christina Williams, boasts spectacular displays of roses.

Location: MAP 6:O9, OS Ref. SP080 604. Located on A435, 2m N of Alcester, 8m NW of Stratford-upon-Avon, 18m from Birmingham Centre.

Contact: Throckmorton family **Garden Tours:** 01789 762542
Fax: 01789 764369 **E-mail:** office@throckmortons.co.uk
Open: Please contact us for up to date opening times.
Admission: House & Garden: Adult £9.40, Child (5–16) £4.70, Family £23.50, Groups (15+) £7.45. Gardens only: Adult £6.50, Child (5–16) £3.25, Family £16.30, Groups (15+) £5.10. Includes a voluntary donation but visitors can choose to pay the standard prices displayed at the property and on the website. Not included in group prices.
Key facts: Partial. WCs. Licensed. Licensed. Guide dogs only.

RAGLEY HALL & GARDENS

Alcester, Warwickshire B49 5NJ

www.ragleyhall.com

Ragley Hall was designed in 1680 and remains the family home of the Marquess and Marchioness of Hertford, managing to retain its family charm despite the thousands of people who visit each year. Ragley offers beautiful gardens, tours of the majestic state rooms, Woodland Walk and Adventure Playground.
Location: MAP 6:O9. OS Ref. SP073 555. Off A46/A435 1m SW of Alcester, From London 100m, M40 via Oxford and Stratford-on-Avon.
Owner: The Marquess of Hertford
Tel: 01789 762090
Fax: 01789 764791
E-mail: ragley@ragleyhall.com
Open: Please see website for details.
Admission: Please see website for details.
Key facts: No video in the house. Access available. Drinks & Light Snacks. By arrangement. Free. In Park on leads.

BADDESLEY CLINTON

Baddesley Clinton, Warwickshire B93 0DQ

A 500 year old moated medieval manor house with hidden secrets! The house and interiors reflect its heyday in the Elizabethan era, when it was a haven for persecuted Catholics – there are three priest holes. The intimate gardens incorporate stewponds, small lake, walled garden, lakeside walk and nature trail.
Location: MAP 6:P8, OS Ref. SP199 715. 3/4 m W of A4141 Warwick/ Birmingham road at Chadwick End.
Owner: National Trust **Contact:** Property Administrator
Tel: 01564 783294 **Fax:** 01564 782706
E-mail: baddesleyclinton@nationaltrust.org.uk
Website: www.nationaltrust.org.uk
Open: 1 Feb–31 Dec, Tue–Sun & BH Mons, 11am–5pm. (2011 opening times).
Admission: Prices tbc. Please visit www.nationaltrust.org.uk.
Key facts: WCs. Licensed. By arrangement. Guide dogs only.

CHARLECOTE PARK

Charlecote Park, Warwick CV35 9ER

Enjoy a day at Charlecote Park, the home of the Lucy family for over 800 years. Built in the 1550's with warm red bricks and decorated in Warwickshire stone. The house has a fascinating history.
Location: MAP 6:P9, OS151, SP263 564. 1m W of Wellesbourne, 5m E of Stratford-upon-Avon.
Owner: National Trust
Contact: Visitor Services Manager
Tel: 01789 470277
Fax: 01789 470544
E-mail: charlecotepark@nationaltrust.org.uk
Open: Please contact for up to date information.
Admission: Please contact for up to date information.
Key facts:

COUGHTON COURT

Alcester, Warwickshire B49 5JA

Home to the Throckmortons for 600 years, this Tudor house stands testament to a family's courage in their beliefs. From high favour to oppression and danger, the Throckmortons were leaders in a dangerous age. Coughton is still a family home: the Throckmorton family live here and manage the stunning gardens.
Location: MAP 6:O9, OS Ref. SP080 604, Located A435, 2m N of Alcester, 8m NW of Stratford-upon-Avon, 18m from Birmingham City Centre.
Contact: National Trust **Tel:** 01789 400777 **Fax:** 01789 765544
E-mail: coughtoncourt@nationaltrust.org.uk **Website:** www.nationaltrust.org.uk
Open: For full opening times please visit our website.
Admission: Gift Aid prices. House and Garden Adult £9.95, Child £5.00, Family £26.00. Gardens only: Adult £6.50, Child £3.25, Family £17.00. Walled Garden: NT members £2.50.
Key facts: Ground floor of house, gardens & restaurant. WC. Licensed. Licensed. Capacity: 70 inside, Covered Courtyard 50. Free introductory talks available most days. Guide dogs only.

HONINGTON HALL

Shipston-on-Stour, Warwickshire CV36 5AA

This fine Caroline manor house was built in the early 1680s for Henry Parker in mellow brickwork, stone quoins and window dressings. Modified in 1751 when an octagonal saloon was inserted. The interior was also lavishly restored around this time and contains exceptional mid-Georgian plasterwork. Set in 15 acres of grounds.
Location: MAP 6:P9, OS Ref. SP261 427. 10m S of Stratford-upon-Avon. 1½ m N of Shipston-on-Stour. Take A3400 towards Stratford, then signed right to Honington.
Owner: Benjamin Wiggin Esq
Contact: Benjamin Wiggin Esq
Tel: 01608 661434
Fax: 01608 663717
Open: By appointment for groups (10+).
Admission: Telephone for details.
Key facts: Obligatory.

PACKWOOD HOUSE

Packwood House, Lapworth, Solihull B94 6AT

Packwood House is originally 16th century; its interiors were extensively restored between the world wars by Graham Baron Ash to create a 20th century evocation of domestic Tudor architecture. It contains a collection of 16th century textiles and furniture. The gardens are renowned for herbaceous borders and collection of yews.
Location: MAP 6:O8. OS Ref. SP174 722. 2m E of Hockley Heath (on A3400), 11m SE of central Birmingham.
Owner: National Trust **Contact:** The Estate Office
Tel: 01564 783294 **Fax:** 01564 782706
E-mail: packwood@nationaltrust.org.uk
Website: www.nationaltrust.org.uk
Open: 1 Feb 2011–31 Oct, Tues–Sun, 11am–5pm with last entry 4.30pm. (2011 opening times).
Admission: Please see website or contact us for up-to-date information.
Key facts: WCs. By arrangement. Guide dogs only. Parkland only.

RYTON GARDENS

Wolston Lane, Ryton on Dunsmore, Coventry, Warwickshire CV8 3LG

Ryton Gardens is set in the heart of England and combines 10 acres of organic gardens buzzing wildlife, brimming with plants, bursting with flowers and abundant in fruit and vegetables. It has been home to the UK's leading charity, Garden Organic for over 25 years.
Location: MAP 7:A8, OS Ref. SP4074.
Owner: Garden Organic **Contact:** Mark Wilkinson
Tel: 024 7630 3517 **Fax:** 024 7663 9229
E-mail: enquiry@gardenorganic.org.uk
Website: www.rytongardens.co.uk
Open: 7 days, 9am–5pm, excluding Christmas Day & Boxing Day.
Admission: Adult £5.50*, Con/student/child £3.50*, Family Ticket £13.20*
*prices include a 10% Gift Aid donation.
Key facts: WCs. Licensed. Licensed. By arrangement. Guide dogs only.

WINTERBOURNE HOUSE AND GARDEN

University of Birmingham, 58 Edgbaston Park Road, Birmingham B15 2RT

www.winterbourne.org.uk

Winterbourne is set in 7 acres of botanic garden, just minutes from Birmingham city centre. Ground floor exhibition spaces tell the history of the previous owners and the garden has a beautiful Japanese bridge, tea house and walled garden, all designed in the Arts and Crafts style.
Location: Minutes away from A38.
Owner: The University of Birmingham
Tel: 0121 414 3003 **E-mail:** enquiries@winterbourne.org.uk
Open: Jan–Mar/Nov–Dec, 10am–4pm weekdays, 11am–4pm weekends. Apr–Oct, 10am–5.30pm weekdays, 11am–5.30pm weekends. We are closed over the Christmas period.
Admission: Adult £4.50, Concession £3.50, Family £14. Group prices on request.
Key facts: Organised professional photography including family or wedding portraiture must be notified to management in advance and will incur a charge. Partial. WCs. Licensed. Licensed. By arrangement. Limited for cars, no coaches. Guide dogs only.

BACK TO BACKS

55–63 Hurst Street, Birmingham B5 4TE

Take an exciting step back into Birmingham's industrial past by visiting the last remaining courtyard of Back to Back houses in Birmingham. Our guided tours tell the stories of ordinary people who made an extraordinary city.
Location: MAP 6:O7, OS Ref. SP071 861. Several car parks within walking distance.
Owner: National Trust
Contact: House & Visitor Services Manager
Tel: 0121 666 7671 (Booking line open Tues–Fri, 10.30am–4pm; Sat/Sun, 10.30am–12 noon)
E-mail: backtobacks@nationaltrust.org.uk
Website: www.nationaltrust.org.uk/backtobacks
Open: Please contact property for all opening hours on 0121 666 7671.
Admission: Please contact property for admission prices on 0121 666 7671.
Key facts: Partial. WCs. Obligatory. Guide dogs only.

BIRMINGHAM BOTANICAL GARDENS AND GLASSHOUSES

Westbourne Road, Edgbaston, Birmingham B15 3TR

Fifteen acres of beautiful landscaped gardens, four glasshouses and 7000 shrubs, plants and trees including rare species. Rose Garden, Alpine Yard, Woodland and Rhododendron Walks, Rock Pool, National Bonsai Collection. Children's playground, aviaries, gallery, bandstand (live music in summer months), tearoom and gift shop. An independent educational charity.
Location: MAP 6:O7. OS Ref. SP048 855. 2m W of city centre. Follow signs to Edgbaston then brown tourist signs. **Owner:** Birmingham Botanical & Horticultural Society **Contact:** Mr James Wheeler **Tel:** 0121 454 1860
Fax: 0121 454 7835 **E-mail:** admin@birminghambotanicalgardens.org.uk
Website: www.birminghambotanicalgardens.org.uk
Open: Daily: 9am–Dusk (7pm latest except pre-booked groups). Suns opening time 10am. Closed Christmas Day. **Admission:** Adult £7.50, Family £22. Groups, Conc. £4.75, Children under 5 FREE.
Key facts: Guide dogs only.

CASTLE BROMWICH HALL GARDENS

Chester Road, Castle Bromwich, Birmingham B36 9BT

A unique example of 17th and 18th century formal garden design within a 10 acre walled area, comprising historic plants, vegetables, herbs and fruit, with a 19th century holly maze.
Location: MAP 6:O6, OS Ref. SP141 899. Off B4114, 5m E of Birmingham City Centre, 1 mile from M6/J5 exit N only.
Owner: Castle Bromwich Hall & Gardens Trust **Contact:** Sue Brain
Tel/Fax: 0121 749 4100 **E-mail:** admin@cbhgt.org.uk
Website: www.cbhgt.org.uk
Open: 1 Apr–31 Oct: Tues–Thurs, 11am–4pm, Sat, Sun, BH Mon 12.30–4.30pm, 1 Nov–31 Mar: Tues, Wed, Thurs, 11am–3pm.
Admission: Summer: Adult £4.75, Concs. £4.25, Child £1.25.
Winter: All Adults £4.25, Child £1.25.
Key facts: WCs. By arrangement. Limited for coaches. On leads.

Drawing Room at Winterbourne House

VISITOR INFORMATION

■ Owner
English Heritage

■ Address
Great Witley
Worcester
WR6 6JT

■ Location
MAP 6:M8
OS150, SO769 649.
10m NW of Worcester
off A443.

■ Contact
Visitor Operations Team
Tel: 01299 896636
E-mail: customers@english-heritage.org.uk

■ Opening Times
Please visit www.english-heritage.org.uk for opening times and the most up-to-date information.

■ Admission

Adult	£6.30
Child	£3.80
Conc.	£5.70
Family	£16.40

Discount for groups (11+).

EH Members Free.

Opening times and prices are valid until 31st March 2012.

■ Special events
There is an exciting events programme available throughout the year, for further details please contact the property or visit the website.

© English Heritage

WITLEY COURT & GARDENS ⌗

www.english-heritage.org.uk/witleycourt

A hundred years ago, Witley Court was one of England's great country houses, hosting many extravagant parties.

A hundred years ago, Witley Court was one of England's great country houses, hosting many extravagant parties. Today it is a spectacular ruin, the result of a devastating fire in 1937.

The vast and rambling remains of the 19th century mansion are surrounded by magnificent landscaped gardens. After a long period of decline, recent major restoration has brought the spectacular gardens back to life.

There are also many woodland walks to enjoy in the North Park, which features trees and shrubs acquired from around the world.

Attached to Witley Court is Great Witley Church, with its amazing Italianate Baroque interior.

The Pool House is a spacious, modern holiday cottage just a short walk away from the romantic ruins of Witley Court.

KEY FACTS

Visitor welcome point. Guidebooks. Hazard. Ovp.

Family learning resources available.

On leads

Holiday cottage available to let.

© English Heritage

© English Heritage

© NTPL / Andrew Butler

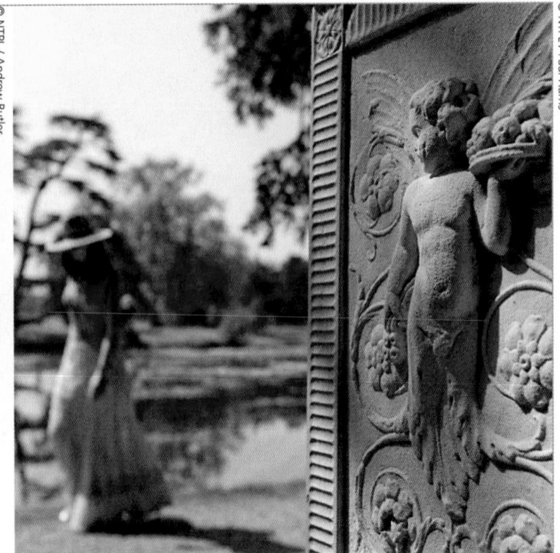

© NTPL / Paul Harris

CROOME

NEAR HIGH GREEN, WORCESTERSHIRE WR8 9DW

www.nationaltrust.org.uk

Explore the ever changing splendour of Croome, a place with so many fascinating stories to discover from the 17th century right up to the 21st century. The serene lakeside garden, with its sumptuous shrubberies, miles of winding paths, enchanting temples and follies, bridges and statues make Croome the perfect place to relax with family and friends. Step into the un-restored mansion house, Croome Court, to discover its chequered past and evocative spaces that have been home to a diverse range of characters and communities for over 400 years. Open for 2012 – Atmospheric Home Shrubbery and the exquisite Rotunda folly.

Location: MAP 6:N9, OS Ref. SO878 448. 8m S of Worcester. Signposted from A38 and B4084.

Owner: National Trust **Contact:** House & Visitor Services Manager

Tel: 01905 371006 **Fax:** 01905 371090

E-mail: croomepark@nationaltrust.org.uk

Open: See National Trust website for full opening times. Park, Restaurant & Shop open every day except 24 & 25 Dec. Garden open every weekend and every day 13 Feb–2 Nov, 10am–5.30pm. House open every weekend and Wed–Mon 13 Feb–2 Nov, 11am–4.30pm, closed Tues. From 26 Dec–1 Jan, Croome fully open 11am–4pm.

Admission: Adult £6.50, Child (6–16) £3.25, Family £16, Group £5.

Key facts: WCs. Licensed. Licensed. By arrangement. On leads.

HARVINGTON HALL

HARVINGTON, KIDDERMINSTER, WORCESTERSHIRE DY10 4LR

www.harvingtonhall.com

Harvington Hall is a moated, medieval and Elizabethan manor house. Many of the rooms have their original Elizabethan wall paintings and the Hall contains the finest series of priest hides in the country. During the 19th century it was stripped of furniture and panelling and the shell was left almost derelict but is now restored. The Hall has walled gardens surrounded by a moat, a gift shop and a tea room serving morning coffees, light lunches and afternoon teas. A programme of events throughout the year including outdoor plays and music, living history weekends, candlelight tours and a pilgrimage is available.

Location: MAP 6:N8, OS Ref. SO877 745. On minor road, 1/2m NE of A450/A448 crossroads at Mustow Green. 3m SE of Kidderminster.

Owner: Roman Catholic Archdiocese of Birmingham

Contact: The Hall Manager **Tel:** 01562 777846 **Fax:** 01562 777190

E-mail: harvingtonhall@btconnect.com

Open: Mar & Oct: Sats & Suns; Apr–Sept: Wed–Sun & BH Mons (closed Good Fri), 11.30am–4pm. Also open throughout the year for pre-booked groups and schools. Occasionally the Hall may be closed for a private function, please ring for up to date information.

Admission: Adult £8, Child (5–16) £5, OAP £7, Family (2 adults & 3 children) £23. Garden and Malt House Visitor Centre: £3.

Special Events: On many weekends the Hall is enhanced by Living History events when the Hall's re-enactment group depict one of the many significant periods throughout its long history.

Key facts: Partial. WCs. Obligatory. Limited for coaches. Guide dogs only.

SPETCHLEY PARK GARDENS

Spetchley Park, Worcester WR5 1RS

www.spetchleygardens.co.uk

Surrounded by glorious countryside and a deer park this 30 acre Victorian paradise, has been lovingly created to boast an enviable collection of plant treasures from every corner of the globe. Whether you are looking for the perfect day out or place to hold your wedding, Spetchley has it all.
Location: MAP 6:N9, OS Ref. SO895 540. 2m E of Worcester on A44. Leave M5/J6/J7.
Owner: Spetchley Gardens Charitable Trust
Contact: Mr RJ Berkeley
Tel: 01453 810303
Fax: 01453 511915
E-mail: hb@spetchleygardens.co.uk
Open: 23 Mar–30 Sept: Wed–Sun & BHs, 11am–6pm. Oct: Sats & Suns, 11am–4pm. (last admission 1hr before closing).
Admission: Adult £6, Child (under 16yrs) Free. Conc. £5.50. Groups (25+): Adult £5.50. Adult Season Ticket £25.
Key facts: Available for filming. Partial. WCs. Licensed. By arrangement. Limited for coaches. Guide dogs only.

THE GREYFRIARS

Worcester WR1 2LZ

Built about 1480 next to a Franciscan friary in the centre of medieval Worcester, this timber-framed house has 17th and late 18th century additions. It was rescued from demolition at the time of the Second World War and was carefully restored. The panelled rooms have noteworthy textiles and interesting furniture.
Location: MAP 6:N9, OS150, SO852 546. Friar Street, in centre of Worcester.
Owner: National Trust
Contact: House and Visitor Services Manager
Tel: 01905 23571
E-mail: greyfriars@nationaltrust.org.uk
Website: www.nationaltrust.org.uk
Open: Please contact for up to date information. Open BH Mons.
Admission: Please contact for up to date information.
Key facts:

HANBURY HALL

Droitwich, Worcestershire WR9 7EA

Completed in 1701, this homely William & Mary-style house is famed for its fine painted ceilings and staircase, and has other fascinating features including an orangery, ice house, pavilions and working mushroom house.
Location: MAP 6:N8, OS150, SO943 637. 4½m E of Droitwich, 4m SE M5/J5.
Owner: National Trust
Contact: The Property Manager
Tel: 01527 821214
Fax: 01527 821251
E-mail: hanburyhall@nationaltrust.org.uk
Website: www.nationaltrust.org.uk
Open: Please contact for up to date information.
Admission: Please contact for up to date information.
Key facts: Partial.

LITTLE MALVERN COURT

Nr Malvern, Worcestershire WR14 4JN

Prior's Hall, associated rooms and cells, c1489. Former Benedictine Monastery. Oak-framed roof, 5 bays. Library, collection of religious vestments and relics. Embroideries and paintings. Gardens: 10 acres of former monastic grounds with spring bulbs, blossom, old fashioned roses and shrubs. Access to Hall only by flight of steps.
Location: MAP 6:M9, OS Ref. SO769 403. 3m S of Great Malvern on Upton-on-Severn Road (A4104).
Owner: Trustees of the late T M Berington **Contact:** Mrs T M Berington
Tel: 01684 892988 **Fax:** 01684 893057
Open: 18 Apr–19 Jul, Weds & Thurs, 2.15–5pm. Open for NGS Sun 18 Mar & Mon 7 May.
Admission: House & Garden: Adult £6, Child £2, Garden only: Adult £5, Child £1. Groups must book, max 30.
Key facts: Garden (partial).

THE TUDOR HOUSE MUSEUM

16 Church Street, Upton-On-Severn, Worcestershire WR8 0HT

Upton past and present, exhibits of local history.
Location: MAP 6:N10, OS Ref. SO852 406. Centre of Upton-on-Severn, 7m SE of Malvern by B4211. **Owner:** Mrs Lavender Beard **Tel:** 01684 592447
Open: Apr–Oct: Daily 2–5pm, including Bank Holidays. Winter: Suns only, 2–4pm.
Admission: Adult £1.50, Conc. £1, Family £2.50.

© Britainonview

Witley Court Gardens

Spetchley Park Gardens

Fairfax House

Helmsley Castle
© English Heritage

Yorkshire & The Humber

Yorkshire

On a grand scale, Castle Howard is one of England's finest private residences with its dramatic interiors, impressive gilded dome and world–renowned collections of furniture, sculpture and paintings. Skipton Castle is a unique fortress that has guarded the gateway to the Yorkshire Dales for over 900 years, while Fairfax House in York is a richly decorated Georgian town house. Outdoors, York Gate Garden is one of Britain's best small gardens, or visit the ruined Helmsley Castle which boasts exceptional medieval architecture. For something a bit different visit The Forbidden Corner, a unique labyrinth of tunnels, chambers, follies and statues in a four acre garden in the heart of the Yorkshire dales.

VISITOR INFORMATION

Owner
Chatsworth Settlement Trustees

Address
Skipton
North Yorkshire
BD23 6EX

Location
MAP 10:O9
OS Ref. SE074 542.
On B6160, N from the junction with A59 Skipton–Harrogate road, 23m from Leeds.

Contact
Moira Smith
Visitor Manager
Tel: 01756 718009
Fax: 01756 710535
E-mail: tourism@boltonabbey.com

Opening Times
All year from 9am.

Admission
Please see www.boltonabbey.com for the most up-to-date information.

Special events
Full programme of events for all the family.

© Chris Northall

BOLTON ABBEY

www.boltonabbey.com

Set in the heart of the Dales, Bolton Abbey is the Yorkshire home of the Duke and Duchess of Devonshire.

Bolton Abbey Estate has long been a magnet for visitors drawn to its breathtaking landscape and excellent facilities. As the name suggests Bolton Abbey was originally a large monastic estate based around the 12th century Priory. Today, the ruins of the Priory, set in an incomparable position overlooking the river Wharfe, will evoke the past glories of the Estate. The restored and thriving Parish Church not only shows that Bolton Abbey is still very much a living community but also provides the perfect point from which to begin a visit and explore this romantic location.

With over 80 miles of paths there is a trail for all abilities. Wander along the woodland and riverside paths, take a moment to admire the views of Barden Tower and be inspired by the fearsome Strid, enjoyed by famous artists such as Turner and Landseer alike. Or cross the exposed heights of the heather moorland and be prepared to be stirred by the spectacular views and abundance of wildlife.

Electric wheelchairs are available to hire April to October giving access to the Priory, riverside, Strid Wood and the Strid.

Bolton Abbey is well known for its hospitality. Why not enjoy the local produce at the award-winning restaurants and tea rooms and indulge in a little retail therapy in the gift shops and delicatessen. Or simply relax and enjoy a picnic.

KEY FACTS

- Filming and Commercial Photography with prior permission only. Choice of gift shops. Disabled parking, toilets and managed footpaths. Pre-booked electric and manual wheelchairs available from April–October. Contact 01756 710663 to book. Choice of tea rooms, cafes, restaurant and outdoor picnic area. Barbecues permitted in designated area of Sandholme car park.
- WCs.
- Licensed.
- Licensed.
- By arrangement.
- On leads.
- Devonshire Arms Country House Hotel & Devonshire Fell Hotel nearby.

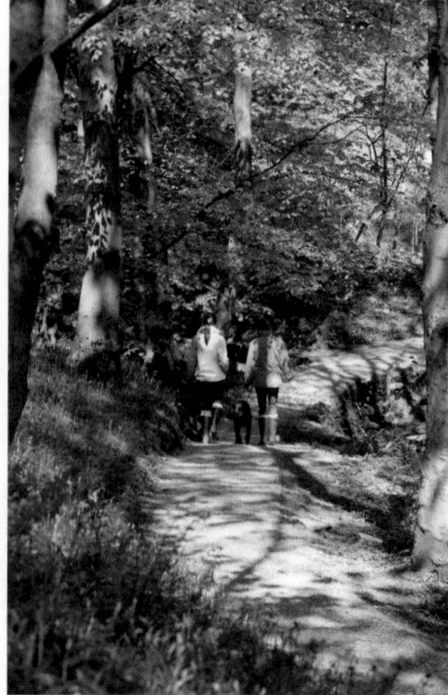

BRODSWORTH HALL & GARDENS ⌗

www.english-heritage.org.uk/brodsworthhall

Time really does stand still at Brodsworth Hall, almost everything has been left exactly as it was.

Explore the changing fortunes of a wealthy Victorian family through the stories of a house and the memories of a home at Brodsworth Hall. This is no glossily restored showpiece, frozen in a single period of manicured grandeur, the hall was 'Conserved as found' and is a mansion which has grown comfortably old over 120 years, revealing a country house as it really was: reflecting its original opulence well-use and patched up in places and full of unexpected family curios.

Built in the Italianate style of the 1860s by the fabulously wealthy Charles Sabine Augustus Thellusson, the hall served as the family home for over 120 years. The pillared, sculpture-lined and sumptuously furnished 'grand rooms' on the ground floor recall the house's Victorian heyday. The Thellusson family's sporting interests, horse racing and yachting, are reflected throughout the house.

In contrast to the house, the extensive gardens have been wonderfully restored to their original horticultural splendour as 'a collection of grand gardens in miniature'. Restoration work continues to reveal new features, along with visitas last enjoyed before World War 1. Explore the enghanted Grove with paths, banks and bridges winding over and under each other revealing an array of different views, which reflect the desires and apsorations of Victorian gentry.

No matter what time of year visited the gardens at Brodsworth Hall are a delight in any season. Brodsworth Hall is available for corporate and private hire.

KEY FACTS

Exhibitions about the family, the servants and the gardens. WCs. No Cameras (house only).

Groups must book. Booked coach parties: 10am–1pm.

220 cars and 3 coaches. Free.

Education Centre. Free if booked in advance.

Gardens, Tearoom and Servants' Wing only.

VISITOR INFORMATION

Owner
English Heritage

Address
Brodsworth Hall
Brodsworth
Nr Doncaster
Yorkshire DN5 7XJ

Location
MAP 11:B12
OS Ref. SE506 070

In Brodsworth, 5m NW of Doncaster off A635. Use A1(M)/J37.

Rail: South Elmsall 4m; Moorthorpe 4.5m; Doncaster 5.5m.

Contact
Visitor Operations Team
Tel: 01302 722598
Fax: 01302 337165
E-mail: brodsworth.hall@english-heritage.org.uk

Opening Times
Please visit www.english-heritage.org.uk for opening times and the most up-to-date information.

Admission
House & Gardens

Adult	£9.00
Child (5–15yrs)	£5.40
Child (under 5yrs)	Free
Conc.	£8.10

Discount for groups (11+).

Gardens only

Adult	£5.50
Child (5–15yrs)	£3.30
Child (under 5yrs)	Free
Conc.	£5.00

EH members Free.

Free admission for tour leaders and coach drivers.

Prices are valid until 31st March 2012.

Special events
150,000 Snowdrops, Bluebells and Daffodils put on a show from February onward.

There is an exciting events programme available throughout the year, for further details please contact the property or visit the website.

VISITOR INFORMATION

Owner
The Hon Simon Howard

Address
Castle Howard
York
North Yorkshire
YO60 7DA

Location
MAP 11:C8
OS Ref. SE716 701

Approaching from S, A64 to Malton, on entering Malton, take Castle Howard Road via Coneysthorpe village.

Rail: London Kings Cross to York 1hr. 50 mins. York to Malton Station 30 mins.

Bus: Service and tour buses from York Station.

Contact
Visitor Services
Tel: 01653 648333
E-mail: house@castlehoward.co.uk

Opening Times
House:
24 March–4 November & 25 November–16 December 2012.
Open daily from 11am (last admission 4pm).

Grounds:
Open all year except Christmas Day, from 10am until 5.30pm (dusk in winter).

Stable Courtyard Gift Shops, Farm Shop, Garden Centre and Cafés:
Open daily all year from 10am until 5pm (4pm in winter) with free admission and parking.

Access to Pretty Wood Pyramid 1 July–31 August.

Special tours to newly restored rooms in the house are available by arrangement.

For more information please contact Castle Howard Estate Office on 01653 648444.

Admission
Annual Passes available

Summer
House & Grounds

Adult	£13.00
Child (5-16yrs)	£7.50
Under 5yrs	Free
Conc.	£11.00

Grounds only

Adult	£8.50
Child (5-16yrs)	£6.00
Under 5yrs	Free
Conc.	£8.00

Winter (when the house is closed) Grounds only

Adult	£6.00
Child (5-16yrs)	£3.00
Under 5yrs	Free

Conference/Function

ROOM	Size	Max Cap
Long Gallery	197' x 24'	200
Grecian Hall	40' x 40'	70

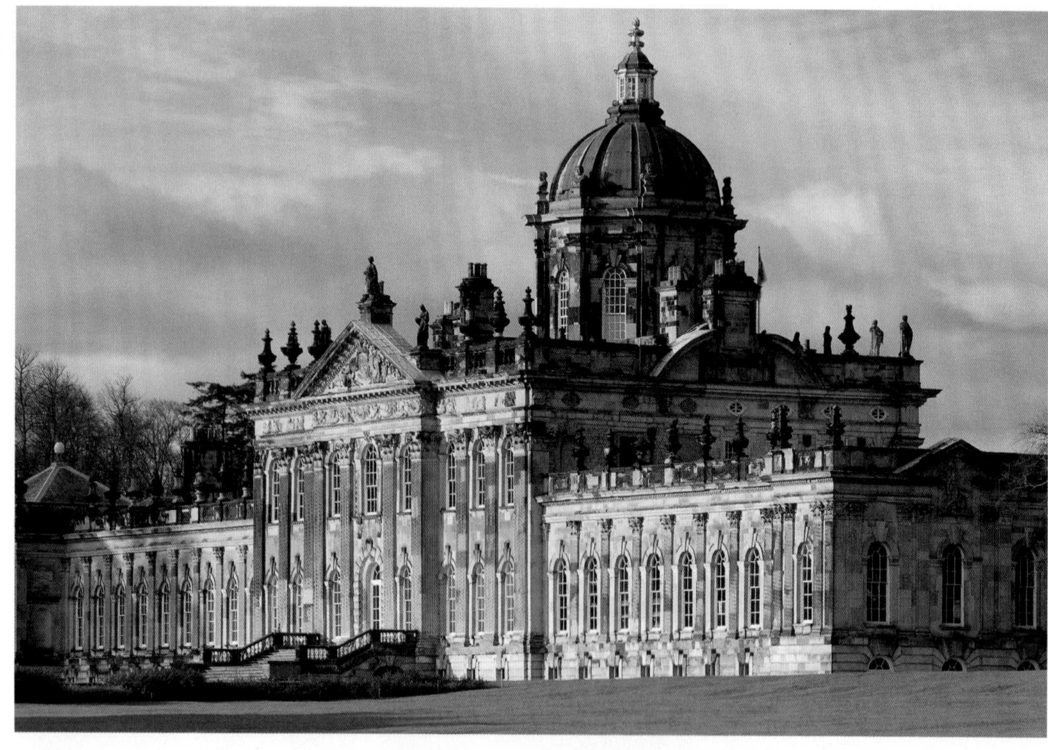

CASTLE HOWARD

www.castlehoward.co.uk

Designed by Sir John Vanbrugh in 1699 Castle Howard is undoubtedly one of Britain's finest private residences.

Built for Charles Howard the 3rd Earl of Carlisle, Castle Howard today remains home to the Howard family. Its dramatic interiors, with impressive painted and gilded dome, contain world – renowned collections – including furniture, porcelain, sculpture and paintings – all gathered by succeeding generations of the family. In each room, listen as friendly and knowledgeable guides share with you the stories of each generation and their influence in shaping the future of Castle Howard.

The High South apartments, which were so tragically destroyed by fire in 1940, are now open to the public. This once bare shell is now a film set – complete with props and painted scenery – following the 2008 film remake of Brideshead Revisited. An accompanying exhibition tells the story of the fire, the extraordinary transformation to movie set, and why Evelyn Waugh's famous novel, was filmed not just once, but twice, at Castle Howard.

Designed on a monumental scale, the breathtaking grounds reflect the grandeur of the house. Featuring statues, lakes, temples and fountains, memorable sights include The Temple of the Four Winds, the Mausoleum and New River Bridge.

Garden enthusiasts will enjoy the 18th century walled garden with its collection of roses and ornamental vegetable garden, while Ray Wood – widely acknowledged as a "rare botanical jewel" – features a unique collection of rare trees, shrubs, rhododendrons, magnolias and azaleas.

Enjoy a changing programme of exhibitions, events and tours throughout the summer. Year round attractions include an adventure playground, self – guided children's trails, and a choice of shops and cafés.

KEY FACTS

- Photography allowed.
- Licensed for civil weddings.
- Access to all areas except High South, Exhibition Wing and Chapel.
- Choice of four cafés.
- Obligatory.
- Free parking.
- School parties welcome.
- Dogs welcome.
- Camping and caravanning.
- Gardens, shops and cafés open all year.
- Full programme for all the family.

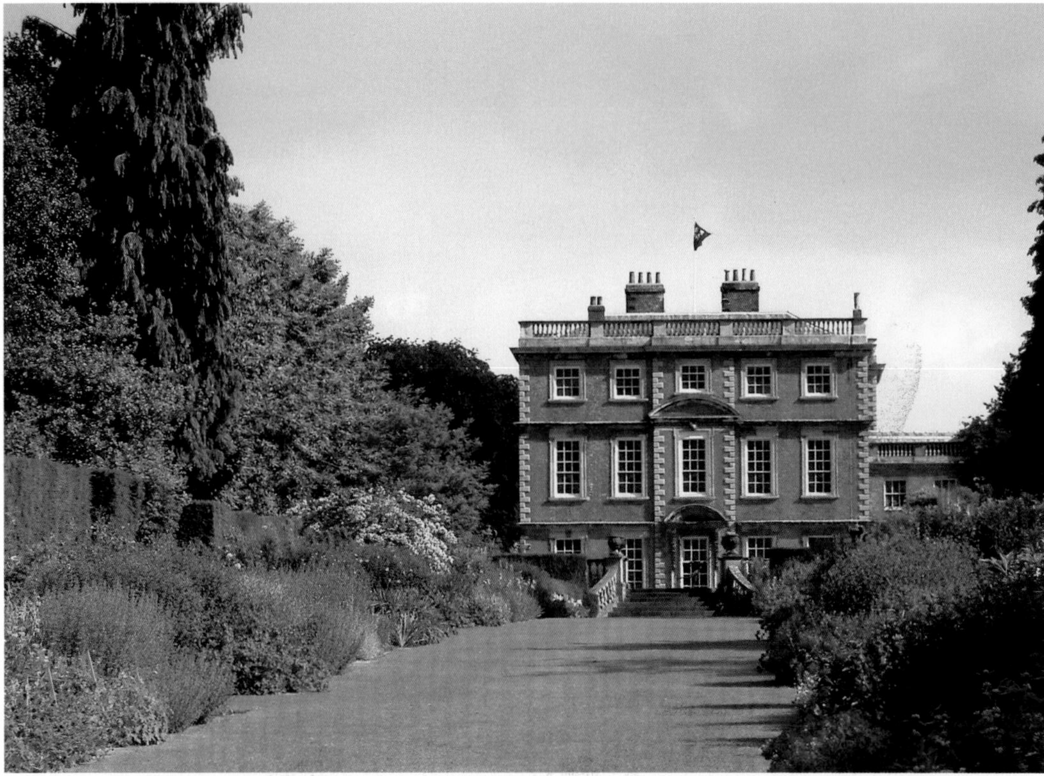

NEWBY HALL & GARDENS

www.newbyhall.com

Newby is a perfect combination of Georgian Grandeur and family home, surrounded by one of Yorkshire's finest gardens.

The home of Richard and Lucinda Compton, Newby Hall is one of England's renowned Adam houses. In the 1760s William Weddell, an ancestor of the Comptons, acquired a magnificent collection of Ancient Roman sculpture and Gobelins tapestries. He commissioned Robert Adam to alter the original Wren designed house and Thomas Chippendale to make furniture. The result is a perfect example of the Georgian 'Age of Elegance' with the atmosphere and ambience of a family home.

Gardens

25 acres of stunning award-winning gardens contain rare and beautiful shrubs and plants, including a National collection of the Genus Cornus (Dogwoods). Newby's famous double herbaceous borders, framed by great bastions of yew hedges, make the perfect walkway to the River Ure. Formal gardens such as the Autumn and Rose Garden, Sylvia's Garden and the Tropical Garden make Newby an inspiring and exciting place to explore. Walking through the curved pergolas leads to the Victorian Rock garden, which is an enchanting magical space for everyone. A well designed adventure garden caters for tots to teens, with a picturesque miniature railway. From 1st June there is an annual exhibition of contemporary sculpture. Newby holds special events, including open air theatre and art exhibitions, throughout the year. See website for details.

The Church of Christ the Consoler, in Newby's grounds, is a Victorian Gothic church built by William Burges. It was commissioned in 1870 by Newby's Lady Mary Vyner, in memory of her youngest son, Frederick after he was kidnapped and later murdered by Greek brigands.

KEY FACTS

- Allow a full day for viewing house and gardens. Suitable for filming and for special events, No indoor photography.
- 'The Shop @ Newby Hall' – Modern British Art and Craftsmanship.
- Wedding receptions & special functions.
- Suitable. WCs.
- Licensed.
- Licensed.
- Obligatory.
- Ample. Hard standing for coaches.
- Welcome. Rates on request. Grantham Room for use as wet weather base subject to availability. Woodland discovery walk, adventure gardens and train rides.

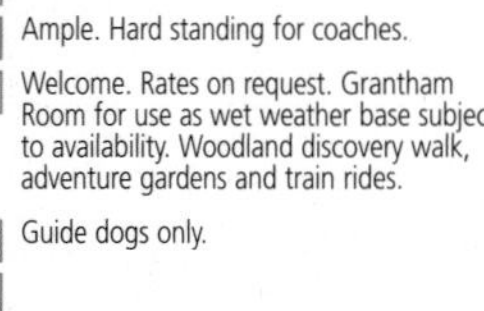

- Guide dogs only.

VISITOR INFORMATION

Owner
Mr Richard Compton

Address
Newby Hall
Ripon
North Yorkshire
HG4 5AE

Location
MAP 11:A8
OS Ref. SE348 675
Midway between London and Edinburgh, 4m W of A1, towards Ripon.
S of Skelton 2m NW of (A1) Boroughbridge.
4m SE of Ripon.
Taxi: Ripon Taxi Rank 01765 601283.

Contact
The Administrator
Tel: 01423 322583
Fax: 01423 324452
Information Hotline: 0845 450 4068
E-mail: info@newbyhall.com

Opening Times
Summer: House*
31 March–30 September.
April, May, June & September:
Tues–Sun & BH Mons;
July–August: Daily
12 noon–5pm.
Last admission 4pm.
*Areas of the House can be closed to the public from time to time, please check website for details.

Garden
Dates as House,
11am–5.30pm.
Last admission 5pm.

Winter
October–end March
Closed.

Admission
(2011 Prices)

House & Garden	
Adult	£12.20
Child/Disabled	£9.50
OAP	£11.20
Group (15+) Adult	£11.20
Child/Disabled	£8.50
OAP	£10.70
Family (2+2)	£41.00
Family (2+3)	£44.00
Garden only	
Adult	£8.70
Child/Disabled	£7.20
OAP	£7.70
Group (15+) Adult	£7.70
Child (4–16yrs)	£6.20
OAP	£7.20
Family (2+2)	£31.00
Family (2+3)	£36.00

Special events
Spring Plant Fair 13 May
Vintage Tractor Rally 9–10 June
Historic Vehicle Rally 15 July
Alfa Romeo Rally 12 August
Darlington Championship Dog Show 14–16 September

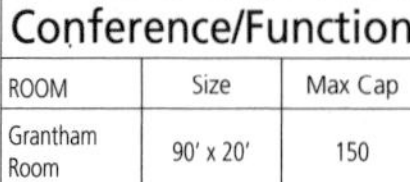

Conference/Function

ROOM	Size	Max Cap
Grantham Room	90' x 20'	150

VISITOR INFORMATION

Owner
English Heritage

Address
Rievaulx
Nr Helmsley
North Yorkshire
YO62 5LB

Location
MAP 11:B7
OS Ref. SE577 850.
In Rievaulx; 21/4m N of Helmsley on minor road off B1257.

Contact
Visitor Operations Team
Tel: 01439 798228
E-mail: rievaulx.abbey@english-heritage.org.uk

Opening Times
please visit www.english-heritage.org.uk for opening times and the most up-to-date information.

Admission

Adult	£5.60
Child	£3.40
Conc.	£5.00

Discount for groups (11+).

Opening times and prices are valid until 31st March 2012.

Special events
There is an exciting events programme available throughout the year, for further details please contact the property or visit the website.

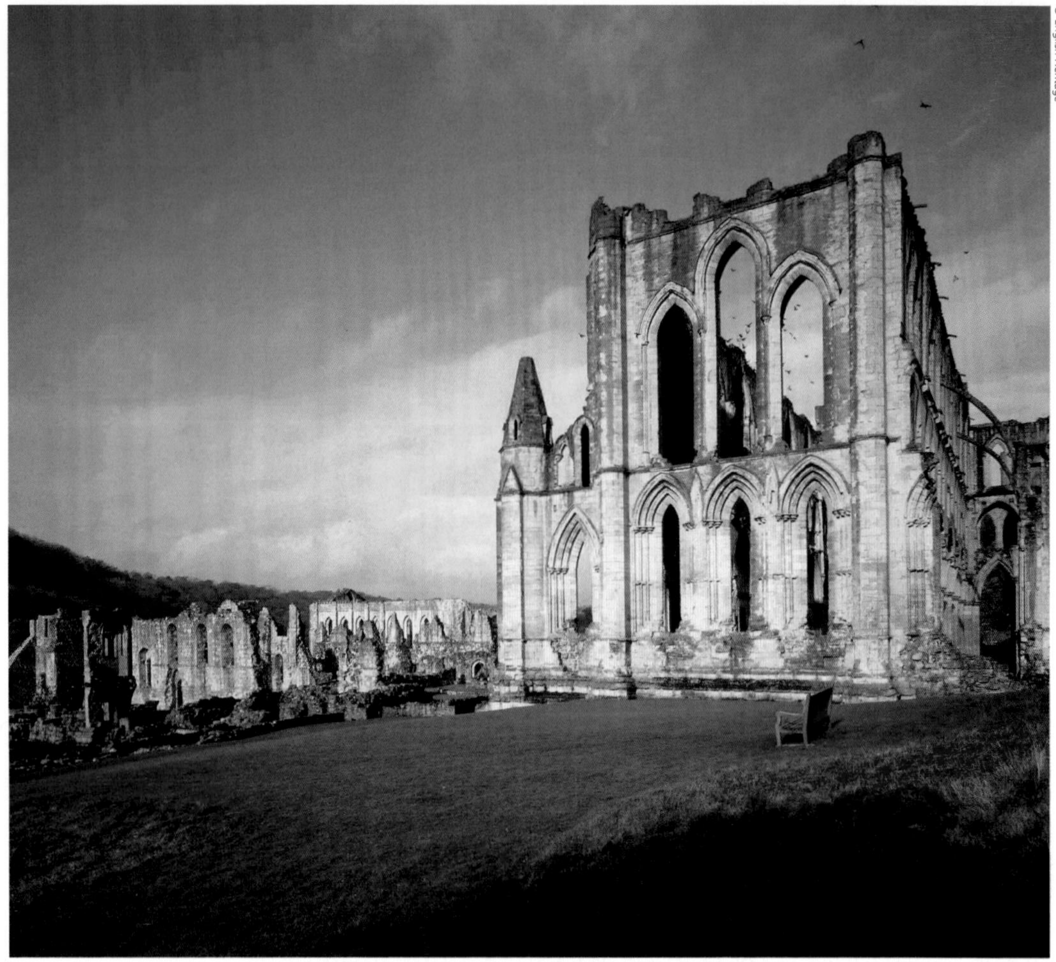

© English Heritage

RIEVAULX ABBEY ⌗

www.english-heritage.org.uk/rievaulx

Rievaulx Abbey is the perfect choice for a peaceful and tranquil day out.

Rievaulx was the first Cistercian Abbey to be founded in the North of England in the 12th century by St Bernard of Clairvaux. Set in a beautiful tranquil valley, it is the most atmospheric and complete of all the ruined abbeys in the region.

"Everywhere peace, everywhere serenity, and a marvellous freedom from the tumult of the world", these words still describe Rievaulx today; written over eight centuries ago by, St Aelred.

An exhibition "The Work of God and Man" explores the agricultural, industrial, spiritual and commercial history of Rievaulx. The tearoom offers delicious Yorkshire fare; made with fresh local produce.

Don't forget to visit the tearoom which has an indoor and outdoor seating area and serves a delicious variety of food, including ingredients grown in the Rievaulx Abbey Garden.

Refectory Cottage was built in the early 20th century for the custodian of the Abbey using reclaimed stone. This well equipped holiday cottage sleeps four, and has a wood-burning stove.

KEY FACTS

WCs.

Audio tours (also available for the visually impaired, those with learning difficulties and in French and German).

Pay and display parking, refundable to EH members and paying visitors upon admission.

On leads.

© English Heritage

© English Heritage

SKIPTON CASTLE

www.skiptoncastle.co.uk

Skipton Castle, over 900 years old, one of the best preserved, most complete medieval castles in England.

Guardian of the gateway to the Yorkshire Dales for over 900 years, this unique fortress is one of the most complete, well-preserved medieval castles in England. Standing on a 40-metre high crag, fully-roofed Skipton Castle was founded around 1090 by Robert de Romille, one of William the Conqueror's Barons, as a fortress in the dangerous northern reaches of the kingdom.

Owned by King Edward I and Edward II, from 1310 it became the stronghold of the Clifford Lords withstanding successive raids by marauding Scots. During the Civil War it was the last Royalist bastion in the North, yielding only after a three-year siege in 1645. 'Slighted' under the orders of Cromwell, the castle was skillfully restored by the redoubtable Lady Anne Clifford and today visitors can climb from the depths of the Dungeon to the top of the Watch Tower, explore the Banqueting Hall, Kitchens, the Bedchamber and even the Privy!

Every period has left its mark, from the Norman entrance and the medieval towers, to the beautiful Tudor courtyard with the great yew tree planted by Lady Anne in 1659.

In the grounds visitors can see the Tudor wing built as a royal wedding present for Lady Eleanor Brandon, niece of Henry VIII, the beautiful Shell Room decorated in the 1620s with shells and Jamaican coral and the ancient medieval chapel of St. John the Evangelist. The Chapel Terrace, with its delightful picnic area, has fine views over the woods and Skipton's lively market town.

KEY FACTS

Unsuitable.

Licensed.

By arrangement.

Large public coach and car park off nearby High Street. Coach drivers' rest room at Castle.

Welcome. Guides available. Teachers free.

On leads.

DESORMAIS

VISITOR INFORMATION

Address

Skipton Castle
Skipton
North Yorkshire
BD23 1AW

Location

MAP 10:09
OS Ref. SD992 520

In the centre of Skipton, at the N end of High Street.

Skipton is 20m W of Harrogate on the A59 and 26m NW of Leeds on A65.

Rail: Regular services from Leeds & Bradford.

Contact

Judith Parker
Tel: 01756 792442
Fax: 01756 796100
E-mail: info@skiptoncastle.co.uk

Opening Times

All year
(closed 25 December)
Mon–Sat: 10am–6pm
Suns: 12 noon–6pm
(October–February 4pm).

Admission

Adult	£6.70
Child (0–4yrs)	Free
Child (5–17yrs)	£4.10
OAP	£6.10
Student (with ID)	£6.10
Family (2+3)	£21.50
Groups (15+)	
Adult	£5.70
Child (0–17yrs)	£4.10

Includes illustrated tour sheet in a choice of nine languages, plus free badge for children.

Groups welcome: Guides available for booked groups at no extra charge.

Special Events

For up-to-date information and coming events, see our website www.skiptoncastle.co.uk

FAIRFAX HOUSE

FAIRFAX HOUSE, CASTLEGATE, YORK YO1 9RN

www.fairfaxhouse.co.uk

Unlock the splendour within the finest Georgian townhouse in England. A classical architectural masterpiece of the 18th century featuring exceptional stuccowork, Fairfax House was the winter home of Viscount Fairfax. Its richly decorated interior was designed by York's most distinguished architect, John Carr. Today, Fairfax House reveals the elegance of city living in Georgian York. The superb collection of 18th century furniture, clocks, paintings and decorative arts perfectly complements the house, bringing it to life and creating a special lived-in feeling. With an exciting programme of events and exhibitions, there is always a reason to come and savour Fairfax House.

Location: MAP 11:B9, OS Ref. SE605 515. In centre of York between Castle Museum and Jorvik Centre.

Owner: York Civic Trust **Contact:** Hannah Phillip

Tel: 01904 655543 **Fax:** 01904 652262

E-mail: info@fairfaxhouse.co.uk

Open: 10 Feb–31 Dec, Tues–Sat & Bank holidays: 10am–5pm. Sat: 11am–5pm. Sun: 12.30–4pm. Mon: Guided tours only 11am & 2pm. Last admission half an hour before stated closing times. Closed 1 Jan–11 Feb & 24–26 Dec.

Admission: Adult £6, Conc. £5, Children under 16 Free with full paying adult. Groups from £4.50 pp. Min payment 10 persons.

Key facts: Suitable for filming. No photography in house. Max. 28 seated. Groups up to 50. Partial. By arrangement. Guide dogs only.

© NTPL / Andrew Butler

© NTPL / Andrew Butler

FOUNTAINS ABBEY & STUDLEY ROYAL

RIPON, NORTH YORKSHIRE HG4 3DY

www.fountainsabbey.org.uk

Come and discover for yourself why Fountains Abbey & Studley Royal is a World Heritage Site. Experience the beauty, history and tranquillity of this inspirational place in the heart of the beautiful North Yorkshire countryside. Explore the spectacular ruin of a 12th century Cistercian Abbey, one of the best surviving examples of a Georgian Water Garden, Elizabethan Manor House, Monastic Watermill and Medieval Deer Park home to over 500 wild deer. Enjoy open-air summer theatre, exhibitions, guided tours, family activities and wildlife walks throughout the year.

Location: MAP 10:P8. OS Ref. SE275 700. Abbey entrance: 4m W of Ripon off B6265. 8m W of A1.

Owner/Contact: National Trust

Tel: 01765 608888

E-mail: info@fountainsabbey.org.uk

Open: Apr–Sept, Daily, 10am–5pm. Oct–Mar, Daily, 10am–4pm or dusk if earlier. Closed 24/25 Dec, & Fris from Nov–Jan. Deer Park: All year, daily during daylight (closed 24/25 Dec).

***Admission:** Adult £9, Child (5–16yrs) £4.85, Family £23, Groups (15+) Adult £7.70. Groups (31+) Adult £7.45. Group discount applicable only with prior booking. Group visits and disabled visitors, please telephone in advance, 01765 643197. *Includes a voluntary donation but visitors can choose to pay the standard prices displayed at the property and on the website. Does not apply to group prices. NT, EH Members & Under 5s Free. The Abbey is owned by the National Trust and maintained by English Heritage. St Mary's Church is owned by English Heritage and managed by the National Trust.

Key facts: Events held throughout the year. Exhibitions. Seminar facilities. Outdoor concerts, meetings, activity days, walks. Two shops. Dinners. WCs. Licensed. Licensed. Free, but seasonal. Groups (please book on 01765 643197), please use Visitor Centre entrance. Audio tour £2. Drivers must book groups. On leads. Fountains Hall, an Elizabethan Mansion is an ideal setting for weddings. For details or a Wedding pack tel: 01765 643198.

MARKENFIELD HALL

NR RIPON, NORTH YORKSHIRE HG4 3AD

www.markenfield.com

"This wonderfully little-altered building is the most complete surviving example of the meduim-sized 14th century country house in England" John Martin Robinson *The Architecture of Northern England*. Tucked privately away down a mile-long winding drive, Markenfield is one of the most astonishing and romantic of Yorkshire's medieval houses: fortified, completely moated, and still privately owned. Winner of the HHA and Sotheby's Finest Restoration Award 2008.

Location: MAP 10:P8, OS Ref. SE294 672. Access from W side of A61. 2½ miles S of the Ripon bypass.

Owner: Mr Ian & Lady Deirdre Curteis **Contact:** The Administrator

Tel: 01765 692303 **Fax:** 01765 607195

E-mail: info@markenfield.com

Open: 6–19 May & 17–30 Jun: daily, 2–5pm. Last entry 4.30pm. Groups all year round by appointment.

Admission: Adult £4, Conc £3. Booked groups (min charge £80).

Key facts: Partial. Obligatory. Limited for coaches. In grounds.

RIPLEY CASTLE

RIPLEY, HARROGATE, NORTH YORKSHIRE HG3 3AY

www.ripleycastle.co.uk

Home of the Ingilby family for 26 generations and Sir Thomas and Lady Ingilby, together with their five children, continue the tradition. Guided tours are amusing and informative. The Tower dates from 1555 and houses splendid armour, books, panelling and a Priest's Secret Hiding Place. The extensive Walled Gardens are a colourful delight every season. In Spring 150,000 flowering bulbs create a blaze of colour through the woodland walks, and also the National Hyacinth Collection whose scent is breathtaking. The Hot Houses have an extensive tropical plant collection. The Kitchen Gardens contain an extensive collection of rare vegetables.

Location: MAP 10:P9, OS Ref. SE283 605. W edge of village. Just off A61 between Harrogate and Ripon.

Owner: Sir Thomas Ingilby Bt

Contact: Tours: Lesley Johnston-Senior, Meetings/Dinners: Jenny Carter

Tel: 01423 770152 **Fax:** 01423 771745 **E-mail:** enquiries@ripleycastle.co.uk

Open: Castle: Easter–end Sept and Halloween Week: Daily. Oct, Nov & Mar: Tues, Thurs, Sat & Sun. 10.30am–3pm. Dec–Feb: Sats & Suns. 10.30am–3pm. Gardens: All year, daily (except Christmas Day and Boxing Day), 10am–5pm (winter 4.30pm).

Admission: All Year: Castle & Gardens: Adult £9, Child (5–16yrs) £5.50, Child under 5yrs Free, OAP £8. Groups (20+): Adult £8, Child (5–16yrs) £5. Gardens only: Adult £6, Child (5–16yrs) £4, OAP £5.50. Groups (20+): Adult £6, Child (5–16yrs) £3.50, Child under 5yrs Free.

Key facts: No photography inside Castle unless by prior written consent. Parkland for outdoor activities & concerts. VIP lunches & dinners (max. 150): unlimited in marquees. Full catering service, wedding receptions, banquets, meetings and activity days. WCs. Licensed. Licensed. Obligatory. Tour time 75 mins. 290 cars – 300 yds from Castle entrance. Coach park 50 yds. Free. Welcome by arrangement, between 10.30am–7.30pm. Guide dogs only. Boar's Head Hotel (AA***) 100 yds. Owned and managed by the estate.

© English Heritage Photo Library

© English Heritage

SCARBOROUGH CASTLE

CASTLE ROAD, SCARBOROUGH, NORTH YORKSHIRE YO11 1HY

www.english-heritage.org.uk/scarborough

Scarborough Castle defends a prominent headland between two bays, with sheer drops to the sea and only a narrow landward approach. Overlooking the town of Scarborough, the castle has witnessed 3000 years of turbulent history from the Bronze Age to WWII. Gain fascinating insights into the past with an exhibition in the Master Gunner's house and see intriguing artefacts from the site. Viewing platforms offer panoramic views of the coast. For younger visitors there are also an investigative story box which helps to visualise and understand the history of the castle.

Location: MAP 11:E7, OS Ref. TA050 892. Castle Road, E of the town centre.

Owner: English Heritage **Contact:** Visitor Operations Team

Tel: 01723 372451

E-mail: scarborough.castle@english-heritage.org.uk

Open: 1 Apr–30 Sep: daily, 10am–6pm. 1 Oct–31 Mar: Thur–Mon, 10am–4pm. Closed 24–26 Dec & 1 Jan.

Admission: Adult £4.80, Child £2.90, Conc. £4.30, Family £12.50. 15% discount for groups (11+). Opening times and prices are valid until 31st March 2012, after this date details are subject to change please visit www.english-heritage.org.uk for the most up-to-date information.

Key facts: WCs. Inclusive. Limited. (pre-booked parking only for disabled visitors, otherwise located in town centre). On leads.

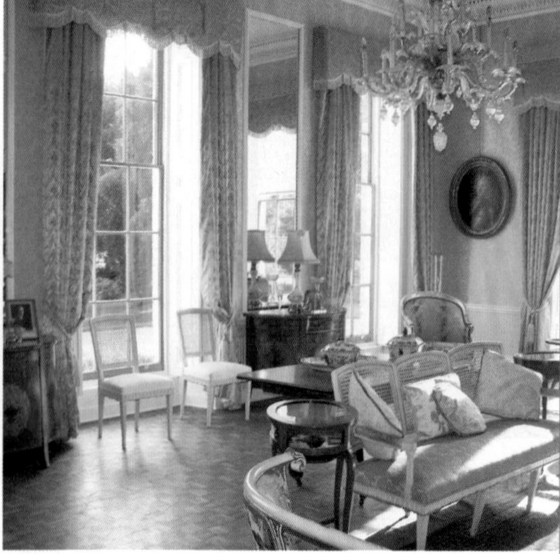

WASSAND HALL

SEATON, HULL, EAST YORKSHIRE HU11 5RJ

www.wassand.co.uk

Fine Regency house 1815 by Thomas Cundy the Elder. Beautifully restored walled gardens, woodland walks, Parks and vistas over Hornsea Mere, part of the Estate since 1580. The Estate was purchased circa 1520 by Dame Jane Constable and has remained in the family to the present day, Mr Rupert Russell being the great nephew of the late Lady Strickland-Constable. The house contains a fine collection of 18/19th century paintings, English and Continental silver, furniture and porcelain. Wassand is very much a family home and retains a very friendly atmosphere. Homemade afternoon teas are served in the conservatory on Open Days.

Location: MAP 11:F9, OS Ref. TA174 460. On the B1244 Seaton–Hornsea Road. Approximately 2m from Hornsea.

Owner/Contact: R E O Russell – Resident Trustee

Tel: 01964 534488 **Fax:** 01964 533334

E-mail: reorussell@lineone.net

Open: 25–28 May; 7–11, 22–26 Jun; 13–14, (Sun 15 Concert House & Garden closed), 28–31 Jul; 3, 5, 6, 24–27 Aug. 2–5pm.

Admission: Hall, all grounds & walks: Adult £5.50, OAP £5, Child (11–15yrs) £3, Child (under 10) Free. Hall: Adult £3.50, OAP £3, Child (11–15yrs) £1.50, Child (under 10) Free. Grounds & Garden: Adult £3.50, OAP £3, Child (11–15yrs) £3, Child (under 10) Free. Guided tours and groups by arrangment – POA.

Key facts: Limited. By arrangement. Ample for cars, limited for coaches. In grounds, on leads.

© English Heritage

© English Heritage

WHITBY ABBEY

WHITBY, NORTH YORKSHIRE YO22 4JT

www.english-heritage.org.uk/whitbyabbey

The dramatic ruins of this once magnificent abbey stand high on the headland over the town of Whitby, on the Yorkshire coast. Founded by St Hilda in AD657, Whitby Abbey soon acquired great influence, before being ransacked by the invading Viking army. It was to be 200 years before the monastic tradition was revived, but yet again the Abbey was plundered, this time following the dissolution. Inspired by detailed archaeological investigation of the site, an interactive visitor centre provides visitors with a chance to discover the Abbey's rich history from St Hilda to Dracula.

Location: MAP 11:D6, OS Ref. NZ904 115. On cliff top E of Whitby.

Owner: English Heritage **Contact:** Visitor Operations Team

Tel: 01947 603568 **E-mail:** customers@english-heritage.org.uk

Open: 1 Apr–30 Sep: daily, 10am–6pm. 1 Oct–31 Mar: Thur–Mon, 10am–4pm. Closed 24–26 Dec & 1 Jan.

Admission: Adult £6, Child £3.60, Conc. £5.40, Family £15.60. EH members Free. Opening times and prices are valid until 31st March 2012, after this date details are subject to change please visit www.english-heritage.org.uk for the most up-to-date information.

Key facts: WCs. From the Whitby harbour area, the Abbey can only be directly reached on foot via the 199 'Abbey steps' (or Caedmon's Trod). Alternatively, a well-signposted road leads from the town outskirts to the cliff-top Abbey. Parking not managed by English Heritage. Charge payable. On leads.

BROUGHTON HALL

Skipton, Yorkshire BD23 3AE

www.broughtonhall.co.uk

Broughton Hall Estate has been nurtured by The Tempest family for over 900 years. The Estate is well known for its hospitality for exclusive use, leisure or corporate events, and holidays.

The Broughton Hall Estate has a sister property, Aldourie Castle Estate, Loch Ness, Scotland. www.aldouriecastle.co.uk.

Location: MAP 10:N9, OS Ref. SD943 507. On A59, 2m W of Skipton.

Owner: The Tempest Family

Contact: The Estate Office

Tel: 01756 799608

Fax: 01756 700357

E-mail: tempest@broughtonhall.co.uk

Open: Tours by arrangement.

Admission: P.O.A

Key facts:

Licensed. Licensed.

By arrangement.

BURTON AGNES HALL & GARDENS

Driffield, East Yorkshire YO25 4NB

www.burtonagnes.com

A magnificent Elizabethan Hall containing treasures collected over four centuries, from the original carving and plasterwork to modern and Impressionist paintings. The Hall is surrounded by lawns and topiary yew. The award-winning gardens contain a maze, potager, jungle garden, campanula collection and colour gardens incorporating giant game boards. Children's corner.

Location: MAP 11:E9, OS Ref. TA103 633. Off A614 between Driffield and Bridlington.

Owner: Burton Agnes Hall Preservation Trust Ltd

Contact: Mr Simon Cunliffe-Lister **Tel:** 01262 490324 **Fax:** 01262 490513

E-mail: office@burtonagnes.com

Open: Gardens, shops & café: Snowdrops 4 Feb–4 March, daily, 11am–4pm. Hall & gardens, shops and café: 1 Apr–31 Oct, daily 11am–5pm. Christmas opening: 14 Nov–22 Dec, daily, 11am–5pm.

Admission: Hall & Gardens: Adult £8, Child £4, OAP £7.50. Gardens only: Adult £5, Child £3, OAP £4.50. 10% reduction for groups of 30+.

Key facts: Gift Shop, Farm Shop and Home and Garden Shop. WCs. Licensed. Licensed. Optional. On leads.

BURTON CONSTABLE

Skirlaugh, East Yorkshire HU11 4LN

www.burtonconstable.com

One of the most fascinating country houses surviving with its historic collections, Burton Constable is a large Elizabethan mansion surrounded by extensive parkland. The interiors of faded splendour are filled with fine furniture, paintings and sculpture, a library of 5,000 books and a remarkable 18th century 'Cabinet of Curiosities'.

Location: MAP 11:E10 OS Ref TA 193 369. Beverley 14m, Hull 10m. Signed from Skirlaugh.

Owner: Burton Constable Foundation **Contact:** Mrs Helen Dewson

Tel: 01964 562400 **Fax:** 01964 563229

E-mail: helendewson@btconnect.com

Open: Easter Sat–28 Oct, Hall: 1–5pm, 24 Nov–9 Dec, 1–4pm, last admission 1 hour before closing. Grounds, Stables & Tea Room: 12.30–5pm. Sat–Thur inc.

Admission: Hall: Adult £6.75, Child £3.50, OAP £6.25, Family £17 (2 ad & 4 ch), Groups 15+ £5.75 each. Grounds only: Adult £3, Child £1.50, Family £8. Season Ticket £16.

Key facts: Photography allowed in house. WCs.

Guide dogs only.

CONSTABLE BURTON HALL GARDENS

Leyburn, North Yorkshire DL8 5LJ

www.constableburton.com

A delightful terraced woodland garden of lilies, ferns, hardy shrubs, roses and wild flowers, attached to a beautiful Palladian house designed by John Carr . Garden trails and herbaceous borders ,Stream garden with large architectural plants and reflection ponds. Stunning seasonal displays of snowdrops and daffodils and annual Tulip festival.

Location: MAP 10:P7, OS Ref. SE164 913. 3m E of Leyburn off the A684.

Owner: M C A Wyvill Esq

Contact: M C A Wyvill Esq

Tel: 01677 450428

Fax: 01677 450622

E-mail: gardens@constableburton.com

Open: Garden only: 24 Mar–28 Sept: daily, 9am–6pm. Closed 25th, 26th, 27th May 2012.

Admission: Adult £4, Child (5–16yrs) 50p, OAP £3.

Key facts: WCs.

Obligatory group tours of house & gardens by arrangement.

Limited for coaches. On leads.

© English Heritage

BYLAND ABBEY

Coxwold, Thirsk, North Yorkshire YO61 4BD

www.english-heritage.org.uk/byland

Once one of the greatest monasteries in England, Byland inspired the design of church buildings throughout the north. An outstanding example of early gothic architecture, it inspired the design of the famous York Minster rose window. The Abbey's collection of medieval floor tiles is a testament to its earlier magnificence.

Location: MAP 11:B8, OS Ref. SE549 789. 2m S of A170 between Thirsk and Helmsley, NE of Coxwold village.

Owner: English Heritage

Contact: Visitor Operations Team

Tel: Byland Abbey: 01347 868614 Abbey Inn: 01347 868204

E-mail: byland.abbey@english-heritage.org.uk

Open: Please see www.english-heritage.org.uk for opening times and the most up-to-date information.

Admission: Adult £4.30, Child £2.60, Conc. £3.90. 15% discount for groups (11+). Opening times and prices are valid until 31st March 2012.

Key facts: WC.

Limited for coaches.

On leads.

© Skyscan / William Cross

DUNCOMBE PARK

Helmsley, North Yorkshire YO62 5EB

www.duncombepark.com

The sweeping grass terraces, towering veteran trees, and classical temples are described by historian Christopher Hussey as 'the most spectacularly beautiful among English landscape conceptions of the 18th century'. Beside superb views over the Rye valley, visitors will discover woodland walks, ornamental parterres, and a 'secret garden' at the Conservatory.

Location: MAP 11:B7, OS Ref. SE604 830. Entrance just off Helmsley Market Square, signed off A170 Thirsk–Scarborough road.

Owner/Contact: Hon. Jake Duncombe

Tel: 01439 770213 **Fax:** 01439 771114 **E-mail:** info@duncombepark.com

Open: Garden Only: 3 Jun–31 Aug, Sun–Fri, 10.30am–5pm. Last admission 4pm. The garden may close for private events and functions – please check website for information.

Admission: Gardens & Parkland: Adult £5, Conc £4.50, Child (5–16yrs) £3, Child (0-5yrs) Free, Groups (15+) £4, Group guided tour £5. Parkland: Adult £3, Child (10–16yrs) £2, Child (0-10yrs) Free.

Key facts: Wedding receptions, conferences, corporate hospitality, country walks, nature reserve, orienteering, film location, product launches, vehicle rallies. Banqueting facilities. For 15+ groups only.

THE FORBIDDEN CORNER

Tupgill Park Estate, Coverham, Nr Middleham, North Yorkshire DL8 4TJ

www.theforbiddencorner.co.uk

A unique labyrinth of tunnels, chambers, follies and surprises created in a four acre garden in the heart of the Yorkshire dales. The Temple of the Underworld, The Eye of the Needle, a large pyramid made of translucent glass paths and passageways that lead nowhere. Extraordinary statues at every turn.

Location: MAP 10:O7, OS Ref. SE094 866. A6108 to Middleham, situated 2½ miles west of Middleham on the Coverham Lane.

Owner: Colin R Armstrong OBE **Contact:** John Reeves

Tel: 01969 640638 **Fax:** 01969 640687

E-mail: forbiddencorner@gmail.com

Open: 1 Apr–31 Oct daily, then every Sun until Christmas. Mon–Sat 12–6pm. Suns & BHs 10am-6pm (or dusk if earlier).

Admission: Please see www.theforbiddencorner.co.uk for the most up to date information.

Key facts: Partial. Limited for coaches. Guide dogs only. Self catering cottages all year.

HOVINGHAM HALL

York, North Yorkshire YO62 4LU

www.hovingham.co.uk

Attractive Palladian family home, designed and built by Thomas Worsley. The childhood home of Katharine Worsley, Duchess of Kent. It is entered through a huge riding school and has beautiful rooms with collections of pictures and furniture. The house has attractive gardens with magnificent Yew hedges and cricket ground.

Location: MAP 11:C8, OS Ref. SE666 756. 18m N of York on Malton/ Helmsley Road (B1257).

Owner: William Worsley

Contact: Mrs Lamprey

Tel: 01653 628771

Fax: 01653 628668

E-mail: office@hovingham.co.uk

Open: 1 Jun–28 Jun inclusive 12.30pm to 4.30pm (last admission 3.30pm).

Admission: Adult £8.50, Conc. £8, Child £4. Gardens only: £4.

Key facts: No photography in house. Partial. WCs. Obligatory. Limited. None for coaches.

© English Heritage

HELMSLEY CASTLE

Castlegate, Helmsley, North Yorkshire YO62 5AB

www.english-heritage.org.uk/helmsley

Explore 900 years of life at Helmsley Castle which boasts some amazing medieval architecture. Discover how the castle evolved from a medieval fortress, to a luxurious Tudor mansion, to a Civil War stronghold and a romantic Victorian ruin. Take an audio tour and see original artefacts excavated from the site.

Location: MAP 11:B7, OS Ref. SE611 836. In Helmsley town.

Owner: English Heritage **Contact:** Visitor Operations Team

Tel/Fax: 01439 770442 **E-mail:** helmsley.castle@english-heritage.org.uk

Open: Please visit www.english-heritage.org.uk for opening times and the most up-to-date information

Admission: Adult £4.80, Child £2.90, Conc £4.30, Family £12.50.
15% discount for groups (11+). Opening times & prices are valid until 31st March 2012.

Key facts: Tourist information located within Castle Visitor Centre. Charged. On leads.

LOTHERTON HALL ESTATE

Aberford, Leeds, West Yorkshire LS25 3EB

www.leeds.gov.uk/lothertonhall

Charming Edwardian country home rich in collections of paintings, furniture, silver, china, costume and oriental art. Beautiful formal, wildflower and wooded grounds, red deer park and one of the country's most impressive and important collections of rare and endangered birds.

Location: MAP 11:B10.
OS Ref. SE450 360.
2½ m E of M1/J47 on B1217 the Towton Road. 13 miles from city centre.

Owner: Leeds City Council

Contact: Michael Thaw

Tel: 0113 2813259

E-mail: lotherton@leeds.gov.uk

Open/Admission: Please check the website or call 0113 2813259 for seasonal opening and admission prices.

Key facts: Obligatory.

MANSION HOUSE

St Helen's Square, York YO1 9QL

www.mansionhouseyork.co.uk

The Mansion House is one of York's great historic treasures and the oldest surviving mayoral residence in the country. The beautiful simplicity of the hallway gives way to the magnificent grandeur of the stateroom. The extensive civic collection ranges from silver chamber pots to medieval ceremonial swords.

Location: MAP 21, OS Ref. SE601 518. Situated in St Helen's Square, close to the post office and to York Minster.

Owner: City of York Council **Contact:** Richard Pollitt **Tel:** 01904 552036
Fax: 01904 551052 **E-mail:** mansionhouse@york.gov.uk

Open: 11am, 12.30pm & 2pm every Thur, Fri & Sat from Mar–Dec. Open all year for pre booked groups for silver, candlelit and spooky stories, behind the scenes and connoisseur tours.

Admission: House tours: Adult £5, Child (up to 16) Free, Conc £4. Pre-booked house *Silver tours, *Behind the scenes, candlelit and spooky stories tours* £8.50 *Connoisseur Tours £12.95. *Includes refreshments.

Key facts: Suitable. WCs. Obligatory. Guide dogs only. please see www.mansionhouseyork.co.uk €

NEWBURGH PRIORY

Coxwold, North Yorkshire YO61 4AS

Home to the Earls of Fauconberg and the Wombwell family the house was built in 1145 with alterations in 1538 and 1720 and contains the tomb of Oliver Cromwell. The beautiful grounds contain a lake, water garden, walled garden, amazing topiary yews and woodland walks set against the White Horse.

Location: MAP 11:B8, OS Ref. SE541 764. 4m E of A19, 18m N of York, 1/2 m E of Coxwold.

Owner: Sir George Wombwell Bt
Contact: Sir George Wombwell Bt
Tel: 01347 868372

Open: 1 Apr–27 Jun, Wed & Sun & Easter Mon BH & Mon 27 Aug. Gardens 2–6pm, House 2.30–4.45pm. Tours every 1/2 hour.
Bus parties by arrangement.

Admission: House & Gardens: Adult £6, Child £2. Gardens only: Adult £3, Child Free. Special tours of private apartments Sunday 1, 15, 22, 29 Apr & BH Mon 9 April £5pp.

Key facts: No photography in house. Partial. Obligatory. Limited for coaches. In grounds, on leads. And wedding receptions.

© English Heritage

MOUNT GRACE PRIORY

Staddlebridge, Nr Northallerton, North Yorkshire DL6 3JG

www.english-heritage.org.uk/mountgracepriory

Set amid woodland, this enchanting monastery is the best preserved Carthusian priory in Britain. Discover how the monks lived 600 years ago in the reconstructed monk's cell and herb plot. The gardens, re-modelled in the Arts & Crafts style, are a haven for the famous 'Priory Stoats'.

Location: MAP11:A7, OS Ref. SE449 985. 12m N of Thirsk, 6m NE of Northallerton on A19.

Owner: English Heritage **Contact:** Visitor Operations Team
Tel: 01609 883494 **E-mail:** mountgrace.priory@english-heritage.org.uk

Open: Please visit www.english-heritage.org.uk for opening times and the most up-to-date information.

Admission: Adult £5, Child £3, Conc. £4.50, Family £13. 15% discount for groups (11+). NT Members Free, (except on event days). Opening times and prices are valid until 31st March 2012.

Key facts: Priors Lodge is a charming single storey stone cottage which nestles against the ancient wall of the original manor house. Available for corporate and private hire.

NOSTELL PRIORY & PARKLAND

Doncaster Road, Wakefield, West Yorkshire WF4 1QE

www.nationaltrust.org.uk

Set in over 350 acres of parkland, Nostell Priory is one of Yorkshire's jewels. It is an architectural treasure by James Paine with later additions by Robert Adam, and an internationally renowned Chippendale Collection.

Location: MAP 11:A11.
OS Ref. SE403 175.
6m SE of Wakefield, off A638.

Owner: National Trust
Contact: Visitor Services Manager
Tel: 01924 863892
E-mail: nostellpriory@nationaltrust.org.uk

Open: Please see website for opening times www.nationaltrust.org.uk.

Admission: Please see website for Admission charges www.nationaltrust.org.uk.

Key facts: Baby facilities. WCs. Licensed. By arrangement. Limited for coaches. On leads.

© English Heritage

RICHMOND CASTLE

Tower St, Richmond, North Yorkshire DL10 4QW

www.english-heritage.org.uk/richmond

Built shortly after 1066 on a rocky promontory high above the River Swale, this is the best preserved castle of such scale and age in Britain. The magnificent keep, with breathtaking views, is reputed to be the place where the legendary King Arthur sleeps.

Location: MAP 10:P6, OS Ref. NZ172 007. In Richmond.

Owner: English Heritage **Contact:** Visitor Operations Team

Tel/Fax: 01748 822493

E-mail: customers@english-heritage.org.uk

Open: Please visit www.english-heritage.org.uk for opening times and the most up-to-date information.

Admission: Adult £4.60, Child £2.80, Conc. £4.10. 15% discount for groups (11+). Opening times and prices are valid until 31st March 2012.

Key facts: Interactive exhibition. WCs. On leads.

RIPON CATHEDRAL

Ripon, North Yorkshire HG4 1QR

Close to the A1 and in the Yorkshire Dales Ripon Cathedral has extended a warm welcome to generations of pilgrims and yet felt the heat of battle for over 1300 years.

From Saxon England to the present day the Cathedral offers rich history, great architecture and acclaimed music.

Location: MAP 10:P8, OS Ref. SE314 711. 5m W signposted off A1, 12m N of Harrogate.

Contact: The Cathedral Office

Tel: 01765 603462 (information on tours etc.)

Open: All year: 8am–6pm.

Admission: Donations: £3.

Pre-booked guided tours available.

Key facts: Guide dogs only. €

SCAMPSTON HALL

Scampston, Malton, North Yorkshire YO17 8NG

www.scampston.co.uk

Scampston is among the best examples of the English country house, combining fine architecture with a wealth of art treasures and set in a 'Capability' Brown parkland. Guided tours around this family home are often welcomed by Sir Charles. Restaurant and disabled facilities in The Walled Garden (see separate entry).

Location: MAP 11:D8, OS Ref. SE865 755. 5m E of Malton, off A64.

Owner: Christopher Legard **Contact:** The Administrator

Tel: 01944 759111

Fax: 01944 758700

E-mail: info@scampston.co.uk

Open: 15 May–15 Jul 2012 , Tue–Fri & Suns & BH Mons. 1–3.45pm. All visits by guided tour. Tours at 1pm, 2pm & 3pm.

Admission: Adults £6, Child (5–16yrs) £3, Under 5s Free. Combined ticket inc. Walled Garden: Adults £11, Child (5–16yrs) £5.50. Groups (15+) by appointment. HHA Friends free admission to house only.

Key facts: Partial. Obligatory.

We are open for a range of special events. Please see website for details.

THE WALLED GARDEN AT SCAMPSTON

Scampston Hall, Malton, North Yorkshire YO17 8NG

www.scampston.co.uk

A contemporary garden with striking perennial meadow planting, plus traditional spring/autumn borders, created by acclaimed designer and plantsman Piet Oudolf. Described in The Times as "a gem". The garden is complemented by an excellent restaurant. "It's bold and beautiful–a must if you are heading to Yorkshire" Toparius.

Location: MAP 11:D8, OS Ref. SE865 755. 5m E of Malton, off A64.

Owner: Sir Charles Legard Bt **Contact:** The Administrator

Tel: 01944 759111 **Fax:** 01944 758700 **E-mail:** info@scampston.co.uk

Open: 6 Apr–28 Oct, Tues–Sun plus BHols. Also Mons in Aug. 10am–5pm, last adm. 4.30pm.

Admission: Adult £6, Child (5–16) £3, Under 5s Free. Groups (15+) welcome by arrangement. Please note: HHA membership does not give access to the Walled Garden.

Key facts: Suitable. WCs. Licensed.

Spring Plant Fair Sunday 10th June, Autumn Plant Fair Sunday 7th October.

SION HILL

Kirby Wiske, Thirsk, North Yorkshire YO7 4EU

www.sionhillhall.co.uk

Sion Hill was designed in 1912 by the renowned York architect Walter H Brierley, 'the Lutyens of the North', receiving an award from the Royal Institute of British Architects as being of 'outstanding architectural merit'. The house is furnished with a fine collection of antique furniture, paintings, ceramics and clocks.

Location: MAP 11:A7, OS Ref. SE373 844. 6m S of Northallerton off A167, signposted. 4m W of Thirsk, 6m E of A1 via A61.

Owner: H W Mawer Trust **Contact:** R M Mallaby

Tel: 01845 587206

Fax: 01845 587486

E-mail: sionhill@btconnect.com

Open: Apr–Oct. Please contact the house for dates, times and booking arrangements. Admission strictly by pre-booked ticket.

Admission: £10 per person to include guided tour and admission to the grounds.

Key facts: No photography in the house. Partial. WC. By arrangement Ample for cars and coaches. Guide dogs only.

STOCKELD PARK

Wetherby, North Yorkshire LS22 4AW

www.stockeldpark.co.uk

A gracious Palladian mansion by James Paine (1763), featuring a magnificent cantilevered staircase in the central oval hall. Surrounded by beautiful gardens and set in 18th century landscaped parkland at the heart of a 2000 acre estate. Popular for filming and photography. Home of The Christmas Adventure. www.thechristmasadventure.com

Location: MAP 11:A9, OS Ref. SE376 497. York 12m, Harrogate 5m, Leeds 12m.

Owner: Mr and Mrs P G F Grant **Contact:** Mr P Grant **Tel:** 01937 586101

Fax: 01937 580084 **E-mail:** enquiries@stockeldpark.co.uk

Open: Privately booked events and tours only. Please contact the Estate Office: 01937 586101.

Admission: Prices on application.

Key facts: Suitable. WCs. Licensed. Licensed. By arrangement. Limited for coaches. Outdoor Activities during Summer and Winter months, October Half Term and Halloween Events, Illuminated Enchanted Forest, Ice Skating at The Christmas Adventure. New for 2012 The Summer Adventure–fun for all the family.

SLEDMERE HOUSE

Sledmere, Driffield East, Yorkshire YO25 3XG

www.sledmerehouse.com

At the heart of the Yorkshire Wolds, Sledmere House exudes 18th century elegance with each room containing decorative plasterwork by Joseph Rose Junior, and examples of the finest craftsmen of the period. A tour of the house culminates in the magnificent Library which overlooks the 'Capability' Brown landscaped park.

Location: MAP 11:D9, OS Ref. SE931 648. Off the A166 between York & Bridlington, 7 miles NW of Driffield.

Owner: Sir Tatton Sykes **Contact:** The House Secretary

Tel: 01377 236637 **Fax:** 01377 236500

E-mail: info@sledmerehouse.com

Open: Fri 6 Apr–Thur 27 Sept please see www.sledmerehouse.com or call 01377 236637 for details of opening.

Admission: House & Gardens: Adult £8, Concessions £7.50, Child £3 (Groups 15+ £7 pp) Family Ticket £18 (2 Adults/2 Children 5-16) Gardens & Park: Adult £5.50, Child £2, RHS members £4.50.

Key facts: No photography in house. Suitable. Obligatory, by arrangement.

SUTTON PARK

Sutton-On-The-Forest, North Yorkshire YO61 1DP

www.statelyhome.co.uk

The Yorkshire home of Sir Reginald and Lady Sheffield. Early Georgian architecture. Magnificent plasterwork by Cortese. Rich collection of 18th century furniture, paintings and porcelain, put together with great style to make a most inviting house. Award winning gardens attract enthusiasts from home and abroad. Yorkshire in Bloom Award 2011.

Location: MAP 11:B9, OS Ref. SE583 646. 8m N of York on B1363 York–Helmsley Road.

Owner: Sir Reginald & Lady Sheffield **Contact:** Administrator

Tel: 01347 810249 **Fax:** 01347 811239 **E-mail:** suttonpark@statelyhome.co.uk

Open: House: Apr–Sep: Wed, Sun & BHs, 1.30–5pm (last tour 4pm). Gardens: Apr–Sep: daily, 11am–5pm. Tearoom: Apr–Sep: Wed–Sun, 11am–5pm. Private groups any other day by appointment.

Admission: House & Garden: Adult £6.50, Child £4, Conc. £5.50. Private Groups (15+): £7. Gardens only: Adult £3.50, Child £1.50, Conc. £3 Caravans: £11 per unit per night.

Key facts: No photography. Lunches & dinners in Dining Room. Partial. WCs. Licensed. Obligatory. Limited for coaches.

WENTWORTH CASTLE GARDENS

Lowe Lane, Stainborough, Barnsley, South Yorkshire S75 3ET

www.wentworthcastle.org

The only Grade 1 listed landscape in South Yorkshire. This historic 18th century 500-acre estate features 26 listed monuments, including two castles, follies, a magnificent 50-acre formal garden containing 100,000 bulbs as well as 3 National Collections – Rhododendrons, Camellias and Magnolias. Shop, Café, Adventure Playground. Tours by arrangement.

Location: MAP 10:P12, OS Ref. SE320 034. 5 mins from M1/J37.

Owner: Wentworth Castle Trust **Contact:** Claire Herring – Director

Tel: 01226 776040 **Fax:** 01226 776042

E-mail: heritagetrust@wentworthcastle.org

Open: All year daily (except Christmas Day): Apr–Sept 10am–5pm, Oct–Mar 10am–4pm.

Admission: (2011 Prices) Garden, Parkland & Playground: Adult £4.95, Conc. £3.95, Child (5–16yrs) £2.95. Guided tours £2.75 extra. Parkland only: Free (£3 car park charge).

Key facts: Partial. WCs. Licensed. By arrangement. Guide dogs only.

TEMPLE NEWSAM ESTATE

Leeds LS15 0AE

www.leeds.gov.uk/templenewsamhouse

One of the great country houses of England, this Tudor-Jacobean mansion was the birthplace of Lord Darnley, husband of Mary Queen of Scots and home to the Ingram family for 300 years. Rich in newly restored interiors, paintings, furniture (including Chippendale), textiles, silver and ceramics. Temple Newsam sits within 1500 acres of grand and beautiful 'Capability' Brown parkland with formal and wooded gardens as well as national plant collections.

Location: MAP 10:P10, OS Ref. SE358 321. 4m E of city centre B6159 or 2m from M1 junction 46. 4 miles from city centre.

Owner: Leeds City Council

Contact: Michael Thaw

Tel: 0113 2647321

E-mail: temple.newsam.house@leeds.gov.uk

Open/Admission: Please check the website or call 0113 2647321 for seasonal opening times and admission prices.

Key facts: Obligatory.

YORK GATE GARDEN

Back Church Lane, Adel, Leeds, West Yorkshire LS16 8DW

www.yorkgate.org.uk

Inspirational one acre garden widely recognized as one of Britain's finest small gardens. A series of smaller gardens with different themes and in contrasting styles are linked by a succession of delightful vistas. Striking architectural features play a key role throughout the garden which is also noted for its exquisite detailing.

Location: MAP 10:P10, OS Ref. 275 403. 2¼m SE of Bramhope. ½m E of A660.

Owner: Perennial **Contact:** The Garden Co-ordinator

Tel: 0113 2678240

Open: Apr–Sept: Thur & Sun, 2–5pm. BH weekends (Apr–Aug) Sun & Mon, 11am–5pm. See website for other dates.

Admission: Standard admission £4.50, Gift Aid admission £5. Child (16yrs & under) Free.

Key facts: Groups must book. By arrangement. Guide dogs only.

ASKE HALL

Richmond, North Yorkshire DL10 5HJ

Tours limited to 15 people per tour. Booking advisable and ID will be required (passport, driving licence etc). For further details contact Mandy Blenkiron. A predominantly Georgian collection of paintings, furniture and porcelain in house which has been the seat of the Dundas family since 1763.

Location: MAP 10:P6, OS Ref. NZ179 035. 4m SW of A1 at Scotch Corner, 2m from the A66, on the B6274.

Owner: Earl of Ronaldshay **Contact:** Mandy Blenkiron

Tel: 01748 822000 **Fax:** 01748 826611

E-mail: mandy.blenkiron@aske.co.uk **Website:** www.aske.co.uk

Open: 6 & 7 Sept 2012 (Heritage Open Days). Tours at 10.00, 11.00 & 12.00.

Admission: Free.

Key facts: Partial. Obligatory. Limited, none for coaches.

BENINGBROUGH HALL & GARDENS

Beningbrough, North Yorkshire YO30 1DD

Imposing 18th century house with new interpretation galleries with the National Portrait Gallery.

Location: MAP 11:B9, OS Ref. SE516 586. 8m NW of York, 3m W of Shipton, 2m SE of Linton-on-Ouse, follow signposted route.

Owner: National Trust

Contact: Visitor Services Manager

Tel: 01904 472027

E-mail: beningbrough@nationaltrust.org.uk

Website: www.nationaltrust.org.uk

Open: Please contact for up to date information.

Admission: Please contact for up to date information.

Key facts: Lift to all floors.

BROCKFIELD HALL

Warthill, York YO19 5XJ

Georgian house (1804) by Peter Atkinson for Benjamin Agar Esq. Mrs. Wood's father was Lord Martin Fitzalan Howard, son of Lady Beaumont of Carlton Towers, Selby. Brockfield also has portraits of her Stapleton family. There is a permanent exhibition of paintings by Staithes Group artists, by appointment outside August.

Location: MAP 11:C9, OS Ref. SE664 550. 5m E of York off A166 or A64.

Owner: Mr & Mrs Simon Wood **Contact:** Simon Wood

Tel: 01904 489362 **E-mail:** simon@brockfieldhall.co.uk

Website: www.brockfieldhall.co.uk

Open: Aug 1–31 inclusive except Mons (open BH Mon), 1–4pm. Conducted tours at 1pm, 2pm & 3pm.

Admission: Adult £7, Child £2.

Key facts: No photography inside house. Partial. By arrangement. In grounds, on leads.

CANNON HALL MUSEUM, PARK & GARDENS

Cawthorne, Barnsley, South Yorkshire S75 4AT

Set in 70 acres of historic parkland and gardens, Cannon Hall now contains collections of fine furniture, old master paintings, stunning glassware and colourful pottery, much of which is displayed in period settings. Plus 'Charge', the Regimental museum of the 13th/18th Royal Hussars (QMO) and the Light Dragoons. Events and education programme and an ideal setting for conferences and Civil wedding ceremonies.

Location: MAP 10:P12, OS Ref. SE272 084. 6m NW of Barnsley of A635. M1/J38.

Owner: Barnsley Metropolitan Borough Council

Tel: 01226 790270 **E-mail:** cannonhall@barnsley.gov.uk

Website: www.barnsley.gov.uk

Open: Please call for opening times.

Admission: Free except for some events. Charge for car parking.

Key facts: Partial. WC. Refreshments available on site. Pre-booked. In grounds, on leads.

KIPLIN HALL

Nr Scorton, Richmond, North Yorkshire DL10 6AT

Jacobean house, now furnished as a comfortable Victorian home, originally built in 1620s by George Calvert, founder of Maryland. 1820s 'Gothic' Wing, redesigned by W. E. Nesfield. Eclectic mix of previous owners' furniture, paintings, portraits and personalia, including Arts and Crafts. Gardens undergoing restoration. Newly opened - 'The Travellers' Bedroom'.

Location: MAP 11:A7, OS Ref. SE274 976. Between Scorton and Northallerton, 5 miles east of the A1, on B6271.

Owner: Kiplin Hall Trustees **Contact:** The Administrator

Tel: 01748 818178 **E-mail:** info@kiplinhall.co.uk **Website:** www.kiplinhall.co.uk

Open: 10am–5pm (Hall opens 2pm) Apr–Oct, Sun–Wed, Good Fri/Easter Sat. Gardens/Tea Room also Feb and Mar, 10am–4pm.

Admission: Hall, Gardens & Grounds: Adult £7.50, Conc. £6.50, Child £3.50, Family (2+3) £20. Gardens/Grounds only: Adult £4.50, Conc. £3.50, Child £1.50, Family (2+3) £10.

Key facts: Partial. WCs. By arrangement. Limited. In grounds.

LEDSTON HALL

Hall Lane, Ledston, Castleford, West Yorkshire WF10 2BB

17th century mansion with some earlier work.

Location: MAP 11:A11, OS Ref. SE437 289. 2m N of Castleford, off A656.

Contact: Helen Bridges **Tel:** 01423 707830 **Fax:** 01423 521373

E-mail: joe.robinson@carterjonas.co.uk **Open:** Exterior only: May–Aug: Mon–Fri, 9am–4pm. Other days by appointment. **Admission:** Free. **Key facts:**

NATIONAL CENTRE FOR EARLY MUSIC

St Margaret's Church, Walmgate, York YO1 9TL

The National Centre for Early Music is based in the medieval church of St Margaret's York. The church boasts a 12th century Romanesque doorway and a 17th century brick tower of considerable note. The Centre hosts concerts, music education activities, conferences, recordings and events.

Location: MAP 21, OS Ref. SE609 515. Inside Walmgate Bar, within the city walls, on the E side of the city.

Owner: York Early Music Foundation **Contact:** Mrs G Baldwin

Tel: 01904 632220 **Fax:** 01904 612631 **E-mail:** info@ncem.co.uk

Website: www.ncem.co.uk

Open: Mon–Fri, 10am–4pm. Also by appointment. Access is necessarily restricted when events are taking place.

Admission: Free, donations welcome.

Key facts: Obligatory. By arrangement. Limited. No coaches.

Fairfax House

NORTON CONYERS

Nr Ripon, North Yorkshire HG4 5EQ

Visited by Charlotte Brontë, Norton Conyers, an original of 'Thornfield Hall', has belonged to the Grahams since 1624. The mid-18th century walled garden retains its original design. Herbaceous borders flanked by yew hedges lead to central pavilion. Unusual hardy plants, PYO fruit, vegetables and seasonal flowers for sale.

Location: MAP 11:A8, OS Ref. SF319 763. 4m NW of Ripon. 3½m from the A1.

Owner: Sir James and Lady Graham **Contact:** Lady Graham

Tel/Fax: 01765 640333 **E-mail:** norton.conyers@btinternet.com

Website: www.weddingsatnortonconyers.co.uk

Open: House closed except for pre-booked groups to view work in progress. For Garden openings please see our website.

Admission: Garden: Individual admission free–donations are welcome. Entrance fee on charity days. Charges for groups by arrangement (min. 10).

Key facts: Pavilion is available for functions: seats up to 20. Partial. WC. By arrangement. Limited for coaches. On leads.

PLUMPTON ROCKS

Plumpton, Knaresborough, North Yorkshire HG5 8NA

Grade II* listed garden extending to over 30 acres including an idyllic lake, dramatic millstone grit rock formation, romantic woodland walks winding through bluebells and rhododendrons. Declared by English Heritage to be of outstanding interest. Painted by Turner. Described by Queen Mary as 'Heaven on earth'.

Location: MAP 11:A9, OS Ref. SE355 535. Between Harrogate and Wetherby on A661, 1m SE of A661 junction with Harrogate southern bypass.

Owner: Robert de Plumpton Hunter

Contact: Robert de Plumpton Hunter

Tel: 01289 382322

Open: Mar–Oct: Sat, Sun & BHs, 11am–6pm.

Admission: Adult £2.50, Child/OAP £1.50. (2010 prices, subject to change).

Key facts: Unsuitable. Limited for coaches. In grounds, on leads.

PARCEVALL HALL GARDENS

Skyreholme, Nr Appletreewick, North Yorkshire BD23 6DE

Nestling in a tranquil and picturesque setting steeped in history, Parcevall Hall Gardens are considered a fine example of the Arts & Crafts movement. Laid out from 1927 onwards by Sir William Milner (1893–1960), whose vision resulted in a unique garden totally in harmony with the surrounding Wharfedale landscape.

Location: MAP 10:O8. OS Ref. SE068 613. 1½m NE of Appletreewick. 12m NNW of Ilkley by B6160 and via Burnsall.

Owner: Walsingham College (Yorkshire Properties) Ltd. **Contact:** Phillip Nelson (Head Gardener) **Tel:** 01756 720311 **Fax:** 01756 720311

E-mail: parcevallhall@btconnect.com **Website:** www.parcevallhallgardens.co.uk

Open: 1 Apr–31 Oct: 10am–6pm.

Admission: Adult £6, Senior Citizens £5, Child Under 12 free. (Prices correct to 31 Oct 2011).

Key facts: By arrangement. On leads.

SHIBDEN HALL

Lister's Road, Halifax, West Yorkshire HX3 6XG

A half-timbered 15th century manor house, the home of Anne Lister, set in picturesque landscaped grounds and estate. The 17th century aisled barn contains a carriage collection and the folk museum depicts local crafts and life in West Yorkshire. Events at Shibden include music, walks, guided tours and craft fairs.

Location: MAP 10:O11. OS Ref. SE106 257. 1.5 m E of Halifax off A58.

Owner: Calderdale MBC **Contact:** Deborah Comyn-Platt

Tel: 01422 352246 **Fax:** 01422 348440

E-mail: shibden.hall@calderdale.gov.uk **Website:** www.calderdale.gov.uk

Open: March to Nov: Mon–Sat, 10am–5pm, Sun, 12 noon–5pm Dec to Feb: Mon–Sat, 10am–4pm, Sun, 12 noon–4pm. Opening hours under review.

Admission: Adult £3.50, Child/Conc. £2.50, Family £10. Car Parking Charges are under review.

Key facts: Suitable. WCs. By arrangement. Guide dogs only.

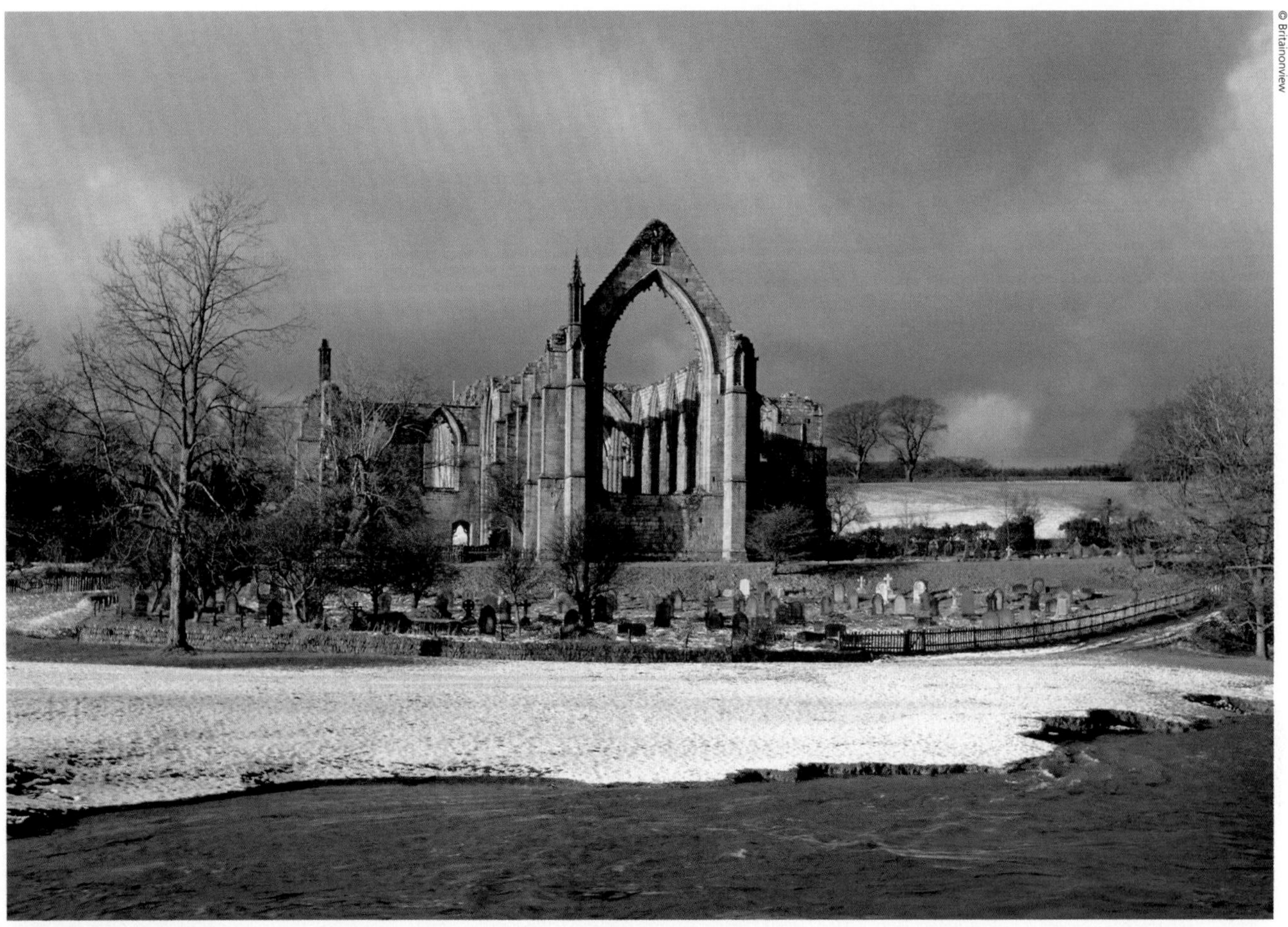

Bolton Abbey in the snow

Cholmondeley Castle

Rydal Mount & Gardens

North West

Cheshire
Cumbria
Lancashire
Merseyside

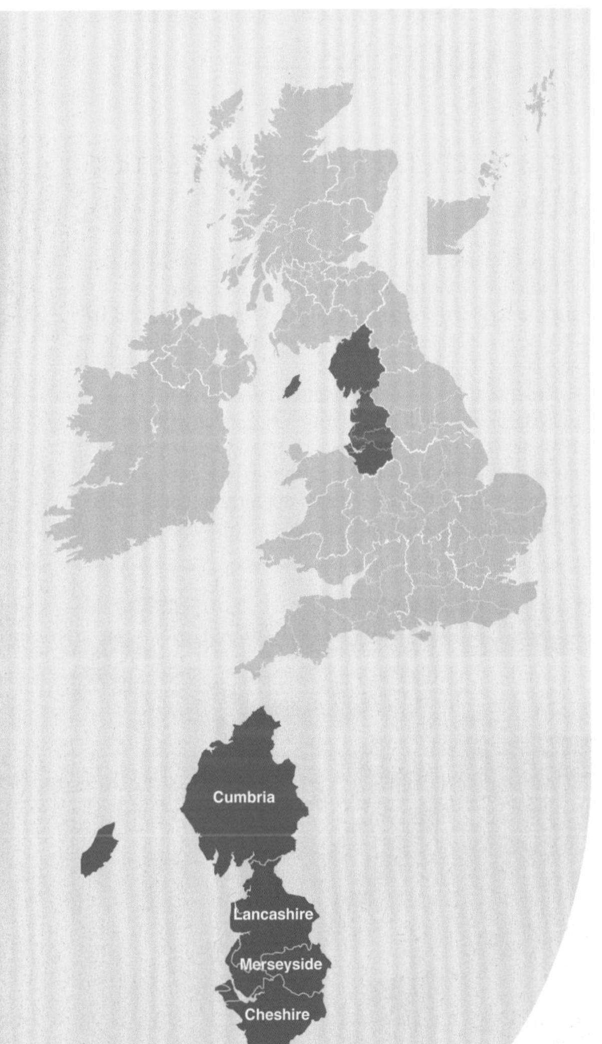
Cumbria
Lancashire
Merseyside
Cheshire

Start in the south of the region where Chester has much more than just its Roman past to offer, including a medieval monastic Cathedral with magnificent architecture. Visit tranquil and romantic Cholmondeley Castle Garden or venture north to Lancashire where Smithills Hall, in 2200 acres of woodland on the edge of the West Pennine Moors, is one of the oldest and best preserved manor houses in the North West. Further north still, Cumbria is dotted with historic properties such as breathtaking Dalemain, and Rydal Mount & Gardens, the picturesque home of William Wordsworth nestling in the beautiful Cumbrian fells.

VISITOR INFORMATION

Owner
Viscount & Viscountess Ashbrook

Address
The Estate Office
Arley
Nr Northwich
Cheshire CW9 6NA

Location
MAP 6:M2
OS Ref. SJ675 809.
5m W Knutsford, 5m from M6/J19 & 20 and M56/J9 & 10.

Contact
Garry Fortune - Estate General Manager
Tel: 01565 777353
Fax: 01565 777465
E-mail: enquiries@arleyhallandgardens.com

Opening Times
31 March–28 October
Gardens: Tuesday–Sunday & BHs, 11am–5pm.
Hall: Tues, Suns & BHs, 12noon–4.30pm.

Admission

Gardens	
Adult	£7.00
Children (5–16yrs)	£2.50
Senior or concession	£6.50
Family (2+2)	£16.50
Groups:	
Adult	£6.50
Concession	£6.00
Children	£2.00
Hall	
Adult	£3.00
Child (5–12yrs)	£2.00
Senior	£2.50
Groups:	
Adult	£2.50
Season tickets	
Individual	£30.00
Joint	£50.00
Family (2+3)	£70.00

Special events
February
Wedding Fair
March
Mothers Day Celebrations
April
Spring Plant Fair
Bluebell Walks
June
Arley Garden Festival
October
Halloween Murder Mystery Evening
December
Christmas Floral Extravaganza

ARLEY HALL & GARDENS

www.arleyhallandgardens.com

Arley is a place of enormous character and charm with visitors struck by the warm, family, intimate atmosphere.

Owned by the current family for over 500 years, Arley is a delightful estate. The award-winning gardens, voted in Europe's top 50 and in Britain's top 10, have been created over 250 years with each generation of the family making its own contribution. The result is a garden of great atmosphere, interest and vitality. Arley is, therefore, a wonderful example of the idea that the best gardens are living works of art. Outstanding features are the renowned double herbaceous border (c1846), the Quercus Ilex and pleached Lime Avenues, Victorian Rootree, walled gardens, yew hedges and shrub rose collection. The family tradition continues today with the current Viscount Ashbrook, who over the last 30 years has created the less formal Grove and Woodland Walk.

One of Cheshire's most charming stately homes, the Hall (Grade II*) was built by the present Viscount Ashbrook's great, great grandfather, Rowland Egerton-Warburton between 1832 and 1885 and is a fine example of the Victorian Jacobean style. From the grandeur of the Gallery to the intimacy of the Library the Hall exudes charm. The Emperor's Room was even home to Prince Louis Napoleon, later Napoleon III of France, in the winter of 1847–48. Arley won the title of 2009 'Small Visitor Atraction of the Year' in the North West and with its new, purpose built conference facility 'Olympia' is also a wonderful, exclusive venue for weddings, corporate functions and private parties.

KEY FACTS

Suitable for weddings, corporate functions, product launches, conferences, filming, photography, concerts and fairs. Photography in Hall by permission & appointment only.

Open while the Garden is open.

Comprehensive set of menus available for entertaining in the Hall and Tudor Barn.

Suitable. WCs.

Licensed.

Licensed.

Welcomed by arrangement.

Free.

On leads.

CAPESTHORNE HALL

www.capesthorne.com

A spectacular venue for weddings, corporate functions, celebrations, park events or simply a fabulous day out.

Capesthorne Hall, set in 100 acres of picturesque Cheshire parkland, has been touched by nearly 1,000 years of English history – Roman legions passed across it, titled Norman families hunted on it and, during the Civil War, a Royalist ancestress helped Charles II to escape after the Battle of Worcester.

The Jacobean-style Hall has a fascinating collection of fine art, marble sculptures, furniture and tapestries. Originally designed by the Smiths of Warwick it was built between 1719 and 1732.

It was altered by Blore in 1837 and partially rebuilt by Salvin in 1861 following a disastrous fire.

The present Squire is Sir William Bromley-Davenport, whose ancestors have owned the estate since Domesday times when they were appointed custodians of the Royal Forest of Macclesfield.

In the grounds near the family Chapel the 18th century Italian Milanese Gates open onto the herbaceous borders and maples which line the beautiful lakeside gardens. But amid the natural spectacle and woodland walks, Capesthorne still offers glimpses of its man-made past … the remains of the Ice House, the Old Boat House and the curious Swallow Hole.

Facilities at the Hall can be hired for corporate occasions and family celebrations including Civil Wedding ceremonies and receptions.

KEY FACTS

- Available for corporate functions, meetings, product launches, promotions, exhibitions, presentations, seminars, activity days, still photography, clay shooting, garden parties, barbecue. No photography in Hall.
- Catering can be provided for groups (full menus on request). Function rooms available for corporate hospitality, meetings and other special events. 'The Butler's Pantry' serves light refreshments.
- Guided tours available for pre-booked parties (except Sunday and Monday).
- 100 cars/20 coaches on hard-standing and unlimited in park, 50 yds from house.
- Licensed for Civil weddings
- Concerts, antiques, craft and game fairs and car shows.

VISITOR INFORMATION

Owner
Sir William and Lady Bromley-Davenport

Address
Capesthorne Hall
Siddington
Macclesfield
Cheshire SK11 9JY

Location
MAP 6:N2
OS Ref. SJ840 727.
5m W of Macclesfield. 30 mins S of Manchester on A34. Near M6, M63 and M62.
Taxi: 01625 533464.
Rail: Macclesfield 5m (2 hrs from London).
Air: Manchester International 20 mins.

Contact
Christine Mountney
Hall Manager
Tel: 01625 861221
Fax: 01625 861619
E-mail: info@capesthorne.com

Opening Times
Summer
April–Oct Suns, Mons & BHs.
Hall
1.30–4pm.
Last admission 3.30pm.
Gardens & Chapel
12 noon–5pm. Groups welcome by appointment.
Caravan Park also open.

Admission
Sundays & BH
Hall, Gardens & Chapel

Adult	£7.50
Child (5–16yrs)	£4.00
Senior	£6.50
Family	£18.50

Gardens & Chapel only

Adult	£5.00
Child (5–16yrs)	£3.00
Senior	£4.00

Hall, Gardens & Chapel
Discounts available for coaches/groups of 20+

Mondays only (Hall, Gardens & Chapel)

Car (max 4)	£12.50
Additional person	£2.50
Minibus (max 12)	£47.50
Coach (max 50)	£95.00

For details see: www.capesthorne.com

Special events
See www.capesthorne.com

ADLINGTON HALL

MACCLESFIELD, CHESHIRE SK10 4LF

www.adlingtonhall.com

Adlington Hall, home of the Leghs from 1315 built on the site of a Hunting Lodge in the Forest of Macclesfield in 1040. Two oaks, part of the original building, remain rooted in the ground supporting the east end of the Great Hall. Between the trees in the Great Hall stands an organ built by 'Father' Bernard Smith. Played on by Handel.

The Gardens laid out over many centuries include a Lime walk planted 1688, Regency rockery surrounding the Shell Cottage. The Wilderness, a Rococo styled landscape garden containing the chinoserie T'Ing House, Pagoda bridge and classical Temple to Diana.

Location: MAP 6:N2. OS Ref. SJ905 804. 5m N of Macclesfield, A523, 13m S of Manchester. London 178m.

Owner: Mrs C J C Legh

Tel: 01625 827595 **Fax:** 01625 820797

E-mail: enquiries@adlingtonhall.com

Open: Sun & Wed afternoons from Easter Sun 8 Apr–Sun 1 Jul (closed Sun 6 May). Open Bank holidays 9 Apr, 4 & 5 Jun. 1.30–5pm

Admission: House & Gardens: Adult £9, Child £5, Student £5, Gardens only: Adult £6, Child FREE, Student FREE, Groups of 20+ £8.50.

Key facts: Suitable for corporate events, product launches, business meetings, conferences, concerts, fashion shows, garden parties, rallies, clay-pigeon shooting, filming and weddings. The Great Hall and Dining Room are available for corporate entertaining. Catering can be arranged. Partial. WCs. By arrangement. For 100 cars and 4 coaches, 100 yds from Hall.

© English Heritage

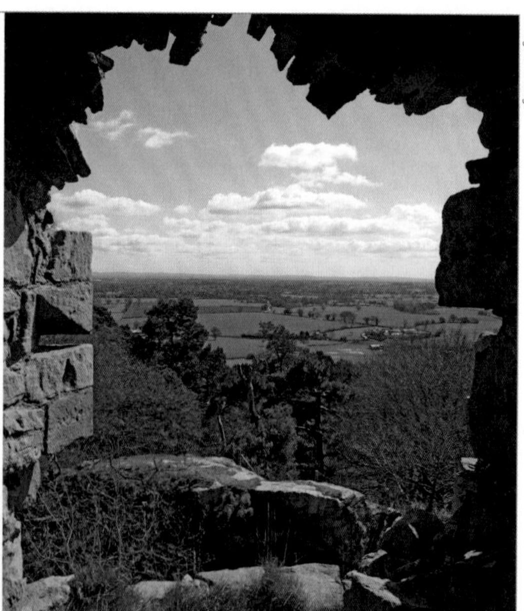

© English Heritage

BEESTON CASTLE

CHAPEL LANE, BEESTON, TARPORLEY, CHESHIRE CW6 9TX

www.english-heritage.org.uk/beestoncastle

Standing majestically on a sheer rocky crag, Beeston offers perhaps the most stunning views of any castle in England as well as fantastic woodland walks in the castle grounds. Its 4,000 year history spans Bronze Age settlement to Iron Age hill fort, to impregnable royal fortress.

Location: MAP 6:L3, OS Ref. SJ537 593. 11m SE of Chester on minor road off A49, or A41. 2m SW of Tarporley.

Owner: English Heritage

Contact: Visitor Operations Team

Tel: 01829 260464

E-mail: beeston.castle@english-heritage.org.uk

Open: Please visit www.english-heritage.org.uk for opening times and the most up-to-date information.

Admission: Adult £5.50, Child £3.30, Conc. £5. 15% discount for groups (11+). EH members Free. Opening times and prices are valid until 31st March 2012.

Key facts: Exhibition. WCs. Partial. The car park is not owned by English Heritage. There is a parking charge of £2-£2.50. On leads.

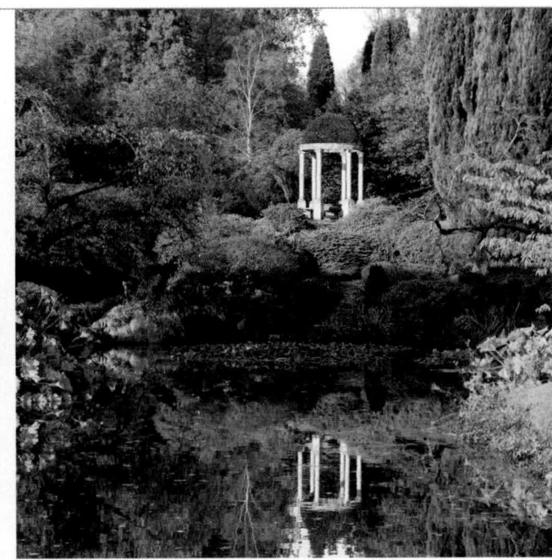

CHOLMONDELEY CASTLE GARDEN

MALPAS, CHESHIRE SY14 8AH

www.cholmondeleycastle.com

Cholmondeley Castle Garden is said by many to be among the most romantically beautiful gardens they have seen. Even the wild orchids, daisies and buttercups take on an aura of glamour in this beautifully landscaped setting with extensive ornamental gardens dominated by a romantic Castle built in 1801 of local sandstone. Visitors can enjoy the tranquil Temple Water Garden, Ruin Water Garden, memorial mosaic designed by Maggy Howarth, Rose garden and many mixed borders. Lakeside walk, picnic area, children's play areas, farm animals, llamas, children's corner, Gift Shop and Tea Room. Private Chapel in the park.

Location: MAP 6:L3, OS Ref. SJ540 515. Off A41 Chester/Whitchurch Rd. & A49 Whitchurch/Tarporley Road. 7m N of Whitchurch.

Owner: The Marchioness of Cholmondeley

Contact: The Secretary

Tel: 01829 720383

Fax: 01829 720877

E-mail: dilys@cholmondeleycastle.co.uk

Open: Sun 1 Apr–Sun 30 Sept 2012, 11am–5pm, Wed, Thur, Sun & Bank hols. Autumn Tints, Sun 14 Sun 21 & Sun 28 Oct. (Castle open for groups only, by pre-arrangement, on limited days).

Admission: Adult £6, Child £3, (reduction for groups to gardens of 25+).

Key facts: Partial. WCs. On leads. For special events please refer to our website www.cholmondeleycastle.com

RODE HALL

CHURCH LANE, SCHOLAR GREEN, CHESHIRE ST7 3QP

www.rodehall.co.uk

The Wilbraham family have lived at Rode since 1669; the present house was constructed in two stages, the earlier two storey wing and stable block around 1705 and the main building was completed in 1752. The house stands in a Repton landscape and the extensive gardens include a woodland garden which has many species of rhododendrons, azaleas, hellebores and climbing roses following snowdrops and daffodils in the early spring. The formal rose garden was designed in 1860; there is a large walled kitchen garden and a new Italian garden. The icehouse in the park has been restored.

Location: MAP 6:M3, OS Ref. SJ819 573. 5m SW of Congleton between the A34 and A50. Kidsgrove railway station 2m NW of Kidsgrove.

Owner/Contact: Sir Richard Baker Wilbraham Bt

Tel: 01270 873237 **Fax:** 01270 882962 **E-mail:** enquiries@rodehall.co.uk

Open: 4 Apr–26 Sep. House only: Wed's and BH's and groups by appointment. Garden only: Tues, Wed and Thurs 12 noon–5pm. Snowdrop walks 28 Jan–11 March daily except Mons, 12noon–4pm.

Admission: House & Garden: Adult £6, Conc £5, Children over 4 £1. Garden only and snowdrop walks: Adult £4, Conc £3, Children over 4 £1.

Key facts: Home-made teas. On leads.

TABLEY HOUSE

KNUTSFORD, CHESHIRE WA16 0HB

www.tableyhouse.co.uk

The finest Palladian House in the North West, Tabley a Grade I listing, was designed by John Carr of York for the Leicester family. Set in landscaped parkland it contains one of the first collections of English paintings, including works of art by Turner, Reynolds, Lawrence, Lely and Dobson. Furniture by Chippendale, Bullock and Gillow and fascinating family memorabilia adorn the rooms. Fine plasterwork by Thomas Oliver and carving by Daniel Shillito and Mathew Bertram. Interesting Tea Room and 17th century Chapel adjoin, including Burne-Jones window.

Location: MAP 6:M2, OS Ref. SJ725 777. M6/J19, A556 S on to A5033. 2m W of Knutsford.

Owner: The University of Manchester **Contact:** The Administrator

Tel: 01565 750151 **Fax:** 01565 653230

E-mail: tableyhouse@btconnect.com

Open: House: Apr–end Oct: Thur–Suns & BHs, 2–5pm. Tea Room: All year Thur–Suns, 11am–6pm. (Tea Room tel: 07804 378504).

Admission: Adult £4. Child/Student £1.50. Groups by arrangement.

Key facts: No photography in galleries. No stilleto heels. Slippers can be provided. By arrangement. Limited for coaches. Guide dogs only. Civil Wedding Licence plus Civil Naming Ceremonies & Re-affirmation of Vows.

CHESTER CATHEDRAL

St. Werburgh Street, Chester, Cheshire CH1 2HU

www.chestercathedral.com

Originally a monastery, Chester Cathedral offers an extraordinary glimpse into the medieval monastic past, with magnificent architecture, amazing woodcarving, a unique ecclesiastical court and colourful stained glass. The visitor can find refreshment in the monks' Refectory where kings once ate and look for unique gifts in our Shop. **Location:** MAP 6:K2, OS Ref. SJ406 665. Chester city centre. **Owner:** Church of England **Contact:** Nicholas Fry **Tel:** 01244 324756 **E-mail:** visits@chestercathedral.com **Open:** Mon–Sat: 9am–5pm. Sun 1–4pm. The Cathedral may be closed on occasion at short notice. Please contact in advance to confirm. **Admission:** Adult £5.50, Concessions £4.50, Groups £4.50, Child (5–16) £2.50, Family £5.50 Up to 3 children, Schools (inc. Guided Tour) £2.50, Pre booked Guided Tours (Min 10) £6.50. **Key facts:** Photography allowed for personal use, not during services. WCs. Licensed. Licensed. By arrangement. Guide dogs only.

DORFOLD HALL

Acton, Nr Nantwich, Cheshire CW5 8LD

Jacobean country house built in 1616 for Ralph Wilbraham. Family home of Mr & Mrs Richard Roundell. Beautiful plaster ceilings and oak panelling. Attractive woodland gardens and summer herbaceous borders.

Location: MAP 6:L3, OS Ref. SJ634 525.
1m W of Nantwich on the A534 Nantwich–Wrexham road.

Owner: Richard Roundell

Contact: Richard Roundell

Tel: 01270 625245

Fax: 01270 628723

E-mail: dorfoldhall@btconnect.com

Open: Apr–Oct: Tue only and BH Mons, 2–5pm.

Admission: Adult £6.50, Child £3.

Key facts: Obligatory.
Limited. Narrow gates with low arch prevent coaches.

GAWSWORTH HALL

Macclesfield, Cheshire SK11 9RN

www.gawsworthhall.com

Fully lived-in Tudor half-timbered manor house with Tilting Ground. Former home of Mary Fitton, Maid of Honour at the Court of Queen Elizabeth I, and the supposed 'Dark Lady' of Shakespeare's sonnets. Fine pictures, sculpture, furniture and beautiful grounds adjoining a medieval church. Open air theatre with covered grandstand, performances in July and August. Yuletide decorations by Barry Grey in December.

Location: MAP 6:N2, OS Ref. SJ892 697. 3m S of Macclesfield on the A536 Congleton to Macclesfield road.
Owner: Mr and Mrs T Richards
Contact: Mr T Richards
Tel: 01260 223456
Fax: 01260 223469
E-mail: gawsworthhall@btinternet.com
Open: Daily 2–5pm in Jul and Aug, other times see website.
Admission: Adult £7, Child £3.50. Groups (20+): £5.
Key facts: Partial. WCs. Licensed. Licensed. Guided tours by arrangement. In grounds.

NORTON PRIORY MUSEUM & GARDENS

Tudor Road, Manor Park, Runcorn, Cheshire WA7 1SX

www.nortonpriory.org

An award winning 40 acre horticultural and wildlife haven in Runcorn, Cheshire with a rich and varied history dating back to 1134. Discover the Museum, Undercroft and Medieval herb garden set in the woodland garden and the restored Georgian walled garden, home to the National Collection of tree quince.

Location: MAP 6:K1, OS Ref. SJ54805 83035. 3m from M56/J11. 2m E of Runcorn.
Owner: The Norton Priory Museum Trust
Contact: Museum & Garden Reception
Tel: 01928 569895 **Fax:** 01928 589266 **E-mail:** info@nortonpriory.org
Open: Open daily 1 Apr–31 Oct. Museum: 10am–5pm. Walled Garden:12–4pm. Open daily 1 Nov–31 Mar. Museum: 12–4pm. Walled Garden closed.
Admission: Adult £5.90 (Gift aid £6.50), Child/Conc. £4.20 (GA £4.65), Family £14.50 (GA £15.95). Groups £4 per person (min 15)
Key facts: Free wheelchair loan - please book in advance. The site is closed 24–26 Dec & 1–11 Jan 2013. WCs. By arrangement.

LYME PARK, HOUSE & GARDEN

Disley, Stockport, Cheshire SK12 2NR

www.nationaltrust.org.uk

At Lyme there is a painting called The Servants' Ball painted at the height of the Edwardian age. It captures Lyme at its best but life would never be the same again. Explore lavish interiors, celebrations, treasures, and beautiful gardens. Enjoy a relaxed visit, experiencing a vanished age.

Location: MAP 6:N2, OS Ref. SJ965 825. Off the A6 at Disley. 6 1/2m SE of Stockport. M60 J1.
Owner: National Trust **Contact:** The Visitor Experience Manager
Tel: 01663 762023 **Fax:** 01663 765035
Open: House: 25 Feb–28 Oct, 11am–5pm, Mon, Tue, Fri–Sun. Garden: 25 Feb–28 Oct, 11am–5pm. Please call for winter opening times.
***Admission:** House & Gardens: Adult £11, Child £5.50, Family £25. Park: Car £5, Coach £20. NT members free. *includes a voluntary donation but visitors can choose to pay the standard prices.
Key facts: No photography in house. Licensed. Licensed. By arrangement. Limited for coaches. In grounds.

PEOVER HALL

Over Peover, Knutsford WA16 9HW

An Elizabethan house dating from 1585. Fine Carolean stables. Mainwaring Chapel, 18th century landscaped park.
Large garden with topiary work, and walled gardens.

Location: MAP 6:M2, OS Ref. SJ772 734. 4m S of Knutsford off A50 at Whipping Stocks Inn.
Owner: Randle Brooks
Contact: I Shepherd
Tel: 01565 632358
Open: May–Aug: Stables & Gardens, Mon & Thu except BHs, 2–5pm. Tours of the House at 2.30 & 3.30pm.
Admission: House, Stables & Gardens: Adult £5.
Stables & Gardens only: Adult £4.
Accompanied children free.
Key facts: Obligatory.

BRAMALL HALL

Bramhall Park, Bramhall, Stockport SK7 3NX

Bramall Hall is a magnificent black and white timber-framed Tudor manor house with Victorian additions, spanning six centuries and set in 70 acres of parkland. It gives a unique insight into the families and servants who have lived and worked there. A great afternoon out.

Location: MAP 6:N1. OS Ref. SJ 890 864. 3/4m N of Bramhall centre, off A5102

Owner: Stockport Metropolitan Borough Council **Contact:** Caroline Egan, House Manager **Tel:** 0161 485 3708 **Fax:** 0161 486 6959

Website: www.bramallhall.org.uk

Open: 1 Apr–31 Oct: Tues–Thur 1–5pm, Fri & Sat 1–4pm, Sun 1–5pm, BHs 11am–5pm.1 Nov–31 Mar: Sat & Sun only 1–4pm, BHs 11am–4pm. Telephone for Christmas openings. Guided Tours 1.15pm & 2.15pm. Self guided tours other times.

Admission: Adult £4.05, Conc. & under 16s £3.05, Stockport Leisure Key and under 5s Free. **Key facts:** No photography inside the Hall. Partial. WCs. By arrangement. Limited for coaches. Dogs allowed in the grounds on leads. Guide dogs only in the house.

TATTON PARK

Knutsford, Cheshire WA16 6QN

A complete historic estate, formerly home to the Egerton family with 1,000 acres of parkland, 200 year old gardens, neo-classical mansion, working rare breed farm, speciality shops, restaurant and full events programme. A perfect day out!

Location: MAP 6:M2, OS Ref. SJ745 815. From M56/J7 follow signs. From M6/ J19, signed on A56 & A50.

Owner: National Trust (Managed by Cheshire East Council)

Tel: 01625 374400 **Info:** 01625 374435 **Fax:** 01625 374403

E-mail: tatton@cheshireeast.gov.uk **Website:** www.tattonpark.org.uk

Open: Park open every day except Mondays in low season.
See www.tattonpark.org.uk or call 01625 374400 for all opening times.

Admission: For prices see website www.tattonpark.org.uk or call 01625 374400.

Key facts: Dinners, dances, weddings and conferences. Licensed. Licensed. By arrangement. Entry Charge applies. See website, 200–300 yds. Meal vouchers for coach drivers. Please book. In grounds. €

Capesthorne Hall

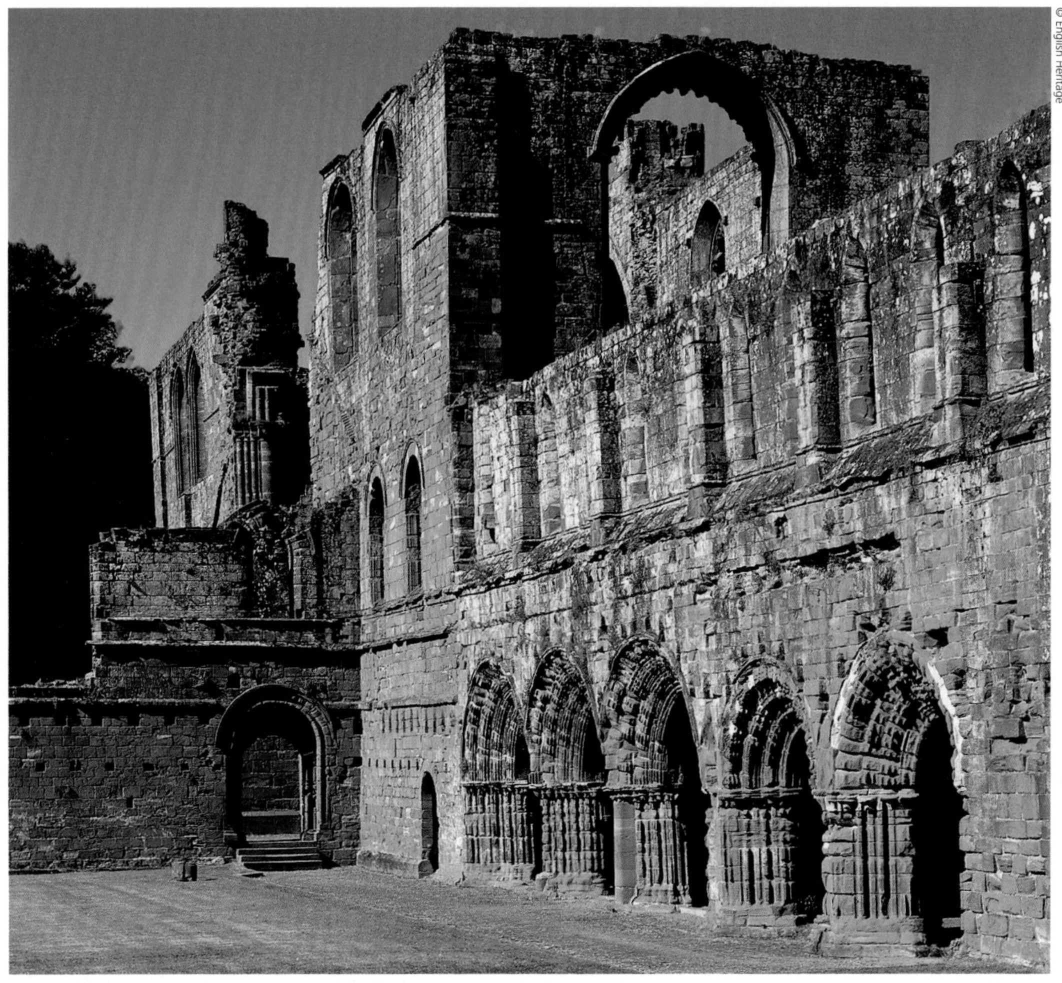
© English Heritage

CARLISLE CASTLE ⌗

www.english-heritage.org.uk/carlisle

Carlisle Castle was a constantly updated working fortress until well within living memory.

Even before the medieval castle was begun, this site was an important Roman fortress. Today, the castle still plays a prominent role as one of Cumbria's best loved landmarks.

The commanding keep, begun during the 12th century by King Henry I of England and completed by King David I of Scotland, is both the oldest part of the Castle and a reminder that Carlisle was a disputed frontier fortress, long commanding the especially turbulent western end of the Anglo-Scottish border. The keep houses displays about the Castle's history, from medieval assaults to the Civil War siege and Bonnie Prince Charlie's Jacobite Rising of 1745-6.

By the time Mary Queen of Scots was imprisoned here 1567-8, Henry VII's updating for heavy artillery had left it's mark on Carlisle.

KEY FACTS

Obligatory.

Disabled parking only.

On leads.

© English Heritage

© English Heritage

VISITOR INFORMATION

Owner
English Heritage

Address
Carlisle
Cumbria
CA3 8UR

Location
MAP 10:K3
OS Ref. NY396 562.
In Carlisle town, at N end of city centre.

Contact
Visitor Operations Team
Tel: 01228 591922
E-mail: customers@english-heritage.org.uk

Opening Times
1 Apr–30 Sep: daily, 9.30am–5pm. 1 Oct–31 Mar: daily, 10am–4pm. Closed 24–26 Dec & 1 Jan.

Admission

Adult	£5.00
Child	£3.00
Conc	£4.50

Discount for groups (11+).
EH members Free.

Opening times and prices are valid until 31st March 2012, please visit www.english-heritage.org.uk for the most up-to-date information.

Special events
There is an exciting events programme available throughout the year, for further details please contact the property or visit the website.

VISITOR INFORMATION

Owner
Mrs Iona Frost Pennington

Address
Muncaster Castle
Ravenglass
Cumbria CA18 1RQ

Location
MAP 10:J7
OS Ref. SD103 965
See our website for details.
A595 1 mile south of Ravenglass.
SatNav CA18 1RD.
Rail: Ravenglass (on Barrow-in-Furness-Carlisle Line) 1½ m.
Air: Manchester 2½ hrs.

Contact
Reception
Tel: 01229 717614
Fax: 01229 717010
E-mail: info@muncaster.co.uk

Opening Times
Full Season
Last Sunday in March–last Sunday in October
Gardens & World Owl Centre open daily 10.30am–6pm (dusk if earlier). Castle open Sunday–Friday 12–4.30pm.
Winter Season
11am–4pm (dusk if earlier).
Castle open reduced hours, please see website or call for details.
Closed in January.
Open for groups, conferences and weddings by appointment.
Darkest Muncaster
Explore the hauntingly beautiful illuminated gardens by night and light, see website or call for more details.
'Meet the Birds'
Daily at 2.30pm,
Full season only.
'Heron Happy Hour'
daily 4.30pm
(winter 3.30pm).

Admission
Castle, Gardens, Owl Centre & MeadowVole Maze
Please see www.muncaster.co.uk for details.
Gardens, Owl Centre & MeadowVole Maze
Please see www.muncaster.co.uk for details.
Special discounts groups (12+).

Special events
See our website www.muncaster.co.uk for details.

Conference/Function

ROOM	Size	Max Cap
Drawing Room		100
Dining Room		50
Family Dining Room		60
Great Hall		100
Old Laundry		120
Library		48
Guard Room		30
Marquee		200

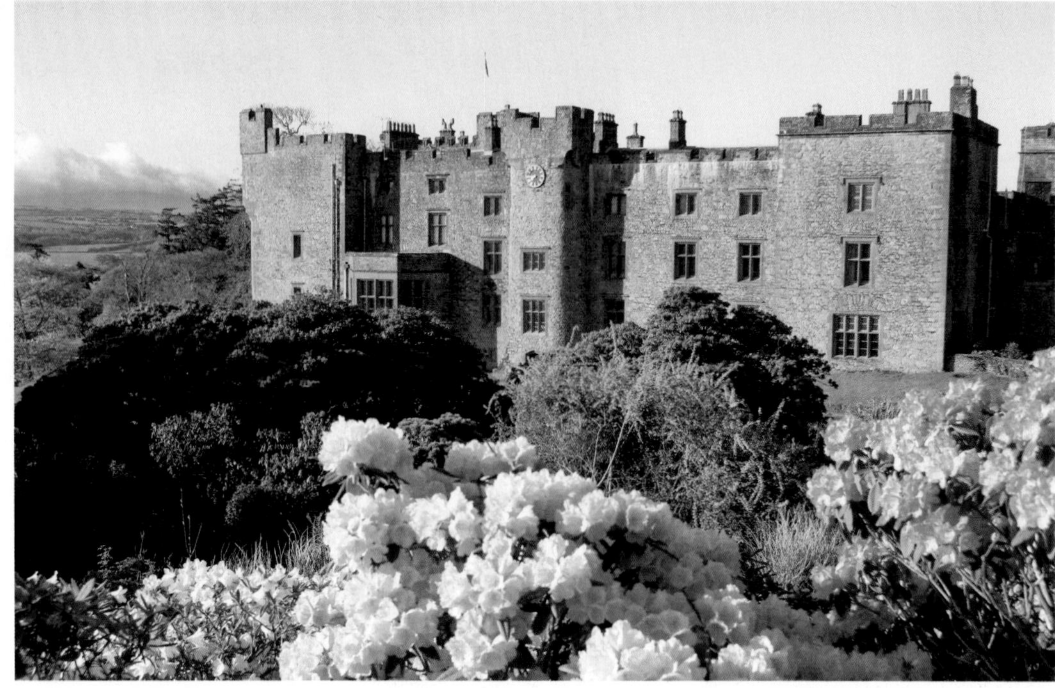

MUNCASTER CASTLE GARDENS & OWL CENTRE

www.muncaster.co.uk

Historic haunted Castle, extensive gardens famous for its rhododendrons, World Owl Centre, yearly event programme, playgounds, shops, cafe and more!

Described by Ruskin as the 'Gateway to Paradise', Muncaster is set in 77 acres of historic woodland Grade 2 listed gardens of the Lake District National Park and is, uniquely, also the start of the famous 'Hadrian's Wall Country'.

With the Georgian Terrace (c.1780), 12th century Church and home to the World Owl Centre (with more than 200 birds on display), the Gardens also house one of Europe's largest collection of rhododendron's amongst the rich and diverse planting of this stunning landscape.

With influences dating back to Roman times, the Castle (the jewel in the crown at Muncaster), is an iconic landmark in our local history. Since 1208 Muncaster has been the family home of the Pennington family and is still a lived in family home to this day. The impressive library, beautiful barrel-vaulted drawing room and exquisite dining room are a real treasure trove of furniture, tapestries, silver, porcelain and interesting stories. Muncaster's beautiful setting is perfect for weddings, team building events, conferences as well as parties and private dining experiences.

4* Guest B&B accommodation is available at the Coachman's Quarters within the Castle Gardens or at the 3* luxurious Pennington Hotel in Ravenglass. The Pennington was formerly a coaching inn and has been recently rennovated in a modern and comfortable style. 3 holiday cottages are also available providing the ideal base for your short break or family holiday.

Whether to relax, wonder, relish or enjoy, your experience will be as unique and personal as the service.

KEY FACTS

- Church. Film location.
-
-
- Wedding receptions and private parties.
- WCs.
- Licensed.
- Licensed.
- Private Castle and Garden Tours.
- Individual audio tour.
- Free Parking. Central Coach parking.
- Conservation and Owl tours available.
- On leads.
-
-
-

DALEMAIN

PENRITH, CUMBRIA CA11 0HB

www.dalemain.com

A fine mixture of mediaeval, Tudor & early Georgian architecture. The present owner's family have lived at Dalemain since 1679 & have collected a wide variety of china, furniture and family portraits. Don't miss Mrs Mouse's House! 5 acres of richly planted herbaceous borders with intriguing & unusual combination of flowers. Highlights are the Rose Walk with over 100 old-fashioned roses & ancient apple trees of named varieties. Tudor Knot Garden. Wild Garden with a profusion of flowering shrubs & wild flowers & in early summer the blue Himalayan Poppies. Giantess Earth Sculpture & newly developed Stumpery in Lobs's Wood.

Location: MAP 10:L5, OS Ref. NY477 269. On A592 1m S of A66. 4m SW of Penrith. London, M1, M6/J40. Edinburgh, A73, M74, M6/J40: 2 1/2 hrs.

Owner: Robert Hasell-McCosh Esq

Contact: Jennifer Little – House Administrator

Tel: 017684 86450 **Fax:** 017684 86223

E-mail: admin@dalemain.com

Open: 1 Apr–1 Nov: Gardens, Tearoom & Gift Shop: Sun–Thur. 10.30am–5pm (4pm in Oct). House open 11.15am–4pm (3pm in Oct). Groups (12+) please book.

Admission: House & Garden: Adult £9.75, Accompanied Children under 16 Free. Gardens only: Adult £6.75, Accompanied Children under 16 Free. Group prices on application.

Key facts: No photography in house. Moorings available on Ullswater. Phone for event enquiries. Partial. WCs. Licensed. Licensed. 1hr tours. German and French translations. Garden tour for groups extra. 50 yds. Guide dogs only.

LEVENS HALL

LEVENS HALL, KENDAL, CUMBRIA LA8 0PD

www.levenshall.co.uk

Levens Hall is an Elizabethan mansion built around a 13th century pele tower. The much loved home of the Bagot family, with fine panelling, plasterwork, Cordova leather wall coverings, paintings by Rubens, Lely and Cuyp, the earliest English patchwork and Wellingtoniana combine with other beautiful objects to form a fascinating collection. The world famous Topiary Gardens were laid out by Monsieur Beaumont from 1694 and his design has remained largely unchanged to this day. Over 90 individual pieces of topiary, some over nine metres high, massive beech hedges and colourful seasonal bedding provide a magnificent visual impact.

Location: MAP 10:L7, OS Ref. SD495 851. 5m S of Kendal on the A6. Exit M6/J36.

Owner: C H Bagot **Contact:** The Administrator **Tel:** 015395 60321

Fax: 015395 60669 **E-mail:** houseopening@levenshall.co.uk

Open: 1 Apr–11 Oct, Sun–Thurs (closed Fris & Sats). Garden, Tea Room, Gift Shop & Plant Centre: 10am–5pm. House: 12 noon–4.30pm (last entry 4pm). Groups (20+) please book.

Admission: House & Gardens or Gardens Only. Please see www.levenshall.co.uk for details. Group Rates on application.

Key facts: No indoor photography. Gift shop. Partial. WCs. Licensed. Licensed. By arrangement. Free on-site parking. Guide dogs only.

© English Heritage

FURNESS ABBEY ⌗

Barrow-in-Furness, Cumbria LA13 0PJ

www.english-heritage.org.uk/furnessabbey

Set in the peaceful 'Valley of Nightshade' are the beautiful red sandstone remains of the wealthy abbey founded in 1123 by Stephen, later King of England. This abbey first belonged to the Order of Savigny and later to the Cistercians. There is a museum and exhibition.

Location: MAP 10:J8, OS Ref. SD218 717. 1$^1/_2$ m N of Barrow-in-Furness off A590.

Owner: English Heritage

Contact: Visitor Operations Staff

Tel: 01229 823420

E-mail: customers@english-heritage.org.uk

Open: Please visit www.english-heritage.org.uk for opening times and the most up-to-date information.

Admission: Adult £3.80, Child £2.30, Conc. £3.40.

15% discount for groups (11+). EH members Free. Opening times & prices are valid until 31st March 2012.

Key facts: WC.

RYDAL MOUNT & GARDENS

Rydal, Cumbria LA22 9LU

www.rydalmount.co.uk

Home of William Wordsworth – England's finest poet. Nestling in the beautiful fells between Lake Windermere and Rydal Water, lies the 'best loved family home' of William Wordsworth from 1813–1850. Experience the splendid historic home of Wordsworth's descendants. Enjoy the beautiful terraced gardens landscaped by the poet. Feel the peaceful relaxed 'romantic' atmosphere and the freedom of wandering through this 'spot of more perfect and enjoyable beauty' as wrote Dr Thomas Arnold.

Location: MAP 10:K6, OS Ref. NY364 063. 1$^1/_2$m N of Ambleside on A591 Grasmere Road.

Owner: Rydal Mount Trustees **Contact:** Peter & Marian Elkington

Tel: 01539 433002 **Fax:** 01539 431738 **E-mail:** info@rydalmount.co.uk

Open: Mar–Oct, daily, 9.30am–5pm. Nov–Feb, Wed–Sun, 11am–4pm. Closed Jan. Garden; Open daily, tearoom; Mar–Oct, 9.30am–5pm. Nov–Feb 11am–4pm.

Admission: Adult £6.75, Child (5-15 yrs) £3.25, Conc. £5.75, Family £16, Gardens only £4.50.

Key facts: No inside photography. Partial. By arrangement. Limited. In grounds, on leads. Guide dogs only in house.

HUTTON-IN-THE-FOREST

Penrith, Cumbria CA11 9TH

www.hutton-in-the-forest.co.uk

The home of Lord Inglewood's family since 1605. Built around a medieval pele tower with 17th, 18th and 19th century additions. Fine collections of furniture, paintings, ceramics and tapestries. Outstanding grounds with terraces, topiary, walled garden, dovecote and woodland walk through magnificent specimen trees.

Location: MAP 10:L5, OS Ref. NY460 358. 6m NW of Penrith & 2.5 m from M6/J41 on B5305.

Owner: Lord Inglewood **Contact:** Pamela Davidson **Tel:** 017684 84449

Fax: 017684 84571 **E-mail:** admin@hutton-in-the-forest.co.uk

Open: 1 Apr–30 Sept 2012. Wed, Thur, Sun, BH Mon, 12.30–4pm. Tearoom as House 11am–4.30pm. Gardens & Grounds: 31 Mar–31 Oct 2012, daily except Sat, 11am–5pm.

Admission: Please see www.hutton-in-the-forest.co.uk or telephone 017684 84449 for details.

Key facts: Picnic area. Gift stall. By arrangement. Partial. WCs. Licensed. Licensed. Obligatory (except Jul/Aug & BHs). On leads.

TULLIE HOUSE MUSEUM & ART GALLERY

Castle Street, Carlisle, Cumbria CA3 8TP

www.tulliehouse.co.uk

Tullie House is Carlisle's finest visitor attraction and boasts a wide range of features, exhibitions and artefacts all bought together in one impressive museum and art gallery. Being the premier attraction in the North West means that Tullie House is recognised for its first class customer service and an exciting, varied events and exhibitions programme. For more information visit our website www.tulliehouse.co.uk

Location: MAP 10:L3, OS Ref. NY399 365.

Open: High Season: 1 Apr–31 Oct, Mon–Sat, 10am–5pm (restaurant open 9.30am). Sun 11am–5pm. **Low Season:** 1 Nov–31 Mar, Mon–Sat 10am–5pm (Galleries close at 4.30pm, restaurant open 9.30am) Sun 12 noon–5pm (Galleries close at 4pm).

Admission: Adults: £5.20, Conc £3.60, 50p for children 5-18 years old and under 5's free.

Key facts:

Available on request. Nearby.

ACORN BANK GARDEN & WATERMILL

Temple Sowerby, Penrith, Cumbria CA10 1SP

17th century walls enclose a herb garden with 250 varieties of medicinal and culinary plants and orchards with traditional fruit trees surrounded by mixed borders. Beyond the walls, paths lead through woodland to the watermill, where the machinery turns most weekend afternoons. House not open. Tearoom serving delicious seasonal food.

Location: MAP 10:M5, OS Ref. NY612 281. Just N of Temple Sowerby, 6m E of Penrith 1m from A66.

Owner: National Trust **Contact:** The Custodian **Tel:** 01768 361893

E-mail: acornbank@nationaltrust.org.uk **Website:** www.nationaltrust.org.uk

Open: 11 Feb–4 Mar, weekends; 10 Mar–4 Nov, daily except Tue, 10am–5pm. Last admission 4.30pm. Tearoom 11am–4.30pm.

Admission: £4.50, Child £2.25, Family £11.25. *includes 10% donation, visitors can choose to pay standard prices displayed at property and website.

Key facts: WCs. By arrangement. Limited. On leads on woodland walks and garden courtyard. Guide dogs only in walled gardens.

BRANTWOOD

Coniston, Cumbria LA21 8AD

Brantwood, the former home of John Ruskin, is the most beautifully situated house in the Lake District. Explore Brantwood's estate and gardens or experience contemporary art in the Severn Studio. Brantwood's bookshop, the Jumping Jenny restaurant and Coach House Craft Gallery combine for a perfect day out.

Location: MAP 10:K7, OS Ref. SD313 959. 2½m from Coniston village on the E side of Coniston Water.

Owner: The Brantwood Trust **Tel:** 01539 441396 **Fax:** 01539 441263

E-mail: enquiries@brantwood.org.uk **Website:** www.brantwood.org.uk

Open: Mid Mar–mid Nov: daily, 11am–5.30pm. Mid Nov–mid Mar: Wed–Sun, 11am–4.30pm.

Admission: Adult £6.30, Child £1.35, Student £5, Family (2+3) £13.15. Garden only: Adult £4.50, Family (2+3) £8.60. Groups: Adult £5.95, Child £1.35, Student £4.50. Gift Aid admission available.

Key facts: No photography in the house. Licensed. Licensed. By arrangement. Limited for coaches. In grounds, on leads.

MIREHOUSE

Keswick, Cumbria CA12 4QE

Melvyn Bragg described Mirehouse as 'Manor from Heaven'. Set in stunning landscape, Mirehouse is a literary house linked with Tennyson and Wordsworth. Live piano music and children's history trail in house. Natural playgrounds, serene bee garden and lakeside walk.

Location: MAP 10:J5, OS Ref. NY235 284. Beside A591, 3.5m N of Keswick. Good bus service.

Owner: James Fryer-Spedding **Contact:** Janaki Spedding **Tel:** 017687 72287

E-mail: info@mirehouse.com **Website:** www.mirehouse.com

Open: Apr–Oct: Gardens & Tearoom: daily, 10am–5pm. House: Suns & Weds, 2–5pm (4.30pm last entry). Groups (15+) welcome by appointment.

Admission: House & Garden: Adult £7, Child £3, Family (2+4) £18. Gardens only: Adult £3.50, Child £1.50.

Key facts: No photography in house. By arrangement. On leads in grounds.

TOWNEND

Troutbeck, Windermere, Cumbria LA23 1LB

The Brownes of Townend were an ordinary farming family, but their home and belongings bring to life over 400 years of extraordinary stories. Townend contains carved woodwork, books, papers, furniture and many items collected by the Browne family who lived here from before 1626 until 1943.

Location: MAP 10:K6, OS Ref. NY407 023. 3m SE of Ambleside at S end of Troutbeck village. 3m N of Windermere.

Owner: National Trust **Contact:** The Custodian **Tel:** 015394 32628

Fax: 015394 32628 **E-mail:** townend@nationaltrust.org.uk

Website: www.nationaltrust.org.uk/townend

Open: 10 Mar–4 Nov, Wed–Sun. Entry by guided tour at 11am & 12noon. Self-guided opening 1pm–5pm, last admission 4.30pm.

Admission: Gift Aid admission: Adult £5.20, Child £2.60, Family £13.

Key facts: Partial. By arrangement. Limited for Cars, no coaches. In grounds.

WORDSWORTH HOUSE AND GARDEN

Main Street, Cockermouth, Cumbria CA13 9RX

This Georgian townhouse was the birthplace of William Wordsworth. Imaginatively presented as his family home in the 1770s, it offers a lively and participative visit with costumed servants, a working kitchen and hands-on rooms. The garden, with terraced walk, has been restored to its 18th century appearance. Talks and tours available.

Location: MAP 10:J5, OS Ref. NY118 307. Main Street, Cockermouth

Owner: National Trust **Contact:** Property staff **Tel:** 01900 824805

Opening Info: 01900 820884 **E-mail:** wordsworthhouse@nationaltrust.org.uk

Website: www.wordsworthhouse.org.uk www.nationaltrust.org.uk

Open: 10 Mar–4 Nov: Sat–Thur, 11am–5pm. Last entry 4pm.

Admission: Adult £6.80, Child £3.45, Family £17.05 (GAOE prices). Pre-booked groups (15+): Adult £6, Child £2.50. Group out of hours £9.

Key facts: Suitable. WCs. By arrangement only. Guide dogs only. Visit our website for events for the whole season, every day is a special day.

© Britainonview

Carlisle Castle

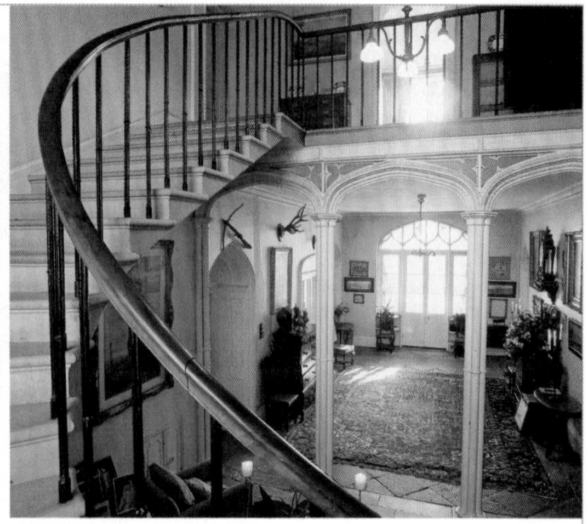

LEIGHTON HALL

CARNFORTH, LANCASHIRE LA5 9ST

www.leightonhall.co.uk

The home of the Reynolds family, is situated in a bowl of parkland, with the Lakeland Fells as a backdrop. The Hall's neo-gothic façade has been superimposed on an 18th century house, built on the ruins of the original medieval house. Mr Reynolds is descended from Adam d'Avranches who built the first house in 1246, as well as from the founder of Gillow & Co of Lancaster. There are many 18th century Gillow pieces, some unique. Fine pictures, clocks, silver and objéts d'art are also on display and Birds of Prey Flying Display are held 3.30pm on open days. The main garden offers herbaceous borders, rose covered walls, the Walled Garden contains flowering shrubs, herb garden and ornamental vegetable garden with Caterpillar Maze, beyond is the Woodland Walk.

Location: MAP 10:L8, OS Ref. SD494 744. 9m N of Lancaster, 10m S of Kendal, 3m N of Carnforth. 1½ m W of A6. 3m from M6/A6/J35, signed from J35A.

Owner: Richard Gillow Reynolds Esq

Contact: Mrs C S Reynolds

Tel: 01524 734474

Fax: 01524 720357

E-mail: info@leightonhall.co.uk

Open: May–Sep, Tue–Fri (also BH Sun & Mon, Suns in Aug) 2–5pm. Booked groups (25+) at any time, all year by arrangement.

Admission: Adult £7.50, Child (5–12 Years) £4.95, Family £23.50, Conc. £6.75, Garden only £4.50. Booked groups (25+): Inside Leighton £6.25, Tea & Tour £12.75, Candelit Tour £12.75, Educational visits for Schools £4.95.

Key facts: No photography in house. Plants for sale. Partial. WCs. Obligatory. Ample for cars and coaches. In Park, on leads.

SMITHILLS HALL

SMITHILLS DEAN ROAD, BOLTON BL1 7NP

www.boltonmuseums.org.uk

Set in 2200 acres of woodland on the edge of the West Pennine Moors, Smithills is one of the oldest, best preserved manor houses in the North West. The earliest part of the hall dates from the 14th century. We provide tours for groups and workshops for schools. The setting is also the perfect backdrop for weddings and business events. The Friends of Smithills Hall work with the council to promote and maintain the hall, why not join them? Bolton also boasts a fantastic museum in the town centre, along with Hall i'th' wood, a Grade 1, 16th century half-timbered building.

Location: OS Ref. SD 697 117. From Bolton town centre, take the A666 north, turn left onto Halliwell Road and follow signs to Smithills Hall.

Owner: Bolton Council **Contact:** Janette Rix, Halls Manager

Tel: 01204 332377

E-mail: museum.customerservices@bolton.gov.uk

Open: Apr–Oct 2011: Tues–Fri & Sun, 12–5pm, last admission at 4pm. Nov–Mar: Please check website.

Admission: Adults £3, Children/concessions £2, Family £7.90 (2 adults and 2 children), Under 5's FREE.

Key facts: Due to the age of the hall there are uneven floors and steps, wheelchair access is to the ground floor only. Partial. WCs. By arrangement. Limited for coaches. Guide dogs only.

BROWSHOLME HALL

Clitheroe, Lancashire BB7 3DE

www.browsholme.com

Built in 1507 and the ancestral Home of the Parker Family, this remarkable Tudor Hall has a major collection of oak furniture and portraits, stained glass and many unusual antiquities including a 'momento mori', civil war arms and armour, even a fragment of a Zeppelin.

Location: MAP 10:M10, OS Ref. SD683 452.
5m NW of Clitheroe off B6243.
Owner: The Parker Family
Contact: Rebecca Clarke, Events Manager
Tel: 01254 827166
E-mail: info@browsholme.com
Open: 1st Sun Apr–Oct, Spring BH 3–4 Jun, 24–28 Jun, 22–26 Jul, 20–30 Aug (not Fri/Sat). Sun 2 Dec.
Admission: Adult £6, OAP & Groups £5.50, Child (under 16) £1.50, Grounds only £2.
Key facts: WCs. Licensed. Obligatory. Guide dogs only.

HOGHTON TOWER

Hoghton, Preston, Lancashire PR5 0SH

www.hoghtontower.co.uk

Hoghton Tower is one of the most dramatic looking houses in northern England. Rebuilt between 1560-1565, it has been the scene of numerous historic events and is an inspirational example of Tudor architecture. Perched on a hilltop, commanding extensive views, its severe exterior surrounds surprisingly elegant and harmonious interiors.

Location: MAP 10:L11. OS Ref. SD622 264. M65/J3. Midway between Preston & Blackburn on A675. **Owner:** Hoghton Tower Preservation Trust
Contact: Office **Tel:** 01254 852986 **Fax:** 01254 852109
E-mail: mail@hoghtontower.co.uk **Open:** Jul, Aug & Sept: Mon–Thur, 11am–4pm. Suns, 1–5pm. BH Suns & Mons excluding Christmas & New Year & Good Friday. Group visits by appointment all year. **Admission:** House Tour and Grounds entry: Adults £7.70, Children £6.60, Retired £6.60 (under 5ys free). Grounds Only (Gardens, Shop and Tearoom): £2.20. Prices vary on event days. Private Tours £7 (min 20). Gift Aid prices.
Key facts: No photography in house. No picnics. Conferences, wedding receptions. Obligatory. No Dogs except guide and hearing dogs. Self Catering. Music/Opera/Theatre/Seminars.

HARRIS MUSEUM & ART GALLERY

Market Square, Preston, Lancashire PR1 2PP

www.harrismuseum.org.uk

Located in the heart of Preston in a beautiful Grade I listed building, the Harris Museum & Art Gallery hosts a wide-ranging programme of exhibitions and events each season. Discover contemporary art, fine art, decorative art and historic collections of national significance. Details online of forthcoming talks, tours and workshops.

Location: MAP 10:L11, OS Ref. SD 54055 29440. Preston City Centre - close to Preston Bus Station Car Park. See website for directions.
Contact: Museum Office
Tel: 01772 258248
Fax: 01772 886764
E-mail: harris.museum@preston.gov.uk
Open: Mon, 11am–5pm, Tue-Sat, 10am–5pm. Closed Suns and BHs.
Admission: Free.
Key facts: Partial. WCs. By arrangement. Guide dogs only.

SAMLESBURY HALL

Preston New Road, Samlesbury, Preston PR5 0UP

www.samlesburyhall.co.uk

Samlesbury Hall is a beautiful oak-timbered medieval manor-house dating from 1325. The Hall is now home to antiques, exhibitions, history rooms, an award-winning restaurant and a growing family of animals within its extensive grounds. It is also available for weddings and events and has a license for civil ceremonies.

Location: MAP 10:L11, OS Ref. SD623 305. Situated between Preston and Blackburn, with easy access from the M6 and M65 motorway networks.
Owner: Samlesbury Hall Trust
Contact: Sharon Jones
Tel: 01254 812010
Fax: 01254 812174
E-mail: info@samlesburyhall.co.uk
Open: Open all year. Sun–Fri 11am–4pm (Closed Sats and occasional Fris).
Admission: Adult £3 Child £1. Prices correct as 2011.
Key facts: WCs. Licensed. Licensed. Limited for coaches. Guide dogs only.

TOWNELEY HALL ART GALLERY & MUSEUMS

Burnley BB11 3RQ

www.towneleyhall.org.uk

Home of the catholic Towneley Family for over 6oo years this historic house contains Burnleys museum and Art gallery.The period rooms contain fine collections of furniture,18th and 19th century paintings. The whalley abbey vestments, family chapel and zoffanys painting of Charles Towneley are some of the highlights.
Location: MAP 10:N10, OS Ref. SD854 309. 1/2m SE of Burnley on E side of Todmorden Road (A671).
Owner: Burnley Borough Council
Contact: Mr. Ken Darwen
Tel: 01282 477130
Fax: 01282 436138
Open: All year: daily except Fri's, 12 noon–5pm. Closed Christmas–New Year.
Admission: Small charge. Guided tours: To be booked for groups.
Key facts: WCs.

BLACKBURN CATHEDRAL

Cathedral Close, Blackburn, Lancashire BB1 5AA

On an historic Saxon site in town centre. The 1826 Parish Church dedicated as the Cathedral in 1926 with new extensions to give a spacious and light interior. Of special interest is 'The Journey', a contemporary version of The Stations of the Cross, by Penny Warden commissioned by the Cathedral.
Location: MAP 10:M11, OS Ref. SD684 280. 9m E of M6/J31, via A59 and A677. Town centre.
Contact: Pauline Rowe
Tel: 01254 503090
Fax: 01254 689666
Website: www.blackburncathedral.com
Open: Daily 9am–5pm.
Admission: Free. Donations invited.
Key facts:

MANCHESTER CATHEDRAL

Manchester M3 1SX

Manchester Cathedral is free of charge and all are welcome. In addition to regular worship and daily offices, there are frequent professional concerts, day schools, organ recitals, guided tours and brass-rubbing. The cathedral contains a wealth of beautiful carvings and has the widest medieval nave in Britain.
Location: MAP 6:N1. OS Ref. SJ838 988. Manchester.
Tel: 0161 833 2220
Fax: 0161 839 6218
Website: www.manchestercathedral.org
Open: Daily. Visitor Centre: Mon–Sat, 9am-4.30pm.
Admission: Donations welcome.
Key facts: Visitor Centre. Dogs are not permitted except for guide dogs.

MARTHOLME

Great Harwood, Blackburn, Lancashire BB6 7UJ

Part of medieval manor house with 17th century additions and Elizabethan gatehouse.
Location: MAP 10:M10, OS Ref. SD753 338. 2m NE of Great Harwood off A680 to Whalley.
Owner: Mr & Mrs T H Codling
Contact: Miss P M Codling
Tel: 01254 886463
Open: May 4–7, 25–27. Jun 1–5, 22–24. Jul 6–7, 27–29. Aug 3–5 24–27. Guided tours at 2pm and 4pm.
Admission: £6. Groups welcome by appointment.
Key facts:

Leighton Hall

MEOLS HALL

Churchtown, Southport, Merseyside PR9 7LZ

17th century house with subsequent additions. Interesting collection of pictures and furniture. Tithe Barn available for wedding ceremonies and receptions all year.
Location: MAP 10:K11, OS Ref. SD365 184. 3m NE of Southport town centre in Churchtown. SE of A565.
Owner: The Hesketh Family **Contact:** Pamela Whelan
Tel: 01704 228326 **Fax:** 01704 507185
E-mail: events@meolshall.com
Website: www.meolshall.com
Open: May Bank Holiday Mon, Mon 4 Jun and from 20 Aug–14 Sept.
Admission: Adult £4, Child £1. Groups welcome but Afternoon Tea is only available for bookings of 25+.
Key facts: Wedding ceremonies and receptions now available in the Tithe Barn.

Hoghton Tower and Garden

The Alnwick Garden

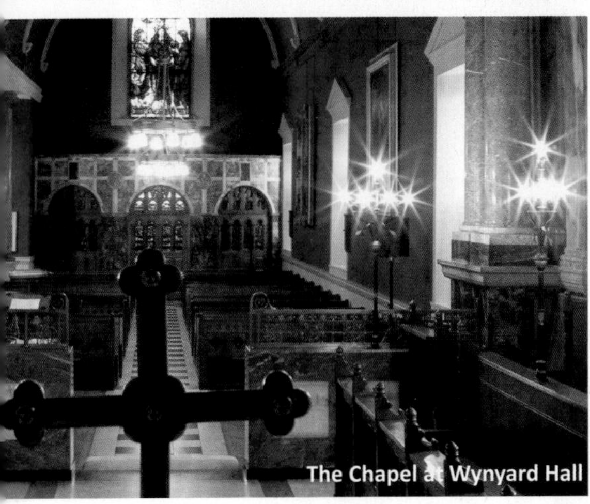
The Chapel at Wynyard Hall

North East

Co. Durham

Northumberland

Tyne & Wear

Northumberland
Tyne & Wear
Co. Durham

The North East is peppered with stately homes, glorious gardens, museums and formidable fortress castles. Visit Durham Cathedral, a World Heritage Site or head further afield to explore the magnificent Barons' Hall, elaborate Octagon Drawing Room and beautiful walled garden at Raby Castle. In Northumberland, experience the atmospheric ruins of Lindisfarne Priory or the impressive Bamburgh Castle which houses over 3000 artefacts, including stunning furniture and artwork. Alnwick Castle has lavish State Rooms, art treasures and entertainment in a beautiful landscape, while the diverse Alnwick Garden has everything from the country's largest collection of European plants in the Ornamental Garden to the intriguing Poison Garden.

VISITOR INFORMATION

Owner
The Lord Barnard

Address
Raby Castle
Staindrop
Darlington
Co. Durham
DL2 3AH

Location
MAP 10:O5
OS Ref. NZ129 218

On A688, 1m N of Staindrop. 8m NE of Barnard Castle, 12m WNW of Darlington.

Bus: Service 85 from Barnard Castle/Staindrop to Raby Castle Gates.

Rail: Darlington Station, 12m.

Air: Durham Tees Valley Airport, 20m.

Contact
Clare Owen / Rachel Milner
Tel: 01833 660202
Fax: 01833 660169
E-mail: admin@rabycastle.com

Opening Times
Castle
Easter weekend: Sat, Sun, Mon. May, June & September: Sun–Wed. July & August: Daily except Sats, 1pm-4.30pm.

Park & Gardens
As Castle, 11am–5.30pm.

Admission
Castle, Park & Gardens

Adult	£10.00
Child (5–15yrs)	£4.50
OAP/Student	£9.00

Family discounts available.

Groups (12+) Adult	£7.50

Park & Gardens

Adult	£6.00
Child (5+)	£2.50
Conc.	£5.00
Groups (12+) Adult	£4.50

Season Tickets available.

VIP Private Guided Tours (20+)*
(incl. reception, tea/coffee in entrance hall)

Adult	£11.00

Standard Private Guided Tours (20+)*

Adult	£8.50

*Please book in advance.

RABY CASTLE

www.rabycastle.com

Discover one of England's finest medieval castles, including walled gardens, deer park, carriage collection and play area.

The magnificent Raby Castle has been home to Lord Barnard's family since 1626, when it was purchased by his ancestor, Sir Henry Vane the Elder, the eminent Statesman and Politician.

The Castle was built mainly in the 14th century by the Nevill family on a site of an earlier Manor House. The Nevills continued to live at Raby until 1569, when after the failure of the Rising of the North, the Castle and its land were forfeited to the Crown. A particular highlight of the Castle is the magnificent Barons' Hall, where 700 knights met to plot The Rising of the North.

Architect John Carr raised the floor level by 3 metres when constructing a carriageway below in the Entrance Hall and later William Burn extended the room by 17 metres over his elaborate Octagon Drawing Room (pictured). Today it houses an impressive Meissen bird collection. Other Raby treasures include fine furniture and artworks with paintings by Munnings, Reynolds, Van Dyck, Batoni, Teniers, Amigoni and Vernet.

There is a large Deer Park with two lakes and a beautiful walled garden with formal lawns, yew hedges and an ornamental pond.

The 18th century Stable block contains a horse-drawn carriage collection including the State Coach last used by the family for the Coronation of Edward VII in 1902. Parts of the stables have been converted into a Gift Shop and Tearooms, where the former stalls have been incorporated to create an atmospheric setting.

KEY FACTS

- Raby Estates venison and game sold in tearooms. No photography or video filming is permitted inside. Colour illustrated guidebook on sale.
- Partial. WCs.
- Licenced.
- By arrangement for groups (20+) or min charge. VIP & Standard Castle Tours available. Tour time 1½ hrs.
- By arrangement (20+), weekday am. £4 a head.
- In grounds.

WYNYARD HALL

WYNYARD, TEES VALLEY TS22 5NF

www.wynyardhall.co.uk

The crown granted tenancy of the Wynyard Estate in 1230 and it has been in use ever since. It wasn't until the tenure of the 3rd Marquess of Londonderry that the Hall became the talk of Europe with guest list including Charles Dickens, Disraeli, Sir Robert Peel, Churchill, King Edward VII, Elizabeth II and 'regular' the Duke of Wellington. Indeed, it inspired Disraeli to remark "I never left London with such a sense of relief and such anticipation of happiness". The House has been sympathetically restored into a Country House Hotel with most of the original features on show.

Location: MAP 11:A5, OS Ref. NZ42544 25984. Easily accessed by A19 and A1 motorways. Within 30-minute drive from Durham, Newcastle upon Tyne and North Yorkshire Moors.

Owner: Cameron Hall Developments Ltd
Contact: Events Office
Tel: 01740 644 811 **Fax:** 01740 644 769
E-mail: enquiries@wynyardhall.co.uk
Open: Day and evening throughout the year.
Admission: Free to guests using dining, hotel or spa facilities. Advance reservation required for groups over 10 guests.
Key facts: The Hall is a functioning 4-star hotel and venue. Rooms offered for private hire may not be available to view - please enquire at Reception on arrival. WCs. Licensed. Licensed. By arrangement. Please visit website.

BARNARD CASTLE

Barnard Castle, Castle House, Durham DL12 8PR

www.english-heritage.org.uk/barnardcastle

Barnard Castle is spectacularly set on a high rock above the river tees. Taking its name from its 12th century founder Bernard de Balliol, this huge and imposing fortress was later developed by the Beauchamp family and Richard III. Richard's boar emblem is carved above a window in the inner ward.

Location: MAP 10:O5, OS92, NZ049 165. In Barnard Castle Town.
Owner: English Heritage
Contact: Visitor Operations Team
Tel: 01833 638212
E-mail: Barnard.Castle@english-heritage.org.uk
Open: Please see www.english-heritage.org.uk for opening times and the most up-to-date information.
Admission: Adult £4.30, Child £2.60, Conc. £3.90. 15% discount for groups (11+). EH members Free. Opening times & prices are valid until 31 Mar 2012.
Key facts: WCs in town. A 'sensory garden' of scented plants and tactile objects. On leads.

© Aerial-Cam

BINCHESTER ROMAN FORT

Bishop Auckland, Co. Durham

www.durham.gov.uk/archaeology

Displayed remains consist of part of commanding officer's house with attached baths-suite which includes one of best preserved examples of a hypocaust (underfloor heating) in whole of Britain. New excavations - both inside fort and in the civil settlement - can be visited weekdays Jun 11–Aug 17. Programme of re-enactment events throughout season; for details see www.durham.gov.uk/archaeology.

Location: MAP 10:P5, OS92 Ref. NZ210 312. 11/2 m N of Bishop Auckland, signposted from A690 Durham–Crook and from A688 Spennymoor–Bishop Auckland roads.
Owner: Durham County Council **Contact:** Archaeology Section
Tel: 01388 663089 / 0191 3708712 (outside opening hours)
Open: Every day, Easter Sat–end Sept, 11am–5pm; Jul & Aug 10am–5pm.
Admission: Adult £2.55, Concession £1.25, Children £1.15, under 4 free.
Key facts: Please note: coaches should approach the fort from lane (Wear Chare) off Bishop Auckland market-place. Except assistance dogs.

DURHAM CATHEDRAL

Durham DH1 3EH

www.durhamcathedral.co.uk

A World Heritage Site. Norman architecture. Burial place of St Cuthbert and the Venerable Bede.
Location: MAP 10:P4, OS Ref. NZ274 422. Durham city centre.
Contact: The Chapter Office
Tel: 0191 3864266
Fax: 0191 3864267
E-mail: enquiries@durhamcathedral.co.uk
Open: Daily 7.30am-6pm (8pm Summer), with Services three times daily.
Admission: Free, donations very welcome.
Groups contact visits@durhamcathedral.co.uk
www.facebook.com/DurhamCathedral
Key facts: Partial. Limited disabled, public parking nearby. Guide dogs only.

Binchester Roman Fort

ROKEBY PARK

Barnard Castle, Co. Durham DL12 9RZ

A Palladian style Country House, built circa 1730. Designed by Sir Thomas Robinson for himself. Acquired in 1769 by JS Morritt in whose family it has remained. The home of a unique collection of needlework pictures by Anne Morritt d.1797. Period furniture and paintings and an unusual print room.
Location: MAP 10:O6, OS ref NZ 080 142. 3m SE of Barnard Castle, N of A66.
Tel: 01609 748612 **E-mail:** admin@rokebypark.com
Website: www.rokebypark.com.
Open: 7 May, 4 Jun–4 Sept: Mons & Tues, 2–5pm (last admission 4.30pm). Groups by appointment.
Admission: Adult £7. Children under 16 Free. Over 60s £6. Students £4. Groups £6 on open days, by arrangement on other days.
Key facts: No photography in house. Ground floor only, no WC. Obligatory by arrangement. Limited for coaches

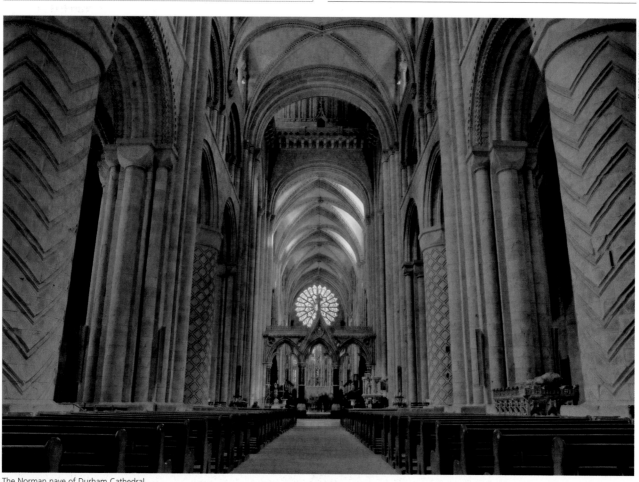

The Norman nave of Durham Cathedral

ALNWICK CASTLE

www.alnwickcastle.com

Set in a stunning landscape designed by 'Capability' Brown, Alnwick Castle is the family home of the Duke of Northumberland.

Owned by his family since 1309, originally built to defend England from the Scots, it now appeals to visitors of all ages. Considered one of the finest castles in England, and known as the 'Windsor of the North'. In the 1760s it was transformed from a fortification into a family home for the First Duke and Duchess. Today Alnwick Castle is an attraction of real significance, with lavish State Rooms, superb art treasures, fun activities and entertainment, all set in a beautiful landscape. Visitors walking through the gates, enter one of the most stunning castles in Europe. The Keep sits magnificently in the spacious grounds, with its medieval towers housing the castle's 14th century dungeon and the entrance to the remarkable State Rooms. The refurbished and restored dining room is worth a visit. Beautifully silked walls, a hand-woven carpet and intricate carved ceiling are among the delights. Important ceramics of the Meissen, Chelsea and Paris factories are impressively displayed in the china gallery. Within the grounds are the museums and towers that tell the story of the Northumberland Fusiliers, the Percy Tenantry Volunteers and an exhibition on the area's fascinating archaeology. Adding to the magic of this castle is an interactive and fun activity area where children can enter the exciting and enchanting world of knights and dragons. Taking the ultimate challenge to win their spurs by facing the monster which rules the kingdom in Dragon's Quest.

KEY FACTS

Conference facilities, events, fairs and exhibitions. Film location hire. No photography inside the castle. No unaccompanied children.

Wedding receptions.

Partial. Parking.

Coffee, light lunches and teas.

Shared with Alnwick Gardens.

Guidebook and worksheet, special rates for children and teachers.

Guide dogs only.

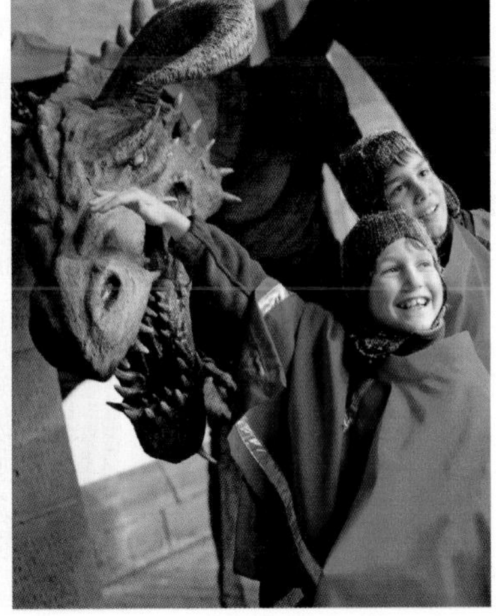

VISITOR INFORMATION

Owner

His Grace the Duke of Northumberland

Address

Estate Office
Alnwick
Northumberland
NE66 1NQ

Location

MAP 14:M11
OS Ref. NU187 135

In Alnwick 1½ m W of A1.
From London 6hrs, Edinburgh 2hrs, Chester 4hrs, Newcastle 40mins
North Sea ferry terminal 30mins.

Bus: From bus station in Alnwick.

Rail: Alnmouth Station 5m.
Kings Cross, London 3½hrs.

Air: Newcastle 40mins.

Contact

Alnwick Castle
Tel: 01665 511172
Group bookings: 01665 511184
Fax: 01665 511169
E-mail: enquiries@alnwickcastle.com

Opening Times

1 April–30 October
Daily, 10am–6pm.
Last admission to State Rooms 4.30pm).

Admission

Adult	£13.00
Child (5–15yrs)	£6.00
Child (under 5yrs)	Free
Conc.	£10.40
Family	£34.00
Booked Groups (14+)	£9.00

(*prices are subject to change).

Seasonal and two day combined tickets with The Alnwick Garden are available.

Conference/Function

ROOM	Size	Max Cap
The Guest Hall	100' x 30'	250

VISITOR INFORMATION

Owner
English Heritage

Address
Belsay
Nr Ponteland
Northumberland
NE20 0DX

Location
MAP 10:O2
OS 87. NZ086 785
In Belsay 14m (22.4 km) NW of Newcastle on SW of A696. 7m NW of Ponteland. Nearest airport and station is Newcastle.

Contact
Visitor Operations Team
Tel: 01661 881636
E-mail: customers@english-heritage.org.uk

Opening Times
please visit www.english-heritage.org.uk for opening times and the most up-to-date information.

Admission

Adult	£7.50
Child	£4.50
Conc.	£6.80
Family	£19.50.

Discount for groups (11+).

Opening times and prices are valid until 31st March 2012.

Special events
There is an exciting events programme available throughout the year, for further details please contact the property or visit the website.

© English Heritage

BELSAY HALL, CASTLE & GARDENS ⌗

www.english-heritage.org.uk/belsay

With so much to see and do, Belsay is one of the best value family days out in north-east England.

Explore the grand medieval castle, later extended to include a magnificent Jacobean mansion and don't miss the stunning views from the top of the tower.

Then it's on to Belsay Hall, an architectural masterpiece with a fabulous 'Pillar Hall'. A true labour of love, the design was inspired by a honeymoon trip to Greece.

Last but not least, there are the huge grounds, packed with an impressive array of shrubs and flowers. See the seasons change in the Grade 1 gardens, with a carpet of Snowdrops in Spring, Rhododendrons and giant Lillies during the Summer, a stunning display of colours in Autumn and even more Rhododendrons in the Winter. The unique Quarry Gardens carry an air of mystery, and not just in the plant species growing there. Tours with the Head Gardener are availble throughout the year, call ahead for details.

The Middleton family created this whole property over seven centuries, and there are facsinating stories at every turn; from the family move from the castle to the hall on Christmas Day 1817, to the pioneering plantsman who introduced exotic species to the Quarry Garden.

Level paths and short grass make the gardens suitable for wheelchairs, and there are plenty of seats around. The tearoom, in the original Victorian kitchens, provides a perfect setting for a break during your visit.

KEY FACTS

© English Heritage

© English Heritage

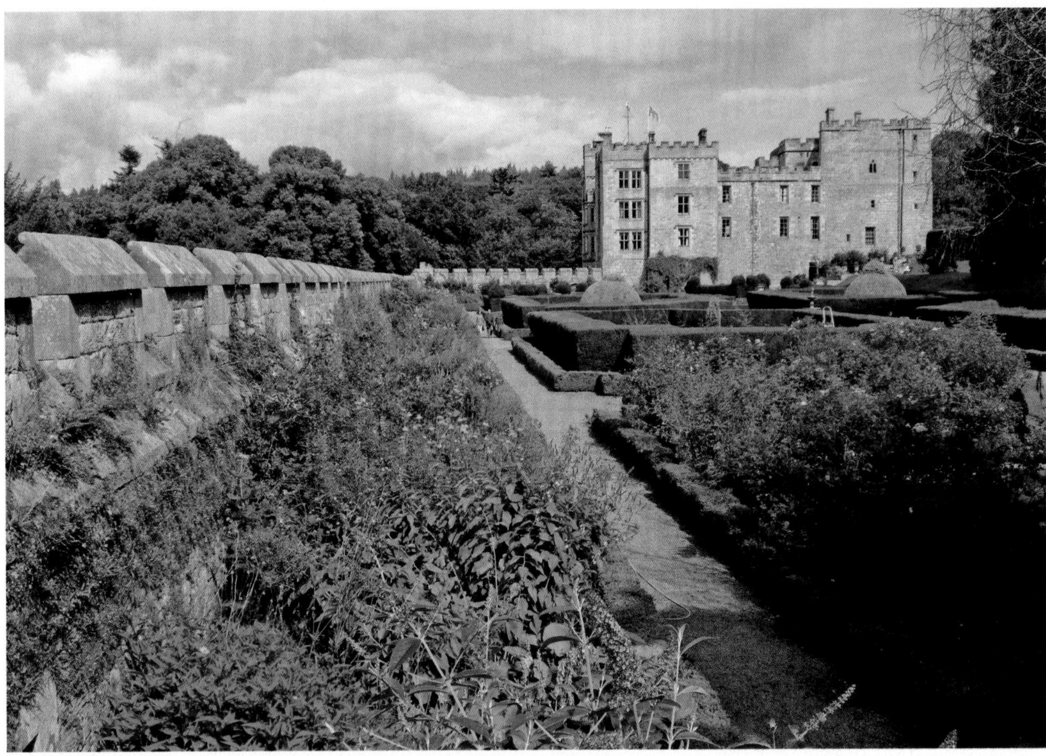

CHILLINGHAM CASTLE

www.chillingham-castle.com

VISITOR INFORMATION

Owner
Sir Humphry Wakefield Bt

Address
Chillingham Castle
Northumberland NE66 5NJ

Location
MAP 14:L11
OS Ref. NU062 258.

45m N of Newcastle between A697 & A1.
2m S of B6348 at Chatton.
6m SE of Wooler.

Rail: Alnmouth or Berwick.

Contact
Administrator
Tel: 01668 215359
Fax: 01668 215463
E-mail: enquiries@chillingham-castle.com

Opening Times
Summer
Easter–31 October Closed Sats, Castle, Garden & Tearoom,12 noon–5pm.

Winter
October–April: Groups & Coach Tours any time by appointment. All function activities available.

Admission

Adult	£8.50
Children	£4.50
Conc.	£7.50
Family Ticket	£21.00

(2 adults and 3 children under 15)

20 minutes from seaside or mountains. 4 stars in Simon Jenkins' "Thousand Best Houses" and the very first of The Independent's "50 Best Castles in Britain & Ireland".

This remarkable and very private castle has been continuously owned by one family line since the 1200s with a visit from Edward I in 1298. You will see alarming dungeons as well as active restoration of complex masonry, metalwork and ornamental plaster as the great halls and state rooms are gradually brought back to life with tapestries, arms and armour and even a torture chamber.

The 1100s stronghold became a fortified castle in 1344, see the original Royal Licence to Crenellate on view. Wrapped in the nation's history Chillingham also occupied a strategic position during Northumberland's bloody border feuds being a resting place to many royal visitors.

Tudor days saw additions but the underlying medievalism has remains. 18th and 19th centuries saw decorative extravagances including Capability Brown lakes and grounds with gardens laid out by Sir Jeffrey Wyatville, fresh from his triumphs at Windsor Castle. Prehistoric Wild Cattle roam the park beyond more rare than mountain gorilla (a separate tour) and never miss the family tomb in the church.

Gardens

With romantic grounds, the castle commands breathtaking views of the surrounding countryside. As you walk to the lake you will see, according to season, drifts of snowdrops, daffodils or bluebells and an astonishing display of rhododendrons. This emphasises the restrained formality of the Elizabethan topiary garden, with its intricately clipped hedges of box and yew. Lawns, the formal gardens and woodland walks are all fully open to the public.

KEY FACTS

Corporate entertainment, lunches, drinks, dinners, wedding ceremonies and receptions.

Partial.

By arrangement.

Avoid Lilburn route, coach parties welcome by prior arrangement. Limited for coaches.

Guide dogs only.

Self catering apartments.

THE ALNWICK GARDEN

Denwick Lane, Alnwick, Northumberland NE66 1YU

www.alnwickgarden.com

Experience the making of one of the most unusual and spectacular public gardens of the 21st century, The Alnwick Garden. This exciting new garden, with the Grand Cascade as its centrepiece, as well as the fascinating Poison Garden and enormous Treehouse, mixes unique and the beautiful in an enchanting landscape.

Location: MAP 14:M11, OS Ref. NU192 132. Just off the A1 at Alnwick, Northumberland.

Owner: The Alnwick Garden Trust **Tel:** 01665 511350 **Fax:** 01665 511351

E-mail: info@alnwickgarden.com

Open: High Season: 1 Apr–30 Oct plus vacation, 10am–6pm. Low Season: 1 Nov–28 Feb except vacation, 10am–4pm. Closed 25 Dec.

Admission: Adult £10, Conc. £8, Child 1p, Group (14+) £7. (Prices are subject to change).

Key facts: WCs. Licensed. By arrangement. Cars & coaches. Guide dogs only.

BAMBURGH CASTLE

Bamburgh, Northumberland NE69 7DF

www.bamburghcastle.com

These formidable stone walls have witnessed dark tales of royal rebellion, bloody battles, spellbinding legends and millionaire benefactors.
With fourteen public rooms and over 3000 artefacts, including arms and armour, porcelain, furniture and artwork. The Armstrong and Aviation artefacts Museum houses artefacts spanning both World Wars as well as others relating to Lord Armstrongs ship building empire on the Tyne.

Location: MAP 14:M10, OS Ref. NU184 351. 42m N of Newcastle-upon-Tyne. 20m S of Berwick-upon-Tweed. 6m E of Belford by B1342 from A1 at Belford.

Owner: Trustees Lord Armstrong dec'd. **Contact:** The Administrator

Tel: 01668 214515 **E-mail:** administrator@bamburghcastle.com

Open: 11 Feb–31 Oct, 10am–5pm. Last Admission 4pm. 1 Nov–15 Feb 2013, Weekends Only, 11–4.30pm, Last Admission 3.30pm. Closed 29 & 30 Dec.

Admission: Adult £9, Senior £8, Child (5-15 yrs) £4 Family £22 (2 Adults & Up to 3 Children) For Group Rates and Bookings please call 01668 214 208.

Key facts: No Flash Photography in the State Rooms. Partial. WCs. Licensed. By arrangement at any time, min charge out of hours £150. 100 cars, coaches park on tarmac drive at entrance. Welcome. Guide provided if requested. Guide dogs only.

LADY WATERFORD HALL & GALLERY

Ford, Berwick-Upon-Tweed TD15 2QA

www.ford-and-etal.co.uk

Situated on the country estate of Ford & Etal, the Hall was built as the village school in 1860. A 'must see venue', it houses a unique collection of magnificent watercolour murals (1861-1883) and smaller original watercolour paintings/sketches by Louisa Waterford, one of the most gifted female artists of her time.

Location: MAP 14:K10, OS Ref. NT945 374. On the B6354, 9m from Berwick-upon-Tweed, midway between Newcastle-upon-Tyne and Edinburgh, close to the A697.

Owner: Ford & Etal Estates **Contact:** Dorien Irving

Tel: 01890 820503 **Fax:** 01890 820384 **E-mail:** tourism@ford-and-etal.co.uk

Open: Mar–Oct: daily, 11am-5pm (see website for details)

Admission: Adult £2.50, Concession/child £2.00, family £7.50. (Prices subject to change). Discounts offered to pre-booked groups of 11+ people.

Key facts: The Hall may occasionally be closed for private functions - please telephone to check before travelling. By arrangement. Limited for coaches. Guide dogs only.

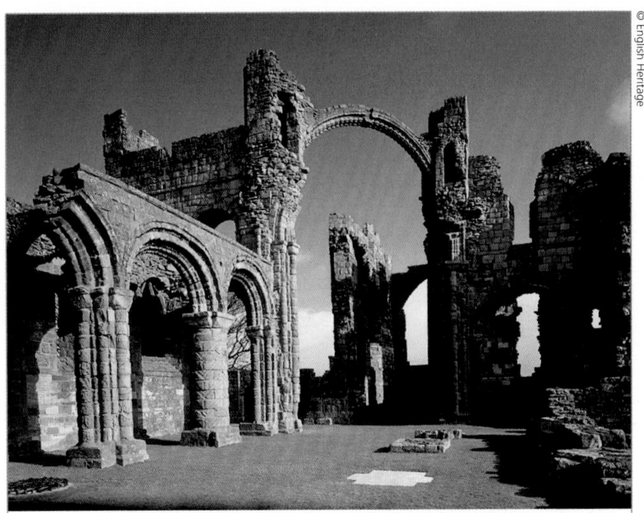

LINDISFARNE PRIORY

Holy Island, Northumberland TD15 2RX

www.english-heritage.org.uk/lindisfarne

Famed as the home and original burial ground of St Cuthbert, this site was one of the most important centres of early Christianity in Anglo-Saxon England. Indulge in the stunning coastal views and atmospheric ruins, then visit the museum for fascinating insight into the lives of the priory's former residents.

Location: MAP 14:L9, OS Ref. NU126 417. On Holy Island, check tide times.

Owner: English Heritage **Contact:** Visitor Operations Team

Tel: 01289 389200 **E-mail:** customers@english-heritage.org.uk

Open: Please see www.english-heritage.org.uk for opening times and the most up-to-date information.

Admission: Adult £4.80, Child £2.90, Conc. £4.30. 15% discount for groups (11+). Opening times and prices are valid until 31 Mar 2012.

Key facts:

SEATON DELAVAL HALL

The Avenue, Seaton Sluice, Northumberland NE26 4QR

www.nationaltrust.org.uk/seatondelavalhall

Seaton Delaval Hall was designed by Sir John Vanbrugh for Admiral George Delaval. It has beautiful formal gardens and is much more than an architectural masterpiece. A new National Trust property, please note that there will be some ongoing building works.

Location: MAP 11:A2. Just off the A190, close to the A19 and 5m from the A1.

Owner: National Trust

Tel: 0191 237 9100 **E-mail:** seatondelavalhall@nationaltrust.org.uk

Open: May–Sept, Thurs–Tues, 11am–5pm; Oct–Apr, Fri–Mon, 11am–3pm. Closed 23–26 Dec. Closed on Weds all year.

Admission: Adult £5, Child £2.25, Family £12.50. Groups by arrangement only.

Key facts: Partial. WCs. By arrangement. Limited for coaches. In grounds.

Bamburgh Castle

WARKWORTH CASTLE

Warkworth, Alnwick, Northumberland NE65 0UJ

www.english-heritage.org.uk/warkworth

The magnificent cross-shaped keep dominates one of the largest, strongest and most impressive fortresses in northern England. This was once home to the powerful Percy family, whose lion badge can still be seen around the castle today. Almost complete, the keep dates mainly from the end of the 14th century.

Location: MAP 14:M12, OS Ref. NU247 058. 7½m S of Alnwick on A1068.

Owner: English Heritage **Contact:** Visitor Operations Team

Tel: 01665 711423 **E-mail:** customers@english-heritage.org.uk

Open: Please visit www.english-heritage.org.uk for opening times and the most up-to-date information.

Admission: Castle: Adult £4.80, Child £2.90, Conc. £4.30, Family £12.50. 15% discount for groups (11+). EH Members free. Opening times and prices are valid until 31 Mar 2012.

Key facts: WC. Partial. Inclusive. On leads.

CAPHEATON HALL

Newcastle-Upon-Tyne NE19 2AB

One of the most fascinating houses in Northumberland, Capheaton was designed by Robert Trollope in 1668 for the Swinburne family. Described by Pevsner as 'one of the most interesting houses of its date and character in England'. Outstanding working kitchen garden with extensive soft fruit glasshouses, conservatory and landscaped park.

Location: MAP 10:O2, OS Ref. NZ038 805. 17m NE of Newcastle off A696.
Owner: W Browne-Swinburne
Contact: Eliza Browne-Swinburne
Tel/Fax: 01830 530159
E-mail: elizab-s@hotmail.co.uk
Open: Open by appointment.
Admission: £8 per adult, Min number 10.
Key facts: Licensed. Obligatory. On leads. Bed & Breakfast Accommodation available.

CHIPCHASE CASTLE

Wark, Hexham, Northumberland NE48 3NT

The castle overlooks the River North Tyne and is set in formal and informal gardens. One walled garden is used as a nursery specialising in unusual perennial plants.

Location: MAP 10:N2, OS Ref. NY882 758. 10m NW of Hexham via A6079 to Chollerton. 2m SE of Wark.
Owner: Mr J R Elkington
Contact: Mr J R Elkington
Tel: 01434 230203
E-mail: info@chipchasecastle.com
Open: Castle: 1–28 Jun, 2–5pm daily. Castle Gardens: Easter–31 Jul, Nursery: Easter–31 Aug, Thurs–Sun Inclusive & Bank Holiday Mons, 10am–5pm.
Admission: Castle £6, Garden £4, concessions available. Nursery Free.
Key facts: Unsuitable. Obligatory for house only.

CRAGSIDE

Rothbury, Morpeth, Northumberland NE65 7PX

Revolutionary home of Lord Armstrong, Victorian inventor and landscape genius, Cragside sits on a rocky crag high above the Debdon Burn. Crammed with ingenious gadgets, it was the first house in the world to be lit with hydro-electricity.

Location: MAP 14:L12, OS Ref. NU073 022. 0.5m NE of Rothbury on B6341.
Owner: National Trust
Contact: Assistant to General Manager
Tel: 01669 620333
Website: www.nationaltrust.org.uk
Open: Opening times vary according to Northumberland school holidays and Bank Holidays. Check NT website for full details.
Admission: Free to NT and NT Scotland members. Check National Trust website for full admission price details.
Key facts: Licensed. On leads.

Britain's Brilliant Heritage
Brought To Life
To find out more visit our website
www.hudsonsheritage.com
HUDSON's
HERITAGE

The Alnwick Garden

LINDISFARNE CASTLE

Holy Island, Berwick-Upon-Tweed, Northumberland TD15 2SH

Built in 1550 to protect Holy Island harbour from attack, the castle was restored and converted into a private house for Edward Hudson by Sir Edwin Lutyens in 1903.

Location: MAP 14:L9, OS Ref. NU136 417. On Holy Island, 3/4m E of village, 6m E of A1 across causeway. Usable at low tide.
Owner: National Trust **Contact:** Property Manager **Tel:** 01289 389244
E-mail: lindisfarne@nationaltrust.org.uk **Website:** www.nationaltrust.org.uk
Open: 11–19 Feb, 10am–3pm, 10 Mar–31 Oct, daily, closed Mons except BH & Aug, 10am–3pm or 12–5pm depending on tides. Alternate weekend openings throughout winter, always 10am–3pm. Telephone, email or visit website for details.
Admission: Adult £6.95, Child £3.50, Family £17.40. Garden only: Adult £1.50, Child Free. Out of hours tours (20+) £9.95 by arrangement.
*Includes a voluntary donation.
Key facts: Emergency toilet only, public WCs in village. NT Shop (in Main St). No parking onsite. In village, 1000m from site.

PRESTON TOWER

Chathill, Northumberland NE67 5DH

Built by Sir Robert Harbottle in 1392, the tower is one of the few survivors of 78 pele towers listed in 1415. The tunnel vaulted rooms provide a realistic picture of a spartan way of life, threatened by "Border Reivers". Two rooms are furnished in contemporary style, displaying historic information.

Location: MAP 14:M11, OS Ref. NU185 253. Follow Historic Property signs on A1 7m N of Alnwick.
Tel: 01665 589227
Website: www.prestontower.co.uk
Open: All year daily, 10am–6pm, or dusk, whichever is earlier.
Admission: Adult £2, Child 50p, Conc. £1.50. Groups £1.50.
Key facts: Grounds.

WALLINGTON

Cambo, Morpeth, Northumberland NE61 4AR

Dating from 1688, Wallington was home to many generations of the Blackett and Trevelyan families, who all left their mark. The result is an impressive, yet friendly, house with a magnificent interior and fine collections.

Location: MAP 10:O2, OS Ref. NZ030 843. Near Cambo, 6m NW of Belsay (A696).
Owner: National Trust
Contact: The Estate Office
Tel: 01670 773600
E-mail: wallington@nationaltrust.org.uk
Website: www.nationaltrust.org.uk
Open: Please contact for up to date information.
Admission: Please contact for up to date information.
Key facts: In grounds, on leads.

SOUTER LIGHTHOUSE

Coast Road, Whitburn, Sunderland, Tyne & Wear SR6 7NH

www.nationaltrust.org.uk

Dramatic red and white lighthouse on rugged coast. Built in 1871, the first in the world to be powered by alternating electric current.

Location: MAP 11:A3, OS Ref. NZ408 641. 2½m S of South Shields on A183. 5m N of Sunderland.

Owner: National Trust

Contact: Operations Manager

Tel: 0191 529 3161

E-mail: souter@nationaltrust.org.uk

Open: 10 Mar–4 Nov: daily except Fri (open Good Fri), 11am–5pm. Last adm 4.30pm.

Admission: Adult £5.50, Child £3.50, Family £14.50. Booked Groups (10+): Adult £4.50, Child £3. NT members Free: membership available from shop. *includes a voluntary donation but visitors can choose to pay the standard prices displayed at the property and on the website.

Key facts: Partial. WCs. Obligatory. In grounds, on leads.

© English Heritage

TYNEMOUTH PRIORY & CASTLE

North Pier, Tynemouth, Tyne & Wear NE30 4BZ

www.english-heritage.org.uk/tynemouth

Set on a steep headland, Tynemouth has always been as much a fortress as a religious site, playing its role in the Civil War and both World Wars. The Life in the Stronghold exhibition tells the story of the 2000 year history, from its original beginnings as an Anglo-Saxon settlement.

Location: MAP 11:A2, OS Ref. NZ373 694. In Tynemouth near North Pier.

Owner: English Heritage **Contact:** Visitor Operations Team

Tel: 0191 257 1090 **E-mail:** customers@english-heritage.org.uk

Open: Please visit www.english-heritage.org.uk for opening times and the most up-to-date information.

Admission: Adult £4.50, Child £2.70, Conc. £4.10, Family £11.70. 15% discount for groups (11+). EH Members free. Opening times and prices are valid until 31 Mar 2012.

Key facts: Available for corporate and private hire. By arrangement.

GIBSIDE

Nr Rowlands Gill, Burnopfield, Newcastle upon Tyne NE16 6BG

Gibside is an 18th century 'forest' landscape garden, created by wealthy coal baron George Bowes, ancestor of the Queen Mother. Gibside is a haven for wildlife with stunning Derwent Valley views, miles of woodland and riverside walks, a spectacular Palladian Chapel and exciting new adventure play area.

Location: MAP 10:P3, OS Ref. NZ172 583. 6m SW of Gateshead, 20m NW of Durham. Entrance on B6314 between Burnopfield and Rowlands Gill.

Owner: National Trust **Contact:** Visitor Services Team **Tel:** 01207 541820

E-mail: gibside@nationaltrust.org.uk **Website:** www.nationaltrust.org.uk/gibside

Open: Gardens, Walks & Stables: 1 Jan–29 Feb: 10am–4pm. 1 Mar–31 Oct: 10am–6pm. 1 Nov–31 Dec: 10am–4pm. Chapel, Café and Shop: close one hour before wider estate. Closed 24 & 25 Dec.

***Admission:** Adult £6.50, Child £4, Family (2 adults+children) £18.50, Family (1 adult+children) £13. Booked groups £5.20. *Includes a Gift Aid donation.

Key facts: WCs. Licensed. Licensed. By arrangement. Limited for coaches. On leads.

© Britainonview

Knight at Mediaeval re-enactment at Tynemouth Priory & Castle

Culzean Castle

Pitmedden Garden

Scotland

- Borders
- South West Scotland, Dumfries & Galloway, Ayrshire & The Isle of Arran
- Edinburgh City, Coast & Countryside
- Greater Glasgow & The Clyde Valley
- Perthshire, Angus & Dundee & The Kingdom of Fife
- West Highlands & Islands, Loch Lomond, Stirling & Trossachs
- Grampian Highlands, Aberdeen & North East Coast
- Highlands & Skye
- Outer Island, Western Isles, Orkney & Shetland

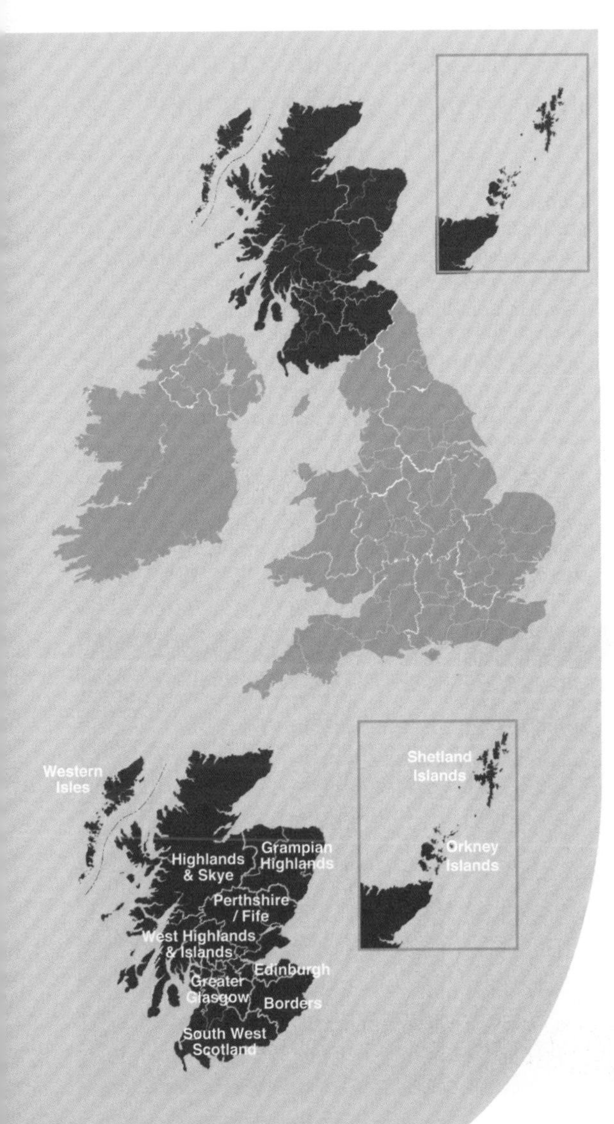
Western Isles
Shetland Islands
Orkney Islands
Highlands & Skye
Grampian Highlands
Perthshire / Fife
West Highlands & Islands
Edinburgh
Greater Glasgow
Borders
South West Scotland

It is hard to beat the drama and sheer variety of Scotland's heritage. An amazing array of grand houses and castles includes Glamis Castle, Hopetoun House, Culzean Castle and Scone Palace, to name but a few. Alloa Tower, one of Scotland's largest surviving medieval towers, The New Lanark World Heritage Site and Robert Burns Birthplace Museum are just a small selection of the treasure trove of historic monuments and museums also to be found in this ancient land.

VISITOR INFORMATION

■ Owner
The Lord Palmer

■ Address
Manderston
Duns
Berwickshire
Scotland TD11 3PP

■ Location
MAP 14:K9
OS Ref. NT810 544
From Edinburgh 47m, 1hr.
11/2 m E of Duns on A6105.
Bus: 400 yds.
Rail: Berwick Station 12m.
Taxi: 07970 221821.
Airport: Edinburgh or Newcastle both 60m or 80 mins.

■ Contact
The Lord and Lady Palmer
Tel: 01361 883450
Secretary: 01361 882636
Fax: 01361 882010
E-mail: palmer@manderston.co.uk

■ Opening Times
Summer 2012
10 May–30 September
Thursday & Sunday only.
Gardens & tearoom open 11.30am.
House opens 1.30–5pm.
Last entry 4.15pm.
BH Mons, late May & late August. Groups welcome all year by appointment.
Winter
September–May
Group visits welcome by appointment.

■ Admission
House & Grounds

Adult	£9.00
Child (under 12yrs)	Free
Groups (15+)	£8.50
Grounds only	£5.00

Open any other day by appointment.

Conference/Function

ROOM	Size	Max Cap
Dining Rm	22' x 35'	100
Ballroom	34' x 21'	150
Hall	22' x 38'	130
Drawing Rm	35' x 21'	150

MANDERSTON

www.manderston.co.uk

Manderston, together with its magnificent stables, stunning marble dairy and 56 acres of immaculate gardens, forms quite a unique ensemble.

Manderston is the supreme country house of Edwardian Scotland: the swansong of its era. Manderston, as it is today, is a product of the best craftsmanship and highest domestic sophistication the Edwardian era had to offer and was completely rebuilt between 1903 and 1905.

Visitors are able to see not only the sumptuous State rooms and bedrooms, decorated in the Adam manner, but also all original domestic offices, in a truly 'upstairs downstairs' atmosphere.

Manderston boasts a unique and recently restored silver staircase. There is a special museum with a nostalgic display of valuable tins made by Huntly and Palmer from 1868 to the present day. Winner of the AA/NPI Bronze Award UK 1994.

Gardens
Outside, the magnificence continues and the combination of formal gardens and picturesque landscapes is a major attraction unique amongst Scottish houses. The stables, still in use, have been described by Horse and Hound as 'probably the finest in all the wide world'. The Marble Dairy and its unusual tower, built to look like a Border Keep, enjoys commanding views. Manderston is often used as a film location but can also cater for corporate events. It is also an ideal retreat for business groups and think-tank weekends. Manderston also lends itself very well to fashion shows, air displays, archery, clay pigeon shooting, equestrian events, garden parties, shows, rallies, filming, product launches and marathons. Two airstrips for light aircraft, approx. 5m, grand piano, billiard table, pheasant shoots, sea angling, salmon fishing, stabling, cricket pitch, tennis court, lake.

KEY FACTS

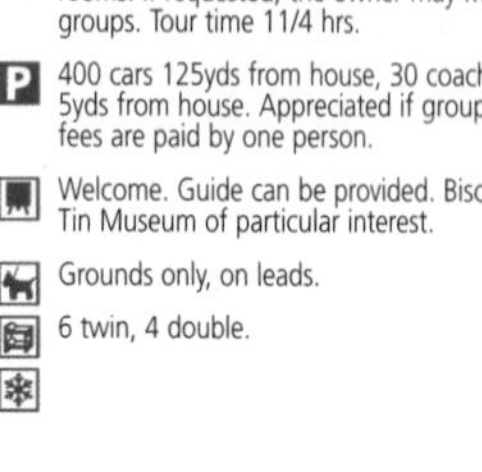

- No photography in house.
- Available. Buffets, lunches and dinners. Wedding receptions.
- Special parking available outside the House.
- Snaffles Tearoom – home made lunches, teas, cakes and tray bakes. Can be booked in advance, menus on request.
- Included. Available in French. Guides in rooms. If requested, the owner may meet groups. Tour time 11/4 hrs.
- 400 cars 125yds from house, 30 coaches 5yds from house. Appreciated if group fees are paid by one person.
- Welcome. Guide can be provided. Biscuit Tin Museum of particular interest.
- Grounds only, on leads.
- 6 twin, 4 double.

ABBOTSFORD

The Abbotsford Trust, Abbotsford, Melrose, Roxburghshire TD6 9BQ

www.scottsabbotsford.co.uk

Much of the stunning gardens and landscape at Abbotsford remain as they were when author Sir Walter Scott created them between 1811 and 1825. New for 2012 Visitor Centre with day time Restaurant & Gift Shop also a free to access exhibition on the life and legacy of Sir Walter Scott. The Historic House will be closed for essential restoration work throughout 2012.
Location: MAP 14:I10, OS Ref. NT508 342. 2 miles from Melrose and Galashiels. Edinburgh 35 miles, Glasgow & Newcastle approx 70 miles. Major routes: A1, A68 and A7 **Owner:** The Abbotsford Trust
Contact: Beverley Rutherford **Tel:** 01896 752043 **Fax:** 01896 752916
E-mail: enquiries@scottsabbotsford.co.uk
Open: Visitors Centre: 18 Apr–30 Sept 2012, 9am–6pm. 1 Oct 2012–31 Mar 2013, 9am–4pm. Gardens: 18 Apr–30 Sept 2012, 9am–6pm. 1 Oct–31 Oct 2012, 9am–4pm.
Admission: Visitor Centre: Free, Gardens: £3.50 (free for children 5 years and under). **Key facts:** Licensed. Gardens. In grounds, on leads. Visitor Centre only.

MELLERSTAIN HOUSE

Mellerstain, Gordon, Berwickshire TD3 6LG

www.mellerstain.com

One of Scotland's great Georgian houses and a unique example of Adam design; the two wings built in 1725 by William Adam, the central block by his son, Robert 1770-78. Rooms boast stunning plasterwork, colourful ceilings and marble fireplaces. The library is considered to be Robert Adam's finest creation.
Location: MAP 14:J10, OS Ref. NT648 392. From Edinburgh A68 to Earlston, turn left 5m, signed.
Owner: The Earl of Haddington
Contact: The Administrator
Tel: 01573 410225
Fax: 01573 410636
E-mail: enquiries@mellerstain.com
Open: From Easter Weekend. May/Jun/Jul/Aug/Sept/Oct: Sun, Mon & Wed. House: 12.30–5pm. Last ticket 4.15pm. Groups anytime by appointment. Tearoom & gardens: 11.30am–5pm.
Admission: See our website or call us.
Key facts: No photography or video cameras. Suitable. WCs. By arrangement On leads.

FLOORS CASTLE

Kelso, Roxburghshire, Scotland TD5 7SF

www.floorscastle.com

Explore the spectacular state rooms with outstanding collections of paintings, tapestries and furniture. Find hidden treasures like the collections of porcelain and oriental ceramics. Enjoy the picturesque grounds and gardens including the beautiful walled gardens. Stop at the Courtyard Restaurant and enjoy a morning coffee or delicious lunch.
Location: MAP 14:J10, OS Ref. NT711 347. From South A68, A698. From North A68, A697/9 In Kelso follow signs.
Owner: His Grace the Duke of Roxburghe **Contact:** Charlotte Newton
Tel: 01573 223333 **Fax:** 01573 226056 **E-mail:** cnewton@floorscastle.com
Open: Summer: Opens Easter Weekend. Please visit our website for more information. Winter: Nov–Mar Closed to the general public, available for events. Please check our website for details.
Admission: Adult £8, Child (5–16yrs) £5, OAP/Student £7, Family £22, Under 5yrs Free.
Key facts: Exclusive lunches & dinners. Partial. WCs. Licensed. By arrangement. On site for cars and coaches. On leads. Please check our website for details.

Gardens at Floors Castle

THIRLESTANE CASTLE

Lauder, Berwickshire TD2 6RU

www.thirlestanecastle.co.uk

Thirlestane Castle was the ancient seat of the Earls and Duke of Lauderdale and is still home to the Maitlands. Thirlestane has exquisite 17th century plasterwork ceilings, a fine portrait collection, historic toys, kitchens and country life exhibitions. Facilities include free parking, café, adventure playground, and woodland picnic tables. Four star STB award; Registered Museum.
Location: MAP 14:I9, OS Ref. NT540 473. Off A68 at Lauder, 28m S of Edinburgh.
Owner: Thirlestane Castle Trust **Contact:** Ian Garner **Tel:** 01578 722430
Fax: 01578 722761 **E-mail:** admin@thirlestanecastle.co.uk
Open: Good Fri, Easter Sun, Mon; 6, 8 & 9 Apr. Suns, Weds & Thurs; 2 May–28 Jun. Also open Bank Holidays; 7 May & 4 & 5 Jun. Every day except Fri & Sats; Jul & Aug. Sun, Wed & Thurs; 2–30 Sept. Open 10am–Last entry into the Castle 3pm. Open all year round for pre-booked groups.
Admission: Castle and Grounds: Adults £10, Children £6, Senior Citizens £8, Family 2+3 £25. Grounds: Adult £3, Children £1.50. Group Castle & Grounds: £8.
Key facts: Woodland walk, children's adventure playground, country life display area. Unsuitable. By arrangement. In grounds, on leads.

TRAQUAIR

Innerleithen, Peeblesshire EH44 6PW

www.traquair.co.uk

Dating back to 1107, Traquair was originally a hunting lodge for the kings and queens of Scotland. Later a refuge for Catholic priests in times of terror the Stuarts of Traquair supported Mary Queen of Scots and the Jacobite cause. Today, Traquair is a unique piece of living history.
Location: MAP 13:H10. OS Ref. NY330 354. On B709 near junction with A72. Edinburgh 1hr, Glasgow 1.5 hrs, Carlisle 1.5 hrs.
Owner/Contact: Catherine Maxwell Stuart, 21st Lady of Traquair
Tel/Fax: 01896 830323 **E-mail:** enquiries@traquair.co.uk
Open: Daily 6 Apr–31 Oct. Weekends only in Nov. Apr–Sept: 11am–5pm; Oct: 11am–4pm; Nov: 11am–3pm.
Admission: House & Grounds: Adult £7.70, Child £4.20, Senior £7, Family (2+3) £22, Groups (20+) Adult £6.70, Child £3.70, Senior £6.20. Grounds only: Adult £4, Concessions £3, Guide book £4.25
Key facts: No photography in house. Exclusive lunches/dinners (max 30) in the Dining Room. Licensed. Licensed. Apr & outside opening hours. Coaches please book. On leads. 3 en suites. B&B.

PAXTON HOUSE, GALLERY & COUNTRY PARK

Berwick-Upon-Tweed TD15 1SZ

Palladian country house by John Adam built 1758. 12 period rooms, magnificent Picture Gallery - Partner of the National Galleries of Scotland, working Georgian kitchen. Grounds, gardens, riverside and woodland walks, red squirrel hide and salmon net fishing museum. Gift shop, tearoom serving home cooked lunches. Ellem Fishing Club exhibition.
Location: MAP 14:K9, OS Ref. NT931 520. 3m west off the A1 Berwick-upon-Tweed bypass on B6461.
Owner: The Paxton Trust **Contact:** Reception **Tel:** 01289 386291
E-mail: info@paxtonhouse.com **Website:** www.paxtonhouse.com
Open: 1 Apr–31 Oct: House: 11am–5pm.Grounds: 10am–sunset. Open to groups/schools all year by appointment.
Admission: Adult £8, Child £3.50, Family £21 Concession £7.50. Grounds only: Adult £5, Child £2, Family £13. Last admission to House 4.30pm.
Key facts: No photography in House. Conferences, weddings. WCs. Obligatory. On leads. €

© Britainonview

The stunning Ballroom at Manderston

DUMFRIES HOUSE

www.dumfries-house.org.uk

A Georgian Gem, nestling within 2,000 acres of scenic Ayrshire countryside in south-west Scotland.

This beautiful Palladian mansion house has been described as an 18th century time-capsule with many of its principal rooms extremely wellpreserved and some of their exquisite contents virtually unchanged for nearly 250 years. Commissioned by William Crichton Dalrymple, the 5th Earl of Dumfries, the House was designed by renowned 18th century architect brothers John, Robert and James Adam and built between 1754 and 1759. Recognised as one of the Adam brothers' masterpieces it remained unseen by the public since it was built 250 years ago until it opened its doors as a visitor attraction in June 2008. The former home of the Marquises of Bute, it was saved for the nation at the eleventh hour by a consortium of organisations and individuals brought together by HRH The Prince Charles, Duke of Rothesay. The house holds the most important collection of works from Thomas Chippendale's 'Director' period. It is widely recognised that Scotland was a testing ground for Thomas Chippendale's early rococco furniture and the Dumfries House collection is regarded as his key project in this area. Dumfries House also holds the most comprehensive range of pieces by Edinburgh furniture makers Alexander Peter, William Mathie and Francis Brodie. Indeed, the Scottish furniture together with the Chippendale collection is of outstanding worldwide historical significance.

KEY FACTS

Pre-booking of tours is recommended (Online at www.dumfries-house.org.uk or via the booking line 01290 551111). Tour times may vary.

Unsuitable. WCs

Obligatory.

Cars ample. Coaches ample.

In grounds. Guide dogs only in the house.

Grounds only.

VISITOR INFORMATION

Owner

The Great Steward of Scotland's Dumfries House Trust

Address

Dumfries House
Cumnock
East Ayrshire
Scotland
KA18 2NJ

Location

MAP 10:I2
OS Ref. NS539 200

Car: Cumnock, East Ayrshire.
Sat Nav KA18 2LN.
Visitors Entrance on Barony Road (B7036).

Rail: Auchinleck.

Air: Prestwick.

Contact

The Wedding & Events Administrator
Tel: 01290 425959
(Booking Line 01290 551111)
Fax: 01290 425464
E-mail: info@dumfries-house.org.uk

Opening Times

Summer season:
March–October (inclusive), Sunday–Friday, 10am–4pm.

Guided tours every 30 minutes.

Winter season:
November–February (inclusive), Saturdays & Sundays, 11am–2pm.

Guided tours every 30 minutes.

Please note: the House is closed for Christmas and New Year.

Please be advised that you should call the Visitor Line on 01290 421742 or go onto www.dumfries-house.org.uk to confirm any House closures before your visit.

For individuals there is no need to pre-book tours – just turn up.

All visitors are advised to call the Visitor Line on 01290 421742 or go onto www.dumfries-house.org.uk to check any House closures prior to their visit.

For groups of 20 or more, please pre-book your chosen tour by contacting Group Bookings on 01290 421742.

Admission

Ticket Price for the House Tour:

Adults:	£8.50
Child (5-16 years):	£4.00
Children under 5	free
Historic Scotland Members: 25% discount	
Art Fund Members:	Free

Special events

Grounds available all year.

House may close for private functions.

Please check with the property before travelling any distance.

Special Events information available at www.dumfries-house.org.uk

House available for private functions and corporate events. Minister license for weddings.

CASTLE KENNEDY & GARDENS

Castle Kennedy, Stranraer, Dumfries and Galloway DG9 8SJ

www.castlekennedygardens.co.uk

Famous 75-acre gardens situated between two large natural lochs. Ruined Castle Kennedy at one end overlooking beautiful herbaceous walled garden; Lochinch Castle at the other. Proximity to the gulf-stream provides an impressive collection of rare trees, including 21 Champion Trees, magnolias, and spectacular rhododendron displays. Guided walks, children's activities, theatre, falconry, gift shop, plant centre – a 'must-visit'.

Location: MAP 9:D3, OS Ref. NX109 610. 3m E of Stranraer on A75.

Owner: The Earl and Countess of Stair **Contact:** Stair Estates

Tel: 01776 702024 / 01581 400225 **Fax:** 01776 706248

E-mail: info@castlekennedygardens.co.uk

Open: Gardens and Tearoom: 1 Apr–31 Oct: daily 10am–5pm. Feb & Mar: Weekends only. Gardens open all year.

Admission: Adult £5, Child £1.50, OAP £3.50. Groups of 20 or more 10% discount.

Key facts: WCs. By arrangement. Limited for coaches. On leads.

KELBURN CASTLE & COUNTRY CENTRE

Fairlie, By Largs, Ayrshire KA29 0BE

www.kelburnestate.com

Kelburn is the home of the Earls of Glasgow and has been in the Boyle family for over 800 years. It is notable for its waterfalls, historic gardens, romantic glen and unique trees. Recently the Castle has been the venue of a major art graffiti project.

Location: MAP 13:B9, OS Ref. NS210 580. A78 to Largs, 2m S of Largs.

Owner: The Earl of Glasgow

Tel: 01475 568685/ 01475 568595

Fax: 01475 568121

E-mail: admin@kelburncountrycentre.com

Open: Country Centre: Easter–Oct: daily. Castle: Jul & Aug. Open by arrangement for groups at other times of the year.

Admission: Country Centre: Adult £7.50, Child/Conc. £5, Family £25. Groups (10+): Adult, £4.50, Conc. £3.50. Castle: £1.75 extra pp.

Key facts: Partial. Licensed. Jul & Aug. By arrangement at other times of the year. In grounds on leads.

CRAIGIEBURN GARDEN

Craigieburn House, Nr Moffat, Dumfriesshire DG10 9LF

A unique six acre garden: woodland, long borders, stunning Himalayan plants, and utter tranquillity. Fine plants for sale. Our Garden Café, open all year, serves irresistible cakes and home baking, delicious lunches and a few touches of the exotic, like our top quality teas imported from China. Dogs very welcome.

Location: MAP 13:G12, OS Ref. NT117 053. NW side of A708 to Selkirk, 2½m E of Moffat.

Owner/Contact: Janet Wheatcroft

Tel: 01683 221250 / 221758

Open: Easter–Oct: Tue–Sun.

Admission: Adult £2.50, Child Free (charges support Sherpa school in Nepal).

Key facts:

Kelburn Castle

AUCHINLECK HOUSE

Ochiltree, Ayrshire KA18 2LR

One of the finest examples of an 18th century Scottish country house, the importance of which is further enhanced by its association with James Boswell, author of The Life of Samuel Johnson. The house has been restored by the Landmark Trust and is let for holidays for 13 people.

Location: MAP 13:C11, OS Ref. NS507 230.

Owner/Contact: The Landmark Trust

Tel: 01628 825925

E-mail: bookings@landmarktrust.org.uk

Website: www.landmarktrust.org.uk

Open: Available for holidays. Parts of the house open Easter–Oct: Wed afternoons. Grounds: dawn–dusk in Spring and Summer.

Admission: By appointment only. Tickets £3 from 01628 825920.

Key facts:

BROUGHTON HOUSE AND GARDEN

12 High Street, Kirkcudbright, Dumfries and Galloway DG6 4JX

Once the home and studio of Scottish artist, EA Hornel, and today visitors can admire many of his paintings and those of his fellow artists. Behind the house is a spectacular Japanese-style garden, with many attractive features.

Location: MAP 9:G4, OS Ref. NX 681 511. In the centre of Kirkcudbright.

Owner: The National Trust for Scotland

Contact: Property Manager

Tel: 0844 493 2246

E-mail: information@nts.org.uk

Website: www.nts.org.uk

Open: House open Apr–Oct; Garden also open Feb & Mar.

Admission: Please see our website or call us for up to date prices.

Key facts: Partial. By arrangement. Guide dogs only.

CRAIGDARROCH HOUSE

Moniaive, Dumfriesshire DG3 4JB

Built by William Adam in 1729, over the old house dating from 14th century (earliest records). The marriage home of Annie Laurie, the heroine of 'the world's greatest lovesong', who married Alexander Fergusson, 14th Laird of Craigdarroch, in 1720 and lived in the house for 33 years.

Location: MAP 9:G1, OS Ref. NX741 909. S side of B729, 2m W of Moniaive, 19m WNW of Dumfries.

Owner: Mrs Carin Sykes

Contact: Mrs Carin Sykes

Tel: 01848 200202

Open: Jul: daily, 2–4pm. Please note: no WCs.

Admission: £3.

CULZEAN CASTLE & COUNTRY PARK

Maybole, Ayrshire KA19 8LE

Robert Adam's 18th century masterpiece - a real 'castle in the air' - is perched on a cliff high above the crashing waves of the Firth of Clyde. The Castle itself boasts a spectacular Oval Staircase, the impressive Armoury and the Circular Saloon, with its panoramic views over the Clyde. The extensive grounds encompass Scotland's first country park where you can explore the deer park, swan pond and miles of woodland walks.

Location: MAP 13:B11, OS Ref. NS232 103. On A719, 4 miles west of Maybole and 12 miles south of Ayr. KA19 8LE.

Owner: The National Trust for Scotland

Tel: 0844 493 2149

E-mail: information@nts.org.uk **Website:** www.nts.org.uk

Open: Garden & Country Park: Open all year. Castle: Apr–Oct. Please see our website or call us for more up to date opening times.

Admission: Please see our website or call us for up to date prices.

Key facts:

GLENMALLOCH LODGE

Newton Stewart, Dumfries And Galloway DG8 6AG

Glenmalloch Lodge represents the aristocratic philanthropy that characterised the Victorian Age. It lies in the middle of a wild glen, with wide views of the surrounding hills. The cottage was built originally not as a lodge, rather as a schoolhouse through the philanthropy of Harriet, Countess of Galloway, before 1842.

Location: MAP 9:F3, OS Ref. NX423 682.

Owner/Contact: The Landmark Trust

Tel: 01628 825925

E-mail: bookings@landmarktrust.org.uk

Website: www.landmarktrust.org.uk

Open: Available for holidays for up to 2 people. Other visits by appointment. Contact the Landmark Trust for details.

Key facts:

RAMMERSCALES

Lockerbie, Dumfriesshire DG11 1LD

Georgian house, with extensive library and fine views over Annandale.

Location: MAP 10:I2, OS Ref. NY080 780. W side of B7020, 3m S of Lochmoben.

Owner: Mr M A Bell Macdonald

Contact: Mr M A Bell Macdonald

Tel: 01387 810229 **Fax:** 01387 810940

E-mail: malcolm@rammerscales.co.uk

Website: www.rammerscales.co.uk

Open: Later half of Jul for 25 days: daily (excluding Sat), 2–5pm. Bus tours by appointment.

Admission: Adult £5, Conc. £2.50.

Key facts: Obligatory.

ROBERT BURNS BIRTHPLACE MUSEUM

Murdoch's Lone, Alloway, Ayr KA7 4PQ

National hero, poet and musician Robert Burns was born in Alloway in 1759. The newly opened Robert Burns Birthplace Museum houses the most important Burns collection in the world and is within easy walking distance of the Burns Cottage, Burns Monument and Garden, Alloway's Auld Kirk and the Brig o'Doon.

Location: MAP 13:B11. OS Ref. NS334 185. In Alloway, 2$^1/_2$ miles south of Ayr.

Tel: 0844 493 2601

E-mail: information@nts.org.uk

Website: www.nts.org.uk

Open: Open all year. Please see our website or call us for more up to date opening times.

Admission: Please see our website or call us for up to date prices.

Key facts:

Dumfries House

VISITOR INFORMATION

■ Owner
The Earl of Rosebery

■ Address
Dalmeny House
South Queensferry
Edinburgh EH30 9TQ

■ Location
MAP 13:G8
OS Ref. NT167 779

From Edinburgh A90, B924, 7m N, A90 1/2m.

On south shore of Firth of Forth.

Bus: From St Andrew Square to Chapel Gate 1m from House.

Rail: Dalmeny station 3m.

Taxi: Hawes Cars 0131 331 1077.

■ Contact
The Administrator
Tel: 0131 331 1888
Fax: 0131 331 1788
E-mail: events@dalmeny.co.uk

■ Opening Times
Summer
3 June–31 July
Sunday–Tuesday afternoons, 2–5pm.

Entry by Guided Tours only. Tours are 2.15pm & 3.30pm.

Winter
Open at other times by appointment only.

■ Admission
Summer

Adult	£7.50
Child (10–16yrs)*	£5.50
OAP	£6.50
Student	£6.50
Groups (20+)	£6.50

DALMENY HOUSE

www.dalmeny.co.uk

Welcome to a family home which contains Scotland's finest French treasurers. Dine in splendor, and enjoy sea-views over superb parkland.

Dalmeny House rejoices in one of the most beautiful and unspoilt settings in Great Britain, yet it is only seven miles from Scotland's capital, Edinburgh, fifteen minutes from Edinburgh airport and less than an hour's drive from Glasgow. It is an eminently suitable venue for group visits, business functions, and special events, including product launches. Outdoor activities, such as off-road driving, can be arranged.

Dalmeny House, the family home of the Earls of Rosebery for over 300 years, boasts superb collections of porcelain and tapestries, fine paintings by Gainsborough, Raeburn, Reynolds and Lawrence, together with the exquisite Mentmore Rothschild collection of 18th century French furniture. There is also the Napoleonic collection, assembled by the 5th Earl of Rosebery, Prime Minister, historian and owner of three Derby winners.

The Hall, Library and Dining Room will lend a memorable sense of occasion to corporate receptions, luncheons and dinners. A wide range of entertainment can also be provided, from a clarsach player to a floodlit pipe band Beating the Retreat.

KEY FACTS

- Fashion shows, product launches, archery, clay pigeon shooting, shows, filming, background photography, and special events. Lectures on House, contents and family history. Helicopter landing area.
- Conferences and functions, buffets, lunches, dinners.
- WCs.
- Obligatory. Special interest tours can be arranged outside normal opening hours.
- 60 cars, 3 coaches. Parking for functions in front of house.
- In grounds.

HOPETOUN HOUSE

www.hopetoun.co.uk

Hopetoun House is a unique gem of Europe's architectural heritage and undoubtedly 'Scotland's Finest Stately Home'.

Situated on the shores of the Firth of Forth, it is one of the most splendid examples of the work of Scottish architects Sir William Bruce and William Adam. The interior of the house, with opulent gilding and classical motifs, reflects the aristocratic grandeur of the early 18th century, whilst its magnificent parkland has fine views across the Forth to the hills of Fife. The house is approached from the Royal Drive, used only by members of the Royal Family, notably King George IV in 1822 and Her Majesty Queen Elizabeth II in 1988. Hopetoun is really two houses in one, the oldest part of the house was designed by Sir William Bruce and built between 1699 and 1707. It shows some of the finest examples in Scotland of carving, wainscotting and ceiling painting. In 1721 William Adam started enlarging the house by adding the magnificent façade, colonnades and grand State apartments which were the focus for social life and entertainment in the 18th century. The house is set in 100 acres of rolling parkland including fine woodland walks, the red deer park, the spring garden with a profusion of wild flowers, and numerous picturesque picnic spots. Hopetoun has been home of the Earls of Hopetoun, later created Marquesses of Linlithgow, since it was built in 1699 and in 1974 a charitable trust was created to preserve the house with its historic contents and surrounding landscape for the benefit of the public for all time.

KEY FACTS

- Private functions, special events, antiques fairs, concerts, Scottish gala evenings, conferences, wedding ceremonies and receptions, grand piano, helicopter landing. No smoking or flash photography in house.
- Receptions, gala dinners.
- Partial.
- Licensed.
- By arrangement.
- Close to the house for cars and coaches. Book if possible, allow 1–2hrs for visit (min).
- Special tours of house and/or grounds for different age/ interest groups.
- No dogs in house, on leads in grounds.

VISITOR INFORMATION

Owner
Hopetoun House Preservation Trust

Address
Hopetoun House
South Queensferry
Edinburgh
West Lothian EH30 9SL

Location
MAP 13:F7
OS Ref. NT089 790
2½m W of Forth Road Bridge.
12m W of Edinburgh (25 mins. drive).
34m E of Glasgow (50 mins. drive).

Contact
Piers de Salis
Tel: 0131 331 2451
Fax: 0131 319 1885
E-mail: marketing@hopetoun.co.uk

Opening Times
Summer
Easter–End September: Daily, 10.30am–5pm. Last admission 4pm.

Winter
By appointment only for Groups (20+).

Admission

House & Grounds	
Adult	£9.20
Child (5–16yrs)*	£4.90
Conc/Student	£8.00
Family (2+2)	£25.00
Groups	£8.00
Grounds only	
Adult	£4.25
Child (5–16yrs)*	£2.50
Conc/Student	£3.70
Family (2+2)	£11.50
Groups	£3.70
School Visits	
Child	£5.50
Teachers	Free

*Under 5yrs Free.

Winter group rates on request.

Admission to Tearoom Free.

Special events
July 28 & 29
Horse Trials

November 23–25
Christmas Shopping Fair

Conference/Function

ROOM	Size	Max Cap
Ballroom	92' x 35'	300
Tapestry Rm	37' x 24'	100
Red Drawing Rm	44' x 24'	100
State Dining Rm	39' x 23'	20
Stables	92' x 22'	200

EDINBURGH CASTLE

CASTLE HILL, EDINBURGH EH1 2NG

www.edinburghcastle.gov.uk

Edinburgh Castle, built on an extinct volcano, dominates the skyline of Scotland's capital city. The castle's wealth of attractions include: The Honours of Scotland - the nation's crown jewels; The Stone of Destiny - coronation stone of Scotland's ancient kings; The Great Hall, Laich Hall and St Margaret's Chapel - remarkable medieval rooms and buildings where royalty and nobles dined and worshipped; Prisons of War Experience – showing what 18th century prison life was like; National War Memorial - commemorating those who died in conflict from World War I onwards; The famous One O'clock Gun - fired daily, except Sundays.

Location: MAP 21, OS Ref. NT252 736. At the top of the Royal Mile in Edinburgh.

Owner: Historic Scotland **Contact:** Executive Manager

Tel: 0131 225 9846

Open: Apr–Sept: daily, 9.30am–6pm. Oct–Mar: daily, 9.30am–5pm. Last ticket 45 mins before closing. Open New Year's Day 11am to 5pm. Closed Christmas Day and Boxing Day.

Admission: Prices range from: Adult £13–£16, Child £6.50–£9.20, Conc. £10–£13. Buy ticket online to beat the queues! Visit www.edinburghcastle.gov.uk for details.

Key facts: Parking only available for drivers with a blue disabled badge. Private evening hire. WCs. Licensed. In 8 languages. Guide dogs only. €

GOSFORD HOUSE

Longniddry, East Lothian EH32 0PX

www.gosfordhouse.co.uk

1791 the 7th Earl of Wemyss, aided by Robert Adam, built one of the grandest houses in Scotland, with a "paradise" of lakes and pleasure grounds. New wings, including the celebrated Marble Hall were added in 1891 by William Young. The house has a fine collection of paintings and furniture.

Location: MAP 14:17, OS Ref. NT453 786. Off A198 2m NE of Longniddry.

Owner: The Earl of Wemyss

Contact: The Earl of Wemyss

Tel: 01875 870201

Open: 4 Aug–15 Sept: Thurs–Sun, 1–4pm. Please check www.gosfordhouse.co.uk for most upto date opening times/days.

Admission: Adult £6, Child £1.

Key facts:

By arrangement.

Limited for coaches.

LENNOXLOVE HOUSE

Haddington, East Lothian EH41 4NZ

www.lennoxlove.com

House to many of Scotland's finest artefacts, including the Death Mask of Mary, Queen of Scots, furniture and porcelain collected by the Douglas, Hamilton and Stewart families. Open to the public and available for events. Lennoxlove lends itself perfectly to intimate parties offering 11 luxury suites for an overnight stay.

Location: MAP 14:I8, OS Ref. NT515 721. 18m E of Edinburgh, 1m S of Haddington.

Owner: Lennoxlove House Ltd **Contact:** Kenneth Buchanan, General Manager

Tel: 01620 828614 **Fax:** 01620 825112 **E-mail:** ken-buchanan@lennoxlove.com

Open: Easter–End of Sept: Weds, Thurs & Suns, 1.30–3.30pm. Guided Tours.

Admission: £5 per adult.

Key facts: 5 star exclusive use house dating back to 14th century. Guided tours. WCs. Licensed. Licensed. Obligatory. Guide dogs only

AMISFIELD MAINS

Nr Haddington, East Lothian EH41 3SA
Georgian farmhouse with gothic barn and cottage.
Location: MAP 14:I8, OS Ref. NT526 755. Between Haddington and East Linton on A199.
Owner: Wemyss and March Estates Management Co Ltd
Contact: M Andrews
Tel: 01875 870201
Fax: 01875 870620
Open: Exterior only: By appointment, Wemyss and March Estates Office, Longniddry, East Lothian EH32 0PY.
Admission: Please contact for details.

BEANSTON

Nr Haddington, East Lothian EH41 3SB
Georgian farmhouse with Georgian orangery.
Location: MAP 14:I8, OS Ref. NT546 763. Between Haddington and East Linton on A199.
Owner: Wemyss and March Estates Management Co Ltd
Contact: M Andrews
Tel: 01875 870201
Fax: 01875 870620
Open: Exterior only: By appointment, Wemyss and March Estates Office, Longniddry, East Lothian EH32 0PY.
Admission: Please contact for details.

HARELAW FARMHOUSE

Nr Longniddry, East Lothian EH32 0PH
Early 19th century 2-storey farmhouse built as an integral part of the steading. Dovecote over entrance arch.
Location: MAP 14:I8, OS Ref. NT450 766. Between Longniddry and Drem on B1377.
Owner: Wemyss and March Estates Management Co Ltd
Contact: M Andrews
Tel: 01875 870201
Fax: 01875 870620
Open: Exteriors only: By appointment, Wemyss and March Estates Office, Longniddry, East Lothian EH32 0PY.
Admission: Please contact for details.

HOUSE OF THE BINNS

Linlithgow, West Lothian EH49 7NA
Historic home of the Dalyell family, it contains a fascination collection of portraits, furniture and procelain revealing their lives and interests through the centuries. In the grounds visitors can enjoy panoramic views over the River Forth.
Location: MAP 13:F7, OS Ref. NT051 786. Off A904, Off A904, 15m W of Edinburgh. 4m E of Linlithgow.
Owner: The National Trust for Scotland
Tel: 0844 493 2127
E-mail: information@nts.org.uk
Website: www.nts.org.uk
Open: House: May–Sept. Please see our website or call us for more up to date opening times.
Admission: Please see our website or call us for up to date prices.
Key facts:

NEWHAILES

Newhailes Road, Musselburgh EH21 6RY
Newhailes is a fine 17th century house with impressive 18th century additions and interiors. Bought in the early 1700s by Sir David Dalrymple, the most remarkable addition was the library, which played host to many famous figures. Much of the original decoration and furnishing has survived, retaining the mellowness of its interiors.
Location: MAP 13:G8, OS Ref. NT327725. On A6095, in Musselburgh.
Tel: 0844 493 2125
E-mail: information@nts.org.uk
Website: www.nts.org.uk
Open: House: Easter weekend & May–Sept. Please see our website or call us for more up to date opening times.
Admission: Please see our website or call us for up to date prices.
Key facts: Visitor centre.

NEWLISTON

Kirkliston, West Lothian EH29 9EB
Late Robert Adam house. 18th century designed landscape, rhododendrons, azaleas and water features. On Sundays there is a ride-on steam model railway from 2–5pm.
Location: MAP 13:G8, OS Ref. NT110 735. 9m W of Edinburgh, 4m S of Forth Road Bridge, off B800.
Owner: Mrs Caroline Maclachlan
Contact: Mrs Caroline Maclachlan
Tel: 0131 333 3231
Open: 2 May–3 Jun: Wed–Sun, 2–6pm. Also by appointment.
Admission: Adult: £3, Children under 12: Free of charge
Key facts: In grounds, on leads.

RED ROW

Aberlady, East Lothian
Terraced Cottages. **Location:** MAP 14:I7, OS Ref. NT464 798. Main Street, Aberlady, East Lothian. **Owner:** Wemyss & March Estates Management Co Ltd
Contact: M Andrews **Tel:** 01875 870201 **Fax:** 01875 870620
Open: Exterior only. By appointment, Wemyss & March Estates Office, Longniddry, East Lothian EH32 0PY. **Admission:** Please contact for details.

Newhailes

ARDGOWAN

2012 Courses at Ardgowan

Join acclaimed experts for our residential courses on art and the history of dining. The seat of Sir Ludovic Shaw Stewart, Ardgowan is a late 18th century Palladian house forty minutes west of Glasgow. Many of the bedrooms have their original Gillows furniture.

Collecting Antique Silver: Secrets of the Experts with Christopher Hartop and Juliet Nusser
April 21st to 23rd

The Art of Dining with Ivan Day
June 9th to 11th

The Hamilton Collections: Mary Queen of Scots, Napoleon and William Beckford
October 6th to 8th

Day visitors also welcome.

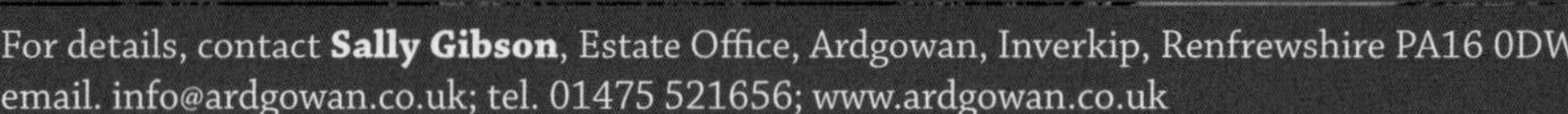

For details, contact **Sally Gibson**, Estate Office, Ardgowan, Inverkip, Renfrewshire PA16 0DW
email. info@ardgowan.co.uk; tel. 01475 521656; www.ardgowan.co.uk

COREHOUSE

Lanark ML11 9TQ

Designed by Sir Edward Blore and built in the 1820s, Corehouse is a pioneering example of the Tudor Architectural Revival in Scotland.

Location: MAP 13:E9, OS Ref. NS882 416. On S bank of the Clyde above the village of Kirkfieldbank.

Owner: Colonel D A S Cranstoun of that Ilk TD

Contact: Estate Office

Tel: 01555 663126

Open: 5–23 May & 8–19 Sept: Sat–Wed. Guided tours: weekdays: 1 & 2pm, weekends: 2 & 3pm. Closed Thurs & Fri.

Admission: Adult £6, Child (under 14yrs)/OAP £3.

Key facts: Partial. Obligatory. Limited. In grounds.

GEILSTON GARDEN

Main Road, Cardross, Dumbarton G82 5HD

A delightful garden, typical of the small country estates on the banks of the Clyde purchased by merchants and industrialists in the 18th and 19th centuries. Attractive features include a walled garden and a burn, winding through the wooded glen.

Location: MAP 13:B7 OS Ref. NS340 783. On A814 at the west end of Cardross.

Tel: 0844 493 2219

E-mail: information@nts.org.uk

Website: www.nts.org.uk

Open: Apr–Oct. Please see our website or call us for more up to date opening times.

Admission: Please see our website or call us for up to date prices.

Key facts: Picnic area. Hot drinks available.

GREENBANK GARDEN

Flenders Road, Clarkston, Glasgow G76 8RB

Within easy reach of city residents, this unique 2.5 acre walled garden contains plants and designs of particular interest to suburban gardeners and includes fountains and a woodland walk.

Location: MAP 13:D8, OS Ref. NS561 566. Off A726.

Tel: 0844 493 2201

E-mail: information@nts.org.uk

Website: www.nts.org.uk

Open: Garden: Open all year. Shop & tearoom: Apr–Oct & weekends ouside these months.

Admission: Please see our website or call us for up to date prices.

Key facts:

HOLMWOOD HOUSE

61-63 Netherlee Road, Cathcart, Glasgow G44 3TU

This unique Villa has been described as Alexander 'Greek' Thomson's finest domestic design. It was built in 1857-8 for James Couper. Many rooms are richly ornamented in wood, plaster and marble. Thomson's original rich room decoration, based on themes from the classical world, is being uncovered and visitors may follow the progress of this continuing conservation work. Attractive riverside grounds, audio tour, exhibition and study rooms.

Location: MAP 13:D8, OS Ref. NS585 597. Off Clarkson Road, 4 miles south of city centre.

Tel: 0844 493 2204 **E-mail:** information@nts.org.uk **Website:** www.nts.org.uk

Open: Apr–Oct. Please see our website or call us for more up to date opening times.

Admission: Please see our website or call us for up to date prices.

Key facts: Picnic area.

NEW LANARK WORLD HERITAGE SITE

New Lanark Mills, Lanark, S Lanarkshire ML11 9DB

Close to the famous Falls of Clyde, this cotton mill village was founded in 1785 and became famous as the site of Robert Owen's radical reforms. Now beautifully restored as both a living community and attraction, the fascinating history of the village has been interpreted in New Lanark Visitor Centre.

Location: MAP 13:E9. OS Ref. NS880 426. 1m S of Lanark.
Owner: New Lanark Trust **Contact:** Trust Office
Tel: 01555 661345 **Fax:** 01555 665738
E-mail: visit@newlanark.org
Website: www.newlanark.org
Open: All year: daily, 10am–5pm (11am–5pm Oct–Mar). Closed 25 Dec & 1 Jan.
Admission: Visitor Centre: Adult £8.50, Concession (senior/student) £7, Child £6. Groups: 1 free/10 booked.
Key facts: Conference facilities. Partial. WC. Visitor Centre wheelchair friendly. Obligatory by arrangement. 5 min walk. In grounds, on leads.

POLLOK HOUSE

Pollok Country Park, 2060 Pollokshaws Road, Glasgow G43 1AT

The present house dates from around 1750 and contains a fine collection of Spanish art, together with furniture and furnishings appropriate to an Edwardian country house. Set within Pollok Country Park, Pollok House's surroundings are a delight to stroll through, perhaps after a wonderful lunch in the Edwardian Kitchen Restaurant.

Location: MAP 13:C8, OS Ref. NS550 616. Off M77, follow signs for Burrell Collection, 3 miles South of Glasgow city centre.
Owner: The National Trust for Scotland
Tel: 0844 4932202
E-mail: information@nts.org.uk
Website: www.nts.org.uk
Open: Open all year. Please see our website or call us for more up to date opening times.
Admission: Please see our website or call us for up to date prices.
Key facts:

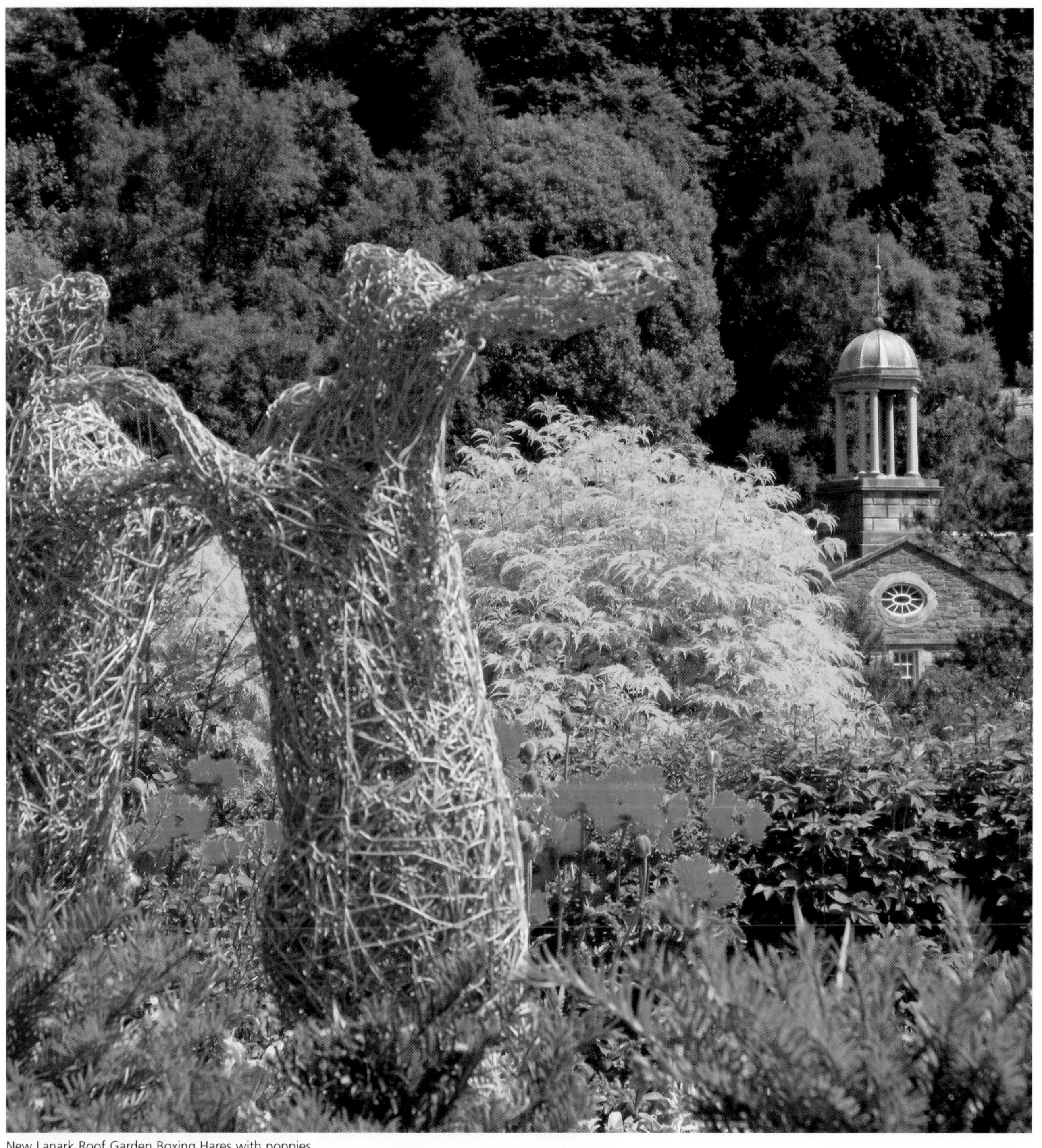

New Lanark Roof Garden Boxing Hares with poppies

VISITOR INFORMATION

Owner
Blair Charitable Trust

Address
Blair Castle
Blair Atholl
Pitlochry
Perthshire PH18 5TL

Location
MAP 13:E3
OS Ref. NN880 660

Car: Just off the main Perth/Inverness road (A9), 35 miles north of Perth. Approximately 90 minutes drive from Edinburgh and Glasgow.

Bus: Elizabeth Yule Service 87 (end March to early Nov), or Stagecoach 83 service from Perth.

Rail: Blair Atholl Station 1m. Serviced by main London Euston to Inverness line.

Contact
Administration Office
Tel: 01796 481207
Fax: 01796 481487
E-mail: bookings@blair-castle.co.uk

Opening Times
Summer:
26 March–26 October, Daily, 9.30am–5.30pm (Last admission to castle tour 4.30pm).

Winter:
3 November–24 March, Sat & Sun, 10.00am–4.00pm (last admission 3.00pm).

Limited opening between Christmas & New Year. Please check website for details.

Admission
House & Grounds

Adult	£9.50
Child (5–16yrs)	£5.70
Senior/Student	£8.10
Family	£25.75
Disabled	£2.85
Groups* (12+)	
Adult	£7.15
Child (5–16yrs)	£5.25
Primary School	£4.30
Senior/Student	£7.15
Disabled	£2.85
Grounds only	
Adult	£5.25
Child (5–16yrs)	£2.40
Senior/Student	£5.25
Family	£13.00
Disabled	Free
Scooter Hire	£3.85
Groups* (12+)	
Adult	£4.30
Child (5–16yrs)	£2.40
Primary School	£2.40
Senior/Student	£4.30
Disabled	Free

*(Groups must book in advance).

Special events
Atholl Highlanders' Parade Saturday 26 May.

Highland Games Sunday 27 May.

Blair Castle International Horse Trials and Country Fair 23–26 August.

Nov–Dec Christmas Castle.

Feb Snowdrop Festival.

Conference/Function

ROOM	Size	Max Cap
Ballroom	88' x 36'	400 or 220 dining
State Dining Room	36' x 26'	150 or 16–50 dining
Banvie Hall	55' x 32'	150

BLAIR CASTLE

www.blair-castle.co.uk

Set in the heart of a breathtaking historic landscape with a fascinating 700 year history just waiting to be discovered.

Nestling like a white jewel in the dramatic Highland Perthshire landscape, Blair Castle has a centuries old history as a strategic stronghold at the gateway to the Grampians and the route north to Inverness.

Famous as the last castle to be held under siege in 1746, Blair Castle is the ancient seat of the Dukes and Earls of Atholl and the home of the Atholl Highlanders, Europe's only remaining private army. More than 30 rooms are on display, full of treasures and alive with the characters and personalities of their former occupants.

Highlights of the visit include: the magnificent ballroom bedecked with 175 pairs of antlers; the superb China Room featuring more than 1700 individual pieces and an ornamental Victorian armoury housing a targe used at the Battle of Culloden. There are also paintings by Sir Edwin Landseer, fine mortlake tapestries and plasterwork by Thomas Clayton.

Weddings and Functions
Civil and religious weddings may be held in the castle and receptions for up to 220 guests can be held in the Ballroom. Banquets, dinners and private functoins are also welcome.

Gardens & Grounds
Blair Castle is at the hub of a breathtaking historic landscape most of which was laid out in the 18th century. It features a beautiful 9 acre walled garden with landscaped ponds, a peaceful wooded grove of some of the country's tallest trees, a ruined Celtic kirk, a red deer park and a whimsical gothic folly. Children will also enjoy the castle's woodland adventure playground.

KEY FACTS

- Photography allowed in Ballroom only.
- Licensed Gift Shop.
- Private functions, civil and religious weddings.
- Partial, WCs.
- Licensed.
- Licensed.
- Guides available when booked in advance.
- 200 cars, 20 coaches. Coach drivers/couriers free, plus meal and shop voucher and information pack.
- Nature walks, ranger service, pony trekking and adventure playground.
- Guide dogs only.
- Civil Wedding Licence.
- Regular winter opening.

GLAMIS CASTLE

www.glamis-castle.co.uk

Visit a Royal home in Diamond Jubilee year.

Glamis Castle is the family home of the Earls of Strathmore and Kinghorne and has been a royal residence since 1372. It was the childhood home of Her Majesty Queen Elizabeth The Queen Mother, the birthplace of Her Royal Highness Princess Margaret and the legendary setting of Shakespeare's play Macbeth. Although the Castle is open to visitors it remains a family home, lived in and loved by the Strathmore family. The Castle, a fivestorey 'L' shaped tower block, was originally a royal hunting lodge. It was remodelled in the 17th century and is built of pink sandstone. It contains the Great Hall, with its magnificent plasterwork ceiling dated 1621, a beautiful family Chapel constructed inside the Castle in 1688, an 18th century billiard room housing what is left of the extensive library once at Glamis, a 19th century dining room containing family portraits and the Royal Apartments which have been used by Her Majesty Queen Elizabeth The Queen Mother. The Castle stands in an extensive park, landscaped towards the end of the 18th century, and contains the beautiful Italian Garden and the Pinetum which reflect the peace and serenity of the Castle and grounds. Glamis is a stunning venue for wedding ceremonies and receptions. The castle provides a magnificent backdrop and accentuates the setting for annual events such as the Highland Games, Vintage Vehicle Extravaganza, the Glamis Prom, and Scotland's Countryside Festival. In winter time it takes on a new atmosphere; hosting popular events and activities at Halloween and Christmas.

KEY FACTS

- Castle Tours, Garden Walks, Exhibitions, Weddings, Fashion Shoots, Product Launches, Highland Games, Royal Memorials, Christmas programme of events Nov–Dec. Music Events, Outdoor Events, Private Receptions/Bespoke Tours.
- Shopping pavilion.
- WCs.
- Licensed.
- Licensed.
- All visits are guided, tour time 50–60 mins.
- Ample parking for coaches/cars. Refreshment vouchers for Drivers & Group Leaders.
- 1 teacher free for every 10 children.
- Guide dogs only.
- By appointment Jan–Mar.
- €

VISITOR INFORMATION

Owner
The Earl of Strathmore & Kinghorne

Address
Estates Office
Glamis By Forfar
Angus DD8 1RJ

Location
MAP 13:H4
OS Ref. NO386 480

Situated just off the A94. From Edinburgh M90, A94, 81miles. From Glasgow M90, A94, 93miles. From Aberdeen A90, A94, 50 miles.

Air: Nearest: Dundee: Aberdeen: Edinburgh: Glasgow.

Bus: Bus no. 20 from Seagate Station in Dundee to Forfar then no. 124 from Forfar to Glamis.

Rail: Dundee Station 12m.

Contact
Castle Administrator, David Broadfoot MBE
Tel: 01307 840393
Fax: 01307 840733
E-mail: enquiries@glamis-castle.co.uk

Opening Times
April–End December, daily, 10am–6pm. Last admission 4.30pm.

November–December, 10.30am–4.30pm. Last admission 3pm.

Extended opening July–August.

Groups & Private Tours are welcome in January–March, by prior arrangement.

Admission

Castle & Grounds:	
Adult	£9.75
Concession	£9.00
Child	£7.25
Family	£28.00
Gardens & Ground visit:	
Adult	£5.75
Concession	£5.25
Child	£3.75
Groups Rate (20+)	
Adult	£8.75
Concession	£8.00
Child (5–16yrs)	£6.25

Drivers and group leaders are admitted free of charge and issued with meal/refreshment voucher.

Special events
Special Events in 2012: Diamond Jubilee Exhibition April–October.

Strathmore Highland Games – June 10

Scottish Transport Extravaganza – July 7 & 8

Scotland's Countryside Festival – July 28 & 29

The Prom at Glamis – August 11

'Macbeth' Outdoor Picnic Play – August 25

Halloween at Glamis – October 27 & 28

Winter programme of events – November–December

www.glamis–castle.co.uk

Conference/Function

ROOM	Size	Max Cap
Dining Room	84 sq.m	90
Restaurant	140 sq.m	100
16th Century Kitchens		40

VISITOR INFORMATION

Owner
The Earl of Mansfield

Address
Scone Palace
Perth
PH2 6BD

Location
MAP 13:G5
OS Ref. NO114 266
From Edinburgh Forth Bridge M90, A93 1hr.
Bus: Regular buses from Perth.
Rail: Perth Station 3m.
Motorway: M90 from Edinburgh.
Taxi: 01738 636777.

Contact
The Administrator
Tel: 01738 552300
Fax: 01738 552588
E-mail: visits@scone-palace.co.uk

Opening Times
Summer
1 April–31 October.
Gates open at 9.30am–last admission 5.00pm, Mon–Fri & Sun.

9.30am–last admission 4.00pm, Sat.

Grounds Only open each Friday during Winter, 10am–4pm.

Evening and Winter tours by appointment.

Please check our website for details of Winter Events.

Admission
Admission prices correct at time of going to print:

Palace & Grounds	
Adult	£10.00
Conc.	£9.00
Child (5–16yrs)	£7.00
Family	£30.00
Groups (20+)	
Adult	£8.95
Conc.	£7.60
Child (5–16yrs)	£6.30
Grounds only	
Adult	£5.80
Conc.	£5.15
Child (5–16yrs)	£4.00
Under 5s Free	

Private Tour £55 supplement.
Season tickets are available.

Special events
2012 Events Include:
29 June–1 July:
The Scottish Game Fair
20–22 July:
80's Rewind Festival
4–5 August:
Orchid Festival.

For details of our 2012 event programme please visit www.scone-palace.co.uk and www.facebook.com/sconepalace

Conference/Function		
ROOM	Size	Max Cap
Long Gallery	140' x 20'	200
Queen Victoria's Rm	20' x 20'	20
Drawing Rm	48' 25'	80
Balvaird Rm	29' x 22'	50/60
Tullibardine Rm	19' x 23'	40/50

SCONE PALACE & GROUNDS

www.scone-palace.co.uk

Scone Palace is home to the Earls of Mansfield and is built on the site of an ancient abbey.

1500 years ago it was the capital of the Pictish kingdom and the centre of the ancient Celtic church. In the intervening years, it has been the seat of parliaments and crowning place of Scottish kings, including Macbeth, Robert the Bruce and Charles II. The State Rooms house a superb collection of objets d'art, including 17th and 18th century ivories, mostly collected by the fourth Earl of Mansfield. Notable works of art are also on display, including paintings by Sir David Wilkie, Sir Joshua Reynolds, and Johann Zoffany. The Library boasts one of Scotland's finest collections of porcelain, including Sèvres, Ludwigsburg and Meissen, whilst the unique 'Vernis Martin' papier mâché may be viewed in the Long Gallery. An audio visual presentation explores centuries of Scone's history.

Gardens
The grounds of the Palace house magnificent collections of shrubs, with woodland walks through the Wild Garden containing David Douglas' original fir and the unique Murray Star Maze. An informative pavilion dedicated to Douglas and other Scottish plant hunters is situated in the Pinetum. A Wildlife Trail way-marked by cartoon character 'Cyril the Squirrel' encourages younger visitors to become nature detectives. There are Highland cattle and peacocks to admire and an adventure play area for children. The 100 acres of mature Policy Parks, flanked by the River Tay, are available for a variety of events, including weddings, corporate and private entertaining.

We also hold events and acticities such as receptions, fashion shows, war games, archery, clay pigeon shooting, equestrian events, garden parties, shooting, fishing, floodlit tattoos, highland games, parkland, helicopter landing, croquet, racecourse, polo field, firework displays, adventure playground.

KEY FACTS

- No photography in state rooms.
- Gift shop & food shop.
- Grand dinners in state rooms (inc. buffets & cocktail parties).
- WCs.
- By Arrangement. Guides in each room. Private tours in French, German, Italian and English by appointment.
- 300 cars and 15 coaches (coaches – booking preferable). Couriers/drivers free meal and admittance.
- Welcome.
- In grounds.
- By Appointment.

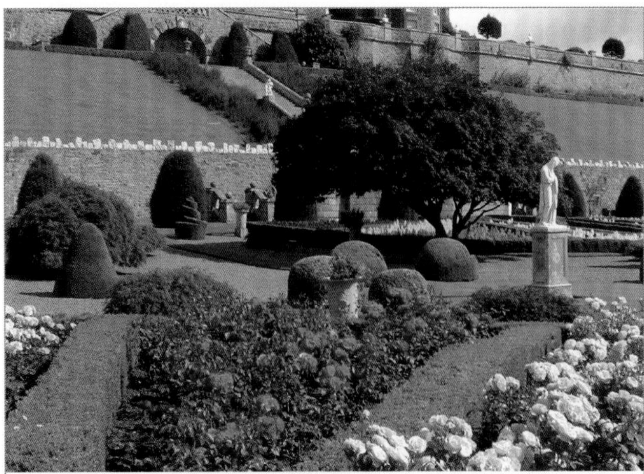

DRUMMOND CASTLE GARDENS

Muthill, Crieff, Perthshire, PH7 4HZ

www.drummondcastlegardens.co.uk

Scotland's most important formal gardens. The Italianate parterre is revealed from a viewpoint at the top of the terrace. First laid out in the 17th century and renewed in the 1950s. The perfect setting to stroll amongst the manicured plantings and absorb the atmosphere of this special place.

Location: MAP 13:E5, OS Ref. NN844 181. 2m S of Crieff off the A822.
Owner: Grimsthorpe & Drummond Castle Trust
Contact: The Caretaker
Tel: 01764 681433
Fax: 01764 681642
E-mail: thegardens@drummondcastle.sol.co.uk
Open: Easter weekend, 1 May–31 Oct: Daily, 1–6pm. Last admission 5pm.
Admission: Adult £5, Child £2, Conc. £4. Groups (20+) 10% discount.
Key facts: Partial. WCs. By arrangement. Limited for coaches. On leads.

BALCARRES

Colinsburgh, Fife KY9 1HN

16th century tower house with 19th century additions by Burn and Bryce. Woodland and terraced gardens.

Location: MAP 14:I6. OS Ref. NO475 044. 0.5m N of Colinsburgh.
Owner: Balcarres Heritage Trust
Contact: Lord Balniel
Tel: 01333 340520
Open: Woodland & Gardens: 1 Mar–30 Sept, 2–5pm. House not open except by written appointment and 1–30 Apr, excluding Sun.
Admission: Adult £7. Garden only: £5.
Key facts: Partial. Obligatory, by arrangement. On leads.

BRANKLYN GARDEN

116 Dundee Road, Perth PH2 7BB

An enchanting garden, established in 1922, with outstanding collections of rhododendrons, alpines, herbaceous and peat-garden plants, which attract gardeners and botanists from all over the world.

Location: MAP 13:F5, OS Ref. NO125 225. Near the centre of Perth, on A85 at 116 Dundee Road, Perth.
Owner: The National Trust for Scotland
Contact: Property Manager
Tel: 0844 493 2193
E-mail: information@nts.org.uk
Website: www.nts.org.uk
Open: Apr–Oct.
Admission: Please see our website or call us for up to date prices.
Key facts: Partial. Limited for cars and coaches. Guide dogs only.

BRECHIN CASTLE

Brechin, Angus DD9 6SG

Dating from 1711 the Castle contains many family pictures and artefacts. Beautiful gardens.

Location: MAP 14:J3, OS Ref. NO593 602. Off A90 on A935.
Owner: Dalhousie Estates
Contact: Mandy Ferries
Tel: 01356 624566
E-mail: mandyferries@dalhousieestates.co.uk
Website: www.dalhousieestates.co.uk
Open: 26 May–24 Jun: guided tours only, 2 & 3.15pm.
Admission: Adult £6. Child under 12 yrs Free.
Key facts: No photography. Partial. Obligatory. Limited for cars and coaches.

CHARLETON HOUSE

Colinsburgh, Leven, Fife KY9 1HG

Location: MAP 14:I6, OS Ref. NO464 036. Off A917. 1m NW of Colinsburgh. 3m NW of Elie.
Tel: 01333 340249 **Fax:** 01333 340583
Open: Sept: daily, 12 noon–3pm. Admission every ½hr with guided tours only.
Admission: £12. **Key facts:** Obligatory.

CORTACHY ESTATE

Cortachy, Kirriemuir, Angus DD8 4LX

Countryside walks including access through woodlands to Airlie Monument on Tulloch Hill with spectacular views of the Angus Glens and Vale of Strathmore. Footpaths are waymarked and colour coded. We are licensed to hold Civil Weddings and can offer wedding reception sites, either a marquee in the grounds or a reception within the Castle.

Location: MAP 13:H3, OS Ref. N0394 596. Off the B955 Glens Road from Kirriemuir.
Owner: Trustees of Airlie Estates **Contact:** Estate Office
Tel: 01575 570108 **Fax:** 01575 540400
E-mail: office@airlieestates.com **Website:** www.airlieestates.com
Open: Walks all year. Gardens 6–9 Apr; 7 & 19 May until 5 Jun 6 & 27 Aug. Last admission 3.30pm.
Admission: Please contact estate office for details.
Key facts: Limited. On leads. We are licensed to hold Civil Weddings and can offer wedding reception sites, either a marquee in the grounds or a reception within the Castle.

DUNNINALD, CASTLE AND GARDENS

Montrose, Angus DD10 9TD

Completed in 1824, Dunninald is a family home, designed by James Gillespie Graham in the gothic revival style. Guided tours explain the collections of furniture, paintings, displays of fine needlework, and memorabilia. In May extensive bluebells carpet the woodlands and in July the walled garden is at its best.

Location: MAP 14:J3, OS Ref. NO705 543. 2 miles south of Montrose, off A92, Usan turning.
Owner: EBJ Stansfeld Esq **Contact:** Mrs M Stansfeld
Tel: 01674 672031 **Fax:** 01674 674860
E-mail: visitorinformation@dunninald.com **Website:** www.dunninald.com
Open: 3 & 4 Mar: Gardens only 12–4pm. 20 May: Gardens only 2–5pm. 28 Jun–29 Jul (excl Mons): Gardens from 12noon, House 1–5pm.
Admission: Adult £6. Concessions £5. Garden only, £3.50. Children U12 Free.
Key facts: No photography in house. Partial. WCs. Obligatory. Limited for coaches. On leads.

FALKLAND PALACE & GARDEN

Falkland, Fife KY15 7BU

The Royal Palace of Falkland, built between 1502 and 1541 and set in the heart of a unique medieval village, was the country residence and hunting lodge of eight Stuart monarchs, including Mary, Queen of Scots. This magnificent Renaissance Palace is famous for its beautiful gardens and for the Real Tennis court, built in 1539.

Location: MAP 13:G6, OS Ref. NO253 075. On A912, 10 miles from M90, junction 8.
Owner: The National Trust for Scotland
Tel: 0844 493 2186
E-mail: information@nts.org.uk
Website: www.nts.org.uk
Open: Mar–Oct. Please see our website or call us for more up to date opening times.
Admission: Please see our website or call us for up to date prices.
Key facts:

GLENEAGLES

Auchterarder, Perthshire PH3 1PJ

Gleneagles has been the home of the Haldane family since the 12th century. The 18th century pavilion is open to the public by written appointment. **Location:** MAP 13:F6, OS Ref. NS931 088. ¾m S of A9 on A823. 2½m S of Auchterarder. **Owner:** Gleneagles 1996 Trust **Contact:** Martin Haldane of Gleneagles **Tel:** 01764 682388. **Open:** By written appointment only. **Key facts:**

HILL OF TARVIT MANSION HOUSE

Cupar, Fife KY15 5PB

The house was rebuilt in 1906 by Sir Robert Lorimer and showcases a notable collection of superb French, Chippendale and vernacular furniture along with paintings by Raeburn, Ramsay and eminent Dutch artists. There is a restored Edwardian laundry set in the midst of a delightful garden, also designed by Lorimer.

Location: MAP 13:F6, OS Ref. NO378 118. Off A916, 2.5m S of Cupar, Fife.
Owner: The National Trust for Scotland
Tel: 0844 493 2185 **E-mail:** information@nts.org.uk **Website:** www.nts.org.uk
Open: Garden: Open all year. House: Apr–Oct. Please see our website or call us for more up to date opening times.
Admission: Please see our website or call us for up to date prices.
Key facts:

HOUSE OF DUN

Montrose, Angus DD10 9LQ

This beautiful Georgian house, overlooking Montrose Basin, was built in 1730 by William Adam. The house features fine furniture, a wonderful art collection and superb plasterwork, a particular and memorable feature. Outside, enjoy the attractive walled garden and woodland walks.

Location: MAP 14:J3, OS Ref. NO670 598. 3m W Montrose on A935.
Owner: The National Trust for Scotland
Tel: 0844 493 2144
E-mail: information@nts.org.uk
Website: www.nts.org.uk
Open: Garden & estate: Open all year, House: Apr-Oct.
Admission: Please see our website or call us for up to date prices.
Key facts:

KELLIE CASTLE & GARDEN

Pittenweem, Fife KY10 2RF

This superb castle was sympathetically restored by the Lorimer family in the late 19th century. It contains magnificent plaster ceilings, painted panelling, furniture designed by Sir Robert Lorimer and a long concealed mural by Phoebe Anne Traquair. The garden features a collection of organically cultivated old-fashioned roses and herbaceous plants.

Location: MAP 14:I6, OS Ref. NO520 052. On B9171, On B9171, 3m from Pittenweem.
Owner: The National Trust for Scotland
Tel: 0844 493 2184
E-mail: information@nts.org.uk
Website: www.nts.org.uk
Open: Garden: All year. Castle: Apr–Oct. Please see our website or call us for more up to date opening times.
Admission: Please see our website or call us for up to date prices.
Key facts:

MEGGINCH CASTLE

Errol, Perthshire PH2 7SW

15th century castle, 1,000 year old yews, flowered parterre, topiary, double walled kitchen garden, astrological garden, heritage orchard. Early 19th century courtyard with Pagoda dovecote, part used as a location for the film Rob Roy.

Location: MAP 13:G5, OS Ref. NO241 245. 8m E of Perth on A90.
Owner: Mr Giles Herdman & The Hon Mrs Drummond-Herdman
Tel: 01821 642222
E-mail: catherine.herdman@gmail.com
Open: Scottish Gardens Scheme. By Appointment. Gardens Only.
Admission: Contact property for details.
Key facts: Partial. By arrangement. Limited for coaches. In grounds, on leads.

MONZIE CASTLE

Crieff, Perthshire PH7 4HD

Built in 1791. Destroyed by fire in 1908 and rebuilt and furnished by Sir Robert Lorimer.

Location: MAP 13:E5, OS Ref. NN873 244. 2m NE of Crieff.
Owner: Mrs C M M Crichton
Contact: Mrs C M M Crichton
Tel: 01764 653110
Open: 12 May–10 Jun: daily, 2–4.30pm. By appointment at other times.
Admission: Adult £5, Child £1. Group rates available, contact property for details.
Key facts:

STOBHALL

Stobhall, Cargill, Perthshire PH2 6DR

Original home of the Drummond chiefs from the 14th century. Romantic cluster of small-scale buildings around a courtyard in a magnificent situation overlooking the River Tay, surrounded by formal and woodland gardens. 17th century painted ceiling in Chapel depicts monarchs of Europe and North Africa on horse (or elephant) back.

Location: MAP 13:G4, OS Ref. NO132 343. 7m N of Perth on A93.
Owner: Viscount Strathallan
E-mail: info@stobhall.com
Website: www.stobhall.com
Open: 30 Jun–29 Jul: Tues–Sun, (closed Mons). Open by tour only: 2, 3 & 4pm.
Admission: Adult £4, Child £2. Large group visits must be booked.
Key facts: Tours to Chapel, Library and Folly. Drawing Room by prior appointment. No internal photography. Partial. Obligatory. Limited. Coaches please book. Guide dogs only.

STRATHTYRUM HOUSE & GARDENS

St Andrews, Fife KY16 9SF

Location: MAP 14:I5, OS Ref: NO490 172. Entrance from the St Andrews/Guardbridge Road which is signposted when open.
Owner: The Strathtyrum Trust
Contact: Henry Cheape
Tel: 01334 473600
E-mail: info@strathtyrumhouse.com
Website: www.strathtyrumhouse.com
Open: 7–11 May, 4–8 Jun, 2–6 Jul, 6–10 Aug, 3–7 Sept: 2–4pm. Guided tours at 2 & 3pm.
Admission: Adult £5, Child + Conc. £2.50.
Key facts: Obligatory. 2pm and 3pm. Free. Guide dogs only.

TULLIBOLE CASTLE

Crook of Devon, Kinross KY13 0QN

Recognised as a classic example of the Scottish tower house. Completed in 1608, the Moncreiff family have lived here since 1747. The Castle is in a parkland setting with ornamental fishponds (moat), a roofless lectarn doocot, with a short walk to a maze, 9th century graveyard and a ruined church.
Location: MAP 13:F6, OS Ref. NO540 888. Located on the B9097 1m E of Crook of Devon. **Owner:** Lord & Lady Moncreiff **Contact:** Lord Moncreiff
Tel: 01577 840236 **E-mail:** visit@tulbol.demon.co.uk
Website: www.tulbol.demon.co.uk
Open: Last week in Aug–30 Sept: Tue–Sun, 1–4pm. Admission every ½ hr with guided tours only. **Admission:** Adult £5.50, Child/Conc. £3.50. Free as part of "Doors Open Day" (last weekend of Sept).
Key facts: Obligatory. Ample for cars but limited for coaches. Guide dogs only. 1 x twin, 1 bed holiday cottage.

Pipe Band at Glamis Castle

VISITOR INFORMATION

■ Owner
Duke of Argyll

■ Address
Inveraray Castle
Inveraray
Argyll PA32 8XE

■ Location
MAP 13:A6
OS Ref. NN100 090.
From Edinburgh 21/2–3hrs via Glasgow. Just NE of Inveraray on A83. W shore of Loch Fyne.
Bus: Bus route stopping point within 0.5m.

■ Contact
Argyll Estates
Tel: 01499 302203
Fax: 01499 302421
E-mail: enquiries@inveraray-castle.com

■ Opening Times
1st April – 31st October
Open 7 days from 10.00 to 17.45
(Last admission 17.00)

■ Admission
Castle & Garden (Group Rate)

Adults	£10.00 (£8.00)
Senior Citizens	£8.50 (£6.80)
Students (on production of student card)	£8.50 (£6.80)
Schools	(£3.80)
Children (under 16)	£6.50 (£5.20)
Family Ticket (2 adults & 2 or more children)	£28.00
Children Under 5	FREE

A 20% discount is allowed on groups of 20 or more persons (as shown in brackets)
Coach/ Car Park Charge per vehicle (for non-Castle visitors) - £2.00

■ Special events
Check website www.inveraray-castle.com for details of forthcoming events.

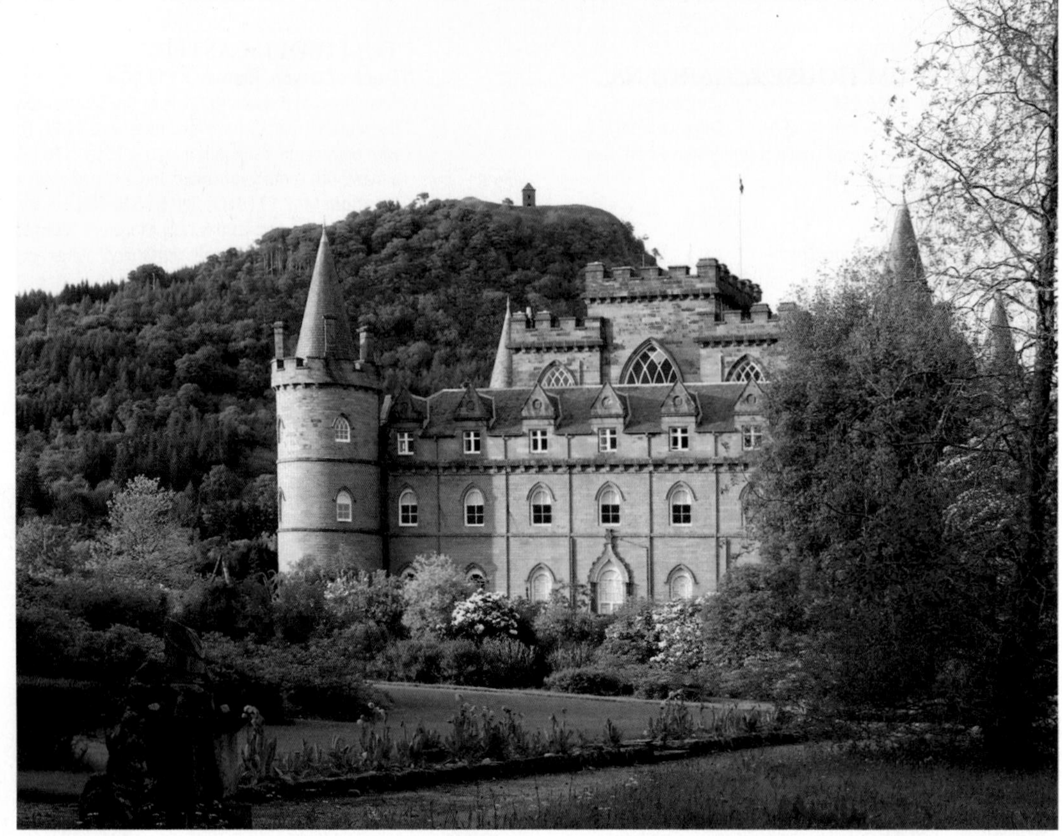

INVERARAY CASTLE & GARDEN

www.inveraray-castle.com

Inveraray Castle & Garden – Home to the Duke & Duchess of Argyll and ancestral home of the Clan Campbell.

The ancient Royal Burgh of Inveraray lies about 60 miles north west of Glasgow by Loch Fyne in an area of spectacular natural beauty. The ruggedness of the highland scenery combines with the sheltered tidal loch, beside which nestles the present Castle built between 1745 and 1790. The Castle is home to the Duke and Duchess of Argyll. The Duke is head of the Clan Campbell and his family have lived in Inveraray since the early 15th century. Designed by Roger Morris and decorated by Robert Mylne, the fairytale exterior belies the grandeur of its gracious interior. The Clerk of Works, William Adam, father of Robert and John, did much of the laying out of the present Royal Burgh, which is an unrivalled example of an early planned town. Visitors enter the famous Armoury Hall containing some 1,300 pieces including Brown Bess muskets, Lochaber axes, 18th century Scottish broadswords, and can see preserved swords from the Battle of Culloden. The fine State Dining Room and Tapestry Drawing Room contain magnificent French tapestries made especially for the Castle, fabulous examples of Scottish, English and French furniture and a wealth of other works of art. The unique collection of china, silver and family artifacts spans the generations which are identified by a genealogical display in the Clan Room.

The castle's private garden which was opened to the public in 2010 for the first time is also not to be missed, especially in springtime with it's stunning displays of rhododendrons and azaleas.

KEY FACTS

No photography. Guide books in French and German translations.

Partial. WCs.

Licensed.

Available for up to 100 people at no additional cost. Groups please book. Tour time: 1 hr.

100 cars. Car/coach park close to Castle.

£3.50 per child. A guide can be provided. Areas of interest include a woodland walk.

Guide dogs only.

STIRLING CASTLE

STIRLING FK8 1EJ

www.stirlingcastle.gov.uk

Experience the newly refurbished Royal Palace where you can explore the richly decorated King's and Queens apartments and meet the characters of the Royal Stewart Court. Younger visitors can get hands on with history in the Palace Vaults. Other highlights include the Great Hall, Chapel Royal, Regimental Museum, Tapestry Studio and the Great Kitchens. Don't miss our guided tour where you can hear tales of the castle's colourful characters and history. Then visit the new castle exhibition in the beautiful surroundings of the Queen Gardens or enjoy an afternoon tea in our Unicorn Café.

Location: MAP 13:E7, OS Ref. NS790 941. Leave the M9 at junction 10. and follow road signs for the castle.

Owner: Historic Scotland
Contact: Duty Manager
Tel: 01786 450 000
Fax: 01786 464 678
Open: Apr–Sept: 9.30am–6pm. Oct–Mar: 9.30am–5pm. Last ticket 45 mins before closing.
Admission: Adult £13, Child £6.50, Conc. £10 (2011 prices). Admission includes free castle tour or audio guide avaialble in six languages.
Key facts: Private hire. Partial. WCs. Licensed. Licensed. Obligatory. Limited for coaches. Guide dogs only. €

DUART CASTLE

Isle Of Mull, Argyll PA64 6AP

www.duartcastle.com

Duart Castle is a 13th century fortress, brought back to life 100 years ago by Sir Fitzroy Maclean. Today, it remains the family home of the Chief of the Clan Maclean. Visitors can explore ancient keeps, dungeons, the banqueting hall, Edwardian state rooms and much more.

Location: MAP 12:O4. OS Ref. NM750 350. Off A849 on the east point of the Isle of Mull.
Owner/Contact: Sir Lachlan Maclean Bt
Tel: 01680 812309 **E-mail:** guide@duartcastle.com
Open: Castle & tea room open from 1 Apr Sun–Thur, 11am–4pm.
Open daily from 1 May (including shop) 10.30am–5.30pm.
Castle closes 18 Oct (tea room & shop close 11 Oct).
Admission: Adult: £5.50, Child (3–14) £2.75, Conc. £4.90, Family (2+2) £13.75.
Key facts: Unsuitable. Obligatory, By arrangement. Guide dogs only. Duart Castle runs a programme of summer events for visitors each year. Previous events have included ceilidhs, treasure hunts, historical re-enactments and much more. See the website for more details.

MOUNT STUART

Isle Of Bute PA20 9LR

www.mountstuart.com

One of the World's finest houses – Mount Stuart, ancestral home of the Marquess of Bute, is a stupendous example of Victorian Gothic, set amidst 300 acres of gloriously landscaped gardens encompassing Victorian Pinetum, arboretum and wondrous woodlands. Spectacular interiors, art collection, kaleidoscopic stained glass, a myriad of intricately carved marble and architectural detail presents both stately opulence and unrivalled imagination.

Location: MAP 13:A9, OS Ref. NS100 600. SW coast of Scotland, 5m S of Rothesay.
Owner: Mount Stuart Trust
Contact: Mount Stuart Office
Tel: 01700 503877
Fax: 01700 505313
E-mail: contactus@mountstuart.com
Open: Open Mar–Oct. Please call or see our website for detailed opening hours.
Key facts: No photography. Ample. Guide dogs only. Exclusive.

ALLOA TOWER

Alloa Park, Alloa FK10 1PP

Fully restored and furnished, this ancestral home of the Earls of Mar is one of Scotland's largest surviving medieval towers. Contains a great collection of family portraits and retains many original features.

Location: MAP 13:E7, OS Ref. NS888 924. Off A907, close to Alloa town centre.
Owner: The National Trust for Scotland
Contact: Property Manager
Tel: 0844 493 2129
E-mail: information@nts.org.uk
Website: www.nts.org.uk
Open: Open Apr–Oct.
Admission: Please see our website or call us for up to date prices.
Key facts: Partial. By arrangement. Limited for cars and coaches.

ARDUAINE GARDEN

Arduaine, Oban PA34 4XQ

This amazing garden boasts spectacular rhododendrons and azaleas in spring and early summer and its perennnial borders are magnificent thoughout the seasons.

Location: MAP 12:O6, OS Ref. NM794 103. Off A816, 20 miles south of Oban, 19 miles north of Lochgilphead.
Owner: The National Trust for Scotland
Contact: Property Manager
Tel: 0844 493 2216
E-mail: information@nts.org.uk
Website: www.nts.org.uk
Open: Garden open all year. Reception centre Apr–Sept.
Admission: Please see our website or call us for up to date prices.
Key facts: Refreshments available in adjacent Loch Melfort Hotel. Licensed. Limited for coaches. Guide dogs only.

CASTLE STALKER

Portnacroish, Appin, Argyll PA38 4BA

Early 15th century tower house and seat of the Stewarts of Appin. Set on an islet 400 yds off the shore of Loch Linnhe. Reputed to have been used by James IV as a hunting lodge. Restored by the late Lt Col Stewart Allward and now retained by his family.

Location: MAP 12:P3, OS Ref. NM930 480. Approx. 20m N of Oban on the A828. On islet 1/4m offshore.
Owner: The Allward Family **Contact:** Messrs R & A Allward
Tel: 01631 730354 & 07789 597442
E-mail: rossallward@madasafish.com **Website:** www.castlestalker.com
Open: 9–13 April; 6–10 Aug; 27–31 Aug; 3–7 Sept; 17–21 Sept. Telephone for appointments. Dependent on tides and weather.
Admission: Adult £10, Child £5.
Key facts: Not suitable for coach parties. Unsuitable. Obligatory. No coaches.

Mount Stuart

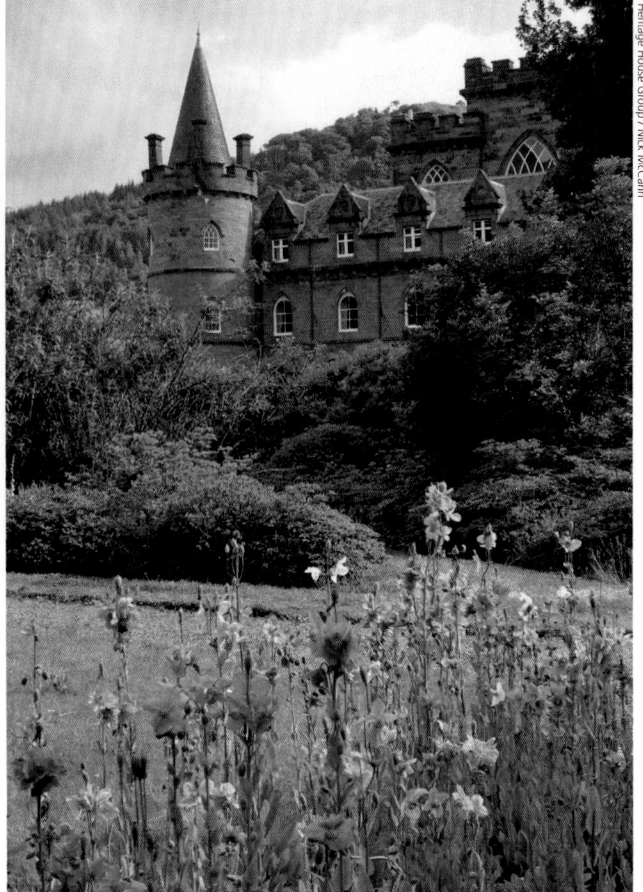

Inverary Castle

CRARAE GARDEN

Inveraray PA32 8YA

A beautiful woodland glen, on the banks of Loch Fyne,with tumbling waterfalls, trees and shrubs from all over the world. Particularly worth visiting in spring and autumn with amazing seasonal colour.

Location: MAP 12:P6. On A83, 10miles south of Inveraray
Owner: The National Trust for Scotland
Tel: 0844 493 2210
E-mail: information@nts.org.uk
Website: www.nts.org.uk
Open: Garden open all year. Visitor centre open Apr–Oct.
Admission: Please see our website or call us for up to date prices.
Key facts: Partial. Guide dogs only.

HILL HOUSE

Upper Colquhoun Street, Helensburgh G84 9AJ

The finest of Charles Rennie Mackintosh's domestic creations, the Hill House dates from 1902. Mackintosh and his wife also designed the interior fittings and decorative schemes.

Location: MAP 13:B7, OS Ref. NS300 838. Off B832, on eastern edge of Helensburgh.
Owner: The National Trust for Scotland
Tel: 0844 493 2210
E-mail: information@nts.org.uk
Website: www.nts.org.uk
Open: House: Apr–Oct. Please see our website or call us for more up to date opening times.
Admission: Please see our website or call us for up to date prices.
Key facts:

DELGATIE CASTLE

Turriff, Aberdeenshire AB53 5TD

www.delgatiecastle.com

"Best Visitor Experience" Award Winner. Dating from 1030 the Castle is steeped in Scottish history yet still has the atmosphere of a lived in home. It has some of the finest painted ceilings in Scotland, Mary Queen of Scots' bed-chamber. Clan Hay Centre. Scottish Home Baking Award Winner.

Location: MAP 17:D9, OS Ref. NJ754 506. Off A947 Aberdeen to Banff Road.

Owner: Delgatie Castle Trust **Contact:** Mrs Joan Johnson

Tel/Fax: 01888 563479 **E-mail:** joan@delgatiecastle.com

Open: Daily, 10am–5pm. Closed Christmas & New Year weeks.

Admission: Adult £6, Child/Conc. £4, Family £16. Groups (10+): £4.

Key facts: No photography. WCs. Home-baking and lunches. By arrangement. Guide dogs only. 6 x houses for self catering. Victorian Christmas Fayre 26/27 Nov and 3/4 Dec 2011. The Castle is decorated throughout with decorations, Christmas trees and much more. Santa is here for the children with a pre-christmas present, crafters in many of the rooms throughout the Castle, staff in period costume. This year will be our 17th year of holding the event.

BALFLUIG CASTLE

Alford, Aberdeenshire AB33 8EJ

Small 16th century tower house, restored in 1967. Its garden and wooded park are surrounded by farmland.

Location: MAP 17:D11, OS Ref. NJ586 151. Alford, Aberdeenshire.

Owner/Contact: Mark Tennant of Balfluig **Tel:** 020 7624 3200 **Open:** Please write to M I Tennant Esq, 30 Abbey Gardens, London NW8 9AT. **Key facts:**

BALMORAL CASTLE (GROUNDS & EXHIBITIONS)

Balmoral, Ballater, Aberdeenshire AB35 5TB

Scottish home to The Royal Family. Ballroom, grounds and exhibitions, large café seating 120, quality gift shop. Excellent for coaches and groups. Holiday cottages, salmon fishing, Land Rover safaris and activity holidays.

Location: MAP 13:G1, OS Ref. NO256 951. Off A93 between Ballater and Braemar. 50m W of Aberdeen.

Owner: Her Majesty The Queen **Contact:** Garry Marsden

Tel/Fax: 013397 42034 **E-mail:** info@balmoralcastle.com

Website: www.balmoralcastle.com

Open: 1 Apr–31 Jul: daily, 10am–5pm, last admission 4.30pm. Nov & Dec: Guided tours available–ring for details.

Admission: Adult £9, Concessions £8, Children (5–16yrs) £5, Family £25 (Audio tour included). Discounts for groups (20+).

Key facts: Suitable. WCs. Licensed. Licensed. By arrangement. In grounds.

BRODIE CASTLE

Forres, Moray IV36 0TE

The lime harled building is a typical 'Z' plan tower house with ornate corbelled battlements and bartizans, with 17th & 19th century additions

Location: MAP 16:P8, OS Ref. NH980 577. Off A96 4.5m W of Forres and 24m E of Inverness.

Owner: The National Trust for Scotland

Tel: 0844 493 2149

E-mail: information@nts.org.uk

Website: www.nts.org.uk

Open: Please see our website or call us for up to date opening times.

Admission: Please see our website or call us for up to date prices.

Key facts:

CRAIG CASTLE

Rhynie, Huntly, Aberdeenshire AB54 4LP

The Castle is built round a courtyard and consists of a 16th century L-shaped Keep, a Georgian house (architect John Adam) and a 19th century addition (architect Archibald Simpson of Aberdeen). The Castle was a Gordon stronghold for 300 years. It has a very fine collection of coats-of-arms.

Location: MAP 17:C10, OS Ref. NJ472 259. 3m W of Rhynie and Lumsden on B9002.

Owner: Mr A J Barlas

Contact: The Property Manager

Tel: 01464 861705

Fax: 01464 861702

Open: May–Sept: Wed & every 2nd weekend in each month, 2–5pm.

Admission: Adult £5, Child £1.

Key facts: Unsuitable. By arrangement. Limited for coaches. Guide dogs only.

CRAIGIEVAR CASTLE

Alford AB33 8JF

This fairytale castle is a fine example of Scottish Baronial architecture and its great tower stands just as it did when completed in 1626. Surrounding the castle are attractive grounds and trails, giving beautiful views of the countryside.

Location: MAP 17:C11, OS Ref. NJ566 095. On A980, 6 miles south of Alford and 15 miles north of Banchory.

Owner: The National Trust for Scotland

Contact: Property Manager

Tel: 0844 493 2174

E-mail: information@nts.org.uk

Website: www.nts.org.uk

Open: Open Apr–Sept. Please see our website or call us for more up to date opening times.

Admission: Please see our website or call us for up to date prices.

Key facts: Obligatory. Guide dogs only.

Balmoral Castle

CRAIGSTON CASTLE

Turriff, Aberdeenshire AB53 5PX

Built in 1607 by John Urquhart Tutor of Cromarty. A sculpted balcony unique in Scottish architecture depicts a piper, two grinning knights and David and Goliath. Remarkable carved oak panels of Scottish kings' biblical heroes, mounted in doors and shutters of the early 17th century.

Location: MAP 17:D8, OS Ref. NJ762 550. On B9105, 4.5m NE of Turriff.
Owner: William Pratesi Urquhart
Contact: The Housekeeper
Tel: 01888 551228
E-mail: wu-gen01@craigston.co.uk
Open: 9–24 Jun 2012, 11–19 Aug 2012: daily 1pm–4pm. Guided house tours: 1pm, 2pm & 3pm. Groups by appointment throughout the year.
Admission: Adult £6, Child £2, Conc. £4. Groups: Adult £5, Child/School £1.
Key facts: Obligatory.

CRATHES CASTLE, GARDEN & ESTATE

Banchory, Aberdeenshire AB31 3QJ

Fairytale-like turrets, gargoyles of fantastic design and the ancient Horn of Leys given in 1323 by Robert the Bruce are just a few of the features of this historic castle. The Crathes gardens and estates are ideal for a family day out. A delight at any time of year, the famous gardens feature great yew hedges and a colourful double herbaceous border. Further afield the 595-acre estate offers six separate trails to enjoy.

Location: MAP 17:D12, OS Ref. NO735 967. On A93, 3 miles east of Banchory. AB31 5QJ.
Owner: The National Trust for Scotland **Tel:** 0844 493 2166
E-mail: information@nts.org.uk **Website:** www.nts.org.uk
Open: Garden & Estate: Open all year. Castle: Daily Apr–Oct. Weekends only Jan–Mar & Nov–Dec.
Admission: Please see our website or call us for up to date prices.
Key facts:

DAVID WELCH WINTER GARDENS – DUTHIE PARK

Polmuir Road, Aberdeen, Grampian Highlands AB11 7TH

One of Europe's largest indoor gardens with many rare and exotic plants on show from all around the world.

Location: MAP 17:E11, OS Ref. NJ97 044. Just N of River Dee, 1m S of city centre.
Owner: Aberdeen City Council
Contact: Alan Findlay
Tel: 01224 585310
Fax: 01224 210532
E-mail: wintergardens@aberdeencity.gov.uk.
Website: www.aberdeencity.gov.uk
Open: All year: daily from 9.30pm.
Admission: Free.
Key facts:

DRUM CASTLE & GARDEN

Drumoak, By Banchory, Aberdeenshire AB31 3EY

The combination of a 13th century square tower, a Jacobean mansion house and the additions of the Victorian lairds make Drum Castle unique among Scottish castles. Enjoy superb furniture and paintings inside and, outside, a beautiful Garden of Historic Roses in the walled garden, woodland trails and children's playground.

Location: MAP 17:D12, OS Ref. NJ796 005. Off A93, 10 miles west of Aberdeen.
Owner: The National Trust for Scotland
Tel: 0844 493 2161
E-mail: information@nts.org.uk
Website: www.nts.org.uk
Open: Grounds: All year. Garden: Apr–Oct. Castle: Apr–Sept.
Admission: Please see our website or call us for up to date prices.
Key facts:

DRUMMUIR CASTLE

Drummuir, By Keith, Banffshire AB55 5JE

Castellated Victorian Gothic-style castle built in 1847 by Admiral Duff. 60ft high lantern tower with fine plasterwork. Family portraits, interesting artefacts and other paintings.

Location: MAP 17:B9, OS Ref. NJ372 442. Midway between Keith (5m) and Dufftown, off the B9014.
Owner: The Gordon-Duff Family
Contact: Alison Noakes
Tel: 01542 810332
Fax: 01542 810302
Open: Sat 1–Sun 30 Sept 2012: daily, 2–5pm (last tour 4.15pm).
Admission: Adult £2, Child £1.50. Pre-arranged groups: Adult £2, Child £1.50.
Key facts: By arrangement. Obligatory.

FYVIE CASTLE & GARDEN

Turriff, Aberdeenshire AB53 8JS

The charm of Fyvie ranges from its 13th century origins to its stunning Edwardian interiors. Superb collection of arms and armour and paintings, including works by Raeburn and Gainsborough. Stroll around the picturesque lake, or visit the restored 1903 racquet court and bowling alley.

Location: MAP 17:D9, OS Ref. NJ764 393. Off A947, 8m south of Turriff.
Owner: The National Trust for Scotland
Tel: 0844 493 2182
E-mail: information@nts.org.uk
Website: www.nts.org.uk
Open: Garden: Open all year. Castle, tearoom & shop: Apr–Oct.
Admission: Please see our website or call us for up to date prices.
Key facts:

HADDO HOUSE

Tarves, Ellon, Aberdeenshire AB41 0ER

Designed by William Adam in 1732, this elegant mansion house has a stunning Victorian interior. Noted for fine furniture and paintings, Haddo also has a terraced garden leading to the Country Park with lakes, walks and monuments. Visits by guided tour only, which can be booked by calling in advance.

Location: MAP 17:E10, OS Ref. NJ868 347. Off B999, 19 miles north of Aberdeen.
Owner: The National Trust for Scotland
Tel: 0844 493 2179
E-mail: information@nts.org.uk
Website: www.nts.org.uk
Open: Please see our website or call us for more up to date opening times.
Admission: Please see our website or call us for up to date prices.
Key facts: Picnic area.

LICKLEYHEAD CASTLE

Auchleven, Insch, Aberdeenshire AB52 6PN

A beautifully restored Laird's Castle, Lickleyhead was built by the Leslies c1450 and extensively renovated in 1629 by John Forbes of Leslie, whose initials are carved above the entrance. It is an almost unspoilt example of the transformation from 'Chateau-fort' to 'Chateau-maison' and boasts many interesting architectural features.

Location: MAP 17:C10, OS Ref. NJ628 237. Auchleven is 2m S of Insch on B992. Twin pillars of castle entrance on left at foot of village.
Owner: The Leslie family **Contact:** Mrs C Leslie **Tel:** 01651 821276
Open: 1, 2 May, 7–11 May, 14–18 May, 21–25 May: 12 noon–2pm. Also Sats only in high season 7 Jul–25 Aug: 12 noon–2pm.
Admission: Free.
Key facts: Unsuitable. Limited. No coaches. In grounds, on leads.

PITMEDDEN GARDEN

Ellon, Aberdeenshire AB41 7PD

In stunning Great Garden, thousands of colourful annual bedding plants make up an elaborate summer spectacle. The adjoining Museum of Farming Life brings the agricultural past to life. Also available: Woodland walks and herb garden.

Location: MAP 17:E10. OS Ref. NJ884 280. On A920 1m W of Pitmedden village & 14m N of Aberdeen.

Owner: The National Trust for Scotland

Tel: 0844 493 2177 **E-mail:** information@nts.org.uk

Website: www.nts.org.uk

Open: May–Sept. Please see our website or call us for more up to date opening times.

Admission: Please see our website or call us for up to date prices.

Key facts:

PROVOST SKENE'S HOUSE

Guestrow, Off Broad Street, Aberdeen AB10 1AS

16th century, Provost Skene's House is one of Aberdeen's few remaining examples of early burgh architecture. Splendid room settings include a suite of Georgian room and an Edwardian nursery.The house also features an important series of religious paintings in the Painted Gallery and changing fashions in the Costume Gallery.

Location: MAP 17:E11, OS Ref. NJ943 064. Aberdeen city centre, off Broad Street.

Owner: Aberdeen City Council

Tel: 01224 641086

E-mail: info@aagm.co.uk

Website: www.aagm.co.uk

Open: Mon–Sat, 10am–5pm, Closed Sun.

Admission: Free.

Key facts: By arrangement. Guide dogs only.

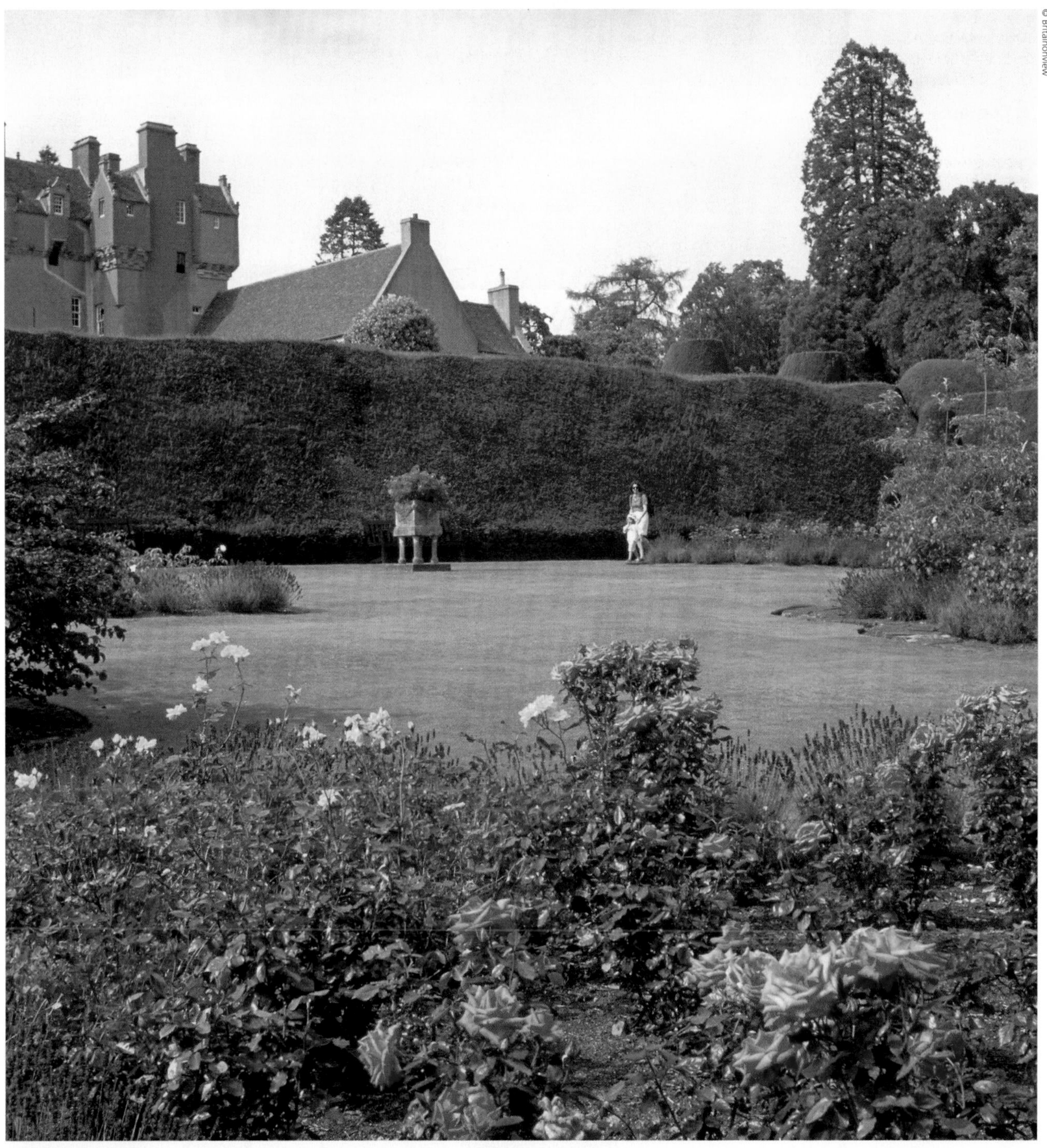

© Britainonview

Crathes Castle & Garden

VISITOR INFORMATION

■ Owner
The Dowager Countess Cawdor

■ Address
Cawdor Castle
Nairn
Scotland IV12 5RD

■ Location
MAP 16:O9
OS Ref. NH850 500

From Edinburgh A9, 3½ hrs, Inverness 20 mins, Nairn 10 mins. Main road: A9, 14m.

Rail: Nairn Station 5m.

Bus: Inverness to Nairn bus route 200 yds.

Taxi: Cawdor Taxis 01667 404315.

Air: Inverness Airport 5m.

■ Contact
General Manager - Brett Gubbins
Tel: 01667 404401
Fax: 01667 404674
E-mail: info@cawdorcastle.com

■ Opening Times
1 May–30 September
Daily: 10am–5.30pm.
Last admission 5pm.

Groups by appointment, admission prices on application.

■ Admission

Adult	£9.50
Child (5–15yrs)	£6.00
OAP	£8.50
Student	£8.50
Family (2+5)	£28.00
Groups	
Adult	£8.00
OAP/Student	£8.50
Garden only	£5.50

RHS Access
May, June, September.

CAWDOR CASTLE

www.cawdorcastle.com

A must see romantic fairy-tale Castle of historical beauty and one of the most outstanding Stately Homes in Scotland.

This splendid romantic castle, dating from the late 14th century, was built as a private fortress by the Thanes of Cawdor, and remains the home of the Cawdor family to this day. The ancient medieval tower was built around the legendary holly tree. Although the house has evolved over 600 years, later additions, mainly of the 17th century, were all built in the Scottish vernacular style with slated roofs over walls and crow-stepped gables of mellow local stone. This style gives Cawdor a strong sense of unity, and the massive, severe exterior belies an intimate interior that gives the place a surprisingly personal, friendly atmosphere. Good furniture, fine portraits and pictures, interesting objects and outstanding tapestries are arranged to please the family rather than to echo fashion or impress.

Memories of Shakespeare's Macbeth give Cawdor an elusive, evocative quality that delights visitors.

Gardens
The flower garden also has a family feel to it, where plants are chosen out of affection rather than affectation. This is a lovely spot between spring and late summer. The walled garden has been restored with a holly maze, paradise garden, knot garden and thistle garden. The wild garden beside its stream leads into beautiful trails through spectacular mature mixed woodland, in which paths are helpfully marked and colour-coded. The Tibetan garden and traditional Scottish vegetable garden are at the Dower House at Auchindoune.

KEY FACTS

- 9 hole golf course, putting green, golf clubs for hire, conferences, whisky tasting, musical entertainments, specialised garden visits. No photography, video taping or tripods inside. No large day sacks inside castle.
- Gift, book and wool shops.
- Lunches, sherry or champagne receptions.
- Visitors may alight at the entrance. WC. Only ground floor accessible.
- Licensed Courtyard Restaurant, May–Oct, groups should book.
- By arrangement.
- 250 cars and 25 coaches.
- £5.50 per child. Room notes, quiz and answer sheet can be provided.
- Guide dogs only in castle and grounds. Dog walking trail available.

€

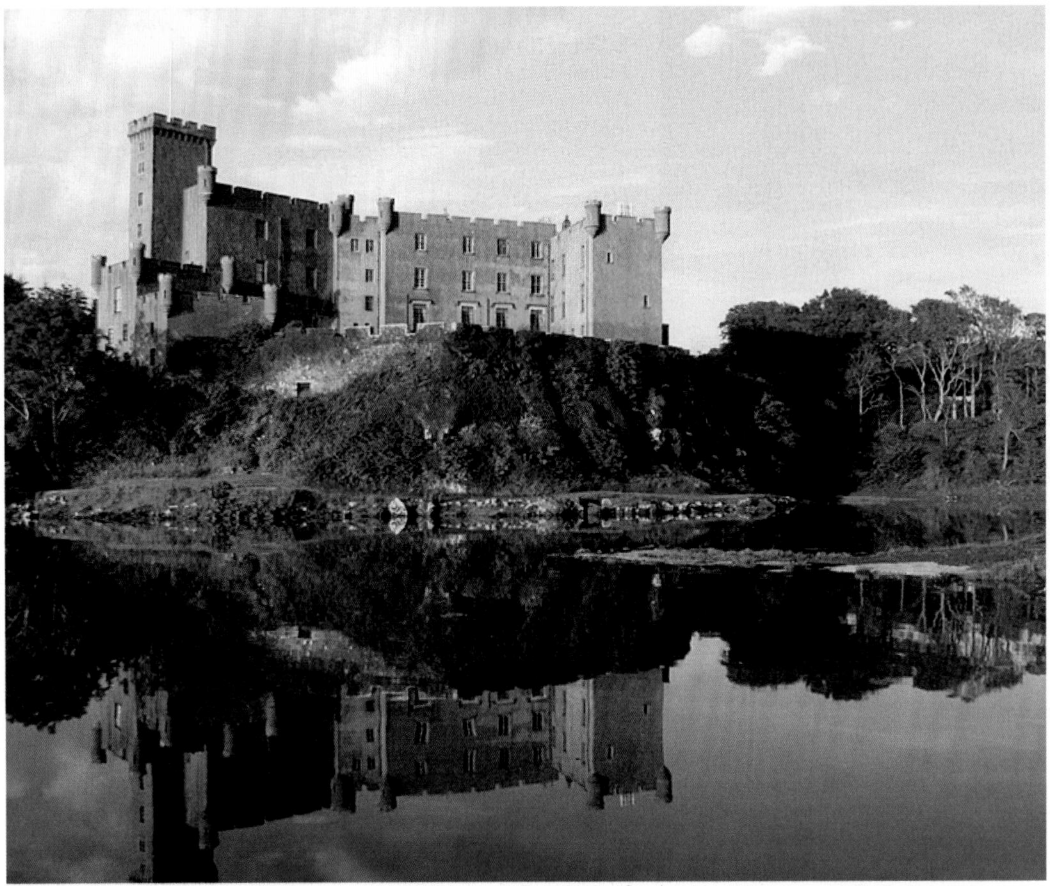

DUNVEGAN CASTLE & GARDENS

www.dunvegancastle.com

Experience living history at Dunvegan Castle, the ancestral home of the Chiefs of Clan MacLeod for 800 years.

Any visit to the Isle of Skye is incomplete without savouring the wealth of history on offer at Dunvegan Castle & Gardens, the ancestral home of the Chiefs of Clan MacLeod for 800 years. Originally designed to keep people out, it was first opened to visitors in 1933 and is one of Skye's most famous landmarks. On display are many fine oil paintings and clan treasures, the most famous of which is the Fairy Flag. Legend has it that this sacred Banner has miraculous powers and when unfurled in battle, the Clan MacLeod will defeat their enemies. Another of the castle's great treasures is the Dunvegan Cup, a unique 'mazer' dating back to the Middle Ages. It was gifted by the O'Neils of Ulster as a token of thanks to one of the Clan's most celebrated Chiefs, Sir Rory Mor, for his support of their cause against the marauding forces of Queen Elizabeth I of England in 1596. Today visitors can enjoy tours of an extraordinary castle and Highland estate steeped in history and Clan legend, delight in the beauty of its formal gardens, take a boat trip onto Loch Dunvegan to see the seal colony, enjoy an appetising meal at the MacLeods Table Cafe or browse in one of its four shops offering a wide choice to suit everyone. Over time, we have given a warm Highland welcome to visitors including Sir Walter Scott, Dr Johnson and Queen Elizabeth II and we look forward to welcoming you.

KEY FACTS

- Boat trips to seal colony. Fishing trips and loch cruises. No photography in the castle.
- Gift and craft shops.
- Partial. WCs.
- MacLeod Table Café (seats 76).
- By appointment. Self Guided.
- 120 cars and 10 coaches. If possible please book. Seal boat trip dependent upon weather.
- Welcome by arrangement. Guide available on request.
- On leads.
- 3 self-catering holiday cottages each sleeping 6.
- Film & TV. A unique location for film, TV or advertising. Check website for details of our events.

VISITOR INFORMATION

Owner
Hugh Macleod of Macleod

Address
Dunvegan Castle
Isle Of Skye
Scotland
IV55 8WF

Location
MAP 15:F9
OS Ref. NG250 480.

1m N of village. NW corner of Skye. Kyle of Lochalsh to Dunvegan via Skye Bridge.

Rail: Inverness to Kyle of Lochalsh

Ferry: Maillaig to Armadale

Contact
Estate Manager
Tel: 01470 521206
Fax: 01470 521205
E-mail: info@dunvegancastle.com

Opening Times
1 April–15 October
Daily: 10am–5.30pm.
Last admission 5pm.
16 October–31 March
Open by appointment weekdays only.
Castle & Gardens closed Christmas and New Year.

Admission

Summer

Castle & Gardens

Adult	£9.50
Child (5–15yrs)	£5.00
Senior/Student/Group (minimum 10 adults)	£7.00
Family Ticket (2 Adults, 3 Children)	£27.00

Gardens only

Adult	£7.50
Child (5–15yrs)	£4.00
Senior/Student/Group	£6.00

Seal Boat Trips

Adult	£6.00
Child (5–15yrs)	£4.00
Senior/Student/Group	£5.00
Infant (under 5yrs)	Free

Loch Cruises & Fishing Trips

Adult	£38.00
Child (5–15yrs)	£28.00

CASTLE OF MEY

Thurso, Caithness KW14 8XH

www.castleofmey.org.uk

The home of The Queen Mother in Caithness. She bought the Castle in 1952, developed the gardens and it became her holiday home because of the beautiful surroundings and the privacy she was always afforded. There is a Visitor Centre with shop and tearoom and an Animal Centre for children.
Location: MAP 17:B2, OS Ref. ND290 739. On A836 between Thurso and John O'Groats, just outside the village of Mey.
Owner: The Queen Elizabeth Castle of Mey Trust
Contact: James Murray
Tel: 01847 851473 **Fax:** 01847 851475
E-mail: enquiries@castleofmey.org.uk
Open: 1 May–30 Sept: daily, 10.20am–last entries 4pm. Closed end of Jul early Aug. Check website or please telephone for details. Coaches in Apr and Oct but please book in advance.
Admission: Adult £10, Child (16yrs and under) £5.50, Conc £9, Family £26. Booked groups (15+): £9. Gardens & grounds only: Adult £5.50.
Key facts: No photography in the Castle. Partial. WCs. Licensed. By arrangement. Guide dogs only.

DUNROBIN CASTLE

Golspie, Sutherland KW10 6SF

www.dunrobincastle.co.uk

Dates from the 13th century with additions in the 17th, 18th and 19th centuries. Wonderful furniture, paintings, library, ceremonial robes and memorabilia. Victorian museum in grounds with a fascinating collection including Pictish stones. Set in fine woodlands overlooking the sea. Magnificent formal gardens, one of few remaining French/Scottish formal parterres.
Location: MAP 16:O6, OS Ref. NC850 010. 50m N of Inverness on A9.
Owner: The Sutherland Dunrobin Trust **Contact:** Scott Morrison
Tel: 01408 633177 **Fax:** 01408 634081 **E-mail:** info@dunrobincastle.co.uk
Open: 1 Apr–15 Oct: Apr, May, Sept & Oct, Mon–Sat, 10.30am–4.30pm, Sun, 12 noon–4.30pm. No Falconry on Suns. Jun, Jul & Aug, daily, 10.30am–5.30pm. Falconry displays every day. Last entry half an hour before closing. Falconry displays at 11.30am & 2pm.
Admission: Adult £9.50, Child £5.50, OAP/Student. £8, Family (2+2) £26. Groups (minimum 10): Rates on request. Rates include falconry display, museum and gardens.
Key facts: Unsuitable for wheelchairs. By arrangement.

BALLINDALLOCH CASTLE

Ballindalloch, Banffshire AB37 9AX

Ballindalloch Castle is a much-loved home, lived in by its original family, the Macpherson-Grants, since 1546. Filled with family memorabilia, including many important 17th century Spanish paintings. Beautiful rock and rose gardens and river walks. The estate is home to the famous Aberdeen-Angus breed of cattle.
Location: MAP 17:A9. OS Ref. NJ178 366. 14 m NE of Grantown-on-Spey on A95. 22 m S of Elgin on A95.
Owner: Mr & Mrs Oliver Russell **Contact:** Mrs Clare Russell **Tel:** 01807 500205
Fax: 01807 500210 **E-mail:** enquiries@ballindallochcastle.co.uk
Website: www.ballindallochcastle.co.uk
Open: Good Fri–30 Sept: 10.30am–4.45pm (last entry). Closed Sats. Coaches outwith season by arrangement.
Admission: House & Grounds: Adult £8, Child (6–16) £4, Conc £6, Family (2+3) £20, Season Ticket £20. (*2011 admission details)
Key facts: Suitable.

EILEAN DONAN CASTLE

Dornie, Kyle Of Lochalsh, Wester Ross IV40 8DX

A fortified site for eight hundred years, Eilean Donan now represents one of Scotland's most iconic images. Located at the point where three great sea lochs meet amidst stunning highland scenery on the main road to Skye. Spiritual home of Clan Macrae with century old links to Clan Mackenzie.
Location: MAP 16:J10, OS Ref. NG880 260. On A87 8m E of Skye Bridge.
Contact: David Win – Castle Keeper
Tel: 01599 555202
Fax: 01599 555262
E-mail: eileandonan@btconnect.com
Website: www.eileandonancastle.com
Open: Open 1 Mar–31 Oct.
Admission: Adult £6, Concession £5, Family £15.
Key facts: Eilean Donan holiday cottage.

THE DOUNE OF ROTHIEMURCHUS

By Aviemore PH22 1QP

The family home of the Grants of Rothiemurchus since 1560, was nearly lost as a ruin and has been under an ambitious repair programme since 1975. As part of the 'Highland Lady' tour you are able to visit a selection of the restored rooms, and the restoration area as well as exploring the haunts of Elizabeth Grant of Rothiemurchus, born 1797 and author of 'Memoirs of a Highland Lady'.
Location: MAP 16:P11, OS Ref. NH900 100. 2m S of Aviemore.
Owner: John Grant of Rothiemurchus, Lord Huntingtower
Contact: Rothiemurchus Centre **Tel:** 01479 812345 **E-mail:** info@rothie.net
Website: www.rothiemurchus.net
Open: Restoration and grounds: Apr–Aug: Mon 10am–12.30pm & 2–4.30pm (or dusk) also 1st Mon in the month in winter excl. Xmas & New Year. House: Wed as part of Highland Lady Tour or by special arrangement excl. Xmas and New Year. Groups by arrangement. **Admission:** Restoration and grounds donation to charity; Tours: £20pp (min 2 people) 2 hours; Groups: On application.
Key facts: Obligatory. Limited. In grounds, on leads.

© Britainonview

Eilean Donan Castle

Dunrobin Castle

Plas Mawr

Llangar Church

Wales

South Wales

Mid Wales

North Wales

North Wales
Mid Wales
South Wales

A small country with a colourful past, Wales is rich in culture and history and is also home to two UNESCO World Heritage sites. The fortified complexes of North Wales – Caernarfon, Conwy, Beaumaris and Harlech are all steeped in ancient history. Also worth a visit are delightful Portmeirion and the fascinating Elizabethan Plas Mawr. The smaller more modest attractions such as Rug Chapel and the nearby medieval Llangar Church are just as interesting. Moving south, Pembroke Castle houses many fascinating displays and exhibitions. Outdoors, the National Botanic Garden Of Wales is 600 acres of extraordinarily beautiful Welsh countryside to explore and Tintern Abbey is a picturesque gothic ruin set against a breathtaking backdrop.

© Welsh Government

CASTELL COCH

Tongwynlais, Cardiff CF15 7JS

www.cadw.wales.gov.uk

A fairytale castle in the woods, Castell Coch embodies a glorious Victorian dream of the Middle Ages. Designed by William Burges as a country retreat for the 3rd Lord Bute, every room and furnishing is brilliantly eccentric, including paintings of Aesop's fables on the drawing room walls.

Location: MAP 2:L1, OS Ref. ST131 826. M4/J32, A470 then signposted. 5m NW of Cardiff city centre.
Owner: In the care of Cadw
Contact: The Custodian
Tel: 029 2081 0101
Open: Mar–Jun: 9.30am–5pm; Jul–Aug: 9.30am–6pm; Sept–Oct 9.30am–5pm; Nov–Feb 10am–4pm, Sun 11am–4pm.
Admission: Adult £3.80, Concessions £3.40, Family £11. Child under 5yrs free. Visit website for details cadw.wales.gov.uk.
Key facts: Toilets. Cycle stands. Baby changing. Induction loop. Partial. Limited for coaches. Assistance dogs only. €

NATIONAL BOTANIC GARDEN OF WALES

Llanarthne, Carmarthenshire SA32 8HG

www.gardenofwales.org.uk

The first botanic garden of the 21st century is becoming an enduring icon for Wales. Extraordinarily beautiful, it has as its centrepiece Lord Foster's stunning Great Glasshouse which shelters a fantastic Mediterranean plant collection. From national nature reserve to Japanese Garden, there are 600 acres of rolling Welsh countryside to explore.

Location: MAP 5:F11, OS Ref. SN159 175. 1/4m from the A48 midway between Cross Hands and Carmarthen. Clearly signposted from A48 and Carmarthen.
Owner: National Botanic Garden of Wales
Contact: David Hardy or Dawn Crisp
Tel: 01558 667149 **Fax:** 01558 668933 **E-mail:** info@gardenofwales.org.uk
Open: Apr–Sept 10am–6pm. Oct–Mar 10am–4.30pm. Closed Christmas Day.
Admission: Adult £8.50, Under 16s £4.50, Under 5s Free, Concessions £7, Family (2+4) £21. Groups (10+): Adult £7.50, Children £3.50, Concessions £6.
Key facts: WCs. Licensed. Licensed. By arrangement. Ample for cars & coaches. Guide dogs only. Excluding Christmas Day.

© Skyscan

FONMON CASTLE

Fonmon, Barry, Vale Of Glamorgan CF62 3ZN

Occupied as a home since the 13th century, this medieval castle has the most stunning Georgian interiors and is surrounded by extensive gardens. Available for weddings, dinners, corporate entertainment and multi-activity days.

Location: MAP 2:L2, OS Ref. ST047 681. 15m W of Cardiff, 1m W of Cardiff airport.
Owner: Sir Brooke Boothby Bt
Contact: Claire Williams
Tel: 01446 710206
Fax: 01446 711687
E-mail: Fonmon_Castle@msn.com
Open: 1 Apr–30 Sept: Tue & Wed, 2–5pm (last tour 4pm). Other times by appointment. Groups: by appointment.
Admission: Adult £5:50, Child Free. (*2011 prices/opening)
Key facts: Conferences. By arrangement (up to 120).

PEMBROKE CASTLE

Pembroke SA71 4LA

www.pembrokecastle.co.uk

Pembroke Castle is situated within minutes of beaches and the breathtaking scenery of the Pembrokeshire Coastal National Park. This early Norman fortress, birthplace of the first Tudor King, houses many fascinating displays and exhibitions. Enjoy a picnic in the beautifully kept grounds, or on the roof of St. Anne's Bastion and take in the views along the estuary. Events throughout July and August please see website.

Location: MAP 5:C12, OS Ref. SM983 016. W end of the main street in Pembroke. **Owner:** Trustees of Pembroke Castle **Contact:** Mr Jon Williams
Tel: 01646 681510 **Fax:** 01646 622260 **E-mail:** info@pembrokecastle.co.uk
Open: All year. 1 Apr–31 Aug: daily 9.30am–6pm. Mar, Sept, & Oct daily, 10am–5pm. Nov–Feb: daily, 10am–4pm. Closed 24–26 Dec & 1 Jan. Brass rubbing centre open Summer months and all year by arrangement.
Admission: Adult £5, Senior/Child £4, Family (2+2) £14, Groups (20+) Adult £4.50, Senior/Child £3.50 **Key facts:** End of May – End of September and all year by arrangement. In grounds, on leads.

RAGLAN CASTLE

Raglan, Monmouthshire NP15 2BT

www.cadw.wales.gov.uk

Undoubtedly the finest late medieval fortress-palace in Britain, begun in the 1430s by Sir William ap Thomas who built the mighty 'Yellow Tower'. His son William, Lord Herbert, created a palatial mansion by adding an impressive gatehouse and many towered walls.

Location: MAP 6:K12, OS Ref. SO415 084. Raglan, NE of Raglan village off A40 (eastbound) and signposted.
Owner: In the care of Cadw
Contact: The Custodian
Tel: 01291 690228
Open: Mar–Jun and Sept–Oct: 9.30am–5pm, Jul and Aug: 9.30am–6pm, Nov–Mar: 10am–4pm, Sun 11am–4pm.
Admission: Adult £3.50, Concessions £3.10, Family £10.10. Child under 5 yrs free. Visit website for details cadw.wales.gov.uk.
Key facts: Toilets. Baby changing. Induction loop. Bluetooth. Partial. WCs. On leads. €

TINTERN ABBEY

Tintern, Monmouthshire NP16 6SE

www.cadw.wales.gov.uk

Tintern is the best-preserved abbey in Wales and ranks among Britain's most beautiful historic sites. The great Gothic abbey church stands almost complete to roof level. Turner sketched and painted here, while Wordsworth drew inspiration from the surroundings.

Location: MAP 6:L12, OS Ref. SO533 000. Tintern via A466, from M4/J23. Chepstow 6m.
Owner: In the care of Cadw **Contact:** The Custodian
Tel: 01291 689251
Open: Mar–Jun & Sept–Oct: 9.30am–5pm; Jul–Aug: 9.30am–6pm; Nov–Feb: Mon-Sat 10am–4pm, Sun 11am–4pm. Visit website for details cadw.wales.gov.uk.
Admission: Adult £3.80, Concessions £3.40, Family £11. Child under 5yrs free. Visit website for details cadw.wales.gov.uk.
Key facts: Induction loop. Toilets. Baby changing. WCs. On leads. €

ABERCAMLAIS HOUSE

Abercamlais, Brecon, Powys LD3 8EY

Splendid Grade I mansion dating from middle ages, altered extensively in early 18th century with 19th century additions, in extensive grounds beside the river Usk. Still in same family ownership and occupation since medieval times. Exceptional octagonal pigeon house, formerly a privy.

Location: MAP 6:I10, OS Ref. SN965 290. 5m W of Brecon on A40.
Owner: Mrs S Ballance
Contact: Mrs S Ballance
Tel: 01874 636206
Fax: 01874 636964
E-mail: info@abercamlais.co.uk
Website: www.abercamlais.co.uk
Open: Apr–Oct: by appointment.
Admission: Adult £5, Child Free.
Key facts: No photography in house. Obligatory. On leads.

BLAENAVON IRONWORKS

North Street, Blaenavon, Blaenau, Gwent NP4 9RN

The famous ironworks at Blaenavon were a milestone in the history of the Industrial Revolution. Visitors can view cottages furnished in three time periods. Recently used for BBC Coalhouse as 'Stack Square'. Part of a World Heritage site.

Location: MAP 6:J11, OS Ref. SO248 092. A4043-follow signs to Big Pit Mining Museum and Blaenavon Ironworks. Cross road to entrance gate.
Owner: In the care of Cadw
Contact: The Custodian
Tel: 01495 792615
Website: www.cadw.wales.gov.uk
Open: 1 Apr–31 Oct: 10am–5pm; 1 Nov–31 Mar: closed Mon–Thurs, 9.30am–4pm, Fri–Sat, 11am–4pm, Sun.
Admission: Free. Under 16s must be accompanied by an adult. Visit website for details cadw.wales.gov.uk.
Key facts: Disabled parking, Toilets, Cycle stands. WCs. Limited for coaches. On leads. €

CAERLEON ROMAN BATHS & AMPHITHEATRE

High Street, Caerleon NP18 1AE

Caerleon is the most varied and fascinating Roman site in Britain – incorporating fortress and baths, well-preserved amphitheatre and a row of barrack blocks, the only examples currently visible in Europe. Enjoy the innovative new displays in the fortress baths.

Location: MAP 2:N1, OS Ref. ST340 905. 4m ENE of Newport by B4596 to Caerleon, M4/J25 (westbound), M4/J26 (eastbound).
Owner: In the care of Cadw **Contact:** The Custodian
Tel: 01633 422518 **Website:** www.cadw.wales.gov.uk
Open: Apr–Oct: 9.30am–5pm; Nov–Mar: Mon–Sat, 9.30am–5pm; Sun 11am–4pm. Closed 24, 25, 26 Dec, 1 Jan.
Admission: Free. Under 16s must be accompanied by an adult. Visit website for details cadw.wales.gov.uk.
Key facts: Video presentation. Baths. Pay and Display. Assistance dogs only. €

CAERPHILLY CASTLE

Caerphilly CF83 1JD

Often threatened, never taken, this vastly impressive castle is much the biggest in Wales. 'Red Gilbert' de Clare, Anglo-Norman Lord of Glamorgan, flooded a valley to create the 30 acre lake, setting his fortress on an artificial island. Famous for its leaning tower and replica siege engines.

Location: MAP 2:L1, OS Ref. ST156 871. Centre of Caerphilly, A468 from Newport, A470, A469 from Cardiff.
Owner: In the care of Cadw **Contact:** The Custodian
Tel: 029 2088 3143
Website: www.cadw.wales.gov.uk
Open: Mar–Jun: 9.30am–5pm; Jul–Aug: 9.30am–6pm; Sept–Oct: 9.30am–5pm; Nov-Feb: 10am–4pm. Sun, 11am–4pm.
Admission: Adults £4, Concessions £3.60, Family £11.60. Child under 5yrs free. Visit website for details cadw.wales.gov.uk.
Key facts: Baby changing, Induction loop, Cycle stands, Disabled visitors can be dropped off by car at the main entrance. WCs. On leads. €

CARREG CENNEN CASTLE ✚

Tir y Castell Farm, Llandeilo, Carmarthenshire SA19 6TS

Spectacularly crowning a remote crag 300 feet above the River Cennen, the castle is unmatched as a wildly romantic fortress sought out by artists and visitors alike. The climb from Rare Breeds Farm is rewarded by breathtaking views and the chance to explore intriguing caves beneath.

Location: MAP 5:G11, OS Ref. SN668 190. Minor roads from A483(T) to Trapp village. 5m SE of A40 at Llandeilo.

Owner: In the care of Cadw **Contact:** The Manager

Tel: 01558 822291 **Website:** www.cadw.wales.gov.uk

Open: 1 Apr–31 Oct: 9.30am–6.30pm; 1 Nov–31 Mar 9.30am–4pm. Closed Christmas Day.

Admission: Adult £4, Concessions £3.50, Family £12. Child under 5 yrs free. Visit website for details cadw.wales.gov.uk.

Key facts: Induction loop. Toilets. Partial. P

CHEPSTOW CASTLE ✚

Chepstow, Monmouthshire NP16 5EY

One of the oldest stone fortifications in Britain. This castle was so powerful that it continued in use until 1690, including an epic Civil War siege. This huge complex, grand castle deserves to be explored; look out for the newly furnished earl's chamber.

Location: MAP 2:O1, OS Ref. ST533 941. Chepstow via A466, B4235 or A48. 11/2m N of M48/J22.

Owner: In the care of Cadw **Contact:** The Custodian

Tel: 01291 624065

Website: www.cadw.wales.gov.uk

Open: Mar–Jun and Sept–Oct: 9.30am–5pm; Jul–Aug: 9.30am–6pm; Nov–Feb: Mon–Sat 10am–4pm, Sun 11am–4pm.

Admission: Adult £4, Concessions £3.60, Family £11.60. Child under 5yrs free. Visit website for details cadw.wales.gov.uk.

Key facts: Induction loop; mobility scooter. P Pay and display. On leads. €

CILGERRAN CASTLE ✚

Cardigan, Pembrokeshire SA43 2SF

Perched high up on a rugged spur above the River Teifi, Cilgerran Castle is one of the most spectacularly sited fortresses in Wales. It dates from the 11th–13th centuries.

Location: MAP 5:D10, OS Ref. SN195 431. Main roads to Cilgerran from A478 and A484. 3½m SSE of Cardigan.

Owner: In the care of Cadw

Contact: The Custodian

Tel: 01239 621339

Website: www.cadw.wales.gov.uk

Open: Apr–Oct: 10am–5pm; Nov–Mar 10am–4pm (free entry). Closed 24, 25, 26 Dec, 1 Jan.

Admission: Adult £3.20, Concessions £2.80, Family £9.20. Child under 5yrs free. Visit website for details cadw.wales.gov.uk.

Key facts: Toilets. Induction loop. Partial. WCs. On leads. €

CORNWALL HOUSE

58 Monnow Street, Monmouth NP25 3EN

Town house, dating back to at least the 17th century. Red brick garden façade in Queen Anne style, dating from 1752. Street façade remodelled in Georgian style (date unknown). Many original features, including fine staircase. Delightful town garden with original walled kitchen garden.

Location: MAP 6:L11, OS Ref. SO506 127. Half way down main shopping street in Monmouth, set back between Boots and WH Smiths.

Owner: Ms Jane Harvey

Contact: Ms Jane Harvey

Tel/Fax: 01600 712031

Open: 31 Mar–Apr 15, 5–7 May, 25–27 Aug, 2, 8 & 9 Sept 2–5pm.

Admission: Adult £4, Conc. £2.

Key facts: Unsuitable. Obligatory. P Public car park nearby. €

CRESSELLY

Kilgetty, Pembrokeshire SA68 0SP

Home of the Allen family for 250 years. The house is of 1770 with matching wings of 1869 and contains good plasterwork and fittings of both periods. The Allens are of particular interest for their close association with the Wedgwood family of Etruria and a long tradition of foxhunting.

Location: MAP 5:C11, OS Ref. SN065 065. W of the A4075.

Owner: H D R Harrison-Allen Esq MFH

Contact: H D R Harrison-Allen Esq MFH

E-mail: hha@cresselly.com

Website: www.cresselly.com

Open: 4–31 Jul Inclusive, 10am–1pm. Guided tours only, on the hour. Coaches and at other times by arrangement.

Admission: Adult £4, no children under 12.

Key facts: Ground floor only. Obligatory. P Coaches by arrangement.

ST DAVIDS BISHOP'S PALACE ✚

St Davids, Pembrokeshire SA62 6PE

The city of St Davids boasts the most impressive medieval bishop's palace in Wales. The palace is lavishly decorated with finely carved stonework and still conveys the power and affluence of the medieval church. Be sure to explore the extensive undercrofts.

Location: MAP 5:B11, OS Ref. SM750 254. A487 to St Davids, minor road past the Cathedral.

Owner: In the care of Cadw

Contact: The Custodian

Tel: 01437 720517

Website: www.cadw.wales.gov.uk

Open: Mar–Jun and Sept–Oct: 9.30am–5pm; Jul–Aug: 9.30am–6pm; Nov–Feb: Mon–Sat, 10am–4pm, Sun 11am–4pm.

Admission: Adult £3.20, Concessions £2.80, Family £9.20. Child under 5yrs free. Visit website for details cadw.wales.gov.uk.

Key facts: Induction loop. Cycle stands. Partial. On leads. €

KIDWELLY CASTLE ✚

Kidwelly, Carmarthenshire SA17 5BQ

A chronicle in stone of medieval fortress technology this strong and splendid castle developed during more than three centuries of Anglo-Welsh warfare. The half-moon shape stems from the original 12th century stockaded fortress, defended by the River Gwendraeth on one side and a deep crescent-shaped ditch on the other.

Location: MAP 5:E12, OS Ref. SN409 070. Kidwelly via A484. Kidwelly Rail Station 1m.

Owner: In the care of Cadw **Contact:** The Custodian

Tel: 01554 890104 **Website:** www.cadw.wales.gov.uk

Open: Mar–Jun: 9.30am–5pm; Jul–Aug: 9.30am–6pm; Sept–Oct: 9.30am–5pm; Nov–Feb: Mon–Sat, 10am–4pm, Sun 11am–4pm.

Admission: Adult £3.50, Concessions £3.10, Family £10.10. Child under 5yrs free. Visit website for details cadw.wales.gov.uk.

Key facts: Baby changing. Induction loop. Toilets. Partial. WCs. P Limited for cars. No coaches. On leads. €

LAMPHEY BISHOP'S PALACE ✚

Lamphey, Pembroke SA71 5NT

Lamphey is home to one of the palaces of the bishops of St Davids, which reached its height of splendour under Bishop Henry de Gower. Today the ruins of this comfortable retreat reflect the power enjoyed by the medieval bishops.

Location: MAP 5:C12, OS Ref. SN018 009. A4139 from Pembroke or Tenby. N of village (A4139).

Owner: In the care of Cadw

Contact: The Custodian

Tel: 01646 672224

Website: www.cadw.wales.gov.uk

Open: Apr–Oct: 10am–5pm. The visitor centre will be closed during winter but the grounds accessible between 10am–4pm.

Admission: Adult £3.20, Concessions £2.80, Family £9.20. Child under 5yrs free. Visit website for details cadw.wales.gov.uk.

Key facts: P On-street parking. On leads. €

LAUGHARNE CASTLE ✤

King Street, Laugharne, Carmarthenshire SA33 4SA

Picturesque Laugharne Castle stands on a low ridge overlooking the wide Taf estuary, one of a string of fortresses controlling the ancient route along the South Wales coast. Inspired Richard Hughes and near to Dylan Thomas' Boathouse.

Location: MAP 5:E11, OS Ref. SN303 107. 4m S of A48 at St Clears via A4066.

Owner: In the care of Cadw

Contact: The Custodian

Tel: 01994 427906

Website: www.cadw.wales.gov.uk

Open: Apr–Oct: 10am–5pm. The monument is closed at all other times.

Admission: Adult £3.20, Concessions £2.80, Family £9.20. Child under 5yrs free. Visit website for details cadw.wales.gov.uk.

Key facts: Induction loop. Partial. Assistance dogs only. €

LLANCAIACH FAWR MANOR

Gelligaer Road, Nelson, Treharris, Caerphilly CF46 6ER

Llancaiach Fawr is a Tudor Manor restored as it was during the Civil War year of 1645. Visitors are guided by the costumed 'servants' who love to chat about the lives of ordinary people in extraordinary times. Visitor Centre provides modern amenities and also caters for weddings, functions and B2B.

Location: MAP 2:M1, OS Ref. ST114 967. S side of B4254, 1m N of A472 at Nelson.

Owner: Caerphilly County Borough Council **Contact:** Marion Anderson

Tel: 01443 412248 **Fax:** 01443 412688

E-mail: llancaiachfawr@caerphilly.gov.uk **Website:** www.llancaiachfawr.co.uk

Open: 10am–5pm, Tue–Sun and BH Mon's all year round.
Closed 24 Dec–1 Jan inclusive.

Admission: £6.50 Adults. £5.50 Conc. £5 Child. £19 Family Ticket (2 ad+ 2ch). Group discounts available (20+).

Key facts: No photography in Manor House. Partial. WCs. Licensed. Licensed. Obligatory. In grounds.

LLANDAFF CATHEDRAL

Llandaff, Cardiff CF5 2LA

Early parts date back to the 12th century, with Christian worship going back 1400 years. The Cathedral suffered serious war damage in 1941 and much restoration was required, under the direction of the late George Pace and includes Jacob Epstein's 'Christ in Majesty'.

Location: MAP 2:L2. OS Ref. ST155 397. Follow the brown signs within the Cardiff area.

Tel: 02920 564554

Website: www.llandaffcathedral.org.uk

Open: Every weekday 8.30am–7pm, Sun 7am–7pm.
www.llandaffcathedral.org.uk for details of daily services.

Admission: Free. Donations accepted.

Key facts: By arrangement.

LLANVIHANGEL COURT

Nr Abergavenny, Monmouthshire NP7 8DH

Grade I Tudor Manor. The home in the 17th century of the Arnolds who built the imposing terraces and stone steps leading to the house. The interior has a fine hall, unusual yew staircase and many 17th century moulded plaster ceilings. Delightful grounds. 17th century features, notably Grade I stables.

Location: MAP 6:K11, OS Ref. SO433 139. 4m N of Abergavenny on A465.

Owner/Contact: Julia Johnson

Tel: 01873 890217

Fax: 01873 890380

E-mail: jclarejohnson@googlemail.com

Website: www.llanvihangel-court.co.uk

Open: Thur 3–Fri 18 May, Sat 18–Mon 27 Aug inclusive, daily 2.30–5.30pm. Last tour 5pm.

Admission: Entry and guide, Adult £5, Child/Conc. £2.50.

Key facts: No inside photography. Partial. Obligatory. No coaches. On leads.

OXWICH CASTLE ✤

Oxwich, Swansea SA3 1NG

Beautifully sited in the lovely Gower peninsula, Oxwich Castle is a striking testament to the pride and ambitions of the Mansel dynasty of Welsh gentry.

Location: MAP 2:I1, OS159 Ref. SS497 864. A4118, 11m SW of Swansea, in Oxwich village.

Owner: In the care of Cadw

Contact: The Custodian

Tel: 01792 390359

Website: www.cadw.wales.gov.uk

Open: Apr–Sept: 10am–5pm. The monument is closed at all other times.

Admission: Adult £2.80, Concessions £2.40, Family £8. Child under 5yrs free. Visit website for details cadw.wales.gov.uk.

Key facts: Baby changing. Toilets. Induction loop. Cycle stands. Partial. No coaches. On leads. €

TREBERFYDD HOUSE

Llangasty, Brecon, Powys LD3 7PX

Stunning Grade I listed house regarded as one of the finest examples of the Gothic Revival movement of the 19th century. Magnificant views of the Black Mountains and set in 10 acres of beautiful landscaped gardens and peaceful woodlands. Home to the same family since it was built in 1852.

Location: MAP 6:I10. OS Ref. OS131 251. From Bwlch take road to Llangors, after 1/4 mile turn left and drive for 2m until Treberfydd sign.

Owner: David Raikes

Tel: 01874 730205

E-mail: info@treberfydd.com

Website: www.treberfydd.com

Open: 21 Jul–19 Aug. Tours of the House: 2 & 4pm. Gardens open: 1–6pm.

Admission: House & Gardens: Adult £5, Child (under 14yrs) Free. Gardens only: £3.

Key facts: On leads.

TREBINSHWN

Nr Brecon, Powys LD3 7PX

16th century mid-sized manor house. Extensively rebuilt 1780. Fine courtyard and walled garden.

Location: MAP 6:I10, OS Ref. SO136 242. 1.5m NW of Bwlch.

Owner: R Watson

Contact: R Watson

Tel: 01874 730653

Fax: 01874 730843

Open: Easter–31 Aug: Mon–Tue, 10am–4.30pm.

Admission: Free.

Key facts:

TREOWEN

Wonastow, Nr Monmouth NP25 4DL

The most important early 17th century gentry house in the county. Particularly fine open well staircase: "massive turned balusters, newel posts, finials and pendants, joined by equally massive and boldly moulded rails, climb in heroic simplicity through all four floors of the house." Elizabethan Architecture, Mark Girouard.

Location: MAP 6:L11, OS Ref. SO461 111. 3m WSW of Monmouth.

Owner: R A & J P Wheelock

Contact: John Wheelock

Tel: 01600 712031

E-mail: john.wheelock@treowen.co.uk

Website: www.treowen.co.uk

Open: Jun–Sep: Fri 10am–4pm. Also 24/25 Mar; 21/22 & 28/29 Apr; 19/20 May; 15/16 Sep; 2–5pm. HHA Friends free Fri only.

Admission: £5 (£3 if appointment made). Groups by appointment only.

Key facts: By arrangement. Entire house let, self-catering. Sleeps 25+.

TRETOWER COURT & CASTLE ✠

Tretower, Crickhowell NP8 1RD

A fine round tower set a short distance from an outstanding late medieval manor house, ranged around a galleried courtyard with a beautiful recreated medieval garden. The kitchens, service rooms and great hall have been decorated and furnished in late 15th century style.

Location: MAP 6:J11, OS Ref. SO187 212. Signposted in Tretower Village, off A479, 3m NW of Crickhowell.

Owner: In the care of Cadw **Contact:** The Custodian

Tel: 01874 730279

Website: www.cadw.wales.gov.uk

Open: Apr-Oct: 10am–5pm; Nov–Mar: Mon–Thurs closed; Fri–Sat: 10am–4pm; Sun 11am–4pm.

Admission: Adult £4, Concessions £3.60, Family £11.60. Under 5yrs free. Visit website for details cadw.wales.gov.uk.

Key facts: Toilets. Induction loop. Cycle stands. Picnic tables. No coaches. Assistance dogs only. €

WEOBLEY CASTLE ✠

Weobley Castle Farm, Llanrhidian SA3 1HB

Perched above the wild northern coast of the beautiful Gower peninsula, Weobley Castle was the home of the knightly de la Bere family. This fortified manor house included a fine hall and private chamber as well as numerous 'garderobes' or toilets, and an early Tudor porch block.

Location: MAP 2:I1, OS Ref. SN477 928. B4271 or B4295 to Llanrhidian Village, then minor road for 1½m.

Owner: In the care of Cadw **Contact:** The Custodian

Tel: 01792 390012

Website: www.cadw.wales.gov.uk

Open: Apr–Oct: 10am–5pm. During winter unstaffed between 10am–4pm. Closed 24, 25, 26 Dec and 1 Jan.

Admission: Adult £2.80, Concessions £2.40, Family £8. Child under 5yrs free. Visit website for details cadw.wales.gov.uk.

Key facts: Toilets. Limited for cars. No coaches. Assistance dogs only.

USK CASTLE

Usk, Monmouthshire NP5 1SD

The best kept secret ever! Romantic ivy-clad medieval castle set above the Usk valley and town. Simon Jenkins: "if ruins must be ruins, let them be like this" – discover them for yourself.

Location: MAP 6:K12, OS Ref. SO3701SE. Up narrow lane off Monmouth Road in Usk, opposite fire station.

Owner: J H L Humphreys **Contact:** Rosie Humphreys

Tel: (01291) 672563

E-mail: info@uskcastle.com

Website: www.uskcastle.com

Open: Castle: open daily; tours, groups, teas by arrangement. Gardens: by arrangement. House: May & BHs 2–5pm, small guided groups.

Admission: Castle: Donation at kiosk. Gardens: £4 for NGS, private visits welcome. House: £6, Child £3.

Key facts: Partial. Obligatory by arrangement. Limited for coaches. In grounds, on leads.

WHITE CASTLE ✠

Llantillio Crossenny, Monmouthshire NP7 8UD

With its high walls and round towers reflected in the still waters of its moat, White Castle is the ideal medieval fortress. Rebuilt in the mid-13th century to counter a threat from Prince Llywelyn the Last. Plenty of wildlife to discover.

Location: MAP 6:K11, OS Ref. SO380 167. By minor road 2m NW from B4233 at A7 Llantilio Crossenny. 8m ENE of Abergavenny.

Owner: In the care of Cadw

Contact: The Custodian

Tel: 01600 780380

Website: www.cadw.wales.gov.uk

Open: 1 Apr–31 Oct: 10am–5pm. Unstaffed between 10am–4pm. Closed 24, 25, 26 Dec and 1 Jan. Visit website for details cadw.wales.gov.uk.

Admission: Adult £2.80, Concessions £2.40, Family £8. Child under 5yrs Free. Visit website for details cadw.wales.gov.uk.

Key facts: Induction loop. Cycle stands. Partial. Limited for cars. No coaches. On leads. €

© Britainonview / Eric Nathan

National Botanic Garden of Wales

THE HALL AT ABBEY-CWM-HIR

Powys LD1 6PH

www.abbeycwmhir.com

In a breathtaking mid Wales setting, The Grade II* listed Hall and its 12 landscaped acres overlook the ruins of the 12th century Cisterian 'Abbey of the Long Valley', in which Llewellyn the Last is buried, and the church. One of Wales' finest examples of Victorian Gothic Revival architecture.

Location: MAP 6:I8, OS Ref. SO054 711. 7m NW of Llandrindod Wells, 6m E of Rhayader, 1m north of Crossgates on A483.

Owner: Paul and Victoria Humpherston **Contact:** Paul Humpherston

Tel: 01597 851727 **E-mail:** info@abbeycwmhir.com

Open: All year daily for prebooked tours only, at 10.30am, 2pm and 7pm for couples, small parties or groups.

Admission: House Tour & Gardens: Adult £15, Child (under 12) £5. Groups (10+) or repeat visitors £13. Gardens only: Adult £5.

Key facts: Visitors are asked to remove outside shoes for the tour of the house, slippers can be provided. Partial. Licensed. Licensed. Obligatory. Ample for cars, limited for coaches. In grounds, on leads.

HAFOD

Hafod Estate, Pontrhydygroes, Ystrad-Meurig, Ceredigion SY25 6DX

Picturesque landscape, one of the most significant in Britain located in a remote valley and improved by Col Thomas Johnes 1780–1816. Ten miles of restored walks featuring cascades, bridges and wonderful views in 500 acres of wood and parkland. The epitome of the Picturesque and Sublime. Georgian Group Award winner.

Location: MAP 5:G8, OS Ref. SN768 736. 15 miles E of Aberystwyth near Devils Bridge, car park, off B4574.

Owner: Forestry Commission Wales **Contact:** The Hafod Trust

Tel: 01974 282568 **Fax:** 01974 282579

E-mail: hafod.estate@forestry.gsi.gov.uk

Website: www.hafod.org

Open: All year, daylight hours.

Admission: Free – guide book available at local shops or website.

Key facts: WC. Obligatory by arrangement. In grounds on leads.

THE JUDGE'S LODGING

Broad Street, Presteigne, Powys LD8 2AD

Explore the fascinating world of the Victorian judges, their servants and felonious guests at this award-winning, totally hands-on historic house. Through sumptuous judge's apartments and the gas-lit servants' quarters below, follow an 'eavesdropping' audio tour featuring actor Robert Hardy. Damp cells, vast courtroom and new interactive local history rooms included.

Location: MAP 6:K8, OS Ref. SO314 644. In town centre, off A44 and A4113. Easy reach from Herefordshire and mid-Wales.

Owner: Powys County Council **Contact:** Gabrielle Rivers **Tel:** 01544 260650

E-mail: info@judgeslodging.org.uk **Website:** www.judgeslodging.org.uk

Open: 1 Mar–31 Oct: Tues–Sun, 10am–5pm. 1 Nov–31 Nov: Wed–Sun, 10am–4pm, 1 Dec–22 Dec: Sat–Sun 10am–4pm. Open BH Mon's.

Admission: Adult £6.50, Child £3.50, Conc. £5.50, Family £17. Groups (10-80): Adult £5.95, Conc. £4.95, Family £16, Schools £4.50.

Key facts: Partial. By arrangement. In town. Guide dogs only

STRATA FLORIDA ABBEY ✤

Ystrad Meurig, Pontrhydfendigaid SY25 6ES

Remotely set in the green, kite-haunted Teifi Valley with the lonely Cambrian mountains as a backdrop, the ruined Cistercian abbey has a wonderful doorway with spiral motifs and preserves a wealth of beautiful medieval tiles. Explore the connections with the princes of Deheubarth and the poet Dafydd ap Gwilym.

Location: MAP 5:H8, OS Ref. SN746 658. Minor road from Pontrhydfendigaid 14m SE of Aberystwyth by the B4340.

Owner: In the care of Cadw **Contact:** The Custodian

Tel: 01974 831261

Website: www.cadw.wales.gov.uk

Open: Apr–Sept: 10am–5pm. Unstaffed between 10am–4pm. Visit website for details cadw.wales.gov.uk.

Admission: Adult £3.20, Concessions £2.80, Family £9.20. Child under 5yrs free. Visit website for details cadw.wales.gov.uk.

Key facts: Induction loop. Partial. Limited for cars. No coaches. On leads. €

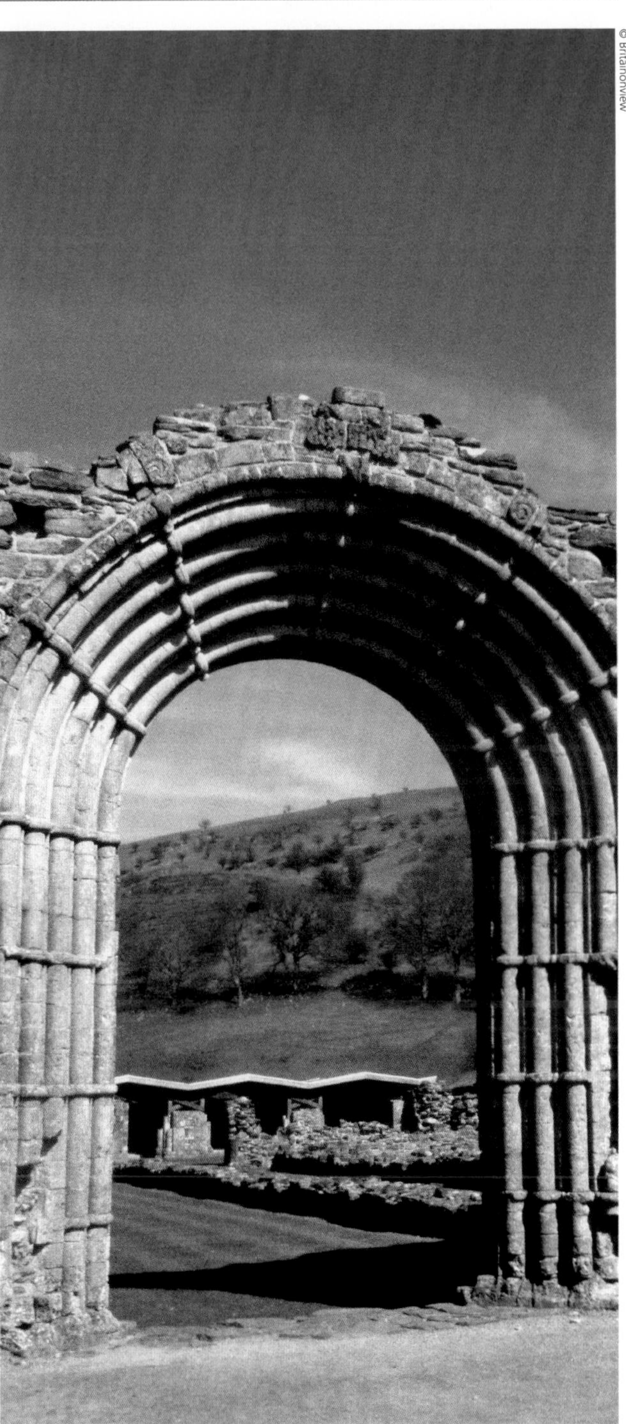

Strata Florida Abbey and the beautifully preserved Norman west doorway

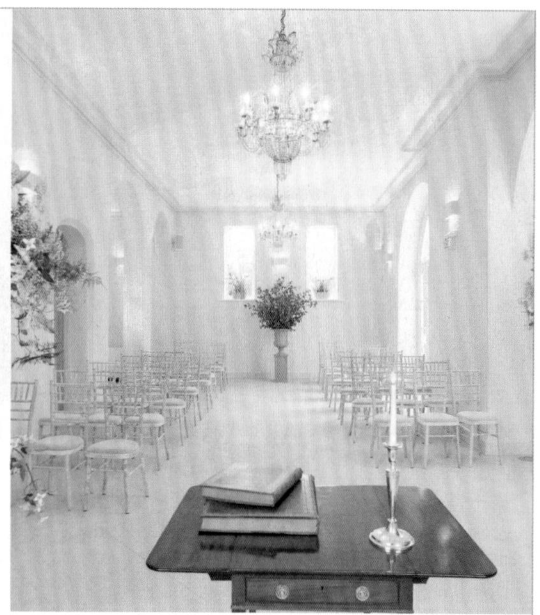

ISCOYD PARK

NR WHITCHURCH, SHROPSHIRE SY13 3AT

www.iscoydpark.com

A red brick Georgian house in an idyllic 18th century parkland setting situated on the Welsh side of the Shropshire/Welsh border. After extensive refurbishment of the house and gardens we are now open for Weddings, parties, photographic and film shoots, conferencing and corporate events of all kinds. The house is only let on an exclusive basis meaning there is never more than one event occurring at any time. We offer a wide range of B&B and self catering accommodation, The Secret Spa and beautiful gardens all within the context of a family home.

Location: MAP 6:L4, OS Ref. SJ504 421. 2m W of Whitchurch off A525.
Owner: Mr P C Godsal
Contact: Mr P L Godsal
Tel: 01948 780785
E-mail: info@iscoydpark.com
Open: House visits by written appointment.
Key facts: Private dinners a speciality. WCs. Licensed. Licensed. Obligatory. Limited for coaches.

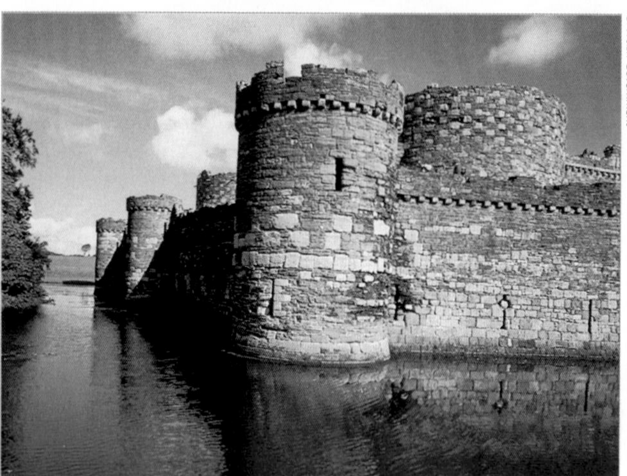

© Welsh Government

BEAUMARIS CASTLE

Beaumaris, Anglesey LL58 8AP

www.cadw.wales.gov.uk

The most technically perfect medieval castle in Britain, standing midway between Caernarfon and Conwy, commanding the old ferry crossing to Anglesey. Part of a World Heritage Inscribed Site.
Location: MAP 5:G2, OS Ref. SH608 762. 5m NE of Menai Bridge (A5) by A545. 7m from Bangor.
Owner: In the care of Cadw
Contact: The Custodian
Tel: 01248 810361
Open: Mar–Jun and Sept–Oct: 9.30am–5pm; Jul–Aug: 9.30am–6pm; Nov–Feb: Mon–Sat, 10am–4pm, Sun 11am–4pm.
Admission: Adult £3.80, Concession £3.40, Family £11, Child under 5yrs Free. Visit website for details cadw.wales.gov.uk.
Key facts: Assistance dogs only. €

© Welsh Government

CAERNARFON CASTLE

Castle Ditch, Caernarfon LL55 2AY

www.cadw.wales.gov.uk

The most famous and perhaps the most impressive castle in Wales, built by Edward I. Distinguished by polygonal towers and colour-banded stone, the castle hosted the 1969 investiture of the current Prince of Wales, HRH Prince Charles. Part of a World Heritage Inscribed site.
Location: MAP 5:F3, OS Ref. SH477 626. In Caernarfon, just W of town centre.
Owner: In the care of Cadw **Contact:** The Custodian **Tel:** 01286 677617
Open: Mar–Jun & Sept–Oct: 9.30am–5pm; Jul–Aug: 9.30am–6pm; Nov–Feb: Mon–Sat 10am–4pm, Sun 11am–4pm.
Visit website for details cadw.wales.gov.uk.
Admission: Adult £5.25, Concessions £4.85, Family £15.35. Child under 5 yrs free. Visit website for details cadw.wales.gov.uk.
Key facts: Induction loop. Toilets. Partial. Assistance dogs only. €

© Welsh Government

CONWY CASTLE ✤

Conwy LL32 8AY

www.cadw.wales.gov.uk

The impressive castle and town walls were built as a single entity by Edward I between 1283 and 1287. Explore both and enjoy the spectacular views. Become a Time Detective and explore the castle. Part of a World Heritage Inscribed site.

Location: MAP 5:H2, OS Ref. SH783 774. Conwy by A55 or B5106.

Owner: In the care of Cadw

Contact: The Custodian

Tel: 01492 592358

Open: Mar–Jun: 9.30am–5pm; Jul–Aug: 9.30am–6pm; Sept–Oct: 9.30am–5pm; Nov–Feb: Mon–Sat, 10am–4pm, Sun 11am–4pm. Visit website for details cadw.wales.gov.uk.

Admission: Adult £4.80, Concessions £4.30, Family £13.90, Child under 5 yrs free. Joint ticket for Conwy Castle and Plas Mawr available. Visit website for details cadw.wales.gov.uk.

Key facts: Induction loop. Toilets. Partial. WCs. By arrangement. Assistance dogs only. €

PENRHYN CASTLE

Bangor, Gwynedd LL57 4HN

www.nationaltrust.org.uk/penrhyncastle

Built by famed architect Thomas Hopper in the 19th century Penrhyn Castle is a fantastical neo-Norman Castle that sits in the glorious surroundings of Snowdonia and the Menai Strait. The Castle is filled with many fascinating objects as well as the rich history of the Pennant family and their guests.

Location: MAP 5:G2. OS Ref. SH602 720. 1m E of Bangor, at Llandygai (J11, A55). **Owner:** National Trust **Tel:** 01248 353084 **Fax:** 01248 371281 **Infoline:** 01248 363219 **E-mail:** penrhyncastle@nationaltrust.org.uk

Open: We are trialing our whole year opening times. As an overview, grounds are open all year, castle from Mar–Nov. Please visit the website for the latest information.

Admission: Castle: Adult £11, Child £5.50, Family £28. Grounds and stable block: Adult £7, Child £3.50. Winter Gardens: Adult £4, Child £1. Christmas weekend: Adult £4, Child £1.

Key facts: No photography in the main castle. Partial. WCs. Licensed. Licensed. By arrangement. Limited for coaches. In grounds.

GWYDIR CASTLE

Llanrwst, Gwynedd LL26 0PN

www.gwydircastle.co.uk

Gwydir Castle is situated in the beautiful Conwy Valley and is set within a Grade I listed, 10 acre garden. Built by the illustrious Wynn family c1500, Gwydir is a fine example of a Tudor courtyard house, incorporating re-used medieval material from the dissolved Abbey of Maenan. Further additions date from c1600 and c1828. The important 1640s panelled Dining Room has now been reinstated, following its repatriation from the New York Metropolitan Museum.

Location: MAP 5:H3, OS Ref. SH795 610. 1/2m W of Llanrwst on B5106.

Owner/Contact: Mr & Mrs Welford

Tel: 01492 641687

E-mail: info@gwydircastle.co.uk

Open: 1 Apr–31 Oct: daily, 10am–4pm. Closed Mons & Sats (except BH weekends). Limited openings at other times. Please telephone for details.

Admission: Adult £5.50, Child £3, Concessions £5. Group discount 10%.

Key facts: Partial. By arrangement. By arrangement. 2 doubles.

© Welsh Government

PLAS MAWR ✤

High Street, Conwy LL32 8DE

www.cadw.wales.gov.uk

The best-preserved Elizabethan town house in Britain, Plas Mawr reflects the status of its builder Robert Wynn. A fascinating house and garden allowing visitors to sample the lives of the Tudor gentry and their servants, Plas Mawr is famous for its colourful plasterwork and authentic furnishings.

Location: MAP 5:H2, OS Ref. SH781 776. Conwy by A55 or B5106 or A547.

Owner: In the care of Cadw

Contact: The Custodian

Tel: 01492 580167

Open: Apr–Sept: Tues–Sun, 9am–5pm; Oct: Tues–Sun, 9.30am–4pm. Visit website for details cadw.wales.gov.uk. Joint ticket available, Plas Mawr and Conwy Castle.

Admission: Adult £5.20, Concessions £4.80, Family £15.20, Child under 5yrs free.

Key facts: Toilets. Induction loop. Partial. Assistance dogs only. €

The spectacular stained glass and entrance hall of Bryn Bras Castle

PORTMEIRION

Portmeirion, Minffordd, Penrhyndeudraeth, Gwynedd LL48 6ER

www.portmeirion-village.com

Clough Williams-Ellis' unique village of listed buildings on the shores of Snowdonia surrounded by a 70 acre sub-tropical woodland with miles of coastal paths. Varied shops and cafes, restaurants and a Hotel. Castell Deudraeth brasserie on the main driveway offers a free entry pass with lunch. Open all year.

Location: MAP 5:F4, OS Ref. SH590 371. Off A487 at Minffordd between Penrhyndeudraeth and Porthmadog.

Owner: Portmeirion Limited

Contact: Mr R Llywelyn

Tel: 01766 772311 **Fax:** 01766 771331

E-mail: enquiries@portmeirion-village.com

Open: All year: daily, 9.30am–7.30pm (5.30pm in winter; Closed 25 Dec.)

Admission: Adults £10, Conc. £9, Children 4–16 years £6, Under 4's free. Half Price Entry 3.30–7.30pm. Family tickets available.

Key facts: Complimentary guided tours available 11am–3pm, 1 Apr–31 Oct. Partial. WCs. Licensed. Licensed. Obligatory. Guide dogs only.

BRYN BRAS CASTLE

Llanrug, Caernarfon, Gwynedd LL55 4RE

Built in the Neo-Romanesque style in c1830, on an earlier structure, and probably designed by Thomas Hopper, it stands in the Snowdonian Range. The tranquil garden includes a hill-walk with fine views of Mt Snowdon, Anglesey and the sea. Bryn Bras, a much loved home, offers a delightful selection of apartments for holidays for twos within the Grade II* listed castle. Many local restaurants, inns.

Location: MAP 5:F3, OS Ref. SH543 625. 1/2m off A4086 at Llanrug, 4 1/2m E of Caernarfon.

Owner: Mr & Mrs N E Gray-Parry

Contact: Marita Gray-Parry

Tel/Fax: 01286 870210

E-mail: holidays@brynbrascastle.co.uk

Website: www.brynbrascastle.co.uk

Open: Only by appointment.

Admission: By arrangement. No children please.

Key facts: Self-catering apartments for two within castle.

CRICCIETH CASTLE

Castle Street, Criccieth, Gwynedd LL52 0DP

Overlooking Cardigan Bay, Criccieth Castle is the most striking of the fortresses built by the Welsh princes. Its inner defences are dominated by a powerful twin-towered gatehouse.

Location: MAP 5:F4, OS Ref. SH500 378. A497 to Criccieth from Porthmadog or Pwllheli.

Owner: In the care of Cadw

Contact: The Custodian

Tel: 01766 522227

Website: www.cadw.wales.gov.uk

Open: Apr–Oct: 10am–5pm; Nov–Mar: Fri & Sat, 9.30am–4pm, Sun, 11am–4pm. Visit website for details cadw.wales.gov.uk.

Admission: Adult £3.20, Concessions £2.80, Family £9.20. Child under 5yrs free. Visit website for details cadw.wales.gov.uk.

Key facts: Induction loop. Toilets. Partial. Limited for cars, no coaches. On leads. €

DENBIGH CASTLE

Denbigh, Denbighshire LL16 3NB

Crowning the summit of a prominent outcrop overlooking the Vale of Clwyd, the principal feature of this spectacular site is the triple-towered great gatehouse dating back to the 13th century. Sections of the town walls are open to visitors. Don't miss Leicester's Church, Denbigh Friary and the Burgess Gate.

Location: MAP 6:I2, OS Ref. SJ052 658. Denbigh via A525, A543 or B5382.

Owner: In the care of Cadw

Contact: The Custodian

Tel: 01745 813385

Website: www.cadw.wales.gov.uk

Open: Apr–31 Oct: 10am–5pm. At all other times unstaffed between 10am and 4pm. Visit website for details cadw.wales.gov.uk.

Admission: Adult £3.20, Concessions £2.80, Family £9.20. Child under 5 yrs free. Visit website for details cadw.wales.gov.uk.

Key facts: Cycle stands. Induction loop. Toilets. Partial. On leads. €

DOLBELYDR

Trefnant, Denbighshire LL16 5AG

A 16th century, Grade II* listed building, a fine example of a 16th century gentry house and has good claim to be the birthplace of the modern Welsh language. It was at Dolbelydr that Henry Salesbury wrote his Grammatica Britannica. Dolbelydr is cared for by The Landmark Trust.

Location: MAP 6:I2, OS Ref. SJ031 709.

Owner/Contact: The Landmark Trust

Tel: 01628 825925

E-mail: bookings@landmarktrust.org.uk

Website: www.landmarktrust.org.uk

Open: Available for holidays for up to 6 people. Open Days on 8 days of the year. Other visits by appointment.

Admission: Free on Open Days and visits by appointment.

Key facts:

DOLWYDDELAN CASTLE

Dolwyddelan, Gwynedd LL25 0JD

Standing proudly on a ridge, the castle remains remarkably intact and visitors cannot fail to be impressed by the great solitary square tower, built by Llywelyn the Great in the early 13th century.

Location: MAP 5:G3, OS Ref. SH722 522. A470(T) Blaenau Ffestiniog to Betws-y-Coed, 1m W of Dolwyddelan.

Owner: In the care of Cadw

Contact: The Custodian

Tel: 01690 750366

Website: www.cadw.wales.gov.uk

Open: Apr–Sept: Mon–Sat, 10am–5pm, Sun 11.30am–4pm; Oct–Mar: Mon–Sat, 10am–4pm, Sun 11.30am–4pm. Visit cadw.wales.gov.uk.

Admission: Adult £2.80, Concessions £2.40, Family £8. Child under 5yrs free. Visit website for details cadw.wales.gov.uk.

Key facts: Assistance dogs only.

Dolbelydr

FFERM

Pontblyddyn, Mold, Flintshire CH7 4HN

17th century farmhouse. Viewing is limited to 7 persons at any one time. Prior booking is recommended. No toilets or refreshments.

Location: MAP 6:J3, OS Ref. SJ279 603. Access from A541 in Pontblyddyn, 3½m SE of Mold.

Owner: Dr M.C. Jones-Mortimer Will Trust

Contact: Miss Miranda Kaufmann

Tel: 01352 770204.

Open: 2nd Wed in every month, 2–5pm. Pre-booking is recommended.

Admission: £4.

Key facts:

HARLECH CASTLE

Castle Square, Harlech LL46 2YH

Set on a towering rock above Tremadog Bay, this seemingly impregnable fortress is the most dramatic of all the castles of Edward I. Discover the castle's connections with Owain Glyndŵr and its importance in Welsh history. Part of a World Heritage Inscribed site.

Location: MAP 5:F4, OS Ref. SH581 312. Harlech, Gwynedd on A496 coast road.

Owner: In the care of Cadw

Contact: The Custodian

Tel: 01766 780552

Website: www.cadw.wales.gov.uk

Open: Mar–Jun: 9.30am–5pm; Jul–Aug: 9.30am–6pm; Sept–Oct: 9.30am–5pm; Nov–Feb: Mon–Sat, 10am–4pm. 11am–4pm Sun. Visit website cadw.wales.gov.uk.

Admission: Adult £3.80, Concessions £3.40, Family £11. Child under 5yrs free. Visit website for details cadw.wales.gov.uk.

Key facts: Induction loop. Toilets. Pay and Display. Cycle stands. Assistance dogs only. €

HARTSHEATH

Pontblyddyn, Mold, Flintshire CH7 4HP

18th and 19th century house set in parkland. Viewing is limited to 7 persons at any one time. Prior booking is recommended. No toilets or refreshments.

Location: MAP 6:J3, OS Ref. SJ287 602. Access from A5104, 3½m SE of Mold between Pontblyddyn and Penyffordd.

Owner: Dr M.C. Jones-Mortimer Will Trust

Contact: Miss Miranda Kaufmann

Tel: 01352 770204

Fax: 01352 770204

Open: 1st, 3rd & 5th Wed in every month, 2–5pm.

Admission: £4.

Key facts:

PLAS BRONDANW GARDENS, CAFÉ & SHOP

Plas Brondanw, Llanfrothen, Gwynedd LL48 6SW

Italianate gardens with topiary.

Location: MAP 5:G4, OS Ref. SH618 423. 3m N of Penrhyndeudraeth off A4085, on Croesor Road.

Owner: Trustees of the Clough Williams-Ellis Foundation.

Tel: 01743 241181 / 07788 425713

E-mail: davinagriffiths@balfours.co.uk

Website: www.brondanw.org

Open: All year: daily, 9.30am–5.30pm. Coaches accepted, please book.

Admission: £3.50 first adult, £2 subsequent adults. Accompanied children free.

Key facts:

PLAS NEWYDD COUNTRY HOUSE AND GARDENS

Llanfairpwll, Anglesey, LL61 6DQ

Set amidst breathtaking scenery with spectacular Snowdonia views. Fine spring garden and Australasian arboretum, summer terrace, massed hydrangeas and Autumn colour. Rhododendron garden April–early June. Elegant 18th century house housing Rex Whistler's largest mural. Waterloo museum contains relics of 1st Marquess of Anglesey. Second-hand bookshop, children's adventure playground.

Location: MAP 5:F2, OS Ref. SH521 696. 2m SW of Llanfairpwll. A55 Junctions 7 and 8a, A4080 to Brynsiencyn. **Owner:** National Trust **Tel:** 01248 714795

Fax: 01248 713673 **E-mail:** plasnewydd@nationaltrust.org.uk

Website: www.nationaltrust.org.uk/plasnewydd

Open: House and garden: 17 Mar–7 Nov, Sat–Wed. Shop, Tea Room & Adventure Playground: All year. **Admission:** NT Members Free. Please ring or see website for details of admission prices for non-members.

Key facts: No indoor flash photography. Licensed. Licensed. By arrangement. Limited for coaches. Guide dogs only.

RHUDDLAN CASTLE

Castle Street, Rhuddlan, Rhyl LL18 5AD

Guarding the ancient ford of the River Clwyd, Rhuddlan was the strongest of Edward I's castles in North-East Wales. Linked to the sea by an astonishing deep water channel nearly 3 miles long, it still proclaims the innovative genius of its architect.

Location: MAP 6:I2, OS Ref. SJ025 779. SW end of Rhuddlan via A525 or A547.

Owner: In the care of Cadw

Contact: The Custodian

Tel: 01745 590777

Website: www.cadw.wales.gov.uk

Open: 1 Apr–31 Oct: 10am–5pm. The monument is closed at all other times.

Admission: Adult £3.20, Concessions £2.80, Family £9.20. Child under 5 yrs go free. Visit website for details cadw.wales.gov.uk.

Key facts: Cycle stands. Toilets. Induction loop. Baby changing. Free childrens' quiz. WCs. Limited for coaches. On leads. €

RUG CHAPEL & LLANGAR OLD PARISH CHURCH

Rug, Corwen, Nr Llangollen LL21 9BT

Prettily set in a wooded landscape, Rug Chapel's exterior gives little hint of the highly decorative and colourful wonders within. Nearby the attractive medieval Llangar Church retains its charming early Georgian furnishings and an important series of wall paintings.

Location: Rug Chapel: MAP 6:I4, OS Ref. SJ065 439. Off A494, 1m N of Corwen. Llangar Church: MAP 6:I4, OS Ref. SJ064 423. 1m S of Corwen.

Owner: In the care of Cadw **Contact:** The Custodian

Tel: 01490 412025 **Website:** www.cadw.wales.gov.uk

Open: Rug Apr–Oct: Wed–Sun, 10am–5pm. Llangar (by arrangement) Apr–Oct: Wed–Sun. Visit website for details cadw.wales.gov.uk.

Admission: Adult £3.80, Concessions £3.40, Family £11. Child under 5 yrs free. Visit website for details cadw.wales.gov.uk.

Key facts: Facilities at Rug Chapel only. Toilets. Cycle stands. Induction loops. WCs. Limited for coaches. Assistance dogs only. €

TOWER

Nercwys Road, Mold, Flintshire CH7 4EW

This Grade I listed building is steeped in Welsh history and bears witness to the continuous warfare of the time. A fascinating place to visit or for overnight stays. Bed and Breakfast graded 5 Star with Visit Wales.

Location: MAP6:J3, OS Ref. SJ240 620. 1m S of Mold. SAT NAV – use CH7 4EF.

Owner/Contact: Charles Wynne-Eyton **Tel:** 01352 700220

E-mail: enquiries@towerwales.co.uk **Website:** www.towerwales.co.uk

Open: 7 May–5 Jun, 27 Aug: 2–4.30pm. Groups welcome at other times by appointment.

Admission: Adult £5, Child £3.

Key facts: Opening dates etc. correct at time of going to press. If travelling significant distance please phone to check details. Partial. Obligatory. Limited for coaches.

VALLE CRUCIS ABBEY ✠

Llangollen, Denbighshire LL20 8DD

Set in a beautiful valley location, Valle Crucis Abbey is the best-preserved medieval monastery in North Wales, enhanced by the only surviving monastic fish pond in Wales.

Location: MAP 6:J4, OS Ref. SJ205 442. B5103 from A5, 2m NW of Llangollen, or A542 from Ruthin.

Owner: In the care of Cadw **Contact:** The Custodian

Tel: 01978 860326 **Website:** www.cadw.wales.gov.uk

Open: Apr–Oct: 10am–5pm. Unstaffed with no admission charge during winter, between 10am–4pm. Visit website for details cadw.wales.gov.uk.

Admission: Adult £2.80, Concessions £2.40, Family £8. Child under 5yrs free. Visit website for details cadw.wales.gov.uk.

Key facts: Induction loop. Limited for cars. On leads. €

WERN ISAF

Penmaen Park, Llanfairfechan LL33 0RN

This Arts and Crafts house was built in 1900 by the architect H L North as his family home and contains much of the original furniture and William Morris fabrics. Situated in a woodland garden with extensive views over the Menai Straits and Conwy Bay.

Location: MAP 5:G2, OS Ref. SH685 753. Off A55 midway between Bangor and Conwy.

Owner: Mrs P J Phillips

Contact: Mrs P J Phillips

Tel: 01248 680437

Open: 3–31 Mar: daily 1–4pm, except Tues.

Admission: Free.

Portmeirion

Antrim Castle Gardens

Ballywalter Park

Ireland

Northern Ireland

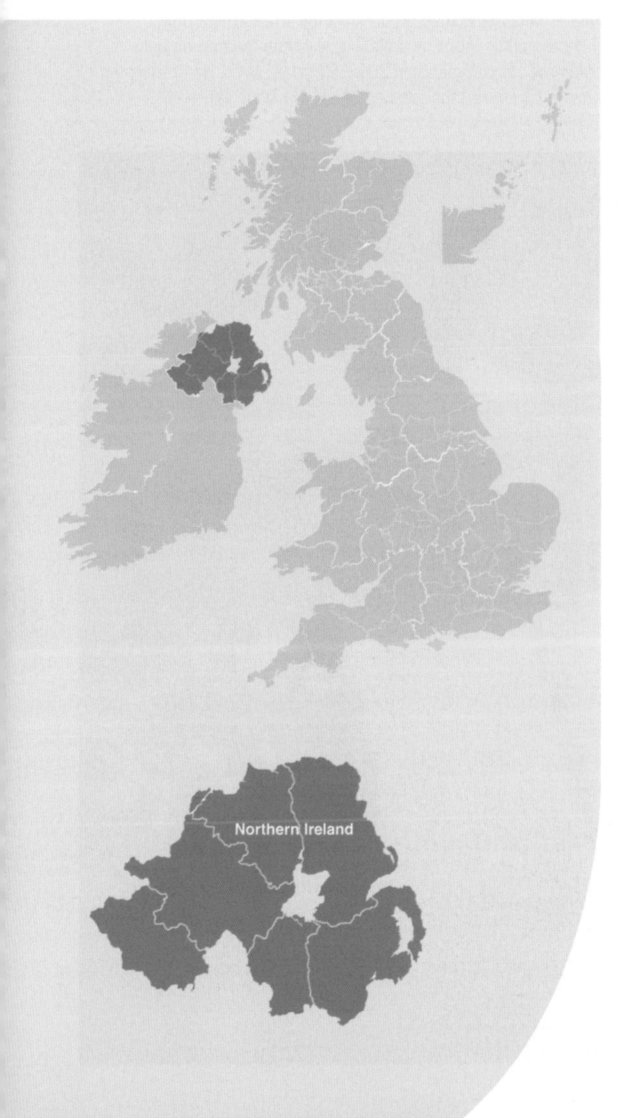
Northern Ireland

Northern Ireland, renowned for many popular outdoor pursuits, also offers visitors an abundance of heritage attractions in a uniquely stunning landscape. From majestic castles and cathedrals to fascinating ancient monuments, there is lots to explore. Ballywalter Park, an Italianate Palazzo style house, is an excellent example with fine collections of original furniture and paintings. At 17th century Antrim Castle Gardens visitors can find 32 acres of ornamental canals, ponds, lime avenues, tunnels and ruins to explore, as well as a Norman motte, artillery fort and restored Italianate tower.

ANTRIM CASTLE GARDENS

RANDALSTOWN ROAD, ANTRIM BT41 4LH

www.antrimcastlegardens.org

Situated adjacent to Antrim Town and nearby Lough Neagh, this 17th century garden retains features of the Anglo-Dutch water garden and formal design styles. The 32 acre gardens comprise ornamental canals, lime avenues with ponds and vistas, and a large reproduction parterre. Later features include a pleasure garden, terrace parterre, tunnels, ruins and landscape structures including a Norman motte, artillery fort, bridge and an restored Italianate tower. A new Garden Heritage exhibition introducing the history of the gardens, the family and the on-going process of restoration is located in Clotworthy House. Arts services occupy the restored Victorian outbuildings.

Location: MAP 18:N4, OS Ref. J186 850. Outside Antrim town centre off A26 on A6.

Owner: Antrim Borough Council

Contact: Sharon Kirk, Garden Heritage Development Officer

Tel: 028 9448 1338

Fax: 028 9448 1344

E-mail: culture@antrim.gov.uk

Open: All year: Mon–Fri, 9.30am–9.30pm (dusk if earlier). Sats, 10am–5pm. Suns, 1–5pm.

Admission: Free. Charge for guided group tours (by arrangement only).

Key facts: Photographic shoots and filming by written permission only. Education programme will commence in 2012. WCs. Licensed. By arrangement. Limited for coaches. On leads.

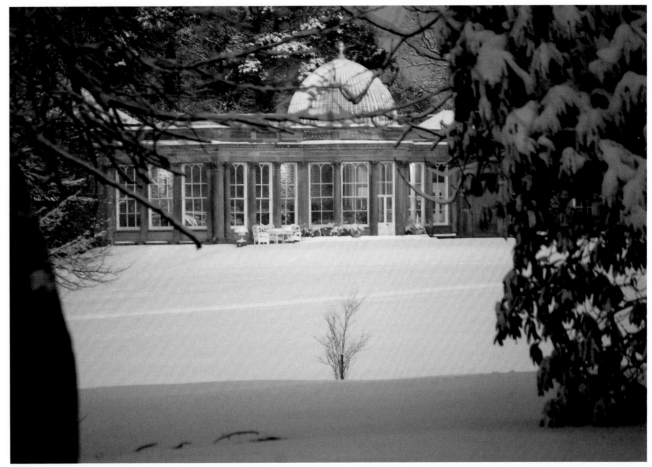

Winter view of conservatory at Ballywalter Park

BALLYWALTER PARK

Ballywalter, Newtownards, Co Down BT22 2PP

www.ballywalterpark.com

Ballywalter Park was built, in the Italianate Palazzo style, by Sir Charles Lanyon for Andrew Mulholland. A Gentleman's wing, was added in 1870 for Andrew's son, John Mulholland, later 1st Baron Dunleath. The house has a fine collection of original furniture and paintings, complemented by contemporary pieces.

Location: MAP 18:P4, OS Ref. J610 723. Off A2 on unclassified road, 1 km S of Ballywalter village.

Owner: The Lord and Lady Dunleath

Contact: Mrs Sharon Graham, The Estate Office

Tel: 028 4275 8264 **Fax:** 028 4275 8818

E-mail: enq@dunleath-estates.co.uk

Open: By prior appointment only; please contact The Estate Office.

Admission: House or Gardens; £8 House & Gardens; £12. Groups (max 50): £8.

Key facts: No photography indoors. Partial. Refreshments by arrangement. Obligatory. Limited for coaches. Guide dogs only. Double, En Suite. €

BARONS COURT

Newtownstewart, Omagh, Co Tyrone BT78 4EZ

The home of the Duke and Duchess of Abercorn, Barons Court was built between 1779 and 1782, and subsequently extensively remodelled by John Soane (1791), William and Richard Morrison (1819–1841), Sir Albert Richardson (1947–49) and David Hicks (1975–76).

Location: MAP 18:M3, OS Ref. H236 382. 5km SW of Newtownstewart.

Contact: The Agent

Tel: 028 8166 1683

Fax: 028 8166 2059

E-mail: info@barons-court.com

Website: www.barons-court.com

Open: By appointment only.

Admission: Adult £9. Groups max. 50.

Key facts: No photography. Partial. By arrangement. €

CASTLE WARD HOUSE & DEMESNE

Strangford, Downpatrick, Co Down BT30 7LS

Situated in a stunning location within an 820 acre walled demesne overlooking Strangford Lough, the lawns rise up to the unique 18th century house and its Gothic façade. This fascinating house features both Gothic and Classical styles of architectural treatment, internally and externally.

Location: MAP 18:P6, OS Ref. J573 498. On A25, 7m from Downpatrick and 1½m from Strangford.

Owner: National Trust **Contact:** Jacqueline Baird, Visitor Services Manager

Tel: 028 4488 1204 **Fax:** 028 4488 1729 **E-mail:** castleward@nationaltrust.org.uk

Website: www.nationaltrust.org.uk/castleward

Open: House: Mid Feb–End Oct. Grounds: All year: daily, 10am–4pm (8pm Apr–Sept).

***Admission:** Grounds/House: Adult £7, Child £3, Family £17.50. Groups: £6. Grounds: Adult £7, Child £3, Family £17.50, Groups £6.

*includes a voluntary donation.

Key facts: WCs. By arrangement. On leads. Caravan park, holiday cottages, basecamp. €

DOWN CATHEDRAL

Cathedral Office, English Street, Downpatrick, County Down BT30 6AB

Built in 1183 as a Benedictine monastery, Down Cathedral is now a Cathedral of the Church of Ireland. Prominent and majestic, the cathedral is believed to have the grave of St Patrick in its grounds. There is also wonderful stained glass and a pulpit and organ of highest quality.

Location: MAP 18:O6. OS Ref. SB583 989. Located in Downpatrick, in the heart of English Street. Follow brown signs.

Owner: Church of Ireland

Contact: Joy Wilkinson

Tel: 028 4461 4922 **Fax:** 028 4461 4452

E-mail: info@downcathedral.org

Website: www.downcathedral.org

Open: Open all year round. Mon–Sat: 9.30am–4.30pm, Sun: 2–4pm.

Admission: Donations. Guided tours by arrangement.

Key facts: By arrangement. Limited for cars and coaches. Guide dogs only.

KILLYLEAGH CASTLE

Killyleagh, Downpatrick, Co Down BT30 9QA

Oldest continually occupied castle in Ireland. Self-catering towers available to sleep 4–13. Swimming pool and tennis court available by arrangement. Access to garden.

Location: MAP 18:P4, OS Ref. J523 529. At the end of the High Street.

Owner/Contact: Mrs G Rowan-Hamilton

Tel/Fax: 028 4482 8261

E-mail: gatehouses@killyleagh.plus.com

Website: www.killyleaghcastle.com

Open: By arrangement.

Admission: Groups (30–50) welcome by arrangement. Usually around £2.50 per adult.

Key facts: No photography in house. Wedding receptions. Unsuitable. Obligatory. No coaches. Guide dogs only.

LARCHFIELD ESTATE BARN & GARDENS

Bailliesmills Road, Lisburn, Co Antrim BT27 6XJ

Just 20 minutes from Belfast City are the converted barn and spectacular walled gardens at Larchfield Estate. A stunning location year round, this venue offers exclusive use for private parties, weddings and corporate events. A private estate, viewings are strictly by appointment only.

Location: MAP 18:O4, OSNI J301 592. 4 Miles S of Lisburn, on the Bailliesmills Road, 10m SW of Belfast, BT27 6XJ.

Owner: Mr & Mrs G Mackie

Contact: Gavin Mackie

Tel: 02892 638 025

E-mail: enquiries@larchfieldestate.co.uk

Website: www.larchfieldestate.co.uk

Open: Not open to general public. Weddings, events and conferences only.

Key facts: WCs. Guide dogs only.

Antrim Castle Gardens

Hartland Abbey

Indexes

©Britainonview/Grant Pritchard

Plant Sales

Properties where plants are offered for sale.

©Britainonview/Joanna Henderson

ENGLAND

EASTERN REGION

HEART OF ENGLAND

YORKSHIRE & THE HUMBER

Hartland Abbey

Hestercombe Gardens
©Claire Reid

Accommodation

Properties where accommodation can be arranged.

Open All Year

Properties and / or their grounds that are open for all or most of the year

The Conservatory
Ballywalter Park

ENGLAND

EASTERN REGION

EAST MIDLANDS

HEART OF ENGLAND

YORKSHIRE & THE HUMBER

Sezincote

Rockingham Castle

Civil Weddings

Properties at which wedding or civil partnership ceremonies can take place

The Gothic Temple
Painshill Park

ENGLAND

Forde Abbey
©English Rose Photography

EASTERN REGION

EAST MIDLANDS

HEART OF ENGLAND

YORKSHIRE & THE HUMBER

WE 2 RI
SIL 9756
Capesthorne Hall

Special Events

Historical re-enactments, festivals, country and craft fairs, concerts, fireworks, car and steam rallies, and much more ...
(Please check dates before visiting)

Beaulieu
©Britainonview

FEBRUARY

12

Hartland Abbey, Devon
Snowdrop Sunday (11am–4pm)

12 & 19

Deene Park, Northamptonshire
Snowdrop Sundays (Gardens Only), 11am–4pm

15 February - 31 March

Blair Castle, Perthshire
Snowdrop Festival

25 - 26

Dalemain, Cumbria
The World's Original Marmalade Festival

February onwards

Brodsworth Hall & Gardens
Yorkshire 150,000 Snowdrops, Bluebells and Daffodils put on a show

MARCH

Abbey House Gardens, Wiltshire
Flowering Crocus, Narcissi, Hellebore, Hyacinth, Camellia

Arley Hall & Gardens, Cheshire
Mothers Day Celebrations

2 - 4

Wilton House, Wiltshire
Antiques Fair

18

Arley Hall & Gardens, Cheshire
Wedding Fair

Hartland Abbey, Devon
Mothering Sunday and Daffodil Day

31 March - 1 April

Boconnoc, Cornwall
Cornwall Garden Society Spring Flower Show

April

Abbey House Gardens, Wiltshire
Flowering Tulips, Primula, Fritillaries

Arley Hall & Gardens, Cheshire
Bluebell Walks

April - October

Glamis Castle, Perthshire
Diamond Jubilee Exhibition

1

Arley Hall & Gardens, Cheshire
Spring Plant Fair

Deene Park, Northamptonshire
Daffodil Day (Gardens Only), 11am–4pm

8

Traquair, Scottish Borders
Easter Egg Extravaganza

Easter

Clovelly, Devon
Easter at Clovelly

8 - 9

Lamport Hall & Gardens, Northamptonshire
Easter Sunday and Monday – Antiques and Collectors Fair

9

Chenies Manor House, Buckinghamshire
Children's egg races, shop, plants for sale

22 & 29

Hartland Abbey, Devon
Bluebell Sundays

29

Beaulieu, Hampshire
Boatjumble

25 April - 7 May (inc.)

Pashley Manor Gardens, Sussex
Tulip Festival

May

Abbey House Gardens, Wiltshire
Flowering Laburnum, Wisteria, Rhododendron, Azaleas, Peonys, Apple blossom, Alliums

Clovelly, Devon
Celebration of Ales & Ciders

5 – 9 May

Hatfield House, Hertfordshire
Living Crafts

7

Penshurst Place & Gardens, Kent
Weald of Kent Craft Show

Chenies Manor House, Buckinghamshire
May Bank Holiday Monday: House & Garden open 2–5pm 'Tulip Festival', Bloms Tulips throughout the House and Gardens

13

Newby Hall & Gardens, Yorkshire
Spring Plant Fair

Pashley Manor Gardens, Sussex
Spring Plant Fair

15 - 16

Boconnoc, Cornwall
Spring Fair

19 - 20

Beaulieu, Hampshire
Spring Autojumble

20

Boconnoc, Cornwall
Dog Show

26

Blair Castle, Perthshire
Atholl Highlanders' Parade

26 May – 5 June (inc.)

Pashley Manor Gardens, Sussex
Sculpture in Particular

26 - 27

Traquair, Scottish Borders
Medieval Fayre

27

Blair Castle, Perthshire
Highland Games

June

Abbey House Gardens, Wiltshire
Flowering Roses, Knifophia, Geraniums, Delphiniums, Poppies, Clematis

Arley Hall & Gardens, Cheshire
Arley Garden Festival

First week in June

Penshurst Place & Gardens, Kent
Glorious Gardens Week. The official reopening of the Double Herbaceous Borders

2 - 3

Beaulieu, Hampshire
Steam Revival (TBC)

3

Stonor, Oxfordshire
VW Owners' Rally

3 - 4

Lamport Hall & Gardens, Northamptonshire
Festival of Country Life

4

Chenies Manor House, Buckinghamshire
House & Garden open 2–5pm / 10am–5pm Carriage Driving Day (contact Shirley Higgins 01923 267919)

6

Deene Park, Northamptonshire
Head Gardener's Tour with Supper, Booking Essential, 6pm

9 - 10

Newby Hall & Gardens, Yorkshire
Vintage Tractor Rally

10

Glamis Castle, Perthshire
Strathmore Highland Games

Rockingham Castle, Northamptonshire
Jousting & Medieval Living History Village

15 - 17

Pashley Manor Gardens, Sussex
Special Rose Weekend

17

Beaulieu, Hampshire
Custom and Hot Rod Festival (TBC)

22 - 24

Boughton Monchelsea Place, Kent
Open Air theatre 'As You Like It'

Pashley Manor Gardens, Sussex
Kitchen Garden Weekend

July

Abbey House Gardens, Wiltshire
Flowering Roses, Lillies, Alstromeria, Astilbes, Hostas, Lavendar, Hydrangea

Clovelly, Devon
Clovelly Maritime Festival

Clovelly, Devon
Lundy Row

Clovelly, Devon
Woolsery Agricultural Show

Goodwood House, Sussex
Festival of Speed

Goodwood House, Sussex
Glorious Goodwood

6 - 8

Boughton Monchelsea Place, Kent
Open Air theatre 'As You Like It'

7 - 8

Glamis Castle, Perthshire
Scottish Transport Extravaganza

15

Beaulieu, Hampshire
Motorcycle Ride-In Day

Chenies Manor House, Buckinghamshire
14th famous Plant & Garden Fair,
70 exhibitors from around the country

Newby Hall & Gardens, Yorkshire
Historic Vehicle Rally

Mid July – Mid August

Pashley Manor Gardens, Sussex
Lily Time

20 - 22

Boconnoc, Cornwall
Steam Fair

28 - 29

Glamis Castle, Perthshire
Scotland's Countryside Festival

Hopetoun House, Edinburgh
Horse Trials

August

Abbey House Gardens, Wiltshire
Flowering Roses, Alstromeria, Salvia,

Clovelly, Devon
Clovelly Gig Regatta

4 - 5

Clovelly, Devon
Lifeboat Weekend

Traquair, Scottish Borders
Traquair Fair

5 – 7

Hatfield House, Hertfordshire
Art in Clay

11

Glamis Castle, Perthshire
The Prom at Glamis

12

Newby Hall & Gardens, Yorkshire
Alfa Romeo Rally

19 – 21

Hatfield House, Hertfordshire
Hatfield House Country Show

23 - 26

Blair Castle, Perthshire
International Horse Trials & Country Fair

Easton Walled Gardens

24 - 27

Stonor, Oxfordshire
Chilterns Craft Fair

25

Glamis Castle, Perthshire
'Macbeth' Outdoor Picnic Play

25 - 27

Pashley Manor Gardens, Sussex
Sussex Guild Craft Show

26 - 27

Rockingham Castle, Northamptonshire
Vikings! Of Middle England

Lamport Hall & Gardens, Northamptonshire
Antiques and Collectors Fair

27

Chenies Manor House, Buckinghamshire
House & Garden open 2–5pm
'Dahlia Festival'

30 August - 2 September

Burghley House, Lincolnshire
The Burghley Horse Trials

August Bank Holiday

The Dorothy Clive Garden, Staffordshire
Plant Hunters' Fair featuring approximately 20 highly acclaimed nurseries including Chelsea and RHS Medal Winners, 10am to 5pm

September

Abbey House Gardens, Wiltshire
Flowering Roses, Salvia

Goodwood House, Sussex
Goodwood Revival

2

Clovelly, Devon
Lobster & Crab Feast

8 - 9

Beaulieu, Hampshire
International Autojumble

14 - 16

Newby Hall & Gardens, Yorkshire
Darlington Championship Dog Show

October

Abbey House Gardens, Wiltshire
Flowering Michaelmas Daisies, Anemones, Salvias fruit, Acers

Arley Hall & Gardens, Cheshire
Halloween Murder Mystery Evening (contact us for details)

Traquair, Scottish Borders
Halloween Experience

1 - 2

Boconnoc, Cornwall
Michaelmas Fair

13 - 14

Lamport Hall & Gardens, Northamptonshire
Autumn Gift and Craft Fair

20

Boconnoc, Cornwall
Scratch Messiah

24 - 25

Chenies Manor House, Buckinghamshire
Spooks and Surprises' - Special scary tour of the house for children, House & Garden open 2–5pm

27

Beaulieu, Hampshire
Fireworks Spectacular

27 - 28

Glamis Castle, Perthshire
Halloween at Glamis

November

Clovelly, Devon
Clovelly Herring Festival

Blair Castle, Perthshire
Christmas Castle

Glamis Castle, Perthshire
Winter programme of events

19 - 23

Rockingham Castle, Northamptonshire
Christmas Eve 1849 - Costumed Tours of the Castle

23 - 25

Hopetoun House, Edinburgh
Christmas Shopping Fair

24 - 25

Traquair, Scottish Borders
Christmas Opening

December

Arley Hall & Gardens, Cheshire
Christmas Floral Extravaganza

Clovelly, Devon
Christmas Lights

Chartwell, Kent
Christmas market

Blair Castle, Perthshire
Christmas Castle

Glamis Castle, Perthshire
Winter programme of events

Arundel Castle
©C&J Willis Photography

Maps

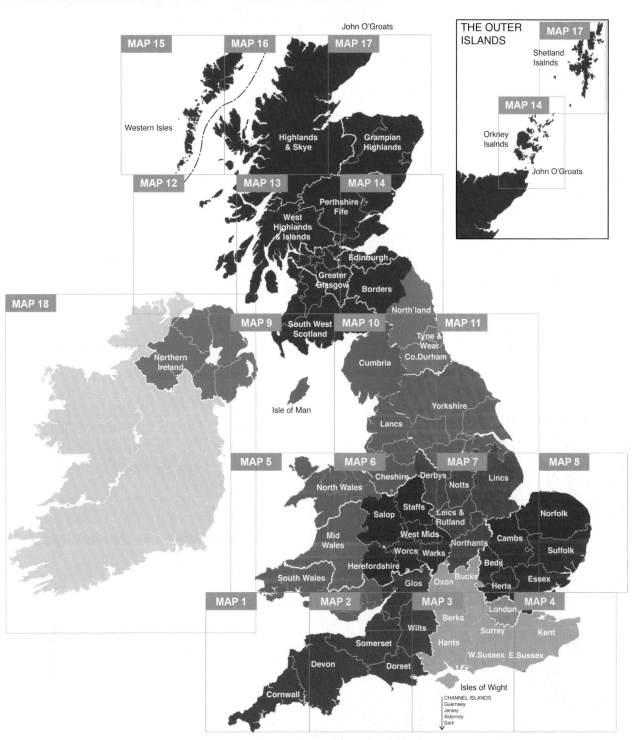

John O'Groats

MAP 15
MAP 16
MAP 17

Western Isles

Highlands & Skye

Grampian Highlands

MAP 12
MAP 13
MAP 14

Perthshire / Fife

West Highlands & Islands

Edinburgh

Greater Glasgow

Borders

MAP 18

North'land

MAP 9
South West Scotland
MAP 10
MAP 11

Tyne & Wear

Northern Ireland

Co.Durham

Cumbria

Isle of Man

Yorkshire

Lancs

MAP 5
MAP 6
MAP 7
MAP 8

Cheshire
Derbys
Lincs
Notts
North Wales
Staffs
Leics & Rutland
Norfolk
Salop
West Mids
Cambs
Mid Wales
Northants
Worcs
Warks
Suffolk
Beds
Herefordshire
South Wales
Bucks
Essex
Glos
Oxon
Herts

MAP 1
MAP 2
MAP 3
MAP 4

London
Berks
Wilts
Surrey
Kent
Hants
Somerset
W.Sussex
E.Sussex
Devon
Dorset
Isles of Wight
Cornwall

CHANNEL ISLANDS
Guernsey
Jersey
Alderney
Sark

THE OUTER ISLANDS
MAP 17
Shetland Isalnds
MAP 14
Orkney Isalnds
John O'Groats

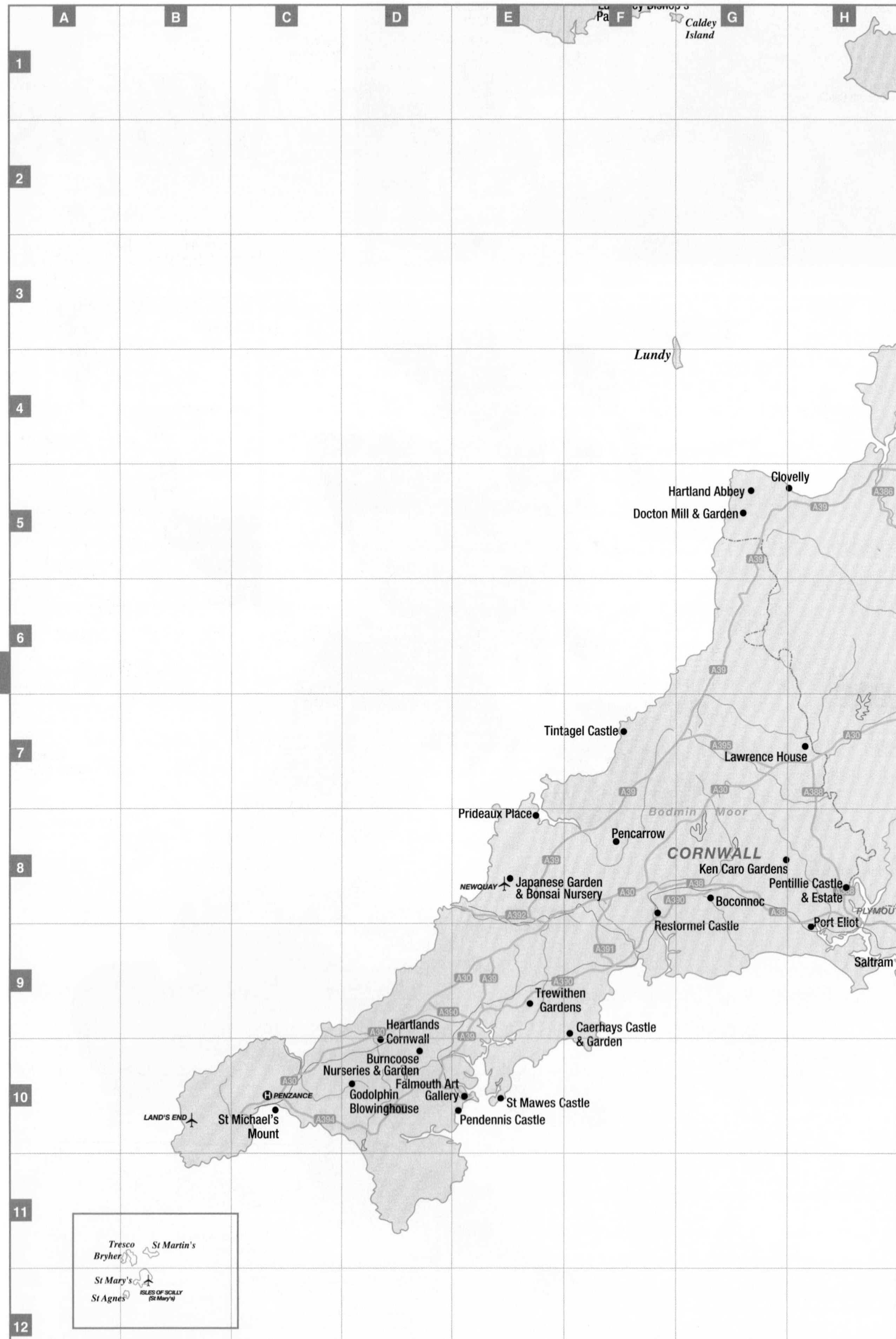
A
B
C
D
E
F
G
H
1
2
3
4
5
6
7
8
9
10
11
12
Caldey Island
Lundy
Clovelly
Hartland Abbey
Docton Mill & Garden
A386
A39
A39
A39
Tintagel Castle
Lawrence House
A395
A30
A39
A30
A388
Bodmin Moor
Prideaux Place
Pencarrow
CORNWALL
A39
Ken Caro Gardens
Pentillie Castle & Estate
NEWQUAY
Japanese Garden & Bonsai Nursery
A30
A38
A390
Boconnoc
A392
Restormel Castle
A38
Port Eliot
PLYMOUTH
A391
Saltram
A30
A39
A390
Trewithen Gardens
A390
Heartlands Cornwall
A30
A39
Caerhays Castle & Garden
Burncoose Nurseries & Garden
A30
Falmouth Art Gallery
PENZANCE
Godolphin Blowinghouse
St Mawes Castle
LAND'S END
St Michael's Mount
A394
Pendennis Castle
Tresco
St Martin's
Bryher
St Mary's
ISLES OF SCILLY (St Mary's)
St Agnes

Weobley Castle
Oxwich Castle
Caerphily Castle
Castell Coch
Llandaff Cathedral
Fonmon Castle
Llancaiach Fawr Manor
Caerleon Roman Baths
Chepstow Castle
Building of Bath Museum
Crowe Hall
Holburne Museum of Art
Peto Gardens at Iford Manor
Farleigh Hungerford Castle
Milton Lodge Gardens
Stoberry House
Nunney Castle
Longleat
Kilver Court Gardens
Glastonbury Abbey
Stourhead
Fairfield
Kentsford Orchard
Dodington Hall
Wyndham
Robin Hood's Hut
Maunsel House
Marwood Hill Garden
Hestercombe Gardens
Muchelney Abbey
Fleet Air Arm Museum
Sandford Orcas Manor House
Sherborne Old Castle
Sherborne Castle
Cothay Manor
Woodlands Castle
Barrington Court
Castle Hill Gardens
Knightshayes Court
Tiverton Castle
Stock Gayland House
Higher Melcombe
Minterne Gardens
Forde Abbey & Gardens
Mapperton
Fursdon House
Downes
Escot Gardens, Maze & Forest Adventure
Athelhampton House & Gardens
Wolfeton House
Okehampton Castle
Custom House Exeter
Great Fulford
Culver House
Cadhay
Sand
Church of Our Lady & St Ignatius
Abbotsbury Subtropical Gardens
Powderham Castle
Ugbrooke
Lulworth Castle & Park
Portland Castle
Buckfast Abbey
Buckland Abbey
House
Shilstone
Dartmouth Castle
Sausmarez Manor
SWANSEA
BRIDGEND
RHONDDA CYNON TAFF
CAERPHILLY
CARDIFF
NEWPORT
VALE OF GLAMORGAN
SOUTH GLOUCESTERSHIRE
BRISTOL
NORTH SOMERSET
SOMERSET
Exmoor
Mendip Hills
Brendon Hills
Polden Hills
Blackdown Hills
DEVON
DORSET
Dartmoor
TORBAY
PLYMOUTH
EXETER
Chesil Beach
Portland Bill
GUERNSEY
MAP 2

MAP 3

A B C D E F G H

1 2 3 4 5 6 7 8 9 10 11 12

Chavenage
TWIGS Community Gardens
Lydiard Park
Milton Manor House
Ardington House
Hughenden
Wildmere Farm Chapel
Stonor
Freeman Mausoleum
Greys Court
Hall Barn
Gothic Temple
Mapledurham & Watermill
Dorney Court
Eton College
St George's Chapel
Frogmore House
Osterley Park
Kew Gdns
Kew Palace
Ham House
Strawberry Hill
Corsham Court
Shaw House
Stratfield Saye House
Great Fosters
Claremont Landscape Garden
Hampton Court
Whitehall
Painshill Park Landscape Garden
Clandon Park & Hatchlands Park
Polesden Lacey
Shalford Mill
Highclere Castle, Gardens & Egyptian Exhibition
Farnham Castle
Goddards
Stonehenge
Great Hall & Queen Eleanor's Garden Winchester Cathedral Winchester City Mill
Northington Grange
Jane Austen's House
Chawton House Library
Gilbert White's House
Old Sarum
Houghton Lodge
Avington Park
Wilton House
Mompesson House
Hinton Ampner Garden
Petworth House & Park
Old Wardour Castle
Norrington Manor
Newhouse
Hamptworth Lodge
King John's House
Broadlands
Sir Harold Hillier Gardens
Woolbeding Gardens
Cowdray Ruins
Uppark
Weald & Downland Open Air Museum
West Dean Gardens
Parham House & Gardens
Bramber Castle
St Mary's
Edmondsham House
Stansted Park
Goodwood House
Denmans
Kingston Lacy
Portchester Castle
St Agatha's Church
Chichester Cathedral
Pallant House
Charles Dickens' Birthplace Museum
Arundel Castle
Arundel Cathedral
Highdown Gardens
Beaulieu
Exbury Gardens
Highcliffe Castle
Osborne House
Nunwell House & Gardens
Yarmouth Castle
Carisbrooke Castle
Clavell Tower
Appuldurcombe House
Isle of Wight

WILTSHIRE
WEST BERKSHIRE
HAMPSHIRE
SURREY
W. SUSSEX
ISLE OF WIGHT
Salisbury Plain
New Forest
Lambourn Downs
The Needles
SWINDON
LYNEHAM
READING
WOKINGHAM
BRACKNELL FOREST
WINDSOR & MAIDENHEAD
HEATHROW
GATWICK
SOUTHAMPTON
PORTSMOUTH
BOURNEMOUTH
POOLE
SHOREHAM

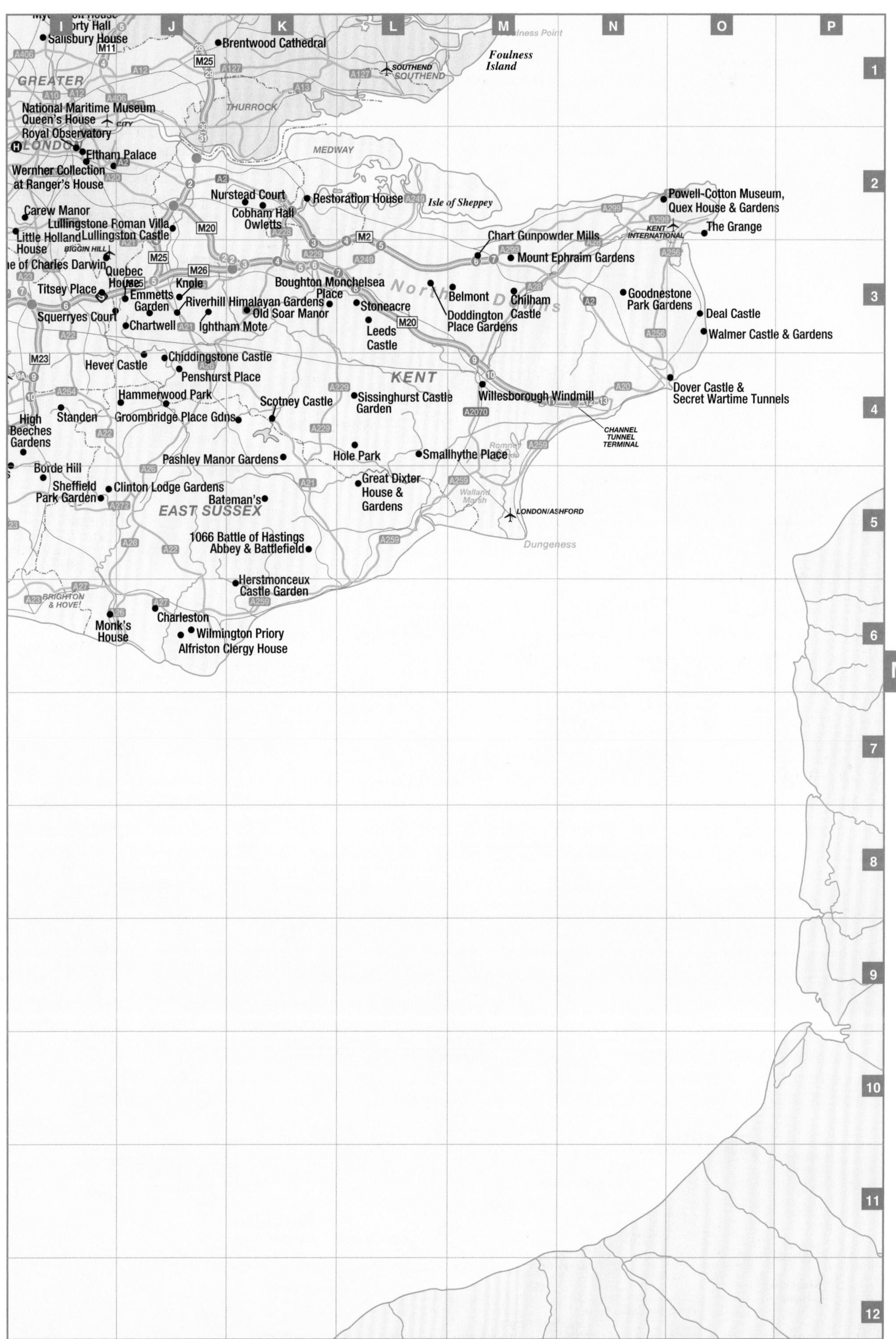
MAP 4
Salisbury House
Brentwood Cathedral
Foulness Island
National Maritime Museum
Queen's House
Royal Observatory
Eltham Palace
Wernher Collection at Ranger's House
Nurstead Court
Cobham Hall
Owletts
Restoration House
Isle of Sheppey
Powell-Cotton Museum, Quex House & Gardens
The Grange
Carew Manor
Lullingstone Roman Villa
Lullingston Castle
Little Holland House
Chart Gunpowder Mills
Mount Ephraim Gardens
Boughton Monchelsea Place
Belmont
Chilham Castle
Goodnestone Park Gardens
Deal Castle
Walmer Castle & Gardens
Titsey Place
Quebec House
Emmetts Garden
Knole
Riverhill Himalayan Gardens
Old Soar Manor
Stoneacre
Leeds Castle
Doddington Place Gardens
Squerryes Court
Chartwell
Ightham Mote
Hever Castle
Chiddingstone Castle
Penshurst Place
KENT
Dover Castle & Secret Wartime Tunnels
Hammerwood Park
Scotney Castle
Sissinghurst Castle Garden
Willesborough Windmill
High Beeches Gardens
Standen
Groombridge Place Gdns
Pashley Manor Gardens
Hole Park
Smallhythe Place
Borde Hill
Sheffield Park Garden
Clinton Lodge Gardens
Great Dixter House & Gardens
Bateman's
EAST SUSSEX
1066 Battle of Hastings Abbey & Battlefield
Herstmonceux Castle Garden
Charleston
Monk's House
Wilmington Priory
Alfriston Clergy House

MAP 5

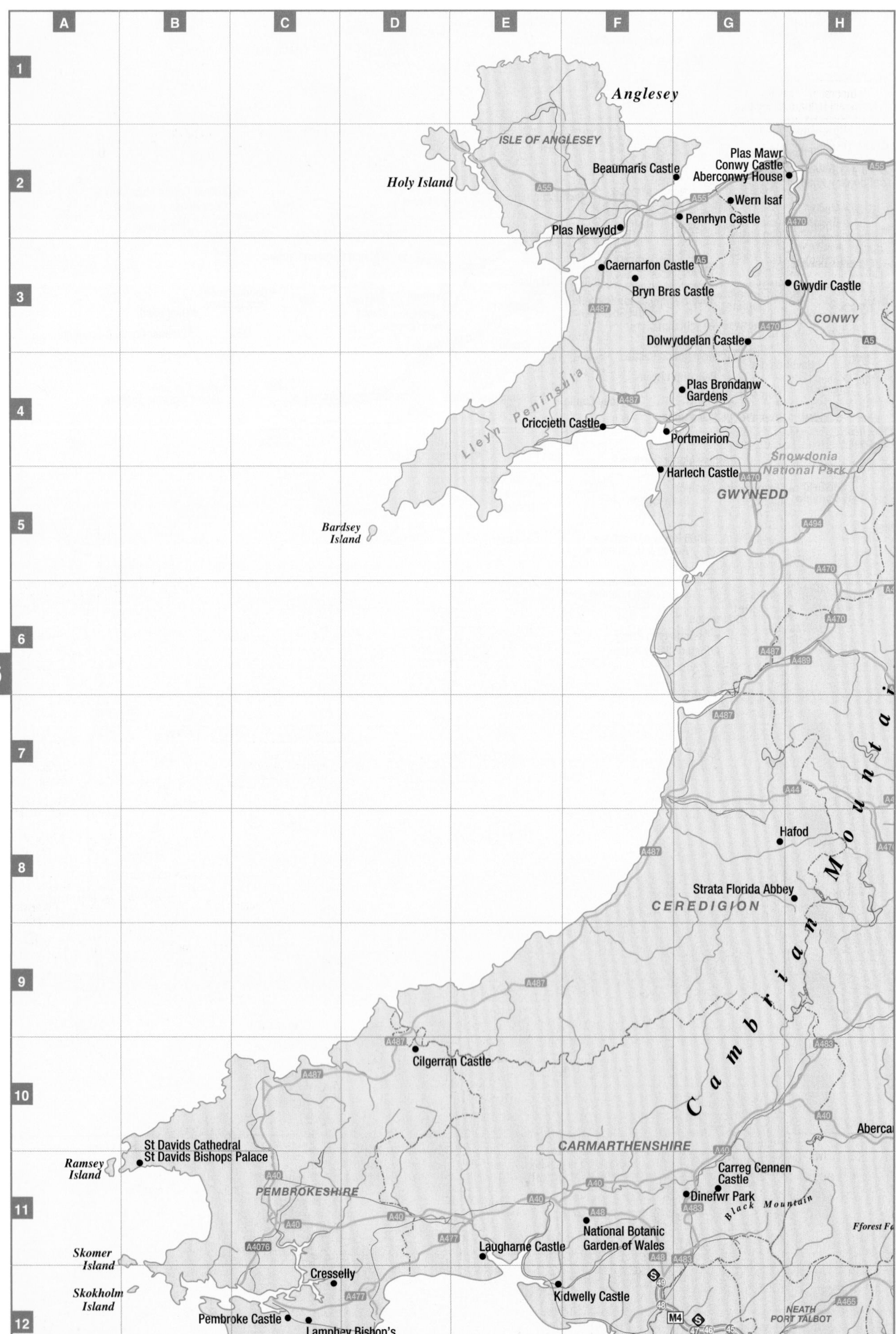
A
B
C
D
E
F
G
H
1
2
3
4
5
6
7
8
9
10
11
12
Anglesey
ISLE OF ANGLESEY
Holy Island
Beaumaris Castle
Plas Mawr
Conwy Castle
Aberconwy House
Wern Isaf
Penrhyn Castle
Plas Newydd
Caernarfon Castle
Bryn Bras Castle
Gwydir Castle
CONWY
Dolwyddelan Castle
Plas Brondanw
Gardens
Lleyn Peninsula
Criccieth Castle
Portmeirion
Snowdonia
National Park
Harlech Castle
GWYNEDD
Bardsey
Island
Hafod
Strata Florida Abbey
CEREDIGION
Cambrian Mountains
Cilgerran Castle
CARMARTHENSHIRE
Aberca
Ramsey
Island
St Davids Cathedral
St Davids Bishops Palace
PEMBROKESHIRE
Carreg Cennen
Castle
Dinefwr Park
Black Mountain
National Botanic
Garden of Wales
Fforest Fa
Skomer
Island
Laugharne Castle
Cresselly
Skokholm
Island
Kidwelly Castle
NEATH
PORT TALBOT
Pembroke Castle
Lamphey Bishop's
Palace
Weobley
A55
A5
A470
A487
A494
A489
A44
A485
A40
A48
A483
A477
A4076
A465
M4

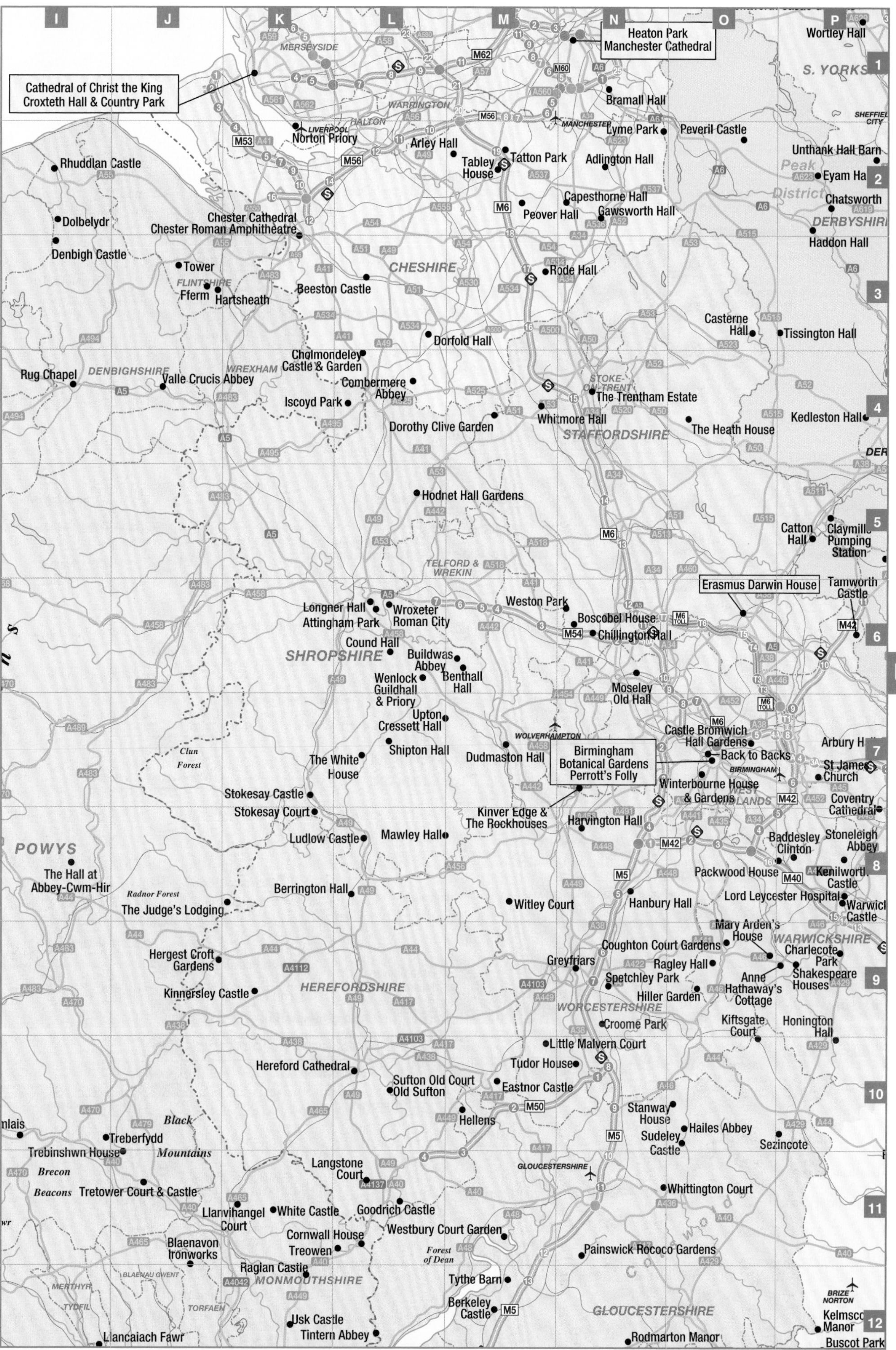

I
J
K
L
M
N
O
P
MAP 6
Heaton Park
Manchester Cathedral
Wortley Hall
S. YORKS
Cathedral of Christ the King
Croxteth Hall & Country Park
MERSEYSIDE
WARRINGTON
HALTON
LIVERPOOL
MANCHESTER
Bramall Hall
Norton Priory
Arley Hall
Lyme Park
Peveril Castle
Unthank Hall Barn
Tatton Park
Tabley House
Adlington Hall
Peak District
Eyam Hall
Rhuddlan Castle
Capesthorne Hall
Peover Hall
Gawsworth Hall
Chatsworth
DERBYSHIRE
Dolbelydr
Chester Cathedral
Chester Roman Amphitheatre
Haddon Hall
Denbigh Castle
Tower
CHESHIRE
Rode Hall
FLINTSHIRE
Fferm
Hartsheath
Beeston Castle
Casterne Hall
Tissington Hall
Dorfold Hall
Cholmondeley Castle & Garden
WREXHAM
DENBIGHSHIRE
Rug Chapel
Valle Crucis Abbey
Combermere Abbey
STOKE-ON-TRENT
The Trentham Estate
Iscoyd Park
Kedleston Hall
Whitmore Hall
Dorothy Clive Garden
The Heath House
STAFFORDSHIRE
Hodnet Hall Gardens
Catton Hall
Claymills Pumping Station
TELFORD & WREKIN
Erasmus Darwin House
Tamworth Castle
Longner Hall
Attingham Park
Wroxeter Roman City
Weston Park
Boscobel House
Chillington Hall
Cound Hall
SHROPSHIRE
Buildwas Abbey
Benthall Hall
Wenlock Guildhall & Priory
Moseley Old Hall
Upton Cressett Hall
WOLVERHAMPTON
Castle Bromwich Hall Gardens
Arbury Hall
Shipton Hall
The White House
Dudmaston Hall
Birmingham Botanical Gardens
Perrott's Folly
Back to Backs
BIRMINGHAM
St James Church
Clun Forest
Stokesay Castle
Stokesay Court
Winterbourne House & Gardens
WEST MIDLANDS
Coventry Cathedral
Kinver Edge & The Rockhouses
Harvington Hall
Ludlow Castle
Mawley Hall
Baddesley Clinton
Stoneleigh Abbey
POWYS
The Hall at Abbey-Cwm-Hir
Packwood House
Kenilworth Castle
Radnor Forest
Berrington Hall
Lord Leycester Hospital
The Judge's Lodging
Witley Court
Hanbury Hall
Warwick Castle
Mary Arden's House
Coughton Court Gardens
WARWICKSHIRE
Charlecote Park
Hergest Croft Gardens
Greyfriars
Ragley Hall
Anne Hathaway's Cottage
Shakespeare Houses
Spetchley Park
Kinnersley Castle
HEREFORDSHIRE
Hiller Garden
WORCESTERSHIRE
Kiftsgate Court
Honington Hall
Croome Park
Little Malvern Court
Hereford Cathedral
Tudor House
Sufton Old Court
Old Sufton
Eastnor Castle
Stanway House
Black Mountains
Hellens
Hailes Abbey
Treberfydd
Sudeley Castle
Sezincote
Trebinshwn House
Langstone Court
Brecon Beacons
Tretower Court & Castle
GLOUCESTERSHIRE
Whittington Court
Llanvihangel Court
White Castle
Goodrich Castle
Westbury Court Garden
Cornwall House
Treowen
Blaenavon Ironworks
Forest of Dean
Painswick Rococo Gardens
Raglan Castle
BLAENAU GWENT
MONMOUTHSHIRE
Tythe Barn
Cotswolds
MERTHYR TYDFIL
BRIZE NORTON
Berkeley Castle
TORFAEN
GLOUCESTERSHIRE
Usk Castle
Tintern Abbey
Kelmscott Manor
Llancaiach Fawr
Rodmarton Manor
Buscot Park

MAP 7

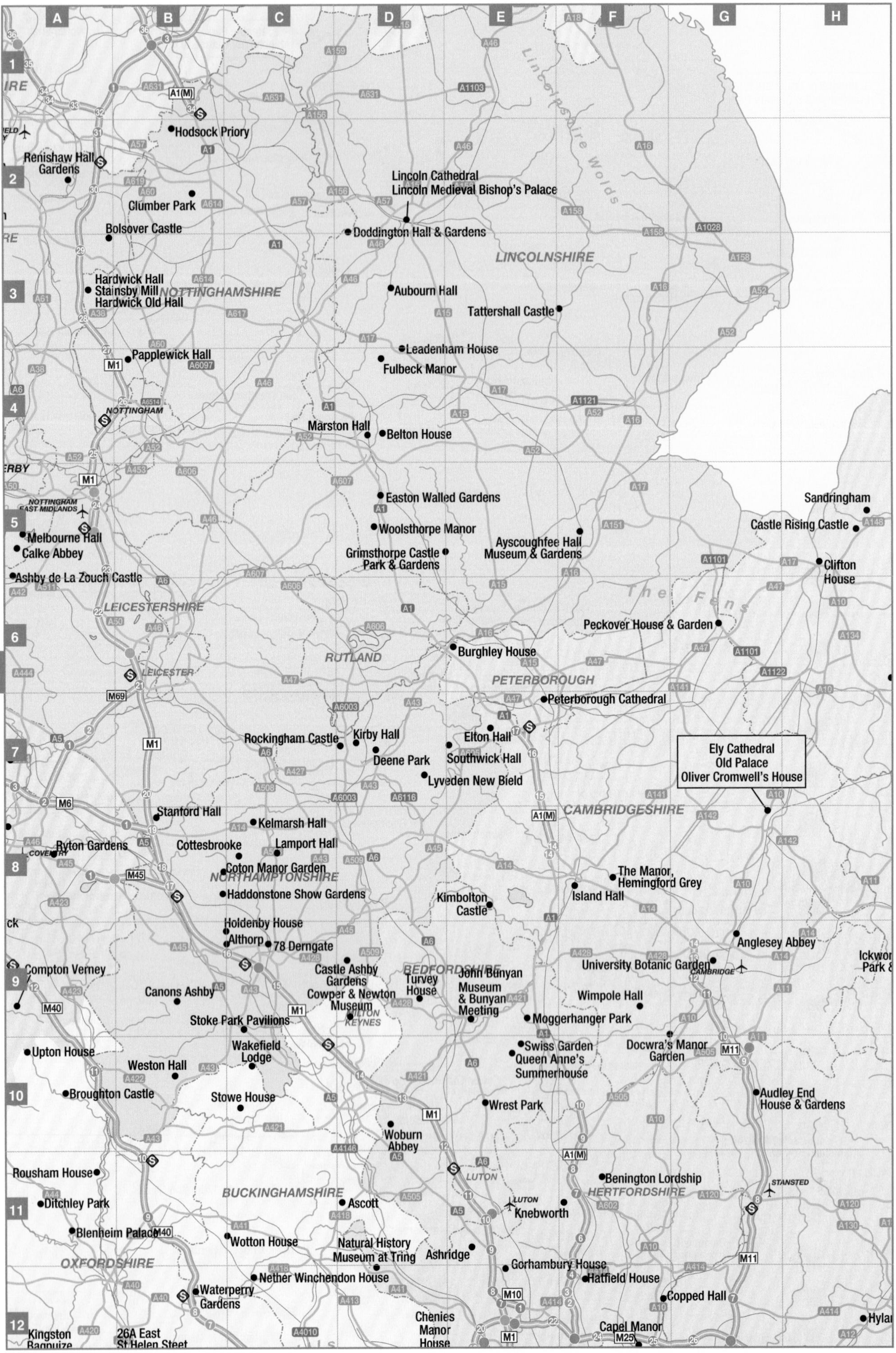

Hodsock Priory
Renishaw Hall Gardens
Clumber Park
Lincoln Cathedral
Lincoln Medieval Bishop's Palace
Bolsover Castle
Doddington Hall & Gardens
LINCOLNSHIRE
Hardwick Hall
Stainsby Mill
Hardwick Old Hall
NOTTINGHAMSHIRE
Aubourn Hall
Tattershall Castle
Leadenham House
Papplewick Hall
Fulbeck Manor
NOTTINGHAM
Marston Hall
Belton House
Easton Walled Gardens
Sandringham
Castle Rising Castle
Melbourne Hall
Woolsthorpe Manor
Calke Abbey
Grimsthorpe Castle Park & Gardens
Ayscoughfee Hall Museum & Gardens
Clifton House
Ashby de La Zouch Castle
The Fens
LEICESTERSHIRE
Peckover House & Garden
Burghley House
RUTLAND
LEICESTER
PETERBOROUGH
Peterborough Cathedral
Rockingham Castle
Kirby Hall
Elton Hall
Deene Park
Southwick Hall
Ely Cathedral
Old Palace
Oliver Cromwell's House
Lyveden New Bield
CAMBRIDGESHIRE
Stanford Hall
Kelmarsh Hall
Ryton Gardens
Cottesbrooke
Lamport Hall
Coton Manor Garden
NORTHAMPTONSHIRE
The Manor, Hemingford Grey
Island Hall
Haddonstone Show Gardens
Kimbolton Castle
Holdenby House
Althorp
78 Derngate
Anglesey Abbey
Compton Verney
Castle Ashby Gardens
BEDFORDSHIRE
Turvey House
John Bunyan Museum & Bunyan Meeting
University Botanic Garden
Canons Ashby
Cowper & Newton Museum
Wimpole Hall
Stoke Park Pavilions
MILTON KEYNES
Moggerhanger Park
Upton House
Wakefield Lodge
Swiss Garden
Queen Anne's Summerhouse
Docwra's Manor Garden
Weston Hall
Broughton Castle
Stowe House
Audley End House & Gardens
Wrest Park
Woburn Abbey
Rousham House
LUTON
Benington Lordship
HERTFORDSHIRE
BUCKINGHAMSHIRE
Ditchley Park
Ascott
Knebworth
Blenheim Palace
Wotton House
Natural History Museum at Tring
Ashridge
OXFORDSHIRE
Gorhambury House
Hatfield House
Nether Winchendon House
Waterperry Gardens
Copped Hall
Chenies Manor House
Capel Manor
Kingston Bagpuize
26A East St Helen Street

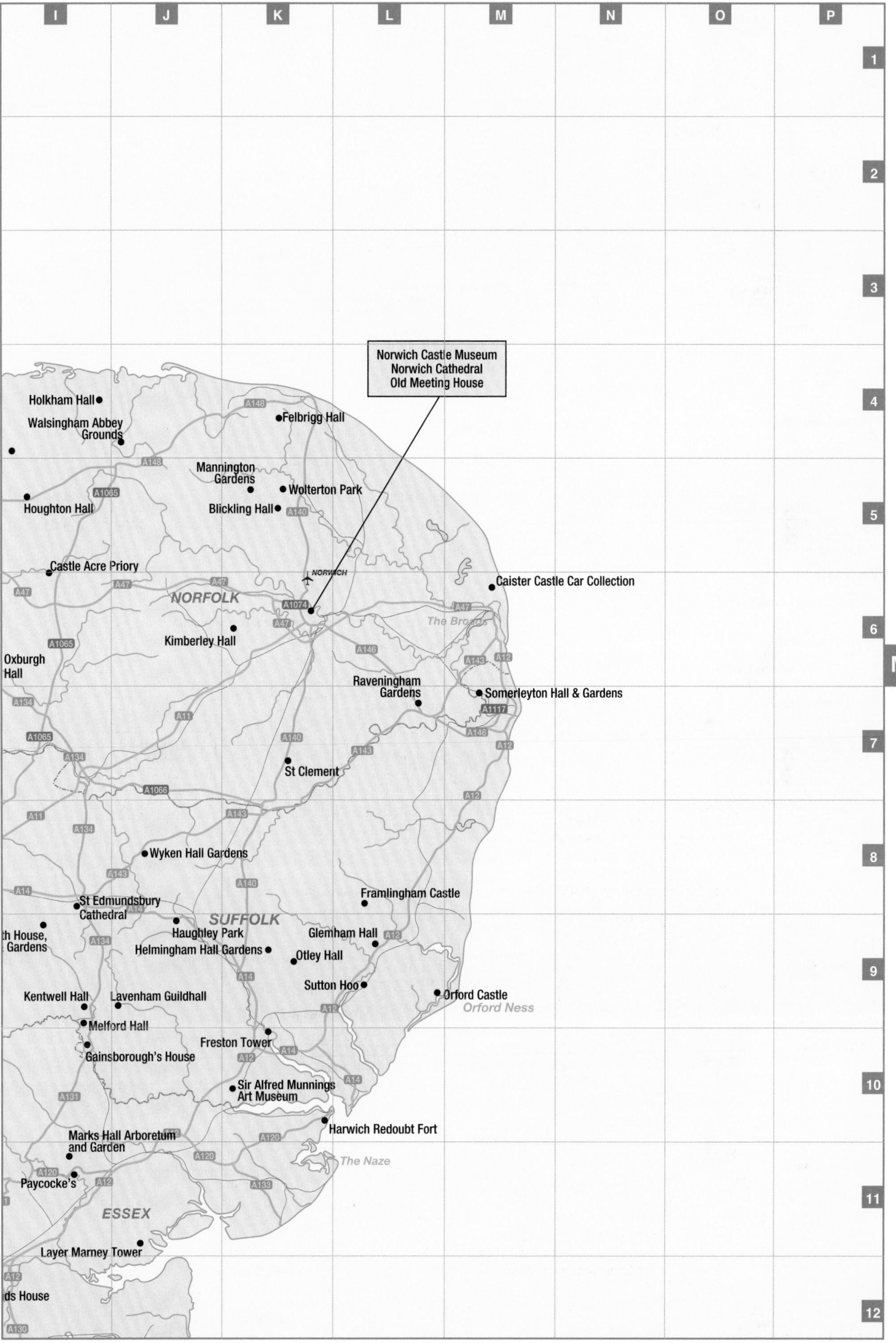
I
J
K
L
M
N
O
P
1
2
3
4
5
6
7
8
9
10
11
12
Norwich Castle Museum
Norwich Cathedral
Old Meeting House
Holkham Hall
Walsingham Abbey Grounds
Felbrigg Hall
Mannington Gardens
Wolterton Park
Houghton Hall
Blickling Hall
Castle Acre Priory
NORWICH
Caister Castle Car Collection
NORFOLK
The Broads
Kimberley Hall
Oxburgh Hall
Raveningham Gardens
Somerleyton Hall & Gardens
St Clement
Wyken Hall Gardens
Framlingham Castle
St Edmundsbury Cathedral
SUFFOLK
Haughley Park
Glemham Hall
Helmingham Hall Gardens
Otley Hall
Sutton Hoo
Orford Castle
Orford Ness
Kentwell Hall
Lavenham Guildhall
Melford Hall
Freston Tower
Gainsborough's House
Sir Alfred Munnings Art Museum
Harwich Redoubt Fort
Marks Hall Arboretum and Garden
The Naze
Paycocke's
ESSEX
Layer Marney Tower
MAP 8

MAP 9

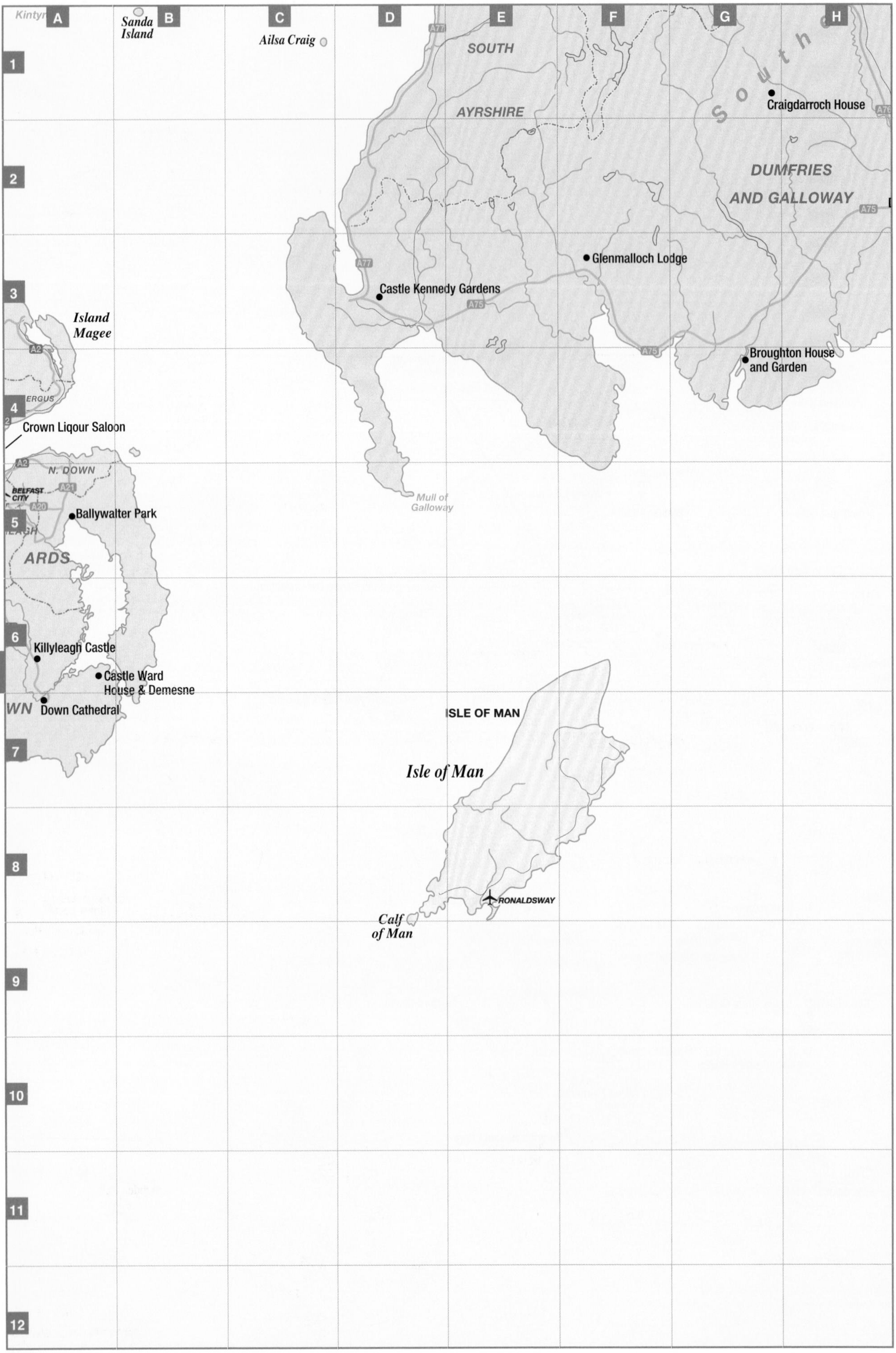

A B C D E F G H

1 2 3 4 5 6 7 8 9 10 11 12

Kintyre
Sanda Island
Ailsa Craig
SOUTH AYRSHIRE
South
Craigdarroch House
DUMFRIES AND GALLOWAY
Glenmalloch Lodge
Castle Kennedy Gardens
Broughton House and Garden
Island Magee
Crown Liqour Saloon
N. DOWN
BELFAST CITY
Ballywalter Park
ARDS
Killyleagh Castle
Castle Ward House & Demesne
Down Cathedral
Mull of Galloway
ISLE OF MAN
Isle of Man
RONALDSWAY
Calf of Man

A77 A75 A2 A21 A20 A76

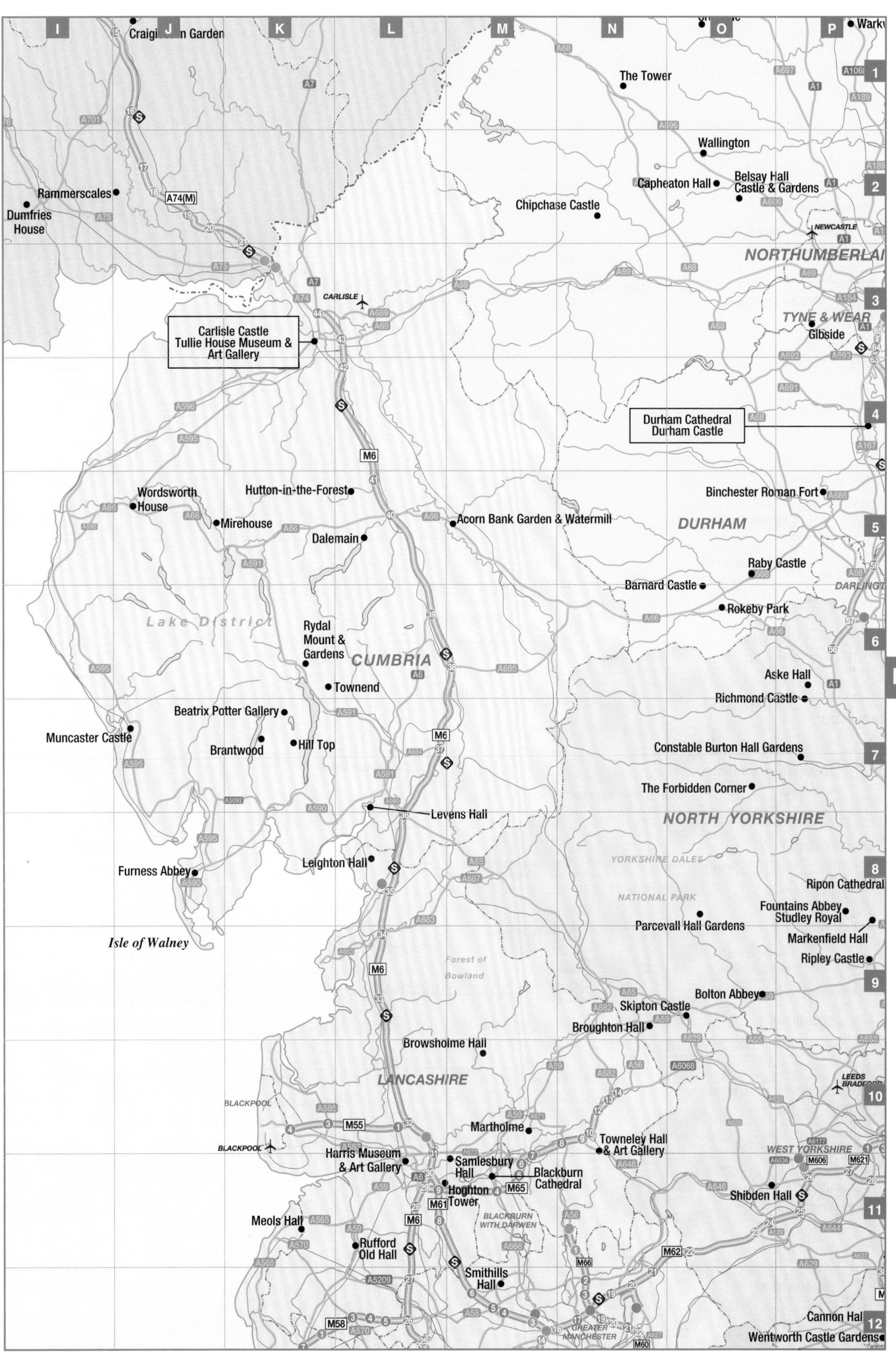

MAP 10
Craigieburn Garden
The Tower
Wallington
Capheaton Hall
Belsay Hall Castle & Gardens
Chipchase Castle
Rammerscales
Dumfries House
NORTHUMBERLAND
CARLISLE
TYNE & WEAR
Gibside
Carlisle Castle Tullie House Museum & Art Gallery
Durham Cathedral Durham Castle
Wordsworth House
Hutton-in-the-Forest
Binchester Roman Fort
Mirehouse
Acorn Bank Garden & Watermill
DURHAM
Dalemain
Raby Castle
Barnard Castle
Rokeby Park
Lake District
Rydal Mount & Gardens
CUMBRIA
Townend
Aske Hall
Richmond Castle
Beatrix Potter Gallery
Muncaster Castle
Brantwood
Hill Top
Constable Burton Hall Gardens
The Forbidden Corner
Levens Hall
NORTH YORKSHIRE
YORKSHIRE DALES
NATIONAL PARK
Leighton Hall
Furness Abbey
Ripon Cathedral
Fountains Abbey Studley Royal
Parcevall Hall Gardens
Markenfield Hall
Isle of Walney
Ripley Castle
Forest of Bowland
Bolton Abbey
Skipton Castle
Broughton Hall
Browsholme Hall
LANCASHIRE
BLACKPOOL
LEEDS BRADFORD
Martholme
Towneley Hall & Art Gallery
Harris Museum & Art Gallery
Samlesbury Hall
Blackburn Cathedral
WEST YORKSHIRE
Hoghton Tower
Shibden Hall
BLACKBURN WITH DARWEN
Meols Hall
Rufford Old Hall
Smithills Hall
GREATER MANCHESTER
Cannon Hall
Wentworth Castle Gardens

MAP 11

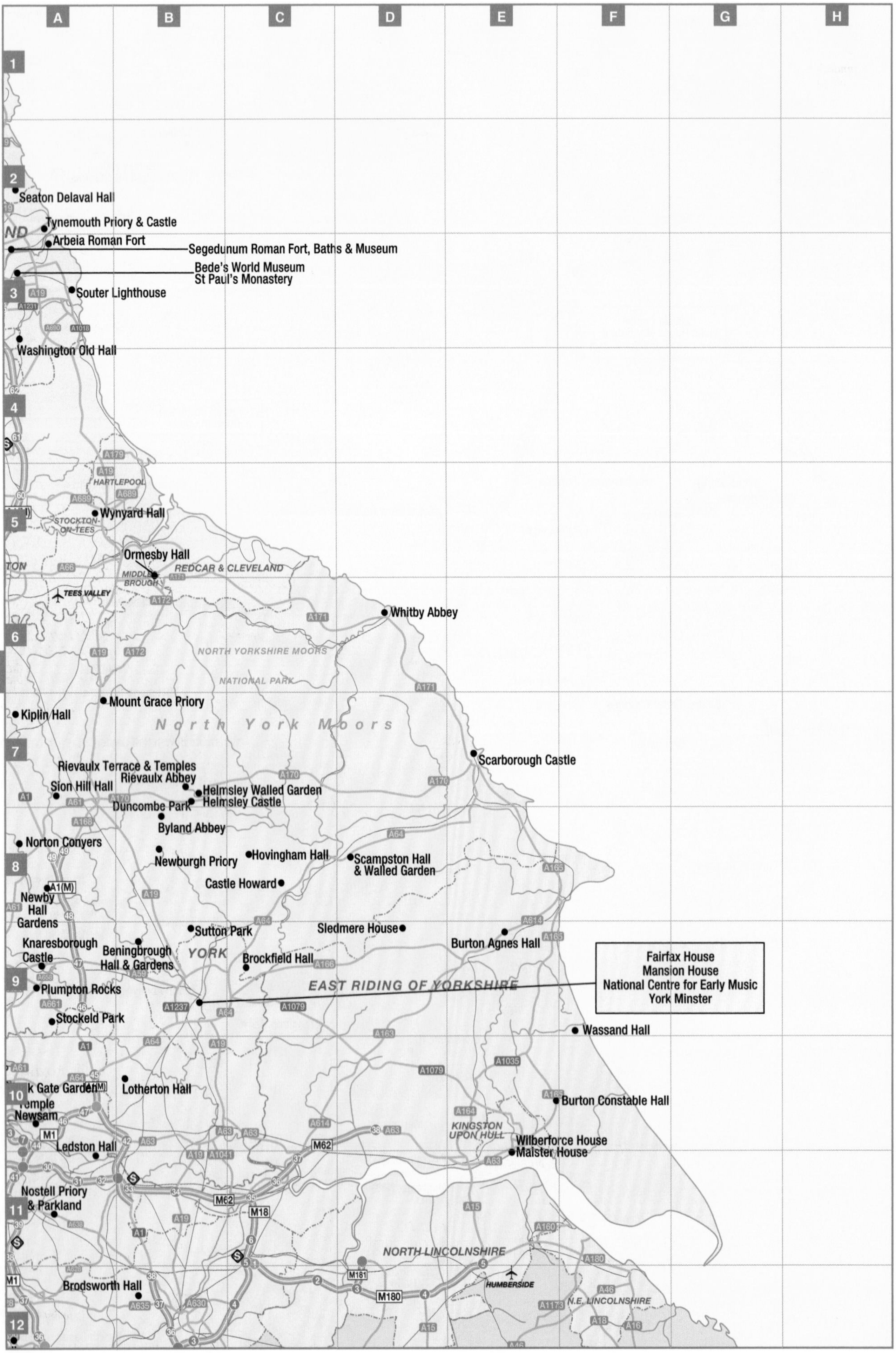

A B C D E F G H

1 2 3 4 5 6 7 8 9 10 11 12

Seaton Delaval Hall
Tynemouth Priory & Castle
Arbeia Roman Fort
Segedunum Roman Fort, Baths & Museum
Bede's World Museum
St Paul's Monastery
Souter Lighthouse
Washington Old Hall
HARTLEPOOL
Wynyard Hall
STOCKTON-ON-TEES
Ormesby Hall
MIDDLESBROUGH
REDCAR & CLEVELAND
TEES VALLEY
Whitby Abbey
NORTH YORKSHIRE MOORS
NATIONAL PARK
Mount Grace Priory
Kiplin Hall
North York Moors
Scarborough Castle
Rievaulx Terrace & Temples
Rievaulx Abbey
Sion Hill Hall
Helmsley Walled Garden
Helmsley Castle
Duncombe Park
Byland Abbey
Norton Conyers
Newburgh Priory
Hovingham Hall
Scampston Hall & Walled Garden
Castle Howard
Newby Hall Gardens
Sutton Park
Sledmere House
Knaresborough Castle
Beningbrough Hall & Gardens
YORK
Brockfield Hall
Burton Agnes Hall
Fairfax House
Mansion House
National Centre for Early Music
York Minster
EAST RIDING OF YORKSHIRE
Plumpton Rocks
Stockeld Park
Wassand Hall
Lotherton Hall
Temple Newsam
Burton Constable Hall
KINGSTON UPON HULL
Ledston Hall
Wilberforce House
Maister House
Nostell Priory & Parkland
NORTH LINCOLNSHIRE
HUMBERSIDE
Brodsworth Hall
N.E. LINCOLNSHIRE

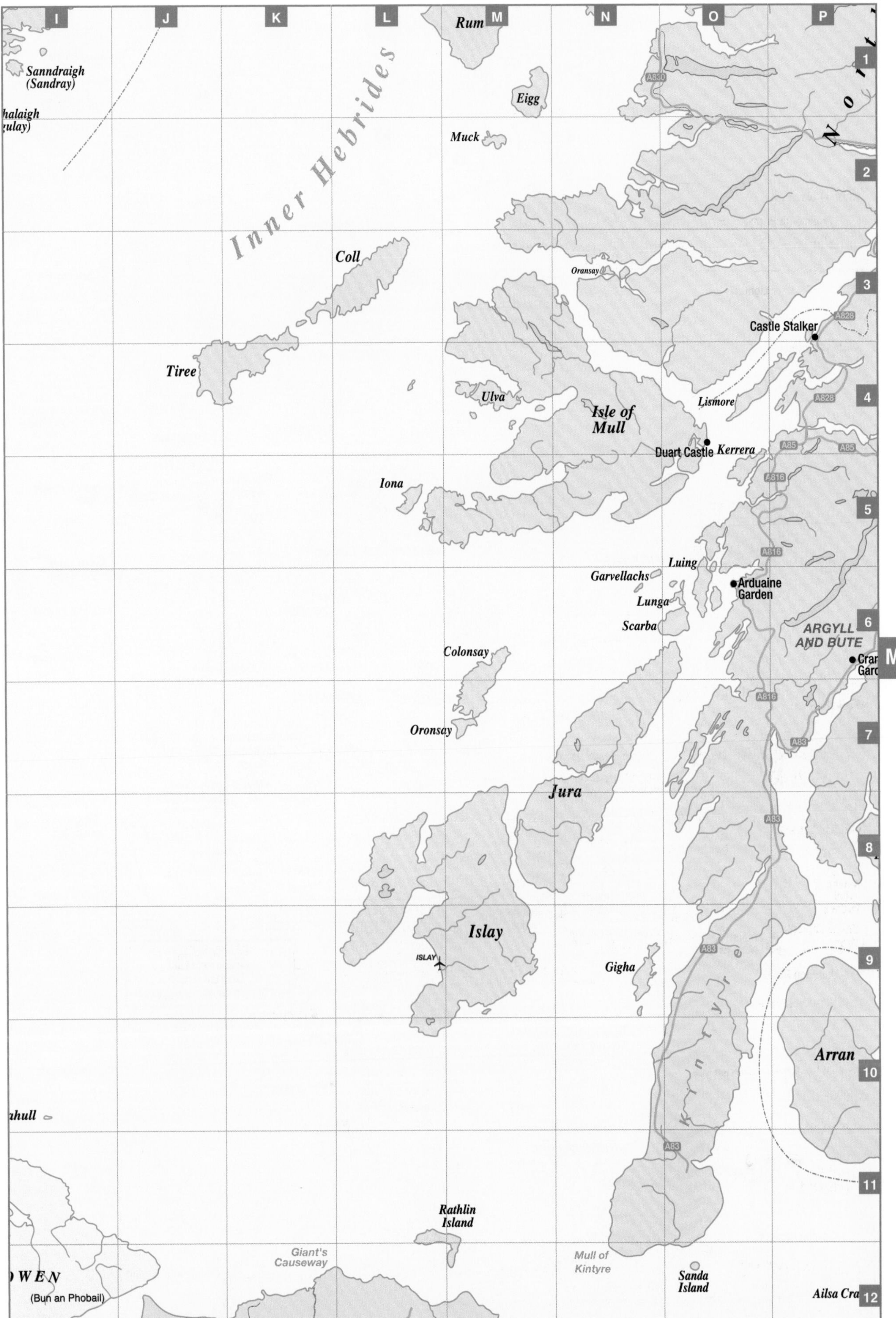

I
J
K
L
M
N
O
P
1
2
3
4
5
6
7
8
9
10
11
12
Rum
Sanndraigh
(Sandray)
Eigg
Muck
Inner Hebrides
Coll
Tiree
Oransay
Castle Stalker
Ulva
Isle of
Mull
Lismore
Duart Castle
Kerrera
Iona
Luing
Garvellachs
Arduaine
Garden
Lunga
Scarba
ARGYLL
AND BUTE
Colonsay
Oronsay
Jura
Islay
ISLAY
Gigha
Kintyre
Arran
Rathlin
Island
Giant's
Causeway
Mull of
Kintyre
Sanda
Island
(Bun an Phobail)
A830
A828
A85
A816
A83

MAP 12

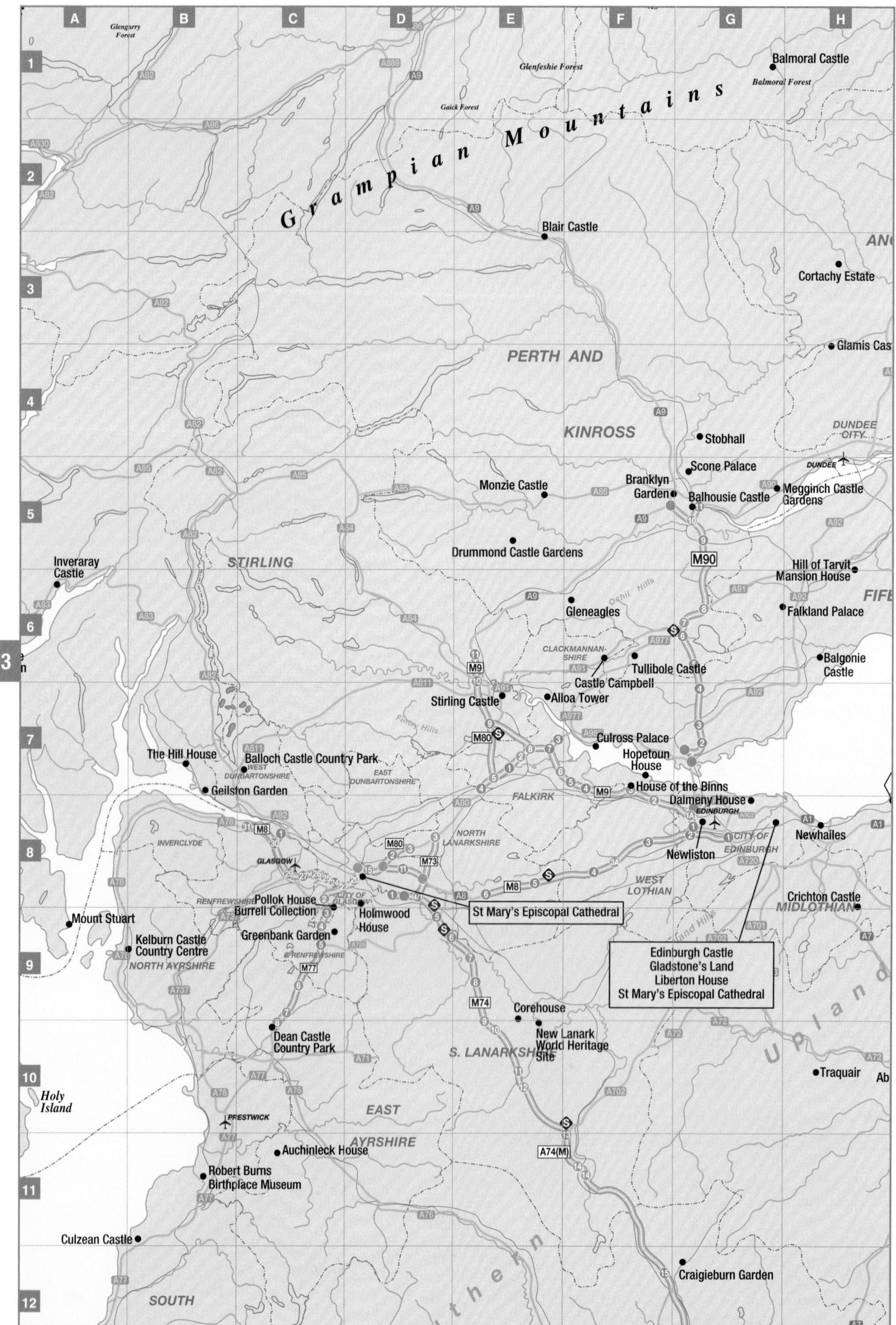
MAP 13
Grampian Mountains
Balmoral Castle
Blair Castle
Cortachy Estate
Glamis Castle
PERTH AND KINROSS
Stobhall
Scone Palace
Monzie Castle
Branklyn Garden
Balhousie Castle
Megginch Castle Gardens
Drummond Castle Gardens
Inveraray Castle
STIRLING
Hill of Tarvit Mansion House
Gleneagles
Falkland Palace
Castle Campbell
Tullibole Castle
Balgonie Castle
Stirling Castle
Alloa Tower
Culross Palace
Hopetoun House
The Hill House
Balloch Castle Country Park
Geilston Garden
House of the Binns
Dalmeny House
Newhailes
Newliston
St Mary's Episcopal Cathedral
Pollok House
Burrell Collection
Holmwood House
Mount Stuart
Greenbank Garden
Kelburn Castle Country Centre
NORTH AYRSHIRE
Crichton Castle
Edinburgh Castle
Gladstone's Land
Liberton House
St Mary's Episcopal Cathedral
Corehouse
New Lanark World Heritage Site
Dean Castle Country Park
S. LANARKSHIRE
Traquair
Holy Island
EAST AYRSHIRE
Auchinleck House
Robert Burns Birthplace Museum
Culzean Castle
Craigieburn Garden
SOUTH

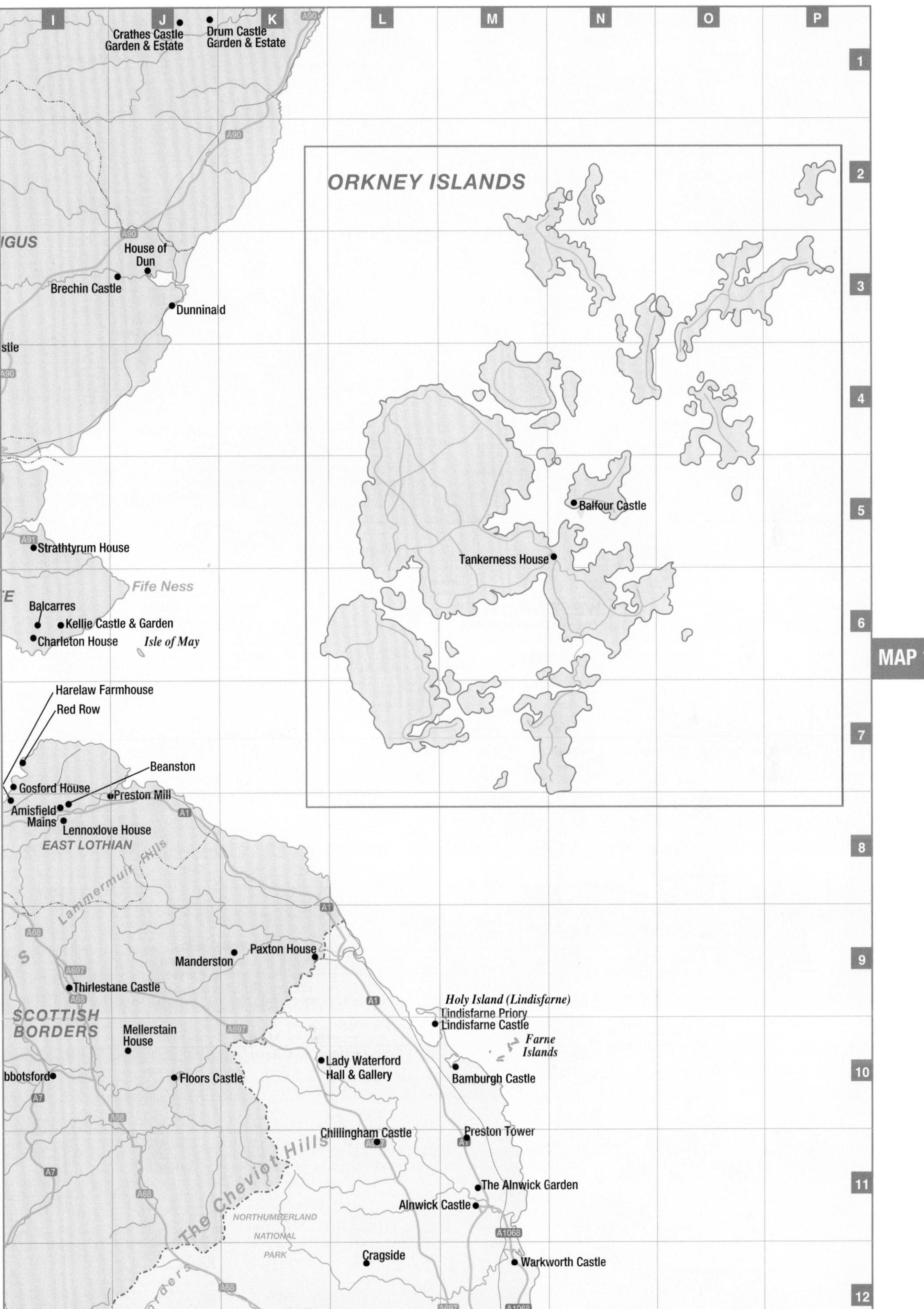
MAP 14
ORKNEY ISLANDS
Balfour Castle
Tankerness House
Crathes Castle Garden & Estate
Drum Castle Garden & Estate
House of Dun
Brechin Castle
Dunninald
Strathtyrum House
Fife Ness
Balcarres
Kellie Castle & Garden
Charleton House
Isle of May
Harelaw Farmhouse
Red Row
Beanston
Gosford House
Preston Mill
Amisfield Mains
Lennoxlove House
EAST LOTHIAN
Lammermuir Hills
Paxton House
Manderston
Thirlestane Castle
SCOTTISH BORDERS
Mellerstain House
Abbotsford
Floors Castle
Holy Island (Lindisfarne)
Lindisfarne Priory
Lindisfarne Castle
Farne Islands
Lady Waterford Hall & Gallery
Bamburgh Castle
Chillingham Castle
Preston Tower
The Cheviot Hills
The Alnwick Garden
Alnwick Castle
NORTHUMBERLAND NATIONAL PARK
Cragside
Warkworth Castle
The Tower

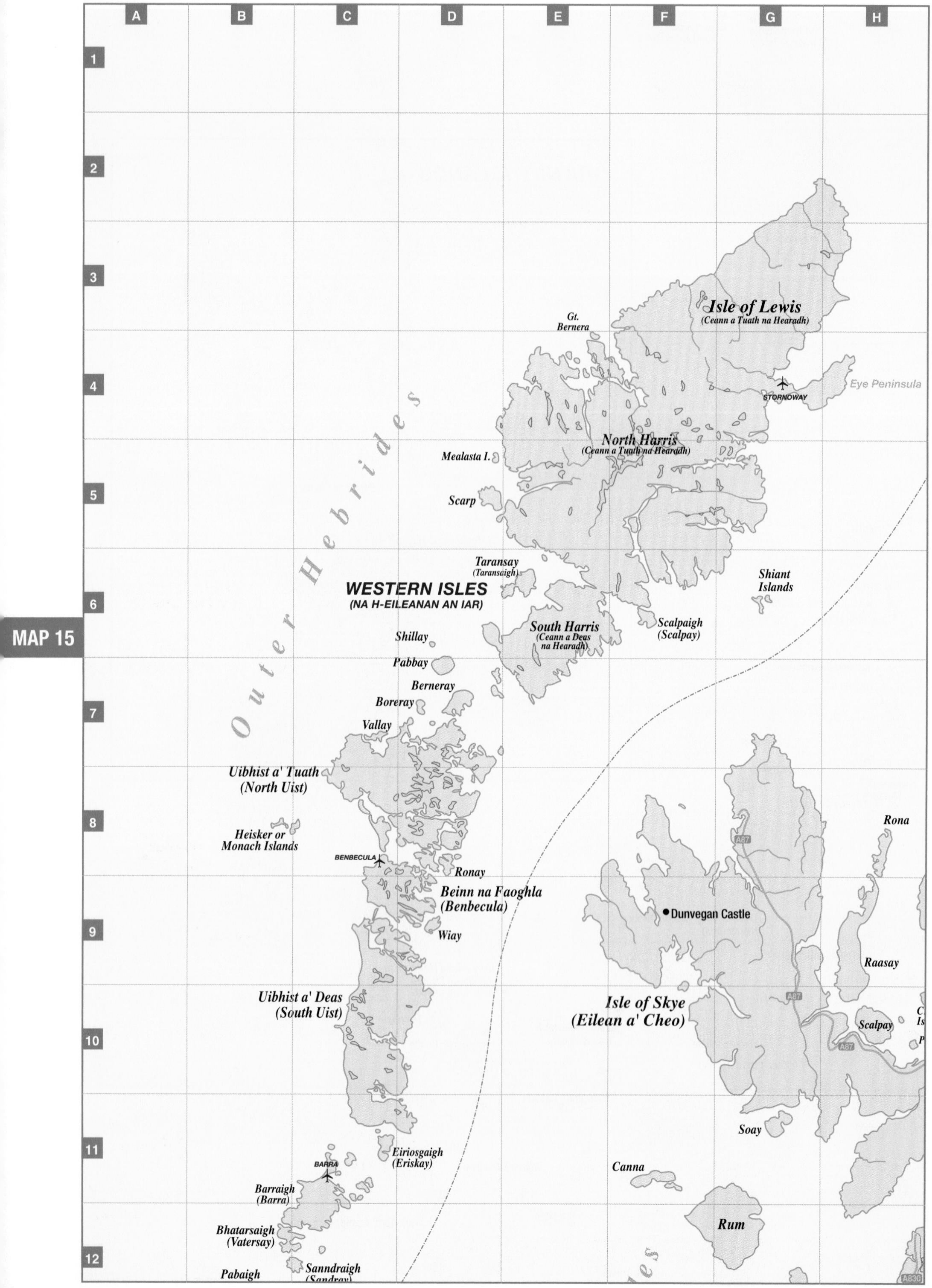

MAP 15

A B C D E F G H

1 2 3 4 5 6 7 8 9 10 11 12

Isle of Lewis
(Ceann a Tuath na Hearadh)

Gt. Bernera

Eye Peninsula

STORNOWAY

North Harris
(Ceann a Tuath na Hearadh)

Mealasta I.

Scarp

Outer Hebrides

Taransay
(Taransaigh)

WESTERN ISLES
(NA H-EILEANAN AN IAR)

Shiant Islands

South Harris
(Ceann a Deas na Hearadh)

Scalpaigh
(Scalpay)

Shillay

Pabbay

Berneray

Boreray

Vallay

Uibhist a' Tuath
(North Uist)

Heisker or Monach Islands

BENBECULA

Ronay

Beinn na Faoghla
(Benbecula)

Wiay

Rona

A87

Dunvegan Castle

Raasay

Uibhist a' Deas
(South Uist)

Isle of Skye
(Eilean a' Cheo)

Scalpay

Soay

Eiriosgaigh
(Eriskay)

BARRA

Canna

Barraigh
(Barra)

Rum

Bhatarsaigh
(Vatersay)

Pabaigh

Sanndraigh
(Sandray)

A830

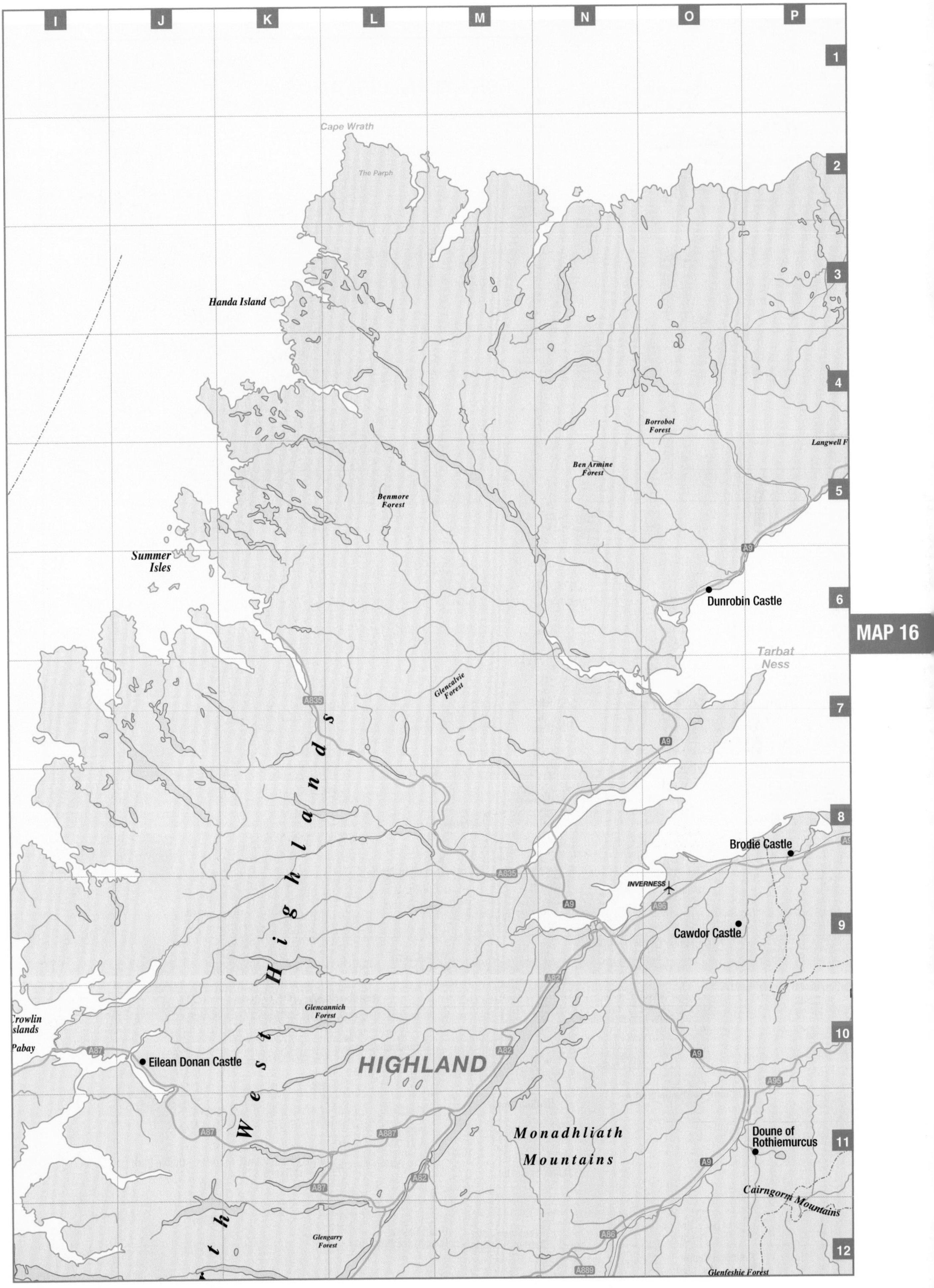

I J K L M N O P

1 2 3 4 5 6 7 8 9 10 11 12

MAP 16

Cape Wrath

The Parph

Handa Island

Borrobol Forest

Langwell F

Ben Armine Forest

Benmore Forest

Summer Isles

A9

Dunrobin Castle

Tarbat Ness

Glencalvie Forest

A835

A9

North West Highlands

Brodie Castle

A835

INVERNESS

A9

A96

Cawdor Castle

A82

Glencannich Forest

Crowlin Islands

Pabay

A87

Eilean Donan Castle

HIGHLAND

A82

A9

A95

Monadhliath Mountains

Doune of Rothiemurcus

A87

A887

A9

A82

A87

Cairngorm Mountains

Glengarry Forest

A86

A889

Glenfeshie Forest

MAP 17

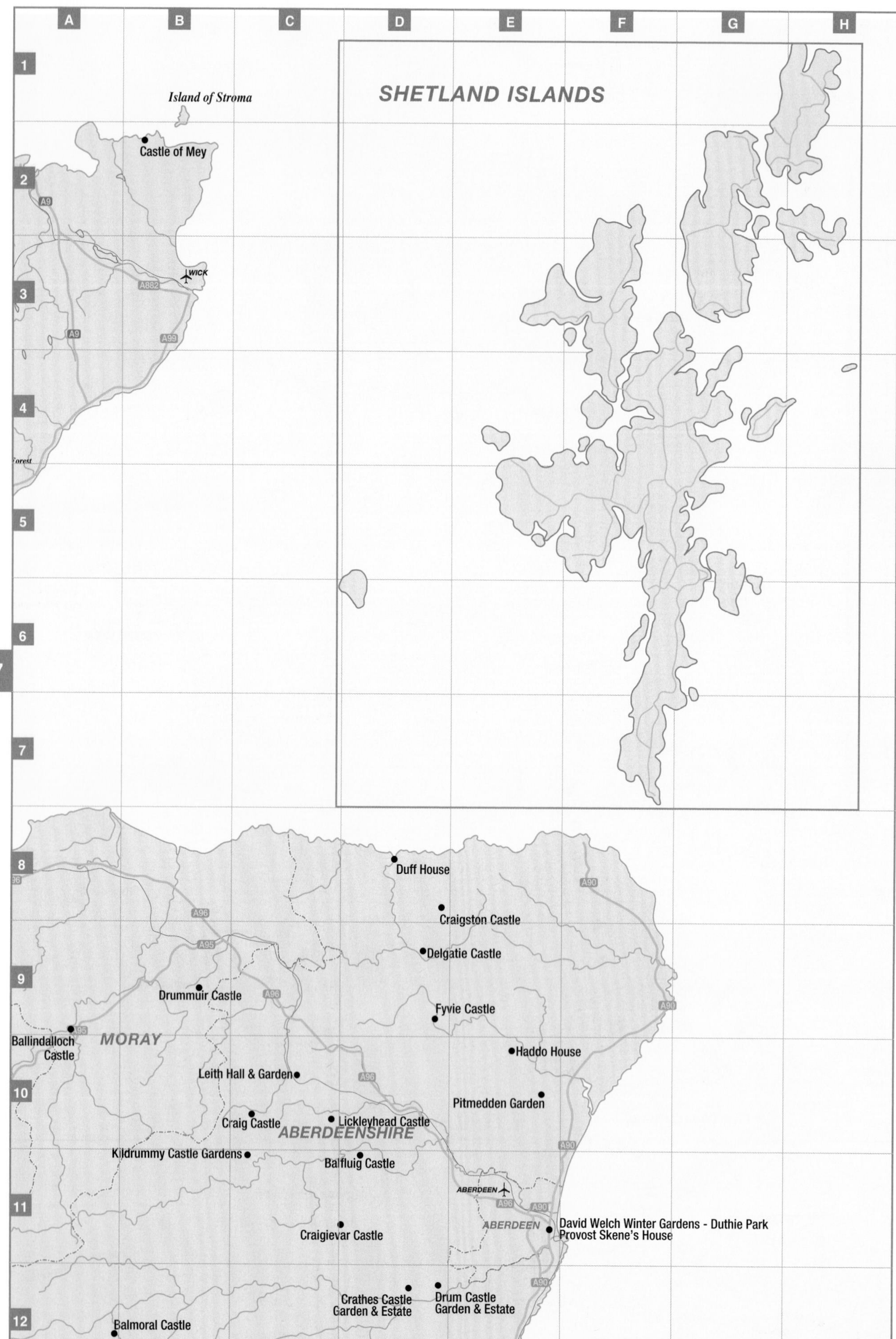
A
B
C
D
E
F
G
H
1
2
3
4
5
6
7
8
9
10
11
12
Island of Stroma
SHETLAND ISLANDS
Castle of Mey
A9
WICK
A882
A9
A99
Duff House
A90
A96
Craigston Castle
A95
Delgatie Castle
Drummuir Castle
A96
A90
Fyvie Castle
A95
Ballindalloch Castle
MORAY
Haddo House
Leith Hall & Garden
A96
Pitmedden Garden
Craig Castle
Lickleyhead Castle
ABERDEENSHIRE
Kildrummy Castle Gardens
Balfluig Castle
A90
ABERDEEN
A96
A90
Craigievar Castle
ABERDEEN
David Welch Winter Gardens - Duthie Park
Provost Skene's House
A90
Crathes Castle Garden & Estate
Drum Castle Garden & Estate
Balmoral Castle

MAP 18

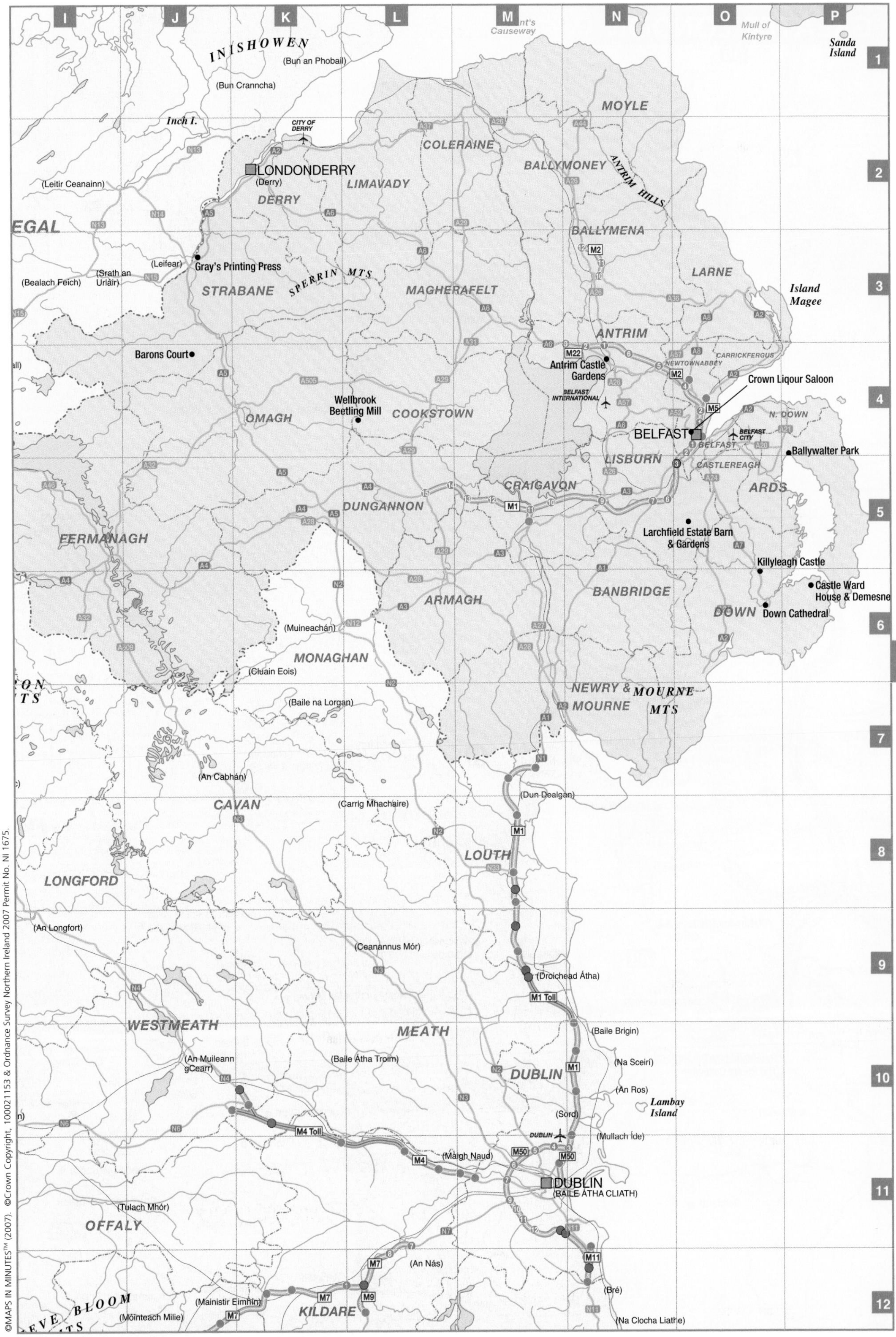

INISHOWEN
LONDONDERRY
(Derry)
DERRY
LIMAVADY
COLERAINE
BALLYMONEY
MOYLE
ANTRIM HILLS
BALLYMENA
LARNE
Island Magee
STRABANE
SPERRIN MTS
MAGHERAFELT
ANTRIM
Gray's Printing Press
Barons Court
Antrim Castle Gardens
Crown Liqour Saloon
Wellbrook Beetling Mill
OMAGH
COOKSTOWN
BELFAST
NEWTOWNABBEY
CARRICKFERGUS
N. DOWN
CASTLEREAGH
Ballywalter Park
LISBURN
CRAIGAVON
ARDS
DUNGANNON
FERMANAGH
Larchfield Estate Barn & Gardens
Killyleagh Castle
Castle Ward House & Demesne
ARMAGH
BANBRIDGE
DOWN
Down Cathedral
MONAGHAN
NEWRY & MOURNE
MOURNE MTS
CAVAN
LOUTH
LONGFORD
WESTMEATH
MEATH
DUBLIN
Lambay Island
DUBLIN
(BAILE ÁTHA CLIATH)
OFFALY
KILDARE
Sanda Island
Mull of Kintyre

GREATER LONDON
MAP 19
D
E
F
G
H
1
2
3
4
5
6
7
8
9
10
11
12
Benington Lordship
Knebworth
Gorhambury House
Hatfield House
Town Hall
Copped Hall
Waltham Abbey Gatehouse & Bridge
Capel Manor
Chenies Manor House
Myddelton House
Brentwood Cathedral
Pitzhanger Manor-house
College
Chiswick House & Gardens
7 Hammersmith Terrace - Home of Emery Walker
Royal Observatory
Queen's House
Wernher Collection At Ranger's House
Osterley Park
Kew Gdns
Syon Park
Kew Palace
The Octagon
Marble Hill House
Eltham Palace
Ham House
Southside House
Strawberry Hill
Great Fosters
Hampton Court
Claremont Landscape Garden
Lullingstone Roman Villa
Lullingston Castle
Whitehall
Honeywood Heritage Centre
Little Holland House
Painshill Park Landscape Garden
Home of Charles Darwin
Quebec House
Hatchlands Park
The Cobbe Collection
alford Mill
Clandon
Polesden Lacey
Emmetts Garden
Knole
Ightham Mote
Squerryes Court
Riverhill Himalayan Gardens
Chartwell
Tonbridge Castle
Goddards
Chiddingstone Castle
Hever Castle
Penshurst Place
Saint Hill Manor
Sackville College
Groombridge Place Gdns
Hammerwood Park
Standen
A6
A5
A1
A10
A41
A414
A602
A120
A413
A406
A12
A13
A40
A102
A4
A30
A316
A3
A205
A2
A20
A24
A232
A21
A22
A23
A217
A25
A26
A264

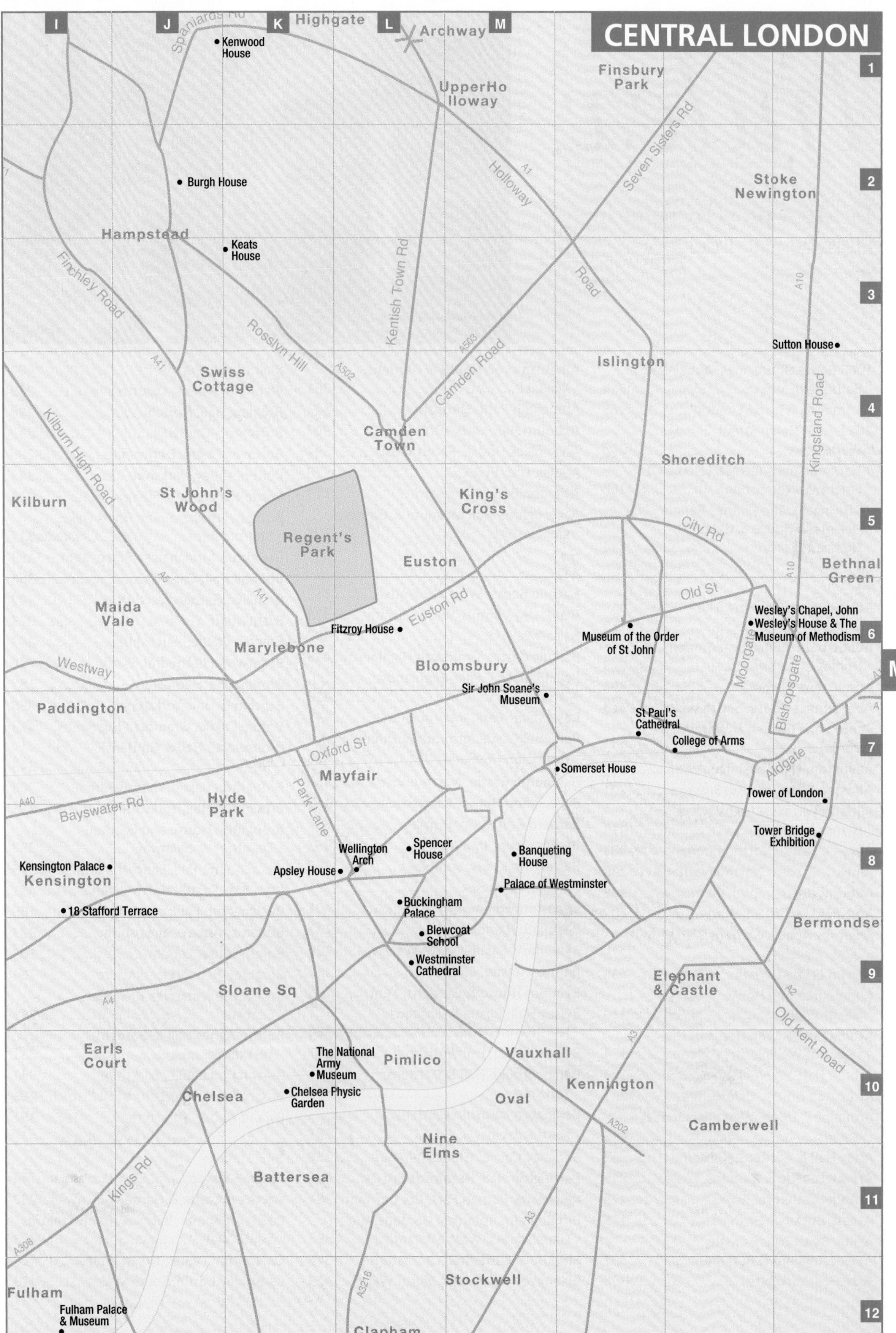

CENTRAL LONDON
MAP 20
I
J
K
L
M
1
2
3
4
5
6
7
8
9
10
11
12
Highgate
Archway
Spaniards Rd
Kenwood House
Finsbury Park
UpperHo lloway
Seven Sisters Rd
Holloway Road
A1
Stoke Newington
Burgh House
Hampstead
Keats House
Finchley Road
Kentish Town Rd
A10
Rosslyn Hill
A502
A503
Camden Road
Sutton House
A41
Swiss Cottage
Islington
Kingsland Road
Camden Town
Kilburn High Road
Shoreditch
Kilburn
St John's Wood
King's Cross
City Rd
Regent's Park
Euston
Bethnal Green
A5
A41
Old St
Maida Vale
Euston Rd
Fitzroy House
Museum of the Order of St John
Wesley's Chapel, John Wesley's House & The Museum of Methodism
Marylebone
Moorgate
Westway
Bloomsbury
Bishopsgate
Sir John Soane's Museum
Paddington
St Paul's Cathedral
College of Arms
Oxford St
Mayfair
Somerset House
Aldgate
A40
Park Lane
Bayswater Rd
Hyde Park
Tower of London
Tower Bridge Exhibition
Wellington Arch
Spencer House
Banqueting House
Kensington Palace
Kensington
Apsley House
Palace of Westminster
Buckingham Palace
18 Stafford Terrace
Blewcoat School
Bermondse
Westminster Cathedral
Elephant & Castle
Sloane Sq
A2
A4
Old Kent Road
A3
Earls Court
The National Army Museum
Pimlico
Vauxhall
Chelsea
Chelsea Physic Garden
Kennington
Oval
A202
Camberwell
Nine Elms
Battersea
Kings Rd
A3
A308
A3216
Stockwell
Fulham
Fulham Palace & Museum
Clapham

Index

Listed by property name in alphabetical order

Apsley House
©English Heritage

D

E

Falkland Palace and Gardens

J

K

L

M

N

O

T

U

V

W

Y

Display Advertisers

©Britainonview

Maps

John O'Groats

MAP 15
MAP 16
MAP 17

Western Isles
Highlands & Skye
Grampian Highlands

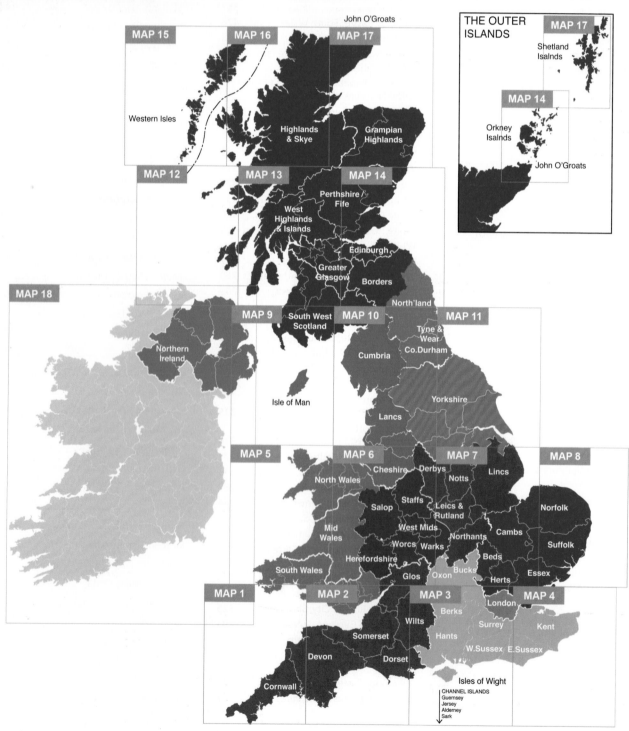

THE OUTER ISLANDS
MAP 17
Shetland Isalnds
MAP 14
Orkney Isalnds
John O'Groats

MAP 12
MAP 13
MAP 14

Perthshire / Fife
West Highlands & Islands
Edinburgh
Greater Glasgow
Borders

MAP 18
North'land
MAP 9
South West Scotland
MAP 10
MAP 11
Tyne & Wear
Northern Ireland
Co.Durham
Cumbria
Isle of Man
Yorkshire
Lancs

MAP 5
MAP 6
MAP 7
MAP 8
Cheshire
Derbys
Lincs
Notts
North Wales
Staffs
Leics & Rutland
Norfolk
Salop
West Mids
Mid Wales
Northants
Cambs
Worcs
Warks
Suffolk
Herefordshire
Beds
South Wales
Bucks
Oxon
Essex
Glos
Herts

MAP 1
MAP 2
MAP 3
MAP 4
London
Berks
Wilts
Surrey
Kent
Somerset
Hants
W.Sussex
E.Sussex
Devon
Dorset
Isles of Wight
Cornwall
CHANNEL ISLANDS
Guernsey
Jersey
Alderney
Sark